CONTENTS

STAR WARS
™

30¢ | 1
CC | JULY
02817

THE GREATEST SPACE-FANTASY FILM OF ALL!

STAR WARS

FABULOUS FIRST ISSUE!

ENTER LUKE SKYWALKER!
WILL HE *SAVE* THE GALAXY--
OR *DESTROY* IT?

MARVEL'S EPIC *OFFICIAL* ADAPTATION OF
THE MONUMENTAL 20ᵀᴴ CENTURY FOX MOVIE!
——A FILM BY GEORGE LUCAS——

LucasFilm PRESENTS: ROY THOMAS SCRIPTER/EDITOR ✶ HOWARD CHAYKIN ILLUSTRATOR ✶ JIM NOVAK LETTERER ✶ ...ADAPTING THE GREATEST SPACE-FANTASY OF ALL!

STAR WARS

ADAPTED FROM THE *GEORGE LUCAS* FILM, A *20th CENTURY-FOX* RELEASE

It is a period of CIVIL WAR in the galaxy.

A brave alliance of UNDERGROUND FREE-DOM FIGHTERS has challenged the tyranny and oppression of the awesome GALACTIC EMPIRE.

To CRUSH the rebellion once and for all, the EMPIRE is constructing a sinister new BATTLE STATION. Powerful enough to destroy an entire planet, its COMPLETION will spell CERTAIN DOOM for the champions of freedom.

Striking from a fortress hidden among the billion stars of the galaxy, REBEL SPACESHIPS have won their first victory in a battle with the powerful IMPERIAL STARFLEET. The Empire fears that ANOTHER defeat could bring a THOUSAND MORE solar systems into the rebellion, and IMPERIAL CONTROL over the galaxy would be LOST FOREVER.

BUT, THAT IS THE NEAR FUTURE.

AT THIS MOMENT:

ABOVE THE YELLOW PLANET TATOOINE, A GIGANTIC IMPERIAL STARSHIP PURSUES A REBEL SPACECRAFT--ITS DEADLY LASER BOLTS DISINTEGRATE THE SMALLER SHIP'S MAIN SOLAR FIN WITH A SOULSEARING SHUDDER...!

MARIE SEVERIN, COLORIST

MOMENTS LATER, GRAPPLING RAYS HAVE JOINED THE TWO VESSELS, AND SUDDENLY THE IMPERIAL TROOPS COME POURING THRU A WIDE-GAPING HOLE...

THIS IS MADNESS, ARTOO!

BEEP BEEP **BEEEP**

AMID THIS CHAOS, IT IS *STRANGE* PERHAPS TO FOCUS NOT UPON THE *HUMANS* ON BOTH SIDES WHO LIVE AND VIOLENTLY DIE...

...BUT UPON A PAIR OF *ROBOTS*, DESIGNATED C-3PO AND R2-D2.

MORE FAMILIARLY: SEE THREEPIO AND ARTOO DETOO.

YES, ARTOO-- I SUPPOSE YOU'RE *RIGHT*... WE SHOULD FLEE THIS WAY... DOWN THE *CORRIDOR*...!

IT LOOKS AS IF THERE IS *NO ESCAPE* FOR THE CAPTAIN THIS TIME! I--

OH! I THINK SOMETHING IS *MELTING!*

THIS IS ALL *YOUR* FAULT!

I SHOULD HAVE KNOWN BETTER THAN TO TRUST THE LOGIC OF A HALF-SIZED THERMO-CAPSULARY DEHOUSING ASSISTER...!

HEY-- WAIT UP! WHERE ARE YOU *GOING?*

WHINE

BELOW, ON THE DEATH-WHITE WASTELAND WHICH IS THE PLANET TATOOINE:

A BRIGHT SPARKLE IN THE MORNING SKY CATCHES A WATCHFUL EYE.

LUKE SKYWALKER LOWERS HIS *MACROBINOCULARS,* STANDING TRANSFIXED FOR A MOMENT.

THEN, HE LEAPS NIMBLY INTO THE NEARBY, RECENTLY-REPAIRED *LANDSPEEDER*...

...AND AIMS THE CRAFT TOWARD THE DISTANT TOWN OF *ANCHORHEAD.*

WHILE, ON THE WOUNDED STARSHIP...

LORD VADER! THE SHIP'S INFORMATION RETRIEVAL SYSTEM HAS BEEN WIPED CLEAN!

THEN THIS REBEL WILL TELL US WHAT WE NEED TO KNOW!

WHERE IS THE DATA YOU INTERCEPTED?

W-WE'RE ON A DIPLOMATIC MISSION--!

LIAR! WHERE ARE THOSE INFORMATION TAPES?

THIS SHIP CARRIES THE CREST OF ALDERAAN! IS ANY OF THE ROYAL FAMILY ON BOARD?

...UNLESS IT BE THE AWFUL UNQUESTIONABLE FINALITY OF A SINGLE GRUESOME SNAPPING SOUND.

THE FOOL IS DEAD!

START TEARING THIS SHIP APART, PIECE BY PIECE, UNTIL YOU HAVE THOSE TAPES!

DARTH VADER, DARK LORD OF THE SITH, TIGHTENS HIS FINGERS ON THE REBEL OFFICER'S THROAT.

BUT, HE STILL RECEIVES NO ANSWER...

AND FIND THE PASSENGERS OF THIS VESSEL!

I WANT THEM-- ALIVE!!

Y-YES, LORD VADER...!

THE IMPERIAL TROOPS FALL ALL OVER EACH OTHER IN THEIR HASTE TO LEAVE--AS MUCH TO ESCAPE THEIR MASTER'S PRESENCE AS TO CARRY OUT HIS ORDERS.

WHILE, NOT FAR DISTANT...

ARTOO! SO THIS IS WHERE YOU VANISHED TO!

THE UNKNOWN GIRL WHO KNEELS BY THE SMALLER ROBOT IS PROBABLY BEAUTIFUL BY HUMAN STANDARDS...

AND, THE NEXT MOMENT, SHE IS GONE, AS IF SHE WERE A PART OF THE THICKENING HAZE...

WELL, ARTOO? WHAT ARE WE GOING TO DO?

WE'LL BE SENT TO THE SPICE MINES OF KESSEL, OR EVEN--

WAIT! WHERE ARE YOU GOING?

BUT, THREEPIO, BEING A ROBOT HIMSELF, TAKES SCANT NOTICE OF HER...

REEEE

REEE

MISSION? WHAT MISSION? WHAT ARE YOU TALKING ABOUT?

HEY! YOU'RE NOT PERMITTED TO GO NEAR THOSE EMERGENCY LIFEPODS!

TWANG!

DON'T YOU CALL ME A MINDLESS PHILOSOPHER, YOU OVERWEIGHT GLOBE OF GREASE!

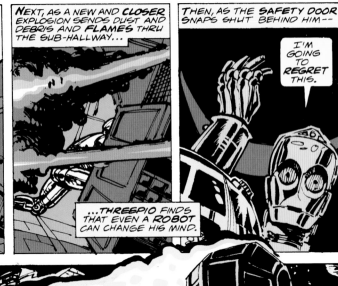

NEXT, AS A NEW AND CLOSER EXPLOSION SENDS DUST AND DEBRIS AND FLAMES THRU THE SUB-HALLWAY...

...THREEPIO FINDS THAT EVEN A ROBOT CAN CHANGE HIS MIND.

THEN, AS THE SAFETY DOOR SNAPS SHUT BEHIND HIM--

I'M GOING TO REGRET THIS.

--THERE IS THE SUDDEN THUNDER OF EXPLODING LATCHES--

--AND THE TINY LIFEPOD EJECTS FROM THE DISABLED STARFIGHTER!

...AS, BACK ABOARD...

THERE'S ONE OF THEM!

SET WEAPONS FOR STUN!

I'VE SET MINE TO KILL!

ZZZZ

THEN, THE YOUNG GIRL STARTS TO FLEE ONCE MORE--

--BUT, UNFORTUNATELY, NOT AT THE LIGHT-SPEED OF A PARALYSIS RAY.

OHHH

FSS

SHE'LL BE ALL RIGHT.

REPORT TO LORD VADER!

I'VE **TOLD** YOU KIDS TO **SLOW DOWN!**

SHREEE

HEY, CAMIE-- DID I HEAR A **YOUNG NOISE BLAST** THRU HERE?

IT WAS JUST **WORMIE** ON ANOTHER **RAMPAGE,** FIXER.

SHAPE IT UP, YOU TWO! I-- **BIGGS!**

WHEN DID **YOU** GET BACK?

JUST **NOW!** I THOUGHT YOU'D BE HERE --CERTAINLY DIDN'T EXPECT YOU TO BE OUT **WORKING!**

HEY, WHAT **HAPPENED?** DIDN'T YOU GET YOUR **COMMISSION?**

WHY, UH--OF **COURSE** I GOT IT! SIGNED ABOARD THE **RAND ECLIPTIC** LAST WEEK.

FIRST MATE **BIGGS DARKLIGHTER** AT YOUR **SERVICE!**

I JUST CAME **BACK** TO SAY **GOODBYE** TO ALL YOU **UNFORTUNATE** LANDLOCKED **SIMPLETONS.**

WAIT! I ALMOST **FORGOT**--

THERE'S A **BATTLE** GOING ON-- RIGHT HERE IN **OUR** SYSTEM! COME AND **LOOK!**

NOT **AGAIN!** FORGET IT, BIGGS-- HE'S ALWAYS--

NO, I **MEAN** IT. COME ON.

UP **THERE!** CAN YOU **SEE**--?

THAT'S **NO** BATTLE, HOT-SHOT. THEY'RE JUST **SITTING** THERE.

PROBABLY A **FREIGHTER-TANKER** REFUELING.

BUT, THERE WAS A LOT OF **FIRING** EARLIER...!

I KEEP **TELLING** YOU, WORMIE--THE REBEL-LION'S A **LONG** WAY FROM HERE; I DOUBT IF THE **EMPIRE** WOULD EVEN **FIGHT** TO KEEP THIS SYSTEM.

BELIEVE ME, LUKE--THIS PLANET IS A **BIG HUNK** OF **NOTHING!**

WHILE, OUT IN SPACE...

LORD VADER! I SHOULD HAVE *KNOWN* --ONLY YOU COULD BE SO *BOLD!*

WELL, THE *IMPERIAL SENATE* WILL NOT SIT *STILL* FOR THIS!

WHEN THEY HEAR YOU'VE ATTACKED A *DIPLOMATIC* --

DON'T PLAY GAMES WITH *ME*, YOUR HIGHNESS!

THIS SHIP PASSED DIRECTLY THRU A *RESTRICTED* SYSTEM.

SEVERAL *TRANSMISSIONS* WERE BEAMED TO THIS SHIP BY *SPIES*, WHO ARE NOW UNFORTUNATELY *DEAD.*

I WANT TO KNOW WHAT HAPPENED TO THOSE *DATA TAPES.*

I DON'T KNOW WHAT YOU'RE *TALKING* ABOUT!

I'M A MEMBER OF THE *IMPERIAL SENATE*, ON A *DIPLOMATIC* MISSION TO --

YOU'RE A PART OF THE *REBEL ALLIANCE* -- AND A *TRAITOR!*

TAKE HER AWAY.

SHE SHOULD BE *DESTROYED*, LORD VADER.

MY DUTY IS TO FIND THE REBELS' *HIDDEN FORTRESS,* COMMANDER.

SHE IS MY ONLY *LINK* TO DISCOVERING ITS LOCATION -- AND I INTEND TO *USE* IT.

MEANWHILE, SEND A *DISTRESS SIGNAL* -- CALL IT A *METEORITE STORM* --

VAPORIZE THIS SHIP; DON'T LEAVE *ANYTHING.*

THEN, INFORM HER *FATHER* AND THE *SENATE* THAT ALL ABOARD WERE *KILLED.*

I'VE BEEN INFORMED THAT A *REPAIR POD* WAS SOMEHOW *JETTISONED* DURING THE FIGHTING.

THE *DATA TAPES* MUST BE HIDDEN IN IT -- SO SEND A DETACHMENT DOWN TO *RETRIEVE* THEM, WITHOUT ATTRACTING *ATTENTION.*

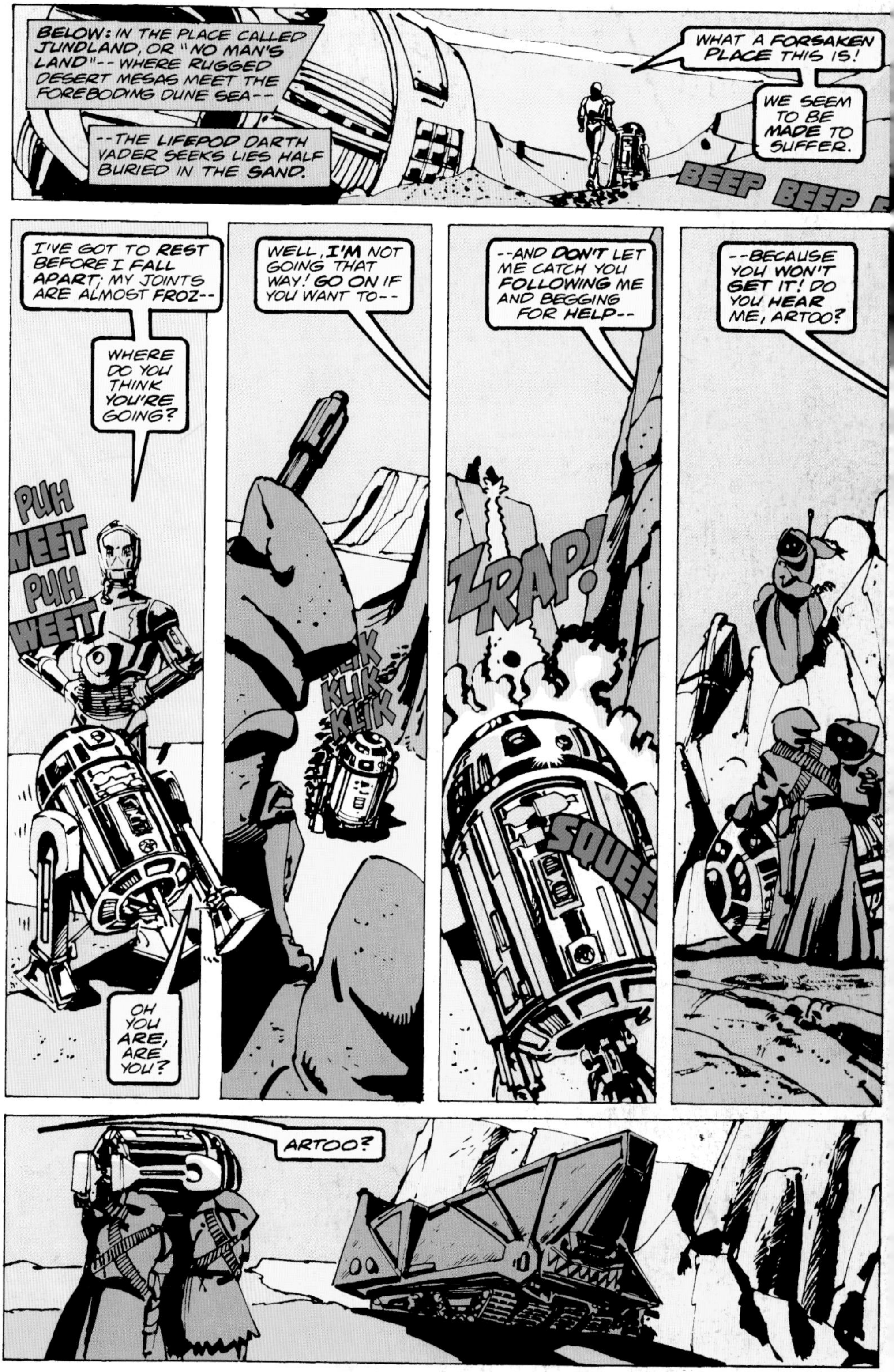
BELOW: IN THE PLACE CALLED JUNDLAND, OR "NO MAN'S LAND"-- WHERE RUGGED DESERT MESAS MEET THE FOREBODING DUNE SEA--
--THE LIFEPOD DARTH VADER SEEKS LIES HALF BURIED IN THE SAND.
WHAT A FORSAKEN PLACE THIS IS!
WE SEEM TO BE MADE TO SUFFER.
BEEP BEEP
I'VE GOT TO REST BEFORE I FALL APART; MY JOINTS ARE ALMOST FROZ--
WHERE DO YOU THINK YOU'RE GOING?
PUH WEET PUH WEET
OH YOU ARE, ARE YOU?
WELL, I'M NOT GOING THAT WAY! GO ON IF YOU WANT TO--
KLIK KLIK
--AND DON'T LET ME CATCH YOU FOLLOWING ME AND BEGGING FOR HELP--
ZRAP!
SQUEEE
--BECAUSE YOU WON'T GET IT! DO YOU HEAR ME, ARTOO?
ARTOO?

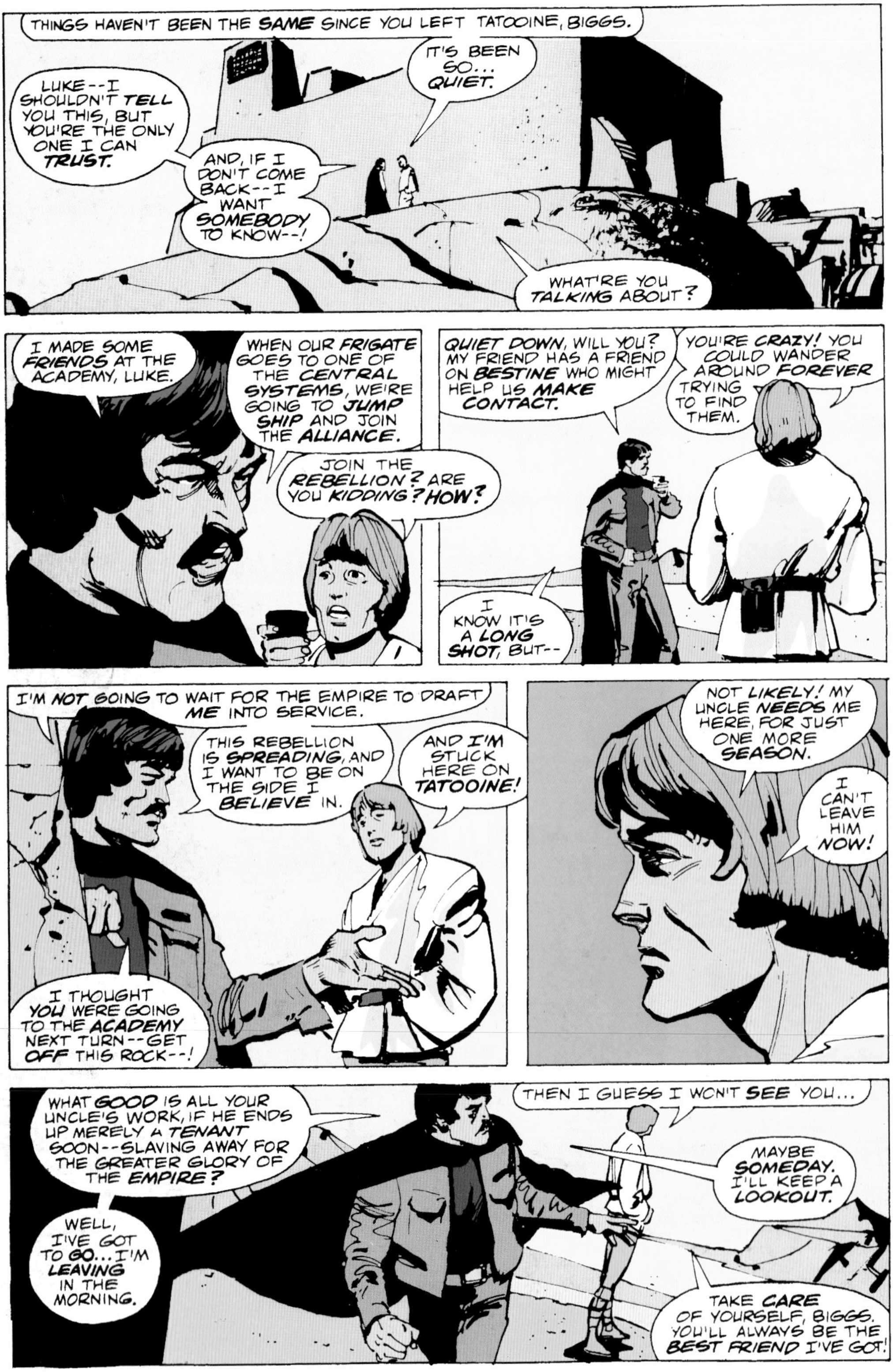
THINGS HAVEN'T BEEN THE SAME SINCE YOU LEFT TATOOINE, BIGGS.
IT'S BEEN SO... QUIET.
LUKE--I SHOULDN'T TELL YOU THIS, BUT YOU'RE THE ONLY ONE I CAN TRUST.
AND, IF I DON'T COME BACK--I WANT SOMEBODY TO KNOW--!
WHAT'RE YOU TALKING ABOUT?
I MADE SOME FRIENDS AT THE ACADEMY, LUKE.
WHEN OUR FRIGATE GOES TO ONE OF THE CENTRAL SYSTEMS, WE'RE GOING TO JUMP SHIP AND JOIN THE ALLIANCE.
JOIN THE REBELLION? ARE YOU KIDDING? HOW?
QUIET DOWN, WILL YOU? MY FRIEND HAS A FRIEND ON BESTINE WHO MIGHT HELP US MAKE CONTACT.
YOU'RE CRAZY! YOU COULD WANDER AROUND FOREVER TRYING TO FIND THEM.
I KNOW IT'S A LONG SHOT, BUT--
I'M NOT GOING TO WAIT FOR THE EMPIRE TO DRAFT ME INTO SERVICE.
THIS REBELLION IS SPREADING, AND I WANT TO BE ON THE SIDE I BELIEVE IN.
AND I'M STUCK HERE ON TATOOINE!
I THOUGHT YOU WERE GOING TO THE ACADEMY NEXT TURN--GET OFF THIS ROCK--!
NOT LIKELY! MY UNCLE NEEDS ME HERE, FOR JUST ONE MORE SEASON.
I CAN'T LEAVE HIM NOW!
WHAT GOOD IS ALL YOUR UNCLE'S WORK, IF HE ENDS UP MERELY A TENANT SOON--SLAVING AWAY FOR THE GREATER GLORY OF THE EMPIRE?
WELL, I'VE GOT TO GO... I'M LEAVING IN THE MORNING.
THEN I GUESS I WON'T SEE YOU...
MAYBE SOMEDAY. I'LL KEEP A LOOKOUT.
TAKE CARE OF YOURSELF, BIGGS. YOU'LL ALWAYS BE THE BEST FRIEND I'VE GOT!

WHILE, IN A SOULLESS IMPERIAL CONFERENCE ROOM, SOMEWHERE IN THE GALAXY...

...I TELL YOU, DARTH VADER HAS GONE TOO FAR!

THIS SITH LORD SENT BY THE EMPEROR WILL BE OUR UNDOING.

THE REBEL ALLIANCE IS MORE DANGEROUS THAN YOU REALIZE!

DANGEROUS TO YOUR STARFLEET, COMMANDER TAGGE -- NOT TO THIS BATTLE-STATION!

YOU'RE A FOOL, ADMIRAL MOTTI!

THE REBELLION WILL CONTINUE TO GAIN SUPPORT IN THE IMPERIAL SENATE, AS LONG AS--

THE IMPERIAL SENATE IS NO LONGER OF ANY CONCERN TO US, GENTLEMEN.

IT'S GRAND MOFF TARKIN-- AND DARTH VADER!

I HAVE JUST RECEIVED WORD THAT THE EMPEROR HAS DISSOLVED THE COUNCIL --PERMANENTLY.

THE LAST REMNANTS OF THE OLD REPUBLIC HAVE BEEN SWEPT AWAY.

THE REGIONAL GOVERNORS NOW HAVE DIRECT CONTROL OVER THEIR TERRITORIES.

IMPOSSIBLE! HOW WILL THE EMPEROR MAINTAIN CONTROL WITHOUT THE BUREAUCRACY?

FEAR WILL KEEP THE LOCAL SYSTEMS IN LINE -- FEAR OF THIS BATTLE-STATION WHICH NEARS COMPLETION.

AND WHAT OF THE REBELLION, GOVERNOR TARKIN?

IF THE REBELS HAVE OBTAINED A COMPLETE TECHNICAL READ-OUT OF THIS BATTLE-STATION, IT IS POSSIBLE-- HOWEVER, UNLIKELY-- --THAT THEY MIGHT FIND A WEAKNESS AND EXPLOIT IT.

THE TECHNICAL DATA YOU REFER TO WILL SOON BE BACK IN OUR HANDS.

13

ANY **ATTACK** MADE AGAINST THIS STATION BY THE REBELS WOULD BE A **USELESS GESTURE,** NO MATTER **WHAT** TECHNICAL DATA THEY'VE OBTAINED.

THIS **BATTLE STATION** IS NOW THE **ULTIMATE POWER** IN THE UNIVERSE!

DON'T BECOME TOO PROUD OF THIS TECHNOLOGICAL **TERROR** YOU'VE CREATED, ADMIRAL MOTTI.

THE ABILITY TO **DESTROY A PLANET** IS INSIGNIFICANT NEXT TO THE **COSMIC FORCE!**

DON'T TRY TO FRIGHTEN US WITH YOUR **SORCERER'S** WAYS, LORD VADER!

YOUR SAD DEVOTION TO THAT **ANCIENT RELIGION** HASN'T HELPED YOU CONJURE UP THOSE STOLEN **DATA TAPES--**

--OR ENABLED YOU TO FIND THE REBELS' **HIDDEN FORTRESS.**

WHY, I HAVE TO **LAUGH**--AH-- ≥CHOKE≥ --CAN'T BREATHE --I--

I FIND YOUR LACK OF FAITH DISTURBING.

ENOUGH OF THIS! VADER-- RELEASE HIM!

THIS BICKERING IS **POINTLESS.**

LORD VADER WILL FIND THE LOCATION OF THE REBEL FORTRESS BY THE TIME THIS STATION IS **OPERATIONAL.**

THEN, WE WILL **CRUSH** THE REBELLION WITH **ONE SWIFT STRIKE!**

AND, BACK ON TATOOINE, ABOARD THE LUMBERING SANDCRAWLER OF THE DESERT-DWELLING JAWAS...

WILL THIS **NEVER** END?

WAKE UP, ARTOO! WAKE UP!

WE'VE STOPPED! WE'RE **DOOMED!**

DO YOU THINK THE JAWAS WILL MELT US DOWN?

WHEET WHEET!

YOU'RE A GREAT COMFORT.

SUDDENLY, THROUGH AN OPENING HATCH, **BLINDING WHITE LIGHT** FILLS THE CHAMBER...

THEY WANT US TO **GO OUTSIDE.**

I WAS **RIGHT!** WE ARE **DOOMED!**

LUKE-- TELL YOUR UNCLE OWEN THAT IF HE GETS A TRANS-LATOR TO BE SURE IT SPEAKS "BOCCE"!

IT LOOKS LIKE WE DON'T HAVE MUCH OF A CHOICE, AUNT BERU, BUT I'LL REMIND HIM.

YES, THIS R2-D2 MODEL WILL DO FINE; THAT OTHER ONE OVER THERE LOOKS READY FOR THE JUNKHEAP.

SAVE YOUR SALES PITCH! YOU-- ROBOT --DO YOU KNOW ETIQUETTE AND PROTOCOL?

DO I KNOW PROTOCOL! WHY, IT'S MY PRIMARY FUNCTION!

I AM WELL VERSED IN THE CUSTOMS AND--

I DON'T NEED A PRO-TOCOL DROID! I NEED A DROID THAT KNOWS SOMETHING ABOUT THE BINARY LANGUAGE OF MOISTURE VAPOR-ATORS.

VAPORATORS! SIR, MY FIRST JOB WAS PRO-GRAMMING BINARY LOAD LIFTERS, A VERY SIMILAR--

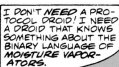

DO YOU SPEAK "BOCCE"?

IT'S LIKE A SEC-OND LANGUAGE FOR ME, SIR. I'M AS FLUENT AS--

SHUT UP!

I'LL TAKE THIS ONE.

SHUTTING UP, SIR.

LUKE, TAKE THEM TO THE GARAGE AND CLEAN THEM UP.

BUT I WAS GOING INTO TOSHI STATION TO--

AFTER YOU'VE FINISHED YOUR CHORES!

UNCLE OWEN--THIS R2 UNIT HAS A BAD MOTIVATOR. LOOK!

SPRING

IF I MIGHT SAY SO, SIR, THIS R2 UNIT IS IN TOP CONDITION --A REAL BARGAIN.

THEN WE'LL TAKE IT--AS A REPLACE-MENT.

I'LL TAKE CARE OF THE JAWAS, LUKE. RUN ALONG.

BLEEP!

DON'T YOU FORGET THIS, ARTOO!

WHY I STICK MY NECK OUT FOR YOU IS BE-YOND MY CAPACITY TO--

BEEP.BEEP.BEEP

15

...IT JUST ISN'T *FAIR!* BIGGS IS RIGHT-- I'LL *NEVER* GET OUT OF HERE!

IS THERE ANYTHING I MIGHT DO TO HELP, SIR?

YES, YOU CAN CALL ME *LUKE!*

HMMM...LOTS OF *CARBON* SCORING HERE. YOU'VE BOTH SEEN A LOT OF *ACTION.*

WELL, MY LITTLE FRIEND, YOU'VE GOT SOMETHING *JAMMED* IN HERE REAL GOOD...

LET'S SEE WHAT-- *OOOOF!*

...OBI-WAN *KENOBI* --HELP ME! YOU'RE MY ONLY HO--

SNAP

WHAT'S *THIS?* A THREE-DIMENSIONAL *HOLOGRAM*-- AND SHE'S *BEAUTIFUL!*

...OBI-WAN *KENOBI* ...HELP ME! YOU'RE MY ONLY HO--

BREEP!

ARTOO SAYS IT'S *NOTHING,* SIR...MERELY A MALFUNCTION. PAY IT NO MIND.

BUT-- WHO *IS* THIS GIRL?

I... THINK SHE WAS A PASSENGER ON OUR *LAST* VOYAGE, SIR, BUT I DON'T--

...OBI-WAN KENOBI...

IS THERE ANY *MORE* TO THIS HOLOGRAM?

OUTH-WHEET

ARTOO SAYS HE'S THE PROPERTY OF OBI-WAN *KENOBI,* AND IT IS A *PRIVATE* MESSAGE FOR HIM.

QUITE FRANKLY, SIR, I DON'T KNOW WHAT HE'S TALKING ABOUT! OUR LAST MASTER WAS CAPTAIN *ANTILLIES...*

I DON'T KNOW ANY *OBI-WAN,* BUT THERE'S AN *OLD BEN KENOBI* WHO LIVES OUT BEYOND THE *DUNE SEA...* SORT OF A *HERMIT.* I WONDER...

HMMM...I WONDER, IF I REMOVE THIS *RESTRAINING BOLT...*

NOW THE HOLOGRAM'S *DISAPPEARED,* GIRL AND ALL!

PLAY BACK THE *ENTIRE* MESSAGE, ARTOO!

MAKE HER COME *BACK!*

I'M SORRY, SIR, BUT HE APPEARS TO HAVE PICKED UP A SLIGHT *FLUTTER.*

PERHAPS *LATER...!*

BOO BEEP BOO BEEP

SOON AFTERWARD, AT DINNER...

UNCLE OWEN -- I THINK THAT *R2 UNIT* MAY BE STOLEN GOODS.

WHAT MAKES YOU THINK *THAT*, LUKE?

THE *DROID* CLAIMS TO BE THE PROPERTY OF SOMEONE CALLED...*OBI-WAN KENOBI!*

I STUMBLED ON A *RECORDING* WHILE I WAS CLEANING HIM...

I THOUGHT HE MIGHT MEAN OLD *BEN* -- THE NAME IS *SIMILAR.* DO YOU KNOW WHAT--?

IT'S A NAME FROM *ANOTHER* TIME, THAT CAN ONLY MEAN *TROUBLE!*

TOMORROW, YOU'LL HAVE THAT *R2* UNIT'S *MEMORY* FLUSHED AND THAT'LL BE THE *END* OF IT.

YOU *STAY* AWAY FROM THAT OLD *WIZARD*, DO YOU HEAR ME? HE'S *DANGEROUS!*

I DON'T CARE *WHERE* THAT DROID CAME FROM; IT BELONGS TO *US* NOW!

BUT, WHAT IF THIS *OBI-WAN* COMES *LOOKING* FOR THE DROID?

HE WON'T! HE *DIED* AT THE SAME TIME AS YOUR *FATHER.* FORGET ABOUT IT.

DID HE *KNOW* MY FATHER?

I SAID *FORGET* IT!

ALL RIGHT-- BUT IF THESE NEW DROIDS *WORK* OUT, I'D LIKE TO TRANSMIT MY APPLICATION TO THE *ACADEMY* THIS YEAR.

YOU MEAN *NEXT TERM* --BEFORE THE *HARVEST*?

YOU'VE GOT *MORE* THAN ENOUGH *DROIDS* TO--

DROIDS CAN'T *REPLACE* YOU, LUKE! IT'S JUST FOR *ONE MORE* SEASON.

FOR THE FIRST TIME, WE'VE GOT A *FORTUNE* COMING INTO OUR HANDS. MAYBE *AFTER* NEXT SEASON...

BUT, THAT MEANS *ANOTHER* YEAR...

THE TIME WILL PASS BEFORE YOU *KNOW* IT.

THAT'S WHAT YOU SAID *LAST* YEAR-- WHEN BIGGS AND TANK LEFT.

WHERE ARE YOU *GOING*?

IT *LOOKS* LIKE I'M GOING *NOWHERE!*

I HAVE TO *FINISH* CLEANING THOSE *DROIDS.*

OWEN, WE CAN'T KEEP HIM HERE *FOREVER!* MOST OF HIS *FRIENDS* ARE GONE...

I'LL MAKE IT *UP* TO HIM NEXT YEAR ...I *PROMISE.*

LUKE'S JUST *NOT A FARMER*, OWEN. HE'S GOT TOO MUCH OF HIS *FATHER* IN HIM.

THAT'S... WHAT I'M *AFRAID* OF....!

THREEPIO! ARTOO! WHERE ARE YOU TWO?

THIS CONTROL BOX WILL POP YOU OUT INTO THE OPEN!

YIPE!

IT-- WASN'T MY FAULT, SIR! PLEASE DON'T DEACTIVATE ME!

I TOLD HIM NOT TO GO, BUT HE'S FAULTY --MALFUNCTIONING.

KEPT BABBLING ON ABOUT HIS "MISSION"!

WHAT WERE YOU HIDING FOR? AND --WHERE'S ARTOO?

OH NO!

MOMENTS LATER, OUTSIDE...

NO SIGN OF HIM, EVEN WITH THESE ELECTRO-BINOCULARS!

UNCLE OWEN'S GOING TO KILL ME FOR THIS.

BEGGING YOUR PARDON, SIR...BUT CAN'T WE GO AFTER HIM?

NOT AT NIGHT! IT'S TOO DANGEROUS WITH ALL THE SANDPEOPLE AROUND. BUT, COME MORNING WE'LL--

LUKE! YOU ABOUT FINISHED WITH THOSE DROIDS?

BE THERE IN A MINUTE, UNCLE OWEN!

BOY, AM I IN FOR IT, IF HE FINDS OUT!

THAT LITTLE R2 DROID IS GOING TO GET ME INTO A LOT OF TROUBLE!

HE EXCELS AT THAT, SIR.

THESE ASTROID DROIDS ARE GETTING TOO MUCH FOR ME; EVEN I CAN'T UNDERSTAND THEIR LOGIC AT TIMES.

HOURS LATER, AS DAWN SLOWLY CREEPS OVER THE SPARSE BUT SPARKLING OASIS WHICH IS OWEN LAR'S HOMESTEAD...

BERU, HAVE YOU SEEN LUKE THIS MORNING?

HE GOT TO WORK EARLY-- TOOK THE NEW DROIDS WITH HIM, I GUESS.

WELL, HE'D BETTER HAVE THOSE CONDENSING UNITS ON THE SOUTH RIDGE BY MIDDAY-- OR THERE'LL BE HELL TO PAY!

18

MEANWHILE, SOME DISTANCE AWAY, FOUR IMPERIAL STORM-TROOPERS MILL ABOUT A FAMILIAR FORM: A HALF-BURIED LIFE-POD...!

THIS IS THE ONE! BUT, THERE ARE NO DATA TAPES HERE, SIR!

IF ONLY WE KNEW WHO WAS IN THAT POD WHEN IT--

HOLD IT!

THIS SMALL PIECE OF METAL I FOUND IN THE SAND--!

DROIDS!

...OLD BEN KENOBI LIVES OUT IN THIS DIRECTION SOMEWHERE, THREEPIO...

BUT, I DON'T SEE HOW ARTOO COULD HAVE--

WAIT! THERE'S SOMETHING DEAD AHEAD ON THE SCANNER!

LOOKS LIKE OUR DROID! HIT IT, THREEPIO!

AS THE TINY LANDSPEEDER GLIDES ACROSS THE DESERT FLOOR, ITS OCCUPANTS ARE UNAWARE OF A DEADLY LASER RIFLE BEING AIMED AT THEM...

MOMENTS, LATER, FOLLOWING A HEATED ARGUMENT IN THEIR BARBARIC TONGUE, THE TWO SAND-PEOPLE--OR TUSKEN RAIDERS AS THEY'RE SOMETIMES CALLED--ARE SCURRYING OVER THE ROCKY TERRAIN...

...TOWARD THEIR TWO ENORMOUS BANTHAS, TETHERED NEARBY.

...AND OF ANOTHER'S HAND, WHICH GRASPS THE GUN BEFORE IT CAN BE FIRED!

MOUNTING THE ELEPHANTINE CREATURES, THEY RIDE OFF DOWN THE RUGGED BLUFF --IN OMINOUS SILENCE.

WHILE, ON THE FLOOR OF A MASSIVE CANYON...

...AND JUST *WHERE* DID YOU THINK *YOU* WERE GOING?

THREEPIO?

TUH-WHEET TUH-WHEE

HE'S STILL TALKING THAT *OBI-WAN KENOBI* JIBBERISH, SIR-- EVEN THOUGH YOU'RE HIS *RIGHTFUL MASTER*, NOW.

ARTOO, YOU'RE FORTUNATE HE DOESN'T BLAST YOU INTO A MILLION PIECES RIGHT HERE!

WELL, COME ON-- IT'S GETTING *LATE!* I ONLY HOPE WE CAN GET *BACK* BEFORE--

WHEE

NOW *WHAT?*

ARTOO SAYS THERE ARE *SEVERAL* CREATURES APPROACHING RAPIDLY FROM THE *SOUTHEAST!*

SANDPEOPLE!

OH MY, SIR...

--OR *WORSE!*

I'VE NEVER BEEN OUT *THIS FAR* BEFORE! THE *WILD THINGS* OUT HERE ARE SAID TO BE *WEIRD*-- AND *SAVAGE!*

HURRY! FROM THIS *RIDGE* WE CAN SCAN THE WHOLE CANYON.

AS YOU KNOW, SIR, SUCH A THING IS *NOT BEYOND* THE REALM OF *POSSIBILITY.*

COME ON, ARTOO!

I JUST HOPE THAT R2 UNIT IS ON THE BLINK!

TWOOT TWOOT

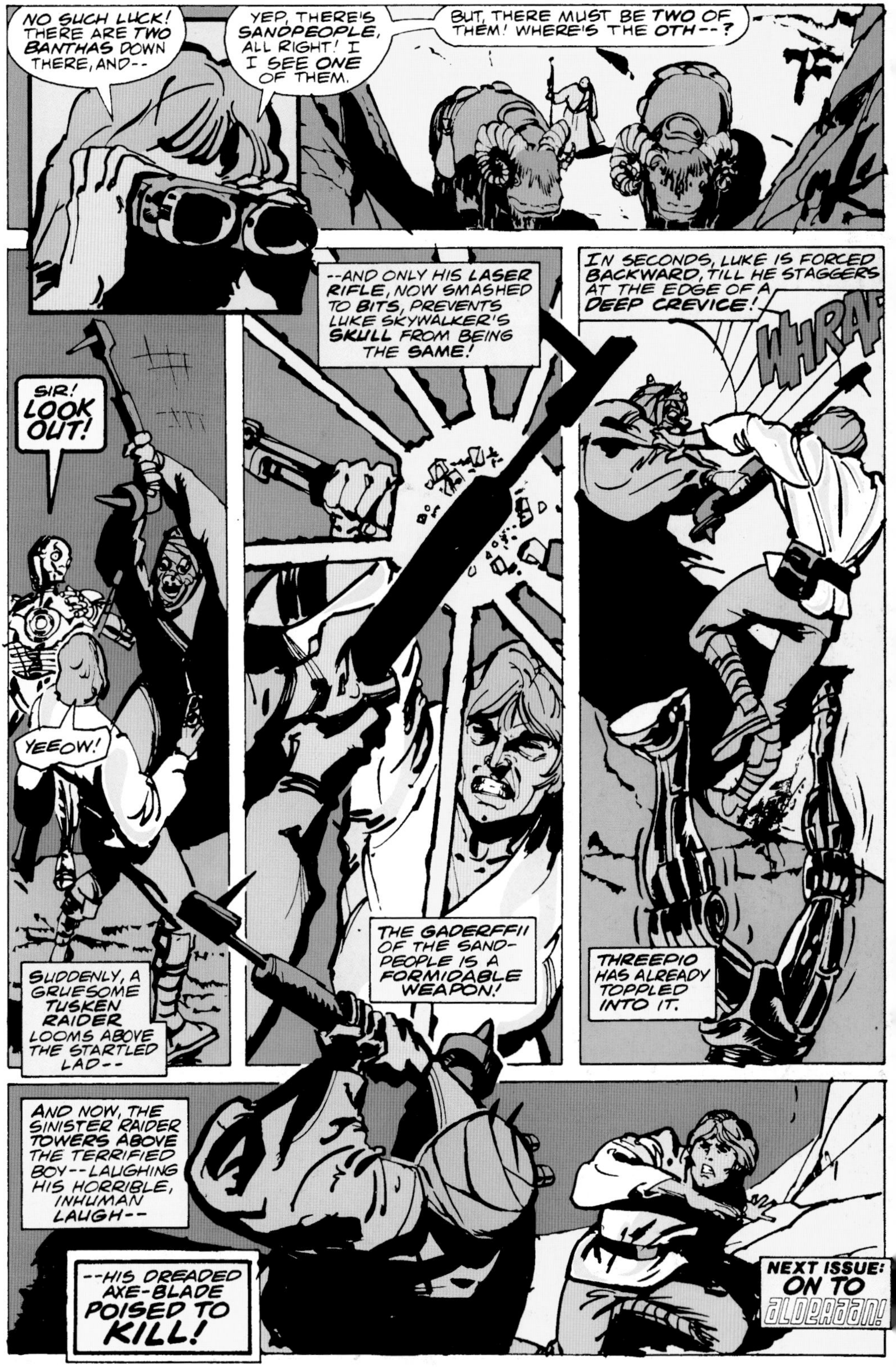
NO SUCH LUCK! THERE ARE TWO BANTHAS DOWN THERE, AND--
YEP, THERE'S SANDPEOPLE, ALL RIGHT! I I SEE ONE OF THEM.
BUT, THERE MUST BE TWO OF THEM! WHERE'S THE OTH--?
SIR! LOOK OUT!
YEEOW!
SUDDENLY, A GRUESOME TUSKEN RAIDER LOOMS ABOVE THE STARTLED LAD--
--AND ONLY HIS LASER RIFLE, NOW SMASHED TO BITS, PREVENTS LUKE SKYWALKER'S SKULL FROM BEING THE SAME!
THE GADERFFII OF THE SAND-PEOPLE IS A FORMIDABLE WEAPON!
IN SECONDS, LUKE IS FORCED BACKWARD, TILL HE STAGGERS AT THE EDGE OF A DEEP CREVICE!
WHRA
THREEPIO HAS ALREADY TOPPLED INTO IT.
AND NOW, THE SINISTER RAIDER TOWERS ABOVE THE TERRIFIED BOY--LAUGHING HIS HORRIBLE, INHUMAN LAUGH--
--HIS DREADED AXE-BLADE POISED TO KILL!
NEXT ISSUE: ON TO ALDERAAN!

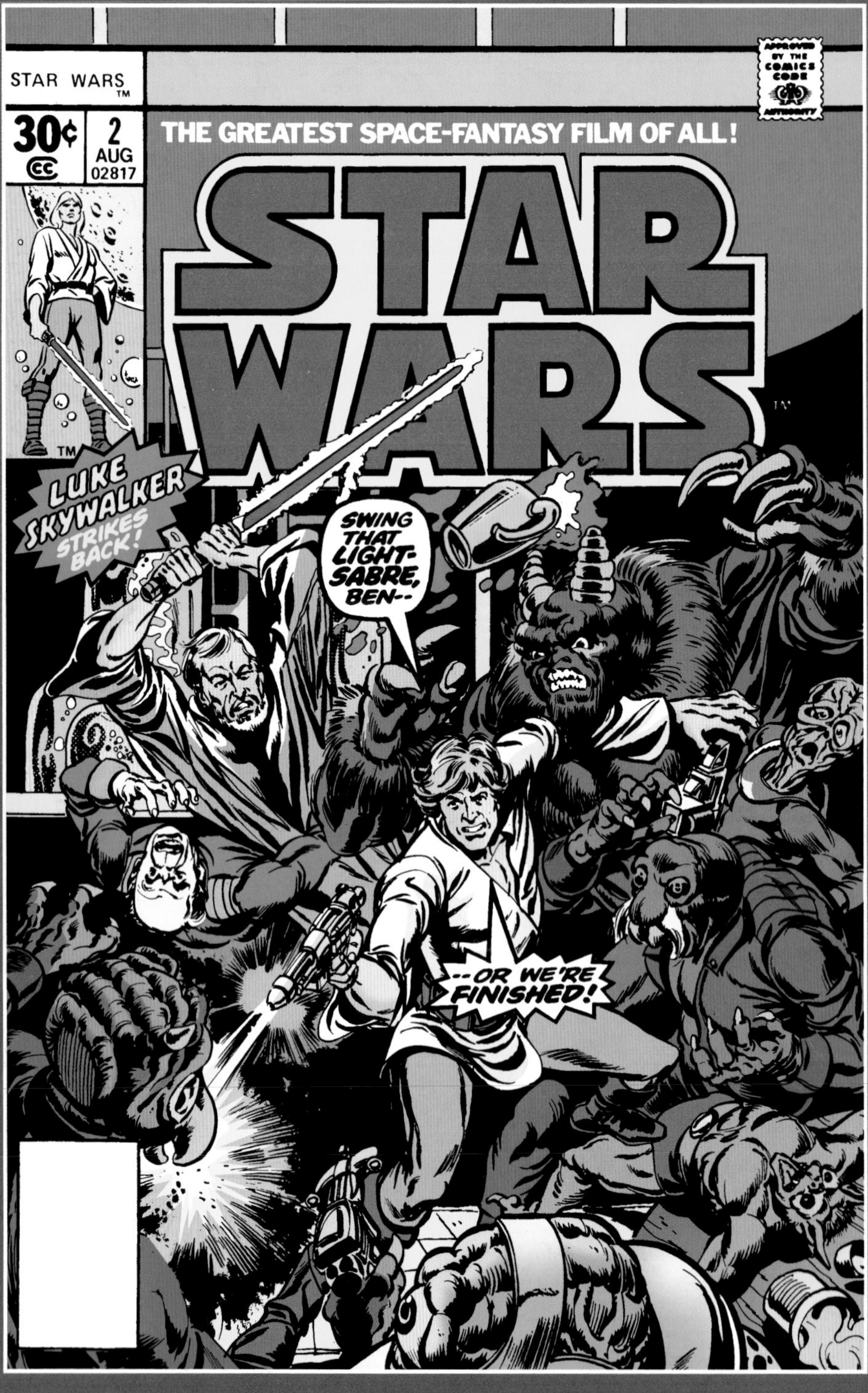
STAR WARS ™
30¢
2
AUG
02817
THE GREATEST SPACE-FANTASY FILM OF ALL!
STAR WARS
LUKE SKYWALKER STRIKES BACK!
SWING THAT LIGHT-SABRE, BEN--
--OR WE'RE FINISHED!

LucasFilm PRESENTS: **STAR WARS** THE GREATEST SPACE FANTASY OF ALL!

ROY THOMAS SCRIPTER / EDITOR   **HOWARD CHAYKIN** ILLUSTRATOR   **STEVE LEIALOHA** EMBELLISHER / COLORIST   **TOM ORZECHOWSKI** LETTERER

--TO *FLEE* IN OBVIOUS TERROR, AS IF BEFORE SOME HORRIBLE *MONSTER!*

BUT, TO THE LITTLE ANDROID *ARTOO DETOO,* THE APPROACHING FIGURE IS *HARDLY MONSTROUS...*

BLEEP?

...BUT ONLY A *MAN,* HIS ANCIENT LEATHERY FACE CRACKED AND WEATHERED BY EXOTIC CLIMATES.

DON'T *WORRY,* LITTLE DROID. HE'LL BE *ALL RIGHT!*

W-WHAT *HAPPENED?* I--*BEN! BEN* KENOBI-- AM I GLAD TO SEE *YOU!*

WHAT BRINGS YOU *OUT* THIS FAR, LUKE?

THAT *DROID* OVER THERE--!

HE CLAIMS TO BE THE PROPERTY OF SOME-ONE CALLED *OBI-WAN KENOBI.*

OBI-WAN...?! NOW *THAT'S* A NAME I HAVEN'T HEARD IN A *LONG* WHILE.

MOST *CURIOUS!*

I THINK MY *UNCLE* KNEW HIM; HE SAYS HE'S *DEAD.*

OH, HE'S *NOT* DEAD, NOT YET... NOT *YET,* HE'S *ME!*

BUT I HAVEN'T GONE BY THE NAME *OBI-WAN* SINCE BEFORE YOU WERE *BORN.*

THEN THIS DROID *DOES* BELONG TO YOU, AS IT *CLAIMS?*

CAN'T REMEMBER EVER *OWNING* A DROID.

BLEET 'N BLEET

MOST *INTERESTING!* BUT, WE'D BEST GET *INSIDE,* BEFORE THE *SANDPEOPLE* RETURN IN GREATER NUMBERS.

ALL RIGHT, BUT I-- THREE-PIO!

WHERE'S MY UNCLE'S *OTHER* DROID?

PUH-WHEET

AIDED BY THE ELECTRONIC WHISTLES AND BEEPS OF LITTLE *ARTOO,* YOUNG LUKE SWIFTLY FINDS A VERY DENTED AND TANGLED *SEE THREEPIO* LYING HALF-BURIED IN THE SAND... *ONE* ARM BROKEN OFF...!

WHERE *AM* I? OH, I'M *SORRY,* SIR...

I MUST HAVE TAKEN A *BAD* STEP.

QUICKLY, SON! THEY'RE ON THE *MOVE!*

SOON, IN BEN KENOBI'S SMALL BUT HOMEY HOVEL...

NOW, LITTLE FRIEND, LET'S SEE IF WE CAN'T FIND WHAT YOU *ARE*--

--AND WHERE YOU *CAME* FROM!

I SAW PART OF A *HOLOGRAPHIC MESSAGE* THAT HE--

I SEEM TO HAVE *FOUND* IT.

GENERAL *OBI-WAN KENOBI*-- I PRESENT MYSELF IN THE NAME OF MY FATHER, *BAIL ANTILLIES*, VICEROY OF *ALDERAAN*.

WHOEVER SHE IS-- SHE'S *TERRIFIC!*

SHE CALLED YOU-- *COMMANDER?* YOU FOUGHT IN THE *CLONE WARS?*

OH *YES*. I WAS ONCE A *JEDI KNIGHT*-- JUST LIKE YOUR *FATHER!*

JEDI KNIGHT? MY FATHER WAS JUST A *NAVIGATOR* ON A *SPICE FREIGHTER*--!

SO YOUR *UNCLE* TOLD YOU.

YEARS AGO, *COMMANDER*, YOU SERVED THE OLD REPUBLIC IN THE *CLONE WARS*; NOW, MY FATHER BEGS YOU TO AID US *AGAIN* IN OUR MOST *DESPERATE* HOUR.

INFORMATION *VITAL* TO THE SURVIVAL OF THE *REBEL ALLIANCE* HAS BEEN PLACED IN THIS *DROID*.

PLEASE SEE THIS *R2 UNIT* DELIVERED *SAFELY* TO *ALDERAAN!* YOU ARE OUR *LAST HOPE*...

MY *MISSION* TO YOU HAS *FAILED*, AND I SHALL BE *CAPTURED*.

YOUR UNCLE *OWEN* DIDN'T AGREE WITH YOUR FATHER'S *IDEALS*-- THOUGHT HE SHOULD HAVE *STAYED* HERE ON *TATOOINE*, AND NOT GOTTEN *INVOLVED*.

HE WAS ALWAYS AFRAID YOUR *FATHER'S* *ADVENTURES* MIGHT *INFLUENCE* YOU.

I WISH I'D *KNOWN* MY FATHER.

THAT *REMINDS* ME: I *HAVE* SOMETHING HERE FOR YOU.

YOUR FATHER WANTED YOU TO *HAVE* THIS-- WHEN YOU WERE *OLD* ENOUGH.

WHAT *IS* IT?

TOUCH THE *BRIGHTLY-COLORED BUTTON* UP THERE BY THE *POMMEL*-- AND YOU'LL *SEE!*

25

AT THE PRESS OF A BUTTON, A METER-LONG BEAM OF BRILLIANT, INTENSE LIGHT APPEARS...

YOUR FATHER'S *LIGHTSABRE*-- THE FORMAL WEAPON OF A *JEDI KNIGHT!*

THE JEDI KNIGHTS WERE THE *GUARDIANS* OF PEACE AND JUSTICE IN THE *OLD REPUBLIC*, AND--

HOW DID MY FATHER *DIE*, BEN?

HE WAS BETRAYED AND *MURDERED* BY A YOUNG JEDI NAMED *DARTH VADER*--

--A BOY I WAS *TRAINING*-- ONE OF MY BRIGHTEST DISCIPLES, MY GREATEST *FAILURE!*

DARTH VADER USED THE POWER OF *"THE FORCE"* FOR EVIL-- TO HELP THE *EMPIRE* HUNT DOWN AND *DESTROY* THE LAST OF THE *JEDI KNIGHTS.*

VADER WAS SEDUCED BY THE *DARK SIDE* OF *"THE FORCE"*-- AND IT *CONSUMED* HIM.

"THE FORCE"?

"THE FORCE" IS AN *ENERGY FIELD* CREATED BY *ALL LIVING THINGS;* IT SURROUNDS, BINDS THE *GALAXY* TOGETHER.

KNOWLEDGE OF *"THE FORCE"* IS WHAT GAVE A *JEDI KNIGHT* HIS POWER.

YOU MUST LEARN THE WAYS OF *"THE FORCE,"* LUKE--

--IF YOU'RE TO COME WITH ME TO *ALDERAAN!*

HUH? *ALDERAAN?*

FLIK!

I'M NOT GOING TO ALDERAAN! I'VE GOT TO GET BACK *HOME!*

I NEED YOUR *HELP*, LUKE; I'M AFRAID I'M GETTING *TOO OLD* FOR THIS SORT OF THING.

SORRY, BUT I CAN'T GET *INVOLVED!* I MEAN, I *HATE* THE *EMPIRE* AND ALL--

BUT, THERE'S NOTHING *I* CAN DO ABOUT IT; IT'S ALL SUCH A *LONG WAY* FROM HERE!

THAT'S YOUR *UNCLE* TALKING.

REMEMBER, *"THE FORCE"* IS WITH *ALL MEN,* BINDING THEM TOGETHER; THE SUFFERING OF *ONE* IS THE SUFFERING OF *ALL!*

I CAN TAKE YOU AS FAR AS *ANCHORHEAD.* YOU CAN GET *TRANSPORT* FROM THERE TO WHEREVER YOU'RE GOING.

YOU MUST DO WHAT YOU *FEEL,* LUKE.

RIGHT NOW, I DON'T FEEL *TOO GOOD!*

26

MEANWHILE, ABOARD THE EMPIRE BATTLE-STATION KNOWN AS *DEATH STAR...*

DARTH VADER!

NOW, YOUR HIGHNESS...

...WE WILL DISCUSS THE LOCATION OF THE *HIDDEN REBEL BASE.*

AS THE CELL DOOR SLIDES ELECTRONICALLY SHUT, THE *FEARFUL SCREAMS* OF PRINCESS LEIA ARE SCARCELY *HEARD* IN THE CORRIDOR OUTSIDE.

WHILE, ON *TATOOINE:*

LOOK, BEN--

THERE'S WHAT'S LEFT OF THE *JAWA SANDCRAWLER* THAT STOPPED BY UNCLE OWEN'S PLACE YESTERDAY!

ALL THE JAWAS--*DEAD!* LOOKS LIKE THE *SANDPEOPLE* DID IT, ALL RIGHT! THERE'S *BANTHA* TRACKS--AND PART OF THOSE *GAFFI* STICKS.

BUT, WE NEVER HEARD OF THEM HITTING SOMETHING THIS *BIG!*

THEY *DIDN'T,* LUKE...BUT WE WERE MEANT TO *THINK* SO.

LOOK AT THESE *BLAST POINTS!* ONLY *IMPERIAL STORMTROOPERS* ARE THIS PRECISE.

THESE ARE THE *SAME* JAWAS WHO SOLD US *ARTOO* AND *THREEPIO.*

IF THEY TRACKED THE *ROBOTS* TO THE *JAWAS,* THEY MAY HAVE LEARNED WHO THEY *SOLD* THEM TO.

AND *THAT* WILL LEAD THEM BACK--

THE TROOPERS MUST HAVE BEEN *LOOKING FOR ARTOO*--BECAUSE OF THE PRINCESS' *MESSAGE!*

--HOME!

BUT, THE NEXT MOMENT, BEN KENOBI IS LEFT *ALONE* WITH TWO SILENT *DROIDS.*

WAIT, LUKE! IT'S TOO *DANGEROUS*--!

AND, BEFORE LONG, LUKE IS RUNNING WILDLY TOWARD THE *SMOKING HOLES* THAT WERE ONCE HIS HOME...

AUNT BERU! UNCLE BEN!

NO!

THEN, HE SUDDENLY SEES TWO *SMOLDERING PILES* WHICH HAD ONCE BEEN HUMAN BEINGS...

NO!

MEANWHILE, THE GRAND MOFF TARKIN-- REGIONAL GOVERNOR OF THIS PORTION OF SPACE-- HAS JOINED *DARTH VADER* AND OTHERS BEFORE A SCREEN WHICH ILLUMINATES THE MANY-STARRED *FACE* OF THE GALAXY...

ALL SYSTEMS ARE *OPERATIONAL* AT LAST! WHAT *COURSE* SHALL WE SET, LORD VADER?

OUR SENATOR-PRINCESS' *RESISTANCE* TO THE *MIND PROBE* IS CONSIDERABLE, ADMIRAL MOTTI.

THUS, IT WILL STILL BE *SOME TIME* BEFORE WE CAN EXTRACT ANY *USEFUL INFORMATION* FROM HER.

PERHAPS PRINCESS LEIA WOULD RESPOND TO AN *ALTERNATIVE* FORM OF PERSUASION.

WHAT DO YOU *MEAN*, GOVERNOR?

I THINK IT IS TIME WE DEMONSTRATED THE *FULL POWER* OF THIS BATTLE-STATION.

SET YOUR COURSE FOR... *ALDERAAN!*

THE *BONFIRE* OF DEAD JAWAS IS STILL *BURNING* BRIGHTLY WHEN LUKE RETURNS TO BEN AND THE ROBOTS...

I *SHARE* YOUR SORROW, LUKE-- STILL, *"THE FORCE"* IS WITH YOU!

IF *YOU* HAD BEEN THERE, YOU WOULD NOW BE *DEAD*--

--AND THE *DROIDS* IN THE HANDS OF THE *EMPIRE!*

BEN-- I WANT TO GO WITH YOU TO *ALDERAAN!*

THERE'S NOTHING *HERE* FOR ME NOW.

I WANT TO LEARN THE WAYS OF *"THE FORCE"*-- TO BECOME A *JEDI*--

--LIKE MY *FATHER!*

LATER, THE SPEEDER BUMPS TO A HALT IN MOS EISLEY SPACEPORT...

WELL, HERE IT *IS*, LAD.

YOU WON'T FIND A MORE *WRETCHED* HIVE OF *VILLAINY!*

UH OH! HERE COME SOME *IMPERIAL TROOPERS...!*

YOU! HOW LONG HAVE YOU HAD THESE *DROIDS?*

Er, uh...

DO YOU COME FROM THE *SOUTH?*

LET US SEE YOUR *IDENTIFICATION!*

YES, ALL RIGHT, I --

ABRUPTLY, BEN KENOBI INTERRUPTS IN A STRANGELY CONTROLLED VOICE...

WE *DON'T* NEED TO SEE HIS IDENTIFICATION.

YOU *DON'T* NEED TO SEE HIS IDENTIFICATION.

THESE *AREN'T* THE DROIDS YOU'RE LOOKING FOR.

THESE *AREN'T* THE DROIDS WE'RE LOOKING FOR.

HE CAN GO ON ABOUT HIS *BUSINESS.*

HE CAN GO ON ABOUT HIS *BUSINESS.*

I CAN'T UNDERSTAND HOW WE GOT BY THOSE TROOPERS! I THOUGHT WE WERE *DEAD!*

"THE FORCE" IS A STRONG INFLUENCE ON THE *MIND...* A POWERFUL *ALLY...*

...THOUGH YOU WILL DISCOVER IT CAN *ALSO* BE A *DANGER.*

DO YOU REALLY THINK WE CAN FIND A *PILOT* WHO'LL TAKE US TO *ALDERAAN --* IN THIS *CANTINA?*

MOST OF THE GOOD FREIGHTER PILOTS FREQUENT HERE -- BUT WATCH YOUR *STEP.*

THIS PLACE CAN BE A LITTLE *ROUGH.*

WITHIN MOMENTS, YOUNG LUKE FINDS OUT WHAT HE MEANT...

NEGOLA DEWAGHI WOOL-DUGGER?!?

Huh--?

HE DOESN'T LIKE YOU.

I'M SORRY...

I DON'T LIKE YOU EITHER!

KATURA VESHTAT! SHADRAAK!

I'M AFRAID I STILL DON'T--

DON'T INSULT US! WE HAVE THE DEATH SENTENCE ON TWELVE SYSTEMS!

MANDYSH MAKORA!

GENTLEMEN! THIS LITTLE ONE ISN'T WORTH THE EFFORT.

COME, LET ME BUY YOU A--

NEGOLA DEWAGHI WOOL-DUGGER?!?

THLAP

UNNFF--!

THEN, AS THE BAD-TEMPERED ALIEN DRAWS A PISTOL--

--AND WHILE THE BARTENDER IS STILL YELLING "NO BLASTERS!"--

--BEN'S OWN LIGHTSABRE COMES SUDDENLY TO LIFE--

FZZT!

GNNG

--AND A WIDE-EYED LUKE SKYWALKER IS ABRUPTLY REMINDED THAT OLD BEN KENOBI WAS ONCE OBI-WAN KENOBI--

--A JEDI KNIGHT!

ONLY WHEN THE TWO AGGRESSORS LIE IN SECTIONS ON THE **FLOOR** DOES THE OLD MAN'S BODY APPEAR TO **RELAX**... OR THE SUGGESTION OF A **SIGH** ESCAPE HIM.

IN A MIXED STATE OF SHOCK AND ADMIRATION, LUKE SKY-WALKER STANDS **SPEECHLESS!**

THEN, WITH A SHUFFLING AND A MANY-TONGUED MUTTERING, THE CANTINA **RETURNS** TO ITS FORMER STATE... SAVE THAT **BEN KENOBI** IS GIVEN A RESPECT-FUL AMOUNT OF SPACE AT THE BAR.

THE WHOLE AFFAIR HAS LASTED ONLY A **FEW SECONDS.**

THEN, AS IF NOTHING HAS HAPPENED, BEN **SPEAKS**...

LUKE...

...THIS IS **CHEWBACCA.** HE'S A **WOOKIEE.**

LUKE HAS **HEARD** ABOUT WOOKIEES, BUT HE NEVER EX-PECTED TO **SEE** ONE, LET ALONE **MEET** ONE.

DESPITE A COMICAL, QUASI-MONKEY FACE, THE SEVEN-FOOT ANTHRO-POID IS ANYTHING **BUT** GENTLE-LOOKING... NOR DOES ITS DEEP-THROATED, UNINTELLIGIBLE **RESPONSE** EASE LUKE'S MIND MUCH:

GRONK

NEITHER DO BEN KENOBI'S *NEXT* WORDS:

HE'S *FIRST MATE* ON A SHIP THAT MIGHT SUIT OUR NEEDS.

THAT'S... *WONDERFUL.*

WHILE, OUTSIDE IN THE *STREET...*

WHAT COULD BE *TAKING* THEM SO LONG?

LOOK! HERE COMES A *PATRON* OF THE CANTINA!

BEEP

NOW HE'S APPROACHING THOSE TWO *IMPERIAL TROOPERS.*

I DON'T LIKE THE *LOOKS* OF THIS, ARTOO.

INSIDE, THE GIANT WOOKIEE ESCORTS BEN AND LUKE TO A *SECLUDED* CORNER...

YOU'RE PRETTY *HANDY* WITH THAT SABRE, OLD MAN.

I'M *HAN SOLO,* CAPTAIN OF THE *MILLENNIUM FALCON;* CHEWIE TELLS ME YOU'RE LOOKING FOR PASSAGE TO THE *ALDERAAN SYSTEM.*

IF IT'S A *FAST* SHIP.

FAST SHIP? YOU MEAN YOU'VE NEVER *HEARD* OF THE *MILLENIUM FALCON?*

SHOULD I?

IT'S THE SHIP THAT MADE THE *KESSEL RUN* IN LESS THAN *12 PAR-SECS!*

I'VE OUTRUN *IMPERIAL STARSHIPS* -- NOT THE *LOCAL* BULK-CRUISERS, MIND YOU-- THESE ARE THE BIG *CORELLIAN* SHIPS I'M TALKING ABOUT.

I THINK SHE'S FAST ENOUGH FOR *YOU,* OLD MAN.

WHAT'S THE *CARGO?*

JUST MYSELF, THE BOY, AND TWO *DROIDS* -- WITH *NO QUESTIONS.*

NO QUESTIONS. *LOCAL* TROUBLE?

LET'S JUST SAY WE'D LIKE TO AVOID ANY *IMPERIAL EN-TANGLEMENTS.*

THESE DAYS, THAT CAN BE A *REAL TRICK.*

TEN THOUSAND-- IN *ADVANCE.*

TEN THOUS--!? WE COULD ALMOST BUY OUR *OWN SHIP* FOR THAT!

BUT COULD YOU *FLY* IT, KID?

YOU *BET* I COULD--!

I'M NOT SUCH A *BAD PILOT* MYSELF! I DON'T--

EASY, LUKE.

WE HAVEN'T THAT MUCH *WITH US.*

BUT WE COULD PAY YOU *2000* NOW, PLUS ANOTHER *15* WHEN WE REACH *ALDERAAN.*

THAT'S *17,000.* ALL RIGHT.

DOCKING BAY *94.* WE CAN TAKE OFF AS SOON AS YOU'RE *READY.*

HMMM... LOOKS LIKE SOMEONE'S TAKING A LOOK AT YOUR *HANDICRAFT,* OLD MAN...!

MOVING TO THE BAR, THE IMPERIAL TROOPERS ASK THE NERVOUS BARTENDER A FEW BRIEF QUESTIONS...

THE BARTENDER HESITATES--BUT A MAN IN HIS POSITION CAN'T AFFORD TROUBLE WITH THE EMPIRE.

HE POINTS OUT A BOOTH NEAR THE BACK OF THE ROOM.

BUT, NO ONE IS SITTING THERE BUT A SPACE-PILOT, OBVIOUSLY ONE WHO DOES NOT POSSESS A LIGHT-SABRE...

...AND A HUGE, STOIC WOOKIEE.

THE BARTENDER SHRUGS HIS SHOULDERS.

I'M AFRAID YOU'LL HAVE TO *SELL YOUR* SPEEDER, LUKE.

IT'S ALL RIGHT. I DON'T THINK I'LL EVER *COME BACK* TO THIS PLANET, ANYWAY!

MEANWHILE, THE *IMPERIAL TROOPERS* HAVE WANDERED ON -- BUT, JUST AS HAN SOLO STARTS TO SLIDE FROM HIS *BOOTH...*

GOING SOMEWHERE, SOLO?

MATTER OF FACT, I WAS JUST GOING TO SEE YOUR *BOSS.* TELL *JABBA* I HAVE HIS *MONEY.*

THAT'S WHAT YOU SAID *YESTERDAY.* NOW IT'S *TOO LATE.*

BUT I'VE REALLY *GOT* THE MONEY THIS TIME!

THEN *HAND IT OVER.*

I HAVEN'T GOT IT *ON ME.*

YOU TELL *JABBA* --

OVER *MY DEAD BODY!*

YOU TELL *JABBA* --

JABBA WOULD RATHER HAVE YOUR *SHIP,* I THINK.

THAT'S THE *IDEA,* SOLO.

NOW, WILL YOU COME *OUTSIDE* WITH ME, OR MUST I FINISH IT H--

SORRY FOR THE *MESS.*

AS, IN A SLEAZY **USED-SPEEDER** LOT...

...HE SAYS THAT PRICE IS THE BEST HE CAN **DO**.

SINCE THE **XP·38** CAME OUT, THIS KIND JUST ISN'T IN **DEMAND**.

IT WILL BE **SUFFICIENT**...

I HAVE ENOUGH TO COVER THE REST. **COME**, LAD.

BEN AND LUKE DO NOT **SEE** THE DARKLY-CLAD CREATURE WHICH MOVES OUT OF THE **SHADOWS** AS THEY PASS...

...AND **WATCHES** THEM INTENTLY AS THEY DISAPPEAR DOWN STILL ANOTHER **ALLEYWAY**.

AT THAT MOMENT, AT **DOCKING BAY 94**...

COME ON OUT, SOLO!

I'VE BEEN **WAITING** FOR YOU, JABBA.

HAN, MY BOY-- THERE ARE TIMES WHEN YOU **DIS-APPOINT** ME.

WHY HAVEN'T YOU **PAID** ME?

AND WHY DID YOU HAVE TO FRY POOR **GREEDO** LIKE THAT-- AFTER ALL WE'VE **BEEN** THRU TOGETHER?

JABBA, THE **NEXT** TIME YOU'VE GOT SOMETHING TO SAY TO ME, DON'T SEND ONE OF YOUR BLASTER-HAPPY **TWERPS**.

COME SEE ME **YOURSELF**.

HAN, *HAN!* IF ONLY YOU HADN'T DUMPED THAT SHIPMENT OF *SPICE!*

WHERE WOULD I BE IF *EVERY* PILOT WHO SMUGGLES FOR ME DUMPED HIS SHIPMENT AT THE FIRST SIGN OF AN *IMPERIAL STARSHIP?*

IT'S NOT GOOD *BUSINESS.*

YOU KNOW, EVEN *I* GET BOARDED *SOME-TIMES,* JABBA; I HAD *NO CHOICE.*

BUT, I'VE GOT A *CHARTER* NOW, AND CAN PAY YOU BACK --PLUS A LITTLE *EXTRA.*

I JUST NEED SOME MORE *TIME.*

PUT YOUR *BLASTERS* AWAY, MEN!

HAN, MY BOY, I'M ONLY DOING THIS BECAUSE YOU'RE THE *BEST,* AND I NEED YOU.

BUT, IF YOU *DISAPPOINT* ME *AGAIN,* I'LL PUT A *PRICE* ON YOUR HEAD SO *LARGE* --

--THAT YOU WON'T BE ABLE TO GO NEAR A *CIVILIZED SYSTEM* AGAIN FOR THE REST OF YOUR *LIFE!*

I'LL PAY YOU, JABBA, BUT *NOT* BECAUSE YOU *THREATEN* ME.

I'LL PAY YOU BECAUSE... IT'S *MY PLEASURE.*

WHILE, ON THE OMINOUS *DEATH STAR...*

WE'VE STARTED TO *SEARCH* THE MOS EISLEY SPACEPORT, LORD VADER..

IT'S JUST A MATTER OF *TIME* BEFORE WE FIND THE *DROIDS!*

SEND IN *MORE* MEN IF YOU HAVE TO!

IT'S HER HOPE OF THAT *DATA* BEING USED AGAINST US THAT ENABLES PRINCESS LEIA TO *RESIST* THE MIND PROBE.

WHEN SHE KNOWS IT HAS BEEN *DE-STROYED,* ONCE AND FOR ALL--SHE WILL *BREAK!*

AT THIS VERY MOMENT, BACK ON TATOOINE, YOUNG **LUKE SKYWALKER** IS VOICING HIS FIRST OPINION OF THE **MILLENNIUM FALCON**...

WHAT A PIECE OF *JUNK*!

THIS SHIP COULDN'T *POSSIBLY* GO ABOVE SUB-LIGHT SPEEDS!

SHE MAY NOT *LOOK* LIKE MUCH, BUT SHE'S GOT IT WHERE IT *COUNTS*...

I'VE ADDED SOME *SPECIAL MODIFICATIONS* MYSELF.

SHE'LL MAKE *POINT FIVE* BEYOND LIGHT SPEED, AND--

Uh oh! WE'RE A LITTLE *RUSHED*--

ZZZAP

SO, IF YOU FOLKS DON'T MIND *HURRYING ABOARD*--

ZZRRAK!

FTIK

FTIK

--WE'LL BE *OFF*!

GET US *OUT* OF HERE!

CHEWIE!

DEFLECTOR SHIELD, QUICK!

GRUNK

ALMOST THE NEXT MOMENT, THE MOTLEY **DENIZENS** OF MOS EISLEY LOOK UP, AND **MURMUR** AMONG THEMSELVES IN A MULTITUDE OF INHUMAN LANGUAGES.

IT WOULD APPEAR THE **MILLENNIUM FALCON** IS OFF FOR **ANOTHER RUN.**

YET, ALMOST AS QUICKLY AS THEY CAN BE NOTICED ON SOLO'S RADAR-SCOPE, A TRIO OF **IMPERIAL STARDESTROYERS** APPEAR, AS IF FROM **NOWHERE...**

OUR **PASSENGERS** MUST BE HOTTER THAN I **THOUGHT,** CHEWIE!

--**GIANT** STARSHIPS WHICH, THOUGH STILL FAR IN THE DISTANCE, ARE FULLY **100 TIMES** THE SIZE OF THE FLEEING FALCON--

--WITH A **FIREPOWER** WHICH DWARFS THE SMALLER SHIP'S NEARLY TO THE POINT OF THE **INFINITESIMAL!**

STAY **SHARP!**

TWO OF THEM ARE TRYING TO **CUT US OFF.**

KRONK

CAN'T YOU **OUTRUN** THEM? I THOUGHT YOU SAID THIS THING WAS **FAST!**

WATCH YOUR **MOUTH,** KID, OR YOU'LL FIND YOURSELF **FLOATING** HOME.

WE'LL BE **SAFE** ENOUGH, ONCE WE'VE MADE THE JUMP INTO **HYPERSPACE.**

PLUS, I KNOW A FEW **MANEUVERS** THAT SHOULD LOSE THEM...!

JUST THEN, THE ENTIRE SPACECRAFT SHUDDERS-- AS A BLINDING EXPLO-SION FLASHES JUST OUTSIDE THE VIEWPORTS--

--AND EVEN A NEAR MISS ALMOST OVERCOMES THE PHOTOTROPHIC SHIELDING!

HERE'S WHERE IT STARTS GETTING INTERESTING!

WELL? HOW LONG BEFORE YOU CAN MAKE THE JUMP TO LIGHT SPEED?

IT'LL TAKE A FEW MINUTES FOR THE NAVI-COMPUTER TO CALCULATE THE COORDINATES.

A FEW MINUTES!? AT THE RATE THEY'RE GAINING--

TRAVELING THRU HYPER-SPACE ISN'T LIKE DUSTING CROPS, BOY!

WITHOUT THE PROPER CALCULATIONS, WE COULD PASS RIGHT THROUGH A STAR, OR BOUNCE TOO NEAR A SUPERNOVA...

... AND THAT WOULD END OUR LITTLE TRIP-- REAL QUICK!

WHAT'S THAT?

WE'RE LOSING A DEFLECTOR SHIELD!

STRAP YOUR-SELVES IN!

WE'RE READY TO MAKE THE JUMP TO LIGHT SPEED!

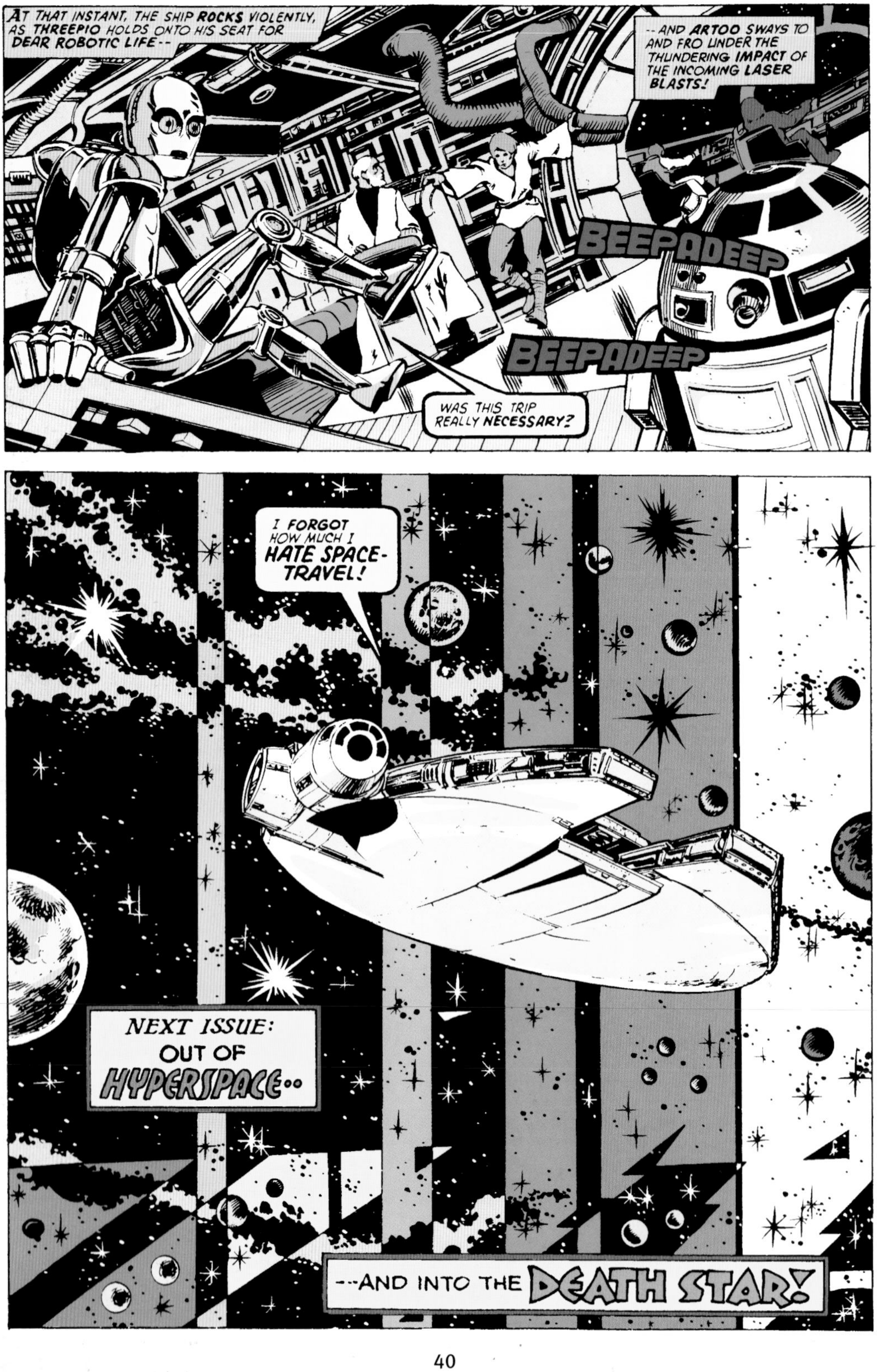
AT THAT INSTANT, THE SHIP ROCKS VIOLENTLY, AS THREEPIO HOLDS ONTO HIS SEAT FOR DEAR ROBOTIC LIFE--
--AND ARTOO SWAYS TO AND FRO UNDER THE THUNDERING IMPACT OF THE INCOMING LASER BLASTS!
BEEPADEEP
BEEPADEEP
WAS THIS TRIP REALLY NECESSARY?
I FORGOT HOW MUCH I HATE SPACE-TRAVEL!
NEXT ISSUE: OUT OF HYPERSPACE..
--AND INTO THE DEATH STAR!

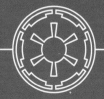

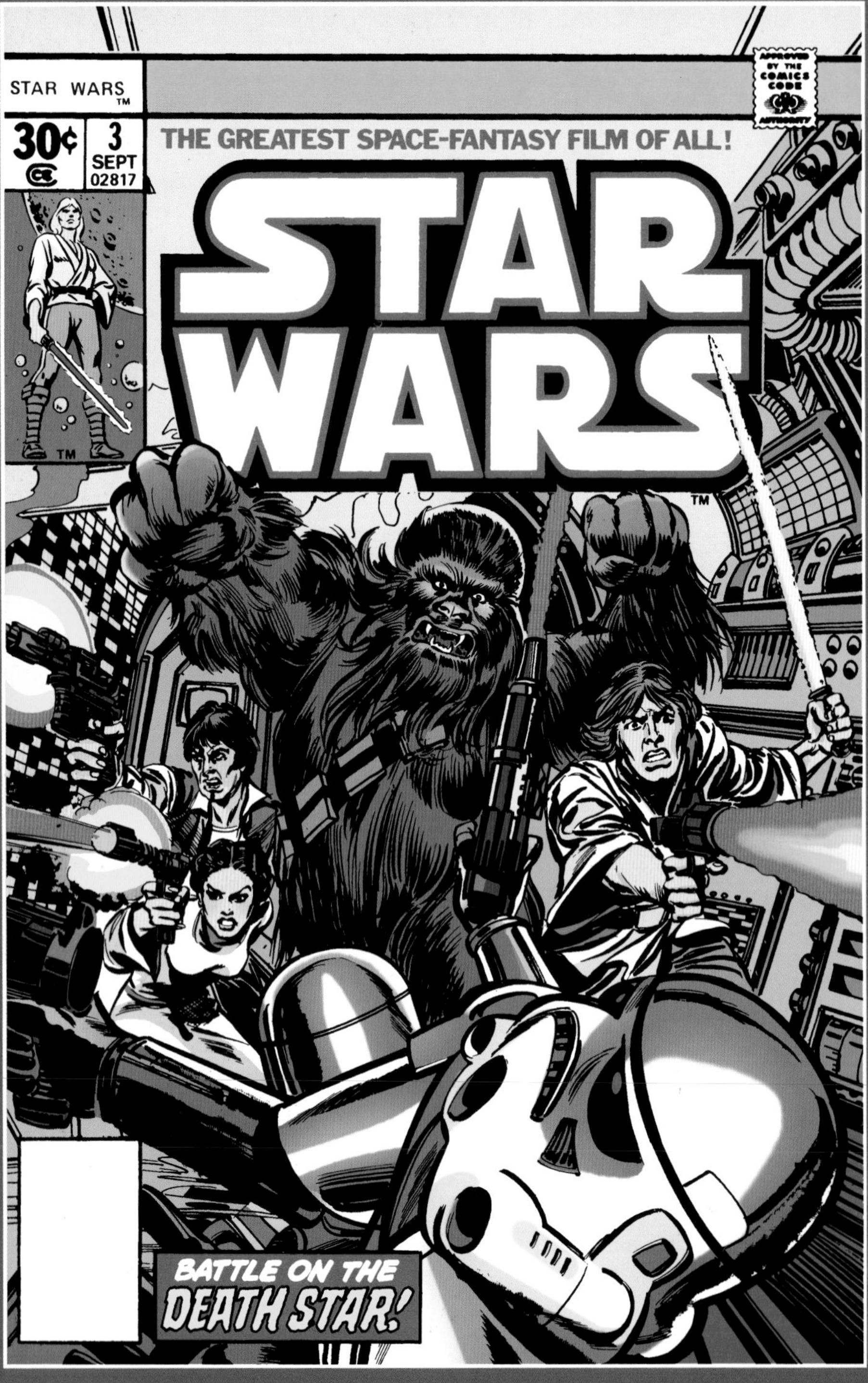

STAR WARS TM
30¢
3 SEPT 02817
APPROVED BY THE COMICS CODE AUTHORITY
THE GREATEST SPACE-FANTASY FILM OF ALL!
STAR WARS TM
BATTLE ON THE DEATH STAR!

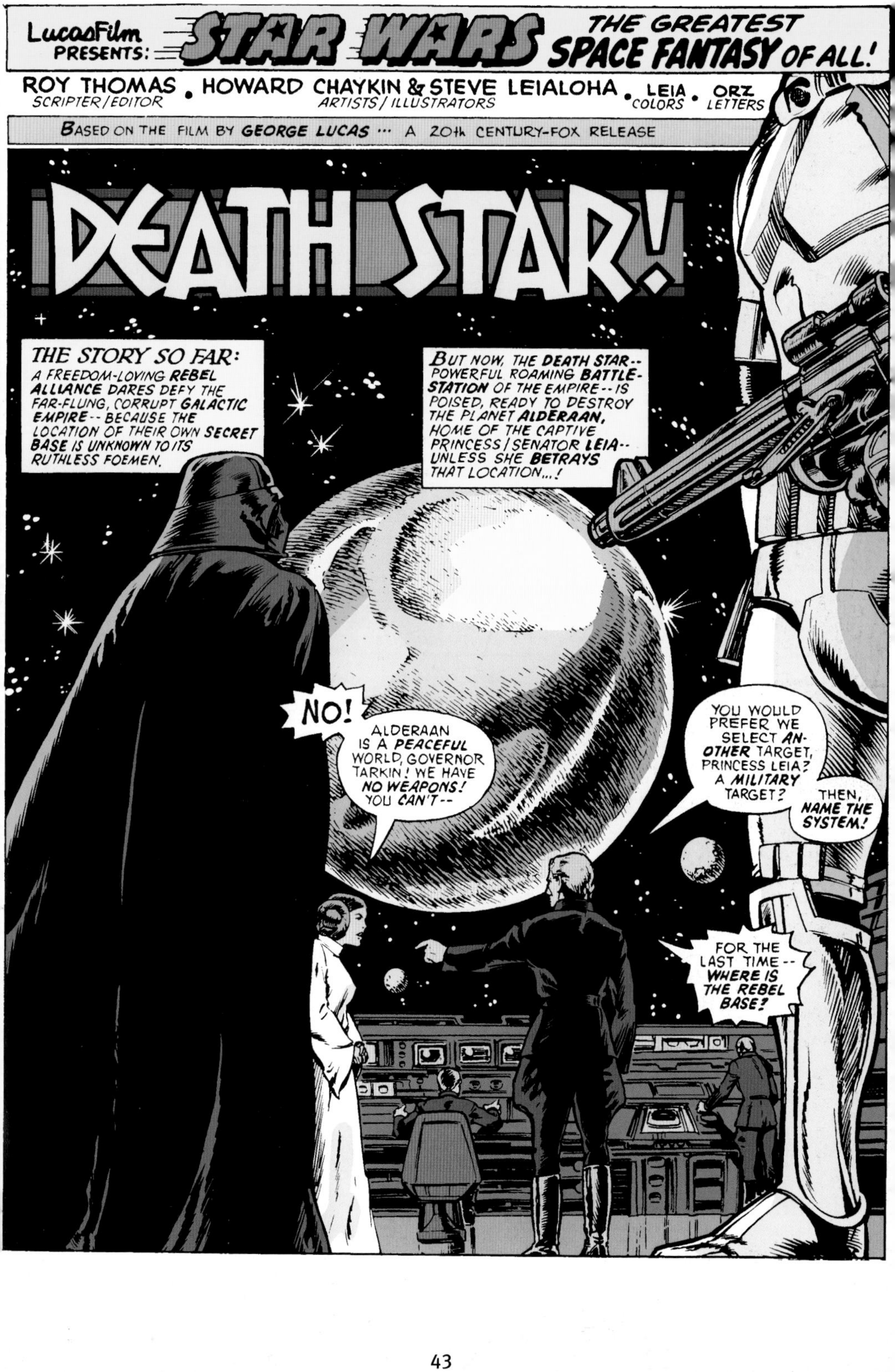
LucasFilm PRESENTS: STAR WARS THE GREATEST SPACE FANTASY OF ALL!
ROY THOMAS SCRIPTER/EDITOR • HOWARD CHAYKIN & STEVE LEIALOHA ARTISTS/ILLUSTRATORS • LEIA COLORS • ORZ LETTERS
BASED ON THE FILM BY GEORGE LUCAS ... A 20th CENTURY-FOX RELEASE
DEATH STAR!
THE STORY SO FAR: A FREEDOM-LOVING REBEL ALLIANCE DARES DEFY THE FAR-FLUNG, CORRUPT GALACTIC EMPIRE -- BECAUSE THE LOCATION OF THEIR OWN SECRET BASE IS UNKNOWN TO ITS RUTHLESS FOEMEN.
BUT NOW, THE DEATH STAR -- POWERFUL ROAMING BATTLE-STATION OF THE EMPIRE -- IS POISED, READY TO DESTROY THE PLANET ALDERAAN, HOME OF THE CAPTIVE PRINCESS/SENATOR LEIA -- UNLESS SHE BETRAYS THAT LOCATION...!
NO!
ALDERAAN IS A PEACEFUL WORLD, GOVERNOR TARKIN! WE HAVE NO WEAPONS! YOU CAN'T --
YOU WOULD PREFER WE SELECT ANOTHER TARGET, PRINCESS LEIA? A MILITARY TARGET?
THEN, NAME THE SYSTEM!
FOR THE LAST TIME -- WHERE IS THE REBEL BASE?

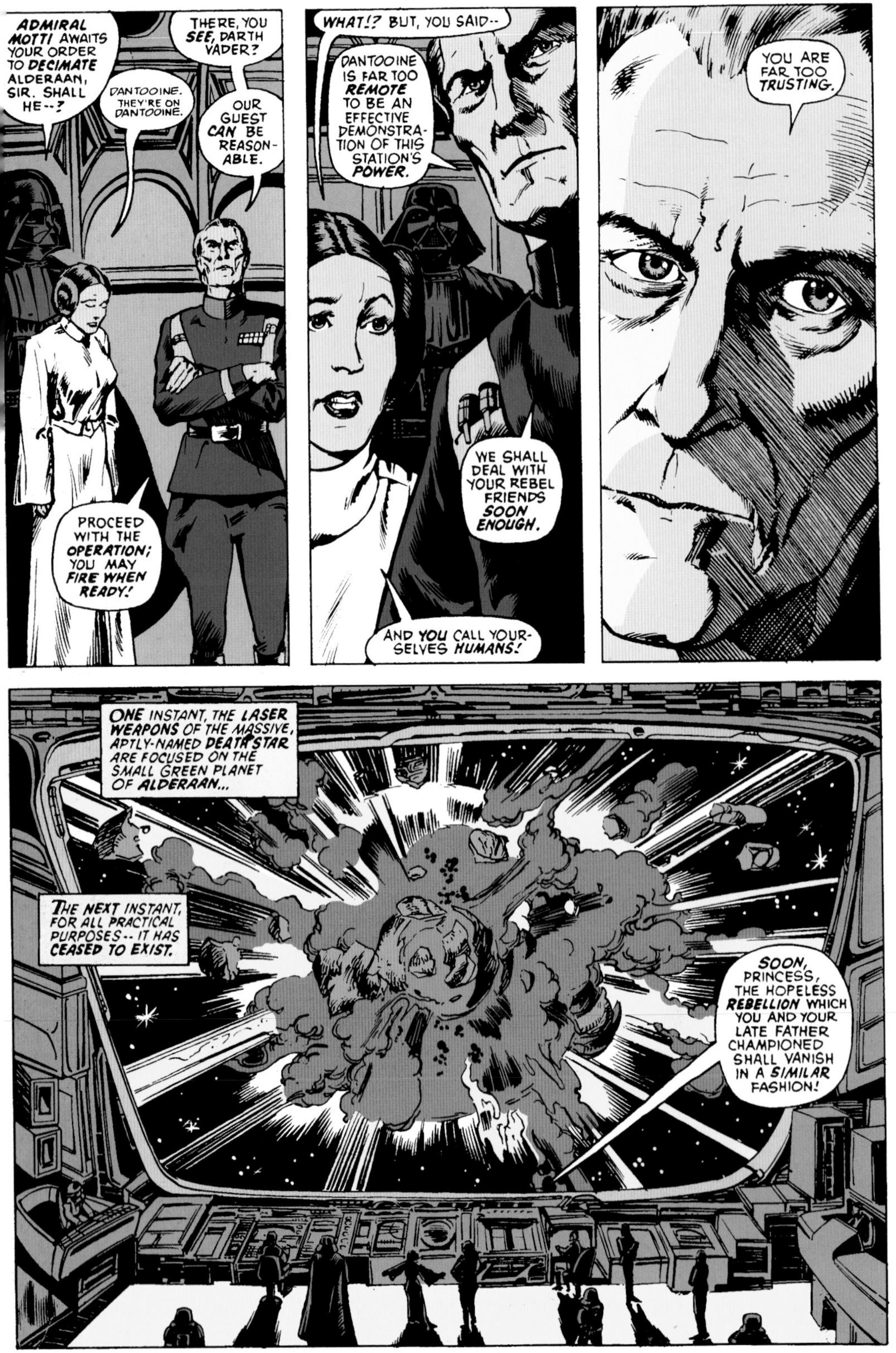
ADMIRAL MOTTI AWAITS YOUR ORDER TO DECIMATE ALDERAAN, SIR. SHALL HE--?
DANTOOINE. THEY'RE ON DANTOOINE.
THERE, YOU SEE, DARTH VADER?
OUR GUEST CAN BE REASONABLE.
PROCEED WITH THE OPERATION; YOU MAY FIRE WHEN READY!
WHAT!? BUT, YOU SAID--
DANTOOINE IS FAR TOO REMOTE TO BE AN EFFECTIVE DEMONSTRATION OF THIS STATION'S POWER.
WE SHALL DEAL WITH YOUR REBEL FRIENDS SOON ENOUGH.
AND YOU CALL YOURSELVES HUMANS!
YOU ARE FAR TOO TRUSTING.
ONE INSTANT, THE LASER WEAPONS OF THE MASSIVE, APTLY-NAMED DEATH STAR ARE FOCUSED ON THE SMALL GREEN PLANET OF ALDERAAN...
THE NEXT INSTANT, FOR ALL PRACTICAL PURPOSES-- IT HAS CEASED TO EXIST.
SOON, PRINCESS, THE HOPELESS REBELLION WHICH YOU AND YOUR LATE FATHER CHAMPIONED SHALL VANISH IN A SIMILAR FASHION!

AND, AT THAT SELFSAME MOMENT, DEEP IN HYPERSPACE...

UNNHH--!

BEN KENOBI-- ARE YOU **ALL RIGHT?**

WHAT'S **WRONG?** YOU LOOK **FAINT!**

I FELT--A SUDDEN GREAT **EBBING** IN "**THE FORCE**," LUKE.

"**THE FORCE**"? YOU MEAN, THAT THING YOU **TALKED** ABOUT--THE **ENERGY** THAT'S GIVEN OUT BY **ALL LIVING THINGS?**

YES. IT WAS LIKE THE **CRY** OF A **BILLION BEINGS**--STOPPING ALL AT ONCE!

IT WAS THE FEELING OF... **DEATH.**

WELL, YOU CAN ALL **STOP WORRYING** ABOUT THOSE **IMPERIAL STARSHIPS** THAT WERE PURSUING US; I **TOLD** YOU WE'D LOSE 'EM. I--

DON'T EVERY-BODY THANK ME AT **ONCE!**

ANYWAY, I **CALCULATE** OUR ARRIVAL ON **ALDERAAN** AT 0200.

HOW'S THE **GAME** COMING, THREEPIO?

OH, ARTOO IS BEATING YOUR MAN **CHEWBACCA** HANDILY, MASTER **SOLO.**

R2 UNITS EXCEL AT GAMES OF MATHEMATI-CAL SKILL, YOU KNOW; HE'S JUST MADE A **MOVE** THAT--

BEEP BEEP

GUH-RUNK! GUH-RONK!

NOW, *NOW!* ARTOO MADE A FAIR MOVE, AND SCREAMING ABOUT IT CAN'T *HELP* YOU.

LET HIM *HAVE* IT! IT'S NOT WISE TO UPSET A *WOOKIEE* LIKE CHEWBACCA!

BUT, SIR, NO ONE WORRIES ABOUT UPSETTING A *DROID!*

THAT'S BECAUSE A *DROID* DOESN'T RIP PEOPLE'S *ARMS* OUT OF THEIR SOCKETS WHEN THEY *LOSE.*

WOOKIEES HAVE BEEN KNOWN TO *DO* THAT.

I SEE YOUR POINT, SIR.

I SUGGEST A NEW STRATEGY, ARTOO. LET... THE WOOKIEE... WIN!

BOOP

MEANWHILE, YOUNG LUKE SKYWALKER IS OTHERWISE OCCUPIED...

YOU'D BEST CONTINUE YOUR EXERCISES, LAD.

YES, BEN KENOBI!

READY LIGHT-SABRE!

LIGHT-SABRE READY!

THEN HERE COMES THE *"REMOTE"!*

WATCH OUT FOR ITS *SENSORS,* LAD! THEY'LL--

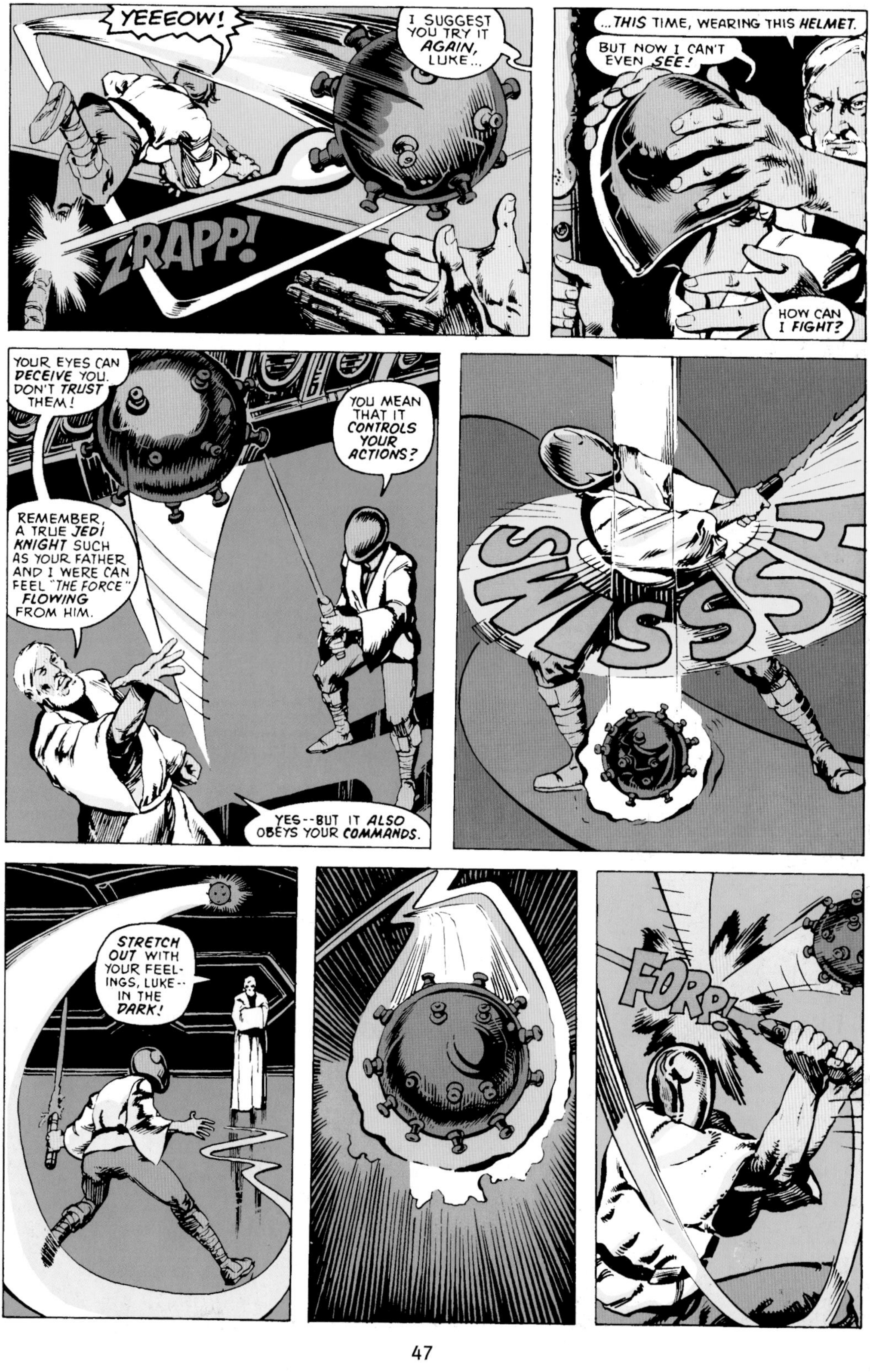
YEEEOW!
I SUGGEST YOU TRY IT AGAIN, LUKE...
ZRAPP!
...THIS TIME, WEARING THIS HELMET.
BUT NOW I CAN'T EVEN SEE!
HOW CAN I FIGHT?
YOUR EYES CAN DECEIVE YOU. DON'T TRUST THEM!
YOU MEAN THAT IT CONTROLS YOUR ACTIONS?
REMEMBER, A TRUE JEDI KNIGHT SUCH AS YOUR FATHER AND I WERE CAN FEEL "THE FORCE" FLOWING FROM HIM.
YES--BUT IT ALSO OBEYS YOUR COMMANDS.
SWISSSH
STRETCH OUT WITH YOUR FEEL-INGS, LUKE-- IN THE DARK!
FORP!

YOU *SEE?* YOU *CAN* DO IT!

HOCUS-POCUS *RELIGIONS* AND ANCIENT *WEAPONS* ARE NO SUBSTITUTE FOR A GOOD *BLASTER* AT YOUR SIDE, KID.

IGNORE HIM, LUKE. HE DOESN'T *BELIEVE* IN "THE FORCE."

MAYBE *NOT,* OLD MAN--

I-- I *DID* FEEL SOMETHING, BEN! I COULD ALMOST *SEE* THE "REMOTE."

BUT I *DO* BELIEVE WE'RE SLOWING DOWN TO *SUB-LIGHT* SPEED.

NEXT STOP, *ALDERAAN!* WE--

WHAT THE--! WE'VE COME OUT OF HYPER-SPACE INTO A *METEOR STORM*-- OR SOME KIND OF *ASTEROID* COLLISION!

OUR *POSITION'S* CORRECT-- ONLY THERE'S *NO ALDERAAN!*

WHAT ARE YOU *TALKING* ABOUT, SOLO? WHERE *IS* IT?

THAT'S WHAT I *AM* TALKING ABOUT, YOUNG-STER-- IT'S *NOT THERE!*

ALDERAAN'S BEEN *BLOWN AWAY*-- TOTALLY!

WAIT-- THERE GOES ONE OF THE IMPERIAL *TIE FIGHTERS*-- BUT WHERE'D IT COME FROM?

THERE ARE *NO* IMPERIAL BASES NEAR HERE!

MAYBE IT *FOLLOWED* US-- THRU *HYPER-SPACE!?*

NO, LUKE. IT'S A SHORT-RANGE FIGHTER.

BUT, IF IT *IDENTIFIES* US-- TELLS OTHERS WE'RE HERE--

NOT IF *I* CAN HELP IT!

CHEWIE-- JAM ITS *TRANSMISSION!*

IT WOULD BE BEST TO LET IT *GO.* IT'S TOO FAR OUT OF *RANGE.*

NOT FOR *LONG!*

HE'S HEADING FOR THAT *SMALL MOON*-- BUT WE'RE *GAINING* ON HIM!

THAT'S NO *MOON*, MR. SOLO. IT'S A *SPACE STATION*.

YOU'RE *CRAZY!* IT'S WAY *TOO BIG* TO BE A--

HOLY--!

I'VE GOT A *BAD FEELING* ABOUT THIS.

YOU'RE RIGHT *THERE*, THREEPIO! *FULL REVERSE*, CHEWIE!

WHY ARE WE STILL MOVING *TOWARD* IT?

CHREE CHREE

LOCK IN THE *AUXILIARY POWER!*

WE'RE CAUGHT IN A *TRACTOR BEAM!* IT'S *DRAGGING US IN!*

YOU MEAN THERE'S *NOTHING* WE CAN--?

BUT--WOULD YOU *LOOK* AT IT, KID--?

I'M *FULL POWER!* IT'S *NO USE*. I'M GOING TO HAVE TO *SHUT DOWN!*

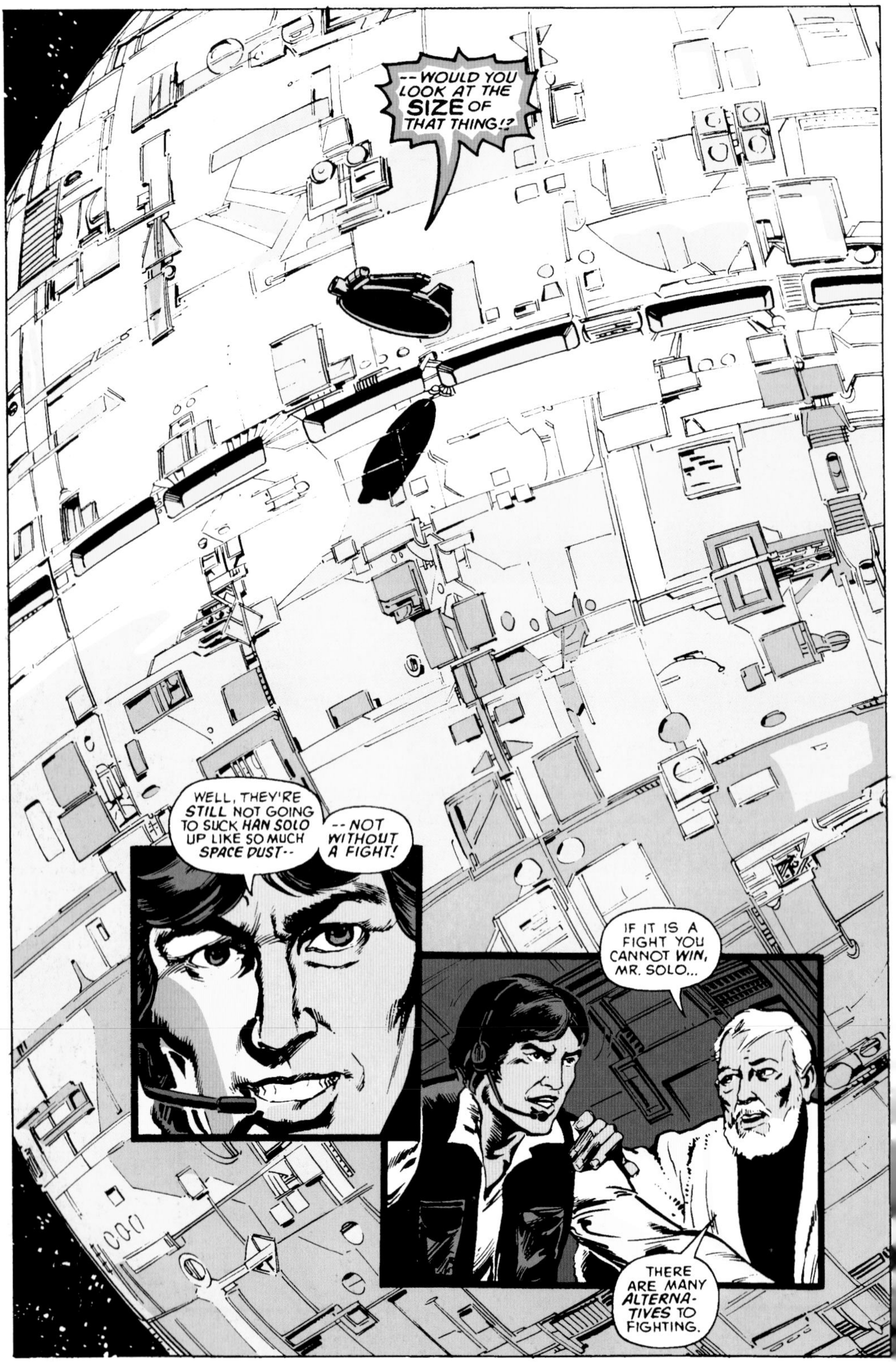
--WOULD YOU LOOK AT THE SIZE OF THAT THING!?
WELL, THEY'RE STILL NOT GOING TO SUCK HAN SOLO UP LIKE SO MUCH SPACE DUST--
--NOT WITHOUT A FIGHT!
IF IT IS A FIGHT YOU CANNOT WIN, MR. SOLO...
THERE ARE MANY ALTERNA-TIVES TO FIGHTING.

AT THAT PRECISE MOMENT, INSIDE THE HUGE STATION...

THE SCOUT SHIPS TO DANTOOINE HAVE FOUND THE REMAINS OF A REBEL BASE, GOVERNOR--AND LORD VADER.

SHE LIED. SHE LIED TO US!

BUT, THEY ESTIMATE IT HAS BEEN DESERTED FOR SOME TIME.

I TOLD YOU SHE WOULD NEVER CONSCIOUSLY BETRAY THE REBELLION--

--UNLESS SHE THOUGHT SHE COULD DESTROY THIS STATION IN THE PROCESS!

TERMINATE HER--IMMEDIATELY!

AND LOSE YOUR ONLY LINK TO THE REBEL BASE?

SHE CAN STILL BE OF VALUE TO US.

I'LL FIND THAT HIDDEN FORTRESS--IF I HAVE TO DESTROY EVERY STAR SYSTEM IN THIS SECTOR!

NO DOUBT, GOVERNOR TARKIN...

...BUT, IN THE MEANTIME, I'VE RECEIVED A REPORT THAT WE HAVE CAPTURED THE SAME CORELLIAN FREIGHTER WHICH BLASTED ITS WAY OUT OF THE QUARANTINE ON MOS EISLEY.

THEY MUST HAVE BEEN TRYING TO RETURN THE STOLEN DATA TAPES TO THE PRINCESS.*

WE MIGHT BE OF SOME HELP THERE...!

* SEE LAST ISSUE. --ROY.

SOON, IN A SPRAWLING HANG-BAY OF THE GREAT DEATH STAR...

NO ONE ABOARD, LORD VADER!

SHIP'S LOG SAYS THE CREW ABANDONED SHIP RIGHT AFTER TAKEOFF.

NO DROIDS ON BOARD, EITHER.

KEEP CHECKING! I SENSE SOMETHING--A PRESENCE, SUCH AS I HAVEN'T FELT SINCE--

HALTING IN MID-SENTENCE, DARTH VADER TURNS QUICKLY--AND EXITS.

AS, INSIDE THE CAPTIVE SHIP...

WHEW! NEVER THOUGHT I'D USE THESE COMPARTMENTS FOR SMUGGLING MYSELF!

THIS WON'T WORK, THOUGH--WE'LL NEVER GET PAST THAT TRACTOR BEAM!

YOU LEAVE THAT TO ME.

YOU'RE A DAMN FOOL!

WHO IS MORE FOOLISH--THE FOOL, OR THE MAN WHO FOLLOWS HIM?

EVEN CRACK IMPERIAL TROOPERS -- THOSE CRUEL, MURDEROUS GUARDIANS OF A FAR-FLUNG GALACTIC EMPIRE -- CANNOT THOROUGHLY SEARCH A WHOLE *FREIGHTER* WITHOUT THE PROPER *SCANNING* EQUIPMENT.

BUT, WHEN A PAIR OF THE ARMORED SOLDIERS CARRY THE HUGE SENSORY APPARATUS *ONTO* THE CAPTURED CORELLIAN SHIP...

...THEY HAVE AN UNEXPECTED *WELCOMING PARTY!*

SHH! HERE THEY COME!

MOMENTS LATER, HIS VISI-SCREEN SHOWING NO GUARDS ON DUTY, A *GANTRY OFFICER* GETS WORRIED...

TX-421! WHY AREN'T YOU AT YOUR POST?

TX-421, DO YOU COPY?

JUST THEN, ONE TROOPER REAPPEARS.

THE MEANING OF HIS HAND SIGNAL IS CLEAR:

TAKE OVER HERE! OBVIOUSLY, WE'VE GOT ANOTHER *BAD* TRANSMITTER.

I'M GOING *DOWN* TO SEE--

--WHAT I CAN -- YYIIII!

THLAP!

NRRLK!

GAROOO!

ZZIK!

WHUMP!

EVEN AS THE TOWERING **CHEWBACCA** FLATTENS THE STARTLED OFFICER WITH A SINGLE BLOW, ANOTHER "*IMPERIAL TROOPER*" APPEARS AT THE DOORWAY...

--TO **BLAST** THE ONE WITHIN, BEFORE HE CAN REACH HIS OWN WEAPON!

BETWEEN HIS *HOWLING* AND YOU *BLASTING* EVERYTHING IN SIGHT, SOLO, IT'S A WONDER THE *ENTIRE* STATION DOESN'T KNOW WE'RE HERE!

LET 'EM *COME!* I DON'T LIKE ALL THIS *SNEAKING* AROUND.

THREEPIO-- PLUG IN THE *R2 UNIT!* HE SHOULD BE ABLE TO READ THE ENTIRE *IMPERIAL COMPUTER NETWORK.*

PLUGGED IN, SIR.

THE TRACTOR BEAM IS COUPLED TO THE MAIN REACTOR IN *SEVEN* LOCATIONS...

WHOOP. BOOP. R-BEEP

MOST OF THE DATA IS *RESTRICTED*, SIR...

BUT HE'LL TRY TO GET WHAT THERE IS TO COME THROUGH ON THE MONITOR.

WITH THE TRACTOR BEAM *OFF*, WE CAN *ZOOM OUT* OF HERE.

WE'RE *WITH* YOU, BEN!

NO, LUKE. I DON'T THINK THERE IS ANY WAY YOU BOYS CAN *HELP* IN THIS.

I MUST GO *ALONE*.

53

WHATEVER YOU *SAY!* I'VE ALREADY DONE MORE THAN *I BARGAINED* FOR ON THIS TRIP!

BEN-- I WANT TO GO *WITH* YOU!

BUT, I THINK PUTTING THAT *TRACTOR BEAM* OUT OF COMMISSION IS GOING TO TAKE MORE THAN YOUR *MAGIC,* OLD MAN.

YOUR DESTINY LIES ALONG A *DIFFERENT* PATH: DELIVER THE *DROIDS* TO THE *REBEL* FORCES.

TRUST YOUR *FEELINGS,* LUKE.

"THE FORCE" IS WITH YOU!

HE'S GONE! I--HEY! WHAT'S WITH ARTOO?

I'M NOT SURE, SIR. HE KEEPS REPEATING: "SHE'S HERE!"

PUH-WHEET! PUH-WHEET! PUH-WHEET!

HE MUST MEAN--THE *PRINCESS!*

AFTER ALL, *SHE'S* THE ONE WHO PUT THAT *HOLOGRAPHIC MESSAGE* INTO HIM BEFORE!*

WE'VE GOT TO *FIND* HER!

*ISSUE #1.--RT.

HOLD IT! PRINCESS? *WHAT* PRINCESS?

THE PRINCESS LEIA, SIR. WE MUST GO RESCUE HER.

I'M NOT GOING ANY-WHERE!

PUH-WHEET! PUH-WHEET!

BUT, I'VE *SEEN* HER, SOLO! SHE'S *BEAUTIFUL!*

SO'S *LIFE.*

SHE'S *RICH!*

SO'S-- HUH? *RICH?*

YES-- AND IF WE *RESCUE* HER, THE *REWARD'LL* BE MORE WEALTH THAN YOU CAN *IMAGINE!*

I DON'T *KNOW!* I CAN IMAGINE QUITE A BIT.

YOU'LL *GET* IT!

WHAT DO *YOU* THINK, CHEWIE?

HNNH!

PUH-WHEET!

ALL RIGHT, KID, BUT YOU'D BETTER BE *RIGHT* ABOUT THIS!

WHAT'S YOUR *PLAN?*

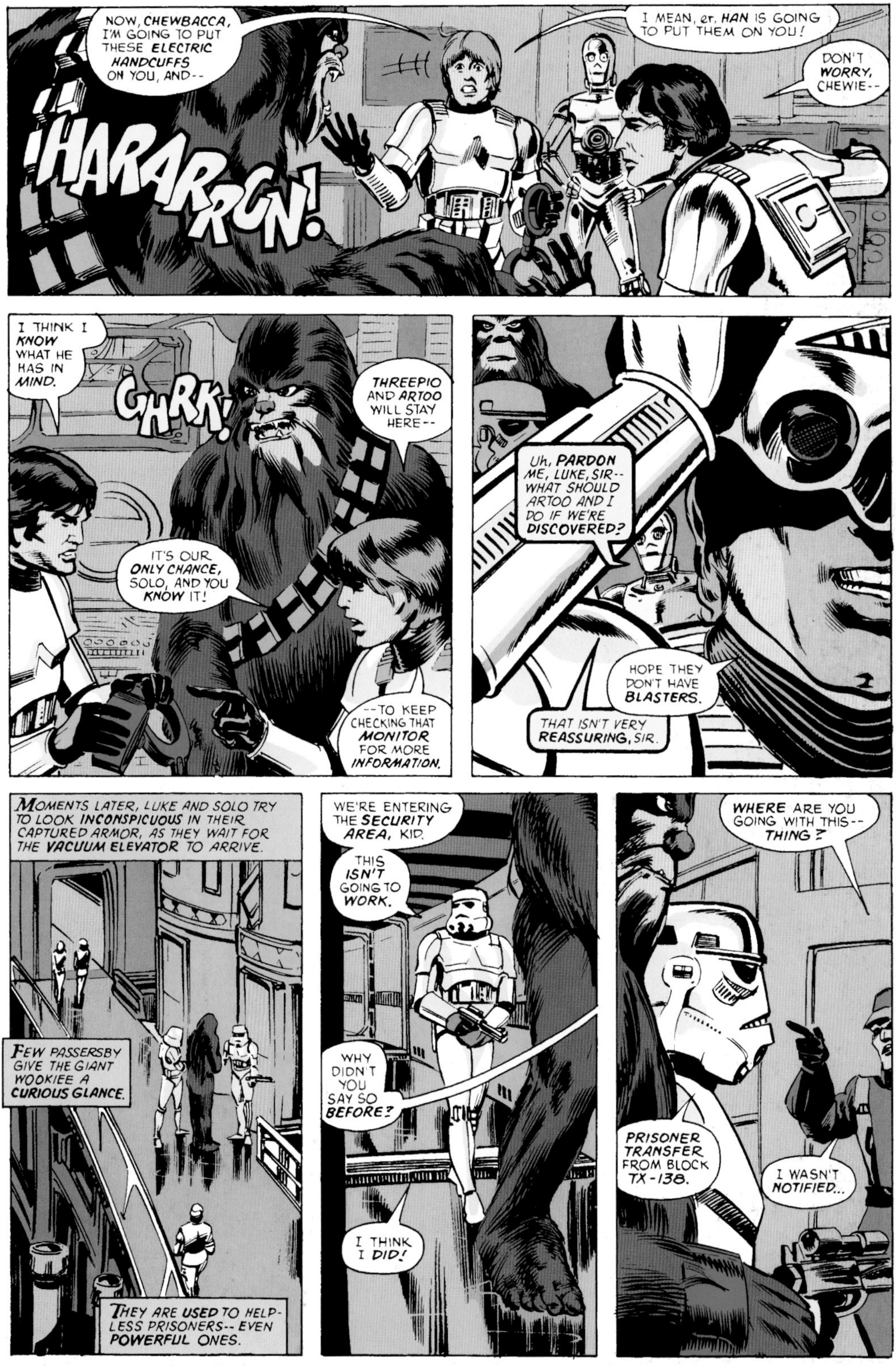

NOW, CHEWBACCA, I'M GOING TO PUT THESE ELECTRIC HANDCUFFS ON YOU, AND--
I MEAN, er, HAN IS GOING TO PUT THEM ON YOU!
DON'T WORRY, CHEWIE--
HARARRRGN!
I THINK I KNOW WHAT HE HAS IN MIND.
GHRK!
THREEPIO AND ARTOO WILL STAY HERE--
IT'S OUR ONLY CHANCE, SOLO, AND YOU KNOW IT!
--TO KEEP CHECKING THAT MONITOR FOR MORE INFORMATION.
Uh, PARDON ME, LUKE, SIR-- WHAT SHOULD ARTOO AND I DO IF WE'RE DISCOVERED?
HOPE THEY DON'T HAVE BLASTERS.
THAT ISN'T VERY REASSURING, SIR.
MOMENTS LATER, LUKE AND SOLO TRY TO LOOK INCONSPICUOUS IN THEIR CAPTURED ARMOR, AS THEY WAIT FOR THE VACUUM ELEVATOR TO ARRIVE.
FEW PASSERSBY GIVE THE GIANT WOOKIEE A CURIOUS GLANCE.
THEY ARE USED TO HELPLESS PRISONERS-- EVEN POWERFUL ONES.
WE'RE ENTERING THE SECURITY AREA, KID.
THIS ISN'T GOING TO WORK.
WHY DIDN'T YOU SAY SO BEFORE?
I THINK I DID!
WHERE ARE YOU GOING WITH THIS-- THING?
PRISONER TRANSFER FROM BLOCK TX-138.
I WASN'T NOTIFIED...

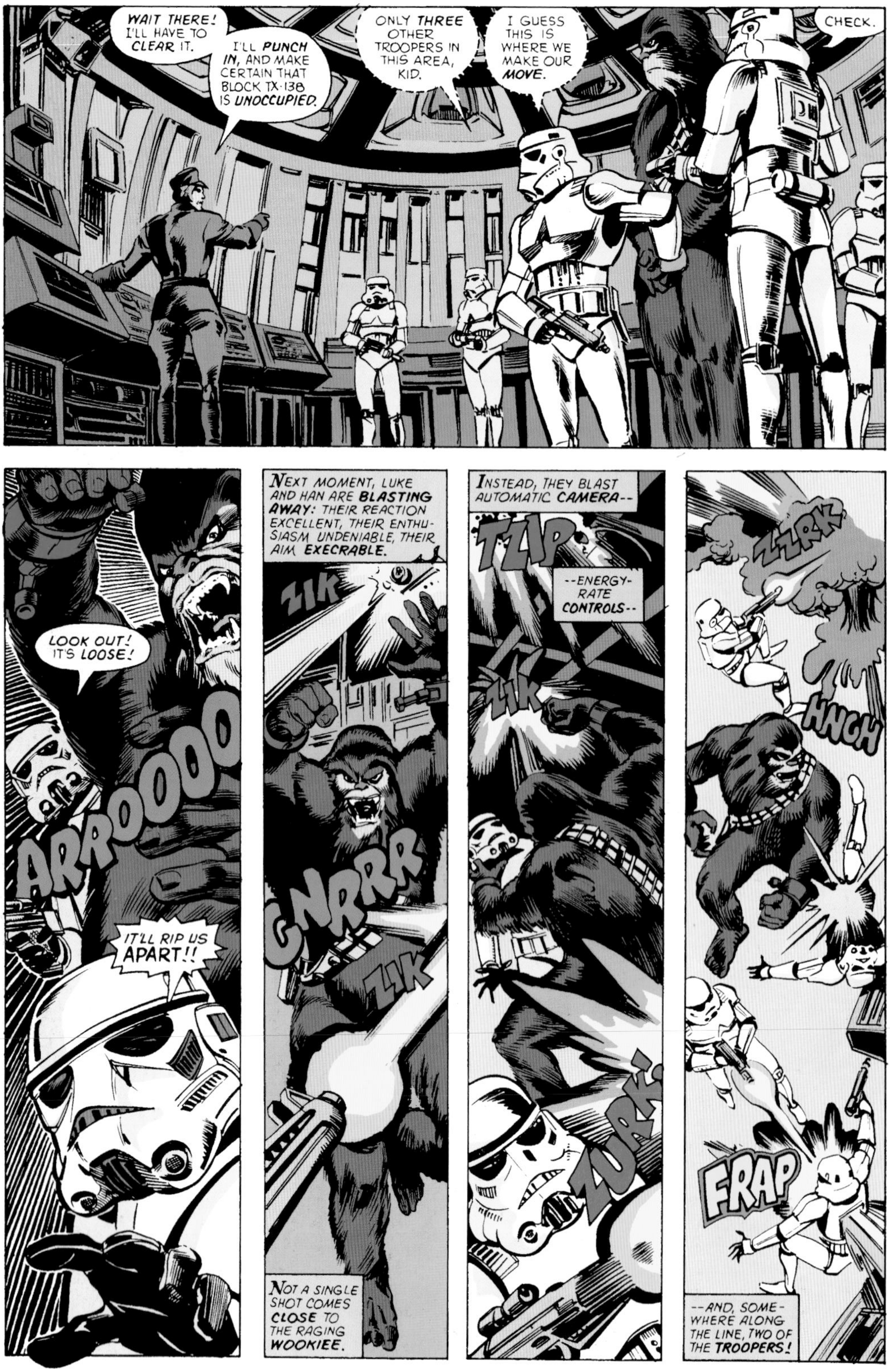
WAIT THERE! I'LL HAVE TO CLEAR IT.
I'LL PUNCH IN, AND MAKE CERTAIN THAT BLOCK TX-138 IS UNOCCUPIED.
ONLY THREE OTHER TROOPERS IN THIS AREA, KID.
I GUESS THIS IS WHERE WE MAKE OUR MOVE.
CHECK.
LOOK OUT! IT'S LOOSE!
ARROOOOO
IT'LL RIP US APART!!
NEXT MOMENT, LUKE AND HAN ARE BLASTING AWAY: THEIR REACTION EXCELLENT, THEIR ENTHUSIASM UNDENIABLE, THEIR AIM EXECRABLE.
ZIK
GNRRR
ZIK
NOT A SINGLE SHOT COMES CLOSE TO THE RAGING WOOKIEE.
INSTEAD, THEY BLAST AUTOMATIC CAMERA--
TZIP
--ENERGY-RATE CONTROLS--
ZIK
ZURK
ZZRK
HNGH
FRAP
--AND, SOMEWHERE ALONG THE LINE, TWO OF THE TROOPERS!

WITHIN SECONDS, A *STAR SYSTEM'S* WORTH OF VALUABLE ELECTRONIC EQUIPMENT IS RENDERED *USELESS...*

SZZRAK

ZIK

AT THIS POINT, THE *REMAINING* TROOPER--TRAINED MORE FOR ACTION THAN RATIONAL ANALYSIS--SUDDENLY REALIZES THE TWO NEWCOMERS ARE *DANGEROUS...*

FZZP!

--AND HE OPENS FIRE!

BUT, IT'S *TOO LATE*--

--AS *HAN SOLO* QUICKLY DEMON-STRATES--!

KZIK

ZZZZ

SOLO! THE *OFFICER IN CHARGE*-- HE'S GOING TO PUSH THE *ALARM SYSTEM*--!

GNARK

THEN *STOP HIM,* KID!

STOP HIM!

'WAY TO GO, KID!

YOU'LL MAKE A SPACE-PIRATE YET!

ZZRAP

NOW, LET'S FIND OUT WHICH CELL THIS *PRINCESS* OF YOURS IS--

HERE IT IS: CELL 2187.

I'LL HOLD THEM *HERE,* KID! YOU GET *MOVING!*

--CURITY CENTER! COME IN, SECURITY CENTER!

Uh...EVERYTHING UNDER *CONTROL.* SLIGHT WEAPON *MALFUNCTION.*

WHAT *HAPPENED?*

WE'RE ALL *FINE,* THANK YOU. HOW ABOUT *YOU?*

WE'RE SENDING A *SQUAD* UP!

Uh...*NEGATIVE!* REACTOR LEAK-- GIVE US A *FEW* MINUTES TO--

IT WAS A *BORING* CONVERSATION, ANYWAY.

WHO *IS* THIS? WHAT'S YOUR *OPERATING*--

B LAM!

WELL, *GET SET,* CHEWIE--

WE'RE GOING TO HAVE *COMPANY!*

ALREADY, YOUNG LUKE HAS REACHED THE **MIDDLE** OF THE LONG CORRIDOR BEYOND--AND COME TO THE CELL DESIGNATED 2187.

HIS COMMANDEERED LASER PISTOL MAKES REASONABLY **FAST** WORK OF IT.

BUT, HE STOPS-- TONGUE-TIED-- WHEN THE SMOKE CLEARS...

Y-YOU'RE-- EVEN **MORE** BEAUTIFUL-- THAN I --

AREN'T YOU A LITTLE **SHORT** FOR A STORM- TROOPER?

WHAT? OH-- THE UNIFORM!

I'VE COME TO **RESCUE** YOU.

I'M LUKE SKYWALKER!

YOU'RE **WHO?**

I'VE COME TO **RESCUE** YOU!

BEN KENOBI IS WITH ME -- AND WE'VE GOT YOUR **DROIDS!**

BEN KENOBI?

WHERE **IS** HE?

OBI-WAN!!

MEANWHILE, IN THE OUTER SECURITY CHAMBER, A SERIES OF EAR-SHATTERING *EXPLOSIONS* TEAR A GAPING *HOLE* IN THE METAL WALL--A HOLE THROUGH WHICH *IMPERIAL TROOPERS* NOW BEGIN TO EMERGE...

BACK, CHEWIE! WE'VE GOT TO *RETREAT!*

ZIK ZIK ZIK

HRNK!

YOU *FOUND* HER, eh?

WELL, WE CAN'T GO BACK *THAT* WAY!

NO, WE CERTAINLY *CAN'T*

IT LOOKS LIKE YOU'VE MANAGED TO *CUT OFF* OUR ONLY *ESCAPE ROUTE!*

Huh? BEGGING YOUR *FORGIVENESS,* YOUR *HIGHNESS* --BUT MAYBE YOU'D PREFER IT BACK IN YOUR *CELL?*

I'D LOVE TO *OBLIGE* YOU, BUT RIGHT NOW--

--*HERE COMES TROUBLE!*

ALL RIGHT, CHEWIE-- STARTING BLASTING!

IF WE *DIE* HERE-- LET'S TAKE A BUNCH OF 'EM WITH US!

THREEPIO! THREEPIO! WE'VE BEEN *CUT OFF!* ARE THERE ANY *OTHER* WAYS OUT??

THREEPIO! WHERE *ARE* YOU?

FTIK ZIK

BUT, LUKE SKYWALKER'S ONLY *ANSWER* IS THE BLAST OF THE *TROOPERS'* LASERS COMING CLOSER--*CLOSER*--!

NEXT ISSUE: **BEN KENOBI** VS. **DARTH VADER** --TO THE **DEATH!**

CHEWIE, HAN SOLO, LUKE SKYWALKER &
PRINCESS LEIA AS SEEN BY ARTIST HOWARD CHAYKIN.

STAR WARS ™

30¢ **4** OCT
CC 02817

THE GREATEST SPACE-FANTASY FILM OF ALL!

™

AT LAST!
THE BATTLE WITH
DARTH VADER™
TO THE **DEATH!!**

NO, LUKE!

HERE I STAND-- THOUGH I MAY **DIE!**

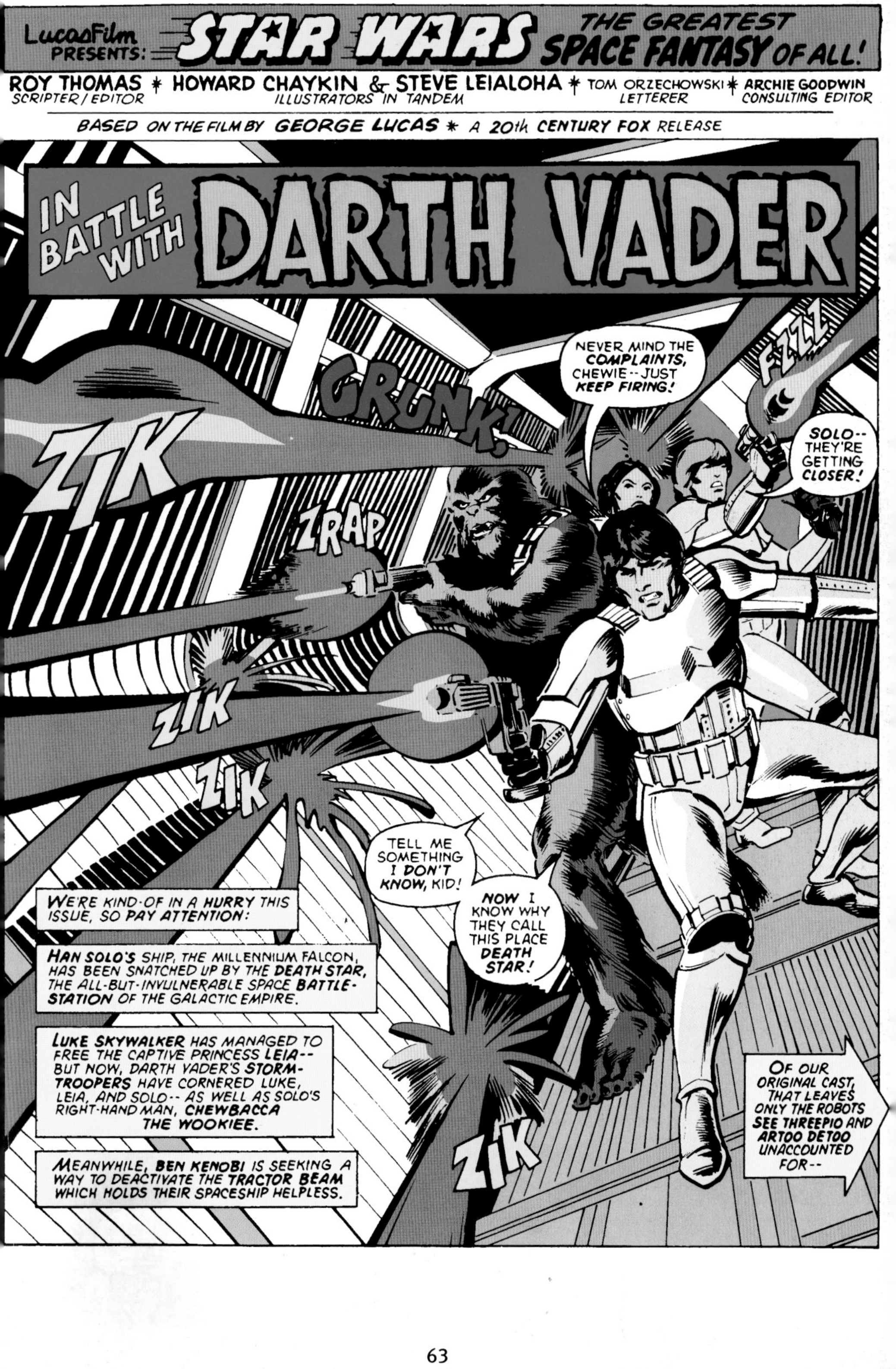
LucasFilm PRESENTS:
STAR WARS
THE GREATEST SPACE FANTASY OF ALL!
ROY THOMAS * SCRIPTER / EDITOR
HOWARD CHAYKIN & STEVE LEIALOHA * ILLUSTRATORS IN TANDEM
TOM ORZECHOWSKI * LETTERER
ARCHIE GOODWIN CONSULTING EDITOR
BASED ON THE FILM BY GEORGE LUCAS * A 20th CENTURY FOX RELEASE
IN BATTLE WITH DARTH VADER
WE'RE KIND-OF IN A HURRY THIS ISSUE, SO PAY ATTENTION:
HAN SOLO'S SHIP, THE MILLENNIUM FALCON, HAS BEEN SNATCHED UP BY THE DEATH STAR, THE ALL-BUT-INVULNERABLE SPACE BATTLE-STATION OF THE GALACTIC EMPIRE.
LUKE SKYWALKER HAS MANAGED TO FREE THE CAPTIVE PRINCESS LEIA-- BUT NOW, DARTH VADER'S STORM-TROOPERS HAVE CORNERED LUKE, LEIA, AND SOLO-- AS WELL AS SOLO'S RIGHT-HAND MAN, CHEWBACCA THE WOOKIEE.
MEANWHILE, BEN KENOBI IS SEEKING A WAY TO DEACTIVATE THE TRACTOR BEAM WHICH HOLDS THEIR SPACESHIP HELPLESS.
ZIK
GRUNK!
ZRAP
NEVER MIND THE COMPLAINTS, CHEWIE-- JUST KEEP FIRING!
FZZZ
SOLO-- THEY'RE GETTING CLOSER!
ZIK
ZIK
TELL ME SOMETHING I DON'T KNOW, KID!
NOW I KNOW WHY THEY CALL THIS PLACE DEATH STAR!
ZIK
OF OUR ORIGINAL CAST, THAT LEAVES ONLY THE ROBOTS SEE THREEPIO AND ARTOO DETOO UNACCOUNTED FOR--

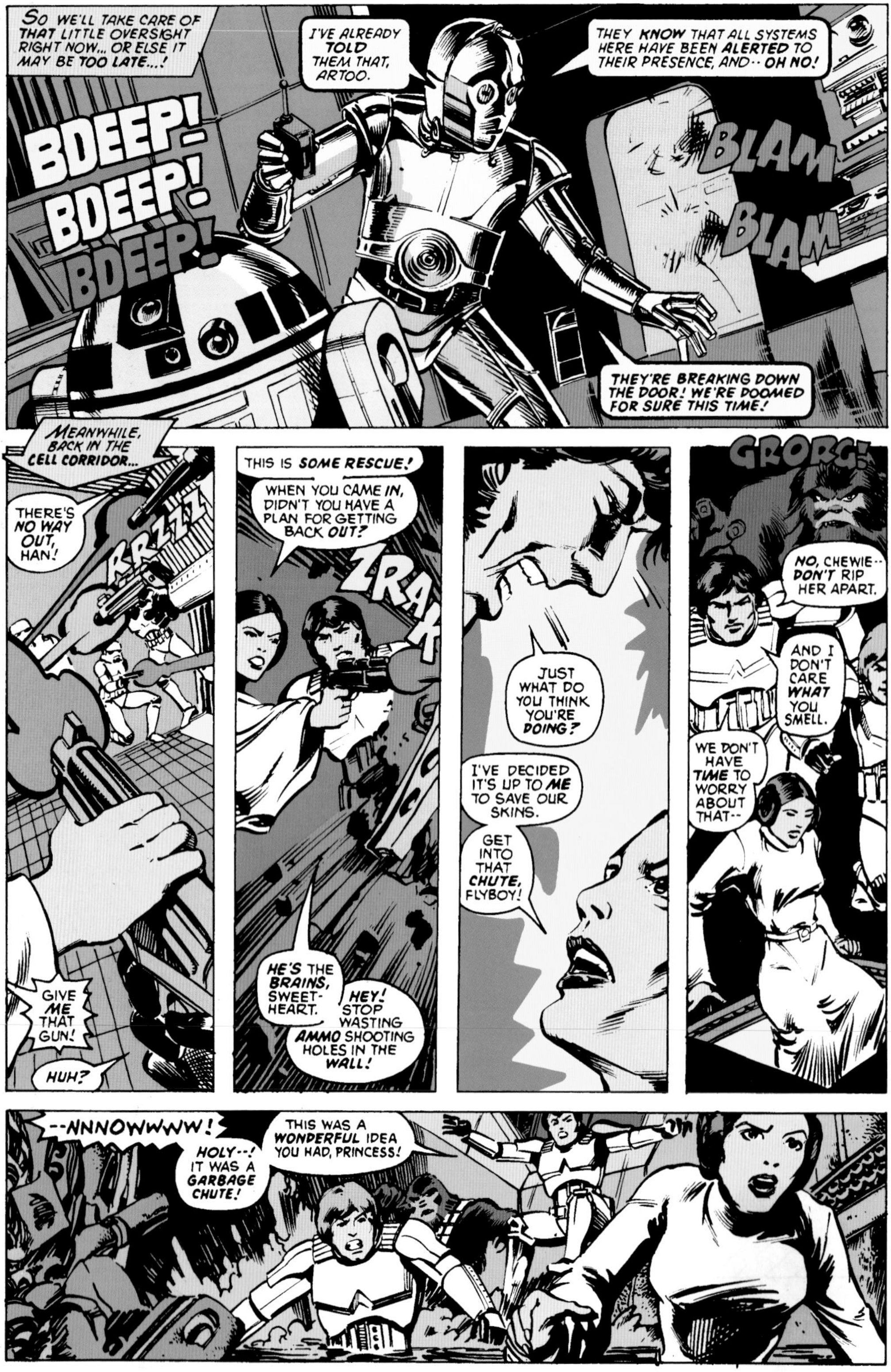
SO WE'LL TAKE CARE OF THAT LITTLE OVERSIGHT RIGHT NOW... OR ELSE IT MAY BE TOO LATE...!
I'VE ALREADY TOLD THEM THAT, ARTOO.
THEY KNOW THAT ALL SYSTEMS HERE HAVE BEEN ALERTED TO THEIR PRESENCE, AND-- OH NO!
BDEEP!-BDEEP!-BDEEP!
BLAM
BLAM
THEY'RE BREAKING DOWN THE DOOR! WE'RE DOOMED FOR SURE THIS TIME!
MEANWHILE, BACK IN THE CELL CORRIDOR...
THERE'S NO WAY OUT, HAN!
KRZZZZ
GIVE ME THAT GUN!
HUH?
THIS IS SOME RESCUE!
WHEN YOU CAME IN, DIDN'T YOU HAVE A PLAN FOR GETTING BACK OUT?
ZRAK
HE'S THE BRAINS, SWEET-HEART.
HEY! STOP WASTING AMMO SHOOTING HOLES IN THE WALL!
JUST WHAT DO YOU THINK YOU'RE DOING?
I'VE DECIDED IT'S UP TO ME TO SAVE OUR SKINS.
GET INTO THAT CHUTE, FLYBOY!
GRORG!
NO, CHEWIE-- DON'T RIP HER APART.
AND I DON'T CARE WHAT YOU SMELL.
WE DON'T HAVE TIME TO WORRY ABOUT THAT--
--NNNOWWWW!
HOLY--! IT WAS A GARBAGE CHUTE!
THIS WAS A WONDERFUL IDEA YOU HAD, PRINCESS!

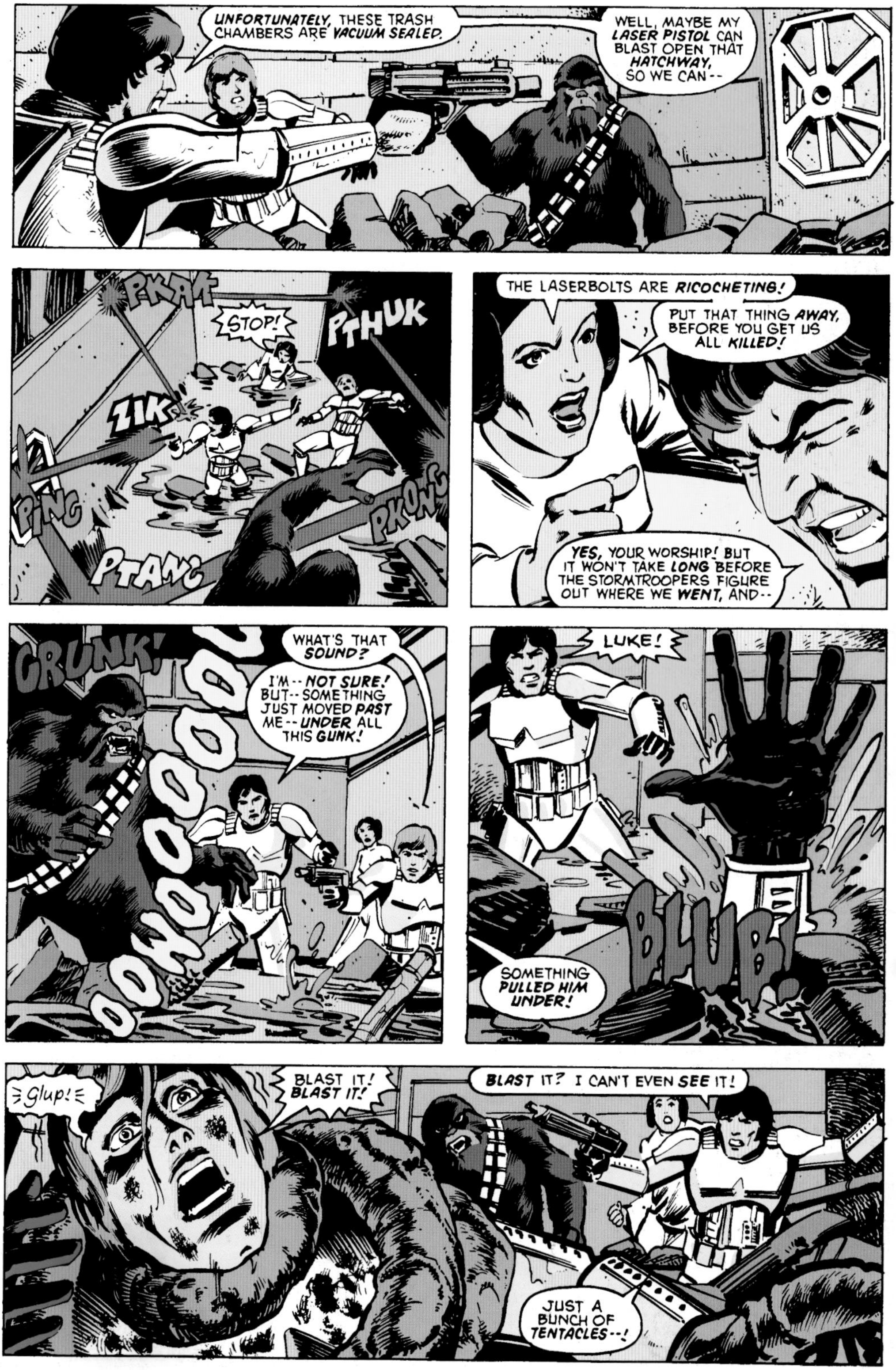
UNFORTUNATELY, THESE TRASH CHAMBERS ARE VACUUM SEALED.
WELL, MAYBE MY LASER PISTOL CAN BLAST OPEN THAT HATCHWAY, SO WE CAN--
PKAK
STOP!
PTHUK
ZIK
PING
PTANG
PKONG
THE LASERBOLTS ARE RICOCHETING!
PUT THAT THING AWAY, BEFORE YOU GET US ALL KILLED!
YES, YOUR WORSHIP! BUT IT WON'T TAKE LONG BEFORE THE STORMTROOPERS FIGURE OUT WHERE WE WENT, AND--
CRUNK!
WHAT'S THAT SOUND?
I'M--NOT SURE! BUT--SOMETHING JUST MOVED PAST ME--UNDER ALL THIS GUNK!
LUKE!
BLUB!
SOMETHING PULLED HIM UNDER!
Glup!
BLAST IT! BLAST IT!
BLAST IT? I CAN'T EVEN SEE IT!
JUST A BUNCH OF TENTACLES--!

GRONK

NOW HE'S BEEN *PULLED BACK* INTO THE MUCK!

NO-- *WAIT!* HE'S COMING BACK *UP!*

IT'S LET HIM GO!

YOU OKAY, KID? WHAT *HAPPENED* TO IT?

I-- *DON'T KNOW!* IT JUST -- DIS-APPEARED!

SPUT

WH-WHAT'S THAT *SOUND?*

RRRRR

THE *WALLS!* THEY'RE *COMING CLOSER!*

I'VE GOT A *VERY BAD FEELING* ABOUT THIS.

MMMB

DON'T JUST *STAND* THERE! TRY TO *BRACE* IT WITH SOMETHING!

KRUNK

NO, I *DON'T THINK* IT'S GOING TO WORK *EITHER,* CHEWIE--

BUT WE'VE GOT TO *TRY!*

BLL

PTAK

THEY'RE *SNAPPING* LIKE *TWIGS!*

LOOKS LIKE WE'VE *HAD* IT-- AND IN OUR STOLEN *STORMTROOPER* OUTFITS YET!

LLL

ARRAG

OUR ONLY *HOPE* ARE THE *DROIDS!*

ARTOO'S PLUGGED INTO THE DEATH STAR'S *MONITORING* SYSTEM! MAYBE HE CAN--

SNAP!

THREEPIO! COME IN, THREEPIO--!

BUT, EVEN AS LUKE'S *MUTED VOICE* IS HEARD, COMING OVER THE *ROBOT'S HAND* COMLINK IN THE *COMMAND OFFICE*--

--OME IN, THREEPIO!

--THE *IMPERIAL STORMTROOPERS* SUCCEED IN BREAKING THROUGH THE *DOOR!*

WHAT? NOBODY *HERE!?*

HELP! *HELP!* LET US *OUT!*

EH? THAT *SUPPLY CABINET*--!

BLAST! IT'S JUST A PAIR OF *DROIDS!*

WHO LOCKED YOU *IN* THERE?

THEY'RE *MAD-MEN,* SIR--THEY'RE HEADING FOR THE *PRISON LEVEL.*

THEY JUST *LEFT!*

IF YOU *HURRY,* YOU MIGHT *CATCH* THEM.

GOOD!

ALL THIS *EXCITEMENT* HAS OVERRUN THE *CIRCUITS* ON MY R2-D2 *COUNTERPART* HERE.

IF YOU DON'T MIND, I'D LIKE TO TAKE HIM DOWN TO *MAINTENANCE.*

BREEP BREEP

PERMISSION *GRANTED.*

ALL RIGHT, MEN--LET'S *GET* THOSE REBELS!

BUT, DOWN BELOW, THE *RELENTLESS WALLS* CLOSING IN ON LUKE SKYWALKER AND COMPANY MAY *NEED* NO HELP...

ONE SURE THING! WE'RE ALL... GOING TO BE... MUCH *THINNER!* ≥Unnh!≤

GRRK!

WHAT'S *HAPPENED* TO *THREEPIO?*

WHY ISN'T HE SENDING US *ESCAPE INSTRUCTIONS?*

RMMBLL

TRY TO BLAST THE **DOOR** AGAIN!

IT'S OUR **ONLY HOPE!**

SZRAP!

THEN WE'RE **SUNK,** PRINCESS -- 'CAUSE IT'S **NO GO!**

MEANWHILE, IN THE **MAIN FORWARD BAY** OF THE DEATH STAR...

THAT'S IT, ARTOO! PLUG YOURSELF INTO THAT **WALL SOCKET** SO I CAN TALK WITH OUR **MASTER** AGAIN, AND --

BEEP BREEP

OH **NO!** IS THAT WHAT'S HAPPENING TO THEM? THAT'S **TERRIBLE!**

THREEPIO! FOR HEAVEN'S SAKE, WHERE **ARE** YOU??

ARE YOU **THERE,** SIR? WE'VE HAD SOME PROBLEMS...

THREEPIO, **SHUT UP** -- AND SHUT DOWN ALL THE **GARBAGE MASHERS** ON THE **DETONATION LEVEL!** DO YOU **COPY?**

OH, MOST **CERTAINLY, SIR!** SHUT THEM **ALL** DOWN, ARTOO!

BDEEK

I ONLY HOPE WE'RE IN **TIME!**

ARTOO! THREEPIO! WE'RE ALL **RIGHT!**

DO YOU **READ** ME? YOU DID **FINE!**

NOW TO SCRAPE THE **MUCK** OFF THIS **HATCH NUMBER,** AND SEE JUST **WHICH** --

3661789

THREEPIO! HAVE ARTOO OPEN THE PRESSURE MAINTENANCE HATCH ON UNIT 36611789!

YES, MASTER. SO GLAD YOU'RE **ALL** RIGHT, SIR.

WHILE, NEARBY, BEN KENOBI HIDES AMID THE EQUIPMENT THAT POWERS THE GREAT TRACTOR BEAM...

...WHICH IN TURN HOLDS HAN SOLO'S SHIP IN THRALL!

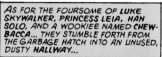

BEN KENOBI: ONCE HE WAS OBI-WAN, OF THE FAMED JEDI KNIGHTS...

NOW HE, LIKE THE OTHERS, IS A FUGITIVE ON BOARD THIS SPRAWLING BATTLE-STATION...

AND, EVEN AS HE MAKES CERTAIN ADJUSTMENTS IN A COMPUTER TERMINAL, AND SEVERAL LIGHTS CHANGE FROM RED TO BLUE...

... THE NET DRAWS TIGHTER!

SECURE THIS ENTRY AREA UNTIL THE ALERT IS CANCELLED!

AS FOR THE FOURSOME OF LUKE SKYWALKER, PRINCESS LEIA, HAN SOLO, AND A WOOKIEE NAMED CHEWBACCA... THEY STUMBLE FORTH FROM THE GARBAGE HATCH INTO AN UNUSED, DUSTY HALLWAY...

DOESN'T THAT THING EVER GIVE UP?

WAIT! SOMEBODY MIGHT HEAR--!

ZAP!

I DON'T KNOW WHO YOU ARE OR WHERE YOU CAME FROM, BUT FROM NOW ON YOU'LL DO AS I TELL YOU!

AND YOU TELL THAT BIG HAIRY WALKING CARPET OF YOURS TO GET OUT OF MY WAY!

RRNK?

LISTEN, YOUR HOLINESS... LET'S GET SOMETHING STRAIGHT:

I TAKE ORDERS FROM ONE PERSON-- ME!

THEN IT'S A WONDER YOU'RE STILL ALIVE!

NO REWARD IS WORTH THIS!

MEANWHILE, BACK IN THE TRACTOR BEAM POWER-GENERATOR TRENCH...

ANY *SIGN* OF ANY OF THEM YET?

NONE!...

...MAYBE *DOWN HERE!*

NEXT MOMENT, HE SLIPS INTO A *MAIN PASSAGEWAY.*

AS, ELSEWHERE...

SEE THREEPIO... DO YOU *COPY?*

I *READ* YOU, SIR.

ARE YOU *SAFE?*

FOR THE *MOMENT*, WE'RE IN THE *MAIN HANGAR*, ACROSS FROM THE SHIP.

WE'RE RIGHT *ABOVE* YOU, THEN.

STAND BY!

Y'KNOW, KID-- GETTING BACK TO THE *FALCON'S* GOING TO BE LIKE FLYING THRU THE *FIVE FIRE RINGS OF FORNAX!*

YOU CAME IN *THAT* THING DOWN THERE?

YES.

YOU'RE *BRAVER* THAN I THOUGHT!

IF YOU'D PREFER TO *STAY HERE*, PRINCESS, I'M SURE IT CAN BE--

Uh oh!

THE *BOYS IN WHITE* ARE BACK!

STOP-- OR WE'LL FIRE!

70

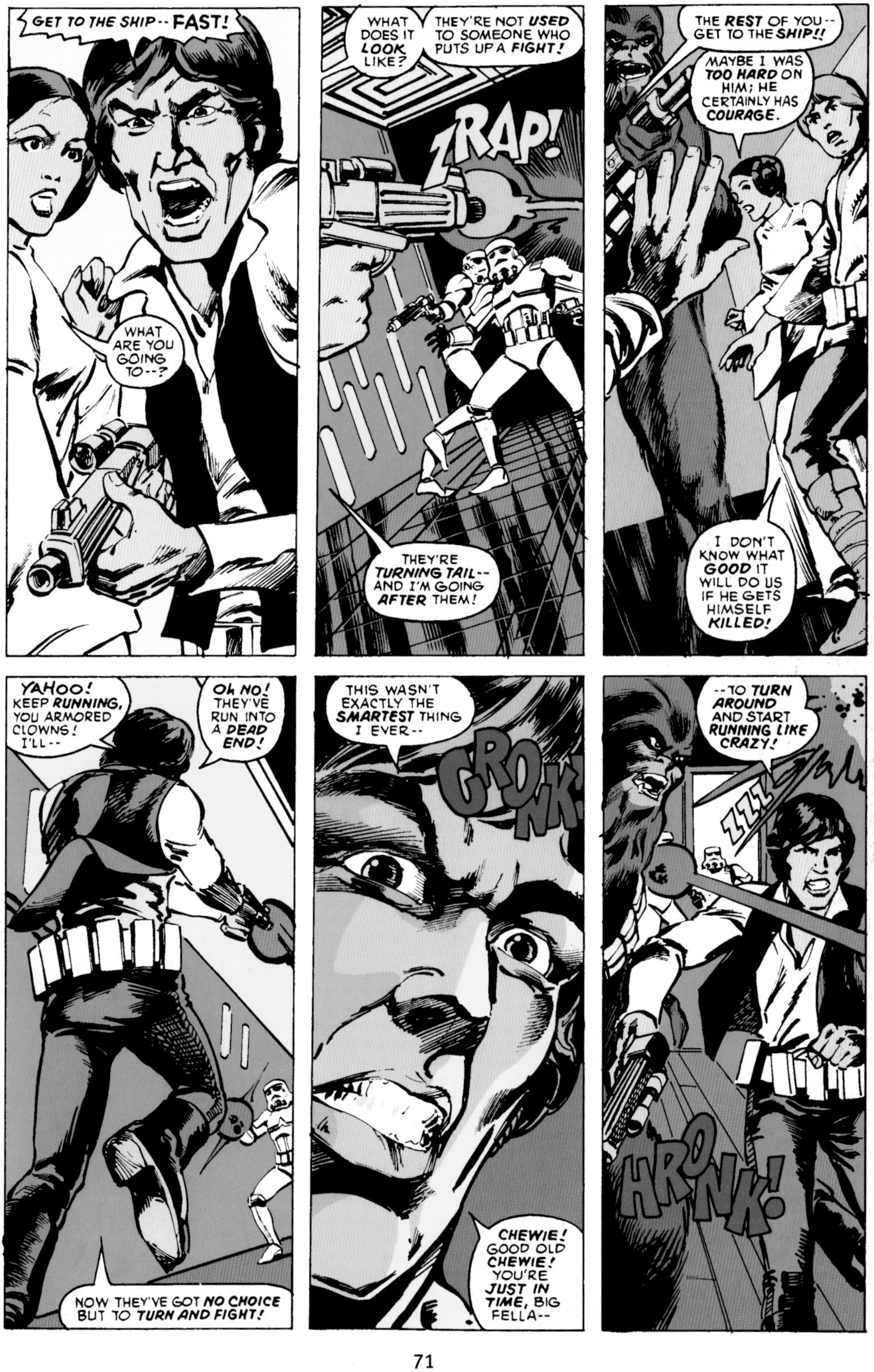
GET TO THE SHIP-- FAST!
WHAT ARE YOU GOING TO--?
WHAT DOES IT LOOK LIKE?
THEY'RE NOT USED TO SOMEONE WHO PUTS UP A FIGHT!
ZRAP!
THEY'RE TURNING TAIL-- AND I'M GOING AFTER THEM!
THE REST OF YOU-- GET TO THE SHIP!!
MAYBE I WAS TOO HARD ON HIM; HE CERTAINLY HAS COURAGE.
I DON'T KNOW WHAT GOOD IT WILL DO US IF HE GETS HIMSELF KILLED!
YAHOO! KEEP RUNNING, YOU ARMORED CLOWNS! I'LL--
Oh NO! THEY'VE RUN INTO A DEAD END!
NOW THEY'VE GOT NO CHOICE BUT TO TURN AND FIGHT!
THIS WASN'T EXACTLY THE SMARTEST THING I EVER--
GRONK!
CHEWIE! GOOD OLD CHEWIE! YOU'RE JUST IN TIME, BIG FELLA--
--TO TURN AROUND AND START RUNNING LIKE CRAZY!
ZZZ
HRONK!

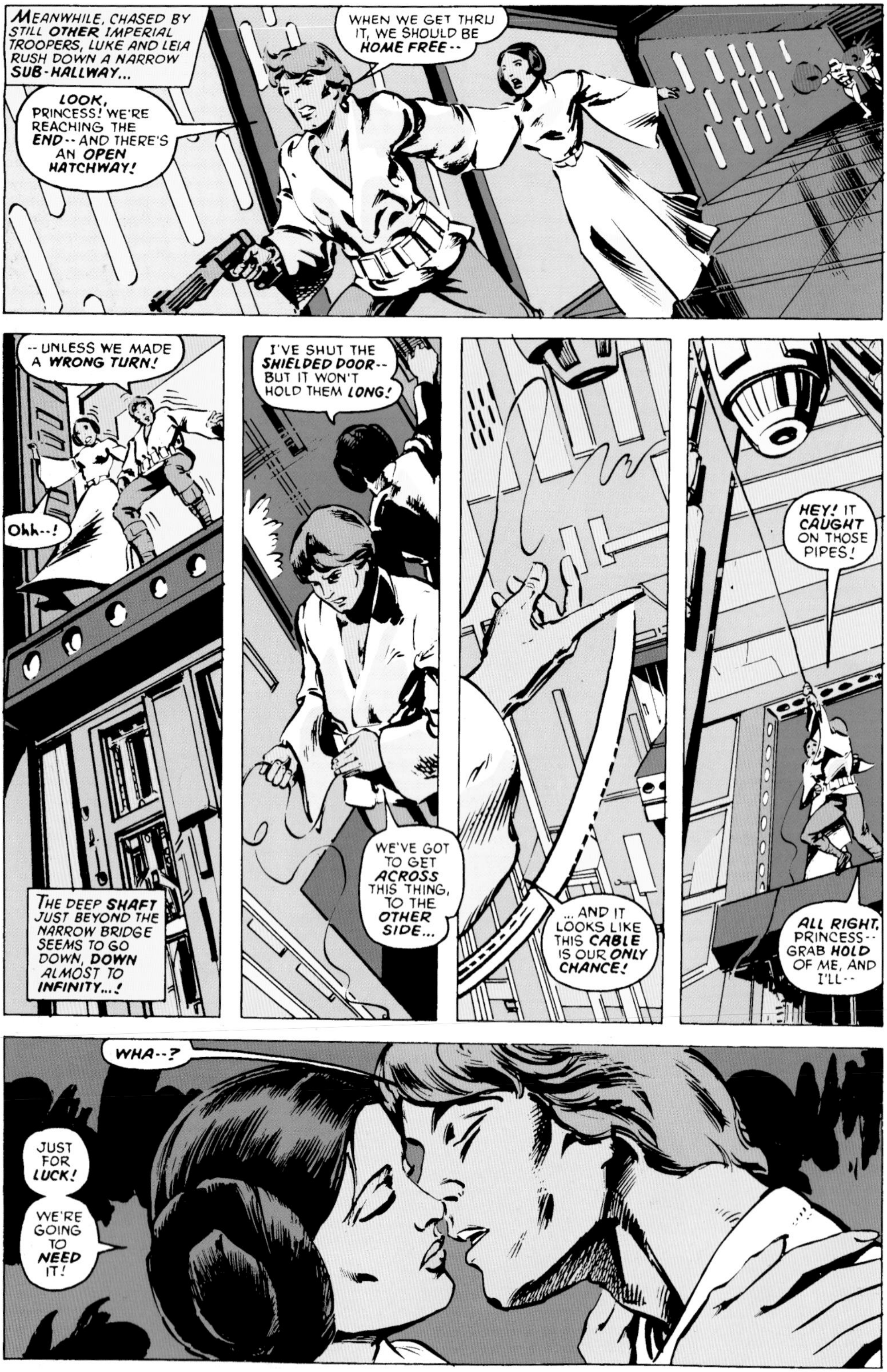
MEANWHILE, CHASED BY STILL OTHER IMPERIAL TROOPERS, LUKE AND LEIA RUSH DOWN A NARROW SUB-HALLWAY...
LOOK, PRINCESS! WE'RE REACHING THE END-- AND THERE'S AN OPEN HATCHWAY!
WHEN WE GET THRU IT, WE SHOULD BE HOME FREE--
-- UNLESS WE MADE A WRONG TURN!
Ohh--!
THE DEEP SHAFT JUST BEYOND THE NARROW BRIDGE SEEMS TO GO DOWN, DOWN ALMOST TO INFINITY...!
I'VE SHUT THE SHIELDED DOOR-- BUT IT WON'T HOLD THEM LONG!
WE'VE GOT TO GET ACROSS THIS THING, TO THE OTHER SIDE...
...AND IT LOOKS LIKE THIS CABLE IS OUR ONLY CHANCE!
HEY! IT CAUGHT ON THOSE PIPES!
ALL RIGHT, PRINCESS-- GRAB HOLD OF ME, AND I'LL--
WHA--?
JUST FOR LUCK!
WE'RE GOING TO NEED IT!

YOU'RE TELLING ME!?

EVEN AS THEY SWING ACROSS, LUKE KNOWS THAT EVEN A SLIGHT *MISCAL-CULATION* IN ARC, AND THEY WILL *MISS* THE OPPOSITE OPEN HATCH-- SLAMMING INTO THE *METAL* AROUND IT!

YET, *LUCK* -- OR *"THE FORCE"* -- IS WITH THEM, AND...

WE *MADE* IT! JUST IN *TIME*, TOO!

THE TROOPS ARE *THRU* THE DOOR BACK THERE!

ZZZ

ZAK!

FRAZK!

WE'VE GOT TO FIND THE *OTHERS!*

LET'S GET *MOVING,* PRINCESS!

BEN KENOBI SEEMS NEARLY A *PART* OF THE PASSAGEWAY IT-SELF, AS A LARGE CLUSTER OF *TROOPERS* HURRIES PAST HIM...

THEN, PAUSING TO MAKE CERTAIN THEY'VE ALL PASSED, HE STARTS DOWN IT *HIMSELF*...

...FAILING TO SEE THE *DARK SILHOU-ETTE* WHICH ECLIPSES THE *LIGHT* FAR BEHIND HIM.

AS FOR **SOLO** AND **CHEWBACCA:**

AHEAD OF THEM, AS THEY'VE RUN, A SERIES OF **SHIELDED DOORS** HAS BEGUN TO **CLOSE** IN FRONT OF THEM.

...**BEHIND** THEM!

THAT OUGHT TO HOLD 'EM FOR A WHILE!

NOW, LET'S GO FIND THE **MILLENNIUM FALCON!**

GNORR

SLAMM

PANTING WITH EXERTION, MAN AND WOOKIEE MANAGE TO MAKE SURE THAT THEY **FINISH** CLOSING...

AT THAT PRECISE MOMENT, BEN HAS ALREADY **FOUND** HAN SOLO'S ANTIQUE BUT STURDY STARSHIP.

WITH EAGER TREAD, HE HURRIES **TOWARD** IT, SURE HE HAS **FREED** IT FROM THE POWERFUL **TRACTOR BEAM** THAT HELD IT...

AND THEN --

YOU!

I HAVE BEEN **WAITING,** OBI-WAN KENOBI; THE **CIRCLE** IS NOW COMPLETED.

WHEN I LEFT YOU, I WAS BUT A **LEARNER;** NOW, I AM THE **MASTER.**

YOU **STILL** HAVE MUCH TO LEARN.

FZIPP!

HIS LIGHTSABRE ACTIVATED, BEN KENOBI MOVES WITH ELEGANT EASE INTO A CLASSICAL OFFENSIVE POSITION...

...AS THE FEARSOME DARK KNIGHT, WEAPON IN HAND, TAKES A DEFENSIVE STANCE.

FOR A MOMENT, THE TWO GALACTIC WARRIORS STAND PERFECTLY STILL, SIZING EACH OTHER UP...

THEN--
YOUR POWERS ARE WEAK, OLD MAN!

YOU SHOULD NEVER HAVE COME BACK!

SZRAK

YOU... ONLY KNOW... HALF "THE FORCE"... VADER...!

YOU PERCEIVE ITS FULL POWER... AS LITTLE AS A SPOON... PERCEIVES THE TASTE OF FOOD!

YET, EVEN AS THEY FIGHT, BEN SEEMS TO BE UNDER IN-CREASING PRESSURE AND STRAIN--AS IF AN INVISIBLE WEIGHT WERE BEING PLACED UPON HIM...

HE MAKES A SUDDEN LUNGE AT HIS FOE--

ZZARP

--BUT IS CHECKED BY A LIGHTNING MOVEMENT OF THE TOWERING ARMORED GIANT!

THEN, HIS SWORD LOCKED WITH VADER'S, BEN BEGINS BACKING INTO THE MASSIVE STARSHIP HANGAR.

THEIR LIGHT-SABERS LOCKED IN MID-AIR, THE TWO POWERFUL WARRIORS STAND MOTIONLESS...

...LIKE TITANS OUT OF SOME LOST TIME!

75

AND, EVEN AS THE FORMER *JEDI KNIGHT* AND *LORD OF THE SITH* JOIN TOGETHER IN THIS GRIM TABLEAU--

IT'S *GOOD* WE'RE ALL *TOGETHER* AGAIN... BUT, THERE ARE SO MANY *STORMTROOPERS* MILLING ABOUT THE *ENTRY RAMP* OF MR. SOLO'S *STARSHIP...!*

LUKE! PRINCESS! WHAT *KEPT* YOU?

WE RAN INTO SOME *OLD FRIENDS.*

IS THE *MILLENNIUM FALCON* ALL RIGHT?

IT'LL GET US *OUT* OF HERE OKAY-- IF WE CAN GET *NEAR* IT, BUT I--

OH-- *WAIT*--

LOOK!

THEN, BEFORE THE *STARTLED EYES* OF HUMANS, DROIDS, AND WOOKIEE--

--*BEN* AND *VADER* EMERGE FROM THE HALLWAYS ON THE *FAR SIDE* OF THE DOCKING BAY--

--STILL LOCKED IN THEIR DEADLY *LIGHTSABRE DUEL!*

PREPARE TO MEET "*THE FORCE*," OBI-WAN.

THIS IS A FIGHT YOU *CANNOT WIN,* DARTH--FOR, I HAVE *GROWN* MUCH SINCE OUR *PARTING*...

IF *MY* BLADE FINDS ITS MARK, YOU WILL *CEASE* TO EXIST.

BUT, IF YOU *CUT ME DOWN*-- I WILL ONLY BECOME MORE *POWERFUL*...!

AS HE SPEAKS, BEN KENOBI SEES *TROOPERS* CHARGING TO- WARD HIM... AND REALIZES HE IS *TRAPPED!*

STILL, HIS TONE IS *DEFIANT*...

HEED MY WORDS!

NOT *THIS* TIME!

I AM THE MASTER NOW!

I-- --DARTH VADER!

ZZRAKK

THE SITH LORD BRINGS HIS *SWORD* DOWN, SEEMINGLY CUTTING HIS ELDER FOE IN *HALF!*

BEN KENOBI'S CLOAK FALLS TO THE FLOOR IN *TWO PARTS*--

--BUT BEN IS *NOT* IN IT!

AND VADER, PUZZLED AT THE OLD MAN'S *DIS-APPEARANCE,* POKES AT THE EMPTY CLOAK.

NEITHER HE NOR THE DISTRACTED *TROOPERS* HAVE SEEN *FIVE FORMS* RACING TOWARD THE *CAPTURED STARSHIP...*

...TILL *LUKE SKYWALKER* REALIZES THAT HE MAY HAVE JUST SEEN *BEN KENOBI'S DEATH!*

BEN!

HE WAS A *BRAVE* OLD GEEZER, I'LL SAY *THAT* FOR HIM!

COME ON, SO HIS SACRIFICE WON'T HAVE BEEN IN *VAIN!*

HURRY, LUKE....!

NO...

LUKE! THAT WON'T--

YOU *KILLED* HIM, YOU DIRTY--

FRAP!

LIKE VENGEFUL *WHITE ROBOTS*--THE MEN WITHIN *SUBMERGED* IN THE CAUSE OF GALACTIC POWER-- THE *STORMTROOPERS* SURGE FORWARD--

--AND, THOUGH LUKE SKY-WALKER FIRES WITH A *SURE AIM* HE WOULD SCARCELY HAVE THOUGHT *POSSIBLE* A FEW DAYS BEFORE, THERE ARE *MORE* OF THEM THAN HE CAN HOPE TO SLAY--!

IT'S *TOO LATE,* LUKE! *COME ABOARD!*

WE'VE GOT TO GO, BE-FORE THEY--

NO!

THEN, SUDDENLY, A *FAMILIAR YET DIFFERENT VOICE* RINGS INTO HIS EARS:

LUKE--!

IT IS *BEN KENOBI'S* VOICE!

STUNNED, LUKE WHIRLS TOWARD THE SOURCE OF THE VOICE--BUT SEES ONLY *PRINCESS LEIA*--!

COME ON!

DID HE *IMAGINE* THE OLD MAN'S EERILY ALTERED VOICE, OR--?

THERE IS NO WAY TO KNOW... FOR THE MOMENT.

SO HE TURNS-- AND *RACES UP* THE RAMP--

--INTO THE *MILLENNIUM FALCON!*

I... I CAN'T BELIEVE HE'S... *GONE!*

BOOP

THEN, EVEN AS HE SLUMPS INTO A SEAT, *HAN SOLO* PULLS BACK ON THE CONTROLS --

-- AND THE SHIP BEGINS TO *MOVE!*

I HOPE THAT *OLD MAN* MANAGED TO KNOCK OUT THAT *TRACTOR BEAM* --

-- OR THIS IS GOING TO BE A *VERY SHORT RIDE!*

THE DULL THUD OF *LASER BOLTS* CAN BE HEARD BOUNCING OFF THE SHIP'S *HULL,* AS THE GIANT *CHEWBACCA* ADJUSTS FOR *TAKEOFF*...!

... HEARD BY ALL, THAT IS, SAVE LUKE SKYWALKER!

HE *CAN'T* BE GONE!

HE JUST... *CAN'T!*

THERE WASN'T ANYTHING *YOU* COULD HAVE DONE, LUKE...!

HOLD ON TIGHT, KIDDIES --

-- 'CAUSE HERE WE GO!

THE NEXT MOMENT, THE PIRATE STARSHIP *POWERS AWAY* FROM THE MASSIVE *DEATH STAR* --

-- AND *DISAPPEARS* INTO THE *VASTNESS* OF SPACE!

NEXT ISSUE: *ESCAPE* TO THE MOONS OF *YAVIN!*

STAR WARS TM
35¢
5 NOV 02817
APPROVED BY THE COMICS CODE AUTHORITY
THE GREATEST SPACE-FANTASY FILM OF ALL!
STAR WARS
LUKE SKYWALKER STRIKES AGAIN!
HURRY, CHEWBACCA! WE'RE BEING ATTACKED BY THE DEATH STAR!
IT'S TOO LATE, KID!
WE'RE FINISHED!
HOBERG: COCKRUM

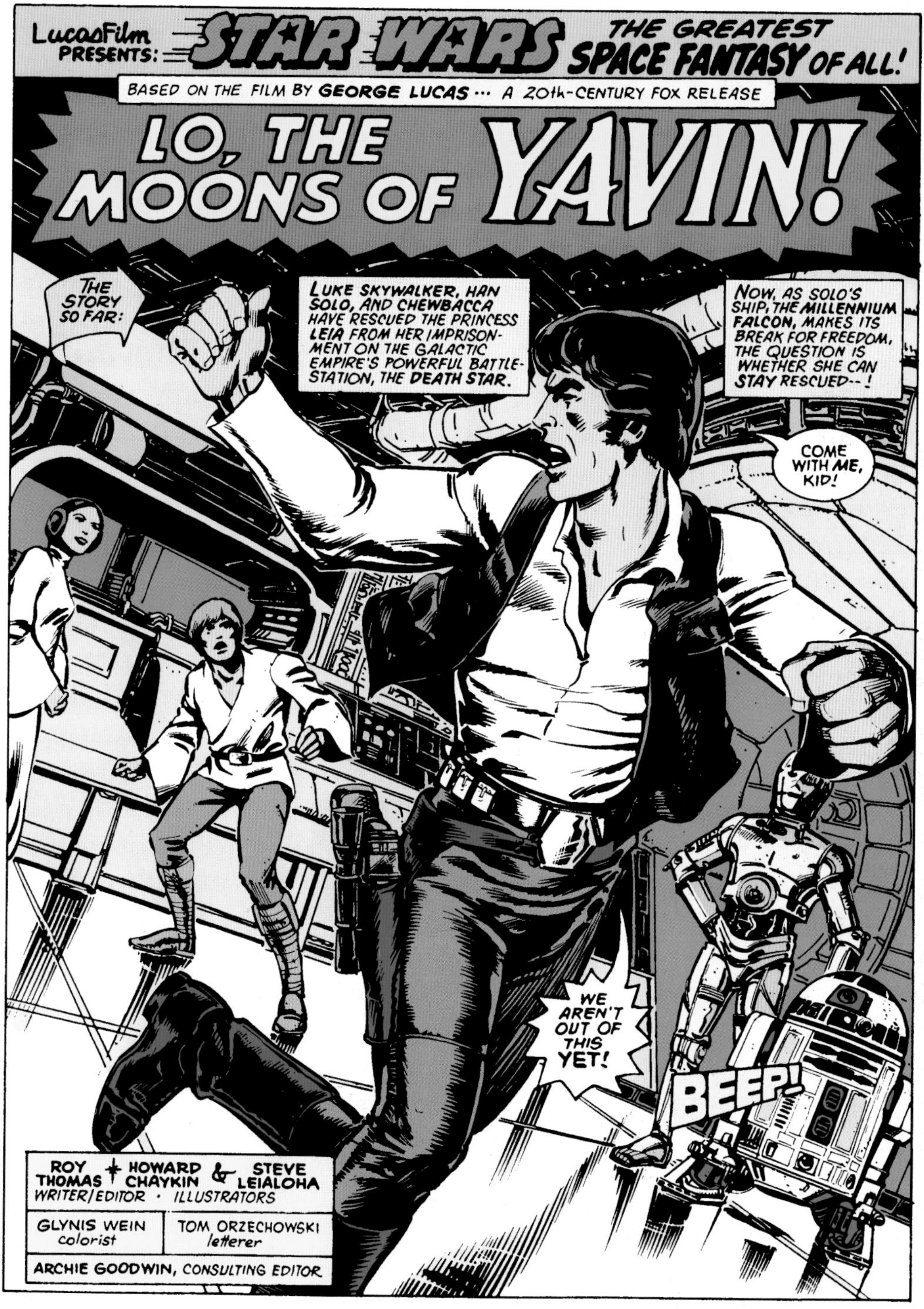
LucasFilm PRESENTS: STAR WARS THE GREATEST SPACE FANTASY OF ALL!
BASED ON THE FILM BY GEORGE LUCAS ... A 20th-CENTURY FOX RELEASE
LO, THE MOONS OF YAVIN!
THE STORY SO FAR:
LUKE SKYWALKER, HAN SOLO, AND CHEWBACCA HAVE RESCUED THE PRINCESS LEIA FROM HER IMPRISONMENT ON THE GALACTIC EMPIRE'S POWERFUL BATTLE-STATION, THE DEATH STAR.
NOW, AS SOLO'S SHIP, THE MILLENNIUM FALCON, MAKES ITS BREAK FOR FREEDOM, THE QUESTION IS WHETHER SHE CAN STAY RESCUED--!
COME WITH ME, KID!
WE AREN'T OUT OF THIS YET!
BEEP!
ROY THOMAS WRITER/EDITOR + HOWARD CHAYKIN & STEVE LEIALOHA ILLUSTRATORS
GLYNIS WEIN colorist
TOM ORZECHOWSKI letterer
ARCHIE GOODWIN, CONSULTING EDITOR

ALMOST INSTANTLY, LUKE FINDS HIMSELF SETTLING INTO THE *LASER CANNON* ON ONE SIDE OF THE FLEEING STARSHIP...

NEVER FIRED *THIS* KIND OF GUN BEFORE!

FOR BEN KENOBI!

BUT, I'VE GOT TO DO IT! *I'VE GOT TO!*

...WHILE, ON THE *OTHER* SIDE, *HAN SOLO'S* THOUGHTS ARE OF MORE *MUNDANE* MATTERS AS HE TAKES HIS *OWN* STATION:

THAT OLD MAN, *KENOBI,* DIED FREEING US FROM THE DEATH STAR'S *BEAM* THAT HELD US.

AND THIS IS *ONE* ERSTWHILE SPACE-SMUGGLER THAT'S GOING TO SEE HE DIDN'T DIE IN *VAIN!*

SIT *TIGHT,* KID, TILL DARTH VADER'S STOOGES *ATTACK* US!

AS FOR OUR *MYSTERIOUS* SPACE PRINCESS, *LEIA ORGANA:*

IT'S *HOPELESS!* WE'RE OUT-NUMBERED-- *OUTGUNNED*--

BUT SOMEHOW, THESE CHARACTERS WHO'RE TRYING TO *RESCUE* ME MIGHT JUST MANAGE TO *PULL IT OFF!*

AND *CHEWBACCA,* THE SEVEN-FOOT, FUR-COVERED *WOOKIEE?*

HIS *THOUGHTS* ARE AS MUCH HIS OWN AS THE STRANGE *LANGUAGE* HE SPEAKS.

THEN, SUDDENLY, *LEIA'S* VOICE RESOUNDS THROUGHOUT THE *MILLENNIUM FALCON*--

HERE COME THE TIE FIGHTERS!

WITHIN THE SHORT-RANGE STARSHIPS OF THE EMPIRE, AIR-GIVING HELMETS HIDE *ALL* LIFE, ALL *EMOTION*...

LUKE, HOWEVER, IS LESS *RELUCTANT* TO SHOW HIS FEELINGS...

MISSED!

BLAST! I'VE GOT TO GET THE HANG OF IT *FAST*-- USE *"THE FORCE"* THAT BEN SHOWED ME *HOW* TO USE--

--OR WE'RE *FINISHED!*

"THE FORCE": THE NAME BEN KENOBI GAVE THE ENERGY FIELD CREATED BY ALL LIVING THINGS-- AND WHICH BINDS THEM TOGETHER.

EARLIER, IT ENABLED LUKE TO WIELD A LIGHTSABRE SKILLFULLY, BY GETTING IN TOUCH WITH HIMSELF-- AND THUS ALL MANKIND.

BUT NOW, AS THE ELUSIVE IMPERIAL SHIPS WEAVE A DEADLY TRAIL ALL AROUND THE MILLENNIUM FALCON...

SOLO! I--CAN'T SEEM TO GET THE RANGE.

KEEP TRYING, KID! HERE THEY COME AGAIN!

YEAH--BUT THEY'RE COMING IN TOO FAST!

AT THAT MOMENT, TWO FIGHTERS DIVE SIMULTANEOUSLY AT THE TWISTING, SPIRALING FREIGHTER, TRYING TO LINE UP THEIR WEAPONS ON IT.

TWIN ENERGY-BOLTS STREAK THROUGH THE BLACK VOID, ZEROING IN FLAWLESSLY ON THE FLEEING SHIP...

... AND THIS TIME, A BOLT PIERCES THE OVERLOADED RAY-DEFLECTORS, TO STRIKE THE SIDE OF THE SHIP!

REEEEEEE

THOUGH STILL PARTIALLY DEFLECTED, IT STILL CARRIES ENOUGH POWER TO BLOW OUT A LARGE CONTROL PANEL.

GAUGES WHINE IN PROTEST AT THE QUANTITY OF LETHAL ENERGY THEY ARE BEING ASKED TO MONITOR AND COMPENSATE FOR...

HROWK

... AND CHEWBACCA'S ANSWERING GRUNTS TO LEIA ARE NOT MUCH HAPPIER.

JUST THEN, *ONE* OF THE TIE FIGHTERS FLOATS DIRECTLY INTO *LUKE'S* SIGHTS.

HIS MOUTH MOVING SLIGHTLY, THE YOUTH *FIRES* AT IT.

NEXT INSTANT, THE INCREDIBLY *AGILE* LITTLE VESSEL DARTS *OUT OF RANGE*--

--ONLY TO PASS *BENEATH* THE *FALCON,* AND INTO *SOLO'S* SIGHTS!

WITHOUT WARNING, THE FIGHTER *ERUPTS* IN AN INCREDIBLE FLASH OF *MULTICOLORED LIGHT!*

WE *DID IT,* KID!

A MOMENT LATER, THEY ARE *FIRING* AGAIN--LUKE STRIVING TO RELAX, TO *BECOME PART* OF HIS WEAPON.

AND THIS TIME--IT *WORKS!*

YET, EVEN AS LUKE FLASHES THE CORELLIAN SMUGGLER A *GRIN OF TRIUMPH*--

WE'RE NOT OUT OF THE WOODS *YET,* SONNY!

THERE'S STILL *THREE MORE* OF THEM!

CORRECTION-- TWO!

ALL RIGHT... TWO, THEN!

BUT WE'VE STILL LOST THE LATERAL CONTROLS FOR THE STARBOARD DEFLECTOR SHIELD!

FRONK!

DON'T WORRY, CREW! SHE'LL HOLD TOGETHER!

YOU HEAR ME, SHIP?!

HOLD TOGETHER!

Uh oh-- HEADS UP, GANG--

HERE THEY COME!

CHEWIE! TRY TO KEEP 'EM ON OUR PORT SIDE! IF WE--

85

SUDDENLY, THE CORELLIAN IS FORCED TO *BREAK OFF,* AS THE TIE-FIGHTER'S DEADLY *ENERGY BOLTS* REACH OUT TOWARD THE *MILLENNIUM FALCON...*

...AND HAN SOLO FINDS OUT THAT *SPACE-MERCENARIES,* TOO, CAN *PRAY!*

ALL IS GRIM SILENCE WITHIN THE FLEEING SMUGGLER-CRAFT...

FOR, THEY KNOW THAT *ONE DIRECT HIT* ON THE SIDE WITHOUT A *DEFLECTOR SHIELD--* SPELLS *DOOM!*

ONE OF THE ENEMY CRAFT SUDDENLY FINDS ITSELF IN *HAN'S GUN-SIGHTS* -- AND IS INSTANTLY *VAPORIZED!*

BUT, AT THE SAME MOMENT, THE *REMAINING* TIE-FIGHTER HEADS FOR THE DEFENSELESS *STARBOARD SIDE* --

-- AND LUKE FINDS HIMSELF FIRING *STEADILY* AT IT, IGNORING THE IMMENSELY POWER-FUL ENERGY IT THROWS AT HIM!

AT THE LAST POSSIBLE INSTANT BEFORE IT PASSES OUT OF RANGE, HE SWINGS HIS WEAPON'S *NOZZLE* MINUTELY--

-- HIS FINGER TIGHTEN-ING CONVULSIVELY ON THE *FIRE CONTROL* --

NOW!

-- AND THE IMPERIAL FIGHTER TURNS INTO A RAPIDLY-EXPANDING CLOUD OF PHOSPHOR-ESCING DUST!

THEN, INSIDE THE FALCON...

WE'VE MADE IT, PRINCESS!

AND THE CRY COMES BACK:

WE'VE MADE IT!!

SO, WHAT DO YOU THINK, SWEETHEART?

NOT A BAD BIT OF RESCUING.

Y'KNOW, SOME-TIMES I AMAZE EVEN MYSELF!

THAT DOESN'T SOUND TOO HARD.

AT LEAST THE INFORMATION IN THE R2 UNIT IS STILL INTACT.

WHAT'S THAT DROID CARRYING THAT'S SO IMPORTANT, ANYWAY?

THE TECHNICAL READ-OUTS OF THAT BATTLE-STATION!

I ONLY HOPE THAT WHEN THE DATA IS ANALYZED, ITS WEAKNESS CAN BE FOUND... AND QUICKLY.

OUR ESCAPE WAS EASY... FAR TOO EASY... TO SUIT ME!

WHILE, BACK ABOARD THE FORMIDABLE BATTLE-STATION KNOWN AS DEATH STAR...

ARE THEY *AWAY?*

THEY HAVE JUST MADE THE JUMP TO *HYPER-SPACE*, GOVERNOR TARKIN.

GOOD. I AM TAKING A *GRAVE CHANCE*, VADER.

THIS HAD BETTER *WORK.*

ARE YOU CERTAIN THAT THE *HOMING BEACON* IS SECURE ABOARD THEIR SHIP--

--SO THAT WE CAN *FOLLOW* THEM WHER-EVER THEY GO-- WHICH WILL DOUBTLESS BE THE MAIN *REBEL BASE?*

HAVE NO *FEAR.*

THIS WILL BE A DAY *LONG* REMEMBERED.

IT HAS SEEN THE END OF THE LAST OF THE *JEDI KNIGHTS*--

AND SOON, *VERY SOON,* IT WILL SEE THE *END OF THE REBELLION* ITSELF!

WHAT DO YOU MEAN... OUR ESCAPE WAS "TOO EASY"!?

THEY LET US ESCAPE... DON'T YOU SEE?

THEY KNOW WE WILL TAKE R2-D2 STRAIGHT TO THE REBEL BASE--AND THEY UNDOUBTABLY MEAN TO TRAIL US THERE!

I ONLY HOPE THE DATA INSIDE ARTOO CAN BE ANALYZED QUICKLY, SO THAT WE CAN FIGHT BACK AGAINST--

CUT THAT "WE" STUFF, PRINCESS! IT'S ALL OVER FOR ME!

I'M NOT DOING THIS FOR YOUR REVOLUTION-- AND I'M NOT DOING IT FOR YOU. I EXPECT TO BE PAID...

... WELL PAID!

YOU NEEDN'T WORRY ABOUT YOUR REWARD.

IF MONEY IS ALL THAT YOU LOVE...

... THAT IS WHAT YOU WILL RECEIVE.

WHAT ELSE IS THERE?

WELL??

HAN SOLO WAITS FOR HIS ANSWER... BUT THERE IS NONE.

YOUR FRIEND IS INDEED A MERCENARY, LUKE...

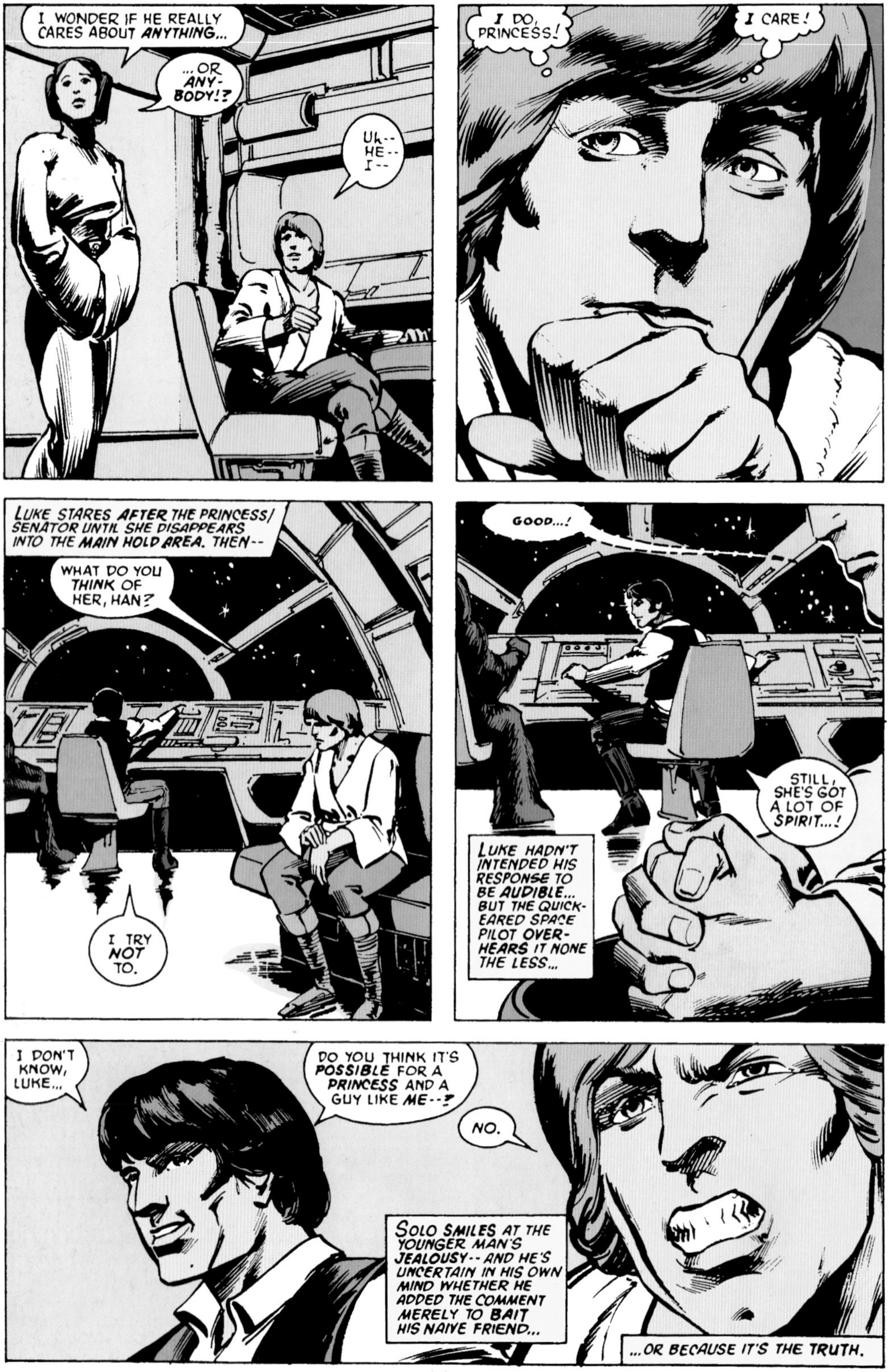
I WONDER IF HE REALLY CARES ABOUT ANYTHING...
...OR ANY-BODY!?
UH-- HE-- I--
I DO, PRINCESS!
I CARE!
LUKE STARES AFTER THE PRINCESS/ SENATOR UNTIL SHE DISAPPEARS INTO THE MAIN HOLD AREA. THEN--
WHAT DO YOU THINK OF HER, HAN?
I TRY NOT TO.
GOOD...!
STILL, SHE'S GOT A LOT OF SPIRIT...!
LUKE HADN'T INTENDED HIS RESPONSE TO BE AUDIBLE... BUT THE QUICK-EARED SPACE PILOT OVER-HEARS IT NONE THE LESS...
I DON'T KNOW, LUKE...
DO YOU THINK IT'S POSSIBLE FOR A PRINCESS AND A GUY LIKE ME--?
NO.
SOLO SMILES AT THE YOUNGER MAN'S JEALOUSY-- AND HE'S UNCERTAIN IN HIS OWN MIND WHETHER HE ADDED THE COMMENT MERELY TO BAIT HIS NAIVE FRIEND...
...OR BECAUSE IT'S THE TRUTH.

THE PLANET YAVIN, A HUGE GAS GIANT, IS NOT A HABITABLE WORLD.

SEVERAL OF YAVIN'S NUMEROUS MOONS, HOWEVER, ARE PLANET-SIZED THEMSELVES... AND THREE OF THESE CAN SUPPORT HUMANOID LIFE.

IT IS TOWARD THE SATELLITE DESIGNATED AS NUMBER FOUR, SHINING EMERALD-LIKE WITH ITS THICK JUNGLES, THAT THE MILLENNIUM FALCON FINALLY DRIFTS...

THE VERY AIR IS HEAVY WITH THE FANTASTIC CRIES OF UNIMAGINABLE CREATURES.

AND, ROTTING IN A FOREST OF GARGANTUAN TREES, AN ANCIENT TEMPLE LIES SHROUDED IN AN EERIE MIST.

BUT, THE ORIGINAL BUILDERS WOULD NOT NOW RECOGNIZE-THE INTERIOR OF THEIR ONCE-MIGHTY EDIFICE.

WITHIN, SEAMED METAL HAS REPLACED ROCK, AND THE BURIED LAYERS FAR BELOW THE SURFACE CONTAIN HANGAR UPON HANGAR OF ONE-MAN FIGHTER SPACECRAFT.

IT IS TOWARD THE UPPERMOST OF THESE HANGARS THAT A LANDSPEEDER NOW STREAKS, WITH THE MAKE-SHIFT CREW OF THE BELEAGUERED FALCON...

... TO DEPOSIT *FIVE* OF THE SIX WHO, A SHORT TIME BEFORE, TOOK ON THE MOST DREAD WEAPON OF THE EVIL *GALACTIC EMPIRE*-- AND SURVIVED.

SCARCELY HAVE THEY *STEPPED OFF* THE LAND-SPEEDER WHEN THE NOISY CLUSTER OF *HUMANS* NEARBY CEASE THEIR CONVERSATION AND RUSH TOWARD THE NOW-HOVERING CRAFT...

PRINCESS LEIA!

THANK THE STARS YOU'RE *SAFE!*

WE HAD FEARED THE *WORST!*

SO DID *WE.*

WE--HEARD ABOUT *ALDERAAN* BEING DESTROYED, AND WE WERE AFRAID YOU WERE *LOST*-- ALONG WITH YOUR PLANET-- AND YOUR *FATHER.*

WE DON'T HAVE *TIME* FOR OUR SORROWS, COMMANDER WILLARD...

THE *DEATH STAR* HAS SURELY *TRACKED* US HERE.

YOU MUST USE THE *INFORMATION* STORED IN THIS *R2 UNIT* TO PLAN OUR *ATTACK* AGAINST IT.

WE'LL DO OUR *BEST.*

YOU *MUST!* IT'S OUR *ONLY HOPE!*

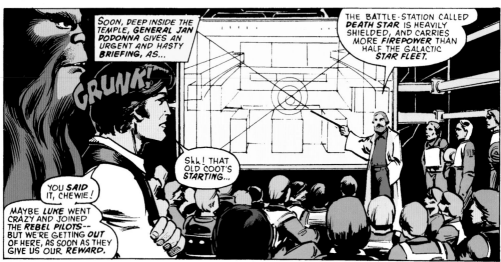

SOON, DEEP INSIDE THE TEMPLE, *GENERAL JAN DODONNA* GIVES AN URGENT AND HASTY BRIEFING, AS...

THE BATTLE-STATION CALLED *DEATH STAR* IS HEAVILY SHIELDED, AND CARRIES MORE *FIREPOWER* THAN HALF THE GALACTIC *STAR FLEET.*

GRUNK!

SHH! THAT OLD COOT'S *STARTING...*

YOU *SAID* IT, CHEWIE!

MAYBE *LUKE* WENT CRAZY AND JOINED THE *REBEL PILOTS*-- BUT WE'RE GETTING *OUT* OF HERE, AS SOON AS THEY GIVE US OUR *REWARD.*

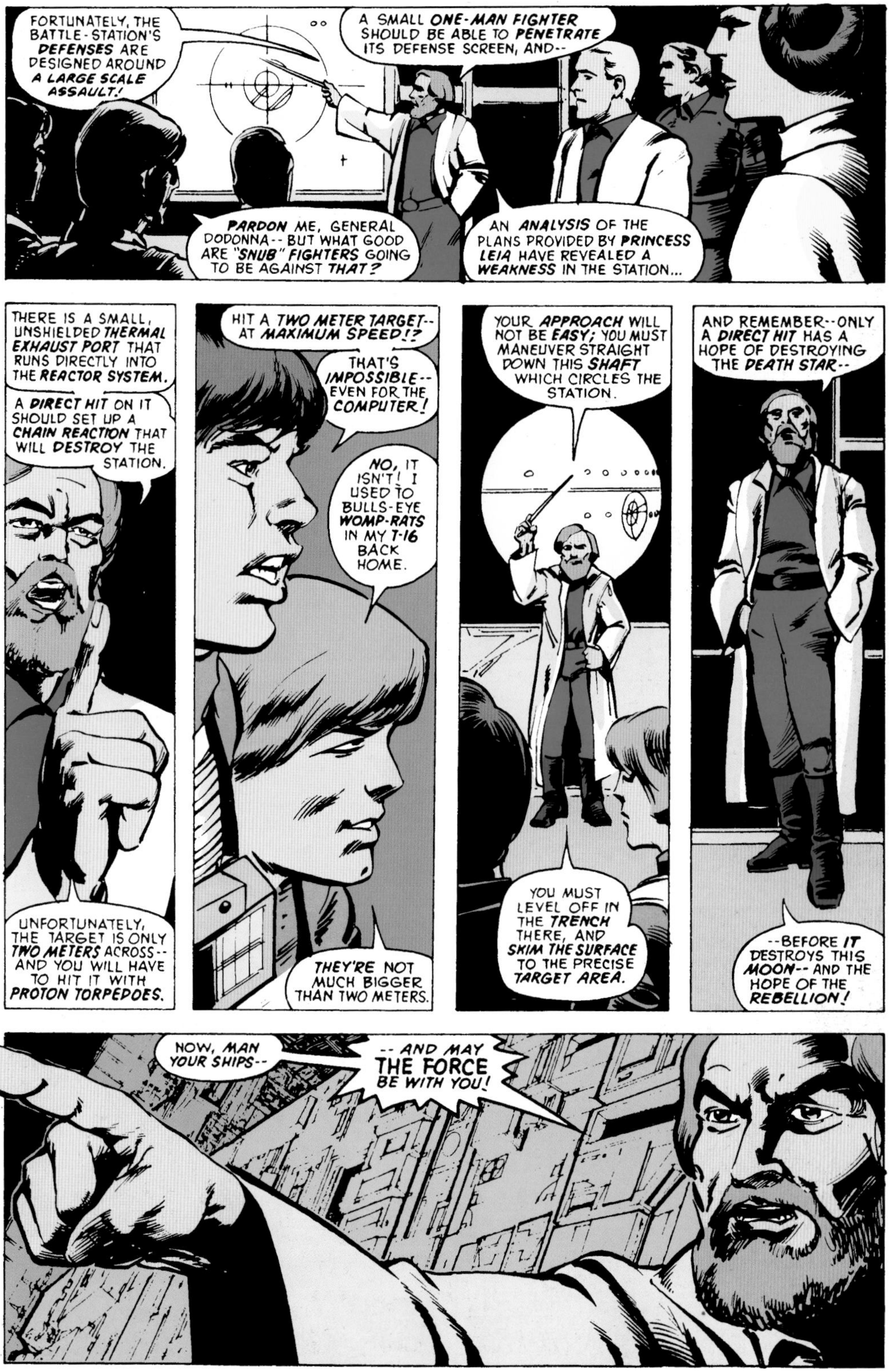

FORTUNATELY, THE BATTLE-STATION'S DEFENSES ARE DESIGNED AROUND A LARGE SCALE ASSAULT!
A SMALL ONE-MAN FIGHTER SHOULD BE ABLE TO PENETRATE ITS DEFENSE SCREEN, AND--
PARDON ME, GENERAL DODONNA-- BUT WHAT GOOD ARE "SNUB" FIGHTERS GOING TO BE AGAINST THAT?
AN ANALYSIS OF THE PLANS PROVIDED BY PRINCESS LEIA HAVE REVEALED A WEAKNESS IN THE STATION...
THERE IS A SMALL, UNSHIELDED THERMAL EXHAUST PORT THAT RUNS DIRECTLY INTO THE REACTOR SYSTEM.
A DIRECT HIT ON IT SHOULD SET UP A CHAIN REACTION THAT WILL DESTROY THE STATION.
UNFORTUNATELY, THE TARGET IS ONLY TWO METERS ACROSS-- AND YOU WILL HAVE TO HIT IT WITH PROTON TORPEDOES.
HIT A TWO METER TARGET-- AT MAXIMUM SPEED!?
THAT'S IMPOSSIBLE-- EVEN FOR THE COMPUTER!
NO, IT ISN'T! I USED TO BULLS-EYE WOMP-RATS IN MY T-16 BACK HOME.
THEY'RE NOT MUCH BIGGER THAN TWO METERS.
YOUR APPROACH WILL NOT BE EASY; YOU MUST MANEUVER STRAIGHT DOWN THIS SHAFT WHICH CIRCLES THE STATION.
YOU MUST LEVEL OFF IN THE TRENCH THERE, AND SKIM THE SURFACE TO THE PRECISE TARGET AREA.
AND REMEMBER--ONLY A DIRECT HIT HAS A HOPE OF DESTROYING THE DEATH STAR--
--BEFORE IT DESTROYS THIS MOON-- AND THE HOPE OF THE REBELLION!
NOW, MAN YOUR SHIPS--
-- AND MAY THE FORCE BE WITH YOU!

MOMENTS LATER, ALONG WITH HUNDREDS OF OTHERS, LUKE, THREEPIO, AND LITTLE ARTOO RUSH INTO THE HUGE SPACE-SHIP HANGAR.

FLIGHT CREWS BUSTLE ABOUT, LOADING LAST-MINUTE ARMAMENT AND UNLOCKING POWER COUPLINGS.

BUT, IT IS TWO DIFFERENT FIGURES THAT SUDDENLY CATCH LUKE SKYWALKER'S STARTLED ATTENTION--

-- THE HUGE WOOKIEE NAMED CHEWBACCA, AND --

HAN! SO YOU GOT YOUR REWARD-- AND YOU'RE LEAVING!

THAT'S RIGHT, KID. I'VE GOT SOME OLD DEBTS TO PAY OFF... AND EVEN IF I DIDN'T, I'D BE A FOOL TO STICK AROUND HERE.

YOU'RE PRETTY GOOD IN A SCRAP YOURSELF...

...SO WHY DON'T YOU COME WITH US?

I COULD USE YOU...!

WHY DON'T YOU LOOK AROUND, HAN?

YOU KNOW WHAT'S ABOUT TO HAPPEN... WHAT THEY'RE UP AGAINST.

THEY COULD USE A GOOD PILOT-- BUT YOU'RE TURNING YOUR BACK ON THEM!

WHAT GOOD'S A REWARD IF YOU'RE NOT AROUND TO SPEND IT?

ATTACKING THAT BATTLE-STATION ISN'T MY IDEA OF COURAGE; IT'S MORE LIKE SUICIDE.

HRUNK

SHUT UP, CHEWIE! I KNOW WHAT I'M DOING.

WELL... TAKE CARE OF YOUR-SELF, HAN...

...BUT, I GUESS THAT'S WHAT YOU'RE BEST AT, ISN'T IT?

LUKE SKYWALKER HARDLY HEARS HAN SOLO'S WHISPERED FAREWELL:

"MAY THE FORCE BE WITH YOU!"

AS LUKE REACHES HIS ASSIGNED SHIP, *PRINCESS LEIA* IS THERE WAITING...

ARE YOU *SURE* THIS IS WHAT YOU *WANT* TO DO, LUKE?

MORE THAN *ANYTHING*.

THEN, WHAT'S *WRONG?*

IT'S *HAN!* I THOUGHT HE'D *CHANGE HIS MIND*...

A MAN MUST FOLLOW HIS *OWN PATH*; NO ONE CAN CHOOSE IT *FOR HIM*.

YEAH... I KNOW. I ONLY WISH... *BEN* WERE HERE.

MAY *"THE FORCE"* BE WITH YOU, LUKE!

LUKE! I DON'T *BELIEVE* IT! HOW'D YOU GET MIXED UP IN THIS?

BIGGS! * I THOUGHT YOU'D BE AROUND HERE SOME- WHERE!

HAVE I GOT SOME *STORIES* TO TELL YOU, OLD BUDDY!

*LUKE'S CHILD- HOOD CHUM, FROM ISH #1. --Roy

ARE YOU *LUKE SKYWALKER?*

SURE *AM*, "BLUE LEADER"!

HAVE YOU BEEN CHECKED OUT ON THE *INCOM T-65?*

WELL, I ... NOT *EXACTLY*, I ... uh...

SIR, *LUKE* HERE IS THE *BEST BUSH- PILOT* IN THE OUTER-RIM TERRITORIES.

I'LL VOUCH FOR HIM!

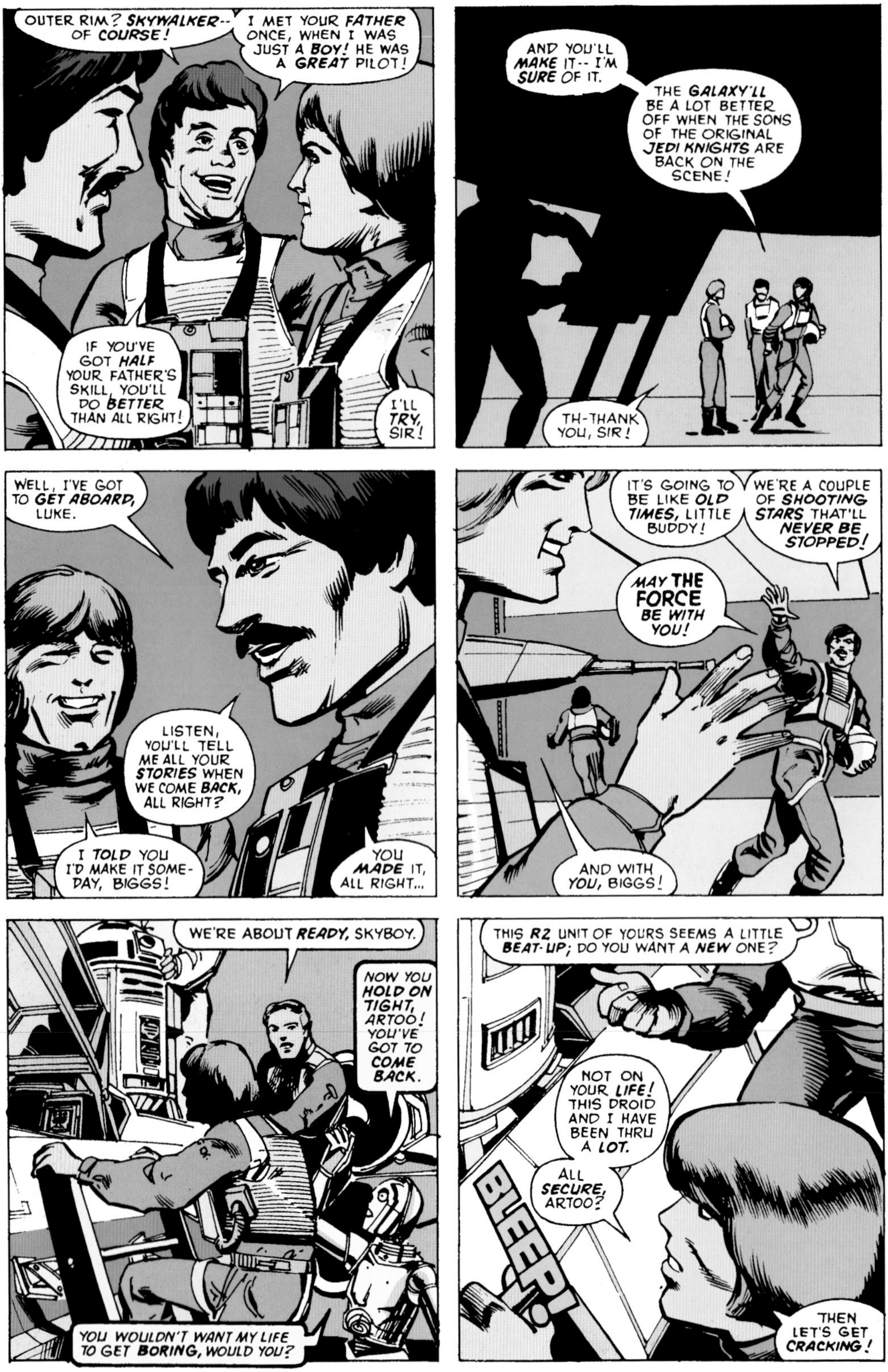
OUTER RIM? SKYWALKER-- OF COURSE!
I MET YOUR FATHER ONCE, WHEN I WAS JUST A BOY! HE WAS A GREAT PILOT!
IF YOU'VE GOT HALF YOUR FATHER'S SKILL, YOU'LL DO BETTER THAN ALL RIGHT!
I'LL TRY, SIR!
AND YOU'LL MAKE IT-- I'M SURE OF IT.
THE GALAXY'LL BE A LOT BETTER OFF WHEN THE SONS OF THE ORIGINAL JEDI KNIGHTS ARE BACK ON THE SCENE!
TH-THANK YOU, SIR!
WELL, I'VE GOT TO GET ABOARD, LUKE.
LISTEN, YOU'LL TELL ME ALL YOUR STORIES WHEN WE COME BACK, ALL RIGHT?
I TOLD YOU I'D MAKE IT SOME-DAY, BIGGS!
YOU MADE IT, ALL RIGHT...
IT'S GOING TO BE LIKE OLD TIMES, LITTLE BUDDY!
WE'RE A COUPLE OF SHOOTING STARS THAT'LL NEVER BE STOPPED!
MAY THE FORCE BE WITH YOU!
AND WITH YOU, BIGGS!
WE'RE ABOUT READY, SKYBOY.
NOW YOU HOLD ON TIGHT, ARTOO! YOU'VE GOT TO COME BACK.
YOU WOULDN'T WANT MY LIFE TO GET BORING, WOULD YOU?
THIS R2 UNIT OF YOURS SEEMS A LITTLE BEAT-UP; DO YOU WANT A NEW ONE?
NOT ON YOUR LIFE! THIS DROID AND I HAVE BEEN THRU A LOT.
ALL SECURE, ARTOO?
BLEEP!
THEN LET'S GET CRACKING!

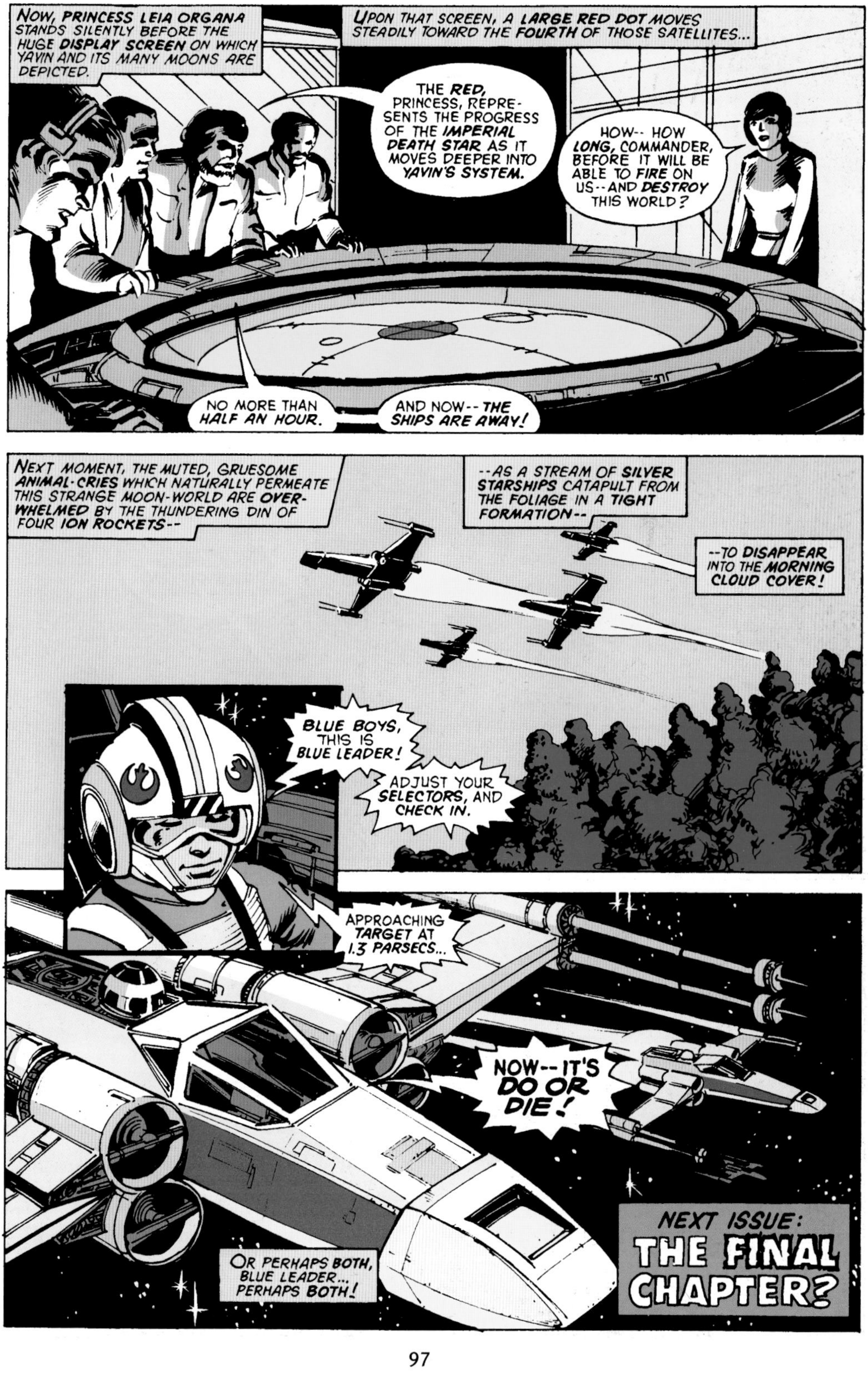
NOW, PRINCESS LEIA ORGANA STANDS SILENTLY BEFORE THE HUGE DISPLAY SCREEN ON WHICH YAVIN AND ITS MANY MOONS ARE DEPICTED.
UPON THAT SCREEN, A LARGE RED DOT MOVES STEADILY TOWARD THE FOURTH OF THOSE SATELLITES...
THE RED, PRINCESS, REPRESENTS THE PROGRESS OF THE IMPERIAL DEATH STAR AS IT MOVES DEEPER INTO YAVIN'S SYSTEM.
HOW-- HOW LONG, COMMANDER, BEFORE IT WILL BE ABLE TO FIRE ON US--AND DESTROY THIS WORLD?
NO MORE THAN HALF AN HOUR.
AND NOW-- THE SHIPS ARE AWAY!
NEXT MOMENT, THE MUTED, GRUESOME ANIMAL-CRIES WHICH NATURALLY PERMEATE THIS STRANGE MOON-WORLD ARE OVERWHELMED BY THE THUNDERING DIN OF FOUR ION ROCKETS--
--AS A STREAM OF SILVER STARSHIPS CATAPULT FROM THE FOLIAGE IN A TIGHT FORMATION--
--TO DISAPPEAR INTO THE MORNING CLOUD COVER!
BLUE BOYS, THIS IS BLUE LEADER!
ADJUST YOUR SELECTORS, AND CHECK IN.
APPROACHING TARGET AT 1.3 PARSECS...
NOW--IT'S DO OR DIE!
OR PERHAPS BOTH, BLUE LEADER... PERHAPS BOTH!
NEXT ISSUE:
THE FINAL CHAPTER?

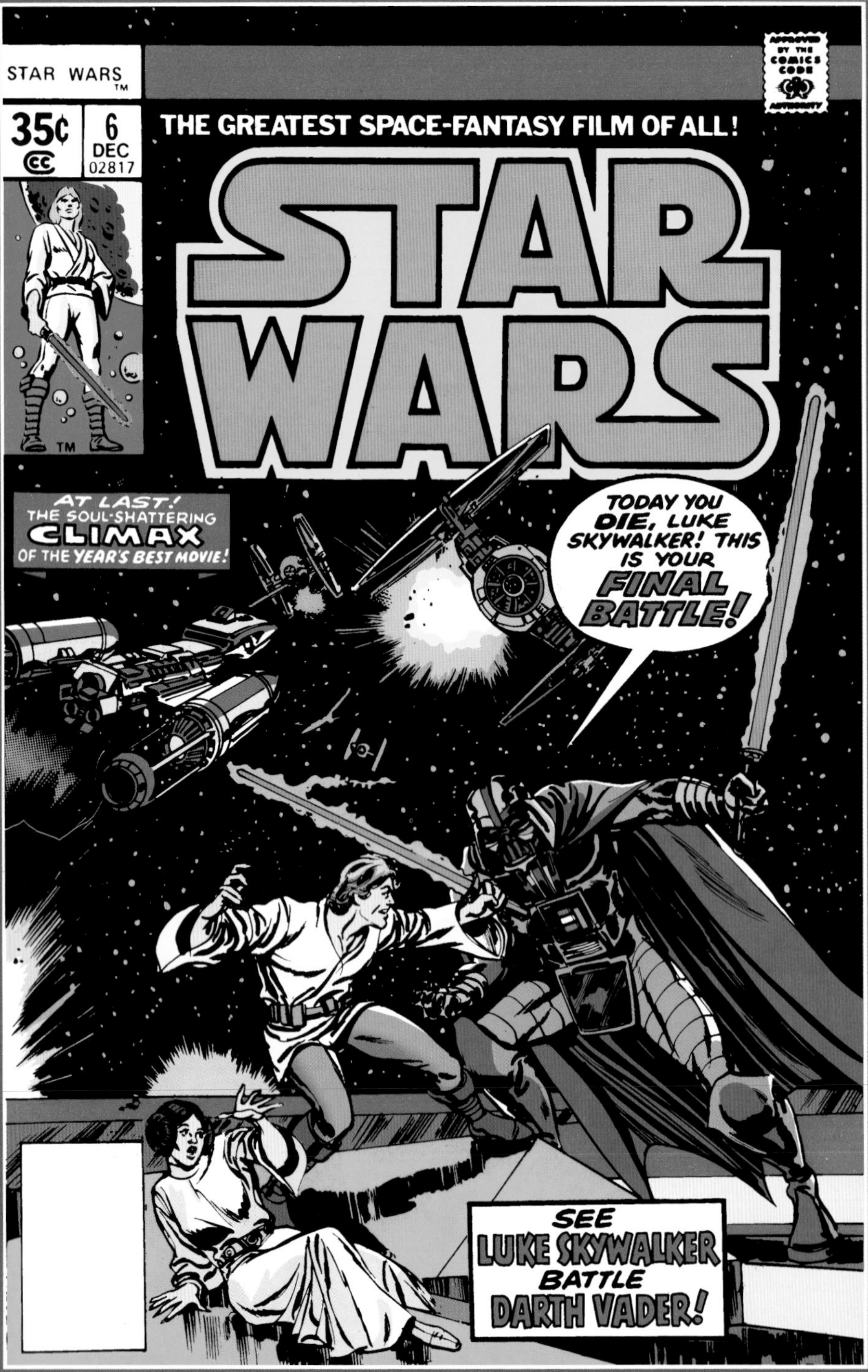
STAR WARS ™
35¢
6 DEC 02817
THE GREATEST SPACE-FANTASY FILM OF ALL!
STAR WARS
AT LAST! THE SOUL-SHATTERING CLIMAX OF THE YEAR'S BEST MOVIE!
TODAY YOU DIE, LUKE SKYWALKER! THIS IS YOUR FINAL BATTLE!
SEE LUKE SKYWALKER BATTLE DARTH VADER!

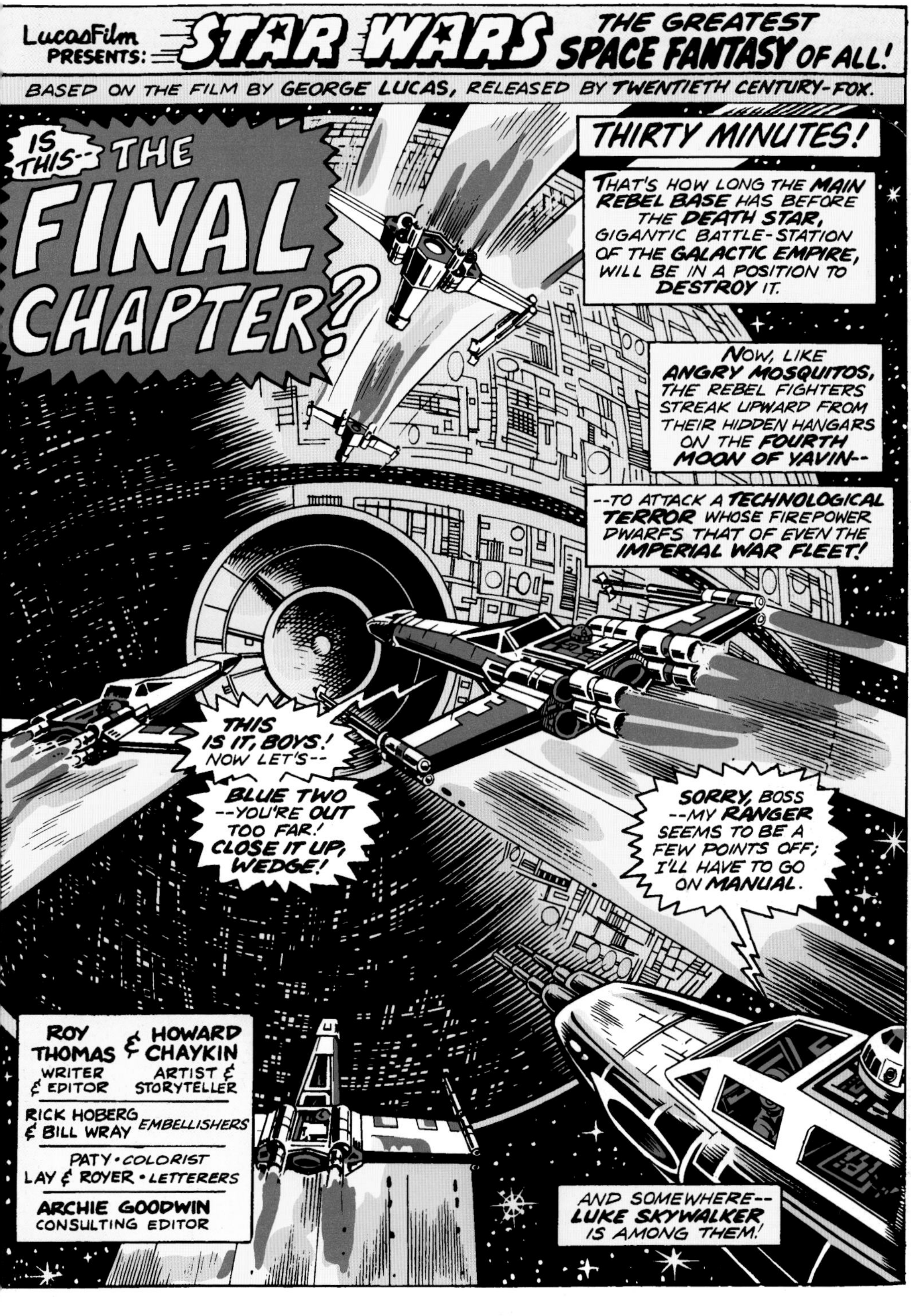
LucasFilm PRESENTS: STAR WARS THE GREATEST SPACE FANTASY OF ALL!
BASED ON THE FILM BY GEORGE LUCAS, RELEASED BY TWENTIETH CENTURY-FOX.
IS THIS-- THE FINAL CHAPTER?
THIRTY MINUTES!
THAT'S HOW LONG THE MAIN REBEL BASE HAS BEFORE THE DEATH STAR, GIGANTIC BATTLE-STATION OF THE GALACTIC EMPIRE, WILL BE IN A POSITION TO DESTROY IT.
NOW, LIKE ANGRY MOSQUITOS, THE REBEL FIGHTERS STREAK UPWARD FROM THEIR HIDDEN HANGARS ON THE FOURTH MOON OF YAVIN--
--TO ATTACK A TECHNOLOGICAL TERROR WHOSE FIREPOWER DWARFS THAT OF EVEN THE IMPERIAL WAR FLEET!
THIS IS IT, BOYS! NOW LET'S--
BLUE TWO --YOU'RE OUT TOO FAR! CLOSE IT UP, WEDGE!
SORRY, BOSS --MY RANGER SEEMS TO BE A FEW POINTS OFF; I'LL HAVE TO GO ON MANUAL.
ROY THOMAS WRITER & EDITOR & HOWARD CHAYKIN ARTIST & STORYTELLER
RICK HOBERG & BILL WRAY EMBELLISHERS
PATY • COLORIST
LAY & ROYER • LETTERERS
ARCHIE GOODWIN CONSULTING EDITOR
AND SOMEWHERE-- LUKE SKYWALKER IS AMONG THEM!

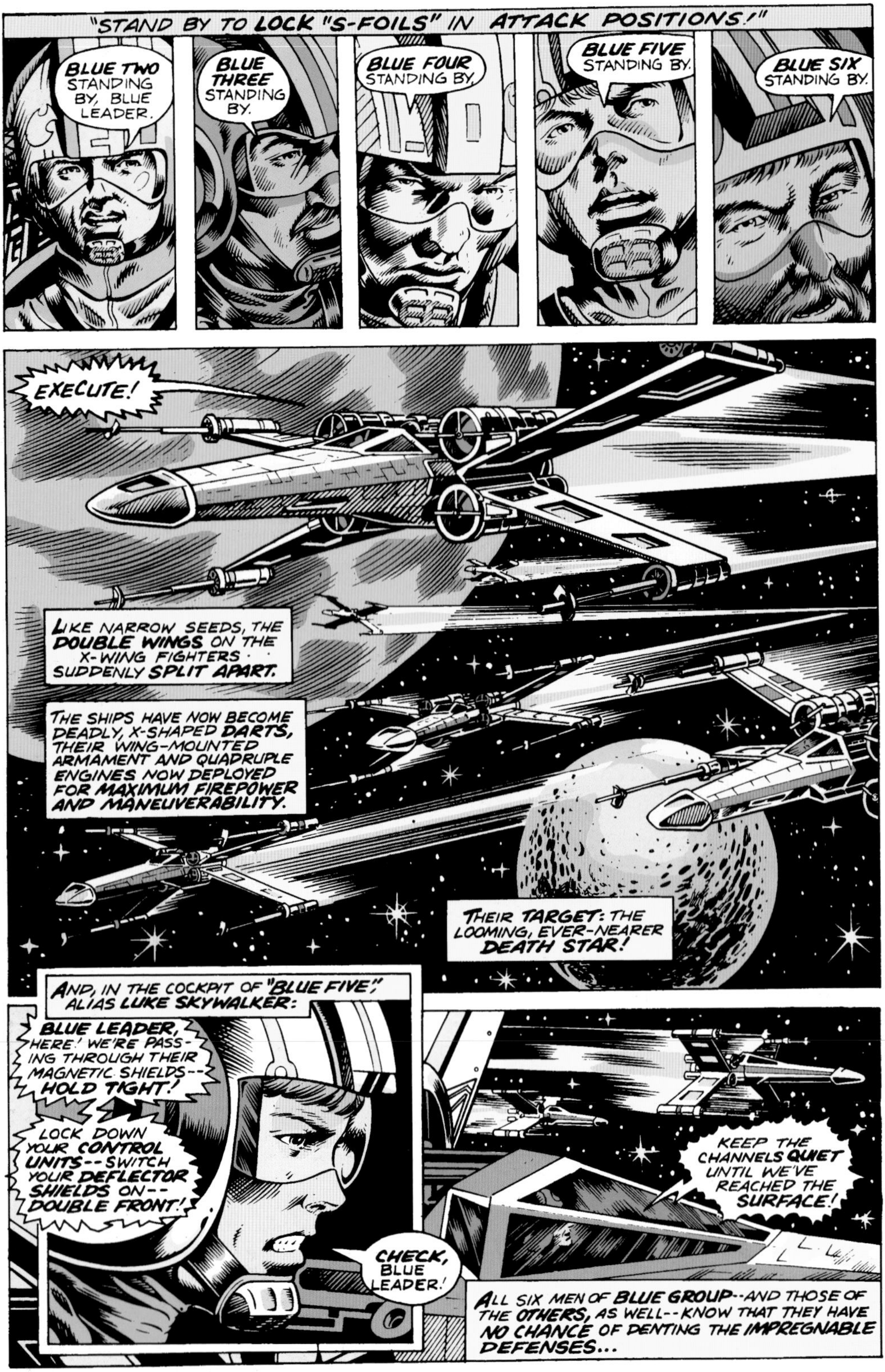
"STAND BY TO LOCK "S-FOILS" IN ATTACK POSITIONS!"
BLUE TWO STANDING BY, BLUE LEADER.
BLUE THREE STANDING BY.
BLUE FOUR STANDING BY.
BLUE FIVE STANDING BY.
BLUE SIX STANDING BY.
EXECUTE!
LIKE NARROW SEEDS, THE DOUBLE WINGS ON THE X-WING FIGHTERS SUDDENLY SPLIT APART.
THE SHIPS HAVE NOW BECOME DEADLY, X-SHAPED DARTS, THEIR WING-MOUNTED ARMAMENT AND QUADRUPLE ENGINES NOW DEPLOYED FOR MAXIMUM FIREPOWER AND MANEUVERABILITY.
THEIR TARGET: THE LOOMING, EVER-NEARER DEATH STAR!
AND, IN THE COCKPIT OF "BLUE FIVE," ALIAS LUKE SKYWALKER:
BLUE LEADER, HERE! WE'RE PASSING THROUGH THEIR MAGNETIC SHIELDS-- HOLD TIGHT!
LOCK DOWN YOUR CONTROL UNITS--SWITCH YOUR DEFLECTOR SHIELDS ON--DOUBLE FRONT!
KEEP THE CHANNELS QUIET UNTIL WE'VE REACHED THE SURFACE!
CHECK, BLUE LEADER!
ALL SIX MEN OF BLUE GROUP--AND THOSE OF THE OTHERS, AS WELL--KNOW THAT THEY HAVE NO CHANCE OF DENTING THE IMPREGNABLE DEFENSES...

YET, THE **REBEL LEADER** SPOKE EARLIER OF ITS **ONE WEAKNESS** WHICH MAY BE EXPLOITED IF THE SPACE-GODS ARE KIND:

"THERE IS A SMALL, UNSHIELDED *THERMAL EXHAUST PORT* THAT RUNS DIRECTLY INTO THE *REACTOR SYSTEM.*

"A *DIRECT HIT* ON IT SHOULD SET UP A *CHAIN REACTION* THAT WILL *DESTROY* THE STATION.

"YOU MUST MANEUVER STRAIGHT DOWN THE *SHAFT* WHICH CIRCLES THE STATION; YOU MUST LEVEL OFF IN THE *TRENCH* THERE, AND *SKIM THE SURFACE* TO THE *PRECISE TARGET AREA.*

"UNFORTUNATELY, THE TARGET IS ONLY *TWO METERS* ACROSS-- AND YOU WILL HAVE TO HIT IT WITH *PROTON TORPEDOES!*"

WHILE, *WITHIN* THE DEATH STAR ITSELF...

REEEEE

THERE GOES THE *ALARM!*

THE *REBELS* ARE COMING OUT TO MEET US IN *FORCE!*

THE *FOOLS!* DON'T THEY *REALIZE* THIS BATTLE-STATION IS NOW THE *ULTIMATE POWER IN THE UNIVERSE?*

WHAT CHANCE DO A FEW *X-WING FIGHTERS* HAVE AGAINST *US?*

THEY'RE *MAD,* THAT'S WHAT THEY ARE!

WHY AREN'T THEY SIMPLY *DE-FENDING* THEMSELVES ON *YAVIN'S FOURTH MOON* AS WE EXPECTED?

NO MATTER! WE'LL BLAST THEM RIGHT OUT OF THE *SKY!*

WITHIN MOMENTS, A *WEB OF ANNIHI-LATION* ENVELOPS THE APPROACHING STATION--

--AS *ENERGY BOLTS* AND *EXPLOSIVE SOLIDS* RIP OUT AT THE ON-COMING *REBEL* CRAFT.

THEN, AS *BLUE GROUP* DRAWS NEAR THE BATTLE-STATION...

BLUE THREE, THIS IS *BLUE FIVE!* HI, BIGGS!

HI YOURSELF, LUKE! WHAT--?

101

I'M GOING IN, BLUE THREE!

COVER ME!

I'M RIGHT BEHIND YOU, BLUE FIVE!

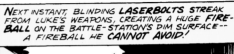

NEXT INSTANT, BLINDING *LASERBOLTS* STREAK FROM LUKE'S WEAPONS, CREATING A HUGE *FIRE-BALL* ON THE BATTLE-STATION'S DIM SURFACE-- A FIREBALL HE *CANNOT* AVOID!

PULL OUT, LUKE! *PULL OUT!*

I-- I CAN'T!!

UNABLE TO *TURN* IN TIME, LUKE'S FIGHTER *PLUNGES INTO* THE EXPANDING BALL OF *SUPER-HEATED GASES* --

--WHERE *LUKE SKYWALKER* KNOWS THE *TERRORS* OF THE DAMNED!

INTENSE HEAT LICKS AT THE STREAKING SPACE-CRAFT--THE *HOT WINDS OF HELL* BUFFET IT TO AND FRO UNTIL LUKE'S *TEETH RATTLE* --

THEN, HE IS *THROUGH* AND *CLEAR* ON THE *OTHER SIDE!*

YOU *ALL RIGHT,* LUKE?

I GOT A LITTLE *COOKED,* BUT I'M *OKAY!*

AND, MOVING AMID THE *CHAOS* WITH THE EMBATTLED *DEATH STAR* IS...*DARTH VADER!*

AT LEAST *THIRTY* REBEL SHIPS, LORD VADER--BUT THEY'RE SO *SMALL,* THEY'RE EVADING OUR *TURBO-LASERS!*

WE COUNT

GET THE CREWS TO THEIR *FIGHTERS,* AND PREPARE TO *LIFT OUT,* IMMEDIATELY!

THIS STATION IS *NOT* DESIGNED TO DO BATTLE WITH SUCH *PUNY, INSIGNIFICANT* SPACE-CRAFT...AND THAT COULD BE ITS *FATAL FLAW!*

WE'LL HAVE TO *DESTROY* THE REBELS, *SHIP TO SHIP!*

YES, LORD VADER!

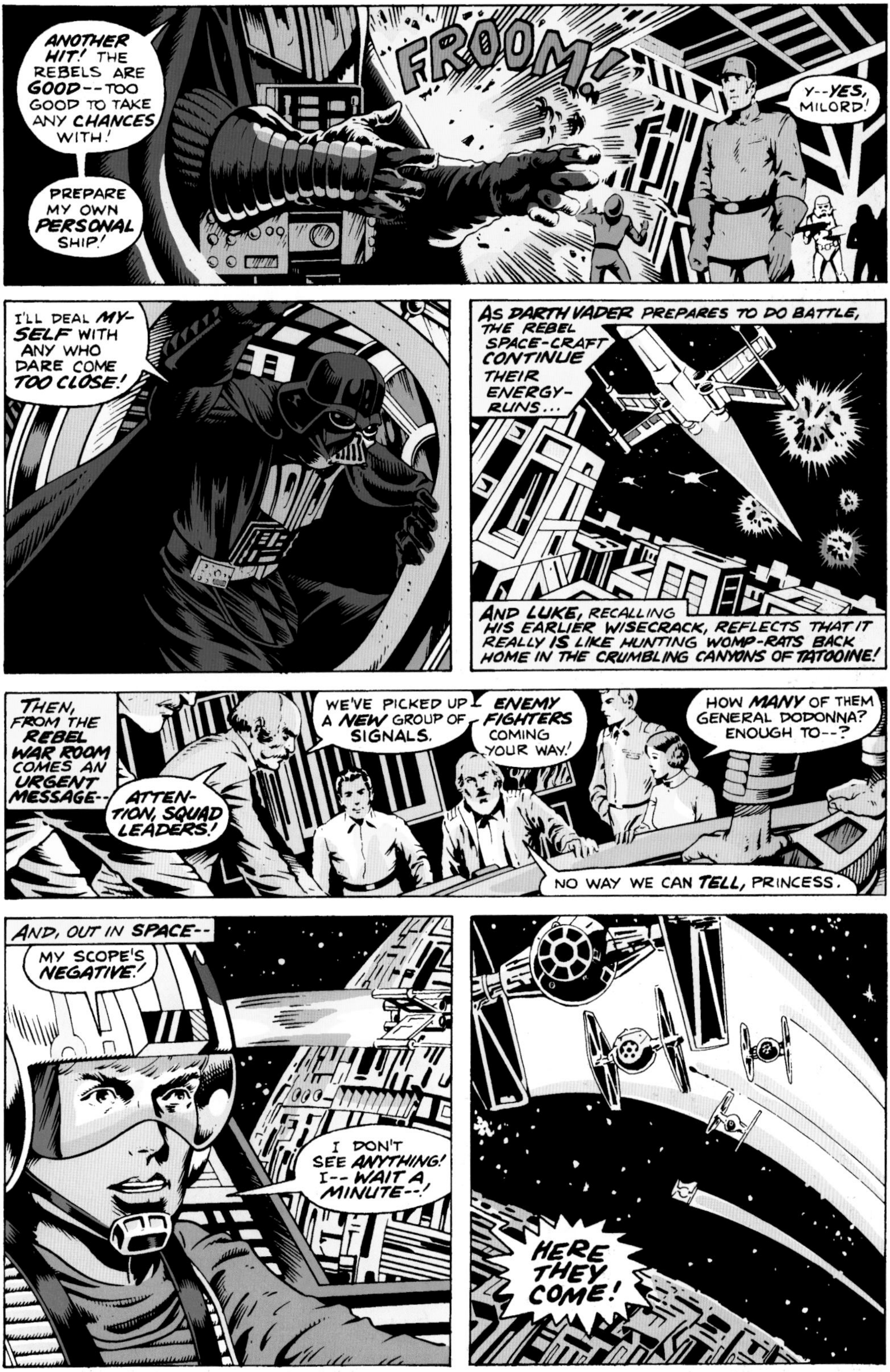
ANOTHER HIT! THE REBELS ARE GOOD--TOO GOOD TO TAKE ANY CHANCES WITH!
PREPARE MY OWN PERSONAL SHIP!
FROOM!
Y--YES, MILORD!
I'LL DEAL MY-SELF WITH ANY WHO DARE COME TOO CLOSE!
AS DARTH VADER PREPARES TO DO BATTLE, THE REBEL SPACE-CRAFT CONTINUE THEIR ENERGY-RUNS...
AND LUKE, RECALLING HIS EARLIER WISECRACK, REFLECTS THAT IT REALLY IS LIKE HUNTING WOMP-RATS BACK HOME IN THE CRUMBLING CANYONS OF TATOOINE!
THEN, FROM THE REBEL WAR ROOM COMES AN URGENT MESSAGE--
ATTEN-TION, SQUAD LEADERS!
WE'VE PICKED UP A NEW GROUP OF SIGNALS.
ENEMY FIGHTERS COMING YOUR WAY!
HOW MANY OF THEM GENERAL DODONNA? ENOUGH TO--?
NO WAY WE CAN TELL, PRINCESS.
AND, OUT IN SPACE--
MY SCOPE'S NEGATIVE!
I DON'T SEE ANYTHING! I--WAIT A MINUTE--!
HERE THEY COME!

I'D FEEL BETTER IF *HAN SOLO* AND *CHEWBACCA* WERE HERE!

BUT, HAN GOT HIS *REWARD* FOR HELPING SAVE THE *PRINCESS*, AND THAT'S ALL HE SEEMS TO--

BIGGS!

LOOK OUT!

THE ENEMY'S SWOOPING *AROUND* US--THEY'RE MORE *MANEUVERABLE* THAN WE *THOUGHT*--!

YOU'VE *PICKED UP* ONE!

WATCH IT!

I CAN'T *SEE* IT! WHERE *IS* HE??

LUKE SKYWALKER *WATCHES* HELPLESSLY AS THE BOYHOOD CHUM'S SHIP SHOOTS *AWAY* FROM THE STATION SURFACE AND OUT INTO *CLEAR SPACE*--

--STILL WITH EACH SUCCESSIVE *ENEMY BOLT* PASSING A BIT *CLOSER* TO HIS HULL!

HE'S ON ME *TIGHT!* I CAN'T *SHAKE* HIM.

I CAN'T *SHAKE* HIM!

HANG ON, BIGGS! I'M COMING IN!

THE NEXT MOMENT, *ELECTRONIC CROSSHAIRS* LINE UP IN LUKE'S GUNSIGHTS--THERE IS A *SMALL EXPLOSION* IN THE VAST SILENCE OF THE COSMOS--

--AND THE *IMPERIAL PILOT* IS VAPORIZED WITH HIS *SHIP!*

GOT HIM!

--AND THE FOLLOWING INSTANT--

THE IMAGE HAS FADED, PRINCESS! THE HIGH-BAND RECEIVE HAS FAILED!

THEN SWITCH TO AUDIO ONLY-- AND DO THE BEST YOU CAN!

OH DEAR! EVEN WITH ARTOO DETOO SERVING AS HIS R2 UNIT, MASTER LUKE IS LIKELY TO BE HURT. I DO WISH HE WOULDN'T TAKE SO MANY CHANCES.

SO DO I, THREE-PIO...

MEANWHILE, HIGH ABOVE, BLUE FOUR HAS BECOME THE FIRST REBEL CRAFT OF BLUE GROUP TO FALL BEFORE THE DEADLY IMPERIAL LASERBOLTS...

...AND LUKE SKYWALKER LOOKS AS IF HE MAY SOON BECOME THE SECOND!

SO DO I!

TIE FIGHTER ON MY TAIL!

CAN'T SHAKE HIM!

BLUE TWO HERE.

I'M ON HIM, LUKE.

HOLD ON!

THE YOUNGEST OF THE REBEL PILOTS DOESN'T HAVE TO WAIT VERY LONG...

PORKINS! DO YOU READ? EJECT! EJECT!

THANKS, WEDGE! I-- WAIT!

BLUE SIX IS HIT!

COME IN, BLUE SIX!

I-I'M OKAY! I CAN HOLD HER! JUST--

THOSE ARE THE LAST WORDS EVER UTTERED BY THE MAN LUKE SKYWALKER KNOWS ONLY AS BLUE SIX.

BUT BIGGS HAS FOUGHT BESIDE LT. TONO PORKINS FOR LONG WEEKS AND MONTHS, AND HE KNOWS SUDDENLY WHAT IT MEANS TO LOSE... A FRIEND.

SO LONG, PIGGY.

YOU WILL BE AVENGED!

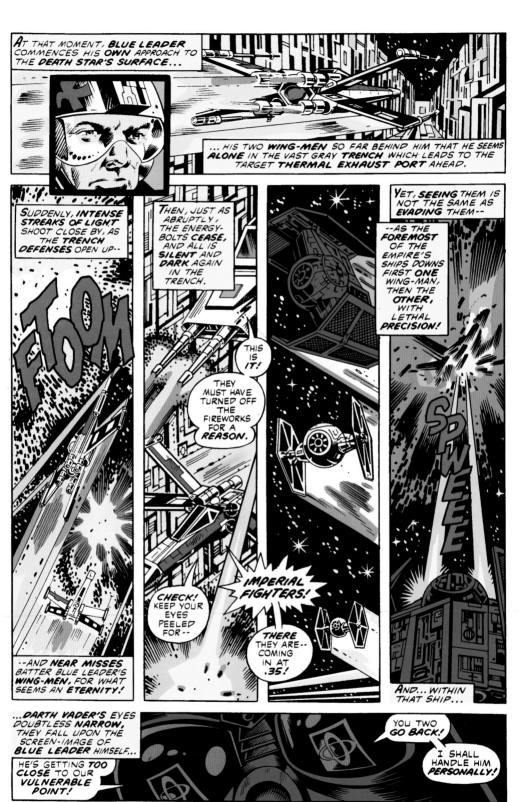

AT THAT MOMENT, BLUE LEADER COMMENCES HIS OWN APPROACH TO THE DEATH STAR'S SURFACE...

... HIS TWO WING-MEN SO FAR BEHIND HIM THAT HE SEEMS ALONE IN THE VAST GRAY TRENCH WHICH LEADS TO THE TARGET THERMAL EXHAUST PORT AHEAD.

SUDDENLY, INTENSE STREAKS OF LIGHT SHOOT CLOSE BY, AS THE TRENCH DEFENSES OPEN UP--

FTOOM

--AND NEAR MISSES BATTER BLUE LEADER'S WING-MEN, FOR WHAT SEEMS AN ETERNITY!

THEN, JUST AS ABRUPTLY, THE ENERGY-BOLTS CEASE, AND ALL IS SILENT AND DARK AGAIN IN THE TRENCH.

THIS IS IT!

THEY MUST HAVE TURNED OFF THE FIREWORKS FOR A REASON.

CHECK! KEEP YOUR EYES PEELED FOR--

IMPERIAL FIGHTERS!

THERE THEY ARE-- COMING IN AT .35!

YET, SEEING THEM IS NOT THE SAME AS EVADING THEM--

--AS THE FOREMOST OF THE EMPIRE'S SHIPS DOWNS FIRST ONE WING-MAN, THEN THE OTHER, WITH LETHAL PRECISION!

SPWEEE

AND... WITHIN THAT SHIP...

...DARTH VADER'S EYES DOUBTLESS NARROW, THEY FALL UPON THE SCREEN-IMAGE OF BLUE LEADER HIMSELF...

HE'S GETTING TOO CLOSE TO OUR VULNERABLE POINT!

YOU TWO GO BACK!

I SHALL HANDLE HIM PERSONALLY!

I'M IN *RANGE!* TARGET IN *SIGHT.*

IF I CAN *JUST--*

NOW!

AAAA

BLUE LEADER'S PROTON TORPEDOES WERE LAUNCHED A MICRO-SECOND BEFORE THE FATAL ENERGY-BOLT FROM THE LORD OF THE SITH SENT HIS SHIP HURTLING DOWNWARD TO SMASH BRILLIANTLY BUT HARMLESSLY AGAINST THE DEATH STAR HULL.

PERHAPS IT IS MERCY, OF A SORT, THAT HE WILL NEVER KNOW THAT HIS TORPEDOES MISSED THE TWO-METER TARGET BY THE MEREST FRACTION.

LOOKING DOWN, LUKE FOR THE FIRST TIME FEELS THE TRUE HELPLESSNESS OF HIS SITUATION...

WE'VE... LOST BLUE LEADER.

HE SCARCELY CARES IF HIS WORDS ARE HEARD BACK ON YAVIN FOUR.

NOW, THERE IS JUST HIMSELF...

...AND WEDGE...

...AND BIGGS.

OKAY, YOU TWO-- THIS IS LUKE-- BLUE FIVE...

CLOSE IT UP! WE'RE GOING IN!!

AND *DEEP INSIDE* THE DEATH STAR...

GOVENOR TARKIN-- I HAVE CHECKED ALL COORDINATES, AS YOU ORDERED... AND I FIND THAT THERE *IS* A DANGER, HOW-EVER *SMALL*.

SHALL I HAVE YOUR *PERSONAL CRAFT* STAND BY FOR POSSIBLE *EVACUATION*?

EVACUATE? *NEVER!*

THE VERY IDEA IS *TREASONOUS.*

WE *SHALL* PREVAIL-- IN THE NAME OF THE *GALACTIC EMPIRE!*

WHILE, OVERHEAD, LUKE SKYWALKER HAS SUDDENLY DISCOVERED THAT ONE OF HIS KEY INSTRUMENTS IS MALFUNCTIONING...

BLAST! IF ARTOO CAN'T PUT ME BACK IN TOUCH WITH *COMPUTER CENTRAL* BACK ON YAVIN-4--

--I'LL HAVE TO AIM THE PROTON TORPEDOES *MANUALLY*, AND THAT'S NOT AS *ACCURATE* AS--

TRUST YOUR FEELINGS, LUKE--!

HUH? *WHO--?*

IT IS A YOUNG-OLD VOICE WHICH SOUNDS IN HIS EARS... A FAMILIAR VOICE...

... A VOICE AT ONCE CALM, CONFIDENT, CONTENTED... AND REASSURING.

A VOICE HE HAS LISTENED TO INTENTLY ON THE DESERT OF TATOOINE... AND ELSEWHERE.

BEN! BEN KENOBI!!

THEN-- MAYBE HE *WASN'T* KILLED BY DARTH VADER'S *LIGHTSABRE,* AFTER ALL!

MAYBE HE *MERGED*, SOMEHOW, WITH *"THE FORCE"*-- AND HE'S HERE *WITH* ME-- *RIGHT NOW!*

THEN MAYBE THERE'S A *CHANCE* FOR US, AT THAT-- EVEN AGAINST *DARTH VADER* AND THE *DEATH STAR!*

WEDGE-- BIGGS-- WE'RE GOING IN-- *FULL THROTTLE!*

IT'LL BE JUST LIKE *BEGGARS' CANYON* BACK HOME!

WE'RE WITH YOU, BOSS!

YOU WORRY ABOUT *TARGET ZERO*-- WE'LL HANDLE THOSE *IMPERIAL FIGHTERS* FOLLOWING US INTO THE *TRENCH!*

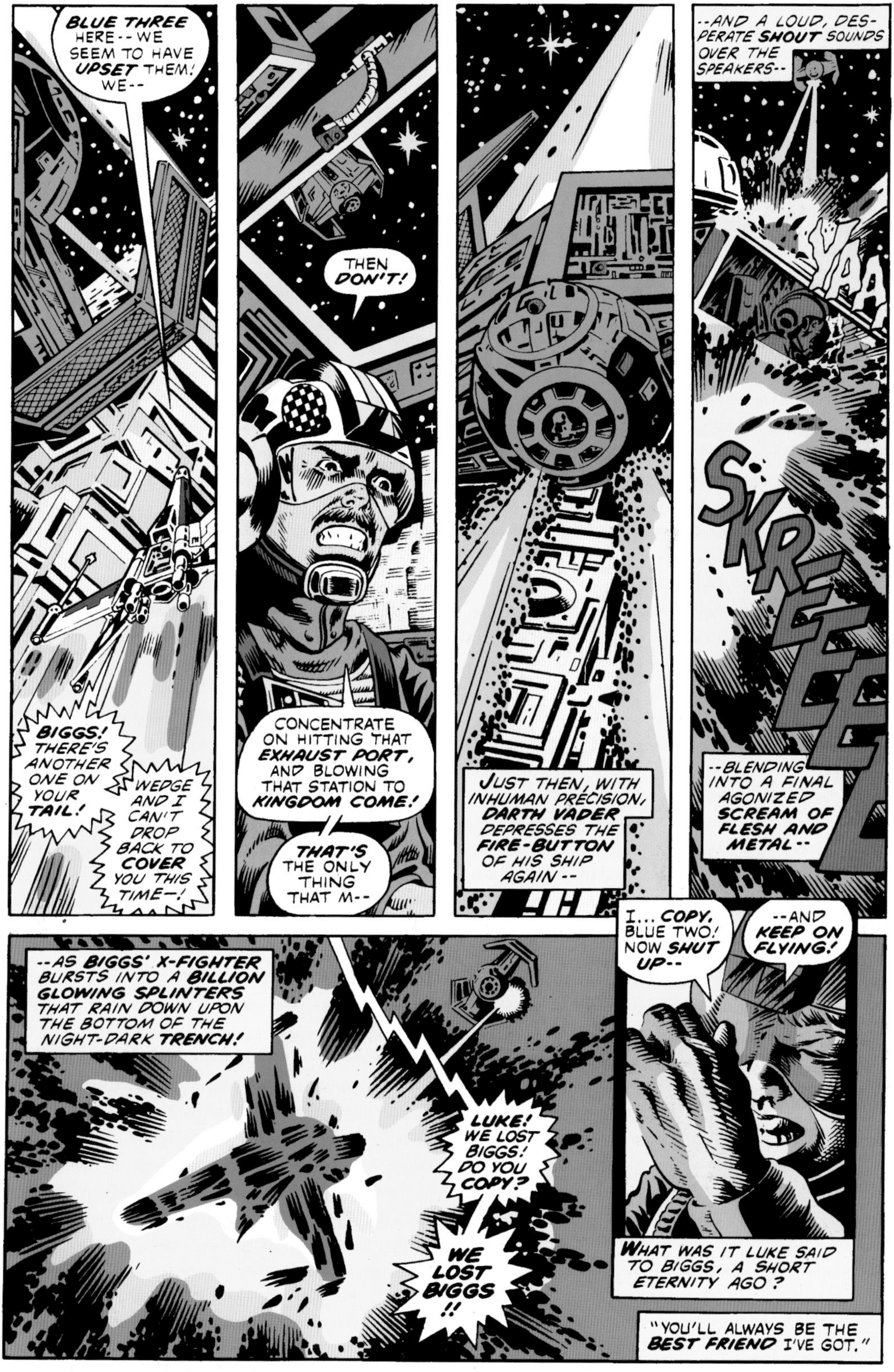

BLUE THREE HERE--WE SEEM TO HAVE UPSET THEM! WE--
BIGGS! THERE'S ANOTHER ONE ON YOUR TAIL!
WEDGE AND I CAN'T DROP BACK TO COVER YOU THIS TIME--!
THEN DON'T!
CONCENTRATE ON HITTING THAT EXHAUST PORT, AND BLOWING THAT STATION TO KINGDOM COME!
THAT'S THE ONLY THING THAT M--
JUST THEN, WITH INHUMAN PRECISION, DARTH VADER DEPRESSES THE FIRE-BUTTON OF HIS SHIP AGAIN --
--AND A LOUD, DESPERATE SHOUT SOUNDS OVER THE SPEAKERS--
SKREEEE
--BLENDING INTO A FINAL AGONIZED SCREAM OF FLESH AND METAL--
--AS BIGGS' X-FIGHTER BURSTS INTO A BILLION GLOWING SPLINTERS THAT RAIN DOWN UPON THE BOTTOM OF THE NIGHT-DARK TRENCH!
LUKE! WE LOST BIGGS! DO YOU COPY?
WE LOST BIGGS!!
I... COPY, BLUE TWO! NOW SHUT UP--
--AND KEEP ON FLYING!
WHAT WAS IT LUKE SAID TO BIGGS, A SHORT ETERNITY AGO?
"YOU'LL ALWAYS BE THE BEST FRIEND I'VE GOT."

NOW, WITH **RED GROUP** BEATEN OFF AND **BLUE GROUP** ALL BUT ANNIHILATED BY ENEMY FIRE, ONLY **LUKE** AND **WEDGE** REMAIN...

CLOSE IT UP, NEDGE! YOU CAN'T DO ANY MORE **GOOD** BACK THERE.

CHECK! BUT-- I'VE **PICKED UP** ONE... AND WHOEVER HE IS, HE'S A **DEVIL** OF A FLYER!

AND, HOT ON WEDGE'S ROCKETING HEELS COMES ...**DARTH VADER!**

HIS **JEDI-BORN INSTINCTS** TELL HIM THAT THE GREAT **BATTLE-STATION** HE SERVES IS ONLY **SECONDS** AWAY FROM BEING ABLE TO **DESTROY** THE REBEL FORTRESS ON **YAVIN-4** ...

...AND NO MERE PAIR OF UPSTARTS MUST BE ALLOWED TO STOP THE **IMPERIAL JUGGERNAUT.**

LUKE-- I'VE GOT A MAL-FUNCTION!

I CAN'T STAY **WITH** YOU.

OKAY, WEDGE, **GET CLEAR,** IF YOU CAN!

SORRY...!

IF HE HAD HOPED TO **LURE** THE **IMPERIAL SHIPS** AWAY, BLUE TWO'S HOPES ARE SWIFTLY **DASHED...**

...AS THEY **IGNORE** HIS SHIP, AND BEAR DOWN ON LUKE'S **FIGHTER**-- GAINING WITH EACH PASSING INSTANT!

HE WILL BE **IN RANGE** IN ANOTHER SECOND!

PREPARE TO FI--

ONE OF THE THREE TIE-FIGHTERS HAS SUDDENLY BECOME AN EXPANDING CYLINDER OF **DECOMPOSING DEBRIS...**

BY THE IMMORTAL GODS OF THE SITH!

LORD VADER! THAT ENERGY-BOLT CAME FROM **ABOVE** US!

BUT, WHO IS **LEFT** TO--?

THEN, FROM **OUT OF YAVIN'S SUN**, OR SO IT SEEMS, COMES A **NEW** THREAT, FOR WHICH THE PURSUING TIE-FIGHTERS ARE **NOT PREPARED**:

A **SPACE-FREIGHTER** THAT DOES NOT **MOVE** LIKE A FREIGHTER, SOMEHOW-- BUT **FASTER**--**SURER**.

ITS NAME IS THE **MILLENNIUM FALCON**--

--AND ITS CAPTAIN, **HAN SOLO**, IS ONE OF THE **BEST PILOTS** IN THE GALAXY!

THE FALCON'S INTERVENTION CAUSES VADER'S WING-MAN TO **VEER OFF** SUDDENLY, STRIKING HIS **LORD'S SHIP** AS HE GOES!

THEN, AS THE WING-CRAFT IS **OBLITERATED** AGAINST THE SIDE OF THE TRENCH, THE **REMAINING** SHIP GOES **SPINNING OFF** INTO THE BLACKNESS--

ABOARD IT, **DARTH VADER** FINDS HIMSELF WHIRLING AROUND, HIS INSTRUMENTS SHATTERED, HIS VESSEL WILDLY **OUT OF CONTROL**--

-- AND HEADING OUT INTO THE ENDLESS REACHES OF **DEEP SPACE**!

THEN, OVER HIS HEADPHONES, LUKE SKYWALKER HEARS STILL **ANOTHER** FAMILIAR, WELCOME VOICE:

YOU'RE **ALL CLEAR**, KID!

NOW **BLOW** THIS THING, SO WE CAN ALL **GO HOME**!

GRONK!

LUKE IS ABOUT TO REPLY WHEN --

LUKE... TRUST ME...!

HE HESITATES A MOMENT. THEN--

BASE ONE TO BLUE FIVE-- YOUR TARGET DEVICE IS OFF! WHAT'S WRONG?

NOTHING! I'M NOT GOING TO USE THE COMPUTER--

I'M SWITCHING TO MANUAL!

MANUAL!? ARE YOU INSANE? YOU CAN'T HIT A TARGET TWO METERS WIDE WITHOUT THE COMPUTER!

BLUE FIVE, ARE YOU THERE? COME IN, BLUE FIVE!

THE YOUNG SPACE-PILOT DOES NOT RESPOND --UNLESS IT IS BY PUSHING A BUTTON ON THE CONTROL-PANEL BEFORE HIM--

--TO HIT A NARROW TARGET LUKE SKYWALKER HAS NOT EVEN SEEN!

AGAIN, THE WORDS OF BEN KENOBI COME TO HIM FROM OUT OF THE RECENT PAST:

"YOUR EYES CAN DECEIVE YOU. DON'T TRUST THEM! STRETCH OUT YOUR FEELINGS!"

HE DID.

GOOD SHOT, KID! THAT WAS ONE IN A MILLION!

GLAD YOU WERE HERE TO SEE IT! NOW, LET'S GET SOME DISTANCE--

--BEFORE THAT THING GOES SUPER-NOVA!

BEHIND THEM, SMALL FLASHES OF FADING LIGHT MARK THE RECEDING BATTLE-STATION...

THEN, WITHOUT WARNING-- THE ETERNAL NIGHT OF SPACE BECOMES, FOR A FEW SECONDS, THE BRIGHTNESS OF DAY!

NO ONE DARES LOOK DIRECTLY AT THE EXPLODING BATTLE- STATION--

--NOT EVEN MULTIPLE SHIELDS SET ON HIGH COULD DIM THAT AWESOME GLARE SUFFICIENTLY TO PREVENT PERMANENT BLINDNESS.

THE UNIVERSE SEEMS FILLED FOR AN INSTANT WITH TRILLIONS OF MICROSCOPIC METAL FRAGMENTS, PROPELLED PAST THE RETREATING SHIPS BY THE LIBERATED ENERGY OF A SMALL ARTIFICIAL SUN.

THE COLLAPSED RESIDUE OF THE DEATH STAR WILL CONTINUE TO CONSUME ITSELF FOR SEVERAL DAYS--

--FORMING, FOR THAT BRIEF SPAN OF TIME, THE MOST IMPRESSIVE TOMBSTONE IN THIS CORNER OF THE COSMOS.

FOLLOWING WEDGE AND HAN TO **TOUCH DOWN** IN THE HANGER ON YAVIN-4, LUKE SOON FINDS HIMSELF IN THE CENTER OF A **CHEERFUL, GLEAMING THRONG** THAT INCLUDES TECHNICIANS AND GENERALS ALIKE...

TECHNICOS! HURRY UP AND SEE TO MY **R2 UNIT** HERE!

HE TOOK SOME BAD **HITS** UP THERE!

OH MY! **ARTOO,** CAN YOU HEAR ME? YOU CAN **REPAIR** HIM, CAN'T YOU?

WE'LL DO OUR **BEST.**

YOU **MUST!**

IF ANY OF **MY** CIRCUITS OR GEARS WILL HELP, I'LL GLADLY **DONATE** THEM!

HAN, YOU OLD SPACE-DEVIL! I **KNEW** YOU'D COME BACK IN TIME TO KEEP ME FROM WINDING UP **SPACE-DUST!**

WELL, I COULDN'T LET A **FLYING FARMBOY** GO UP AGAINST THE DEATH STAR ALL BY **HIMSELF,** COULD I?

BESIDES, I DIDN'T WANT YOU TO GET ALL THE **CREDIT!**

AND, AS THEY LAUGH, A **LITHE FIGURE,** ROBES FLOWING, RUSHES UP TO EMBRACE LUKE IN A VERY **UNSENATORIAL** FASHION.

YOU **DID** IT, LUKE!

YOU DID IT!!

AND **YOU,** YOU BIG **CORELLIAN**--I KNEW THERE WAS **MORE** TO YOU THAN **MONEY!**

ONCE IN A WHILE, PRINCESS--

ONCE IN A WHILE!

GAZING **UPWARD** TOWARD THE CEILING, **LUKE SKYWALKER** THINKS FOR A PASSING MOMENT HE HEARS SOMETHING OVERHEAD...

...SOMETHING FAINTLY LIKE A **GRATIFIED SIGH.**

OF COURSE, IT IS PROBABLY ONLY THE INTRUDING **HOT WIND** OF A STEAMING **JUNGLE WORLD**...

BUT, LUKE PREFERS TO THINK **OTHERWISE.**

Epilogue: IN THE VAST AND ANCIENT CHAMBER, THE **BANNERS OF MANY WORLDS** FLUTTER... WORLDS WHICH HAVE **LENT SUPPORT** TO THE REBEL ALLIANCE DURING ITS MOST DIFFICULT DAYS.

TODAY, HUNDREDS OF **REBEL TROOPS AND TECHNICIANS** STAND ASSEMBLED IN PRESSED UNIFORMS AND POLISHED SEMI-ARMOR, TO HONOR THOSE WHO STOOD AGAINST THE MIGHT OF THE GALACTIC EMPIRE.

AND, AT THE **FAR END** OF AN OPEN AISLE, STANDS A **VISION IN WHITE**--

--THE PRINCESS **LEIA ORGANA.**

IT TAKES A FULL **MINUTE** FOR THE **TRIO OF FIGURES** AT THE OTHER END TO COVER THE DISTANCE TO THE **RAISED DAIS** WHERE SHE STANDS...

...AND SEVERAL TIMES, IT SEEMS AS IF THE **GIGANTIC, FURRY ONE** WILL BOLT AND **RUN!**

THEN, WORDLESSLY, PRINCESS LEIA PLACES **GOLD MEDALLIONS** FIRST AROUND **HAN SOLO'S** NECK...THEN LUKE SKYWALKER'S.

CHEWBACCA THE WOOKIEE, TOO, WILL HAVE HIS **OWN** MEDAL...BUT HE WILL HAVE TO PUT IT ON **HIMSELF.**

FEW SPACE-PRINCESSES ARE **THAT** TALL.

THEN, JOINED BY A FULLY-REPAIRED **ARTOO DETOO** AND A BEAMING **SEE THREEPIO**...

--THEY STAND AWASH IN THE **CHEERS AND SHOUTS** OF A GRATEFUL ALLIANCE!

WHAT THE **FUTURE** HOLDS FOR THESE SIX **DARING SOULS,** ONLY **TIME** AND THE **SPACE-WINDS** KNOW.

BUT, FOR TODAY... FOR NOW..., THEY ARE **CONTENT.**

NEXT ISSUE: A **NEW** ADVENTURE OF THE **STAR WARRIORS!**

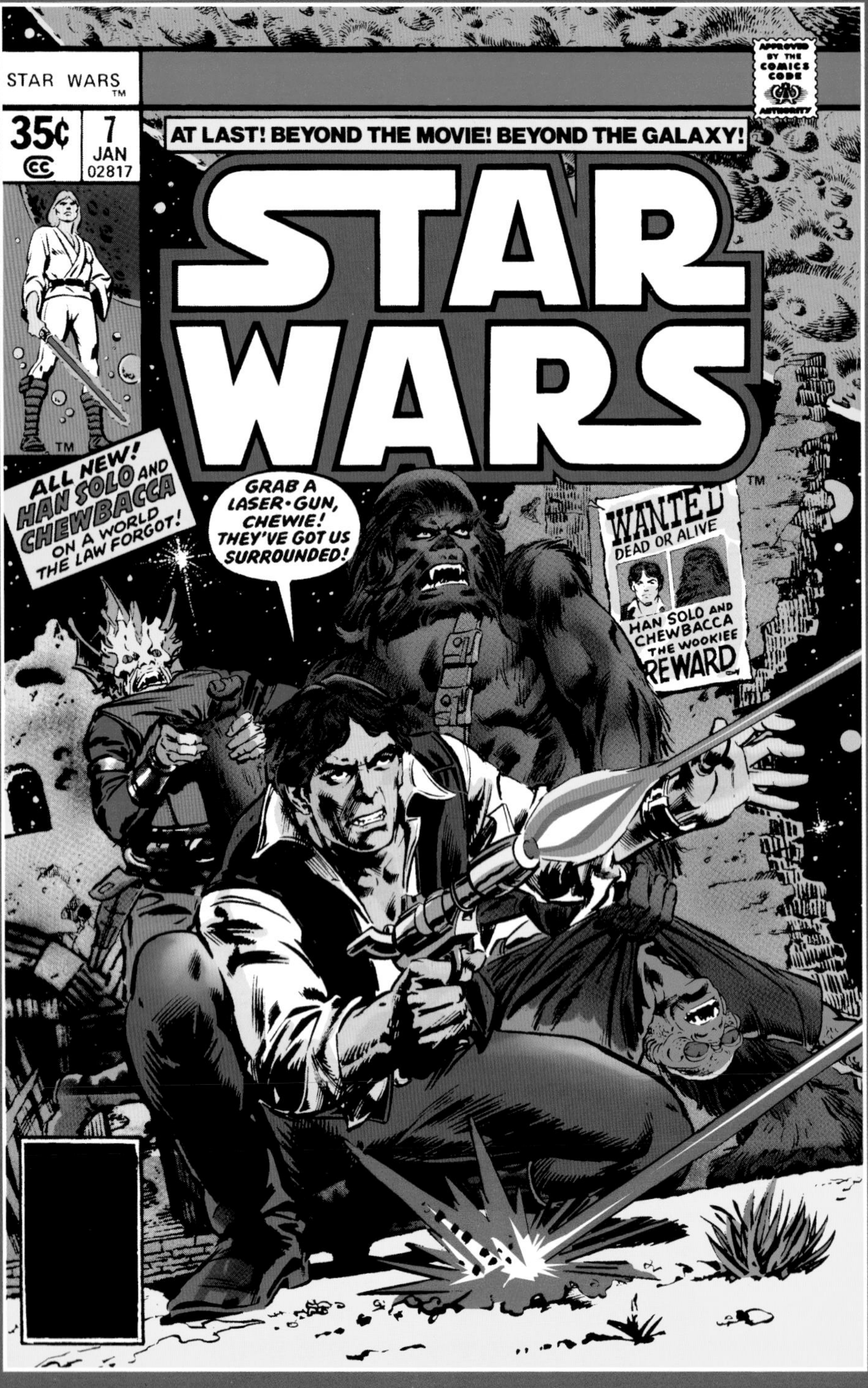
STAR WARS ™
35¢
7
JAN
02817
APPROVED BY THE COMICS CODE AUTHORITY
AT LAST! BEYOND THE MOVIE! BEYOND THE GALAXY!
STAR WARS ™
ALL NEW! HAN SOLO AND CHEWBACCA ON A WORLD THE LAW FORGOT!
GRAB A LASER-GUN, CHEWIE! THEY'VE GOT US SURROUNDED!
WANTED
DEAD OR ALIVE
HAN SOLO AND CHEWBACCA THE WOOKIEE
REWARD

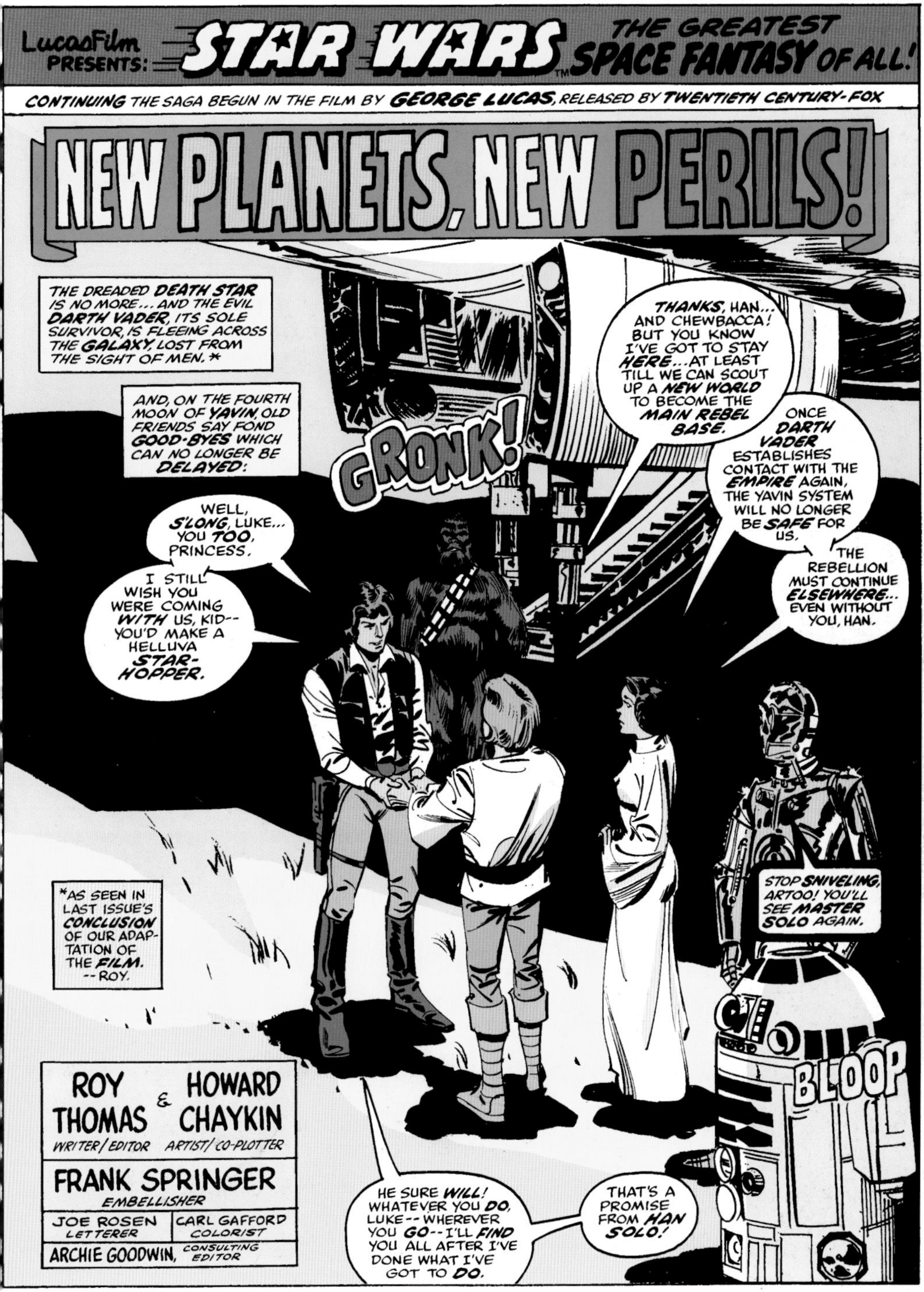

LucasFilm PRESENTS: STAR WARS™ THE GREATEST SPACE FANTASY OF ALL!
CONTINUING THE SAGA BEGUN IN THE FILM BY GEORGE LUCAS, RELEASED BY TWENTIETH CENTURY-FOX
NEW PLANETS, NEW PERILS!
THE DREADED DEATH STAR IS NO MORE... AND THE EVIL DARTH VADER, ITS SOLE SURVIVOR, IS FLEEING ACROSS THE GALAXY, LOST FROM THE SIGHT OF MEN.*
AND, ON THE FOURTH MOON OF YAVIN, OLD FRIENDS SAY FOND GOOD-BYES WHICH CAN NO LONGER BE DELAYED:
GRONK!
WELL, S'LONG, LUKE... YOU TOO, PRINCESS.
I STILL WISH YOU WERE COMING WITH US, KID-- YOU'D MAKE A HELLUVA STAR-HOPPER.
THANKS, HAN... AND CHEWBACCA! BUT YOU KNOW I'VE GOT TO STAY HERE... AT LEAST TILL WE CAN SCOUT UP A NEW WORLD TO BECOME THE MAIN REBEL BASE.
ONCE DARTH VADER ESTABLISHES CONTACT WITH THE EMPIRE AGAIN, THE YAVIN SYSTEM WILL NO LONGER BE SAFE FOR US.
THE REBELLION MUST CONTINUE ELSEWHERE... EVEN WITHOUT YOU, HAN.
*AS SEEN IN LAST ISSUE'S CONCLUSION OF OUR ADAPTATION OF THE FILM. --ROY.
STOP SNIVELING, ARTOO! YOU'LL SEE MASTER SOLO AGAIN.
BLOOP
ROY THOMAS WRITER/EDITOR & HOWARD CHAYKIN ARTIST/CO-PLOTTER
FRANK SPRINGER EMBELLISHER
JOE ROSEN LETTERER
CARL GAFFORD COLORIST
ARCHIE GOODWIN, CONSULTING EDITOR
HE SURE WILL! WHATEVER YOU DO, LUKE-- WHEREVER YOU GO-- I'LL FIND YOU ALL AFTER I'VE DONE WHAT I'VE GOT TO DO.
THAT'S A PROMISE FROM HAN SOLO!

MOMENTS LATER, THE *MILLENNIUM FALCON* STREAKS SKYWARD, TILL FIRST THE SATELLITE, THEN YAVIN, THEN YAVIN'S FIERY *SUN* IS LOST TO VIEW...

...ONE MORE FLICKERING *POINT OF FLAME* IN AN VAST BLACK *OCEAN.*

WELL, CHEWIE... WE'RE *ON OUR WAY!*

GUH-RUK!

YEAH, I *KNOW!* AFTER ALL THAT *BATTLE ACTION,* I'D GIVE MY *STAR-SPURS* TO STAY THERE AND HELP PRINCESS LEIA RE-GROUP THE *REBELS.*

BUT YOU *FORGET,* WE'VE BOTH GOT A *PRICE* ON OUR HEADS--

--OR AT LEAST WE *WILL* HAVE, IF WE DON'T GET BACK TO *DANTOOINE* AND PAY *JABBA THE HUT* THE MONEY WE PROMISED HIM!*

*ISSUE #2. -- R.T.

GET A *SMUGGLING CZAR* ON YOUR TAIL, OL' BUDDY, AND EVEN A *GALACTIC WAR* WON'T SAVE YOU!

AS SOON AS THE CRATERS COOLED, *JABBA*'D HAVE US BOTH *ZAPPED* BY ONE OF HIS BLASTER-HAPPY *BONGOS!*

URK!

YEAH, I *THOUGHT* YOU'D SEE IT MY WAY.

SO, SET 'EM FOR *TATOOINE...* NEXT STOP, *MOS EISLEY* SPACEPORT...

"..THOUGH WE'VE A FEW MORE *LIGHT-YEARS* TO GO BEFORE WE EVEN CUT TO *HYPER-SPACE!*"

118

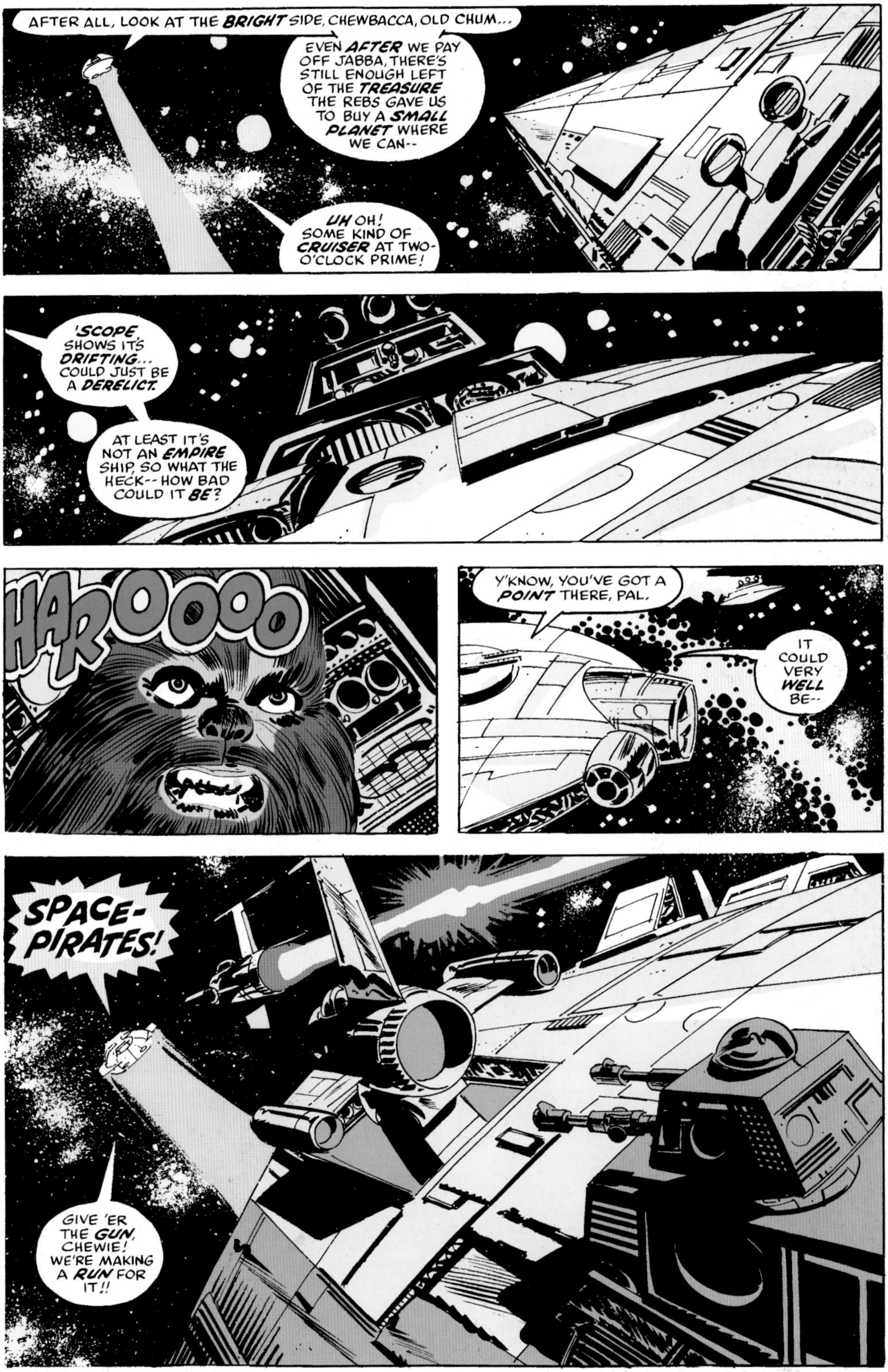
AFTER ALL, LOOK AT THE BRIGHT SIDE, CHEWBACCA, OLD CHUM...
EVEN AFTER WE PAY OFF JABBA, THERE'S STILL ENOUGH LEFT OF THE TREASURE THE REBS GAVE US TO BUY A SMALL PLANET WHERE WE CAN--
UH OH! SOME KIND OF CRUISER AT TWO-O'CLOCK PRIME!
'SCOPE SHOWS IT'S DRIFTING... COULD JUST BE A DERELICT.
AT LEAST IT'S NOT AN EMPIRE SHIP, SO WHAT THE HECK-- HOW BAD COULD IT BE?
HAROOOO
Y'KNOW, YOU'VE GOT A POINT THERE, PAL.
IT COULD VERY WELL BE--
SPACE-PIRATES!
GIVE 'ER THE GUN, CHEWIE! WE'RE MAKING A RUN FOR IT!!

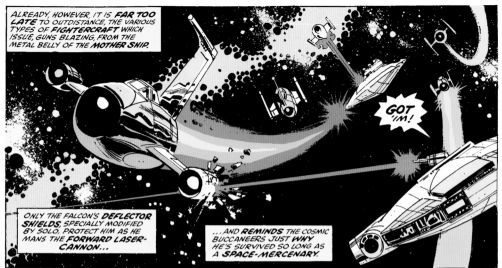

ALREADY, HOWEVER, IT IS *FAR TOO LATE* TO OUTDISTANCE, THE VARIOUS TYPES OF *FIGHTERCRAFT* WHICH ISSUE, GUNS BLAZING, FROM THE METAL BELLY OF THE *MOTHER SHIP.*

GOT 'IM!

ONLY THE FALCON'S *DEFLECTOR SHIELDS,* SPECIALLY MODIFIED BY SOLO, PROTECT HIM AS HE MANS THE *FORWARD LASER-CANNON...*

...AND *REMINDS* THE COSMIC BUCCANEERS JUST *WHY* HE'S SURVIVED SO LONG AS A *SPACE-MERCENARY.*

YET, ALL THE *WHILE...*

...THE GIANT *CRUISER* MOVES INTO *POSITION...*

...SO THAT, MOMENTS LATER...

BLAST IT! *TRACTOR BEAM'S* GOT US!

SHE'S *SWALLOWING* US UP FOR *BOARDING!*

HRUNK!

YOU'RE NOT AS MAD AS *I* AM, CHEWIE!

SERVES ME *RIGHT* FOR THINKING ABOUT *MONEY* WHEN I SHOULD'VE BEEN CHECKING THE *'SCOPE.*

TO BE SWALLOWED UP BY THE *DEATH STAR* WAS ONE THING*...BUT *SPACE-PIRATES*--!

*ISH #3. --ROY.

X-WINGERS...TIE-FIGHTERS...*EVERY* KIND OF SMALL BATTLE-SPACER I'VE *SEEN!*

I DON'T KNOW *WHO* OUR OVER-EAGER *HOST* IS, BUT ONE THING'S CERTAIN:

HE SURE *GETS AROUND!*

AND *I'VE* BEEN FROM *ONE* END OF THE GALAXY TO THE *OTHER!*

IT'S *WELL* PERHAPS, THAT HE *HAS...*

...FOR, WITHIN MINUTES, THE MILLENNIUM FALCON HAS ITS FIRST, IF UNWELCOME PASSENGERS SINCE LUKE SKYWALKER, BEN KENOBI, AND COMPANY.

THOUGH ALL ARE MORE OR LESS HUMAN, THEY ARE AS VARIED IN PLANETARY ORIGIN AS THEY ARE INVARIABLY GRIM.

THE GARB OF BOTH CIVILIZED AND SEMI-CIVILIZED STAR-SYSTEMS SPARKLES IN THE CORRIDORS... RAY-GUNS GLITTER NEXT TO ARCHAIC CUTLASSES. THERE IS EVEN THE WHITE, STOIC ARMOR OF A FALLEN STORMTROOPER, STRANGELY OUT OF PLACE.

AND, STRIDING THRU ALL THE DIN AND CLAMOR... A RED-BEARDED MAN IN BLACK.

YEAH, IT'S MOMENT-OF-TRUTH TIME, ALL RIGHT, FURRY BUDDY.

DO WE MAKE A STAND FOR IT, OR--?

GRONK!

I'M AFRAID THAT CHOICE HAS ALREADY BEEN MADE... FOR BOTH OF YOU.

DROP IT, STAR-HOPPERS... BEFORE I DROP YOU!

THAT'S BETTER! HE'S ALL YOURS, CAP'N.

NICE WORK, JOLLI.

I'M GLAD HE DIDN'T FORCE YOU TO KILL HIM.

I'D HATE TO HAVE TO BURY THE ILLUSTRIOUS HAN SOLO.

WELL THEN THERE NOW, IF IT ISN'T CRIMSON JACK!

LONG TIME, NO SEE-- BUT NOT LONG ENOUGH.

STILL A JOKER, EH, SOLO?

I GET BY.

BUT WHEN DID A SECOND-CLASS SCAVENGER LIKE YOU PICK UP EVEN A CAST-OFF CRUISER? LAST I RECALL YOU WERE STILL AMBUSHING SPICE-CARAVANS ON THE OUTER RIM.

WE'VE WASTED ENOUGH TIME, CAP'N. LET ME BLAST A HOLE IN 'EM.

AND I SEE THE COMPANY YOU KEEP IS AS CHARMING AS EVER.

WHERE'D YOU PICK UP MISS SUNSHINE, JACK?

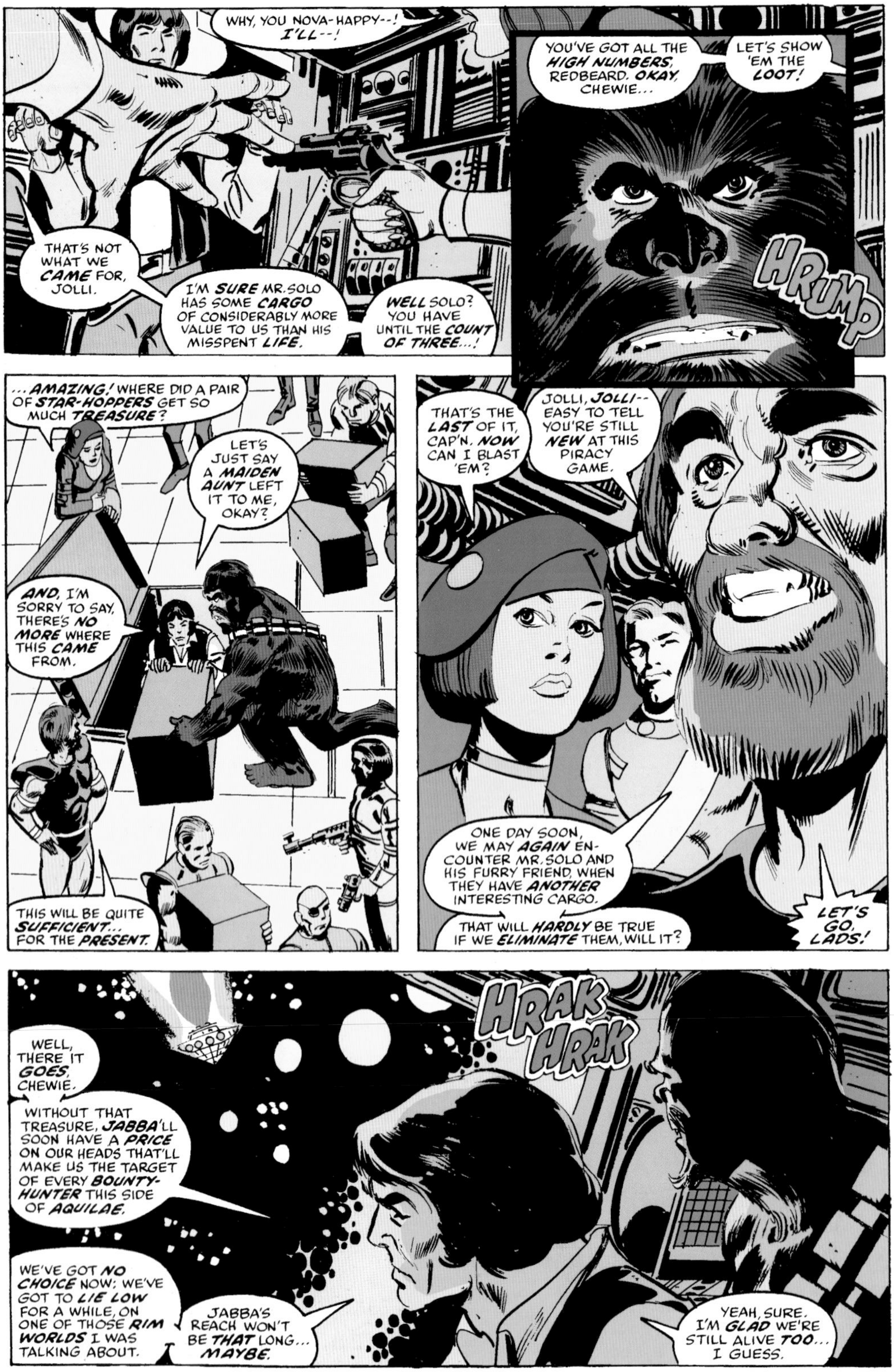
WHY, YOU NOVA-HAPPY--! I'LL--!
THAT'S NOT WHAT WE CAME FOR, JOLLI.
I'M SURE MR. SOLO HAS SOME CARGO OF CONSIDERABLY MORE VALUE TO US THAN HIS MISSPENT LIFE.
WELL SOLO? YOU HAVE UNTIL THE COUNT OF THREE...!
YOU'VE GOT ALL THE HIGH NUMBERS, REDBEARD. OKAY, CHEWIE...
LET'S SHOW 'EM THE LOOT!
HRUMP
...AMAZING! WHERE DID A PAIR OF STAR-HOPPERS GET SO MUCH TREASURE?
LET'S JUST SAY A MAIDEN AUNT LEFT IT TO ME, OKAY?
AND, I'M SORRY TO SAY, THERE'S NO MORE WHERE THIS CAME FROM.
THIS WILL BE QUITE SUFFICIENT... FOR THE PRESENT.
THAT'S THE LAST OF IT, CAP'N. NOW CAN I BLAST 'EM?
JOLLI, JOLLI-- EASY TO TELL YOU'RE STILL NEW AT THIS PIRACY GAME.
ONE DAY SOON, WE MAY AGAIN EN-COUNTER MR. SOLO AND HIS FURRY FRIEND, WHEN THEY HAVE ANOTHER INTERESTING CARGO.
THAT WILL HARDLY BE TRUE IF WE ELIMINATE THEM, WILL IT?
LET'S GO, LADS!
HRAK HRAK
WELL, THERE IT GOES, CHEWIE.
WITHOUT THAT TREASURE, JABBA'LL SOON HAVE A PRICE ON OUR HEADS THAT'LL MAKE US THE TARGET OF EVERY BOUNTY-HUNTER THIS SIDE OF AQUILAE.
WE'VE GOT NO CHOICE NOW; WE'VE GOT TO LIE LOW FOR A WHILE, ON ONE OF THOSE RIM WORLDS I WAS TALKING ABOUT.
JABBA'S REACH WON'T BE THAT LONG... MAYBE.
YEAH, SURE. I'M GLAD WE'RE STILL ALIVE TOO... I GUESS.

ADUBA-3 IS ON RELATIVELY FEW *STAR-CHARTS*...AND WITH *GOOD REASON.*

SOME YEARS BACK, IT WAS THE SITE OF A *CHROMIUM RUSH* WHICH TURNED OUT TO BE LARGELY *FALSE ALARM*... THE RESULT OF *MINE-SEEDING* BY GREEDY SPECULATORS.

SINCE THEN, THOSE STAR-TRADERS WHO STILL *RE-MEMBER* IT MOSTLY TURN UP THEIR *NOSES* AT THE MENTION OF ITS *NAME.*

STILL, FOR A PAIR OF WEARY *SPACE-PILOTS* TEMPORARILY ON THE *LAM*...

...EVEN *ITS* BARREN WASTES HAVE CERTAIN *POSSIBILITIES.*

WELL, HERE WE *ARE*, CHEWIE -- *HOME SWEET HOME* FOR A WHILE...

...THAT IS, IF THE *LOCALS* HAVE ANY EMPLOYMENT FOR A COUPLE OF INCOGNITO *PLANET-JUMPERS.*

GUH-RUNK!

YEAH, I *KNOW!* THERE'S USUALLY MORE *PEOPLE* AROUND IN A *SPACEPORT TOWN* LIKE THIS...

AND *THAT* SEEMS TO BE THE REASON WE DIDN'T *SEE* ANYBODY BEFORE,

SOME KIND OF *COMMOTION* GOING ON NEAR THE LOCAL *CANTINA!*

APPARENTLY THE GUYS ON THE *GROUND* ARE UNHAPPY WITH THAT *INSECT-GUY* UP ON THE *BANTHA* ABOUT SOMETHING.

WHAT SAY WE GET A LITTLE *CLOSER*?

HEY! ISN'T THE *BUGGIE* DRESSED LIKE SOME KIND OF *PRIEST*?

CAN'T IDENTIFY THE EXACT *RELIGION;* I GUESS I SHOULDN'T HAVE SKIPPED SO MUCH *SUNDAY SCHOOL* AS A KID.

CLOTH OR *NO*-- PULL THAT BUGGIE *DOWN* FROM THERE!

HE AIN'T PUTTING NO *BORGS* IN OUR MOUND!

YEAH! IF HE *LIKES* BORGS SO MUCH, LET 'IM DRAG THE CARCASS BACK TO THE *MISSION!*

EVEN AS SOLO AND CHEWBACCA *APPROACH,* THE INSECT-LIKE ALIEN *DESCENDS* FROM THE BANTHA'S BROAD, HAIRY BACK...

BUT, BEFORE HE CAN *SPEAK*--

--ONE OF THE ANGRY *CROWD* SEEKS TO LAY *HANDS* ON HIM.

THAT PROVES TO HAVE BEEN AN *ERROR IN JUDGMENT.*

THRAP!

HOWEVER, BEFORE HE CAN *RE-MOUNT* HIS HUGE BEAST OF BURDEN--

I'VE GOT 'IM, BOYS!

I *STILL* DON'T KNOW WHAT'S *GOING* ON HERE, CHEWIE-- BUT, IF YOU'LL *JOIN* ME--

ROUGH HIM UP!

GRONK

YEAH, I KIND'A *THOUGHT* YOU WOULD!

SHOW 'IM WE MEAN *BUSINESS!*

THE SPACEPORT ALIENS ARE **SPACERS**, MOSTLY... A FEW MEDIOCRE **PILOTS**. THE REST **NAVIGATORS** OR **CREW-MEN** IN BETWEEN ASSIGNMENTS.

NONE OF THEM HAS HAD THE EXPERIENCE IN **HAND-TO-HAND COMBAT** AND GENERAL **ROUGH-HOUSING** THAT HAN SOLO HAS...

AND MOST **CERTAINLY** NONE OF THEM HAS EVER STOOD UP TO A **WOOKIEE**.

IN SHORT ORDER, THE UNEQUAL BATTLE IS **OVER**...

...AND **HAN SOLO** TURNS TO THE SHAKEN **INSECTOID** BEFORE HIM:

YOU **ALL RIGHT**, PERA? *

YES, MY FI. *

THEY MEANT ME **NO HARM**... NOT **REALLY**. PLEASE, DO NOT **HURT** THEM!

I DON'T BEAR ANY GRUDGES, PERA...

*PERA IS HIGH GALACTIC FOR MALE PARENT; FI MEANS MALE CHILD.
--ROY.

...BUT, THEY'D BETTER GIVE MY FRIEND **CHEW-BACCA** A WIDE BERTH FOR A WHILE!

GUH-RARRR

IF THERE'S A MANLIKE ALIEN ANYWHERE IN THE **GALAXY** THAT CAN TAKE ON AN **ANGRY WOOKIEE** AND LIVE TO TELL THE TALE, I'VE SURE NEVER **SEEN** HIM!

AND, EVIDENTLY, I'M NOT *ABOUT* TO!

NOW, PERA, WHAT'S THE *DISPUTE*? AND WHO'S THE GUY ON THE *TRAVOIS*?

HE IS A *BORG* WHO DIED LAST NIGHT. YOU KNOW THE *TERM*, I'M SURE...

HALF *HUMAN*...HALF MECHANICAL *DROID*.

YET, THE *MAN* HALF OF HIM HAD A *SOUL*... OR SO *MY* FAITH BELIEVES.

THE *SPACERS*, AS YOU KNOW, HAVE AN AGE-OLD *PREJUDICE* AGAINST ANY KIND OF *ROBOT*, AND REFUSE TO LET HIM BE BURIED ON *SPACERS'* HILL, AS IS HIS *RIGHT* AS A ONETIME PILOT.

WILL *YOU* BURY HIM THERE, OUTSIDE THE CITY?

LISTEN, PERA, WE'VE DONE *ENOUGH* FOR ONE--

HE HAD THIS SMALL *SACK OF COINS* UPON HIS PERSON WHEN HE DIED.

BY *TRADITION*, IT BELONGS TO THE ONE WHO *BURIES* HIM.

BORG, OL' BUDDY...

YOU JUST BOUGHT YOURSELF A *LAST RESTING-PLACE*.

Y'KNOW, CHEWIE, *SPACERS* ARE A *WEIRD* LOT.

HALF OF 'EM HAVEN'T GOT ANYTHING MORE IN *COMMON* WITH EACH OTHER THAN THE SAME NUMBER OF *EYES*...MAYBE NOT EVEN *THAT*.

BUT SHOW 'EM A GUY WHO'S PART *MACHINE* LIKE THE *SHIPS* THEY FLY, AND ALL OF A SUDDEN THEY'RE ONE BIG HAPPY BIGOTED *FAMILY*.

OH WELL... ALL THE BETTER FOR *US*, EH?

AT LEAST WE'LL HAVE ENOUGH MONEY TO *GET BY* HERE FOR A WHILE, IF WE DON'T GET A *LASER-BOLT* IN OUR BACK-SIDES.

URNG!

YEAH, I *KNOW*... BUT AT LEAST THEY'RE FOLLOW-ING US AT A *DISTANCE*, AND NOT REACHING FOR THEIR *BLASTERS*.

JUST KEEP LEADING THE BANTHA AT A *NICE, EVEN PACE*, AND COULD BE WE'LL GET THRU THIS WITHOUT A *FLARE-UP*.

PLEASANT *HOPES*, HAN SOLO...

AND, IN TRUTH, *NONE* OF THE SPACERS WOULD DARE MAKE A *FACE-TO-FACE* CHALLENGE...

BUT, A *STONE* HURLED FROM WITHIN A *CROWD* IS ANOTHER MATTER!

NRLK!

OWWW--!

GO ON BACK WHERE YOU *CAME* FROM, YOU DIRTY *BORG-LICKERS!*

GRRARG!

EASY, CHEWIE! YOU MAY BE AS STRONG AS A WHOLE FREIGHTER-LOAD OF *SWAMP-CATS*, BUT WE'RE STILL *OUTNUMBERED* TEN TO ONE!

JUST *LOOK FIERCE*, KEEP YOUR *GUN LOW*--

--AND MAYBE THEY'LL LET US *PASS*.

ULP! AND THEN AGAIN-- *MAYBE NOT!*

NEXT INSTANT, EVEN AS HAN SOLO IS *YANKED* BY A TALL SPACER FROM HIS HIGH PERCH --

--THE *INSECTOID PRIEST* IS BACK, THOUGH WHERE HE *CAME* FROM, NONE COULD *SAY.*

SPACER AFTER SPACER *GOES DOWN* BEFORE CHEWBACCA'S FURRY FISTS--

ROORG!

--YET, BECAUSE THE WOOKIEE *PULLS HIS PUNCHES*, SOME OF THEM GET BACK *UP* AGAIN.

AND, MEAN-WHILE--

SO FAR, SO *GOOD!*

THEY'RE *MAD*, BUT THEY'RE NOT *KILLERS!* AND, AS LONG AS THEY DON'T TRY ANYTHING *LETHAL*, THERE'S STILL A CHANCE WE CAN--

WHOOPS! LOOKS LIKE I SPOKE *TOO SOON!*

THERE'S ONE IN *EVERY CROWD!* NO WAY I CAN DODGE THAT *SIKURDIAN BATTLE-AXE*--

WHTT

--SO I DON'T HAVE ANY *CHOICE!*

CHEWBACCA, HOWEVER, IS NOT AS *SQUEAMISH* AS HIS CORELLIAN CAPTAIN--

AND, AS SOON AS HE SEES *FIRST BLOOD*--

--HIS *WOOKIEE NATURE* MANIFESTS ITSELF IN ITS *USUAL MANNER.*

FRZZZZ

128

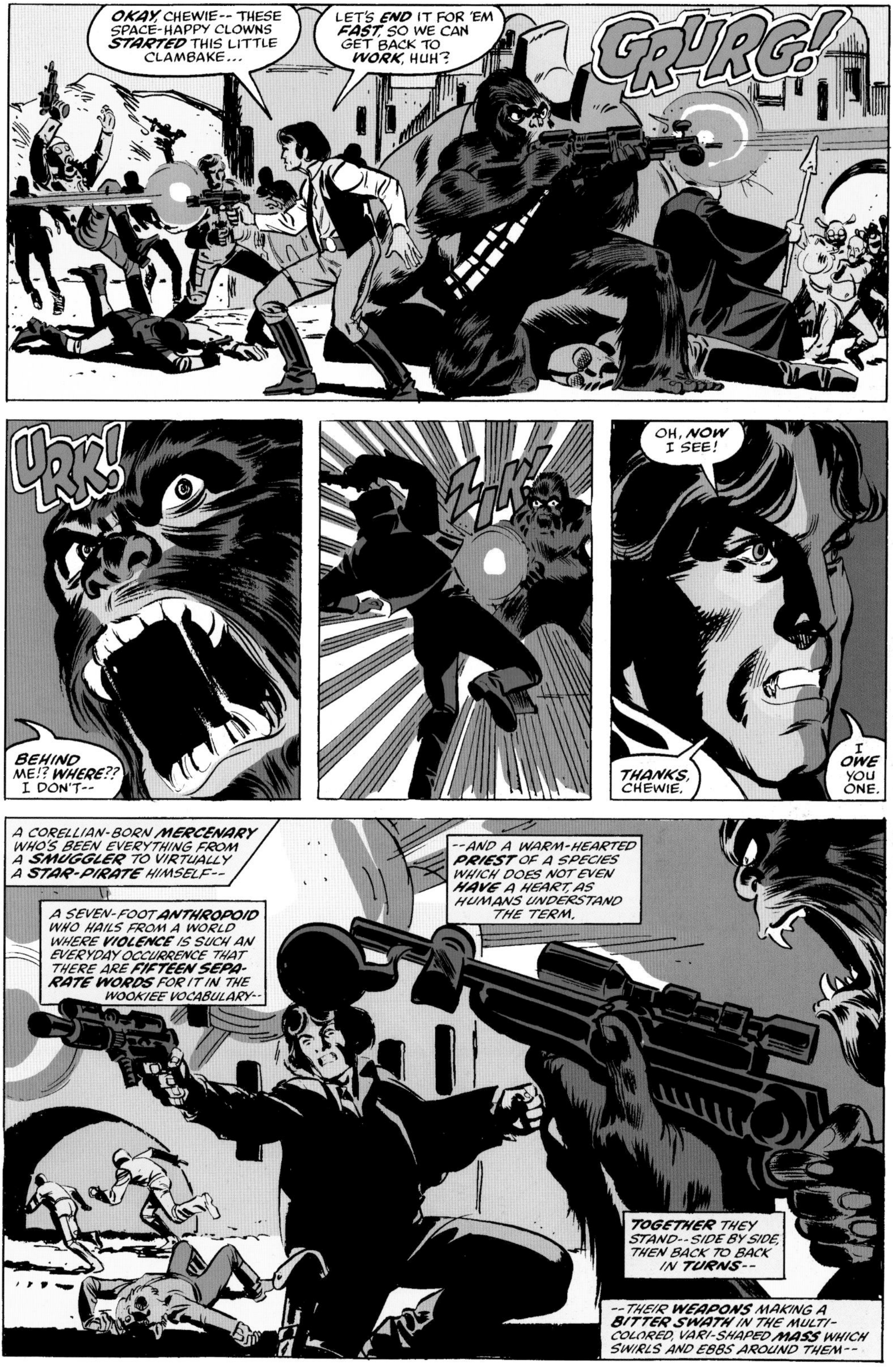
OKAY, CHEWIE-- THESE SPACE-HAPPY CLOWNS STARTED THIS LITTLE CLAMBAKE...
LET'S END IT FOR 'EM FAST, SO WE CAN GET BACK TO WORK, HUH?
GRURG!
URK!
BEHIND ME!? WHERE?? I DON'T--
ZZIK!
OH, NOW I SEE!
THANKS, CHEWIE.
I OWE YOU ONE.
A CORELLIAN-BORN MERCENARY WHO'S BEEN EVERYTHING FROM A SMUGGLER TO VIRTUALLY A STAR-PIRATE HIMSELF--
A SEVEN-FOOT ANTHROPOID WHO HAILS FROM A WORLD WHERE VIOLENCE IS SUCH AN EVERYDAY OCCURRENCE THAT THERE ARE FIFTEEN SEPARATE WORDS FOR IT IN THE WOOKIEE VOCABULARY--
--AND A WARM-HEARTED PRIEST OF A SPECIES WHICH DOES NOT EVEN HAVE A HEART, AS HUMANS UNDERSTAND THE TERM.
TOGETHER THEY STAND--SIDE BY SIDE, THEN BACK TO BACK IN TURNS--
--THEIR WEAPONS MAKING A BITTER SWATH IN THE MULTI-COLORED, VARI-SHAPED MASS WHICH SWIRLS AND EBBS AROUND THEM--

--UNTIL THE *FIRST* OF THE SPACERS TURNS TAIL TO *FLEE*--

--TO BE SWIFTLY JOINED BY *OTHERS* OF HIS ILK.

NOT JUST *YET*, CHEWIE...

DON'T LET YOUR GUARD DOWN *YET!*

THEY *COULD* STILL TRY TO PICK US OFF FROM THE *SHADOWS*--

--THOUGH I *DON'T* THINK THAT'S QUITE WHAT THEY'VE GOT ON THEIR *MIND.*

HROOG!

YEAH, I GUESS YOU'RE *RIGHT.*

THEY'VE *HAD* IT.

NOW, WHERE'S THE *PERA?* I DON'T--

OH.

BEGONE, DEFILERS OF THE *SACRED WAY!*

S'MYT!

WELL, PERA, LOOKS LIKE WE'VE *WON* THAT BORG'S RIGHT TO BE BURIED ON *SPACERS' HILL.*

ONLY THING IS, *SOME* OF THE STAR-HOPPERS SPRAWLED AROUND HERE ARE GOING TO BE *JOINING* HIM, COME THE MORROW.

VIOLENCE EVER *BEGETS* VIOLENCE, OUTWORLDER.

AS MY *HOLY-BOOK* SAYS: "FOR EVERY *SIN* THERE IS AN EQUAL AND POSITIVE *RETRIBUTION.*"

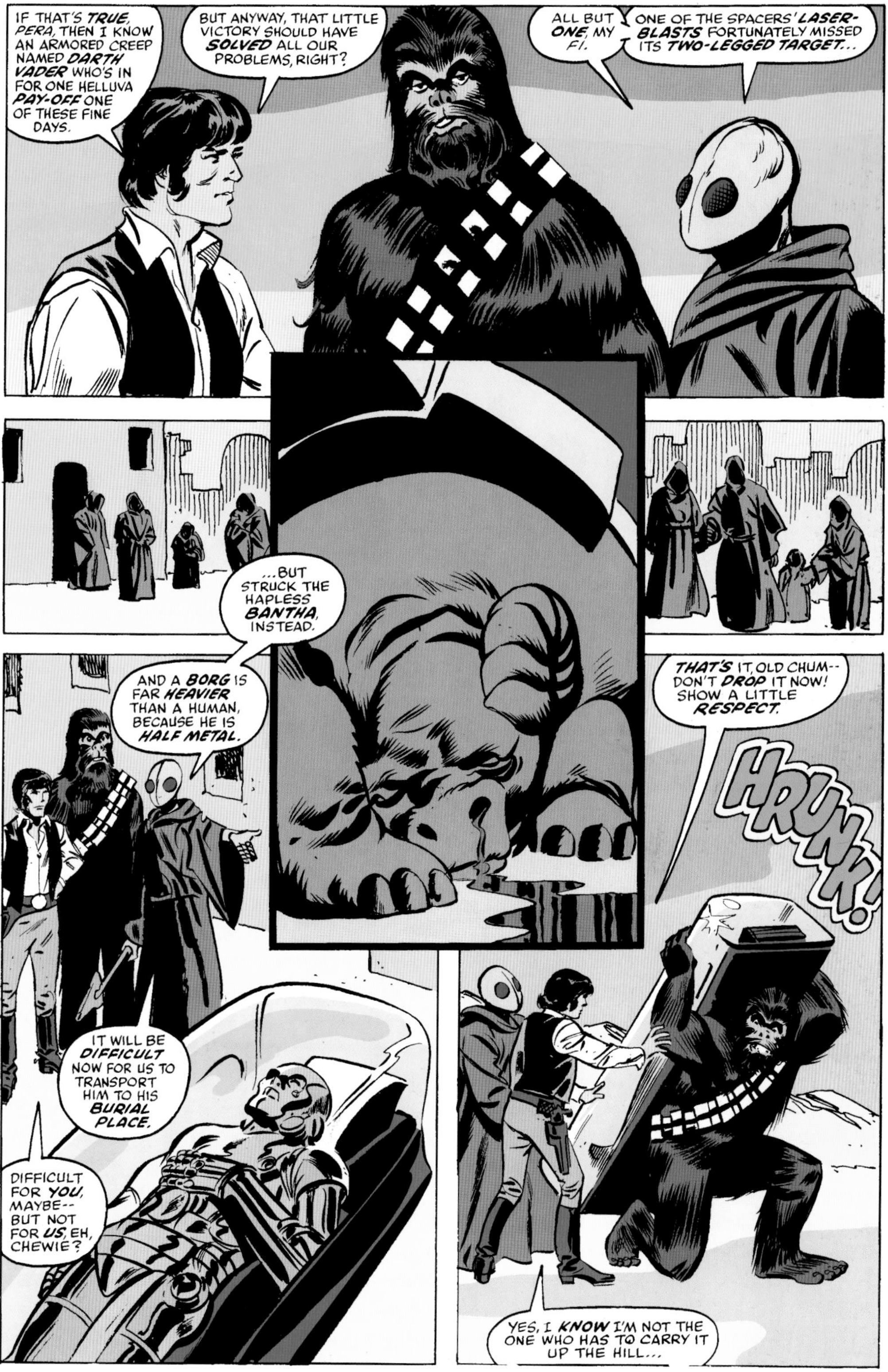
IF THAT'S TRUE, PERA, THEN I KNOW AN ARMORED CREEP NAMED DARTH VADER WHO'S IN FOR ONE HELLUVA PAY-OFF ONE OF THESE FINE DAYS.
BUT ANYWAY, THAT LITTLE VICTORY SHOULD HAVE SOLVED ALL OUR PROBLEMS, RIGHT?
ALL BUT ONE, MY FI.
ONE OF THE SPACERS' LASER-BLASTS FORTUNATELY MISSED ITS TWO-LEGGED TARGET...
...BUT STRUCK THE HAPLESS BANTHA, INSTEAD.
AND A BORG IS FAR HEAVIER THAN A HUMAN, BECAUSE HE IS HALF METAL.
IT WILL BE DIFFICULT NOW FOR US TO TRANSPORT HIM TO HIS BURIAL PLACE.
DIFFICULT FOR YOU, MAYBE-- BUT NOT FOR US, EH, CHEWIE?
THAT'S IT, OLD CHUM-- DON'T DROP IT NOW! SHOW A LITTLE RESPECT.
HRUNK!
YES, I KNOW I'M NOT THE ONE WHO HAS TO CARRY IT UP THE HILL...

...BUT *SOMEBODY* HAS TO PLAY *BRING-UP-THE-REAR*, RIGHT?

HRUNK!

YOU ALREADY *SAID* THAT!

WITH THE *INSECTOID* IN THE LEAD, THE STRANGE ASSEMBLAGE PROCEEDS SLOWLY UP THE CURVE OF THE *BURIAL MOUND*...

...TO A PLACE WHERE THE DREAMS OF *MEN* AND *MONSTERS* ALIKE HAVE ALL COME TO THE SAME, SAD *END* COUNTLESS LIGHT YEARS DISTANT FROM THE WORLDS THEY ONCE CALLED *HOME.*

AND, IF THE *GODS OF SPACE* ARE WATCHING OVER THE PRIEST'S EERIE, CHIRP-LIKE CHANTING, THEY GIVE *NO SIGN.*

BUT THEN, THEY NEVER PROMISED THEY *WOULD.*

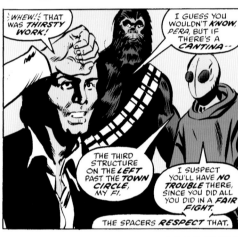

WHEW! THAT WAS *THIRSTY* WORK!

I GUESS YOU WOULDN'T *KNOW,* PERA, BUT IF THERE'S A *CANTINA*--

THE THIRD STRUCTURE ON THE *LEFT* PAST THE *TOWN CIRCLE,* MY FI.

I SUSPECT YOU'LL HAVE *NO TROUBLE* THERE, SINCE YOU DID ALL YOU DID IN A *FAIR FIGHT.*

THE SPACERS *RESPECT* THAT.

SOON AFTERWARD, IN THE SPACEPORT BELOW...

CHNOOP

I COULDN'T AGREE WITH YOU *MORE,* PAL...

I COULD REALLY GET TO LIKE IT HERE, *TOO!*

RIGHT *NOW,* THOUGH, I THINK WE COULD STILL USE A BIT MORE *GOOD WILL* FROM THE *CLIENTELE,*

BARTENDER! ANOTHER ROUND FOR THE *HOUSE*--

--ON ME AND MY *WOOKIEE* FRIEND HERE!

NEXT ISSUE: **TROUBLE IN PARADISE!**

STAR WARS ™

35¢
CC
8
FEB
02817

AT LAST! BEYOND THE MOVIE! BEYOND THE GALAXY!

STAR WARS

EIGHT AGAINST A WORLD!

EXTRA!

IN THIS ISSUE:
THE DEADLY
MISSION OF
LUKE
SKYWALKER!

APPROVED
BY THE
COMICS
CODE
AUTHORITY

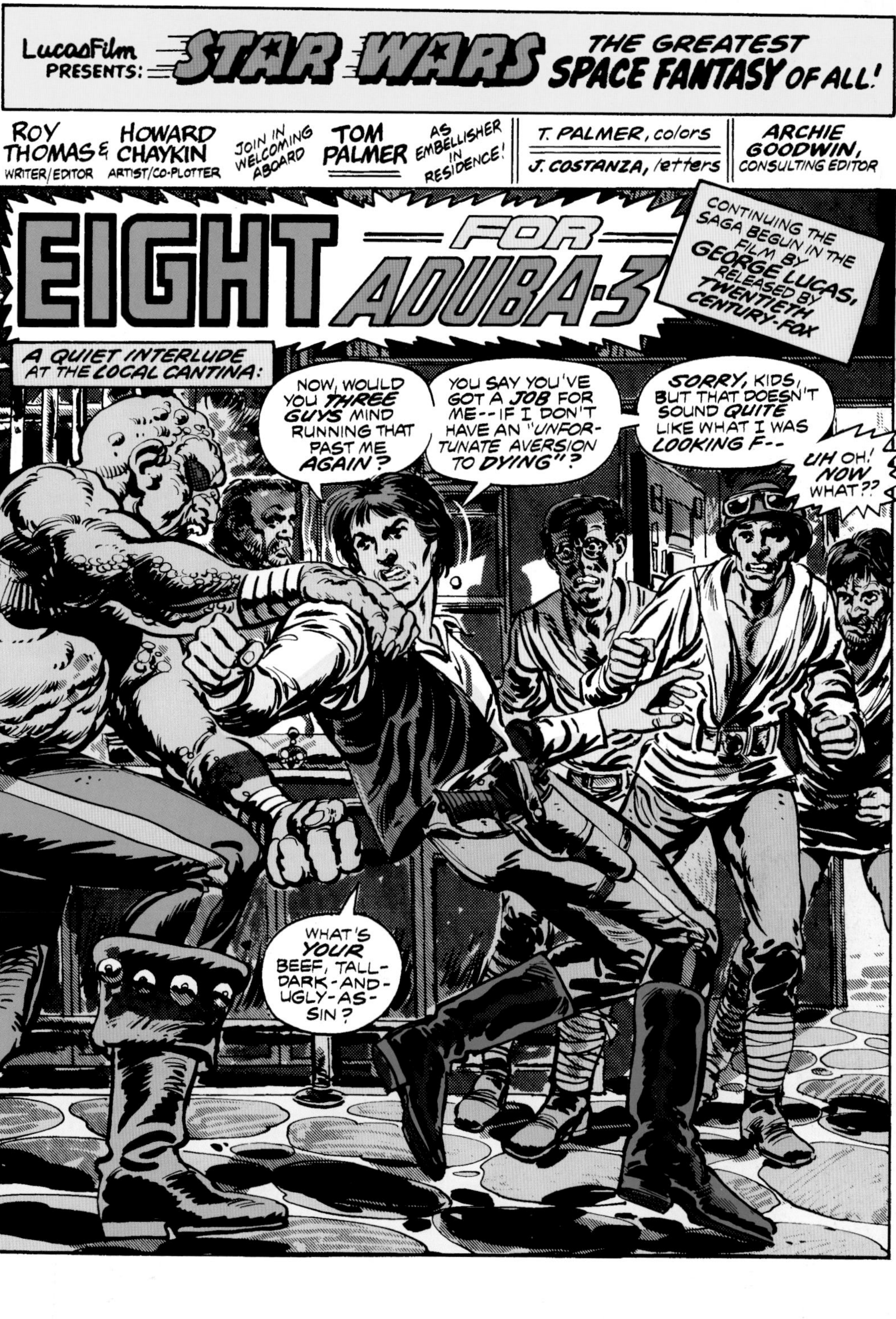
LucasFilm PRESENTS: STAR WARS THE GREATEST SPACE FANTASY OF ALL!
ROY THOMAS & HOWARD CHAYKIN
WRITER/EDITOR ARTIST/CO-PLOTTER
JOIN IN WELCOMING ABOARD TOM PALMER AS EMBELLISHER IN RESIDENCE!
T. PALMER, colors
J. COSTANZA, letters
ARCHIE GOODWIN, CONSULTING EDITOR
EIGHT FOR ADUBA-3
CONTINUING THE SAGA BEGUN IN THE FILM BY GEORGE LUCAS, RELEASED BY TWENTIETH CENTURY-FOX
A QUIET INTERLUDE AT THE LOCAL CANTINA:
NOW, WOULD YOU THREE GUYS MIND RUNNING THAT PAST ME AGAIN?
YOU SAY YOU'VE GOT A JOB FOR ME--IF I DON'T HAVE AN "UNFORTUNATE AVERSION TO DYING"?
SORRY, KIDS, BUT THAT DOESN'T SOUND QUITE LIKE WHAT I WAS LOOKING F--
UH OH! NOW WHAT??
WHAT'S YOUR BEEF, TALL-DARK-AND-UGLY-AS-SIN?

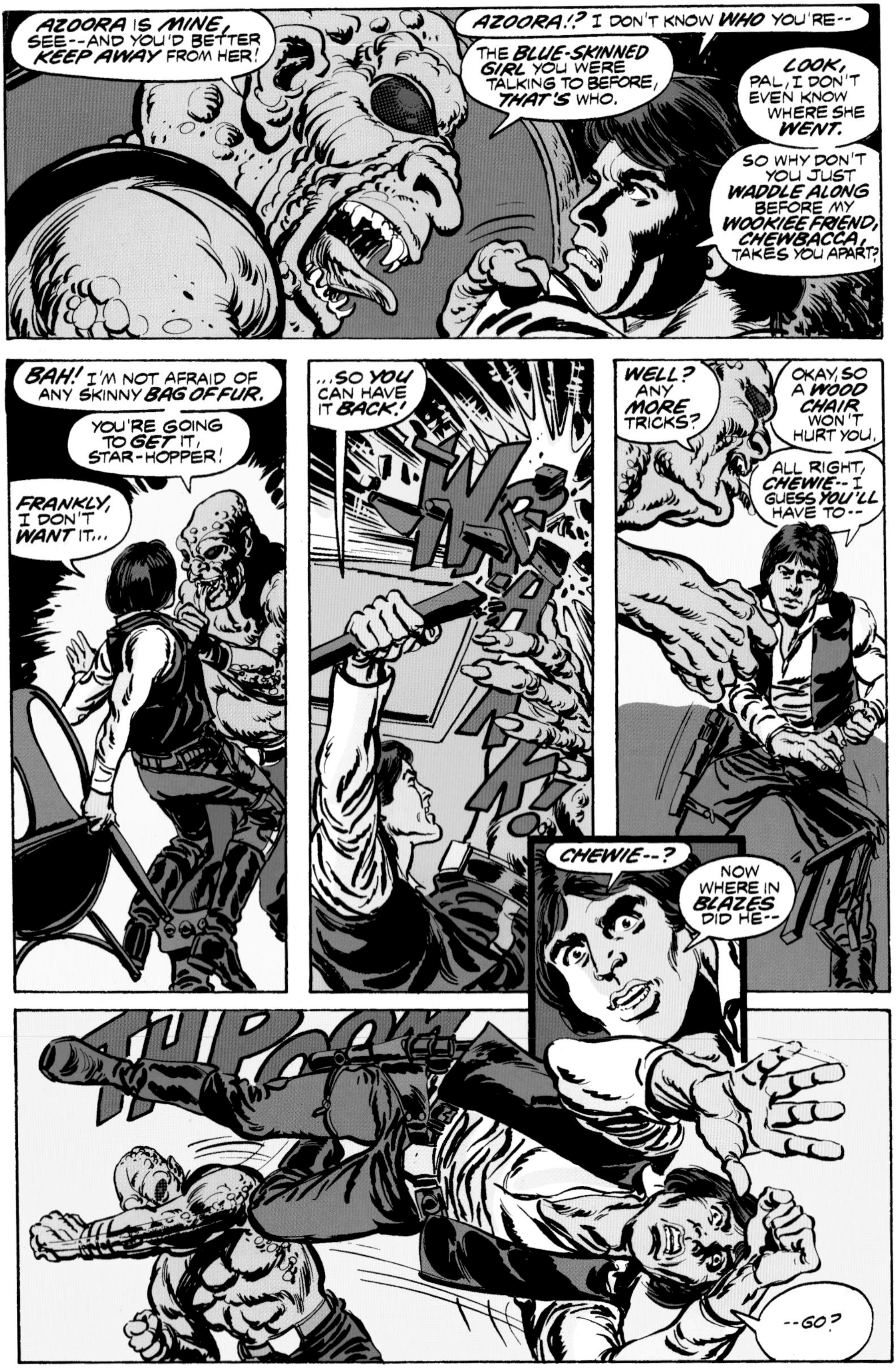
AZOORA IS MINE, SEE--AND YOU'D BETTER KEEP AWAY FROM HER!
AZOORA!? I DON'T KNOW WHO YOU'RE--
THE BLUE-SKINNED GIRL YOU WERE TALKING TO BEFORE, THAT'S WHO.
LOOK, PAL, I DON'T EVEN KNOW WHERE SHE WENT.
SO WHY DON'T YOU JUST WADDLE ALONG BEFORE MY WOOKIEE FRIEND, CHEWBACCA, TAKES YOU APART?
BAH! I'M NOT AFRAID OF ANY SKINNY BAG OF FUR.
YOU'RE GOING TO GET IT, STAR-HOPPER!
FRANKLY, I DON'T WANT IT...
...SO YOU CAN HAVE IT BACK!
WRAKK!
WELL? ANY MORE TRICKS?
OKAY, SO A WOOD CHAIR WON'T HURT YOU.
ALL RIGHT, CHEWIE-- I GUESS YOU'LL HAVE TO--
CHEWIE--?
NOW WHERE IN BLAZES DID HE--
--GO?

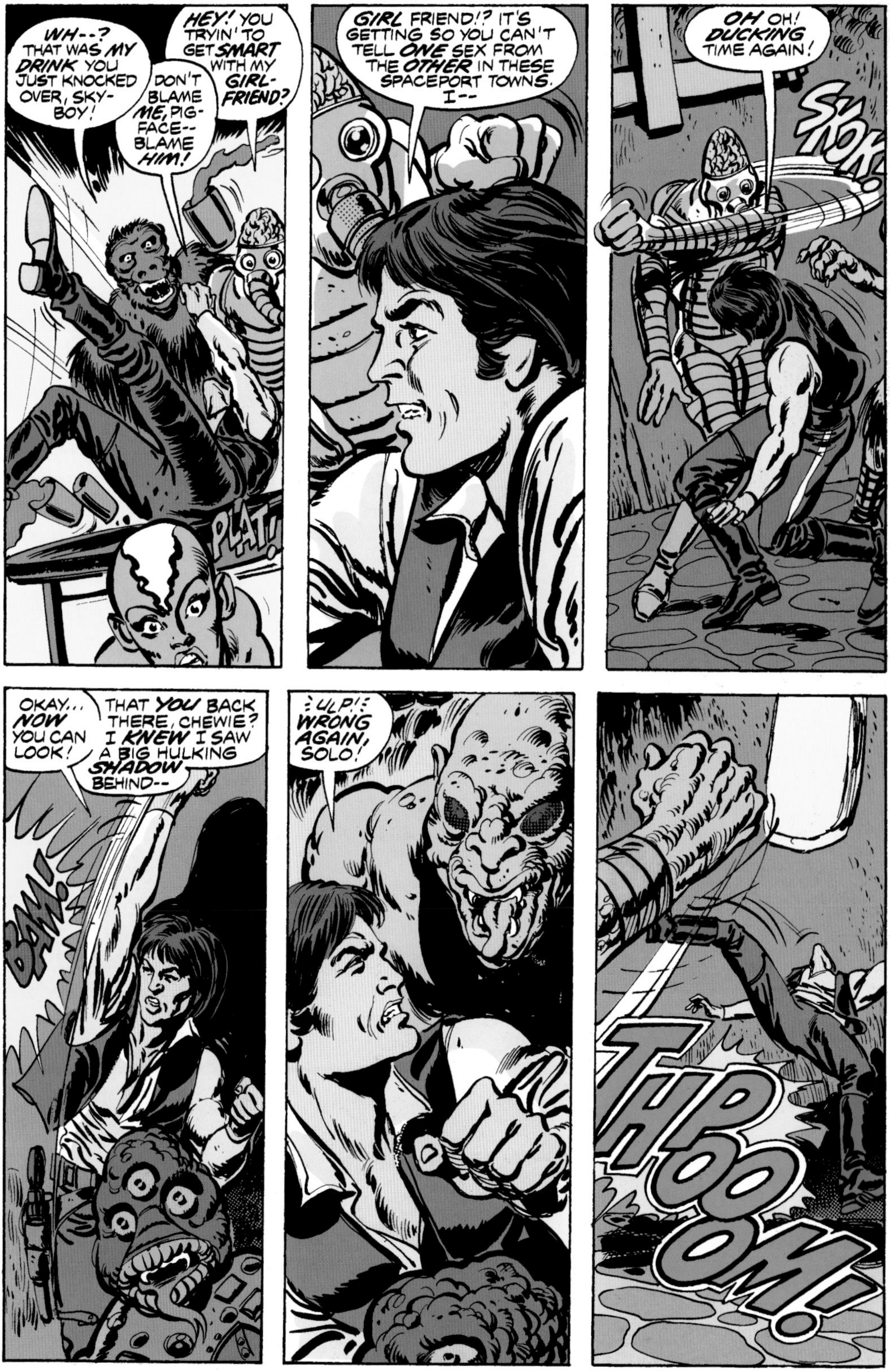
WH--? THAT WAS MY DRINK YOU JUST KNOCKED OVER, SKY-BOY!
HEY! YOU TRYIN' TO GET SMART WITH MY GIRL-FRIEND?
DON'T BLAME ME, PIG-FACE-- BLAME HIM!
PLAT!
GIRL FRIEND!? IT'S GETTING SO YOU CAN'T TELL ONE SEX FROM THE OTHER IN THESE SPACEPORT TOWNS. I--
OH OH! DUCKING TIME AGAIN!
SKOK!
OKAY... NOW YOU CAN LOOK!
THAT YOU BACK THERE, CHEWIE? I KNEW I SAW A BIG HULKING SHADOW BEHIND--
BAM!
ULP! WRONG AGAIN, SOLO!
THOOOM!

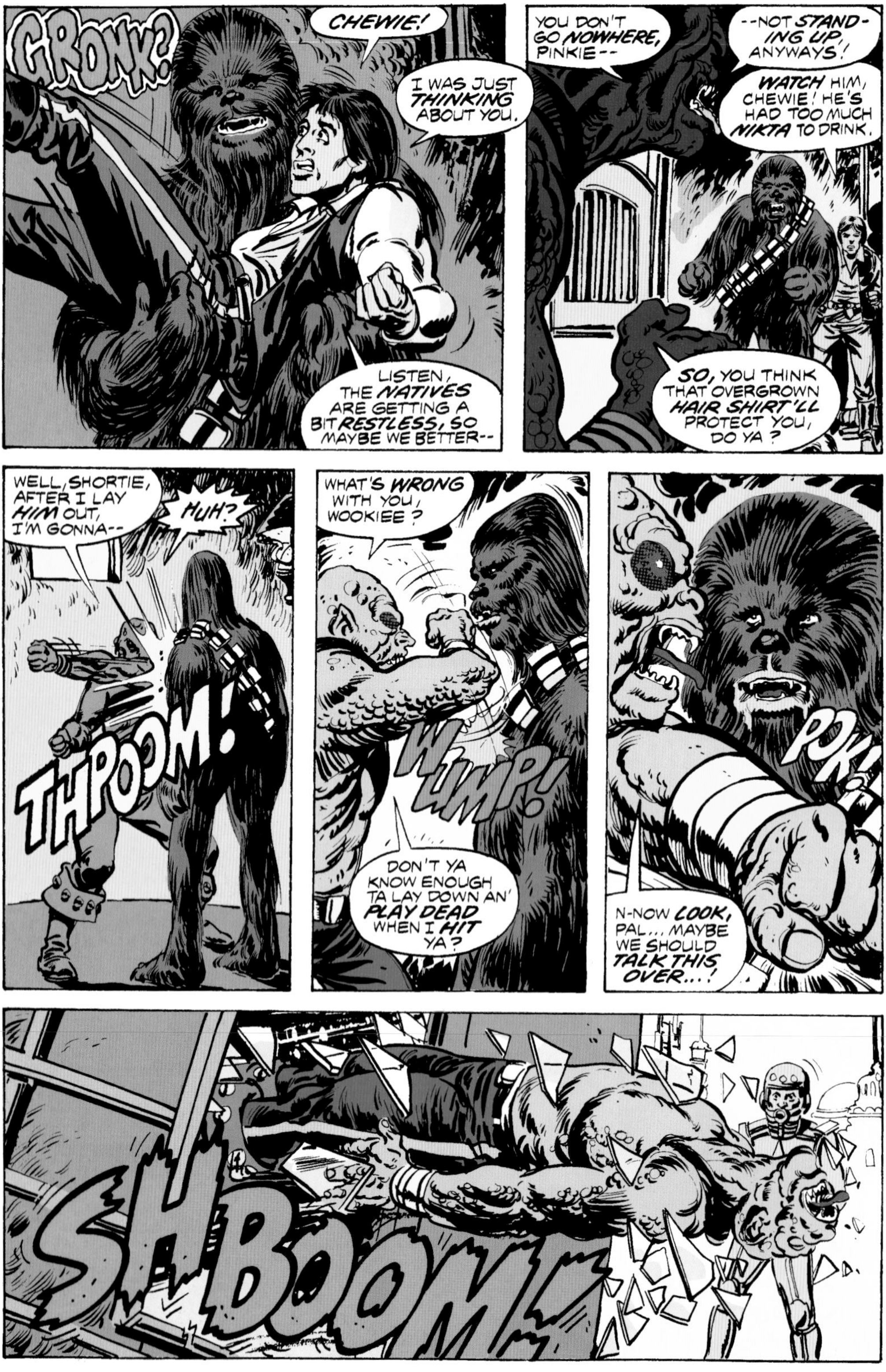
GRONK?
CHEWIE!
I WAS JUST THINKING ABOUT YOU.
LISTEN, THE NATIVES ARE GETTING A BIT RESTLESS, SO MAYBE WE BETTER--
YOU DON'T GO NOWHERE, PINKIE--
--NOT STANDING UP, ANYWAYS!
WATCH HIM, CHEWIE! HE'S HAD TOO MUCH NIKTA TO DRINK.
SO, YOU THINK THAT OVERGROWN HAIR SHIRT'LL PROTECT YOU, DO YA?
WELL, SHORTIE, AFTER I LAY HIM OUT, I'M GONNA--
MUH?
THPOOM!
WHAT'S WRONG WITH YOU, WOOKIEE?
WUMP!
DON'T YA KNOW ENOUGH TA LAY DOWN AN' PLAY DEAD WHEN I HIT YA?
POK!
N-NOW LOOK, PAL... MAYBE WE SHOULD TALK THIS OVER...!
SHBOOM!

AS SWIFTLY AS IT *BEGAN*, THE BATTLE *ROYAL* IS *OVER*...

GRRONK!

NO GRUDGES, NOW, OLD BUDDY.

AFTER ALL, WE *WON*, DIDN'T WE?

AND, AS IS *USUAL* IN SUCH CASES, THE *VICTORS* ARE THE ONES WHO ARE LEFT *STANDING*.

NOW, WHAT SAY WE GO SEE WHY THOSE *PEASANT TYPES* JUST OFFERED US A *JOB*?

WE COULD *USE* ONE Y'KNOW.

NOW, FRIEND, AS YOU WERE SAYING, BEFORE WE WERE SO CRUDELY *INTERRUPTED*..?

WE ARE LOWLY *FARMERS* FROM A VILLAGE IN THE *POORER PARTS* OF THIS PLANET...

THAT'S WHAT I CALL STARTING OUT AT THE *BOTTOM!*

BEG *PARDON*, SIR?

SORRY. GUESS I'LL HAVE TO *SHELVE* MY SENSE OF HUMOR FOR A WHILE, EH, CHEWIE?

ANYWAY ...WHAT'S YOUR *PROBLEM*, LITTLE *FRIEND*?

MY NAME IS *RAMIZ*, AND I WAS *SELECTED* TO COME HERE WITH THE OTHERS TO FIND,... I DO NOT KNOW QUITE HOW TO *SAY* IT,...

...A *CHAMPION*...A *PROTECTOR*, SO TO SPEAK!

SO FAR, I LIKE THE *SOUND* OF IT.

HRUK?

I WAS JUST *GETTING* TO THAT, CHEWIE.

MY FURRY *FIRST MATE* WANTS TO KNOW JUST *WHO* OR *WHAT* YOU WANT US TO PROTECT YOU *FROM*.

HE IS A *DEVIL*,...HE AND HIS *MEN!*

UH OH! SOUNDS LIKE WE'RE *OUTNUMBERED* BEFORE WE EVEN *START*.

BUT, WE ARE DIRELY IN *NEED* OF A CHAMPION, MASTER SOLO,...

"...SOMEONE WHO WILL DEFEND US FROM THE *CLOUD-RIDERS*, AND FROM *SERJI-X!*"

"HE AND HIS MEN-- *OUTLAWS* WHO LIVE IN THE MIST-SHROUDED *HILLS* OUTSIDE OUR VILLAGE-- COME FORTH EACH YEAR AT ABOUT THIS TIME TO *EXACT TRIBUTE* FROM US, WHO HAVE BARELY ENOUGH TO FEED *OURSELVES!*"

"AYE, THAT IS THE NAME OF THEIR LEADER-- *SERJI-X ARROGANTUS* --THE *ARROGANT ONE!*"

"THEY STAMPEDE OUR *BANTHAS,* WHICH WE RAISE FOR *FOOD* AND *TRANSPORTATION*..."

"IF WE TRY TO *RESIST,* THEY WILL *BURN* OUR MEAGRE CROPS, WHICH SCARCELY FEED US WELL IN THE *BEST* OF YEARS..."

"AND THEY CARRY OFF OUR *WIVES,* OUR *DAUGHTERS*...MERELY TO *AMUSE* THEMSELVES!"

I HAVE SAID THAT THEY ARE *DEVILS,* MASTER SOLO...AND THERE IS NO *OTHER* WORD THAT FITS THEM SO *WELL.*

WE HAVE *LITTLE MONEY,* BUT WE CAN OFFER YOU *FOOD*...AND *SHELTER.*

YOU *MUST* HELP US, MASTERS...OR OUR VILLAGE WILL SOON *CEASE TO BE!*

140

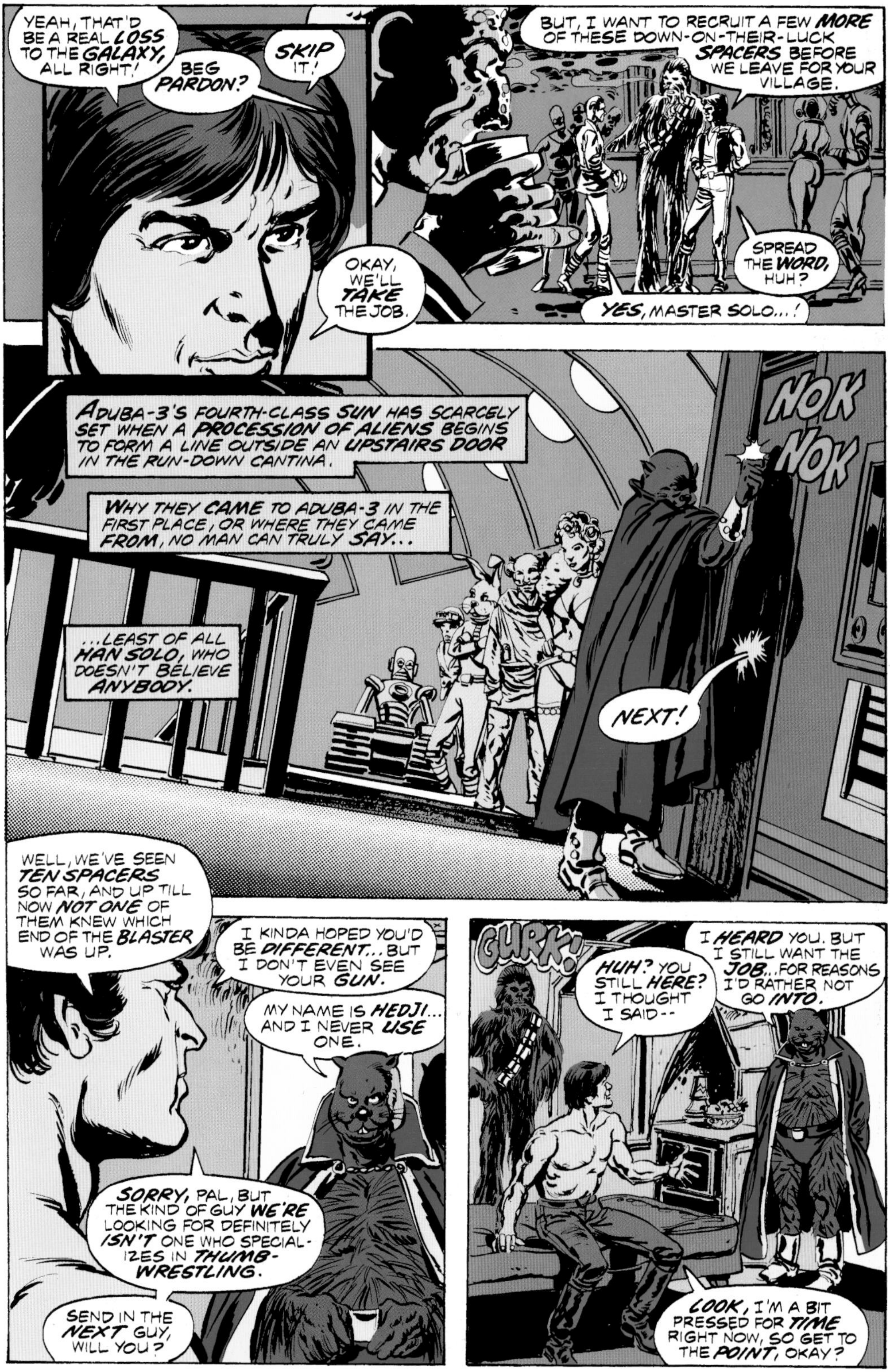
YEAH, THAT'D BE A REAL LOSS TO THE GALAXY, ALL RIGHT!
BEG PARDON?
SKIP IT!
OKAY, WE'LL TAKE THE JOB.
BUT, I WANT TO RECRUIT A FEW MORE OF THESE DOWN-ON-THEIR-LUCK SPACERS BEFORE WE LEAVE FOR YOUR VILLAGE.
SPREAD THE WORD, HUH?
YES, MASTER SOLO...!
ADUBA-3'S FOURTH-CLASS SUN HAS SCARCELY SET WHEN A PROCESSION OF ALIENS BEGINS TO FORM A LINE OUTSIDE AN UPSTAIRS DOOR IN THE RUN-DOWN CANTINA.
WHY THEY CAME TO ADUBA-3 IN THE FIRST PLACE, OR WHERE THEY CAME FROM, NO MAN CAN TRULY SAY...
...LEAST OF ALL HAN SOLO, WHO DOESN'T BELIEVE ANYBODY.
NOK NOK
NEXT!
WELL, WE'VE SEEN TEN SPACERS SO FAR, AND UP TILL NOW NOT ONE OF THEM KNEW WHICH END OF THE BLASTER WAS UP.
I KINDA HOPED YOU'D BE DIFFERENT... BUT I DON'T EVEN SEE YOUR GUN.
MY NAME IS HEDJI... AND I NEVER USE ONE.
SORRY, PAL, BUT THE KIND OF GUY WE'RE LOOKING FOR DEFINITELY ISN'T ONE WHO SPECIAL-IZES IN THUMB-WRESTLING.
SEND IN THE NEXT GUY, WILL YOU?
GURK!
HUH? YOU STILL HERE? I THOUGHT I SAID--
I HEARD YOU. BUT I STILL WANT THE JOB... FOR REASONS I'D RATHER NOT GO INTO.
LOOK, I'M A BIT PRESSED FOR TIME RIGHT NOW, SO GET TO THE POINT, OKAY?

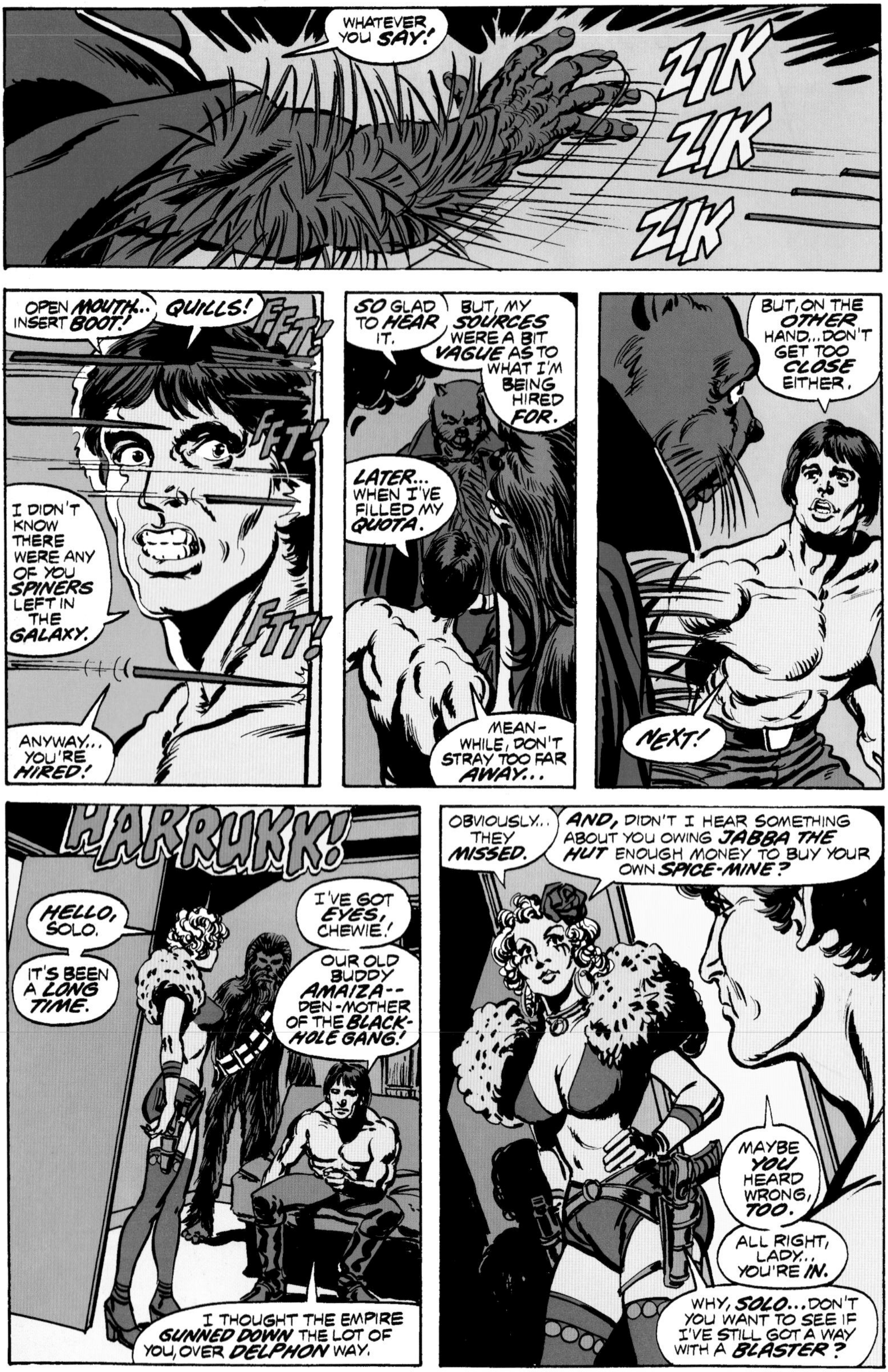
WHATEVER YOU SAY!
ZIK
ZIK
ZIK
OPEN MOUTH.. INSERT BOOT!
QUILLS!
FFT!
FFT!
I DIDN'T KNOW THERE WERE ANY OF YOU SPINERS LEFT IN THE GALAXY.
FTT!
ANYWAY... YOU'RE HIRED!
SO GLAD TO HEAR IT.
BUT, MY SOURCES WERE A BIT VAGUE AS TO WHAT I'M BEING HIRED FOR.
LATER... WHEN I'VE FILLED MY QUOTA.
MEAN-WHILE, DON'T STRAY TOO FAR AWAY...
BUT, ON THE OTHER HAND... DON'T GET TOO CLOSE EITHER.
NEXT!
HARRUKK!
HELLO, SOLO.
IT'S BEEN A LONG TIME.
I'VE GOT EYES, CHEWIE!
OUR OLD BUDDY AMAIZA-- DEN-MOTHER OF THE BLACK-HOLE GANG!
I THOUGHT THE EMPIRE GUNNED DOWN THE LOT OF YOU, OVER DELPHON WAY.
OBVIOUSLY.. THEY MISSED.
AND, DIDN'T I HEAR SOMETHING ABOUT YOU OWING JABBA THE HUT ENOUGH MONEY TO BUY YOUR OWN SPICE-MINE?
MAYBE YOU HEARD WRONG, TOO.
ALL RIGHT, LADY... YOU'RE IN.
WHY, SOLO... DON'T YOU WANT TO SEE IF I'VE STILL GOT A WAY WITH A BLASTER?

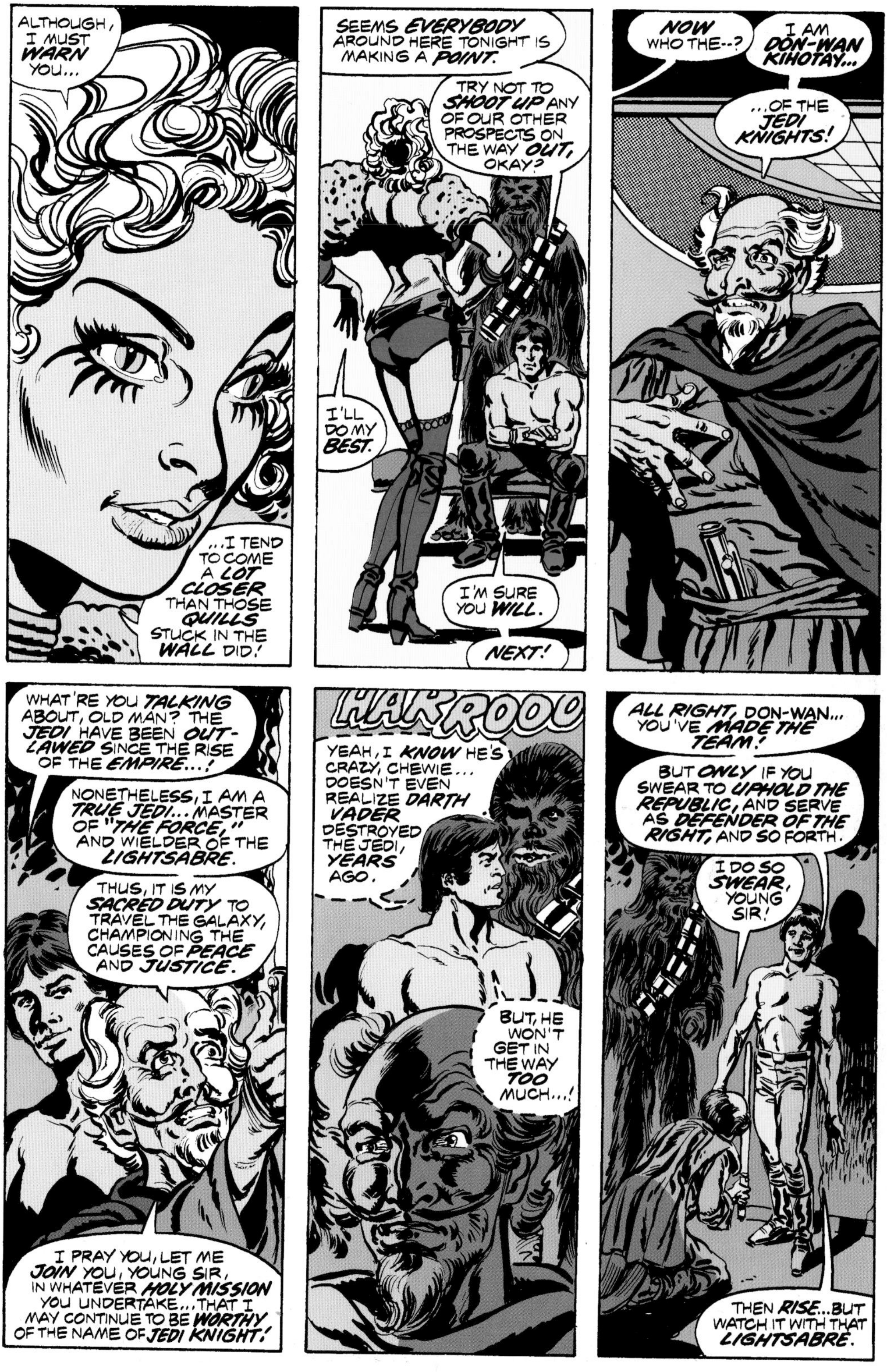
ALTHOUGH, I MUST WARN YOU...
...I TEND TO COME A LOT CLOSER THAN THOSE QUILLS STUCK IN THE WALL DID!
SEEMS EVERYBODY AROUND HERE TONIGHT IS MAKING A POINT.
TRY NOT TO SHOOT UP ANY OF OUR OTHER PROSPECTS ON THE WAY OUT, OKAY?
I'LL DO MY BEST.
I'M SURE YOU WILL.
NEXT!
NOW WHO THE--?
I AM DON-WAN KIHOTAY...
...OF THE JEDI KNIGHTS!
WHAT'RE YOU TALKING ABOUT, OLD MAN? THE JEDI HAVE BEEN OUTLAWED SINCE THE RISE OF THE EMPIRE...!
NONETHELESS, I AM A TRUE JEDI... MASTER OF "THE FORCE," AND WIELDER OF THE LIGHTSABRE.
THUS, IT IS MY SACRED DUTY TO TRAVEL THE GALAXY, CHAMPIONING THE CAUSES OF PEACE AND JUSTICE.
I PRAY YOU, LET ME JOIN YOU, YOUNG SIR, IN WHATEVER HOLY MISSION YOU UNDERTAKE... THAT I MAY CONTINUE TO BE WORTHY OF THE NAME OF JEDI KNIGHT!
HARROOO
YEAH, I KNOW HE'S CRAZY, CHEWIE... DOESN'T EVEN REALIZE DARTH VADER DESTROYED THE JEDI, YEARS AGO.
BUT, HE WON'T GET IN THE WAY TOO MUCH...!
ALL RIGHT, DON-WAN... YOU'VE MADE THE TEAM!
BUT ONLY IF YOU SWEAR TO UPHOLD THE REPUBLIC, AND SERVE AS DEFENDER OF THE RIGHT, AND SO FORTH.
I DO SO SWEAR, YOUNG SIR!
THEN RISE...BUT WATCH IT WITH THAT LIGHTSABRE.

MY *ETERNAL THANKS*, YOUNG SIR! *DON-WAN KIHOTAY* WILL NOT LET YOU *DOWN*.

THAT'S *PEACHY!* NOW *MOVE* IT, POPS-- WE AIN'T GOT *ALL NIGHT* OUT HERE IN THE LOBBY, Y'KNOW.

OH, WELL, LEASTWAYS I'M *NEXT*, SO WE CAN FINALLY GET THIS SHOW ON THE ROAD BEFORE *SUN-UP*.

OUTTA MY WAY, RODENT! I JUST FOUND OUT THAT *NEW GUY* IS HIRIN' *SPACERS*...

AND I WANT SOME *MONEY* SO'S I CAN GET OFF THIS *ROCK*!

I AIN'T NO *RODENT*, CAP'N...

AN' I'M *NEXT IN LINE*, SO WHY DONTCHA JUST--

WHOM

:URG.!

YOU MEAN YOU *WAS* NEXT!

NOW, OPEN *UP* IN THERE, PAL, AND LET ME--

'SCUZE ME, JUNIOR...

...BUT I REALLY GOTTA *INSIST* THAT YOU HAUL YOUR WART-COVERED CARCASS BACK TO THE END'A THE *LINE*, Y'KNOW?

BLAST OFF, RODENT-- OR THERE'S PLENTY *MORE* FISTS WHERE *THAT* ONE CAME FROM!

I AIN'T ABOUT TO *DOUBT* IT, PAL.

BUT, LIKE I SAID *BEFORE*...

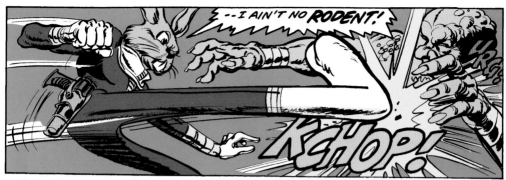

--I AIN'T NO *RODENT!*

KCHOP!

I'M MORE WHAT YA CALL YER BASIC *LEPUS CARNIVORUS*-- A *MEAT-EATIN'*, ROCKET-RIDIN' *RABBIT* TA YOU, JUNIOR!

OH *YEAH*-- AN' GIVE MY *REGARDS* TA THE BOYS IN THE *BAR!*

I *SAW* THAT, RABBIT...

WELL, HOORAY FOR *YOUR* SIDE! YOU MUST'A BEEN EATIN' YOUR *SPACE-CARROTS*...NEVER COULD *STAND* 'EM, MYSELF! I'M--

I *HEARD:* A *MEAT-EATER...* ONE THAT NEEDS A *JOB* RIGHT?

WELL, I AIN'T STANDIN' OUT HERE FOR THE *DECOR.*

YOU GOT *ANOTHER* NAME BESIDES--?

JAXXON. YOU CAN CALL ME *JAX* FOR SHORT...WHICH I *AIN'T.*

OKAY, JAX... I'LL SEND *CHEWBACCA* DOWN FOR YOU AND THE OTHERS LATER.

NOW, SON... WHAT'S A *YOUNGSTER* LIKE YOU DOING IN LINE?

I MEAN, THE *FREE-FOR-ALL* I'VE GOT LINED UP DOESN'T NEED ANOTHER *MASCOT.*

AND THAT *TRACTOR-ROBOT* TREADING HIS WAY UP THE STAIRS BEHIND YOU... HE *YOURS?*

HE SURE *IS!* MY HANDLE'S *JIMM*, BUT I CALL MYSELF THE *STARKILLER KID!*

AND YOU CAN BET I'M GONNA *LIVE UP* TO THAT HANDLE--IF I CAN EVER GET OFF THIS CRUMMY *PLANET.*

WHILE *I*, SIR, AM *FE-9Q...* FAMILIARLY KNOWN AS *EFFIE...*

AND I DON'T BELONG TO *ANYONE...* MOST ESPECIAL-LY NOT TO ANYONE WHO CALLS HIMSELF THE *STARKILLER KID!*

DON'T PAY HIM ANY *MIND*, SOLO! HE GETS *UPPITTY* SOMETIMES, BUT HE'S REALLY *DEVOTED* TO ME... LIKE A *PET*.

MORE LIKE A *LANDSPEEDER* IS DEVOTED TO THE MAN BEHIND THE *STEERING WHEEL*!

WE CAN *ALWAYS* USE A GOOD *ROBOT*, SON.

BUT GIVE ME *THREE* GOOD REASONS WHY WE SHOULD TAKE *YOU* ALONG!

AH-HAH!

SHUT UP, *EFFIE*!

BECAUSE I'VE STUCK ON *ADUBA-3* ALL MY *LIFE*, AND IF I DON'T GET *OFF* IT, I'M GONNA GO *NUTS*... THAT'S WHY!

EVER *FIRED* THAT BLASTER AT ANYTHING BIGGER THAN A *SAND-RAT*?

SURE... *LOTS* OF TIMES, AT-- AT--

DUNE-CACTUSES, RIGHT?

WELL, *YEAH*-- BUT JUST GIVE ME A *CHANCE*, AND I'LL--

WHOA! PUT ON YOUR *RETRO-ROCKETS*!

YOU KNOW, YOU REMIND ME OF *ANOTHER* COCKY KID I USED TO KNOW... NAME OF *LUKE SKYWALKER*.

IT HASN'T BEEN ALL THAT LONG SINCE I *SAW* HIM, BUT THINGS WERE MOVING *PRETTY FAST* WHEN I LEFT.

I WONDER WHAT *HE'S* UP TO, RIGHT ABOUT NOW...!

AND, EVEN AS HAN SOLO *MUSES*...

...EVENTS *ARE* MOVING QUICKLY ON THE *FOURTH MOON* OF THE DISTANT PLANET *YAVIN*, UN-NUMBERED LIGHT-YEARS AWAY.

FOR, SINCE THE DESTRUCTION OF THE GALACTIC EMPIRE'S DREADED *DEATH STAR*, THE *REBELS* ON THAT VERDANT WORLD HAVE BEEN ON CONSTANT *VIGIL*...

...THOUGH ONLY A FEW TELLTALE *RECON-TOWERS*, JUTTING UP OUT OF THE THICK JUNGLE, WOULD GIVE THEM *AWAY*.

WHILE, BENEATH THE SURFACE OF *YAVIN-4*...

OH, *LUKE*... I WISH ANYONE BUT *YOU* WERE GOING...!

AS DO WE *ALL*, YOUR MAJESTY... BUT, *NO ONE* HERE HAS PROVEN HIMSELF AS GOOD A *STAR-PILOT* AS YOUNG *LUKE*...

AND SKILLED, FAST *FLYING* IS JUST WHAT WE *NEED* AT THIS MOMENT IN TIME!

I WON'T LET YOU *DOWN*, GENERAL DODONNA!

NOW *HURRY ABOARD,* ARTOO! MASTER LUKE DOESN'T HAVE *ALL DAY,* YOU KNOW.

BEEP

ARE YOU *SURE* YOU KNOW WHAT YOU'RE LETTING YOURSELF *IN* FOR, LUKE?

I'M NO *HERO,* PRINCESS...

BUT THEN, IT DOESN'T *TAKE* A HERO TO FIGURE OUT THAT THE *GALACTIC EMPIRE'S* GOT TO BE *STOPPED...*

AND THE *REBELS* ARE THE ONLY CHANCE WE'VE *GOT!*

DARTH VADER KNOWS WE'RE *HERE* NOW...

...SO *THREEPIO,* ARTOO, AND I HAD BETTER SCOUT UP ANOTHER HID-ING-PLACE FOR THE REBELS --*FAST!*

YOU'LL BE HEAR-ING FROM ME SOONER THAN YOU *THINK!*

I'M *SURE* I WILL, LUKE... *MAY THE FORCE BE WITH YOU!*

AND WITH *YOU,* PRINCESS!

IF ONLY *I* COULD BE GOING *WITH* HIM, GENERAL...!

YOUR PLACE IS *HERE,* YOUR HIGHNESS... WITH THE *REBELS.*

NOW THAT YOUR *FATHER* IS DEAD, YOU ARE NEEDED BOTH AS A *LEADER...* AND AS A *SYMBOL.*

PRINCESS LEIA THINKS MOMENTAR-ILY OF HER *FATHER,* SLAIN BY THE EMPIRE, AS *LUKE'S* STARSHIP PASSES SWIFTLY FROM SIGHT...

...OUT OF THE GRAVITY FIELDS OF BOTH YAVIN AND ITS FOURTH *MOON,* AND INTO THE *VASTNESS* OF SPACE...

...AS HAN SOLO'S *MILLENNIUM FALCON* DID, NOT SO MANY DAYS BEFORE.

HOW DID I GET *MIXED UP* IN ALL THIS *WAR* STUFF, ANYWAY?

I MEAN, MAYBE I GOT *LUCKY* AND BLEW UP THE *DEATH STAR* --BUT I'M STILL JUST A *FARM-BOY,* FRESH OFF A BACKWATER WORLD LIKE *TATOOINE!*

AW, WHO'RE YOU *KIDDIN',* SKYWALKER?

YOU KNOW YOU DIDN'T HAVE ANY *CHOICE* --NOT ONCE YOU LEARNED YOUR *FATHER* WAS ONE OF THE *JEDI KNIGHTS*--

--EVEN FOUGHT ALONGSIDE *BEN KENOBI* IN THE *CLONE WARS!*

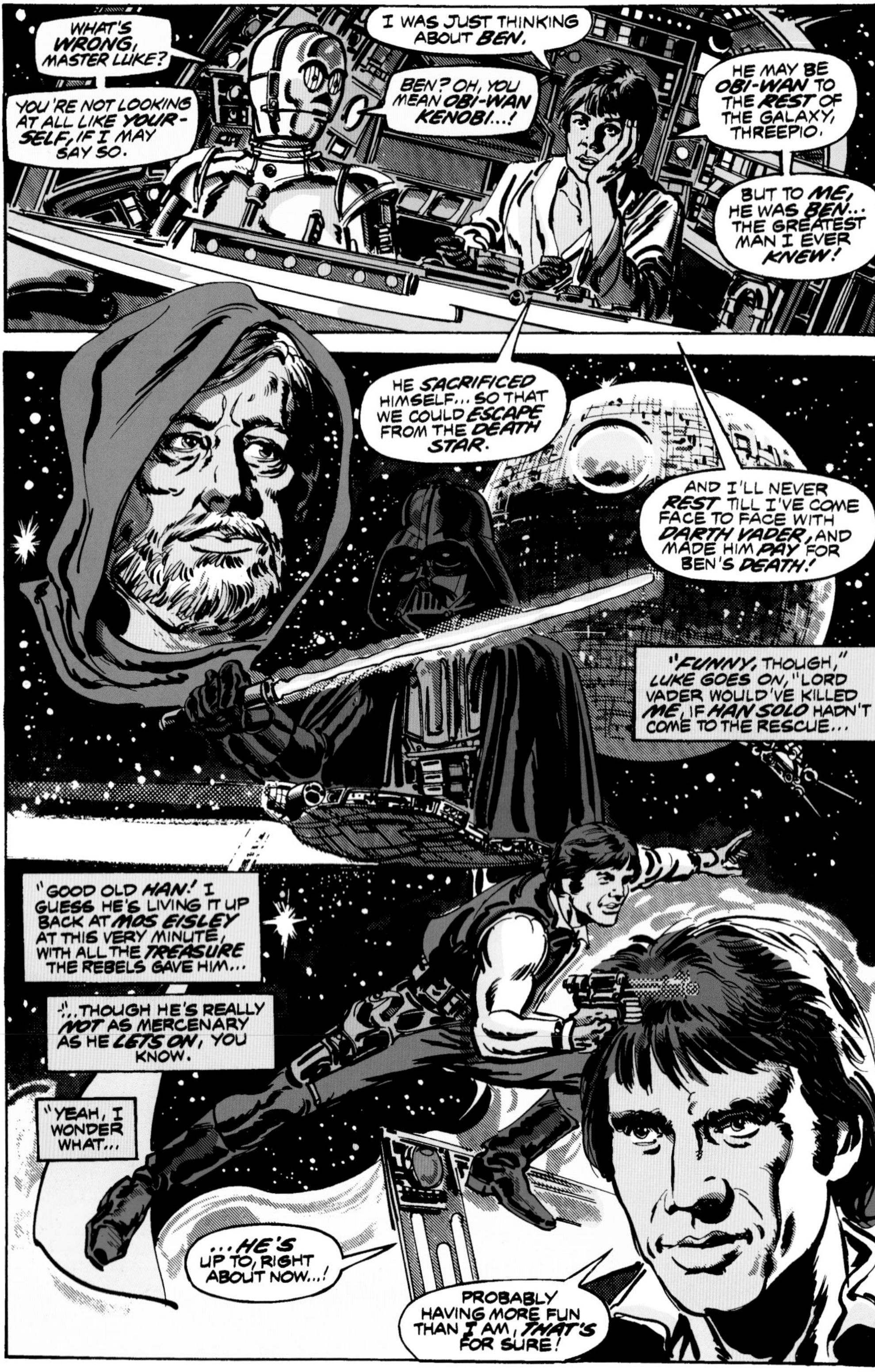
WHAT'S WRONG, MASTER LUKE?
YOU'RE NOT LOOKING AT ALL LIKE YOURSELF, IF I MAY SAY SO.
I WAS JUST THINKING ABOUT BEN.
BEN? OH, YOU MEAN OBI-WAN KENOBI...!
HE MAY BE OBI-WAN TO THE REST OF THE GALAXY, THREEPIO.
BUT TO ME, HE WAS BEN... THE GREATEST MAN I EVER KNEW!
HE SACRIFICED HIMSELF... SO THAT WE COULD ESCAPE FROM THE DEATH STAR.
AND I'LL NEVER REST TILL I'VE COME FACE TO FACE WITH DARTH VADER, AND MADE HIM PAY FOR BEN'S DEATH!
"FUNNY, THOUGH," LUKE GOES ON, "LORD VADER WOULD'VE KILLED ME, IF HAN SOLO HADN'T COME TO THE RESCUE...
"GOOD OLD HAN! I GUESS HE'S LIVING IT UP BACK AT MOS EISLEY AT THIS VERY MINUTE, WITH ALL THE TREASURE THE REBELS GAVE HIM...
"...THOUGH HE'S REALLY NOT AS MERCENARY AS HE LETS ON, YOU KNOW.
"YEAH, I WONDER WHAT...
...HE'S UP TO, RIGHT ABOUT NOW...!
PROBABLY HAVING MORE FUN THAN I AM, THAT'S FOR SURE!

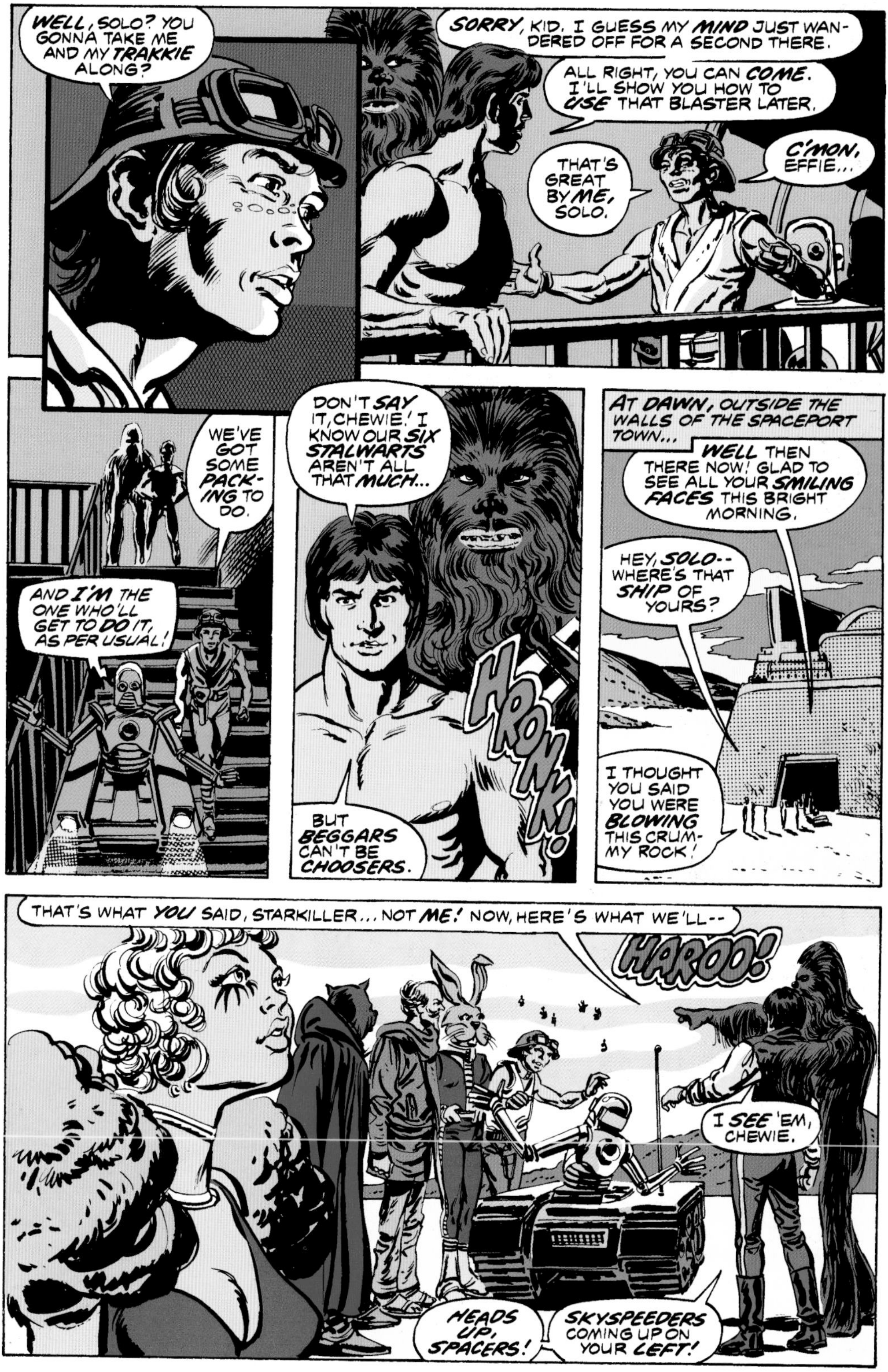
WELL, SOLO? YOU GONNA TAKE ME AND MY TRAKKIE ALONG?
SORRY, KID. I GUESS MY MIND JUST WANDERED OFF FOR A SECOND THERE.
ALL RIGHT, YOU CAN COME. I'LL SHOW YOU HOW TO USE THAT BLASTER LATER.
THAT'S GREAT BY ME, SOLO.
C'MON, EFFIE...
WE'VE GOT SOME PACKING TO DO.
AND I'M THE ONE WHO'LL GET TO DO IT, AS PER USUAL!
DON'T SAY IT, CHEWIE! I KNOW OUR SIX STALWARTS AREN'T ALL THAT MUCH...
HRONNK!
BUT BEGGARS CAN'T BE CHOOSERS.
AT DAWN, OUTSIDE THE WALLS OF THE SPACEPORT TOWN...
WELL THEN THERE NOW! GLAD TO SEE ALL YOUR SMILING FACES THIS BRIGHT MORNING.
HEY, SOLO-- WHERE'S THAT SHIP OF YOURS?
I THOUGHT YOU SAID YOU WERE BLOWING THIS CRUMMY ROCK!
THAT'S WHAT YOU SAID, STARKILLER... NOT ME! NOW, HERE'S WHAT WE'LL--
HAROO!
I SEE 'EM, CHEWIE.
HEADS UP, SPACERS!
SKYSPEEDERS COMING UP ON YOUR LEFT!

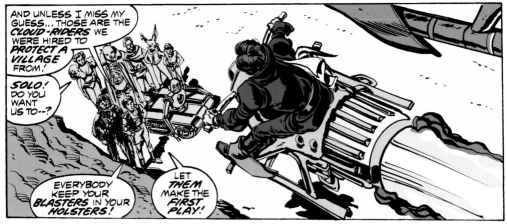

AND UNLESS I MISS MY GUESS... THOSE ARE THE *CLOUD-RIDERS* WE WERE HIRED TO *PROTECT A VILLAGE* FROM!

SOLO! DO YOU WANT US TO--?

EVERYBODY KEEP YOUR *BLASTERS* IN YOUR HOLSTERS!

LET *THEM* MAKE THE *FIRST PLAY!*

THERE'S ONLY *SIX* OF 'EM! WE COULD--

DO *WHAT?* HALF OUR GUYS DON'T EVEN *USE* BLASTERS.

NO, IT'S OBVIOUS THEY *HEARD* ABOUT US, AND CAME TO HAVE A LITTLE *TALK...*

...AND IT'S EASY TO SEE *WHO* TIPPED THEM *OFF!*

HELLO, GRUE-SOME! BEAT UP ANY *LAME BRUSH-MICE* ON YOUR WAY TO TELL THE *BIG BOYS?*

A *SPACER'S* GOT TO *GET BY* THE BEST WAY HE CAN, STAR-HOPPER!

JUST DON'T PRESS YOUR *LUCK,* OR I'LL--

YOU WILL *NOT* FIRE, WARTO, UNLESS *I* GIVE THE WORD!

WELL, MR. SOLO?

MAY I ASSUME WE MEET UNDER A *FLAG OF TRUCE?*

I'M FRESH OUT OF *BANDANAS,* BUT YOU'RE *ON* SERJI-X...

YOU ARE *SERJI-X ARROGANTUS,* AREN'T YOU?

AN *UNFORTUNATE* TITLE, FOR ONE OF SUCH *DELICATE SENSIBILITIES* AS I.

BUT, WE HAVE COME A *LONG WAY,* SO LET US NOT *BANDY WORDS,* EH?

YOU HAVE BEEN APPROACHED BY *FARMERS* FROM A *CERTAIN VILLAGE...* TO WHICH THEY HAVE ALREADY *RETURNED.*

FORGET YOUR MISSION, I AM PREPARED TO OFFER YOU A *MINIMAL SUM...*

...THOUGH I'M SURE IT WILL BE *MORE* THAN THOSE IGNOR-ANT *PEONS* CAN GIVE YOU.

THEY'RE GIVING US *ALL THEY CAN,* FRIEND... AND THAT'S THE *BEST* PAY I'VE EVER *HAD.*

A *SAND-RAT* LIKE *YOU* COULD NEVER *BEGIN* TO MATCH THEIR PRICE.

NOW *I'VE* GOT AN IDEA: HOW'S ABOUT YOU AND YOUR MEN LEAVE THAT VILLAGE *ALONE* THIS YEAR, AND WE WON'T HAVE ANY *TROUBLE!*

SUCH UNEXPECTED *BRAVADO*--FROM ONE WHO LEADS *WOMEN, CHILDREN,* AND *STARSHIP REJECTS!*

IF I HAD *KNOWN,* I WOULD HAVE STAYED IN THE MOUNTAINS --*LAUGHING.*

YEAH? WELL, TRYING LAUGHING THIS *BLASTER* OFF, YOU LOUSY BANDIT! I'LL--

AMAIZA! I *READ* YOU, SOLO--

--LOUD AND *CLEAR!*

SO, ALREADY YOU FIGHT AMONG *YOURSELVES!* AND WITH *THIS* FORCE YOU TRY TO FRIGHTEN *SERJI-X?*

THOM

YOU'VE HAD YOUR *SAY,* FRIEND, NOW, WHY DON'T YOU AND YOUR CLOUD-RIDERS GO HOME AND *PLAY?*

BUT I'D STEER CLEAR OF THAT *PEASANT VILLAGE,* IF I WERE YOU.

YOU ARE *NOT* ME, STAR-PILOT.

AND IF YOU *PERSIST,* YOU WILL SOON BE *NOTHING...*

... JUST ONE MORE *LIFELESS CORPSE,* TWISTING IN THE *DESERT WIND!*

URRK!

YEAH, MAYBE WE *HAVE* BITTEN OFF MORE THAN WE CAN CHEW THIS TIME, OLD BUDDY... I DON'T KNOW.

WELL, LET'S GET *MOVING,* STAR-HOPPERS!

WE'VE GOT SOME *BANTHA-RIDING* TO DO.!!

NEXT: *SHOWDOWN* ON A BARREN WORLD!

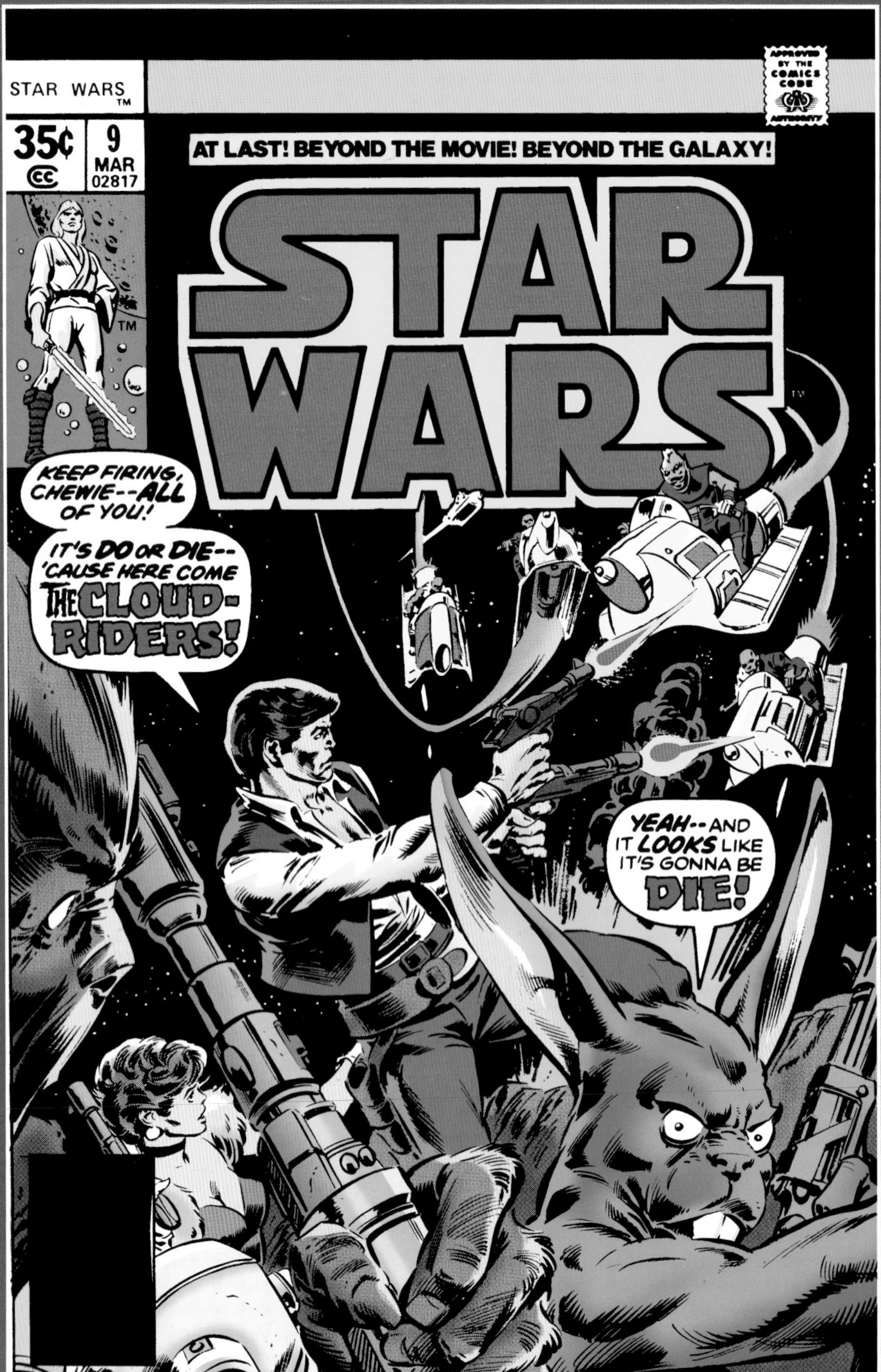
STAR WARS TM
35¢
9
MAR
02817
APPROVED BY THE COMICS CODE AUTHORITY
AT LAST! BEYOND THE MOVIE! BEYOND THE GALAXY!
STAR WARS
KEEP FIRING, CHEWIE--ALL OF YOU!
IT'S DO OR DIE--'CAUSE HERE COME THE CLOUD-RIDERS!
YEAH--AND IT LOOKS LIKE IT'S GONNA BE DIE!

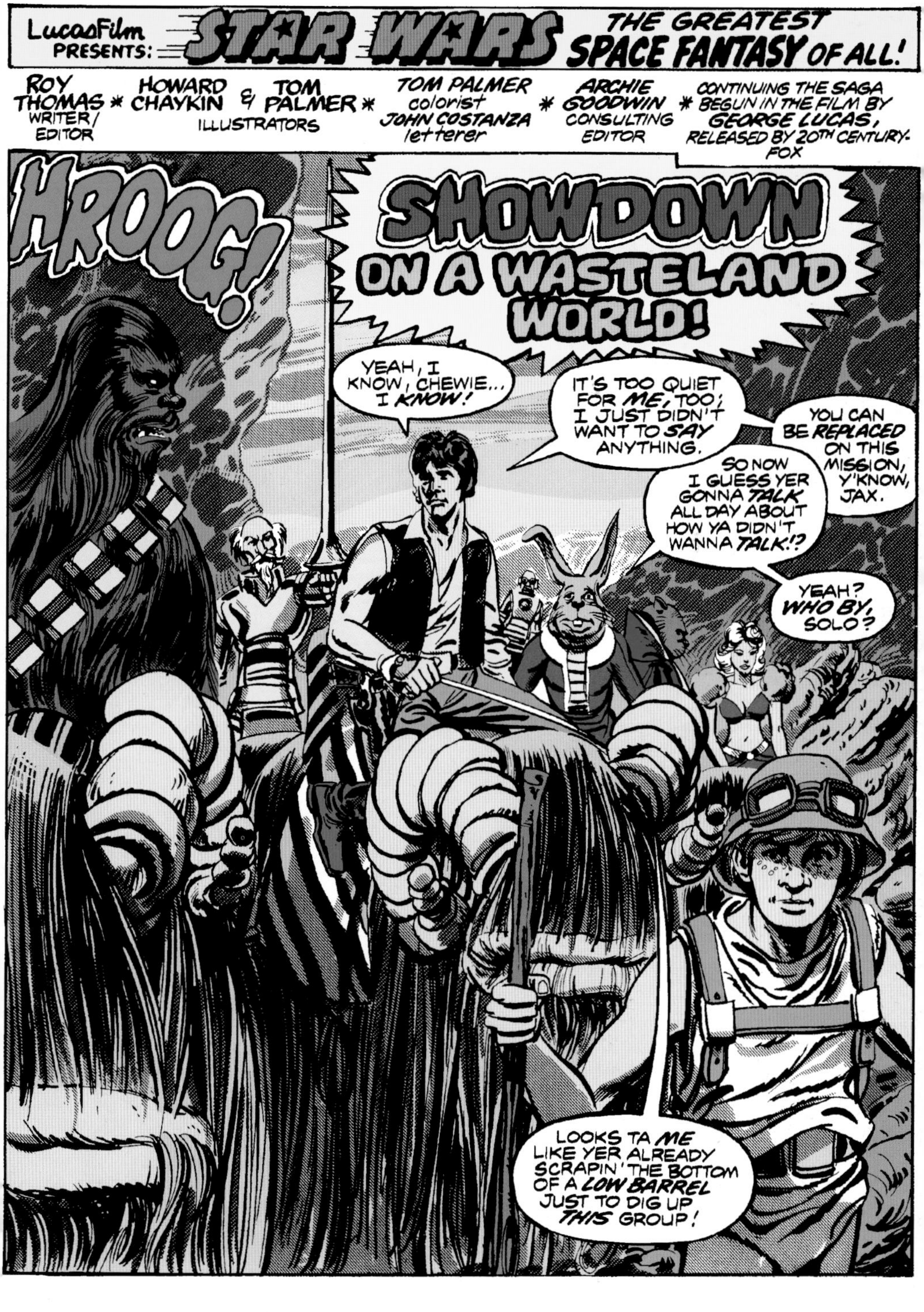
LucasFilm PRESENTS: STAR WARS THE GREATEST SPACE FANTASY OF ALL!
ROY THOMAS WRITER/EDITOR
HOWARD CHAYKIN & TOM PALMER ILLUSTRATORS
TOM PALMER colorist
JOHN COSTANZA letterer
ARCHIE GOODWIN CONSULTING EDITOR
CONTINUING THE SAGA BEGUN IN THE FILM BY GEORGE LUCAS, RELEASED BY 20TH CENTURY-FOX
HROOG!
SHOWDOWN ON A WASTELAND WORLD!
YEAH, I KNOW, CHEWIE... I KNOW!
IT'S TOO QUIET FOR ME, TOO; I JUST DIDN'T WANT TO SAY ANYTHING.
YOU CAN BE REPLACED ON THIS MISSION, Y'KNOW, JAX.
SO NOW I GUESS YER GONNA TALK ALL DAY ABOUT HOW YA DIDN'T WANNA TALK!?
YEAH? WHO BY, SOLO?
LOOKS TA ME LIKE YER ALREADY SCRAPIN' THE BOTTOM OF A LOW BARREL JUST TO DIG UP THIS GROUP!

HE'S *RIGHT*, SOLO--AND YOU *KNOW* IT!

HOW'D YOU GET *INTO* THIS MESS, ANYHOW--LEADING *CHEWBACCA* AND *SIX BASICALLY-SCRUFFY SPACERS* INTO WHAT'S BOUND TO BE A BATTLE WITH A BUNCH OF *BANDITS* WHO OUTNUMBER US *FIVE TO ONE?*

I THOUGHT I WAS ALL OVER THAT *IDEALISTIC* NONSENSE; I MEAN, A FEW MONTHS BACK, I WAS *SMUG-GLING SPICE* FOR A LOWLIFE NAMED *JABBA THE HUT.*

YOU CAN'T *GET* MUCH LESS IDEALISTIC THAN *THAT!*

THEN, I GOT TANGLED UP WITH *LUKE SKYWALKER* AND *PRINCESS LEIA*--AND I ACTUALLY ENDED UP *TURNING NOBLE* FOR A MINUTE THERE.

'COURSE, I TRIED TO *RE-ESTABLISH* MYSELF IN THE *SPACE MERCENARY* COMMUNITY BY PAYING *JABBA* BACK WHAT I OWED HIM--ONLY TO GET AMBUSHED BY *SPACE-PIRATES*--

--WHO TOOK THE *TREASURE* LEIA'S REBELS GAVE US, AND LEFT US WITH NOTHING BUT THE *MILLEN-NIUM FALCON* AND THE *PRICE* JABBA'S PUT ON OUR HEADS!

"YEAH, THAT'S HOW CHEWIE AND I WOUND UP ON THIS HELLHOLE CALLED *ADUBA-3,* ALL RIGHT--AGREEING TO PROTECT A BUNCH OF PEASANTS FROM A *BANDIT* TYPE NAMED *SERJI-X.*

"FAR AS I CAN SEE, THIS JOB'S NOT GOING TO *PAY* US ANYTHING MORE THAN *ALL THE CACTUS WE CAN EAT...*

"AND WE HAD TO GO THRU A *BARROOM BRAWL* OR TWO TO GET THE JOB, AT *THAT!*

SOLO

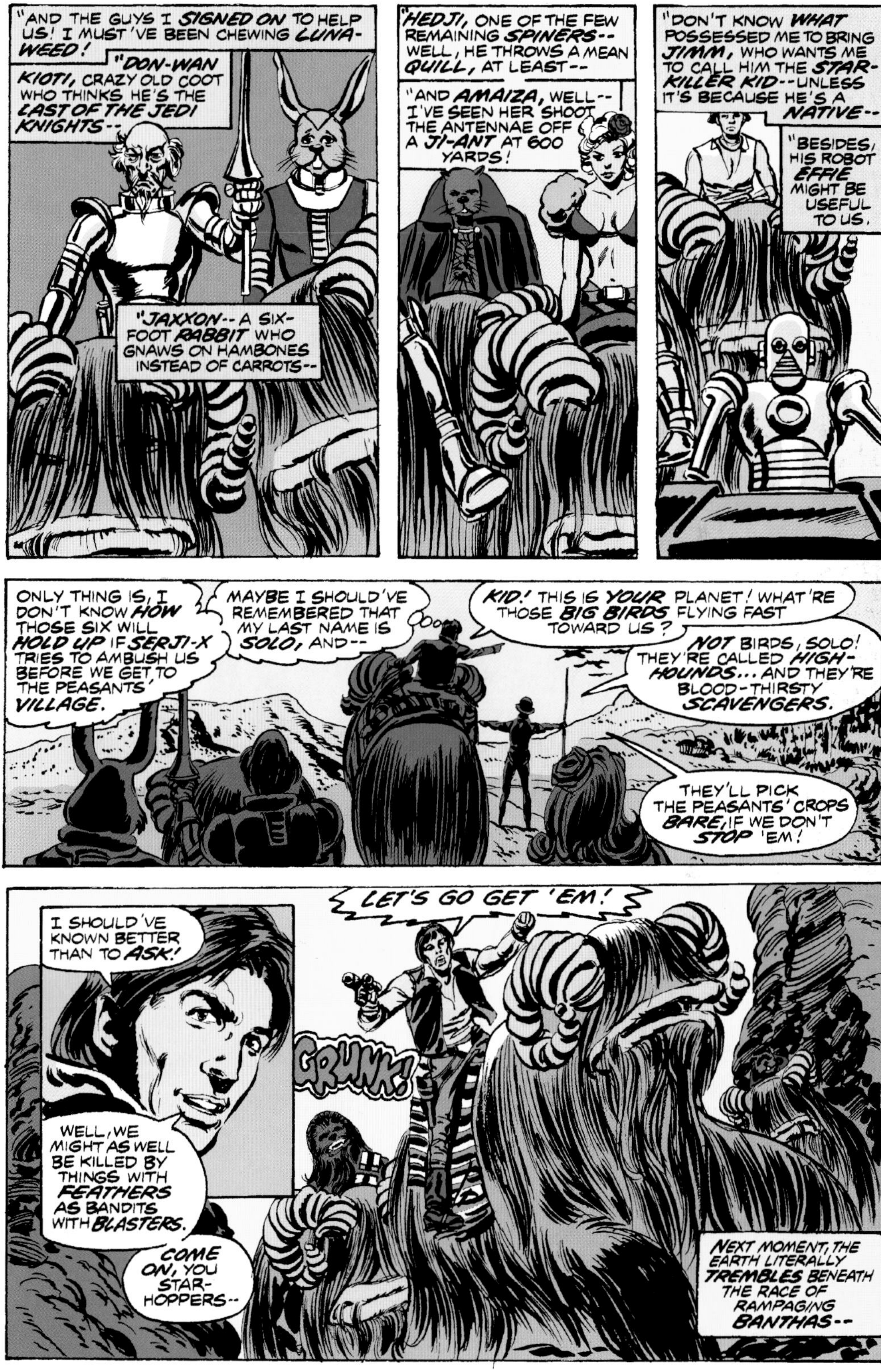

"AND THE GUYS I SIGNED ON TO HELP US! I MUST'VE BEEN CHEWING LUNA-WEED!
"DON-WAN KIOTI, CRAZY OLD COOT WHO THINKS HE'S THE LAST OF THE JEDI KNIGHTS--
"JAXXON-- A SIX-FOOT RABBIT WHO GNAWS ON HAMBONES INSTEAD OF CARROTS--
"HEDJI, ONE OF THE FEW REMAINING SPINERS-- WELL, HE THROWS A MEAN QUILL, AT LEAST--
"AND AMAIZA, WELL-- I'VE SEEN HER SHOOT THE ANTENNAE OFF A JI-ANT AT 600 YARDS!
"DON'T KNOW WHAT POSSESSED ME TO BRING JIMM, WHO WANTS ME TO CALL HIM THE STAR-KILLER KID-- UNLESS IT'S BECAUSE HE'S A NATIVE--
"BESIDES, HIS ROBOT EFFIE MIGHT BE USEFUL TO US.
ONLY THING IS, I DON'T KNOW HOW THOSE SIX WILL HOLD UP IF SERJI-X TRIES TO AMBUSH US BEFORE WE GET TO THE PEASANTS' VILLAGE.
MAYBE I SHOULD'VE REMEMBERED THAT MY LAST NAME IS SOLO, AND--
KID! THIS IS YOUR PLANET! WHAT'RE THOSE BIG BIRDS FLYING FAST TOWARD US?
NOT BIRDS, SOLO! THEY'RE CALLED HIGH-HOUNDS... AND THEY'RE BLOOD-THIRSTY SCAVENGERS.
THEY'LL PICK THE PEASANTS' CROPS BARE, IF WE DON'T STOP 'EM!
I SHOULD'VE KNOWN BETTER THAN TO ASK!
LET'S GO GET 'EM!
WELL, WE MIGHT AS WELL BE KILLED BY THINGS WITH FEATHERS AS BANDITS WITH BLASTERS.
COME ON, YOU STAR-HOPPERS--
GRUNK!
NEXT MOMENT, THE EARTH LITERALLY TREMBLES BENEATH THE RACE OF RAMPAGING BANTHAS--

--AS UP AHEAD, A NUMBER OF THE PLANET'S *HUMAN* INHABITANT'S ARE BEING BESIEGED BY SHRIEKING, *QUASI-HUMAN MONSTERS ON THE WING*--

NOR DID ANY MERE *SCARECROW* EVER SUFFICE AGAINST SUCH *BLOODTHIRSTY* SCAVENGERS AS THESE!

SKRAWW

YET, IF *STRAW MEN* WOULD PROVE USELESS AGAINST CREATURES WHICH FEED ON THE *MAZE-STALKS* WHICH ARE *ADUBA-3'S* STAPLE CROP...

--THERE ARE OTHER WAYS.

OKAY, GUYS! NOW WE KNOW THOSE *BIRDIES AREN'T* IMMUNE TO A WELL-AIMED *BLASTER.*

TIME TO GET IN SOME *TARGET PRACTICE* WHILE WE'RE WAITING FOR *SERJI-X* AND HIS BOYS!

THUS, GUNS BLAZING, THE AMAZING *EIGHT WADE* INTO THE VERY MIDST OF THE UNEVEN FRAY--

--AND PROCEED TO *UNBALANCE* IT IN A *BRAND NEW WAY!*

AMAIZA, ONCE A MEMBER OF THE DREADED *BLACK-HOLE GANG,* IS WANTED DEAD OR ALIVE IN *SIX STAR-SYSTEMS...*

...AND IT *ISN'T* FOR THE WAY SHE *THREADS* A NEEDLE.

MEANWHILE, *JAXXON*--*JAX* FOR SHORT, WHICH HE *ISN'T*--BRINGS DOWN A HIGH-HOUND WITH *EACH* OF THE GUNS HE WIELDS.

AS FOR THE SPINER CALLED *HEDJI,* WHO REFRAINS FROM USING A BLASTER AT ALL...

...HE HAS BUT TO *FLEX HIS MUSCLES* IN A PRECISE, PRE-DETERMINED WAY...

...TO TURN THE *FOREMOST* OF THE MARAUDING MAN-HAWKS INTO A FORMERLY *LIVING* PIN-CUSHION!

AS FOR "THE LAST OF THE JEDI KNIGHTS"...

FIE UPON YOU, FOUL FEATHERY FIEND--

IN THE NAME OF *JUSTICE*, LET THIS PLANET BE *CLEANSED* OF SUCH FILTH AS YOU AND YOUR BRETHREN!

I'M NOT SURE WHAT YOU JUST *SAID*, OLD MAN-- BUT I'M WITH YOU IN *SPIRIT!*

WHILE *I* DO ALL THE ACTUAL *WORK...*

ZKIK!

...AS PER *USUAL.*

POW!

Y'KNOW *AMAIZA--* WHEN THIS BABY-SITTIN' MISSION'S OVER, HOWZABOUT YOU AN' ME *TEAMIN' UP?* I GOT A HUNCH WE COULD MAKE BEAUTIFUL *BLASTER-MUSIC* TOGETHER.

NO *THANKS*, BUCK-TOOTH!

NO OFFENSE, BUT IF I HUNG AROUND WITH A GUY WHO LOOKS LIKE A *BIG GREEN RABBIT*, FOLKS MIGHT START TO *TALK*, AND--

SOLO! OVER THERE TO YOUR *RIGHT--!*

THANKS, LADY! I SEE HER--

--ONE OF THE *LOCALS*, BEING CHASED BY A *HIGH-HOUND!*

EEEE

BUT-- EVEN IF I *TAKE HIM OUT* AT THIS RANGE, HE'S STILL LIABLE TO *CRASH* RIGHT INTO HER!

AND, INDEED, THE GIRL HAS ALREADY *CLOSED HER EYES*-- CONSIGNING HER SOUL TO WHATEVER *GODS* SHE MAY WORSHIP--

FLAK!

--WHEN, *SUDDENLY*--

HERE, STONE-FACE! TRY CHEWING ON A *LASER BEAM* FOR A WHILE!

NOT THAT IT'LL BE TOO EASY WITH *NO TEETH*--

OHH!

OR, FOR THAT MATTER --*NO HEAD!*

NEXT MOMENT, THEIR RANKS SORELY *DEPLETED*, THE GROTESQUE *SCAVENGERS* TAKE TO THE *AIR* ONCE MORE...

...AND, IN A FEW SECONDS, ARE *LOST TO SIGHT*.

I HOPE *SERJI-X* AND HIS *CLOUD-RIDERS* GIVE UP AS--

WELL THEN THERE NOW! THINGS ARE LOOKING *UP* ON ADUBA-3!

I--I *THANK* YOU, KIND STRANGER, FOR *RESCUING* ME-- BUT, I DON'T *UNDERSTAND*--

YOU *WILL*, LADY-- IF WE *STICK AROUND* LONG ENOUGH.

MAYBE THIS PLACE *IS* WORTH SAVING, AFTER *ALL*.

A FEW MINUTES LATER, AT THE VILLAGE ITSELF...

SORRY WE DIDN'T GET HERE *SOONER*, PEOPLE... BUT WE HAD A LITTLE TROUBLE GETTING THE *SPACEPORT CROWD* TO LOAN ME THESE *BANTHAS* WITH MY *STARSHIP* AS SECURITY...

AS YOU MAY *SUPPOSE*, HAN SOLO, WORD OF YOUR COMING *PRECEDED* YOU.

YOUR DA--? UH, LET ME HELP YOU *DOWN*, MISS.

NOR COULD YOU HAVE COME AT A MORE *OPPORTUNE* MOMENT, THAN IN TIME TO SAVE MY *DAUGHTER*.

I SEE THIS ISN'T THE BEST TIME TO *CONTIN-UE* OUR LITTLE DISCUSSION.

HRARK!

NO *CRACKS*, CHEWIE! OKAY, YOU STAR-HOPPERS...

THESE NICE FOLKS SAY WE CAN STABLE OUR *BANTHAS* BEHIND THIS BUILDING.

YEAH? I WONDER WHERE THEY'LL STABLE *US?*

DON'T *MAKE FUN* OF MY PEOPLE, GREENIE!

REMEMBER-- I WAS *BORN* IN THIS VILLAGE... EVEN IF I'VE BEEN TRYING TO *FORGET* IT.

THEN, WHEN THE RELATIVELY SMALL BANTHAS ARE SECURELY *TETHERED*...

NOW, MAYBE IT'S TIME FOR SOME *INTRODUCTIONS*, AND A FEW MORE DETAILS ABOUT *SERJI-X*...?

I AM *ONCHO*, WHOM THE VILLAGERS HAVE CHOSEN AS THEIR *SPOKESMAN.*

MY DAUGHTER, WHOM YOU SAVED, IS NAMED *MERRI.*

FORGET IT! YOUR EMISSARIES IN THE SPACEPORT PROMISED YOU'D EVENTUALLY *PAY* US WHAT LITTLE YOU COULD TO *PROTECT* YOUR VILLAGE, DIDN'T THEY?

LET'S JUST FIGURE THAT WE GOT AN *EARLY START.*

I SHALL BE *EVER* IN YOUR *DEBT* FOR--

WELL, PICTURE *THAT!* HAN SOLO, LAST OF THE RED-HOT *SPACE-SMUGGLERS*...,

...GOING SOFT OVER A *GIRL* NOT MUCH BIGGER THAN A *WODANIAN WOOD-SPRITE!*

AMAIZA, DID ANYBODY EVER TELL YOU THAT YOU *TALK* TOO MUCH?

ONE GUY... *ONCE.*

LAST I *HEARD*, HIS *WIDOW* WAS LIVING IT UP ON *BESTINE* WITH HIS *DEATH-BENEFITS.*

SERVE ME RIGHT FOR GIVING YOU AN *OPENING.*

SOON....

THEY'RE WILLING AND *ABLE*, CHEWIE-- BUT WHEN THOSE *SKY-BANDITS* COME ROARING IN--

-- IT'S GONNA TAKE MORE THAN *GOOD INTENTIONS* TO TURN BACK *THOSE* BLASTER-HAPPY CLOWNS!

ALL RIGHT, "SPRITES"-- 'CAUSE I'VE GOT TO HAVE *SOMETHING* TO CALL YOU-- LET'S GET TO *WORK!*

WHEN *SERJI-X* SHOWS UP NEXT TIME, WE WANT TO BE *READY* FOR HIM!

TIME IS AN ALL BUT *MEANINGLESS* CONCEPT IN THE VAST *SEA OF STARS.*

YET, IF SUCH A WORD A *"MEANWHILE"* CAN HAVE ANY RELEVANCE AT ALL, THEN *THIS* IS WHAT IS HAPPENING AT THE SELFSAME MOMENT ON THE *FOURTH MOON* OF THE DISTANT PLANET *YAVIN...*

...OR, RATHER, *BENEATH THE SURFACE* OF THE JUNGLE-INFESTED SATELLITE?

I DON'T *LIKE* IT, GENERAL DODONNA!

WE SHOULD HAVE HEARD FROM *LUKE* BY NOW!

YOU *LIKE* THIS YOUNG MAN *"LUKE SKYWALKER,"* DON'T YOU, HIGHNESS?

AS MUCH AS ONE WITH MY *RESPONSIBILITES* CAN AFFORD TO LIKE *ANYONE* IN THESE TROUBLED TIMES.

OH, IF ONLY I COULD HAVE GONE *WITH* HIM AND HIS *DROIDS!*

LUKE, LUKE-- WHERE *ARE* YOU??

FOR *US*, HOWEVER, THE EXIGENCIES OF TIME AND SPACE *DO NOT EXIST.*

THUS, LET US SKIP LIGHTLY ACROSS THE *VOID OF SPACE,* TO WHERE THE SMALL STAR-CRAFT OF *LUKE SKYWALKER* HAS JUST GONE INTO ORBIT AROUND AN UNNAMED PLANET OF THE STAR-SUN *DREXEL...*

WELL, THREEPIO... ARTOO... THIS IS *IT!*

BEGGING YOUR *PARDON,* MASTER LUKE, BUT AS YOU KNOW, *SPACE TRAVEL* IS HARDLY MY SPECIALTY...OR EVEN ANYTHING I LIKE VERY MUCH.

WOULD YOU MIND *ELABOR-ATING...?*

GLADLY! WE WERE SENT HERE TO FIND A *NEW WORLD* FOR THE *REBELS* TO MIGRATE TO, BEFORE *DARTH VADER* SENDS THE WHOLE *IMPERIAL WAR-FLEET* AGAINST THEM.

WHREET?

YES, ARTOO,...IT *DOES* SOUND AS IF HE'S FOUND WHAT HE'S LOOKING FOR, DOESN'T IT?

YOU BET YOUR *CARBON SCORING MARKS* I HAVE!

AND THAT'S NOT *ALL--*

THE TIME'S COME TO BREAK *TRANS-CEIVER SILENCE* LONG ENOUGH TO TELL *PRINCESS LEIA* ABOUT IT!

OH, DON'T BE SUCH A *WORRY-DROID!*

BRIEF PERIODS OF *INSTANTANEOUS* COMMUNICATION WON'T ENDANGER OUR LOCATION...

...NOT SO LONG AS THE *ION-SCRAMBLER* IS OPERATING TO *CONFUSE* THE ENEMY.

ISN'T THAT *RIGHT,* MASTER LUKE?

THAT'S THE *THEORY,* THREEPIO. NOW I--

BREEF BREEF

WAIT! I'M RAISING THE *REBEL BASE,* AND--

PRINCESS! IT'S GREAT TO *SEE* YOU AGAIN!

AND *YOU* LUKE. ARE YOU *ALL RIGHT?*

HAVE YOU FOUND A NEW *SAFE-HAVEN* FOR OUR *REBEL FORCE?*

TIME IS *RUN-NING SHORT.*

YEAH, I THINK I *HAVE,* YOUR HIGH-NESS. IT'S A PLANET IN THE *DREXEL* SYSTEM, THAT--

NOW WHAT IN BLAZES--?

NO! IT--IT ISN'T *POSSIBLE!* IT--

LUKE--!

LUKE!?

THE *IMAGE* IS *GONE!*

MORE *POWER,* ENSIGN! YOU'VE GOT TO GIVE ME MORE *RE-CEIVING POWER!*

NO USE, YOUR HIGHNESS!

HE'S *STOPPED SENDING!*

AND THERE'S *NO WAY* TO RE-ESTABLISH CONTACT FROM *THIS* END.

WE'VE *LOST* HIM!

IF WE EVEN *KEEP SENDING,* SOME STRAY *EMPIRE* SHIP IS LIABLE TO--

THEN *STOP* SENDING!

PRINCESS LEIA-- WHERE ARE YOU--?

I'M GOING TO DO WHAT I *WANTED* TO DO IN THE *FIRST* PLACE-- WHAT I WAS *TALKED OUT* OF DOING.

I'M GOING TO *FIND LUKE SKYWALKER*-- NO MATTER *WHAT!!*

BOLD WORDS *INDEED* FOR ONE WHOSE STATION IN LIFE WOULD *USUALLY* HAVE HER DELIBERATING ON MATTERS OF *STATE...*

BUT WHILE PRINCESS LEIA CONTEMPLATES JUST *HOW* TO FIND ONE PERSON LOST IN THE VASTNESS OF *SPACE--*

--THE *TENSION* ON ADUBA-3 IS *WELLING* LIKE A THING *ALIVE...*

OKAY THEN, YOU MISFITS! IT'S NOT GONNA BE *LONG* BEFORE THE *FIREWORKS* START POPPING!

SO YOU WANNA *HURRY UP* WITH UNLOADING THOSE *WEAPONS* AN' *POWER PACKS?*

I DON'T THINK *SERJI-X* IS GONNA *WAIT* FOR US!

WAIT, YOUNG MAN! I WOULD HAVE *WORDS* WITH YOU BEFORE YOU--

NO, GRAND- FATHER! NOT *NOW!*

HUH? *GRAND- FATHER?!* LISTEN, OLD MAN--

--IT'S NOT *SAFE* SNEAKING UP LIKE THAT ON A GUY WITH A TEMPERA- MENTAL *BLASTER!*

LUCKY FOR YOU I HEARD MERRI CALL YOU *GRANDPA,* OR YOUR *OLD AGE* MIGHT'A GOT CUT *SHORT!*

SO WHAT D'YA WANT? BUT MAKE IT QUICK-- 'CAUSE I'M SORTA *BUSY* RIGHT NOW!

I AM HERE TO TELL YOU THAT THE HELP OF YOU AND YOUR COM- PANIONS IS NOT *NEEDED* HERE!

LISTEN, OLD-TIMER! TIME'S A' WASTING, SO...

YOU THINK I AM *JESTING,* YOUNG MAN! BUT IT HAS BEEN MANY *DECADES* SINCE I HAVE SPOKE *LIGHTLY!*

I TELL YOU IN ALL *SOBRIETY* THAT WE DO NOT *NEED* YOU OR YOUR ALIEN HORDE TO DRIVE THOSE *OUTLAWS* FROM OUR VILLAGE!

"WHY SHED THE LIFE FLUIDS OF YOUR *FRIENDS,* WHEN THERE IS A *SIMPLER* SOLUTION TO MY PEOPLE'S PROBLEM--

"--A *MYSTICAL* SOLUTION I ONCE BEHELD IN MY *YOUTH!*"

FIRST OF ALL, NOT ALL THOSE CHARACTERS ARE MY *FRIENDS!* AND *SECOND,* THEY KNEW WHAT THEY WERE GETTING INTO WHEN THEY *TOOK* THIS JOB!

AND THIRD, I OUTGREW *FAIRY TALES* BY THE TIME I COULD TALK!

NO, HEAR ME, MER- CENARY!

MAYBE SOME *OTHER* TIME, ALL RIGHT?

THEN YOU WILL *NOT* LISTEN! GRAND- DAUGHTER...TAKE HIDING BEFORE *SERGI-X* COMES--

--WHILE *I* DO WHAT I WAS *BORN* TO DO... *ALONE!*

PLEASE *IGNORE* THE OLD ONE, HAN SOLO!

HE FANCIES HIMSELF AS A *MYSTIC*... A *SHAMAN*...CAPABLE OF SUMMONING SOME LEGENDARY *MONSTER* TO SAVE OUR VILLAGE!

UH, *YEAH!* WELL TELL YOU WHAT, ONCHO! AFTER WE'VE USED UP OUR *LAST SHOT*--

--THEN *MAYBE* WE'LL TAKE THE CODGER UP ON HIS OFFER! BUT FOR *NOW*--

--ALL YOU HEROES *READY?* BLASTERS AT FULL POWER... *QUILLS SHARPENED* AND ALL THAT?

READY WHEN- EVER *YOU* GIVE THE WORD, SOLO!

ME AN' MY *ROBOT'S* READY, LEADER MAN!

FRONK!

SPEAK FOR *YOURSELF,* JUVENILE!

READY! AND IF WHAT THEY SAY ABOUT US RABBITS HAVIN' *GOOD* EYES IS *TRUE*--

--THEN I SUGGEST WE GET *UP* OFF OUR FANNIES AN' COTTON TAILS--

--'CAUSE I GOT A HUNCH *TROUBLE'S* ON THE WAY...

"*BIG* TROUBLE--

KR-BLAZZ!

"--AN' IT'S COMIN' AT US *HARD* AN' *FAST!*"

163

I HOPE YOU PEASANTS *APPRECIATE* OUR SPECTACU-LAR *ENTRANCE* THIS YEAR! BUT WE HADDA *TOP* OUR *LAST* APPEARANCE IN YOUR SQUALID VILLAGE--

--WHEN WE SIMPLY *CRASHED INTO* A FEW OF YOUR *DWELL-INGS!* REMEMBER? *HARRRR!!*

BUT YOU *KNOW* WHY WE'RE HERE, SO LET'S NOT WASTE ANYMORE OF MY *VALUABLE TIME!*

YOU CAN START DOLIN' OUT THE *TRIBUTE* YOU'VE BEEN SAVIN' UP FOR US ALL YEAR! *RIGHT?!*

AND THAT INCLUDES THE *CREAM* OF YOUR CROP, WHO JUST REACH-ED THE AGE I *LIKE* THEM! YOU KNOW, WHAT'S-HER-NAME--?

"--MERRI!" LIKE *HELL* YOU'RE TAKING ANYMORE OUTA THIS VILLAGE, *ARROGANTUS!*

AND IF YOU THINK YOU'RE GONNA LAY ONE GRIMY *FINGER* ON THAT GIRL--

-- GONNA BE OVER MY *SMOKING BONES!!*

ALL RIGHT, STAR-JUMPERS! LET'S *LET 'EM HAVE IT!!*

SO, THE HIRED GUNS DID NOT TAKE MY *WARN-ING!*

THEY ARE STILL *HERE!*

ALL RIGHT, THEN, IF THESE SPACE-RATS ARE SO ANXIOUS TO *DIE*--

"-- LET'S GIVE THEM WHAT THEY WANT!"

Y'KNOW, MAYBE THIS *WASN'T* SUCH A BRIGHT IDEA!

AT LEAST WHEN WE FOUGHT THE *DEATH STAR,* WE WERE IN *SHIPS!*

BUT *HERE,* THOSE OUTLAWS CAN PICK US OFF LIKE SITTING *WOMP-RATS!*

RIGHT NOW I SURE WISH WE HAD SOME'A THAT *FORCE* I KEEP HEARING ABOUT!

BUT THERE ARE OTHER, THOUGH *LESSER,* "FORCES" ON HAN SOLO'S SIDE--

SPANG!

URK?

--LIKE THE *ROBOTIC* FORCE THAT BRINGS A *METAL ARM* TO SNATCH A LOW-FLYING *SKYSPEEDER.*

"OR THAT IN THE SHAG-COVERED ARMS OF AN ENRAGED SEVEN-FOOT, *WOOKIEE!*

N-NO, YOU M-MONSTER! LET ME GO!!

BASH!

OBVIOUSLY, SUCH FORCES CANNOT *COMPARE* WITH THAT WHICH BINDS TOGETHER THE GALAXY.

YET, IN THEIR OWN, IMMEDIATE WAY...

...THEY ARE EFFECTIVE.

GRONK!

YOU KNOW, *CHEWBACCA!* WE MAKE AN EFFECTIVE *TEAM* AND--

WHAT'S THAT YOU SAID, *EFFIE?* CAN'T HEAR YOU ABOVE ALL THIS *SHOOTIN'!!*

MORE OUTLAWS.. SNEAKING UP FROM THE *REAR!*

BLASK!

I AM JUST A *TRACTOR-ROBOT* ...NOT REALLY *PROGRAMMED* FOR THIS SORT OF THING!

BUT EVEN THOUGH THE *STARKILLER KID* IS *NOT* MY MASTER, I CANNOT LET HIM BE *SHOT DOWN* BY THAT OUTLAW'S WEAPON--

EFFIE!!

--EVEN THOUGH IT MEANS MY...

BZZ--ZAK!

THOUGH THE ROBOT FE9O CLAIMED NEITHER TO BE SERVANT NOR PET TO THE STARKILLER KID...PERHAPS HE WAS SOMETHING MORE...

...THEIR RELATION-SHIP NOT UNLIKE THAT SHARED BY HAN SOLO AND...

CHEWIE--!!

AMAIZA...DON-WAN... YOU THREE BETTER PROTECT OUR REAR!!

YEAH! THAT'S A SIMPLE ENOUGH ORDER TO GIVE, HOT-SHOT!

BUT THESE SPACE-UGLIES ARE ALSO COMIN' AT US FROM EVERY OTHER DIRECTION!

TAKE CARE, FAIR MAIDEN! BEHIND YOU--

UGHNN! I APPRECIATE THE COMPLI-MENT, DON-WAN--

--BUT NOW I NEED YOUR HELP A HELLUVA LOT MORE!

SO IF YOU REALLY KNOW HOW TO USE THAT LIGHT-SABRE OF YOURS--

AYE, IN THE NAME OF RIGHTEOUS-NESS, USE IT I SHALL!

SHE SEES THE BLADELIKE BEAM APPEAR AT THE TOUCH OF A BUTTON...

AND SHE WONDERS IF THIS *MADMAN* CAN ACTUALLY *WIELD* THE LEGENDARY WEAPON OF THE JEDI-KNIGHTS...

YAAARRGG!!

HE *CAN*...

MAY YOU *PERISH,* YOU SCUM WHO WOULD DARE *TAINT* THE FLESH OF THIS *LADY* MOST *FAIR!!*

HE'S *NOT BAD* FOR AN OLD-TIMER! BUT HE'S NOT *FAST* ENOUGH--

--AND THERE'S A *SKYSPEEDER* ZOOMING DOWN, TOO *FAST* FOR ME TO GET HIM BEFORE--

ARRGHH!!

KAZZZ!

KASSH!

FAREWELL, COMELY DAMSEL! AT LEAST *YOU* SHALL... *LIVE...!*

FROM THE CORNER OF HIS EYE, HAN SOLO SEES THE VALIANT OLD MAN *DROP,* BUT EULOGIES MUST *WAIT...*

THAT'S *TWO* OF US DOWN... AND THERE SEEMS TO BE NO *LETTING UP* OF THE OUTLAW FORCES!

BUT AT LEAST WE SEEM TO HAVE KNOCKED OFF THE LAST OF THOSE *SNEAK* ATTACKERS, SO--

UH, OH! LOOKS LIKE BIG MOUTH *SOLO* SPOKE TOO *SOON!*

HEDJI-- TO YOUR *RIGHT...!!*

I'M NO *AMATEUR,* HAN SOLO!

BUT THANKS ANYWAY FOR THE *WARNING!*

ZIK

ZIK

ZIK

YEAH?! WELL SOMEBODY OUGHTA WARN *GRANDPA* OUT THERE IT AIN'T *HEALTHY* WAVIN' HIS *ARMS* LIKE THAT--

--'LESS HE *LIKES* MAKIN' HISSELF AN EASY *TARGET!*

BUT THE SHAMAN SEEMS NOT TO *HEAR* THE NOISES OF BATTLE. FOR HIS MIND IS SOMEWHERE *ELSE*--

DON'T KNOW WHAT GRAMPS IS *HOWLING* ABOUT.' AND RIGHT NOW I'M TOO BUSY TO *CARE!*

BOFF!

--HIS THOUGHTS BURNING THROUGH *SOLID STONE* WITH THE EASE AND INTENSITY OF A *LIGHT-SABRE--*

--UNTIL AN ALMOST INHUMAN *SHRIEK* ISSUES FROM HIS MOUTH!

THERE! THAT TAKES CARE OF THE LAST OF THOSE *SNEAK* ATTACKERS FAR AS I CAN TELL.'

BUT OUR *MAIN* ATTACK'S STILL COMING FROM THE *SKY!*

ZAK!

HEY, *JAXXON!* HOW'S OUR *AMMUNITION* HOLDING OUT?!

WELL, UNLESS YOU GOT SOME TRICK *EXTRA* LONG FEET STASHED AWAY, YOU'D BETTER KEEP *SHOOTING!*

SHA-BRAK!

YIIIII!!

YAAAHOOOO!! YOU SEE *THAT,* RABBIT--?

TALK ABOUT FLYING RIGHT *INTO* THE LINE OF FIRE.!!

AIN'T *COMPLAININ',* SOLO.' AN' IF I RUN OUTA *POWER,* I CAN ALWAYS *KICK* THOSE RIDERS OUTA THE CLOUDS!

NO ONE HAS YET NOTICED THAT THE OLD SHAMAN HAS *RELAXED* HIS CONCENTRATION...

...OR THAT HE NOW *SPEAKS.*

EMERGE FROM YOUR BED-CHAMBERS OF STONE! *SAVE* US WHOSE ANCESTORS ONCE *WOR-SHIPPED* YOU!

HEAR ME, SLUMBERING ONE!

I BEG YOU *AWAKEN* AS YOU DID IN DECADES *PAST!* OUR MINDS ARE NOW *LINKED TOGETHER AS ONE!*

WHEN THE ROCK BEGINS TO SHIFT, EVEN *HAN SOLO* MUST TAKE NOTICE !

OH, *HELL!* IF WE DIDN'T HAVE *ENOUGH* TO WORRY ABOUT.!!

THE **CARNAGE** OF BATTLE CONTINUES, WITH BLASTERS BARKING THEIR MINIATURE **EXPLOSIONS**...AND WITH THE SKIES ABLAZE WITH THE DEBRIS OF ERUPTING **SKYSPEEDERS.**

BUT, SOMEHOW, **SERJI-X ARROGANTUS** AND HIS SURLY BAND OCCUPY **SECOND PLACE** IN HAN SOLO'S PRIORITIES--

GREE-AARGH!

--AS HE STARES **DUMBFOUNDEDLY** WHILE THE MOUNTAIN ITSELF IS TORN ASUNDER-- FROM WITHIN...

QUITE OBVIOUSLY, THE **REAL BATTLE'S** YET TO BEGIN!!

NEXT ISSUE: **DAY** OF THE **BEHEMOTH!**

169

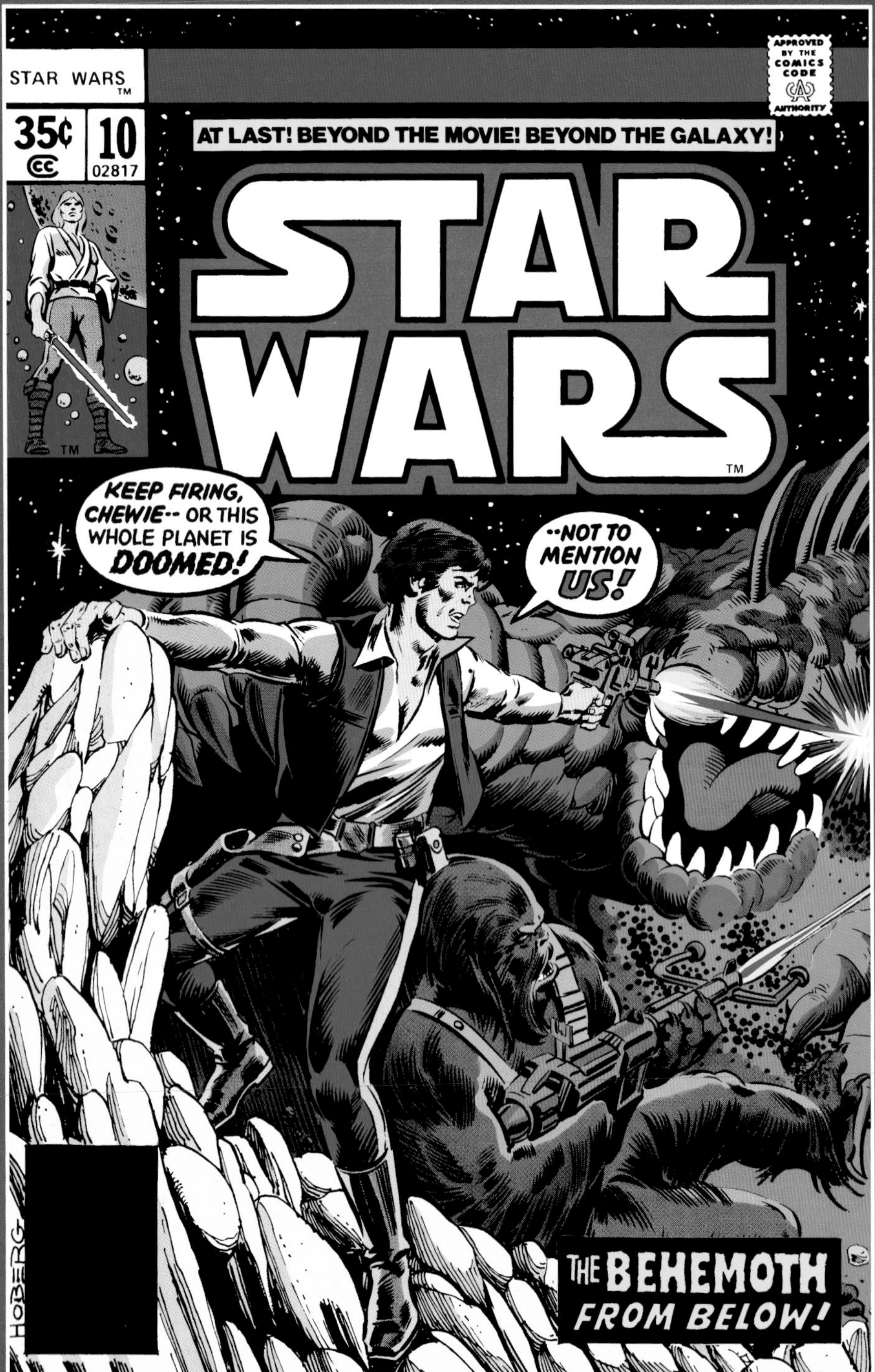
STAR WARS TM
35¢
10
02817
APPROVED BY THE COMICS CODE AUTHORITY
AT LAST! BEYOND THE MOVIE! BEYOND THE GALAXY!
STAR WARS TM
KEEP FIRING, CHEWIE-- OR THIS WHOLE PLANET IS DOOMED!
--NOT TO MENTION US!
THE BEHEMOTH FROM BELOW!
HOBERG

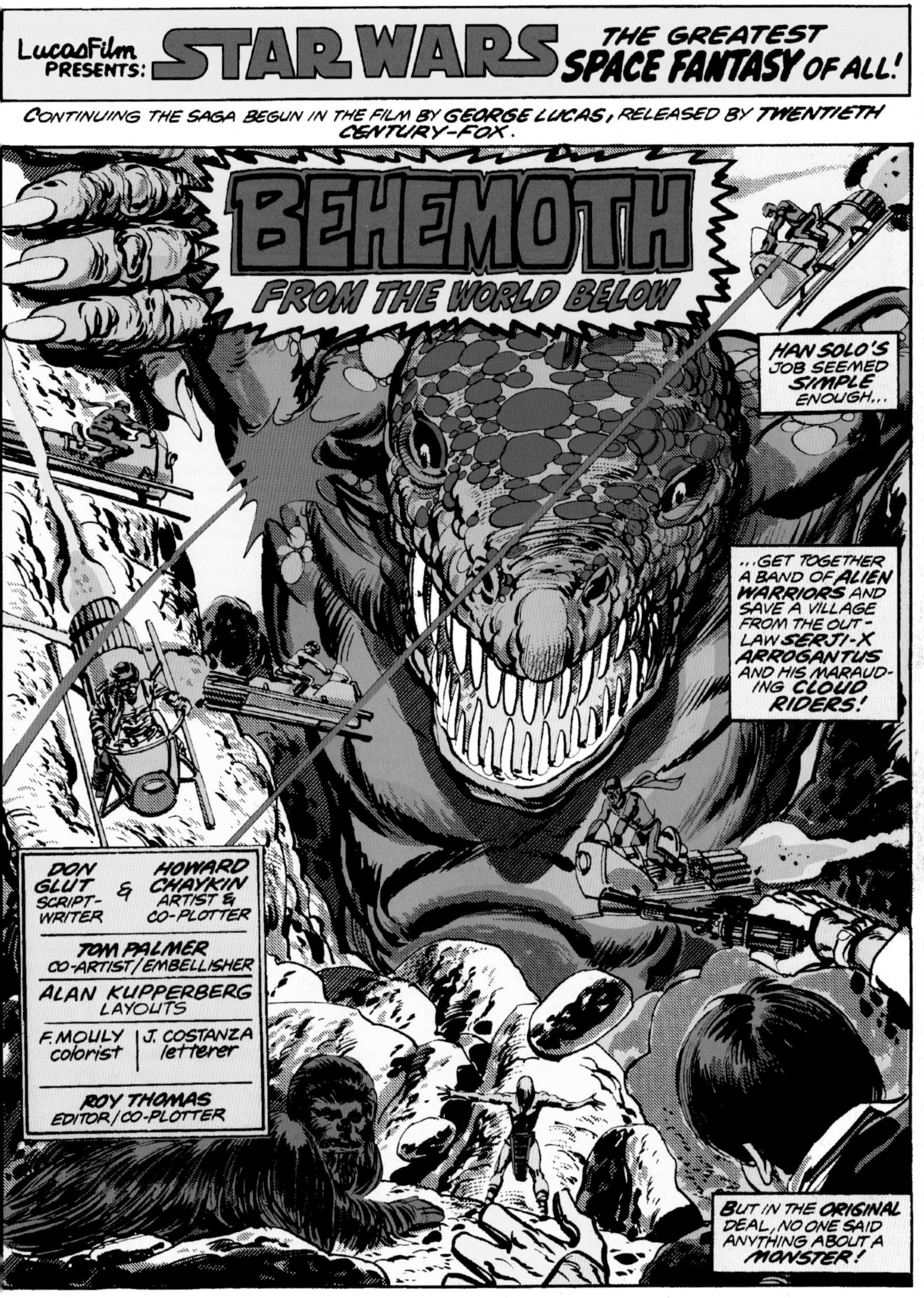

LucasFilm PRESENTS: STAR WARS THE GREATEST SPACE FANTASY OF ALL!
CONTINUING THE SAGA BEGUN IN THE FILM BY GEORGE LUCAS, RELEASED BY TWENTIETH CENTURY-FOX.
BEHEMOTH FROM THE WORLD BELOW
HAN SOLO'S JOB SEEMED SIMPLE ENOUGH...
...GET TOGETHER A BAND OF ALIEN WARRIORS AND SAVE A VILLAGE FROM THE OUT-LAW SERJI-X ARROGANTUS AND HIS MARAUD-ING CLOUD RIDERS!
DON GLUT SCRIPT-WRITER & HOWARD CHAYKIN ARTIST & CO-PLOTTER
TOM PALMER CO-ARTIST/EMBELLISHER
ALAN KUPPERBERG LAYOUTS
F. MOULY colorist
J. COSTANZA letterer
ROY THOMAS EDITOR/CO-PLOTTER
BUT IN THE ORIGINAL DEAL, NO ONE SAID ANYTHING ABOUT A MONSTER!

BUT THEN, EVERYONE ASSUMED THE OLD SHAMAN TO BE A SENILE *FOOL*--

--INCAPABLE OF *ACTUALLY* SUMMONING FORTH A SCALY *BEHEMOTH* LOST IN THE ROCK AND LEGEND OF *ADUBA-3*--*

SWI-...SPLAK!

* LAST ISSUE. --ROY.

--FOR THE SIMPLE PURPOSE OF LASHING OUT AND *DESTROYING* THIS BAND OF SURLY OUTLAWS...

...ESPECIALLY THEIR LEADER, *SERJI-X*... THE *ARROGANT ONE!*

I REMEMBER HEARING *STORIES* ABOUT THIS BEASTIE WHEN I WAS A *YOUTH!*

AND *ONE THING* ABOUT THOSE STORIES *STICKS OUT* IN MY MIND...

IF WE DON'T *DO* SOMETHING, IT JUST ISN'T GONNA GO *AWAY!* AND YOU KNOW WHAT *THAT* MEANS...

NO MORE *TRIBUTE* FROM THIS VILLAGE... NO MORE FEMALE *AMUSEMENTS!*

SO COME *ON*, MEN! LET'S GET RID OF THE BIG--

BZZ-ZAK!

BUT SERJI-X BEGINS TO WONDER HOW *FEASIBLE* THAT MIGHT BE, AS ONE-BY-ONE HIS MEN *FALL* TO THE BEAST!

FRONK!

DON'T ASK *ME*, CHEWBACCA! THIS WASN'T IN THE ORIGINAL *PROGRAM!*

NOW WHAT, SOLO?! IF THAT BEHEMOTH'S *SIZE* AND *STRENGTH* WEREN'T BAD ENOUGH--

YEAH, I *KNOW*, HEDJI! IT'S COME EQUIPPED WITH SOME KIND OF BUILT-IN *BLASTER!*

"WELL," SAYS SOLO TO THE *SPINER*, "BE THANKFUL FOR *ONE* THING...

...THAT THE MONSTER HASN'T ATTACKED *US*--

--BUT ONLY THE ONES THE SHAMAN *SUMMONED* HIM TO FIGHT...

"...SERJI-X AND HIS STINKING *CUTTHROATS!!*"

INDEED, THE BEHEMOTH SEEMS NOT EVEN TO *NOTICE* THE PRESENCE OF HAN SOLO AND HIS SMALL ARMY OF MERCENARIES...

KRUNK!

HEY?! WHAT'S THE THING DOIN' *NOW??*

GREE-ARR!!

YY////////////!!

IT'S CREATING A *LANDSLIDE!* THAT'S WHAT! *LOOK OUT--*

--AN' *MOVE THOSE SKYSPEEDERS!!*

173

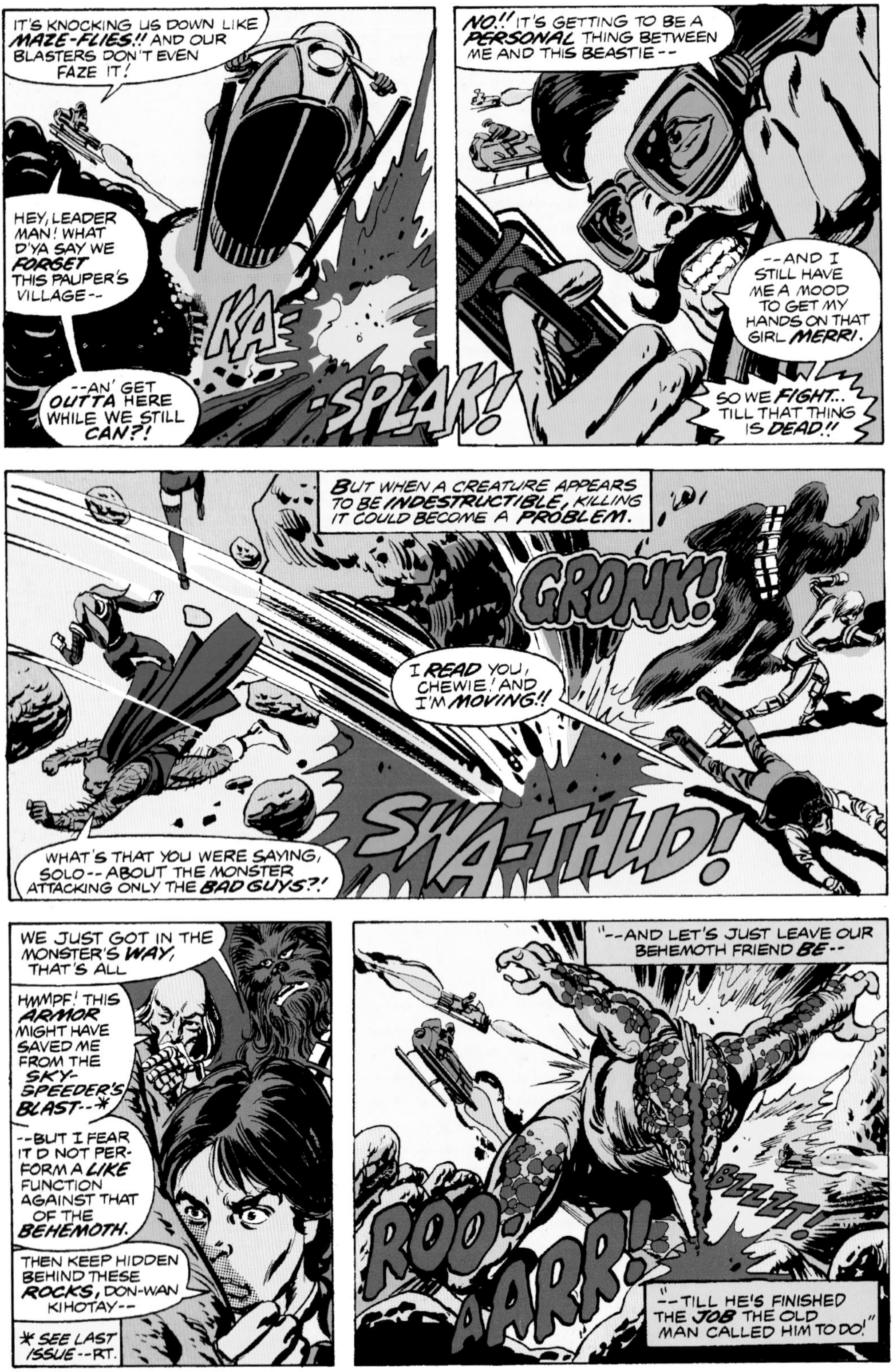
IT'S KNOCKING US DOWN LIKE MAZE-FLIES!! AND OUR BLASTERS DON'T EVEN FAZE IT!
HEY, LEADER MAN! WHAT D'YA SAY WE FORGET THIS PAUPER'S VILLAGE--
--AN' GET OUTTA HERE WHILE WE STILL CAN?!
KA-SPLAK!
NO!! IT'S GETTING TO BE A PERSONAL THING BETWEEN ME AND THIS BEASTIE--
--AND I STILL HAVE ME A MOOD TO GET MY HANDS ON THAT GIRL MERRI.
SO WE FIGHT... TILL THAT THING IS DEAD!!
BUT WHEN A CREATURE APPEARS TO BE INDESTRUCTIBLE, KILLING IT COULD BECOME A PROBLEM.
GRONK!
I READ YOU, CHEWIE! AND I'M MOVING!!
SWA-THUD!
WHAT'S THAT YOU WERE SAYING, SOLO-- ABOUT THE MONSTER ATTACKING ONLY THE BAD GUYS?!
WE JUST GOT IN THE MONSTER'S WAY, THAT'S ALL
HMMPF! THIS ARMOR MIGHT HAVE SAVED ME FROM THE SKY-SPEEDER'S BLAST--*
--BUT I FEAR IT D NOT PERFORM A LIKE FUNCTION AGAINST THAT OF THE BEHEMOTH.
THEN KEEP HIDDEN BEHIND THESE ROCKS, DON-WAN KIHOTAY--
* SEE LAST ISSUE--RT.
"--AND LET'S JUST LEAVE OUR BEHEMOTH FRIEND BE--
ROOAARR!
BZZZT!
"--TILL HE'S FINISHED THE JOB THE OLD MAN CALLED HIM TO DO!"

THERE'S ONLY A *FEW* OF MY MEN *LEFT!* AND WITHOUT THEM, I MIGHT AS WELL JUST *SURRENDER* TO THOSE MERCENARIES.

BUT *SERGI-X ARROGANTUS* SURRENDERS TO *NOBODY!! NEVER!!*

AND SINCE MY MEN HAVE THEIR *HANDS* FULL'A TROUBLE RIGHT ABOUT NOW--

--SEEMS LIKE I'LL HAVE TO KILL THE BEASTIE *MYSELF!!*

THAT OLD *CODGER*...FOR *YEARS* HE'S BEEN BABBLING ABOUT BEING ABLE TO CONTROL A LEGENDARY *MONSTER!*

LOOKS TO ME LIKE HE WASN'T JUST CHEWING THE *LUNA-WEED!* THERE HE IS, CONTROLLING IT LIKE A *MAESTRO!*

ALL RIGHT, SINCE WE CAN'T SEEM TO EVEN *SCRATCH* THAT BEASTIE'S HIDE--

--IT APPEARS I'LL HAVE TO ATTACK IT THE *ONLY* WAY IT'LL DO ANY *GOOD!*

THAT'S IT, OLD MAN! KEEP STANDING THERE IN *ONE SPOT*--

--AND YOU'LL MAKE A *PERFECT TARGET!*

BROO-SH!

THE SHAMAN *DOESN'T* MOVE. BUT SERGI-X ARROGANTUS NEVER QUITE *KNOWS* IF HE *STRIKES* HIM OR NOT...

...AS BOTH *SHAMAN* AND *OUTLAW CHIEF* ARE TRAMPLED BY A SINGLE *GARGANTUAN FOOT!*

WDMP!

SPLAT!

AND, WITHOUT THEIR LEADER--

--THE FEW REMAINING CLOUD-RIDERS ARE QUICK TO FALL.

GUESS THAT'S THE END OF THOSE OUT-LAWS!

BUT WHAT ABOUT THE BEHEMOTH?

WELL, WHAT ABOUT IT?

WITH THE OLD MAN DEAD, IT COULD MEAN BAD NEWS FOR MY ENTIRE VILLAGE--

--AND EVERY-ONE IN IT!

THE STAR-KILLER KID AIN'T JUST SUPPOSIN', SOLO!

I THINK YOU'RE GETTING MY MESS-AGE, JAXXON!

WITHOUT THE SHAMAN TO CALL THE SHOTS, THAT BEHEMOTH'S STARTIN' TO GET REALLY MAD!

AND THIS TIME I DON'T THINK IT'S GONNA BE SO PARTICULAR ABOUT WHO IT STOMPS!

HOLD IT THERE, SOLO! WE DIDN'T SIGN ON TO THIS LITTLE BLAST-PARTY OF YOURS TO FIGHT ANY MONSTER!

WE'RE BEING PAID TO GET RID OF SERJI-X AND HIS CRONIES--

--AND SINCE I DON'T SEEM TO SEE THEM AROUND ANYMORE...

LISTEN TO ME-- ALL OF YOU SPACE FREAKS!!

WE DIDN'T EARN THE PAY WE'RE GETTING FOR THIS JOB! THE BEHEMOTH DID!

HMMPF! SOME PAY!

AND IF YOU WANT TO GET EVEN THAT, THERE'D BETTER BE A VILLAGE LEFT STANDING TO PAY US!

BESIDES, I'M GETTING TO LIKE SOME OF THE LOCAL FOLK IN THIS TOWN.

AWWRIGHT, AWWRIGHT ALREADY! SO WE KNOW YOU'RE A LITTLE SOFT ON THAT MERRI FEMALE.

SO YOU TWO CAN STAND AROUND ARGUIN' ABOUT IT!

BUT Y'KNOW HOW US ROCKET-RABBIT TYPES ARE:

WE JUST CAN'T STAND STILL!!

JAXXON!!

AND SINCE I ALWAYS SAY, "NEVER SEND A MAN OUT TO DO A *RAB-BIT'S* JOB--"

NO *WAIT*, JAXXON--!!

BZ-ZZAK!

GROARR!

THE **LEPUS CARNIVORUS** *IS FAST--POSSIBLY THE* **SWIFTEST BIPED** *ON ALL OF* **ADUBA-3**...

BUT IT'S NOT EASY FOR EVEN A HUMANOID **RABBIT** *TO OUT-SPRINT THE MONSTER'S WELL-AIMED* **ENERGY BLASTS**...

THAT LAST SHOT ALMOST TOOK OFF THE RABBIT'S *TAIL*!

BUT EVEN THOUGH IT *MISSED* HIM, THE BURST HIT THE ROCK WALL AND--

CRUM-MBL!

HEAVENLY *HUTCHES*! ROCKS KNOCKED THE *GUN* OUT 'A MY HAND!!

GOT TO *REACH* THE CRUMMY THING BEFORE--

LEAVE THE BLASTER, JAX!

AND TAKE COVER BETWEEN THE *ROCKS*! YOU'LL *NEVER*--

ALREADY *HAVE*, AMAIZA! BUT DID THESE FLOPPY EARS 'A MINE DETECT A LITTLE *AFFECTION* IN YOUR VOICE?

HMMMMM?!

NAWWW! LIKE MY MOTHER TOLD ALL *EIGHTY* OF US KIDS--

IT'D *NEVER* WORK OUT! MARRY A *NICE* GIRL FROM A NICE *BURROW*, AN'--

WHOOOOEEEE!! ALMOST DIDN'T *SEE* THAT ONE!

MAYBE I OUGHT'A GET MY *EYES* CHECKED IF WE EVER GET OUT 'A THIS MESS!

KWUMP!

...WHICH JAXXON BEGINS TO *DOUBT,* AS HE HEARS A PORTENTIOUS *RUMBLE* FROM ABOVE...

MOVE THAT TAILLESS *FANNY* OF YOURS, TOOTS--

--'CAUSE *JUNIOR* HERE'S STARTED A BLAMED *LAND-SLIDE!*

COME ON, *CHEWIE!* GET THAT SEVEN-FOOT *WOOKIEE CARCASS* OF YOURS MOVING AT TOP SPEED!

YOU *OKAY*, LADY?

JUST TWISTED MY *ANKLE!* BUT I'LL LIVE!

HRUG!

HOW ABOUT YOU, *JAXXON?*

GOT THE *WIND* KNOCKED OUTTA ME... AND MUSSED UP MY *TAIL!* BUT OTHERWISE...

ALL RIGHT! THEN, BEFORE THE ROCKS START FALLING AGAIN... CHEWIE, TAKE AMAIZA WHERE IT'S *SAFE*--

--BUT DON'T *SQUEEZE* TOO HARD!

LOOK, GROUP! IF WE'RE GONNA *KILL* THAT WALKING *HUNK OF POWER*, WE'RE GONNA HAVE TO DO IT AS A *TEAM.*

EVERYBODY GET BEHIND THESE *ROCKS!*

THEN, IF WE CAN KEEP OUT OF THE MONSTER'S *WAY* LONG ENOUGH TO PLAN SOME KIND OF GROUP *ATTACK*--

INDEED, THEY BE *FOOLS* TO THINK THAT SUCH A DRAGON MIGHT BE SLAIN BY *THEIR* CRUDE METHODS--

--FOR IT RE-QUIRES THE SKILLS OF ONE TRAINED IN THE HOLY ORDER OF THE *JEDI KNIGHTS!*

O9OPS!! WE'LL DO OUR PLANNING *LATER!*

BLAZT!

'CAUSE RIGHT NOW, GUESS WHO'S *BACK?!*

RUNK!

DIDN'T MEAN THAT *LITERALLY,* CHEWIE!

OKAY, HEROES-- GET YOURSELVES OUT OF SIGHT AND DO IT *FAST!*

THE BEHEMOTH'S SHOOTING THOSE *RAYS* AT US AGAIN!

BUT IF IT DOESN'T *SEE* US FOR A WHILE, MAYBE IT'LL THINK IT *GOT* US!

THEN MAYBE WE'LL BUY THE *TIME* TO--

SCRATCH THAT PLAN! THE THING'S READY TO BLAST US *AGAIN!* AND IT'S AIMING RIGHT FOR THAT WA--

BRM-MMBL!!

ANOTHER LANDSLIDE!!

GRK!

IF ANYBODY EVER TOLD ME I'D HAVE 'TA DO *THIS* MUCH RUNNIN' ON THIS MISSION, I'D OF--

HEY, *CHEWBACCA*-- LET *GO!*

I CAN MOVE OUTTA THE WAY *MYSELF,* Y'KNOW!

THE BEHEMOTH *DOESN'T GIVE UP,* DOES IT?!

NO? WELL, NEITHER DO *WE!* AND I'M GETTING AN IDEA HOW WE MIGHT *GET RID* OF THAT NIGHTMARE!

BUT IT'S GONNA TAKE DON-WAN'S *LIGHT-SABRE* TO DO IT

YOU *HEAR* ME, DON-WAN? YOU NEVER TOLD HOW YOU *GOT* A JEDI KNIGHT'S WEAPON, BUT IT STILL--

DON-WAN..?

OH NO! *LOOK!!* WE'VE GOT TO HELP HIM!

BUT WHAT HAN SOLO HAS JUST SEEN MEANS *NOTHING* TO THE PILOT OF A SMALL SPACE CRUISER--

--WHICH NOW STREAKS FROM THE DENSE *JUNGLE* GROWTH OF THE *FOURTH SATELLITE* OF THE PLANET *YAVIN*--

--TO BE SWALLOWED BY SILENT *SPACE...*

I NEVER SHOULD HAVE *LISTENED* TO GENERAL DODONNA AND THE OTHERS! I SHOULD HAVE DONE THIS *RIGHT AWAY!*

THE *PILOT:* PRINCESS LEIA, A MEMBER OF THE *IMPERIAL SENATE...*

HER MISSION...?

SOMETHING'S HAPPENED TO *LUKE* AND I'M GOING TO *FIND* HIM --

--EVEN IF I'VE GOT TO DO IT *ALONE!*

HE'D GONE OFF WITH THE TWO *ROBOTS* TO FIND A NEW *PLANET* FOR THE *REBELS...*

AND THEN, JUST AS HE *SAW* SOMETHING AND WAS ABOUT TO *TELL* US WHAT IT *WAS--*

--WE *LOST* ALL *COMMUNICATION* WITH HIM!*

AND THERE WAS *NO WAY* FOR US TO MAKE *CONTACT* WITH HIM AGAIN!

*LAST ISSUE AGAIN. --ROY.

BUT IF I CAN FIND THE POINT LUKE WAS AT WHEN WE LAST *HEARD* FROM HIM, MAYBE THERE'LL BE *SOMETHING* I CAN DO!

I *CAN'T* JUST LET HIM BE *SWALLOWED UP*-- ONE MORE CASUALTY OF THE REBELLION AGAINST THE *EMPIRE!*

IT'S TOO BAD *HAN SOLO* HAD TO ROCKET OFF TO SPEND HIS *REWARD MONEY!**

I COULD *USE* THAT STAR-HOPPER'S *HELP* RIGHT ABOUT NOW!

**STAR WARS #7.--R.T.*

HELP?!

A JEDI KNIGHT NEEDS THE HELP OF *NO ONE*--LEAST OF ALL A MERCENARY SUCH AS *HAN SOLO!*

ALL THAT I NEED IS THE *LIGHTSABRE* HELD IN MY *STEADY HAND...*

...AND THE *COURAGE* AND *SKILL* TO USE IT!

HOLD, BEHEMOTH! AND, IF YOU DARE, *FACE ME!*

GRRRRR!

WHETHER IT IS THE SOUND OF THE OLD MAN'S *VOICE* OR THE PULSATING *WEAPON* THAT HE HOLDS--

--*SOMETHING* ATTRACTS THE BEHEMOTH'S ATTENTION!

LOOK! YOU SEE WHAT THAT CRAZY OLD FOOL IS *DOING?!*

SURE DO! HE'S LEADING THAT MONSTER *AWAY* FROM US... SO'S HE CAN FACE IT *ALONE!*

MAYBE HE'S *NOT* SO CRAZY! MAYBE HE REALLY *WAS* A JEDI KNIGHT--

--AND KNOWS SOMETHING *WE DON'T!*

YEAH! LIKE HOW TO GET YOURSELF *KILLED* IN ONE EASY *LESSON!*

YOU HEAR THEIR *JEERS,* BEHEMOTH? THEY THINK DON-WAN KIHOTAY TO BE TOO *OLD* FOR THE NOBLE ART OF *COMBAT!*

YET EVEN ONE OF SO *ADVANCED* YEARS IS STILL AS *ONE* WITH THE *FORCE*--

--WHICH PERMITS EVEN *THESE* STIFF AND WEARY BONES--

--TO EVADE *WHATEVER* HELL-SPAWNED BOLTS YOU MIGHT HURL TOWARD ME!!

BZ-ZAM!

AND *NOW*, BEHEMOTH, THE TIME FOR A *FINAL CONFLICT* IS UPON US!

NEEDLESS TO ADD--

--BUT *ONE* OF US SHALL EMERGE FROM THE BATTLE *ALIVE!!*

BOLDLY, THE AGED WOULD-BE KNIGHT STALKS TOWARD THE BEHEMOTH--

--AND, IF ONLY FOR MOMENTS, THE MONSTER *PAUSES*, ITS SCALY HEAD *LIFTING.*

YOU *SEE* THAT??!

THE MONSTER'S REACTING *FUNNY.* THE CLOSER HE GETS WITH THAT *LIGHT-SABRE!*

THEN I THINK MY HUNCH IS *RIGHT!* I THINK IT'S--

--HEY, *HEDJI... SPINER...*WHERE DO YOU THINK *YOU'RE* GOING!

WHERE *YOU* SHOULD *ALL* HAVE BEEN BY NOW, HAN SOLO--

--TO HELP AN OLD WARRIOR WHO'S PUT HIS OWN *LIFE* ON THE LINE TO SAVE *ALL* OF US!

LISTEN TO ME, DON-WAN! MAYBE YOU *DID* STUMBLE ONTO A *LIGHTSABRE* SOMEWHERE, AFTER THE EMPIRE HAD *CRUSHED* THE REAL JEDI KNIGHTS--

--AND MAYBE IT *WARPED* YOU INTO THINKING *YOU* WERE A JEDI--

--BUT YOU'RE NOT *FAST* ENOUGH TO KEEP AVOIDING THOSE *BOLTS!*

KEEP BACK! NO ONE... NEITHER *MAN* NOR *SPINER...* MUST INTERFERE WITH A *JEDI KNIGHT'S* TASK!

SLAYING THE BEAST IS *MY* MISSION! AND SLAY HIM I *SHALL!!*

I *TRIED* TO REASON WITH YOU, KIHOTAY--BUT YOU WOULDN'T *LISTEN!* ALL RIGHT THEN, *DON'T*--

ZLIK ZLIK

YOU'RE *GETTING* MY HELP WHETHER YOU WANT IT OR *NOT!*

THERE ARE BUT *FEW* SPINERS REMAINING IN THE GALAXY.

BUT THOSE THAT *DO* REMAIN CAN FIRE THEIR BODY-QUILLS WITH *ASTOUNDING ACCURACY...*

FTT!

FTT!

FTT!

USUALLY, ANY *ONE* OF THESE QUILLS WOULD BRING *INSTANT DEATH* TO ITS VICTIM...

CRAZ-- ZLL!

YET, *THIS* TIME--

--A WHOLE *BARRAGE* OF THE NEEDLE-LIKE WEAPONS ONLY FURTHER *ANGER* THE BEHEMOTH!

WHHUUUU!!!!

ZZ-- BLAM!

THE QUILLS DIDN'T DO MUCH *GOOD*, DID THEY?!

HANG THE QUILLS! IT'S THAT *LIGHTSABRE* THAT'S GETTING THAT MONSTER ALL RILED UP!

DON'T YOU ALL SEE WHAT'S *HAPPENING?*

THE SWORD'S ACTING LIKE AN OLD-FASHIONED *LIGHTNING ROD*--

--INTERFERING WITH THAT ENERGY BEAM THE CREATURE SHOOTS FROM ITS *FIN!*

"EVEN A *DUMB BRUTE* LIKE THAT CAN *SENSE* THAT THE LIGHTSABRE'S A *THREAT* TO ITS LIFE," SHOUTS SOLO.

"THAT'S WHY THE *CLOSER* DON-WAN GETS, THE *CRAZIER* THE BEHEMOTH ACTS!"

"BUT THE OLD GUY'S TOO *SLOW!* IF I COULD RUN *FAST* ENOUGH, MAYBE *I* COULD --"

CRONK?!

URK!!

EVEN *I* READ *THAT* ONE, CHEWBACCA! *DO* IT!!

WHICH THE TOWERING *WOOKIEE* DOES... WITH *INCREDIBLE* SPEED...

HEEEEY, YOU STUFFED--

SURE! WITH THOSE STOVE-PIPE *LEGS* OF YOURS AND THE *SPEED* THAT COMES WITH 'EM--

OH, I *GET* YOU!

GREEA-

-ARRG!

--WE JUST MIGHT *SAVE* THE OLD MADMAN *YET!!*

A FEW MORE STRIDES OF THOSE GREAT SHAGGY LEGS, AND...

OKAY, PAL! SET ME *DOWN!*

LISTEN, DON-WAN, I APPRECIATE THE *HEROICS!* BUT EVEN THOUGH YOUR *INTENTIONS* ARE GOOD--

--YOU'RE JUST NOT *MAKING* IT!

HAN SOLO!! BUT WHY ARE YOU INTERRUPTING MY *HOLY TASK?!*

You've **GOT** something I **NEED**, friend--and I just stopped by to **BORROW** it!

N-NO! YOU COMMIT **BLASPHEMY!**

Perhaps, and though Don-wan Ki/hotay tries in vain to TEAR the lightsabre from Solo's grasp--

--again, the task is BEYOND one of his years...

NEVER USED ONE OF THESE GADGETS BEFORE! AND **I'M** CERTAINLY NO **JEDI KNIGHT!**

BUT I'VE USED MOST **OTHER** HANDWEAPONS--

--SO MAYBE **THIS** BABY WON'T GIVE ME **TOO** MUCH TROUBLE! MAYBE.

*SEEMS I REMEMBER **HEARING** ONCE ABOUT A JEDI KILLING A MONSTER SOMETHING LIKE THIS WITH A **LIGHTSABRE**...*

...SOMETHING ABOUT THE **LIGHT-BLADE** COUNTERACTING THE **ENERGY**--

--THAT POWERS THE MONSTER'S **FIN BOLTS** AND--

HOLY BEEK-MONKEYS!! THAT WAS **CLOSE!!**

ALL RIGHT, UGLY! I'VE NO MORE TIME TO **FOOL AROUND** WITH YOU!

IT'S ABOUT TIME I FIND OUT IF THAT **IDEA** OF MINE IS **RIGHT** OR **WRONG!**

THEN, THRUSTING WITH A WEAPON HE HAS NEVER WIELDED BEFORE--

*--HAN SOLO MAKES A SUDDEN **DASH** TOWARD THE CREATURE'S CHEST.*

*A MOMENT LATER, THE MONSTER GOES **BERSERK**--*

*--LASHING AND BLASTING AT **EVERYTHING**...*

ROARING HIDEOUSLY...

TAKE COVER!!

DON'T KNOW IF I DID THE BEHEMOTH ANY **DAMAGE!**

BUT I SURE AS BLAZES GOT IT **MAD!!**

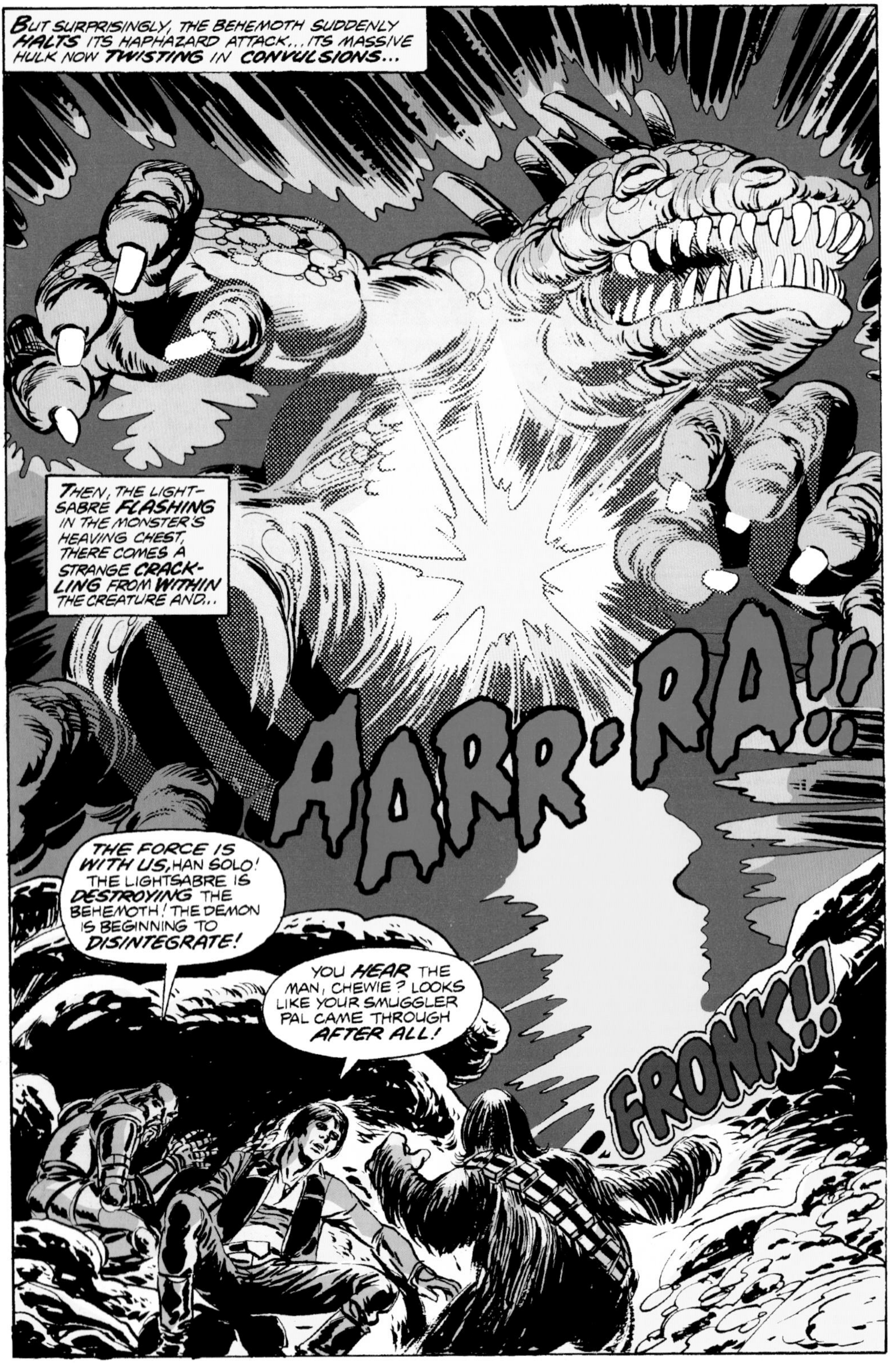
BUT SURPRISINGLY, THE BEHEMOTH SUDDENLY HALTS ITS HAPHAZARD ATTACK... ITS MASSIVE HULK NOW TWISTING IN CONVULSIONS...
THEN, THE LIGHT-SABRE FLASHING IN THE MONSTER'S HEAVING CHEST, THERE COMES A STRANGE CRACKLING FROM WITHIN THE CREATURE AND...
AARR-RA!!
THE FORCE IS WITH US, HAN SOLO! THE LIGHTSABRE IS DESTROYING THE BEHEMOTH! THE DEMON IS BEGINNING TO DISINTEGRATE!
YOU HEAR THE MAN, CHEWIE? LOOKS LIKE YOUR SMUGGLER PAL CAME THROUGH AFTER ALL!
FRONK!!

WHEN THE LAST FADING IMAGE OF THE BEHEMOTH IS *SWEPT AWAY* BY THE WINDS OF *ADUBA-3*...

GUESS IT'S ALL *OVER*, HEROES!

NOT *QUITE*, LEADER-MAN! MY *POCKETS* ARE STILL *EMPTY*!

THEY WON'T BE, SOON AS THE PEASANTS *PAY* US!

SPEAKING OF WHICH... HERE THEY *COME*!

GREAT! THEN AFTER I GET *MY* SHARE, I CAN FINALLY GET *OFF* THIS CRUMMY PLANET--

--BEFORE I TOTALLY CRACK... UP?

HELLO, JIMM! I SAW WHAT YOU *DID* TODAY! YOU WERE VERY *BRAVE*!

B-BUT, YOU NEVER EVEN *LOOKED* AT ME BEFORE! THAT'S *ONE'A* THE REASONS I,...

I'M LOOKING *NOW*, JIMM!

AND PERHAPS I CAN SOMEHOW *CHANGE* YOUR MIND ABOUT *LEAVING* OUR LITTLE VILLAGE!

BUT *FIRST*--

--*THANK* YOU, HAN SOLO...

HUH?!

...FOR SAVING OUR VILLAGE... AND ALSO BRINGING OUT THE *MAN* IN THE *STAR-KILLER* "KID"!

AFTER THE MEAGER *PAYMENTS* HAVE BEEN MADE ...

...AND *FIVE* WEARY HEROES RETURN TO THEIR *BANTHA* MOUNTS...

SO I *DIDN'T* GET THE GIRL! WHO CARES?! SHE WAS KIND OF YOUNG *ANYWAY*!

AT LEAST NOW I CAN AFFORD TO GET THE *MILLENNIUM FALCON* OUT OF *HOCK*!

AND IF ONLY FOR A MINUTE, I GOT A LITTLE FEELING OF WHAT IT'S LIKE--

--TO BE A *JEDI KNIGHT*!

SEE YOU *AROUND*, SOLO! DROP BY THE *VILLAGE* SOMETIME! *HEAR*?

NEXT ISSUE: *STAR WARS* CONTINUES WITH THE *SEARCH FOR* LUKE SKYWALKER!

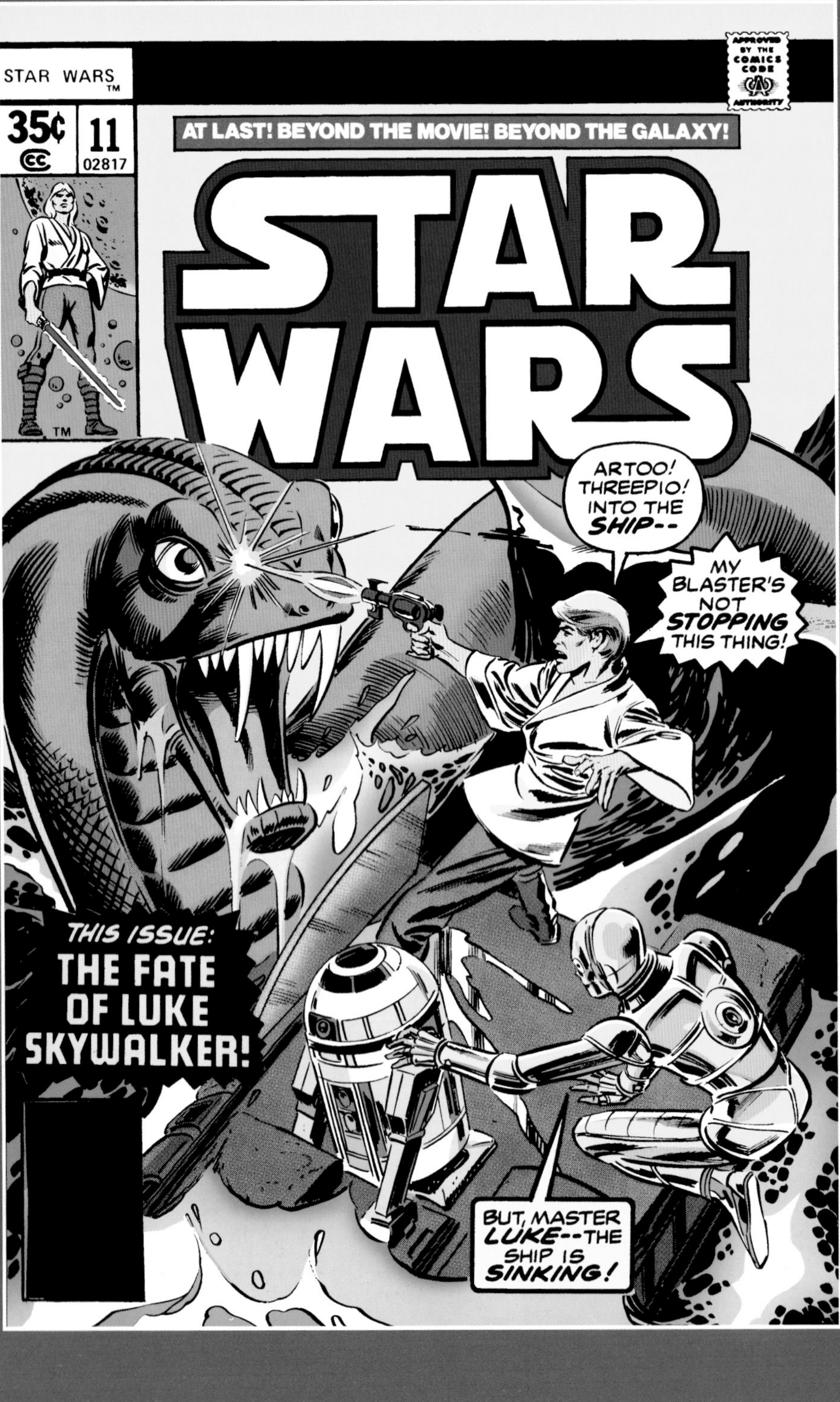

STAR WARS ™
35¢
CC
11
02817
APPROVED BY THE COMICS CODE AUTHORITY
AT LAST! BEYOND THE MOVIE! BEYOND THE GALAXY!
STAR WARS
™
ARTOO! THREEPIO! INTO THE SHIP--
MY BLASTER'S NOT STOPPING THIS THING!
THIS ISSUE: THE FATE OF LUKE SKYWALKER!
BUT, MASTER LUKE--THE SHIP IS SINKING!

Long ago in a galaxy far, far away. . .there exists a state of cosmic *civil war*. A brave alliance of *underground freedom fighters* has challenged the tyranny and oppression of the awesome *Galactic Empire*. This is their story!

LucasFilm PRESENTS: **STAR WARS**™ THE GREATEST **SPACE FANTASY** OF ALL!

CONTINUING THE SAGA BEGUN IN THE FILM BY *GEORGE LUCAS* RELEASED BY *TWENTIETH CENTURY-FOX*

ARCHIE GOODWIN WRITER / EDITOR • **CARMINE INFANTINO** & **TERRY AUSTIN** ARTISTS • **JOE ROSEN**, LETTERER **JANICE COHEN**, COLORIST • **ROY THOMAS** CONSULTING EDITOR

STAR SEARCH!

THE PLANET IS CALLED *ADUBA-3*. IT IS A BACKWATER WORLD, ONE OF THE MANY ON THE GALACTIC RIM, TOO POOR, TOO DISTANT FOR THE *EMPIRE'S* DARK INTEREST...

THE SHIP IS THE *MILLENNIUM FALCON*. TO SOME IT MIGHT SEEM A BATTERED, ORDINARY *FREIGHTER*... IF THEY HAD NEVER SMUGGLED SPICE ON THE *KESSEL RUN*...

...OR CHALLENGED THE TIE FIGHTER OF SITH LORD, *DARTH VADER*, IN THE BATTLE OF THE *DEATH STAR*...

BETTER SAY GOOD-BYE WHILE YOU CAN, CHEWIE... I'M COMPUTING FOR THE JUMP TO HYPERSPACE.

THAT HUNK OF ROCK AND SAND WASN'T MUCH--

--BUT IT WAS HOME SWEET HOME FOR A LITTLE WHILE. WHEN YOU'VE A PRICE ON YOUR HEAD LIKE WE DO... THAT'S AS MUCH AS YOU CAN EXPECT OF ANY PLACE!

GROWK!

YEAH, YOU'RE RIGHT. WE MADE SOME INTERESTING ACQUAINTANCES THERE, TOO! QUITE A CREW, REALLY... CONSIDERING I FIRST HAD THEM ALL PEGGED AS DOWN AND DEFINITELY OUT STAR-HOPPERS!*

* SEE ISSUE #8-- ARCH

"JIMM, THE STARKILLER KID... HIS ROBOT, EFFIE... AMAIZA, OUR LADY FRIEND FROM THE BLACK HOLE GANG... JAXXON, WHO LOOKED LIKE A BUNNY AND FOUGHT LIKE A TIGER... DON-WAN KIHOTAY CRAZY OLD TIMER WHO THOUGHT HE WAS A JEDI KNIGHT... AND HEDJI, THE QUILL-THROWING SPINER...

"PRETTY MOTLEY ASSORTMENT... EVEN WHEN YOU ADD ONE CORRELLIAN SPACE ACE LIKE ME AND A FRIENDLY NEIGHBORHOOD WOOKIEE LIKE YOURSELF, CHEWBACCA. STILL...

"...WE CAME THROUGH AS CHAMPIONS FOR THOSE FARMER-TYPES AGAINST THE CLOUD RIDERS... BUT AT A PRICE, AND A DAMN HIGH ONE!"

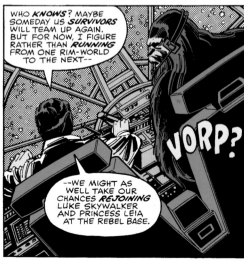

WHO KNOWS? MAYBE SOMEDAY US SURVIVORS WILL TEAM UP AGAIN. BUT FOR NOW, I FIGURE RATHER THAN RUNNING FROM ONE RIM-WORLD TO THE NEXT--

VORP?

--WE MIGHT AS WELL TAKE OUR CHANCES REJOINING LUKE SKYWALKER AND PRINCESS LEIA AT THE REBEL BASE.

NO, NOT BECAUSE I *MISS* THEM! DON'T LET A FEW GOOD DEEDS MAKE YOU THINK I'M GOING *SOFT*... IT'S SHREWD *STRATEGY*, THAT'S ALL!

I'M NOT *ABOUT* TO LOSE MY STANDING AS A *MERCENARY!*

NOW HANG ONTO YOUR *FUR*... WE'RE GOING TO POP INTO *LIGHT SPEED.*

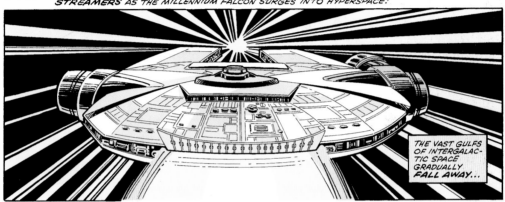

HAN SOLO'S *FINGERS* MOVE OVER THE CONTROLS... AND SUDDENLY THE STARS BECOME DOPPLER-DISTORTED *STREAMERS* AS THE MILLENNIUM FALCON SURGES INTO HYPERSPACE!

THE VAST GULFS OF INTERGALAC- TIC SPACE GRADUALLY *FALL AWAY*...

UNTIL...

DROPPING BACK TO *SUB-LIGHT*, CHEWIE, WE'RE STILL WELL *SHY* OF THE YAVIN SYSTEM... BUT IF *IMPERIAL FORCES* HAVE SHOWN UP THERE AGAIN--*

-- WE WON'T *HELP* BY POPPING UP RIGHT IN THE *MIDDLE* OF THEM!

*AS THEY DID WITH THE *DEATH STAR* IN ISSUES #5 & 6 --ARCH.

BUT FIRST CHECK OF THE SPACEWAYS ABOUT THEM REVEALS *NOTHING*. THEN...

URROWK!

I *SEE* THE SCOPE, CHEWIE! *CRUISER* COMING ON US... AT *BATTLE SPEED!* HIT THE *DEFLECTORS* AND GET READY TO--

WAIT A MINUTE!

THAT'S NOT ONE OF THE *EMPIRE* SHIPS! IT'S OUR OLD *PIRATE* PAL... *CRIMSON JACK!*

THE ONE WHO MADE OFF WITH OUR *TREASURE*, BIG BUDDY!

IT CAN'T BE A *COINCIDENCE!* THAT FORTUNE-HUNGRY *PARASITE* MUST'VE PLANTED SOME KIND OF *TRACER* ABOARD THE *FIRST* TIME HE GRABBED US! *

I *HATE* DIRTY TRICKS LIKE THAT... PARTICULARLY WHEN *I* DON'T PULL THEM *FIRST!*

THERE'S HIS *WARNING SHOT!* SHUT 'ER *DOWN,* CHEWIE... I'VE GOT AN *IDEA!*

*BACK IN *STAR WARS* #7-- ARCHIE*

AND SHORTLY, TRACTOR BEAMS HAUL THE MILLENNIUM FALCON INTO THE GIANT CRAFT'S HOLD. THERE, A WAITING HORDE SWARMS EAGERLY ABOARD...

WELL, WELL... *SOLO!* MY LITTLE PLAYMATE, *JOLLI,* SAID I'D WASTED MY TRACER... SAID YOU'D NEVER BE *STUPID* ENOUGH TO STRAY INTO *MY* SECTOR AGAIN!

BUT I *PRIDE* MYSELF ON RECOGNIZING A *STEADY* CUSTOMER!

THIS TIME HE'S COME *EMPTY-HANDED,* CAP'N! THERE'S *NOTHING* HERE TO BUY THE LIVES OF HIM AND THAT HULKIN' *FURBALL!*

WURK?

NO *PROBLEM,* PAL...THE REBELS COULD *USE* A CRUISER LIKE THIS. I'M GOING TO PLAY ON OL' JACK'S *GREED* TO BRING HIM RIGHT *TO* THEM!

WE'LL PROBABLY GET *REWARDED* ALL *OVER* AGAIN LIKE WHEN WE RESCUED THE *PRINCESS* AND--

UH-OH!

I *SEE* IT... BUT I DON'T *BELIEVE* IT.

WURG!

DON'T JUMP TO *CONCLUSIONS,* CHEWIE--

--BUT, YEAH, THIS *MAY* MEAN A VERY *LARGE CRIMP* IN MY PLAN!

STILL AN EVER-READY EYE FOR THE *LADIES,* EH, SOLO? EVEN WITH YOUR *TAIL* IN A SLING...!

WELL, THIS IS A *SPECIAL* ONE, ALL RIGHT. PRINCESS *AND* SENATOR, NO LESS.

AND *REBEL* BESIDES! I FIGURE THE ALLIANCE WILL PAY A SMART *RANSOM* FOR HER... ONLY *SHE* WON'T TELL ME WHERE THEIR *BASE* IS!

SO YOU CAN THEN *SELL* THAT INFORMATION TO THE *EMPIRE?* THIS CRUISER WILL *RUST* AROUND YOUR *EARS* BEFORE I TELL YOU *ANYTHING!*

SPUNKY, ISN'T SHE, MR. SOLO? WE CAUGHT HER ALL *ALONE,* HOPPING ACROSS THE VOID... NERVY, BUT *FOOLISH.*

OF COURSE, THE RIGHT *EXAMPLE* COULD *CURE* THE PRINCESS' FOOLISHNESS. THAT'S WHERE *YOU* AND YOUR *WOOKIEE FRIEND* COME IN, MY BOY.

JOLLI, YOU AND THE LADS SET YOUR BLASTERS AT *SLOW BURN!* WE'RE GOING TO *FRY* A PAIR OF PENNILESS STAR-ROVERS--

--TO *DEMONSTRATE* WHAT'S IN STORE FOR LEIA ORGANA HERE IF SHE DOESN'T *COOPERATE!*

GRURK!

NOT ON YOUR *LIFE,* MISTER... WHICH IS ABOUT TO BECOME *SHORT, HOT* AND *VERY UNHAPPY!*

WAIT A *MINUTE,* JACK--

VRAWK!

DOWN, CHEWIE!

I NEED TIME TO *TALK*... AND *YOU'RE* GONNA HAVE TO *BUY* IT FOR ME!

THE GIANT WOOKIEE *NEEDS* NO FURTHER INSTRUCTIONS! WITH SPEED SEEMINGLY *IMPOSSIBLE* FOR HIS GREAT BULK, HE IS UP AGAIN AND *MOVING*...

...*MOVING* INTO BLASTS MEANT TO KILL *SLOWLY*...

WHUNG!

ROWRR!

...AND CHEWBACCA HAS NO INTENTION OF STANDING *STILL* FOR THAT!

GREAT *GOING*, FIRST MATE!

GOTTA CHANGE THIS SETTING *FAST*, THEN--

CALL OFF THE *HOUNDS*, JACK! YOU'VE GOT THE MEN AND FIRE-POWER TO TAKE US *OUT*--

--BUT IT'LL BE ROUGH GLOATING WITHOUT A *HEAD*!

A WORTHWHILE *POINT*, MR. SOLO... IF MY MEN DON'T PICK *YOU* OFF *FIRST*.

YOU CAN PROBABLY GET A FEW MOMENTS *DISCUSSION* OUT OF IT BEFORE SOMEONE *TRIES*.

BUT IF CHEWIE AND I DIE *NOW*, YOU'LL MISS OUT ON THE *TREASURE*... PLUS A BLOODLESS AND *EASY WAY* TO GET WHAT YOU WANT FROM THE PRINCESS!

WHAT TREASURE, SOLO...? WE TOOK THAT FROM YOU *LAST* TIME.

AND *I CRIED* A LOT ABOUT IT, REDBEARD! THEN I REALIZED THERE *WAS* A WAY TO GET *MORE*... BUT IT'D TAKE A *CRUISER* TO PULL IT OFF! WHY DO YOU THINK I *LET* YOU GRAB THE MILLENNIUM FALCON--

SOME DAY, JACK, WE'RE GOING TO TALK WHEN YOU DON'T *HAVE* ANY MEN--

--WITHOUT EVEN A *CHASE*, JACK? I WAS *COMING* TO YOU WITH THIS *PROPOSITION* ANYWAY!

SOLO, I *TRUST* YOU ABOUT AS MUCH AS I'D TRUST RIDING A *SPICE-KEG* THROUGH A *METEOR SWARM*--

BUT YOU'VE INTRIGUED ME ENOUGH TO GIVE YOU A *REPRIEVE*... AND A *FREE MEAL*.

AND SOME TIME *LATER* IN THE PIRATE MASTER'S QUARTERS, A *FEAST* IS UNDERWAY... AS IS A GREAT DEAL OF *FAST TALKING* BY THE SKIPPER OF THE MILLENNIUM FALCON.

...REALIZE I'M IN A POOR *BARGAINING POSITION*, JACK, SO I'M WILLING TO *SETTLE* FOR A FIFTY-FIFTY SPLIT.

I'LL FILL YOUR *FACE* WITH THE BUSINESS END OF MY *BLASTER*, YOU CORRELLIAN CONNIVER!

CAP'N, HOW MUCH *LONGER* ARE WE GOING TO PUT UP WITH HIS *SPACE GAS*?!

YOU PROVIDE THE *ATTACK FORCE*... I PROVIDE THE LOOT'S *LOCATION*. JOLLI, FILL MY *CUP* AGAIN, WILL YOU, SWEETHEART?

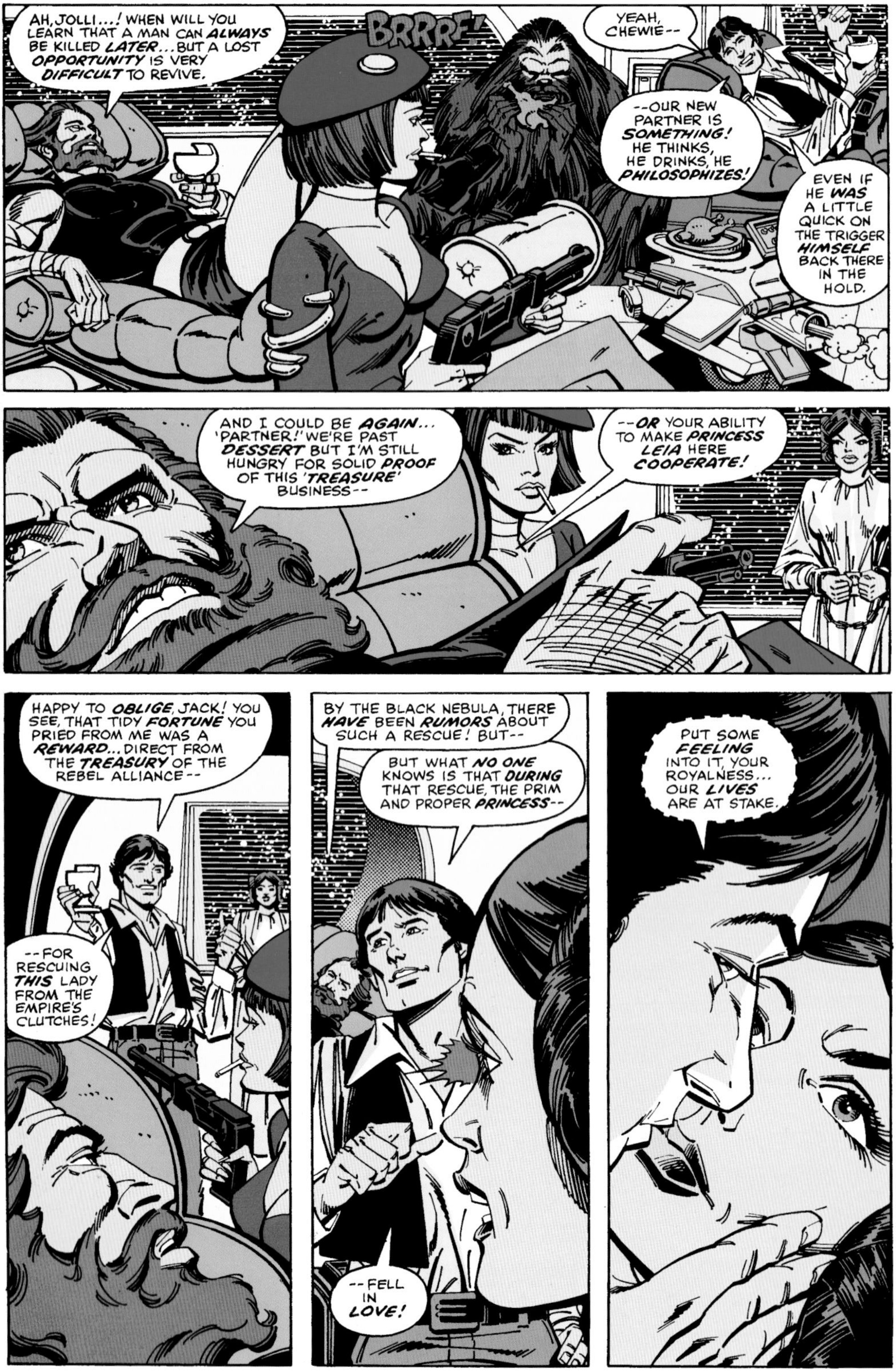
AH, JOLLI...! WHEN WILL YOU LEARN THAT A MAN CAN ALWAYS BE KILLED LATER... BUT A LOST OPPORTUNITY IS VERY DIFFICULT TO REVIVE.
BRRRF!
YEAH, CHEWIE--
--OUR NEW PARTNER IS SOMETHING! HE THINKS, HE DRINKS, HE PHILOSOPHIZES!
EVEN IF HE WAS A LITTLE QUICK ON THE TRIGGER HIMSELF BACK THERE IN THE HOLD.
AND I COULD BE AGAIN... 'PARTNER!' WE'RE PAST DESSERT BUT I'M STILL HUNGRY FOR SOLID PROOF OF THIS 'TREASURE' BUSINESS--
--OR YOUR ABILITY TO MAKE PRINCESS LEIA HERE COOPERATE!
HAPPY TO OBLIGE, JACK! YOU SEE, THAT TIDY FORTUNE YOU PRIED FROM ME WAS A REWARD... DIRECT FROM THE TREASURY OF THE REBEL ALLIANCE--
--FOR RESCUING THIS LADY FROM THE EMPIRE'S CLUTCHES!
BY THE BLACK NEBULA, THERE HAVE BEEN RUMORS ABOUT SUCH A RESCUE! BUT--
BUT WHAT NO ONE KNOWS IS THAT DURING THAT RESCUE, THE PRIM AND PROPER PRINCESS--
--FELL IN LOVE!
PUT SOME FEELING INTO IT, YOUR ROYALNESS... OUR LIVES ARE AT STAKE.

THANKS FOR KEEPING *SILENT* UP TILL NOW... I *KNOW* IT GOES AGAINST YOUR NATURE NOT TO BE SCREAMING ABOUT WHAT I'M DOING *WRONG.*

ACTUALLY, I'VE BEEN *SPEECH-LESS*--

--IT'S *LONG* ENOUGH SINCE ESCAPING THE *DEATH STAR* THAT I'D FORGOTTEN JUST HOW *MUDDLED* YOUR RESCUES GET!

JUST *WHAT* IS THIS SUP-POSED TO *ACCOMPLISH*...?

I'M NOT *SURE*, BUT AT LEAST IT'S *FUN!* AND THE *MORE* FRIEND JACK HAS TO *THINK* ABOUT, THE *LONGER* HE'LL KEEP US *ALIVE!*

THEN ALLOW *ME* TO MAKE A CONTRI-BUTION--

HOW *DARE* YOU, HAN SOLO?! HOW DARE YOU *BETRAY* MY FEELINGS FOR YOU?!

WRAP!

WUD!

I CAN'T *STOP* YOU FROM LEADING THESE VERMIN TO OUR *TREASURY* IN THE *DREXEL SYSTEM*... YOU ALREADY *KNOW* THE APPROACH THROUGH ITS *DEFENSE GRID.*

BUT *LUKE SKYWALKER* IS THERE, TOO... THAT MEANS SOME *SURPRISES* IN STORE FOR YOU!

CAPTAIN... I'D LIKE TO *RETURN* TO MY *CELL!*

TAKE HER *BACK,* JOLLI.

AND AS THE *SOLE SURVIVOR* OF THE PLANET ALDERAAN'S RULING HOUSE IS LED AWAY...

I DOUBT YOU'LL *EVER* CHARM THAT *FIRE-BRAND* INTO COOPERATION, SOLO... BUT SHE'LL BE A VALUABLE *HOSTAGE* IF THIS *SKYWALKER* GIVES US TROUBLE.

WHO *IS* HE ANYWAY?

UH... SORT OF A *RIVAL*... REALLY GETS *AROUND*...

...IT *SEEMS.*

197

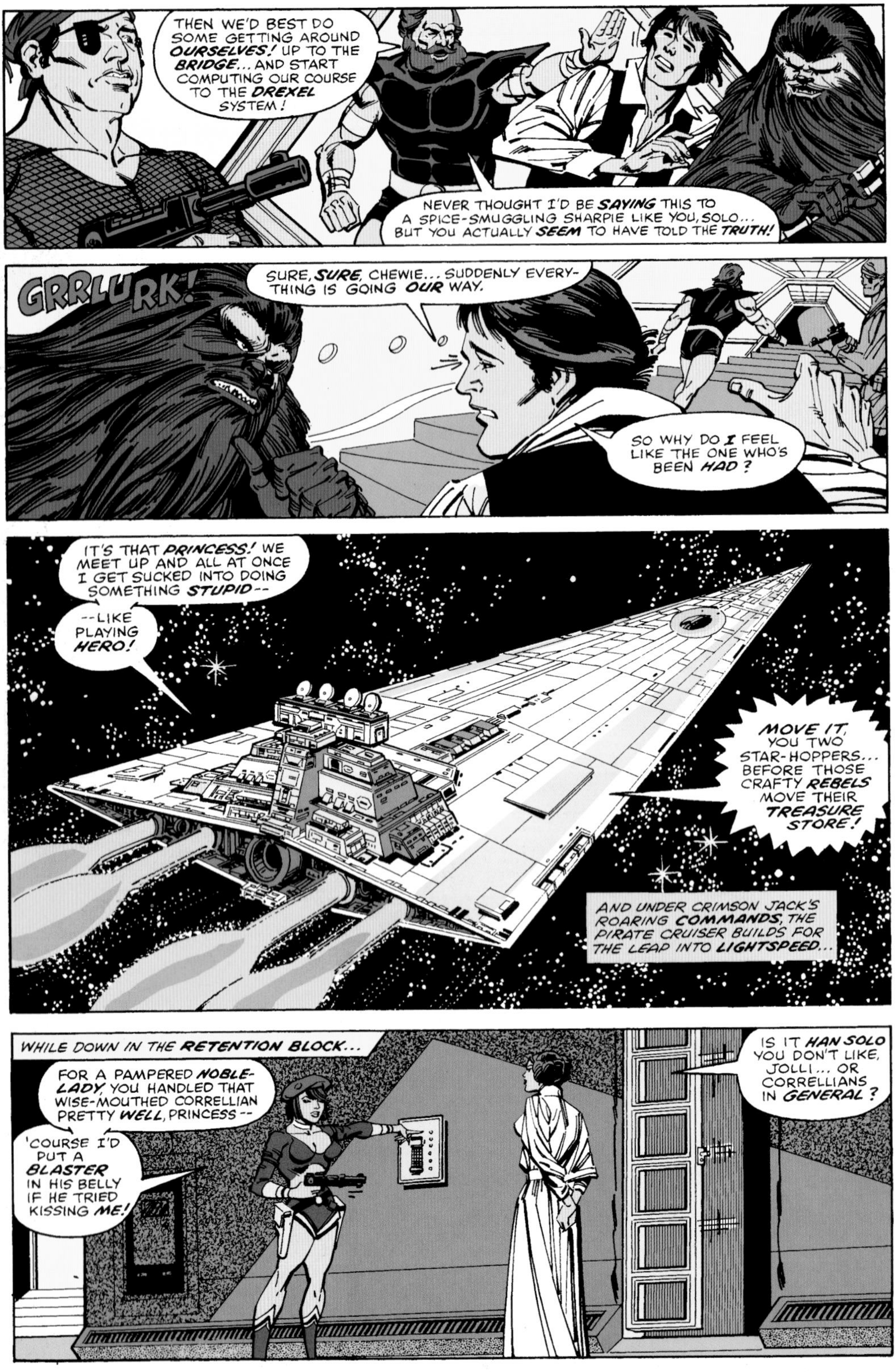

THEN WE'D BEST DO SOME GETTING AROUND OURSELVES! UP TO THE BRIDGE... AND START COMPUTING OUR COURSE TO THE DREXEL SYSTEM!
NEVER THOUGHT I'D BE SAYING THIS TO A SPICE-SMUGGLING SHARPIE LIKE YOU, SOLO... BUT YOU ACTUALLY SEEM TO HAVE TOLD THE TRUTH!
GRRLURK!
SURE, SURE, CHEWIE... SUDDENLY EVERYTHING IS GOING OUR WAY.
SO WHY DO I FEEL LIKE THE ONE WHO'S BEEN HAD?
IT'S THAT PRINCESS! WE MEET UP AND ALL AT ONCE I GET SUCKED INTO DOING SOMETHING STUPID--
--LIKE PLAYING HERO!
MOVE IT, YOU TWO STAR-HOPPERS... BEFORE THOSE CRAFTY REBELS MOVE THEIR TREASURE STORE!
AND UNDER CRIMSON JACK'S ROARING COMMANDS, THE PIRATE CRUISER BUILDS FOR THE LEAP INTO LIGHTSPEED...
WHILE DOWN IN THE RETENTION BLOCK...
FOR A PAMPERED NOBLE-LADY, YOU HANDLED THAT WISE-MOUTHED CORRELLIAN PRETTY WELL, PRINCESS --
'COURSE I'D PUT A BLASTER IN HIS BELLY IF HE TRIED KISSING ME!
IS IT HAN SOLO YOU DON'T LIKE, JOLLI... OR CORRELLIANS IN GENERAL?

IT'S *MEN*, LADY... THE WHOLE BLASTED *BREED!* A SMOOTH-TALKIN' *HANDSOME* ONE IS NO BETTER THAN ANY OTHER... AND MAYBE *WORSE!*

THERE *ARE* GOOD MEN, JOLLI... A *PIRATE* VESSEL MAY NOT BE THE BEST PLACE TO *FIND* THEM.

CERTAINLY, I'VE HAD MY *PROBLEMS* WITH MISTER SOLO. STILL--

--HE *DOES* KISS WELL.

ZISP

WELL, WHAT DOES A HIGH, MUCKETY-MUCK REBEL *PRINCESS* KNOW ABOUT ANYTHING *ANYWAY?!*

KLONG

KEEP YOUR THOUGHTS ON MEN AND KISSING TO *YOURSELF!*

THE LADY PIRATE STORMS FROM THE DETENTION AREA, *DISTURBED* BY HER OWN ANGER, UNCERTAIN *WHY* IT SUDDENLY ERUPTED...

...LEAVING PRINCESS LEIA ORGANA ALONE IN THE DARKNESS WITH HER *OWN* THOUGHTS.

RIGHT NOW SHE HAS *MANY*, FROM THE DESTRUCTION OF HER HOME WORLD *ALDERAAN*, TO THE PROBLEMS OF WARRING AGAINST A STILL-STRONG *EMPIRE*, TO HER OWN IMMEDIATE *PERIL*. YET *MOSTLY*, HER MIND FLIES TO VISIONS OF *ONE* YOUNG MAN...

...A FARM-BOY OF THE DESERT WORLD *TATOOINE* TURNED *STAR-WARRIOR*--

--*LUKE SKYWALKER!*

OH, LUKE... *LUKE!* IF ONLY YOU HADN'T VOLUNTEERED FOR THAT *SCOUTING* MISSION--

--THEN WE'D *BOTH* BE SAFE BACK AT OUR *MAIN BASE* ON THE FOURTH MOON OF *YAVIN.*

"BUT AFTER THE BATTLE OF THE *DEATH STAR,* THERE WAS NO WAY TO BE *CERTAIN* WHETHER OR NOT DARTH VADER HAD SUCCEEDED IN REPORTING OUR *POSITION* TO EMPIRE FORCES...

WE *HAVE* TO SEEK A NEW *HIDING PLACE,* YOUR MAJESTY... AND YOUNG SKYWALKER *HAS* PROVEN HIMSELF ONE OF OUR *BEST* STAR-PILOTS.

AND I'M NEEDED *HERE*... AS BOTH *SYMBOL* AND *LEADER* OF THE REBEL ALLIANCE. I *UNDERSTAND,* GENERAL DODONNA--

--BUT I *STILL* WISH I WERE GOING *WITH* HIM!

"AT LEAST I COULD TAKE COMFORT THAT YOU WEREN'T *ALONE*... THAT YOU HAD *COMPANIONS,* THE LOYAL *DROIDS,* ARTOO DETOO AND SEE THREEPIO. BUT WHEN AT LAST YOU MADE *TRANSCEIVER COMMUNICATION*...

I THINK I'VE FOUND A NEW *SAFE HAVEN,* PRINCESS! IT'S A PLANET IN THE *DREXEL* SYSTEM, THAT--

NO! IT-- IT ISN'T *POSSIBLE!* IT--

WHAT'S *HAPPENING?!* WE'RE LOSING *CONTACT!*

"IT WAS *NEVER* REGAINED! *SOMETHING* HAPPENED TO YOU AND YOUR SHIP WHILE ORBITING AN *UNNAMED PLANET* THERE IN THE *DREXEL* STAR SYSTEM! AND I *KNEW*--

"-- I COULDN'T *REST* OR *THINK* OF MY DUTIES UNTIL I FOUND OUT *WHAT!*

"SO I SET OFF IN *SEARCH* FOR YOU, LUKE--"

--AND GOT CAPTURED BY *CRIMSON JACK* INSTEAD!

BUT IF *HAN SOLO* JUST PICKS UP ON THE *HINTS* I GAVE... THE SEARCH WILL STILL GO *ON,* LUKE! IT *MUST!*

MEANWHILE, ON THE HUGE SPACECRAFT'S *BRIDGE*...

THIS *DREXEL* SYSTEM IS LITTLE MORE THAN A *NAME* TO ME, SOLO... AND OUR *CHART PRINT-OUTS* DON'T HAVE MUCH DATA EITHER.

YOU'VE BEEN WORKING THE SAME SECTORS *TOO LONG*, JACK... MAKES FOR COMFORTABLE *PIRATING* BUT NARROWS YOUR VIEW OF THE *UNIVERSE*.

32·5 12 75·0 67·8

SPACE-HOPPING FORCES US TO KEEP A MUCH MORE *DETAILED* SET OF CHARTS ABOARD THE *FALCON*.

WURFLE

OKAY TO HAVE *CHEWIE* TAP IN OUR COMPUTER-SYSTEM WITH YOURS SO WE CAN *DRAW* ON THEM?

SO LONG AS YOUR HIRSUTE FIRST MATE DOESN'T MIND AN *ESCORT*... OR THE POSSIBILITY OF BEING *SLAIN* BY THEM IF HE TRIES ANYTHING *SUSPICIOUS*!

GROWF!

NO *PROBLEM*, JACK. AS CHEWIE SAYS--

-- WHAT'S THE FUN IN BEING *PARTNERS* IF YOU CAN'T *TRUST* ONE ANOTHER?

DON'T WORRY ABOUT THE *WOOKIEE*, JACK... HE'LL ONLY DO WHAT HE'S *SUPPOSED* TO.

MEANTIME, LET ME GET STARTED ON THE *PRELIMINARY* COMPUTATIONS. IT'S A *LONG HOP* TO THE DREXEL SYSTEM--

--AND IT'S ONE OF THE *FEW* PLACES IN THIS GALAXY I'VE NEVER *BEEN* BEFORE! BUT WHY UPSET MY RED-BEARDED BUDDY WITH *THAT* TIDBIT OF INFORMATION?

OR THE FACT THAT ANY STAR-FARING OLD-TIMER I EVER *TALKED* TO SAID IT'S A SPOT TO BE AVOIDED LIKE A *BLACK HOLE!*

I DON'T KNOW WHAT LUKE SKYWALKER IS *DOING* THERE... BUT THE *PRINCESS* CERTAINLY SET THINGS UP SO WE'RE *ALL* ABOUT TO FIND OUT!

YEAH, KID! *WHEREVER* YOU ARE AND WHATEVER *MESS* YOU'RE IN--

"--YOU'RE ABOUT TO HAVE *LOTS* OF *COMPANY!*"

ARTOO! THREEPIO! BACK INSIDE THE *SHIP!* THE CHARGE IN MY BLASTER HAS GOTTEN TOO *WEAK*--

--THESE SHOTS WON'T *STOP* IT!

VEEBREEP!

YOU *HEARD* MASTER LUKE, ARTOO DETOO--

--I'M QUITE SURE HE'S ALREADY *AWARE* THE SHIP IS *SINKING!*

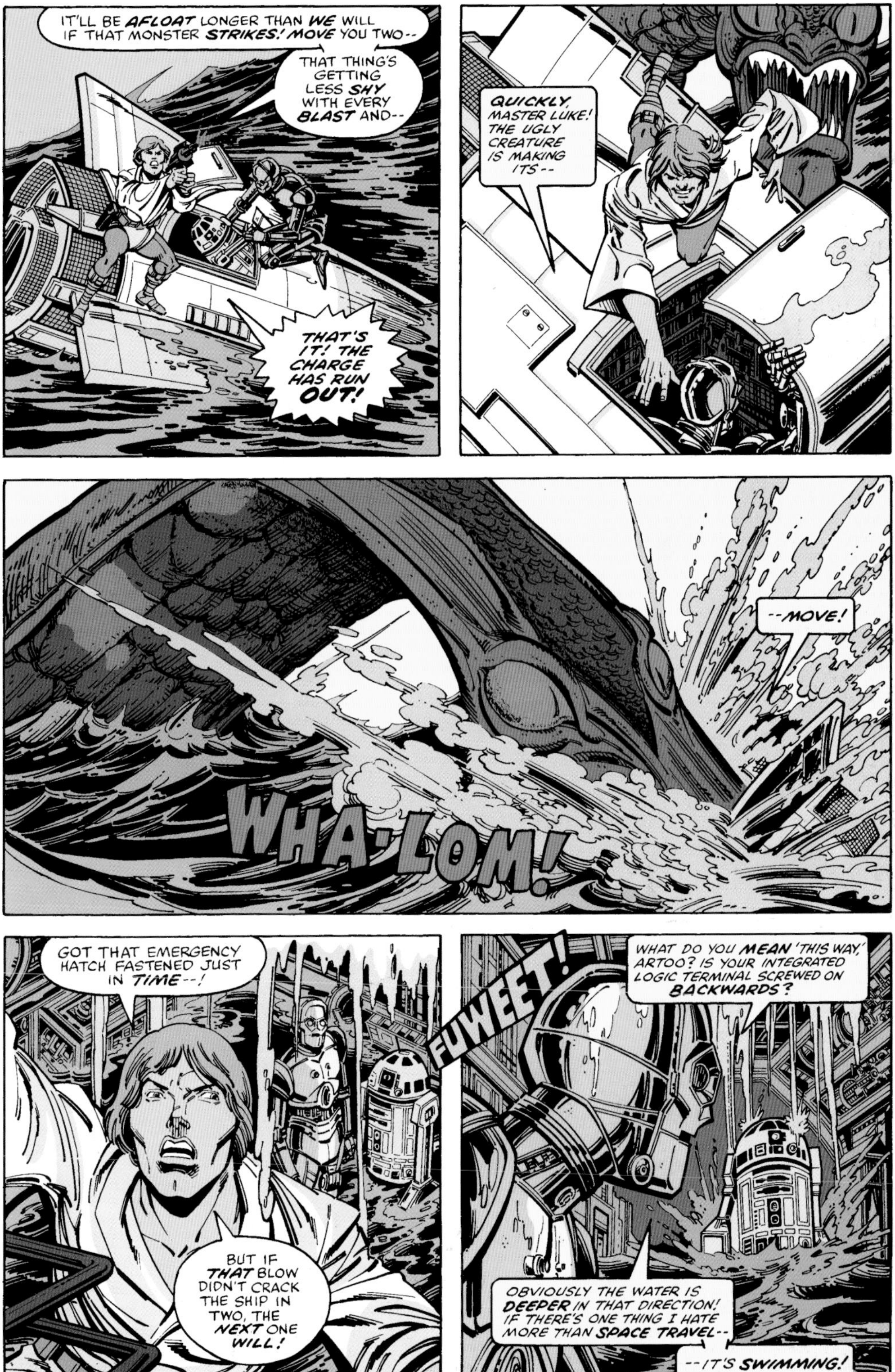
IT'LL BE AFLOAT LONGER THAN WE WILL IF THAT MONSTER STRIKES! MOVE YOU TWO--
THAT THING'S GETTING LESS SHY WITH EVERY BLAST AND--
THAT'S IT! THE CHARGE HAS RUN OUT!
QUICKLY, MASTER LUKE! THE UGLY CREATURE IS MAKING ITS--
--MOVE!
WHA-LOM!
GOT THAT EMERGENCY HATCH FASTENED JUST IN TIME--!
BUT IF THAT BLOW DIDN'T CRACK THE SHIP IN TWO, THE NEXT ONE WILL!
FUWEET!
WHAT DO YOU MEAN 'THIS WAY,' ARTOO? IS YOUR INTEGRATED LOGIC TERMINAL SCREWED ON BACKWARDS?
OBVIOUSLY THE WATER IS DEEPER IN THAT DIRECTION! IF THERE'S ONE THING I HATE MORE THAN SPACE TRAVEL--
--IT'S SWIMMING!

I THINK I KNOW WHAT HE'S UP TO, THREEPIO. FOLLOW HIM!
EXACTLY AS I WAS ABOUT TO SUGGEST, SIR! MAY AS WELL HUMOR THE STUBBORN LITTLE DROID--
--MAKE HIS LAST MOMENTS BEFORE SHORT-CIRCUITING HAPPY ONES AND--
ARTOO! NOW WHAT ARE YOU DOING?
HE'S OPENING THE LIFE POD CHAMBER! INSIDE... BEFORE IT FLOODS!
THINGS ARE HAPPENING ENTIRELY TOO FAST FOR MY COMPREHENSION REACTORS!
ONE MOMENT WE'RE SAFELY ORBITING THIS PLANET... THE NEXT, ALL SYSTEMS GO DEAD AND WE CRASH-GLIDE INTO SEEMINGLY ENDLESS OCEAN...! THEN THAT CREATURE--
SEAL THE SAFETY DOOR, ARTOO! AND PRAY THIS POD CAN STILL--
--EJECT!
CHONG!
AND LONG MOMENTS LATER, WHEN THE POD HAS BOBBED TO THE SURFACE...
CAN YOU SEE ANYTHING, MASTER LUKE?
THE END OF OUR SPACECRAFT, THREEPIO! THAT KING-SIZE WATERWORM IS ABOUT TO APPLY THE FINISHING TOUCHES!
AT LEAST WE PUT SOME DISTANCE BETWEEN US SO THAT--WAIT A MINUTE!

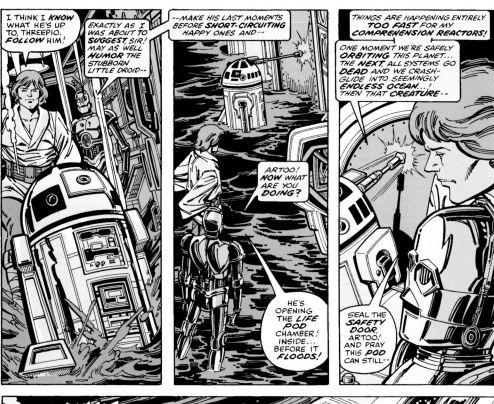

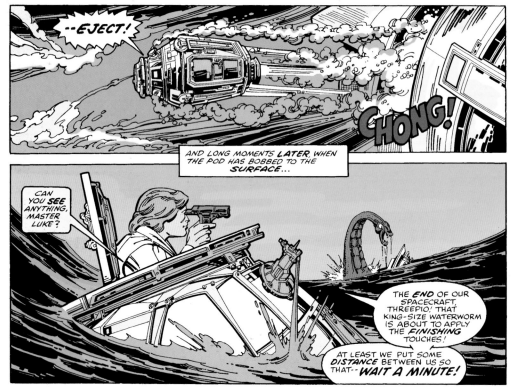

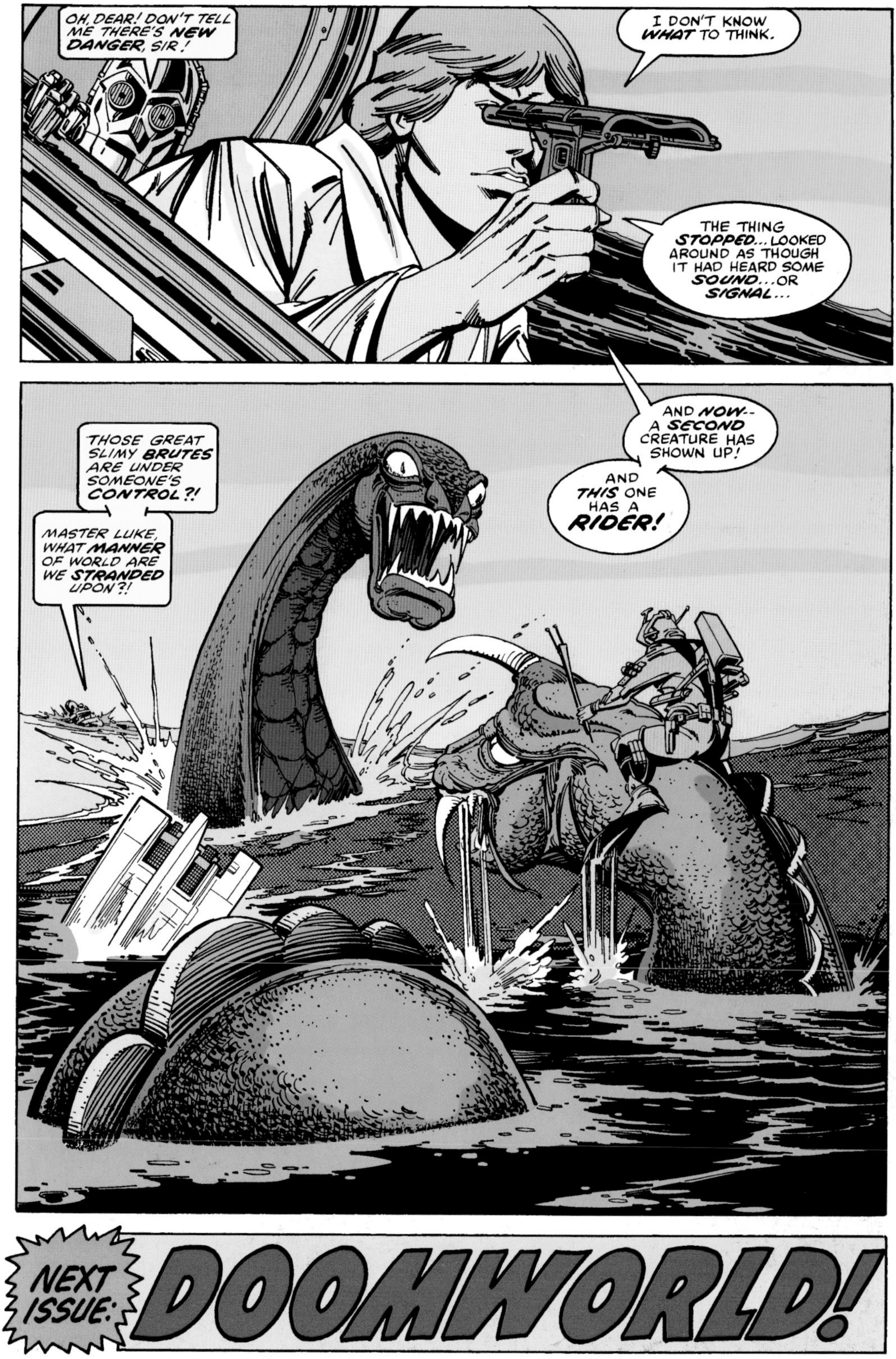
OH, DEAR! DON'T TELL ME THERE'S NEW DANGER, SIR!
I DON'T KNOW WHAT TO THINK.
THE THING STOPPED... LOOKED AROUND AS THOUGH IT HAD HEARD SOME SOUND... OR SIGNAL...
AND NOW-- A SECOND CREATURE HAS SHOWN UP!
AND THIS ONE HAS A RIDER!
THOSE GREAT SLIMY BRUTES ARE UNDER SOMEONE'S CONTROL?!
MASTER LUKE, WHAT MANNER OF WORLD ARE WE STRANDED UPON?!
NEXT ISSUE:
DOOMWORLD!

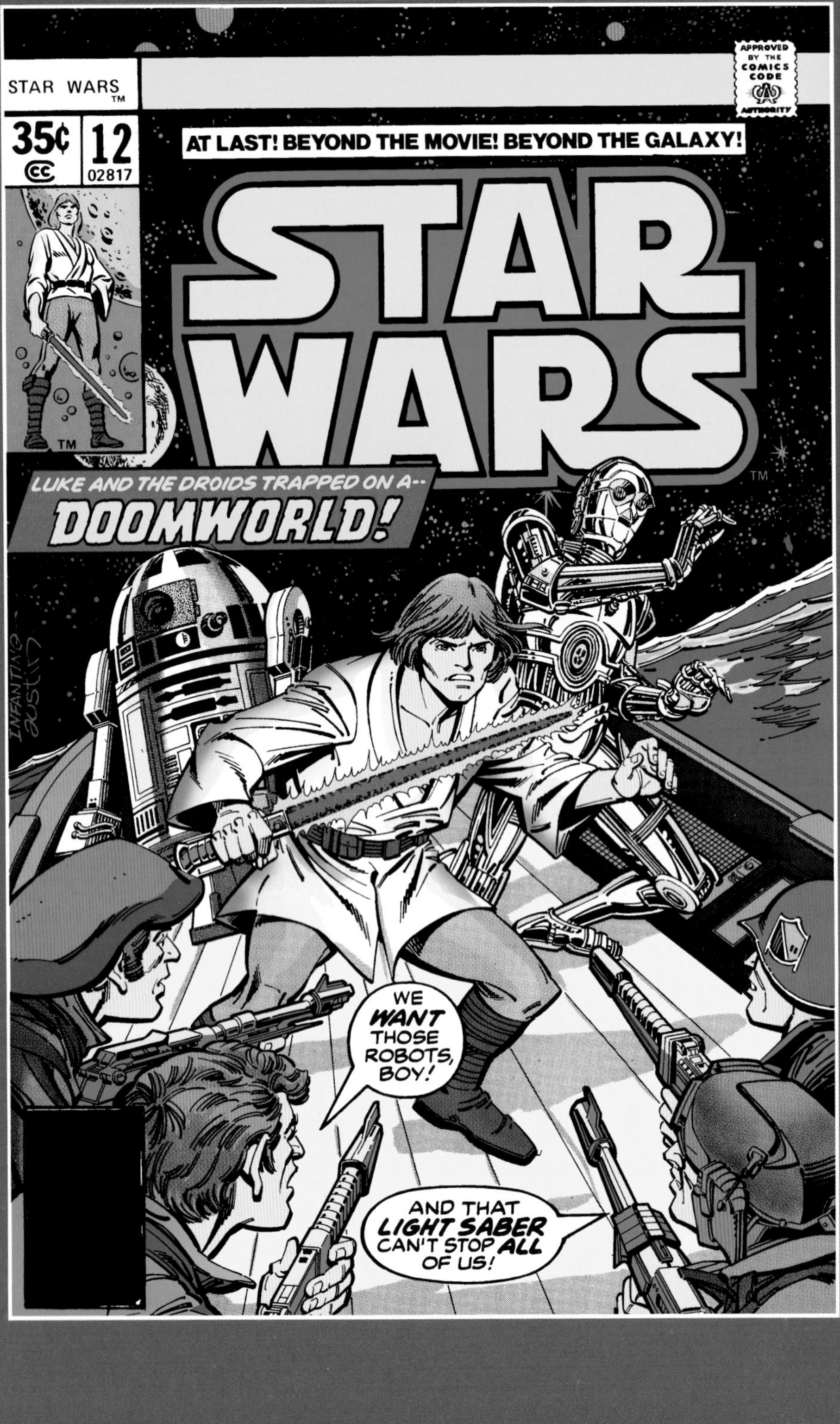
STAR WARS TM
35¢
12
02817
APPROVED BY THE COMICS CODE AUTHORITY
AT LAST! BEYOND THE MOVIE! BEYOND THE GALAXY!
STAR WARS
LUKE AND THE DROIDS TRAPPED ON A--
DOOMWORLD!
WE WANT THOSE ROBOTS, BOY!
AND THAT LIGHT SABER CAN'T STOP ALL OF US!

Long ago in a galaxy far, far away. . .there exists a state of cosmic *civil war*. A brave alliance of *underground freedom fighters* has challenged the tyranny and oppression of the awesome *Galactic Empire*. This is their story!

LucasFilm PRESENTS: **STAR WARS** ™ THE GREATEST **SPACE FANTASY** OF ALL!

CONTINUING THE SAGA BEGUN IN THE FILM *BY GEORGE LUCAS* RELEASED BY *TWENTIETH CENTURY FOX.*

ARCHIE GOODWIN WRITER/EDITOR • CARMINE INFANTINO & TERRY AUSTIN ARTISTS • JOHN COSTANZA letterer • JANICE COHEN colorist • JIM SHOOTER consulting editor

THE REBEL ALLIANCE HAS SENT LUKE SKYWALKER TO FIND A *NEW LOCATION* FOR THEIR MAIN BASE AFTER THE BATTLE OF THE *DEATH STAR*. ✱ BUT *HERE*, ON THIS UNNAMED PLANET OF THE STAR-SUN *DREXEL*, LUKE HAS FOUND INSTEAD WHAT MAY BE FOR HIM AND THE TWO DROIDS, ARTOO-DEETOO AND SEE-THREEPIO, A...

THE *RIDER* CONTROLLING THAT *ONE* MONSTER HAS DONE *SOMETHING* TO THE OTHER ONE TOO! IT'S NO LONGER *ATTACKING* OUR SHIP... IT'S *PUSHING* IT!

OH, DEAR! IS THAT *GOOD* OR *BAD* AS FAR AS WE'RE--

I KNOW IT'S *FANTASTIC*, THREE-PIO, B-BUT... I THINK THEY'RE OUT TO *SALVAGE* OUR SPACECRAFT!

EXCUSE ME, SIR. *ARTOO* IS RAISING SOME SORT OF *COMMOTION.*

FLWEET

HE CLAIMS HIS *SENSORS* ARE DETECTING SOME SORT OF *MECHANIZED CRAFT* IN THE AREA.

FRANKLY, MASTER LUKE, I THINK SPLASHING AROUND IN THE *WATER* BEFORE WE ABANDONED SHIP* MAY HAVE CORRODED HIS *PERCEPTION FILAMENTS* BECAUSE I DON'T DETECT--

WAIT, THREEPIO! *BEHIND* US... ON THE *HORIZON...*

LAST ISSUE-- ARCH.

HYDRA-CRAFT! DON'T KNOW WHAT THEY'RE *CALLED* HERE... BUT THEY'RE SKIMMING OVER THE *WATER* JUST LIKE I USED TO WHIP AROUND *TATOOINE* IN MY OLD *LANDSPEEDER!*

BEGGING YOUR *PARDON*, SIR, BUT ISN'T THAT A RATHER *AWKWARD* ANALOGY--

-- SINCE THERE DOESN'T SEEM TO **BE** ANY LAND?

WHATEVER THEY ARE, THREEPIO, THEY'RE **ARMED** --

--AND **OPENING FIRE** ON THOSE SEA MONSTERS WITH **US** CAUGHT IN THE **MIDDLE!**

THE AIR IS FILLED WITH THE WHINE AND CRACKLE OF LASER BOLTS...

...AS THE MONSTER'S RIDER WAVES HIS STRANGE STAFF ALOFT, NO NOTICEABLE SOUND OR SIGNAL ISSUES FROM IT...

YET BOTH HIS SERPENTINE STEED...

...AND ITS DRAGON-LIKE COUNTERPART RESPOND AS IMMEDIATELY AS IF SPURRED!

FOR A MOMENT, THEY ARE *LOST* IN THE WINE-DARK DEPTHS. *THEN*, AS THEIR ARMED ATTACKERS SURGE STEADILY FORWARD...

WHA-LUD!

BUT THE TWO *OTHER* CRAFTS ARE NOT SO EASILY *CAUGHT*. WHEELING SHARPLY IN THE FOAMING WATERS, THEY BRING THEIR *GUNS* TO BEAR!

CIRCLE THE MISERABLE SEA SPAWN! HE'S GONNA *PAY* FOR WIPIN' OUT THAT *HYDRA-SKIMMER!*

CATCH 'IM IN A *CROSSFIRE!*

AN' KEEP A *SHARP EYE* OUT FOR--

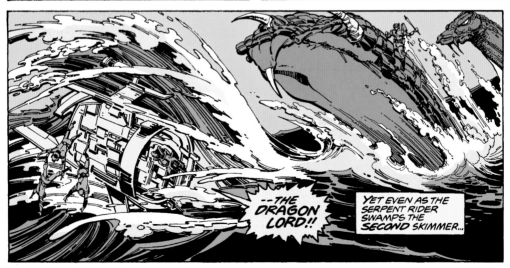

--THE *DRAGON LORD!!*

YET EVEN AS THE SERPENT RIDER SWAMPS THE *SECOND SKIMMER...*

WE'VE *GOT* 'IM! A FEW MORE BLASTS AN' HE'S *DONE!*

BUT THE RIDER DOESN'T *WAIT* FOR THAT. WITH THE TWO WOUNDED CREATURES AT HIS COMMAND... HE *RETREATS.*

STOP *FIRIN'!* THEY'RE OUT OF *RANGE!* RUNNIN' OFF LIKE WHIPPED *WOMP RATS!*

SOME WHIPPIN'... COST US *TWO SKIMMERS* AN' WE GOT *NOTHIN'* TO SHOW FOR IT!

DON'T BE SO *CERTAIN!* THE BIG PRIZE MAY HAVE *SUNK*... BUT *SOMETHING'S* BOBBIN' ABOUT OUT THERE.

AND IT'S *GLEAMIN'* LIKE METAL!

METAL?!

SHOOT OUT THE *MAGNETIC GRAPPLES*... ON THE *DOUBLE!*

CHOOM!

CHOOM!

AND AS THE GRAPPLES THUD AGAINST THE LIFE POD'S HULL...

THREEPIO, I THINK WE'RE *RESCUED*... LIKE IT OR NOT.

WHY IS IT, SIR, I HAVE THE FEELING IT'S GOING TO BE *NOT?*

MOMENTS LATER, THE GOLDEN-HUED TRANSLA-TOR DROID'S *FEELING* IS PUT TO THE TEST... AS THE POD IS HAULED ONTO THE HYDRA-CRAFT.

BLAZES! THAT IRON *STEW POT* STILL HAS A FEW PIECES OF *MEAT* IN IT!

BUT... ONE OF 'EM'S WEARIN' A *METAL SUIT!*

THAT'S NO *SUIT,* FOOL! HAVE YOU FORGOTTEN *ALL* YOUR OFF-WORLD LORE--?

THE YOUNG STAR-HOPPER IS TRAVELIN' WITH A GENUINE *ROBOT!* THAT *SMALLER* PIECE OF NUTS AN' BOLTS BESIDE 'IM IS *ONE* TOO!

AN' EITHER OF 'EM HOLDS ENOUGH *COMPONENTS* TO MAKE THE *GOVERNOR* FOR-GIVE US THEM LOST SKIMMERS.

CHUCK THE BOY BACK TO THE *FISHES*--

--THEN TEAR APART THE *MACHINES* SO THEY DON'T CAUSE *TROUBLE!*

NOW *WAIT* A MINUTE--

I SAID *WAIT!*

A L-LIGHT SABER! THE BARE-FACED LITTLE PUP IS A *JEDI!*

VRAMMMM

JEDI! EVEN IN THIS MOMENT OF DANGER, LUKE THRILLS TO THE WORD... AND WISHES IT WAS TRUE. WISHES THAT LIKE HIS FATHER, WHOSE SABER HE WIELDS, AND LIKE OBI WAN KENOBI, THE MAN WHO TRAINED HIM...

...HE TOO WAS A JEDI KNIGHT.

BUT I'M NOT...

"...BEN KENOBI WAS THE LAST OF THAT PROUD LINE. AND HE HAD BARELY STARTED TEACHING ME ABOUT THE FORCE WHEN HE FELL DUELING DARTH VADER. YET... SOMETIMES...

"...I STILL FEEL AS IF HE'S WITH ME."

AT LEAST HIS WORDS CERTAINLY ARE: "TRY TO DIVORCE YOUR ACTIONS FROM CONSCIOUS CONTROL--

SWOOOMP

"STRETCH OUT WITH YOUR FEELINGS--"

JUMP! IF THAT LASER BLADE EVEN TOUCHES YOU... YOU'RE SLICED SEA CABBAGE!

HE CAN'T SWING IT EVERY WAY AT ONCE! COME AT 'IM FAST FROM ALL SIDES!

HE'S RIGHT, ARTOO! POOR MASTER LUKE! WE'RE CERTAINLY DOOMED THIS TI--

BADEEP

ARTOO! YOU'RE LEAKING LUBRICANT ONTO THE DECK! SOMEONE COULD--

--SLIP!

AND BEFORE *MORE* OF THE SKIMMER CREW CAN MOVE IN ON HIM...

...LUKE *LEAPS* TOWARD THE CRAFT'S *HELM!*

WRAK!

ALL RIGHT! *ENOUGH!* ANY MORE MOVES AGAINST *ME* OR THE *DROIDS*--

--AND I USE MY LIGHT SABER TO *FUSE* THESE CONTROLS INTO A MOLTEN *LUMP!*

EASY NOW, *LAD!* THAT'D LEAVE US *STRANDED...* AT THE MERCY OF ANY *DRAGON LORD* WHO HAPPENED ALONG.

I WANT TO *TALK* TO THIS "GOVERNOR" OF YOURS--

THEN HEAVE YOUR *WEAPONS* OVER THE SIDE,... AND START ACTING *FRIENDLY!*

--AND I WANT MY *FRIENDS* AND I IN *ONE PIECE* WHEN WE DO!

LUKE'S ORDER IS OBEYED *SULLENLY...* BUT IT *IS* OBEYED.

AND THE AGING CRAFT STARTS *FORWARD* TOWARD THE DISTANT HORIZON...

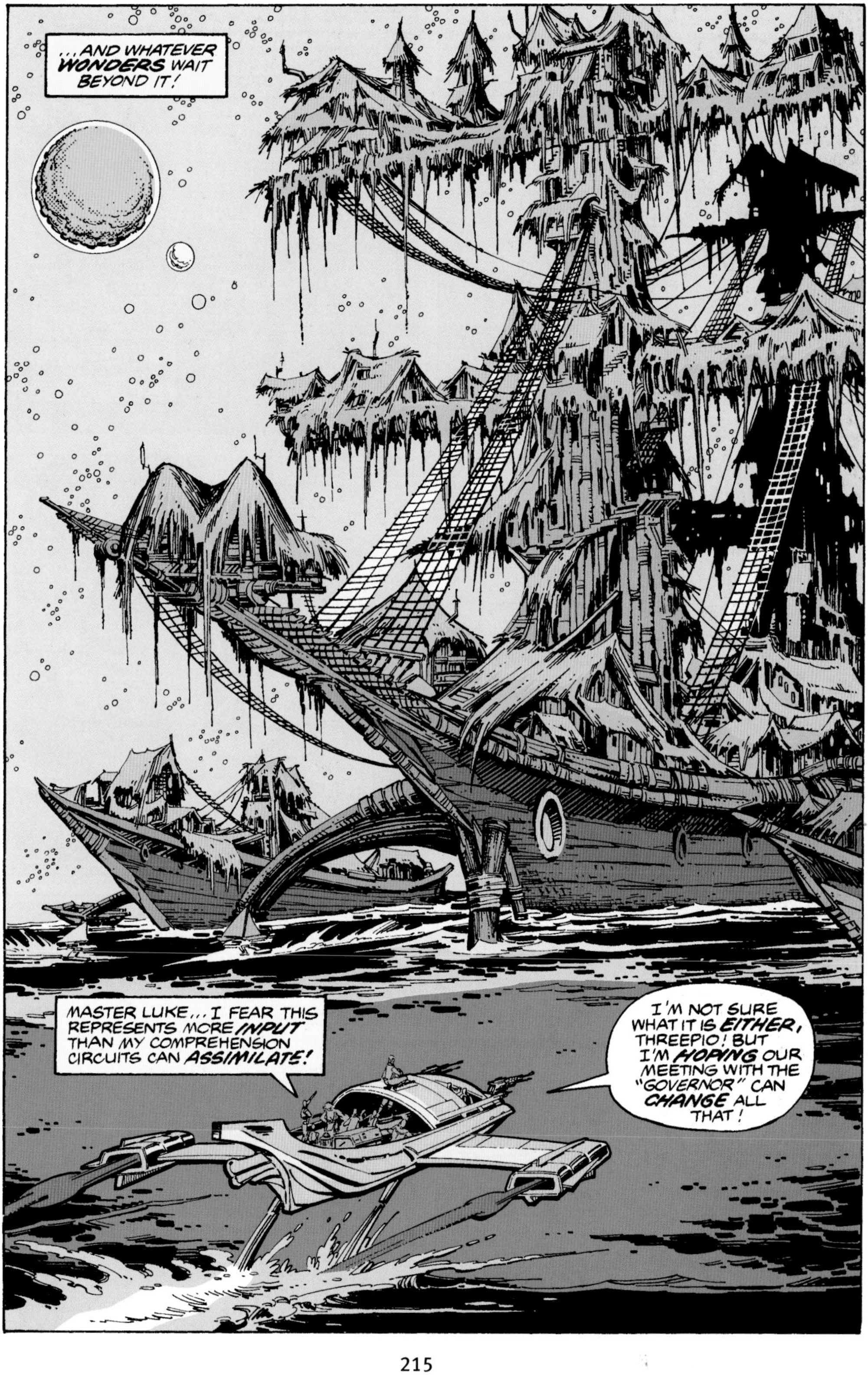
...AND WHATEVER WONDERS WAIT BEYOND IT!
MASTER LUKE... I FEAR THIS REPRESENTS MORE INPUT THAN MY COMPREHENSION CIRCUITS CAN ASSIMILATE!
I'M NOT SURE WHAT IT IS EITHER, THREEPIO! BUT I'M HOPING OUR MEETING WITH THE "GOVERNOR" CAN CHANGE ALL THAT!

WHEN WE FIRST CAME WITHIN *SCANNING DISTANCE* OF THIS WATER WORLD, OUR SHIP'S INSTRUMENTS PICKED UP WHAT I *THOUGHT* WAS A LARGE *LAND MASS*--

EVIDENTLY, IT WAS... T-THIS!

I *RECALL*, SIR, WE HOPED IT MIGHT SERVE AS A NEW *REBEL BASE*--

--NOW I ONLY HOPE IT DOESN'T SERVE AS OUR *FINAL RESTING SPOT*.

BADOOP

NO, ARTOO, BY THAT I *DON'T* MEAN AN EXTENDED *LUBRICATION BATH!*

DON'T *WORRY*, THREEPIO. I THINK I CAN TALK SOME *SENSE* INTO THE PERSON IN CHARGE.

AT LEAST... IT MAKES SENSE TO *ME*.

YOU'LL HAVE YOUR *CHANCE*, SONNY! THAT'S *GOVERNOR QUARG* WAITIN' ON THE DOCK!

BUT US SHOWIN' UP SHY *TWO SKIMMERS* AIN'T LIKELY TO HAVE 'IM IN A *RECEPTIVE MOOD!*

AND AS THE CRAFT TIES UP...

GUARDS! *SEIZE* EVERYONE ABOARD! I WANT THEM *HANGED* AS TRAITORS! IN OUR *WAR* WITH THE DRAGON LORDS--

--MEN ARE EXPENDABLE. *SKIMMERS* DEFINITELY ARE *NOT!*

WAIT, YOUR HONOR--

-- JUST *LOOK* WHAT WE BROUGHT *BACK* WITH US!

ROBOTS! THEY *MORE* THAN MAKE UP FOR THOSE BROKEN DOWN *SKIMMERS* YOUR HONOR!

AYE, SIR! THEY COULDN'T HAVE *LASTED* ANOTHER MISSION *ANYWAY!*

PERHAPS, I'LL HAVE THE *MASTER MACHINE-SMITH* STRIP DOWN YOUR CATCH AND *JUDGE* ITS VALUE.

THEN I'LL DECIDE ABOUT *YOU.*

GOVERNOR QUARG, YOU'D BETTER HEAR *ME* OUT BEFORE YOU DECIDE *ANYTHING!*

I DON'T THINK THERE'S A *SOUL* ON THIS WHOLE *FLOATING MESS* OF YOURS WHO KNOWS WHAT THESE DROIDS ARE *REALLY* WORTH... AND *IN ONE PIECE!*

WELL *SAID,* SIR!

WHO IN THE THREE MOONS IS *THIS?!*

FOUND 'IM *WITH* THE ROBOTS, YOUR HONOR. HE SWINGS A *LIGHT SABER* JUST LIKE ONE 'A THEM *JEDI KNIGHTS* THE HISTORIES TELL ABOUT.

THERE'S FAR *MORE* TO BEING A JEDI THAN *THAT*... OR SO MY *FATHER* ALWAYS INSISTED. HE LIKENED THEM TO *WARRIOR PRIESTS* --

-- OR *WIZARDS!* BUT, OF COURSE, HE *HATED* AND *FEARED* THEM TOO!

I'M NOT A *FOOL* LIKE FATHER, MY *RUDE* YOUNG FRIEND, BUT YOU'VE SPURRED MY *CURIOUSITY* ENOUGH TO HEAR YOU OUT.

OF COURSE, IF I DON'T *LIKE* WHAT I HEAR... YOU'LL BE THE *FIRST ONE* HANGED.

GUARDS! BRING HIM AND HIS METALLIC FRIENDS *WITH* US.

AS THE GUARDS' *BLASTERS* FOLLOW HIM, LUKE *SHEATHS* HIS SABER AND MOVES WITH HIS COMPANIONS UP ONTO THE DOCK...

THIS WAY, BOY... AND *QUICKLY!* SHIP'S *GOVERNOR* HAS BETTER THINGS TO DO THAN ENTERTAINING OFF-WORLD *FLOTSAM.*

ARE YOU GOING TO *TELL* ME SOMETHING OR *NOT?!*

BROTHER! WHAT I WOULDN'T GIVE NOW FOR *HAN SOLO'S* GIFT OF GAB... OR AT VERY LEAST, HIS *SELF CONFIDENCE!*

BETTER *YET* I'D LIKE TO SEE THE *MILLENNIUM FALCON* ROARING DOWN TO BLAST US *OUT* OF THIS!

*AND CURIOUSLY ENOUGH, THAT **WISH** IS NOT SO FAR-FETCHED AS LUKE **FEELS** AS THE GREAT WOODEN DOOR SLAMS DOWN BEHIND HIM. FOR SOME **LIGHT YEARS** DISTANCE...*

...A MIGHTY *BATTLE CRUISER* IS MAKING THE JUMP INTO HYPERSPACE. IT'S DESTINATION IS THE *DREXEL SYSTEM...*

*IN ITS **HOLD** IS HAN SOLO'S CORELLIAN SMUGGLING SHIP, THE **MILLENNIUM FALCON**...*

...AND ON ITS *BRIDGE* IS HAN SOLO HIMSELF, FEELING UNCHARACTER-ISTICALLY *TENSE*.

HOW DO I GET MYSELF *INTO* SITUATIONS LIKE THIS? RUNNING A HALF-BAKED *BLUFF* ON *CRIMSON JACK*, ONE OF THE DEADLIEST *SPACE PIRATES* GOING--

--WHILE HEADING TOWARD A *STAR SYSTEM* MOST OLD-TIMERS SAY SHOULD BE *AVOIDED* LIKE A HERD OF STAMPEDING *BANTHAS*--

--WITH THE *PRINCESS* WHO *MASTERMINDED* THIS MOVE LOCKED BELOW DECKS WAITING TO BE *RESCUED*!

WHATEVER HAPPENED TO THE *GOOD OLD DAYS* WHEN I WAS A SIMPLE *SMUGGLER*... AND ONLY HAD TO WORRY ABOUT OUTRUNNING *EMPIRE SHIPS* AND BEING *MURDERED* BY DISGRUNTLED EMPLOYERS LIKE *JABBA THE HUT?*

PROBLEMS, MR. SOLO--?

I'D *HATE* TO THINK MY NEW *PARTNER* HAS ANYTHING ON HIS MIND HE'S NOT *SHARING* WITH ME.

WELL, I DIDN'T WANT TO HURT YOUR *FEELINGS*, JACK, BUT THIS TAIL-HEAVY *BATTLE-WAGON*--

--GOES INTO *WARP* WITH ALL THE GRACE OF A VERULLIAN *LAND SLUG*.

IT HAS THE SIZE AND FIRE-POWER TO DO ALL *I* REQUIRE, MR. SOLO--

--THOUGH I WILL ADMIT IT SAW SOME RATHER *HARD SERVICE* JUST BEFORE I *ACQUIRED* IT FROM THE *IMPERIAL FLEET.*

QUITE AN *ACCOMPLISHMENT,* JACK... HOW *DID* YOU PULL THAT OFF?

"BY BEING IN THE RIGHT *PLACE* AT THE RIGHT *TIME,* SOLO... SHORTLY *AFTER* THE REBEL ALLIANCE WON THEIR FIRST BIG *VICTORY* OVER EMPIRE FORCES. THERE WERE MANY *CASUALTIES...*

"...AND THIS CRUISER WAS *ONE* OF THEM. SHE APPARENTLY *ESCAPED* THE MAIN BATTLE... ONLY TO DRIFT HELPLESSLY WHEN HER *REACTORS* WENT OUT.

"WHICH IS WHEN *ME* AND *MINE* HAPPENED UPON HERE!

"THEY MANAGED TO PUT A TRIO OF *TIE FIGHTERS* INTO DESPERATE ACTION AGAINST US...

"BUT IT WAS A LAST DITCH *EFFORT...* AND MY LADS WERE *UP* TO THE CHALLENGE.

"THE EARLIER COMBAT HAD TAKEN OUT MOST OF HER *CREW.* WE BOARDED TO *LIGHT RESISTANCE,* INTENDING TO SCAVAGE AND RUN. THEN I STARTED *NOTICING...*

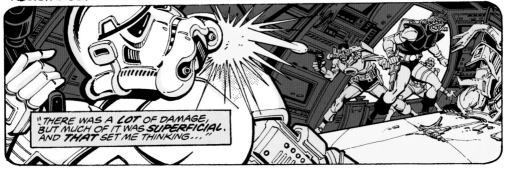

"THERE WAS A *LOT* OF DAMAGE, BUT MUCH OF IT WAS *SUPERFICIAL.* AND *THAT* SET ME THINKING..."

"WHY *ABANDON* HER, IF SHE COULD BE *RECLAIMED* INSTEAD?" JACK, I NEVER THOUGHT I'D *SEE* IT... A PIRATE WITH *VISION!*

BUT THE *COST--!* EVEN FOR A MAN MODERATELY *SUCCESSFUL* AT HIS TRADE LIKE YOU.

I FOUND *BACKERS*, MY BOY...WILLING TO COME IN FOR A *SHARE* IN FUTURE *PROFITS*.

THEN...YOU'RE PRACTICALLY A *CORPORATION!* IMPRESSIVE... BUT WHERE'S THE *ROMANCE?*

I'LL LEAVE *THAT* TO STAR-HOPPERS LIKE YOURSELF, MR. SOLO. I'VE AMBITIONS *BEYOND* BEING A PIRATE--

AND THAT *REBEL TREASURY* YOU'RE LEADING US TO IN THE *DREXEL SYSTEM* WILL BE A NICE *SHORT CUT* TOWARD *REALIZING* THEM.

LET'S HOPE YOU NEVER FIND OUT THAT *PARTICULAR* SHORT CUT IS A FIGMENT OF PRINCESS LEIA'S *IMAGINATION!*

CAP'N! CAP'N!

THERE'S *TROUBLE* ON THE *OBSERVATION DECK*, SIR! JOLLI'S GONE *CRAZY!*

JOLLI?! WHAT'S GOTTEN INTO THAT BLOOD-THIRSTY LITTLE *SPITFIRE* NOW?

YOU WORTHLESS BAG OF *NEBULA DUST!* I'LL *FRY* YOU FOR DARING TO LAY A *HAND* ON ME!

BACK OFF, WOMAN! *YOU'RE* THE ONE WHO STARTED THE TALK ABOUT *KISSIN'--*

ME AN' MY MATES JUST TRIED TO *OBLIGE!*

221

MEANWHILE, IN THE COCKPIT OF THE *MILLENNIUM FALCON*, AT REST IN THE CRUISER'S HOLD, A CERTAIN ONE HUNDRED YEAR OLD *WOOKIEE* FINISHES HIS ASSIGNED TASK...

TIME TO DROP INTO *SUB-LIGHT SPEED,* MR. SOLO.

NOW WE'LL SEE HOW ACCURATE THOSE *CHARTS* ARE THAT YOU HAD FED INTO OUR COMPUTER FROM THE *FALCON'S.*

THERE YOU *ARE,* JACK! *DREXEL...!* AND IT'S ONE *PLANET.*

NOBODY KEEPS MORE *DETAILED CHARTS* THAN AN OLD STAR-ROVER LIKE *ME.*

NOT SO *FAST,* "PARTNER!" SOMETHING'S *WRONG!*

ACCORDING TO OUR *SCANNERS*...THAT'S A *WATER WORLD!* THE REBELS COULDN'T *POSSIBLY* HAVE A TREASURY THERE!

WELL, SOLO...? I'M WAITING TO *HEAR* ABOUT THIS...BUT *NOT* VERY *LONG.*

JACK...! EVERYTHING'S *OKAY!*

JUST GET THE *PRINCESS* UP HERE AND I'LL *PROVE* THAT TO YOU.

OR *DIE* TRYING...!

NEXT ISSUE: **DAY** OF THE **DRAGON LORDS!**

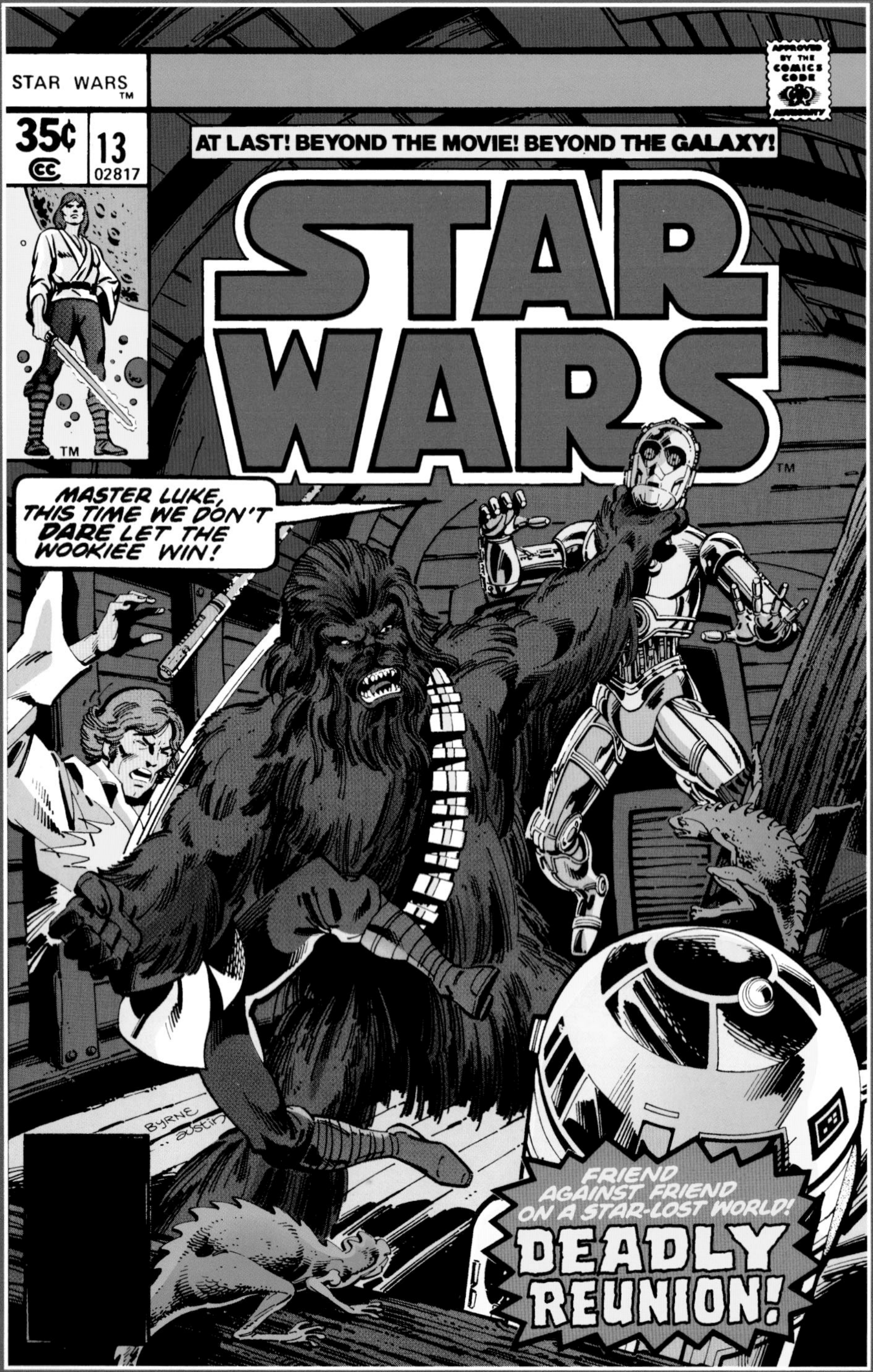
STAR WARS™
35¢
13
02817
APPROVED BY THE COMICS CODE AUTHORITY
AT LAST! BEYOND THE MOVIE! BEYOND THE GALAXY!
STAR WARS™
MASTER LUKE, THIS TIME WE DON'T DARE LET THE WOOKIEE WIN!
BYRNE austin
FRIEND AGAINST FRIEND ON A STAR-LOST WORLD!
DEADLY REUNION!

Long ago in a galaxy far, far away. . .there exists a state of cosmic *civil war*. A brave alliance of *underground freedom fighters* has challenged the tyranny and oppression of the awesome *Galactic Empire*. This is their story!

LucasFilm PRESENTS: **STAR WARS** *THE GREATEST* **SPACE FANTASY** *OF ALL!*

CONTINUING THE SAGA BEGUN IN THE FILM BY GEORGE LUCAS RELEASED BY TWENTIETH CENTURY FOX.

DAY OF THE DRAGON LORDS!

THE SHIP IS AS BIG AS A CITY. IT ENDLESSLY SAILS THE VAST OCEAN THAT IS THE **SURFACE** OF THIS UN-NAMED PLANET IN THE **DREXEL SYSTEM.**

A SCOUTING MISSION FOR THE REBEL ALLIANCE HAS **BROUGHT** LUKE SKYWALKER HERE... A MYSTERIOUS ACCIDENT HAS **TRAPPED** HIM. AND **NOW**... ONLY HIS **WITS** ARE KEEPING HIM **ALIVE!**

SHIP'S **POLICY,** MY YOUNG FRIEND, IS TO **SLAY** ALL OFF-WORLDERS... AND TO **CANNIBALIZE** ALL METAL AND MACHINERY.

AND **MY** JOB, SKYWALKER, IS TO **ENFORCE** THAT POLICY!

ARCHIE GOODWIN	CARMINE INFANTINO & TERRY AUSTIN	RICK PARKER	JANICE COHEN	JIM SHOOTER
WRITER/EDITOR	ARTISTS	LETTERER	COLORIST	CONSULTING EDITOR

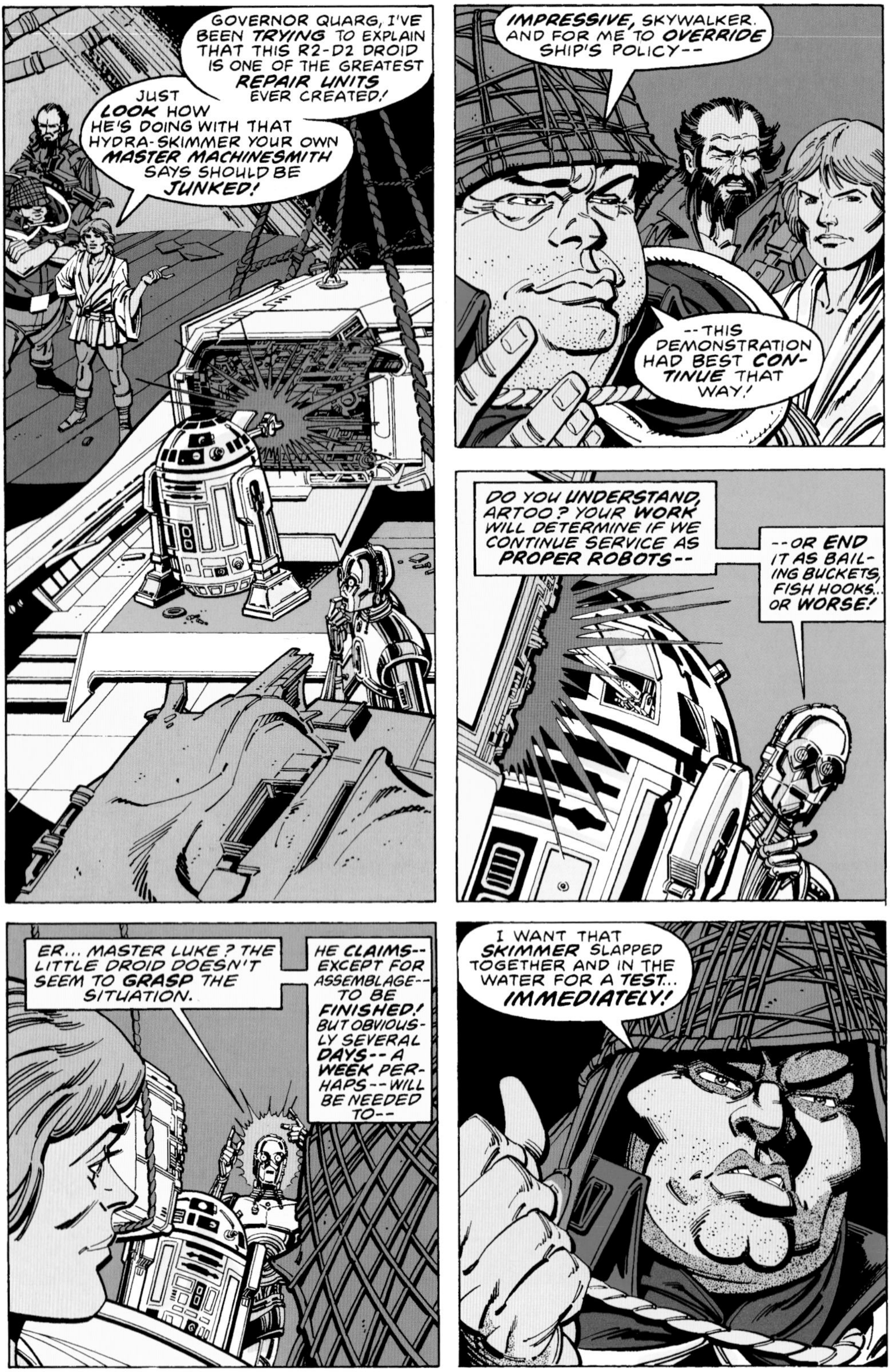
GOVERNOR QUARG, I'VE BEEN TRYING TO EXPLAIN THAT THIS R2-D2 DROID IS ONE OF THE GREATEST REPAIR UNITS EVER CREATED!
JUST LOOK HOW HE'S DOING WITH THAT HYDRA-SKIMMER YOUR OWN MASTER MACHINESMITH SAYS SHOULD BE JUNKED!
IMPRESSIVE, SKYWALKER. AND FOR ME TO OVERRIDE SHIP'S POLICY--
--THIS DEMONSTRATION HAD BEST CONTINUE THAT WAY!
DO YOU UNDERSTAND, ARTOO? YOUR WORK WILL DETERMINE IF WE CONTINUE SERVICE AS PROPER ROBOTS--
--OR END IT AS BAILING BUCKETS, FISH HOOKS... OR WORSE!
ER... MASTER LUKE? THE LITTLE DROID DOESN'T SEEM TO GRASP THE SITUATION.
HE CLAIMS--EXCEPT FOR ASSEMBLAGE--TO BE FINISHED! BUT OBVIOUSLY SEVERAL DAYS--A WEEK PERHAPS--WILL BE NEEDED TO--
I WANT THAT SKIMMER SLAPPED TOGETHER AND IN THE WATER FOR A TEST... IMMEDIATELY!

AND MUCH **SOONER** THAN SEE-THREEPIO WOULD PREFER, THE HASTILY REPAIRED SEA-CRAFT BOBS IN THE WAVES OFF THE SPRAWLING CITY-SHIP'S **STERN**... WITH **LUKE** AT ITS HELM!

WE'RE AT WAR WITH THE **DRAGON LORDS**, SKYWALKER, IF YOU AND THESE DROIDS CAN MAKE A WORTHLESS SKIMMER **COMBAT READY**... YOUR FUTURES ARE **SECURE**!

THAT FLOAT ON THE HORIZON IS YOUR **TARGET**... SINK IT AND I'LL BE QUITE **SATISFIED**.

SOUNDS EASY. BUT MECHANICS AND MAINTENANCE SURE AREN'T THESE PEOPLE'S **STRONG POINT**! I COULD TELL BY THE WAY THEIR SKIMMERS **PERFORMED** WHILE BATTLING THOSE SEA-DRAGONS. *

LET'S HOPE THIS OVERNIGHT WATER WAGON ISN'T **TOO FAR GONE** FOR ARTOO'S REPAIRS TO **HOLD UP**!

*LAST ISSUE--ARCHIE.

BUT WHATEVER **PROBLEMS** AWAIT... **STARTING** ISN'T ONE OF THEM.

WELL, AT LEAST YOU GOT **THAT MUCH** RIGHT, ARTOO! BUT FRANKLY, I FEEL YOUR **RESETTING** OF THE **LASER CANNON FEED SYSTEM** WAS DONE FAR TOO **SWIFTLY** AND --

NAME-CALLING DOES NOT MAKE IT ANY LESS **TRUE**.

WEE DOOP

BEET

THAT FLOAT IS A **SOLID MASS** OF LOGS! FULLY-FUNCTIONING **LASERS** COULD STILL SLICE 'EM LIKE **BUTTER** --

--BUT THESE CANNONS OBVIOUSLY HAVEN'T BEEN **FULLY**- FUNCTIONING FOR **YEARS**!

ARTOO'S REPAIRS WILL **HELP**... BUT IT'S GOING TO TAKE SOME BEGGAR'S CANYON STYLE **SHARPSHOOTING** TO GET THE JOB DONE!

I'LL CIRCLE ONCE TO PICK OUT THE **KEY STRESS POINTS**, THEN --

227

THEN YOU'LL BE *DEAD*, BOY!

AN' I WON'T HAVE TO *WORRY* ABOUT SOME BAREFACED *OFF-WORLDER* AND A COUPLE OF *MECHANICALS* REPLACIN' ME AS MASTER *MACHINESMITH*!

CORDED MUSCLES TIGHTEN AGAINST LUKE'S THROAT, CUTTING OFF *AIR*, THE FLOW OF *BLOOD*...

CAN'T *STOP* HIM...! HE'S TOO *BIG*...TOO *STRONG*...! I'VE *HAD* IT... UNLESS...

THE ONE-TIME MOISTURE-FARMER-NOW-STAR-WARRIOR *KICKS* OUT AT THE SKIMMER'S CONTROLS...

...AND *MISSES*!

LUKE'S VISION *BLURS*. HIS MIND *REELS*. HE DESPERATELY KICKS AGAIN...

...AND *CONNECTS* WITH THE SWITCH FOR THE *BRAKING JETS*! FOR THE FORWARD-SPEEDING *SKIMMER*...IT'S LIKE HITTING A *WALL*!

LUKE IS PREPARED FOR THE RESULT...

...THE MASTER MACHINESMITH *ISN'T*!

BUT LUKE HAS NO *TIME* TO THINK ABOUT HIS JETTISONED *FOE*... AS HE FIGHTS TO RE-GAIN *CONTROL* OF THE WILDLY TUMB-LING *CRAFT!*

STRAIN'S TEARING THIS BUCKET OF BOLTS *APART!* GOTTA THROW ALL THE POWER INTO THE *STARBOARD REPULSOR TURBO*--!

THAT'LL EITHER *STRAIGHT-EN* HER OUT... OR *FINISH* 'ER OFF!

IT IS A SITUATION WHERE *SOMETHING* HAS TO GIVE, AND WITH A WILD SHRIEK OF RENDING METAL... SOMETHING *DOES!*

CANOPY'S GONE! BUT EV-ERYTHING ELSE IS *HOLDING*... I'M BACK IN *BUSI-NESS!*

SPRAANG!

AND THAT BUSINESS *CENTERS* ON A GREAT MASS OF FLOATING LOGS. SWIFTLY, LUKE TURNS THE HYDRA-SKIMMER-- AND ITS *LASER-CANNONS*-- TO THE TASK!

VRAK-KOW!

GUNS STILL *DON'T* PACK THE *PUNCH* THEY SHOULD... WOULDN'T WANT TO GO UP AGAINST *IMPERIAL STORMTROOPERS* WITH `EM...

BUT CONSIDERING WHAT HE HAD TO *WORK* WITH... ARTOO DID *JUST FINE!*

CONGRATULATIONS, SKYWALKER! YOU'VE WON A **DEFINITE PLACE** ON THE SHIP.

IF YOU AND YOUR DROIDS **CONTINUE** TO PERFORM AS I'VE WITNESSED... YOU'LL BE **MASTER MACHINESMITH** FOR A LIFE-TIME.

SIR, I DIDN'T WANT TO TAKE ANYONE ELSE'S **JOB**...JUST TO PROVE THAT THREEPIO, ARTOO, AND I COULD BE OF **SERVICE**--

--SO THAT IN **TIME**, YOU MIGHT HELP US **GET OFF** THIS WORLD.

LET'S GET YOUR MECHANICAL FRIENDS **SETTLED**, MY BOY...THEN I'LL **EXPLAIN** SOME THINGS.

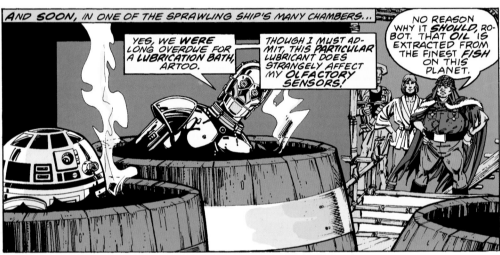

AND **SOON**, IN ONE OF THE SPRAWLING SHIP'S MANY CHAMBERS...

YES, WE **WERE** LONG OVERDUE FOR A **LUBRICATION BATH**, ARTOO.

THOUGH I MUST ADMIT, THIS **PARTICULAR** LUBRICANT DOES STRANGELY AFFECT MY **OLFACTORY** SENSORS!

NO REASON WHY IT **SHOULD**, ROBOT. THAT **OIL** IS EXTRACTED FROM THE FINEST **FISH** ON THIS PLANET.

NO DOUBT THE SMELL IS AN **ACQUIRED PERCEPTION**, SIR. IN TIME, I'LL--

AWAY! SHOO! SCAT!

HERE! WHAT ARE YOU **DOING**, YOU REPULSIVE LITTLE CREATURE?!

IT'S A **LIZARD!** THEY LIKE **FISH**. HARMLESS NUISANCES--

--BUT THEY SWARM OVER OUR VESSEL LIKE **BARNACLES!** THERE'S **MUCH** ABOUT SHIPBOARD LIFE FOR YOU AND YOUR COMPANIONS TO **LEARN**, SKYWALKER.

BUT LET'S START WITH CERTAIN **BASICS**. COME UP ON **DECK**.

THERE, SKYWALKER! THE MOST **BASIC LESSON** OF ALL--

THE PRICE OF **NOT PLEASING** YOUR GOVERNOR!

THAT'S THE **MASTER MACHINESMITH**... THE MAN WHO ATTACKED ME!

THE ACT OF A DESPERATE FOOL... WHO SENSED HIS **USEFULNESS** WAS AT AN END.

HE WAS **WRONG**. HE'S ACTUALLY QUITE USEFUL NOW... AS A **WARNING** TO OTHERS!

THIS PUDGY MADMAN DOESN'T HAVE A **VOICE** LIKE DARTH VADER... BUT HIS **HEART'S** SURE IN THE SAME PLACE!

GOT TO KEEP MY **TEMPER**... APPEAR TO GO **ALONG** WITH HIM UNTIL THE DROIDS AND I CAN FIND SOME WAY TO **ESCAPE!**

YOU'RE **SILENT**, BOY... **IMPRESSED**, I TAKE IT. GOOD!

I'M BREAKING A **RULE** TO LET YOU SURVIVE... I DON'T WANT ANY **BETRAYALS.**

THAT RULE WAS MADE BY MY **FATHER** AND HIS GENERATION WHEN THEY FIRST **CAME** TO THIS WORLD OF WATER ...**FLEEING** THE REPUBLIC!

THE **REPUBLIC**...! THE **OLD** REPUBLIC...! I--IT'S JUST A **MEMORY** NOW... REPLACED BY THE **EMPIRE!**

THEN WHATEVER **HELL** DEAR FATHER'S IN, HE MUST BE **PLEASED--**

"...HE NEVER QUITE **FORGAVE** THE REPUBLIC FOR **ENDING** HIS RATHER PROFITABLE GOVERNORSHIP.

"**FATHER** GOVERNED THE KORTEEN ASTEROID BELT, USING HIS **AUTHORITY** TO COVER HIS CITIZENS' PARTIALLY TO...

"... **SPACE-WRECKING!**

"THE BELT'S DENIZENS, SUPPOSEDLY MINERS, USED *SONIC JAMMING DEVICES* TO DISRUPT STARSHIP DRIVES AND SEND THE HELPLESS CRAFTS *CRASHING* INTO THE ASTEROIDS...

"...WHERE THEY COULD BE *STRIPPED* OF ALL *CARGO*.

"*NATURALLY*, MY FATHER *SHARED* IN EACH WRECK'S *PROFITS*.

"AND LUST FOR EVEN *MORE* OF THOSE PROFITS LED TO DEVELOPMENT OF MORE POWERFUL AND EFFECTIVE *JAMMERS*. BUT THE INFLUX OF SPECIAL EQUIPMENT AND TECHNICIANS NEEDED TO *ACCOMPLISH* THIS IN TIME ATTRACTED *OTHER* INTEREST...

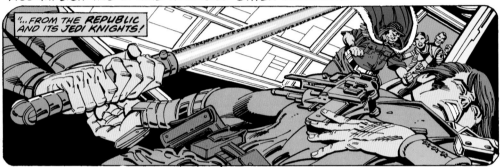

"...FROM THE *REPUBLIC* AND ITS *JEDI KNIGHTS!*

"*FATHER* AND A BAND OF FOLLOWERS *ESCAPED*... IF TUMBLING OUT OF WARP IN A LASER-BLASTED SPACECRAFT AND LIMPING INTO THE *DREXEL SYSTEM* CAN PROPERLY BE *CALLED* ESCAPE.

"THE PROSPECT WAS NOT SO *BLEAK* AS IT FIRST APPEARED. THERE WERE UNDERSEA FORESTS, SHELL AND CORAL FOR CONSTRUCTION MATERIALS... PLANT, FISH, AND REPTILE LIFE FOR *FOOD*.

"AND LIKE IT OR NOT... THEY *HAD* TO MAKE THIS OCEAN-SMOTHERED PLANET THEIR *HOME*.

"ONLY *METAL*, VITAL TO MAINTENANCE OF EQUIPMENT AND WEAPONS, WAS *MISSING*...

"...BUT **WRECKERS** THAT THEY WERE, MY FATHER AND THOSE ORIGINAL SETTLERS MANAGED TO ACQUIRE EVEN **THAT**... THOUGH NEVER IN SUFFICIENT **QUANTITY**. AND FOR **US**, METAL **REMAINS** MORE PRECIOUS THAN GEMS!"

"...AND A **REVOLT** BY THE SHIP'S **TECHNICIANS!** THEY CLAIMED WRECKER **POLICIES** WERE SOMEHOW **CAUSING** THE DRAGON'S ATTACKS!"

"EVEN SO, AROUND THE REMNANTS OF THEIR ORIGINAL SPACECRAFT, THIS **SHIP** GREW AND THRIVED...

"...EXCEPT FOR **TWO FACTORS!** MOUNTING **ATTACKS** FROM THE GREAT **SEA-DRAGONS**...

"MY FATHER **SQUASHED** THE UPRISING, BUT--IN THE MOST **FOOLISH MOVE** OF HIS LIFE-- FAILED TO **KILL** THE RING-LEADERS."

"STUPIDLY, HE SET THEM **ADRIFT,** INTENDING THAT THEY PERISH SLOWLY ON THE ENDLESS SEA...

"INSTEAD, THEY **SURVIVED,** TO BECOME OUR DEADLIEST ENEMY...**THE DRAGON LORDS!**

"FOR THE TECHNOS HAD DISCOVERED THAT **SOUND WAVES** AFFECT THE GREAT MONSTERS! AND WITH A DEVICE THEY CALL A **SONIC-STAFF,** THEY SEEMINGLY **CONTROL** THE CREATURES...

"...AND **DIRECT** THEM AGAINST **US!**"

SO LET'S HAVE NO TALK OF **LEAVING** THE PLANET, SKYWALKER! I **NEED** YOU AND YOUR DROIDS FOR MY **WAR**--

A WAR TO WIN **FINAL CONTROL** OF THIS WORLD ONCE AND FOR **ALL!** A WAR--

GOVERNOR QUARG! THE TRACKING CREW REPORTS SOMETHING **BIG** IS ON THE WAY--

--BIGGER THAN WE'VE **EVER** ENCOUNTERED, YOUR HONOR!

REACHING THE TRACKING CREW INVOLVES A DESCENT TO THE SHIP'S *LOWEST* LEVEL...

...AND ANOTHER *REVELATION* FOR LUKE!

THIS IS... A *SPACECRAFT SECTION!* FROM THE SHIP THAT *BROUGHT* YOUR *FATHER* HERE...?!

YOURS... AND *ALL* OTHERS THAT STRAY INTO THE DREXEL SYSTEM.

AND THIS *EQUIPMENT* IS ALL PART OF THE *MOST POWERFUL SONIC-JAMMER* FATHER'S WRECKING PROFITS COULD BUY!

HE MANAGED TO *ESCAPE* WITH IT FROM THE ASTER-OID BELT... WE'VE BEEN PUTTING IT TO *GOOD USE* EVER SINCE!

Y-YOU'RE *STILL* SHIP-*WRECKERS!* THIS IS HOW *MY* SHIP WAS BROUGHT DOWN!

PERHAPS NOT THIS TIME, SIR! THE THING THAT WE'RE GETTIN' *EARLY READINGS* ON COULD BE BIG AS *WE* ARE!

THEN WE'LL SALVAGE *METAL* ENOUGH TO LAST A LIFE-TIME, FOOL! *STRIKE* THE MOMENT IT'S IN *RANGE!*

I ONLY KNOW OF *ONE CRAFT* THAT LARGE... AN *IMPERIAL CRUISER!*

"BUT *WHAT* WOULD BRING AN EMPIRE WARSHIP INTO AN OUT OF THE WAY SYSTEM LIKE *THIS*...?"

ANSWER: *GREED!* THE GREED OF A RED-BEARDED SPACE PIRATE NAMED *CRIMSON JACK*, WHO LONG AGO 'LIBERATED' THIS CRUISER FROM IMPERIAL HANDS... *

...AND WHO NOW *SUSPECTS* THAT HIS GREED HAS ALLOWED A CERTAIN *COR-RELLIAN SMUGGLER* TO SOMEHOW PLAY HIM FOR A *FOOL!*

A *WATER WORLD!* THE REBEL ALLIANCE COULDN'T *POSSIBLY* HAVE THEIR *TREASURY* THERE, SOLO!

RELAX YOUR *TRIGGER FINGER*, JACK! I'M GOING TO *PROVE* HOW *WRONG* YOU ARE--

*AS EXPLAINED IN *DETAIL* LAST ISSUE--ARCHIE.

-- JUST AS *SOON* AS YOUR LITTLE HELPER, *JOLLI,* BRINGS *PRINCESS LEIA* HERE TO THE BRIDGE.

WHICH BUYS ME ABOUT THREE MORE MINUTES TO *THINK* OF SOMETHING--

-- IF *JACK* DOESN'T RUN OUT OF PATIENCE *BEFORE* THEN.'

MEANWHILE, ON A *LIFT* COMING UP FROM THE MASSIVE SHIP'S *DETENTION LEVEL...*

I THINK THAT HIGH 'N' MIGHTY *HAN SOLO'S* ABOUT TO LEARN ALL HIS CHARM AN' SMOOTH TALK WON'T *HELP* HIM MUCH LONGER!

JOLLI, HAVE YOU EVEN CON-SIDERED THAT *SOMETIMES* WHEN WE SEEM TO *HATE* SOME-ONE--

--IT'S TO *HIDE* THE FACT THAT WE'RE REALLY *ATTRACTED* TO THEM?

WHAT?! THE *ONLY* THING *I'M* CONSIDER-ING IS USING THIS *BLASTER* IF YOU KEEP *TALKING* LIKE THAT!

NOW *MOVE!* CAP'N JACK DOESN'T WANT TO ORBIT SOME BALL OF WATER *FOREVER* WAITING AROUND!

WE'RE IN *ORBIT...?* THEN HE SHOULDN'T HAVE TO *WAIT* FOR LONG--

AND EVEN AS PRINCESS LEIA IS *SPEAKING...*

CAP'N! NOW THAT THE PLANET'S *ROTATED* MORE... THE SCANNERS *ARE* PICKING UP SOME-THING BESIDES *WATER!*

SEEMS TO BE AN *ISLAND* OR--

IT TAKES A *BIG MAN* TO ADMIT HE'S *WRONG,* JACK... BUT I BET *YOU* CAN DO IT TOO!

SHUT UP, SOLO! I WANT TO HEAR MORE ABOUT--

BUT WHAT CRIMSON JACK HEARS *NEXT* IS THE SOUND OF CHAOS... AS SOMETHING *GRABS* HIS SHIP AND *SHAKES* IT.'

WE'RE LOSING *POWER!* ALL SYS-TEMS *FAILING!* INCLUDING *ARTI-FICIAL GRAVITY!*

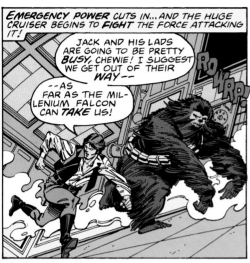

EMERGENCY POWER CUTS IN... AND THE HUGE CRUISER BEGINS TO FIGHT THE FORCE ATTACKING IT!

JACK AND HIS LADS ARE GOING TO BE PRETTY BUSY, CHEWIE! I SUGGEST WE GET OUT OF THEIR WAY--

--AS FAR AS THE MILLENIUM FALCON CAN TAKE US!

ROWRF!

THE PRINCESS? YEAH, YEAH... I SUPPOSE WE'LL HAVE TO PULL HER FEATHERS OUT OF THE FIRE AS USUAL!

LET'S HOPE THIS WEIRD ATTACK HASN'T LEFT HER WANDERING IN HYSTERICS.

ONLY AS FAR AS SOME UNCONSCIOUS GUARDS... IN CASE SOMEONE ELSE FORGOT TO GRAB WEAPONS!

BUT OF COURSE, I SUSPECTED SOMETHING WAS GOING TO HAPPEN... AND WAS PREPARED TO DITCH JOLLI WHEN IT DID!

NOW LET'S GET TO YOUR SHIP FAST! IF YOU HAVE ANY QUESTIONS, I'LL EXPLAIN ON THE WAY!

Y'KNOW, CHEWIE... I THINK I'D PREFER HYSTERICS.

BUT WHAT HAN SOLO GETS, AS THE TRIO REACHES THE VESSEL'S HOLD, IS... A PITCHED BATTLE!

MOST OF THE PIRATES ARE FIGHTING TO SAVE THE CRUISER! WE'LL BE FINE ONCE THIS BUNCH IS OUT OF THE WAY!

GREAT! I WAS BEGINNING TO THINK WE MIGHT BE IN TROUBLE!

...WITH THE *MILLENNIUM FALCON* SOARING *FREE!*

PRINCESS, EVERY *INSTINCT* IN MY SMUGGLER'S SOUL IS SCREAMIN: *GET WHILE THE GETTIN'S GOOD--*

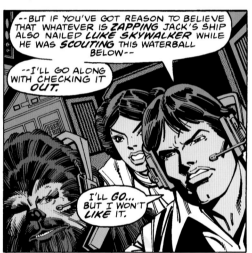

--BUT IF YOU'VE GOT REASON TO BELIEVE THAT WHATEVER IS *ZAPPING* JACK'S SHIP ALSO NAILED *LUKE SKYWALKER* WHILE HE WAS *SCOUTING* THIS WATERBALL BELOW--

--I'LL GO ALONG WITH CHECKING IT *OUT.*

I'LL *GO...* BUT I WON'T *LIKE* IT.

OTHERS ARE FINDING THINGS THEY DON'T LIKE ...OTHERS SUCH AS *GOVERNOR QUARG.*

WHY ISN'T THAT SHIP *DOWN* BY NOW, YOU WORTHLESS INCOMPETENTS! *WHY ISN'T IT DOWN?!*

YOUR HONOR... IT'S TOO *BIG!* TOO *POWERFUL!* THE *JAMMER* CAN'T--

DON'T *TELL* ME THAT! YOU'RE DOING SOMETHING *WRONG!* ARE YOU IN SYMPATHY WITH YOUR *FELLOW TECHNOS--?*

THOSE *TRAITORS* WHO BECAME THE *DRAGON LORDS!*

N-NO, SIR,...! BUT THE EQUIPMENT'S ALREADY AT *POWER FREQUENCIES* WE'VE NEVER RISKED BEFORE! THE *STRAIN* COULD--

GOVERNOR! THE *LOOKOUTS* HAVE *SIGHTED* SOME-THING--

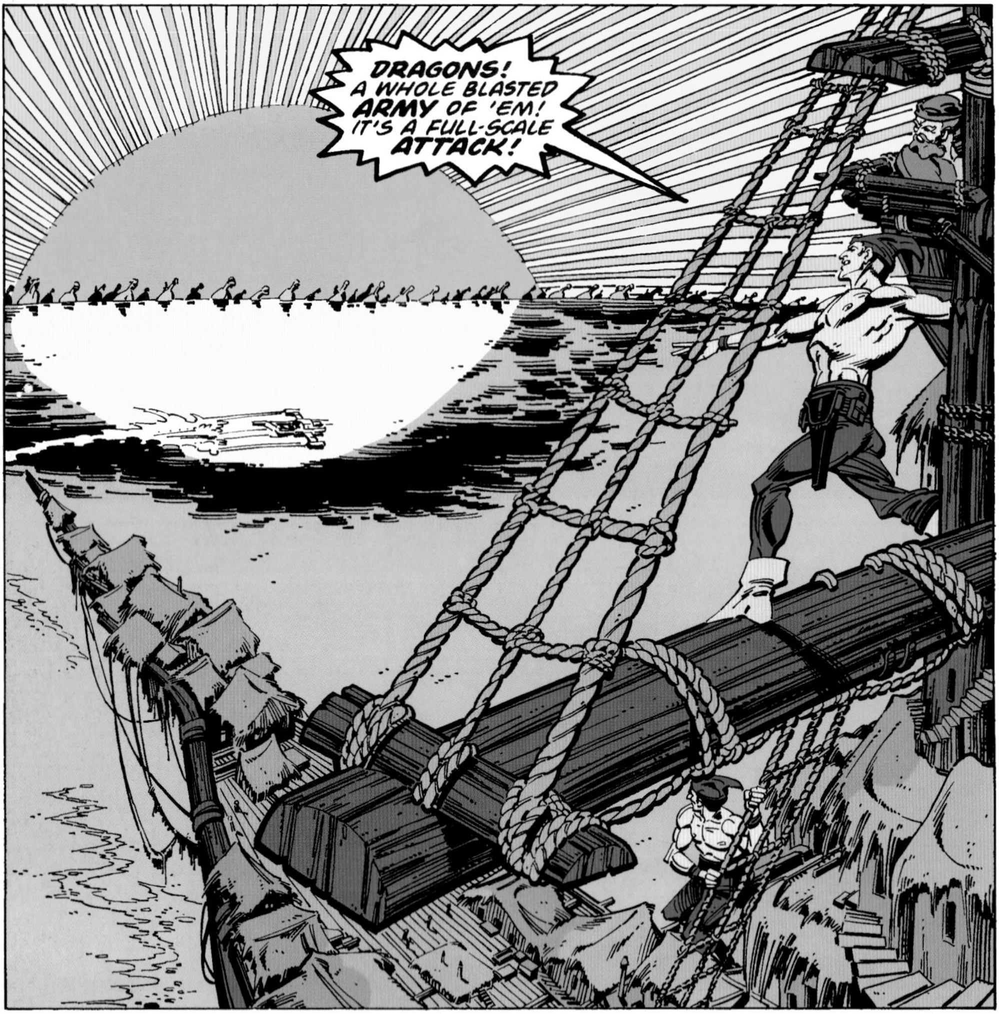
DRAGONS! A WHOLE BLASTED ARMY OF 'EM! IT'S A FULL-SCALE ATTACK!

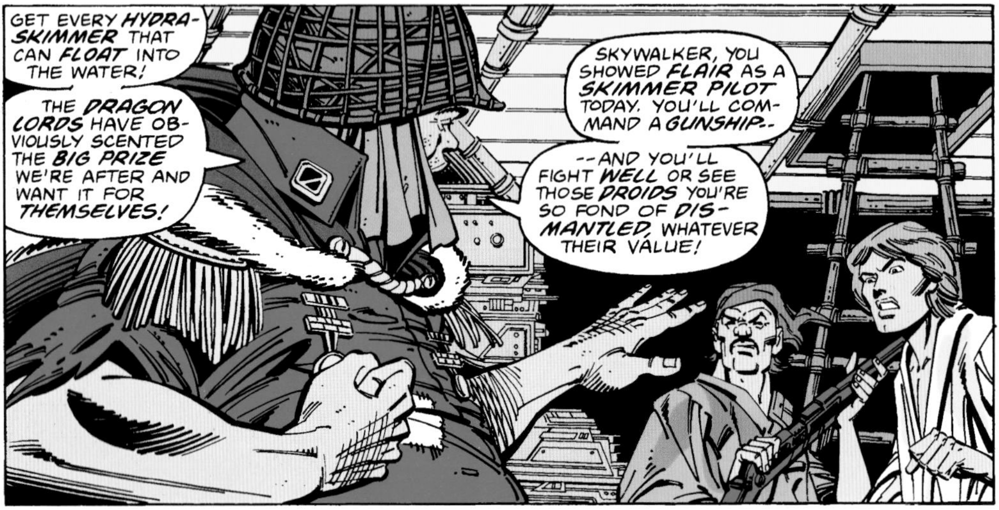
GET EVERY HYDRA-SKIMMER THAT CAN FLOAT INTO THE WATER!
THE DRAGON LORDS HAVE OBVIOUSLY SCENTED THE BIG PRIZE WE'RE AFTER AND WANT IT FOR THEMSELVES!
SKYWALKER, YOU SHOWED FLAIR AS A SKIMMER PILOT TODAY. YOU'LL COMMAND A GUNSHIP--
--AND YOU'LL FIGHT WELL OR SEE THOSE DROIDS YOU'RE SO FOND OF DISMANTLED, WHATEVER THEIR VALUE!

AND *SOON*, LUKE FINDS HIMSELF IN THE MIDST OF A BATTLE HE DOES NOT *WANT* TO FIGHT!

THESE CREATURES ARE *FRENZIED!* LIKE THE ONE WHO ATTACKED US WHEN WE FIRST *CRASHED* HERE!*

EVEN THE ONES CARRYING *DRAGON LORDS* SEEM WILD... OUT OF *CONTROL!*

*BACK IN *STAR WARS* #11 --ARCH.

LIKE IT OR *NOT*... I'VE NO CHOICE *BUT* TO FIGHT BACK! OR ELSE--

HEY! SOMETHING'S MAKING THEM *TURN!* W-WHAT--?!

HAN SOLO! WHAT HAVE YOU *DONE?!*

PRINCESS, I THINK WE'VE JUST *INTERRUPTED* SOMEBODY'S *WAR!*

EVEN *YOU* SHOULD BE ABLE TO MAKE A BETTER *LANDING* THAN THAT!

STOP REVVING YOUR *REACTORS,* YOUR ROYAL-NESS! I DIDN'T HAVE MUCH *CHOICE!*

WE'RE NEAR THE *SOURCE* OF THE BEAM LOCKED-IN ON CRIMSON JACK'S *CRUISER*... THERE'S ENOUGH *THROW OUT* FROM IT DOWN *HERE* TO AFFECT OUR *DRIVE,* TOO!

NOT TO *WORRY!* THE FALCON CAN *FLOAT* FOREVER. BUT UNTIL THAT FORCE *STOPS*... WE WON'T BE *FLYING* ANYWHERE!

BEFORE THE *FIGHTING* PICKS UP AGAIN, LET'S SHOW THE GUYS IN BOATS WE'RE *FRIENDLY.*

THEY LOOK EASIER TO *TALK* WITH THAN THOSE OVERSIZED *SEA SNAKES!*

BUT APPEARANCES ON THIS WATERWORLD ARE *DECEIVING*...

239

...NO ONE KNOWS THIS BETTER THAN *LUKE!* REMEMBERING GOVERNOR QUARG'S *RULE* OF *SAVING* METAL AND *SLAYING* SURVIVORS, HE RACES TO *CUT OFF* THE LEAD SKIMMER...

...AND FINDS HIS AGING, AILING CRAFT *CANNOT* DO IT!

NO!

LUKE SKYWALKER HAS SEEN HIS *AUNT* AND *UNCLE* DEAD BY THE *EMPIRE'S* HAND, HAS WATCHED *OBI-WAN KENOBI* APPARENTLY FALL BEFORE THE SITH LORD, *DARTH VADER.* NOW, TO SEE A *LASER BOLT* LASH AT TWO FRIENDS AND THE REBEL PRINCESS HE HOLDS DEAR *DRIVES* HIM...

....INTO RAGING *ACTION* WITHOUT THOUGHT OF THE CONSEQUENCES!

SLAMMING THROUGH THE WRECKAGE OF THE SKIMMER HE'S *DESTROYED,* LUKE NEARS THE FALCON...

I SAW *SOMEONE* FALL OVER HERE...!

LEIA...?! HAN...?

CHEWBAC--

WROWL!

WOOKIEES ARE NOT *SOPHIS-TICATED.* SOMEONE IN A *SKIMMER* TRIED TO *KILL* HIM... SO ANYONE IN A SKIM-MER IS *SUSPECT!*

IT WOULD TAKE SOMEONE CHEWIE *TRUSTS* SUCH AS HAN *SOLO* TO CALM HIM DOWN. BUT HAN SOLO IS *MISSING* NOW!

THERE *ARE,* HOWEVER, MANY MORE *SKIMMERS.* MOST OF THEIR CREWS *SAW* WHAT LUKE DID...

...AND MEAN TO *REPAY* HIM!

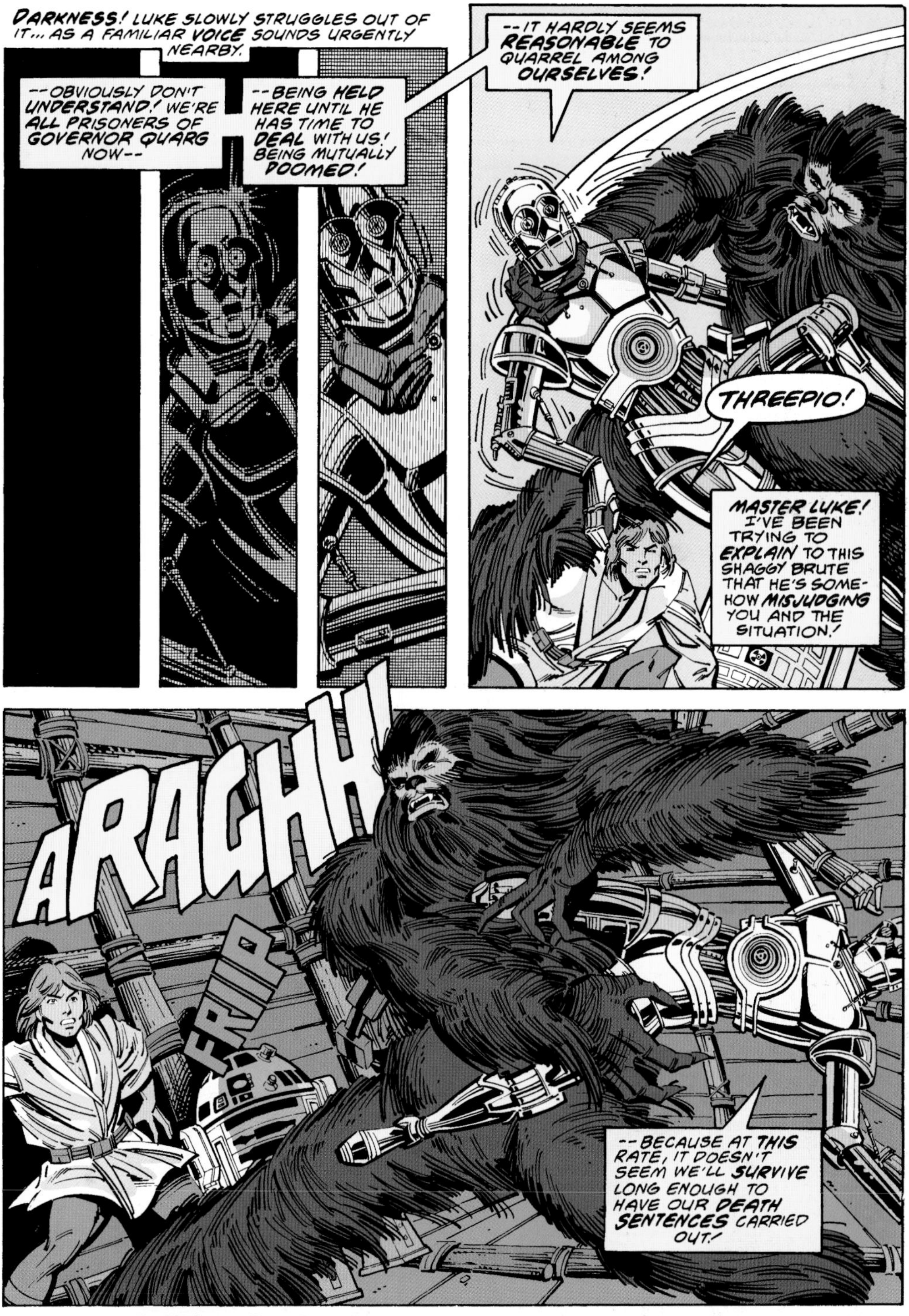
DARKNESS! LUKE SLOWLY STRUGGLES OUT OF IT... AS A FAMILIAR VOICE SOUNDS URGENTLY NEARBY.
--OBVIOUSLY DON'T UNDERSTAND! WE'RE ALL PRISONERS OF GOVERNOR QUARG NOW--
--BEING HELD HERE UNTIL HE HAS TIME TO DEAL WITH US! BEING MUTUALLY DOOMED!
--IT HARDLY SEEMS REASONABLE TO QUARREL AMONG OURSELVES!
THREEPIO!
MASTER LUKE! I'VE BEEN TRYING TO EXPLAIN TO THIS SHAGGY BRUTE THAT HE'S SOMEHOW MISJUDGING YOU AND THE SITUATION!
ARAGHH!
FRIIP
--BECAUSE AT THIS RATE, IT DOESN'T SEEM WE'LL SURVIVE LONG ENOUGH TO HAVE OUR DEATH SENTENCES CARRIED OUT!

NEXT ISSUE: CALL IT ARMAGEDDON!

STAR WARS ™

35¢

14
AUG
02817

AT LAST! BEYOND THE MOVIE! BEYOND THE GALAXY!

STAR WARS

THE SOUND OF ARMAGEDDON!

Long ago in a galaxy far, far away. . .there exists a state of cosmic *civil war*. A brave alliance of *underground freedom fighters* has challenged the tyranny and oppression of the awesome *Galactic Empire*. This is their story!

LucasFilm PRESENTS: STAR WARS THE GREATEST SPACE FANTASY OF ALL!

CONTINUING THE SAGA BEGUN IN THE FILM BY GEORGE LUCAS RELEASED BY 20th CENTURY-FOX

ARCHIE GOODWIN • WRITER/EDITOR

CARMINE INFANTINO and TERRY AUSTIN • ARTISTS

DENISE WOHL • LETTERER

JANICE COHEN • COLORIST

JAMES SHOOTER • CONSULTING EDITOR

THE SOUND OF ARMAGEDDON!

IT'S *HOPELESS*, ARTOO! NOTHING *ANY* OF US SAYS IS *REACHING* CHEWBACCA! HE'S CONVINCED MASTER LUKE PLAYED A *PART* IN HAN SOLO'S *DEATH*--

--AND HE WON'T *STOP* UNTIL HE TEARS *US* AND THIS ENTIRE *SHIP'S PRISON* TO PIECES!

THREEPIO! QUIT *TALKING* AND *HELP* ME!

"*WHAT* DO YOU *CALL* SOMEONE WHO FIGHTS AN ENRAGED WOOKIEE BAREHANDED?" "*DEAD.*"--OLD CANTINA JOKE.

LUKE SKYWALKER IS NOT *DEAD* YET. BUT HE'D BE THE *FIRST* TO ADMIT THAT THINGS DON'T LOOK *HOPEFUL* HERE ON THIS OBSCURE *WATERWORLD* OF THE STAR-SUN, *DREXEL.* FOR EVEN IF HE AND CHEWIE *RESOLVE* THEIR MIS-UNDERSTANDING...

...THEIR *FIGHT* IS BUT ONE SMALL, BARELY RELATED *INCIDENT* IN A MUCH, MUCH *WIDER WAR!*

AND JUST OUTSIDE THE HULL OF THE GREAT CITY-SHIP THAT *HOLDS* THEM, THAT WAR GOES ON IN ALL ITS *FURY*--

THE SEA DRAGONS ARE IN A *FRENZY*, GOVERNOR QUARG.... NO MATTER *WHAT* DAMAGE WE INFLICT, THEY *KEEP COMING!*

SOMEHOW, THEIR *MASTERS* KNOW I'M ONTO THE GREATEST *PRIZE* OF *ALL*, COMMANDER--

-- AND ARE WILLING TO *DESTROY* THEMSELVES TRYING TO *WREST* IT FROM ME!

BUT, YOUR *HONOR* .... IT'S *US* THAT'S *BEING DESTROYED* IF THINGS KEEP GOING AS THEY *ARE* .... WE WON'T HAVE A SKIMMER *LEFT!*

WE'VE GOT TO SET *SAIL*, SIR! MOVE THE *SHIP* BEFORE--

--AS SERPENT-RIDING *DRAGON LORDS* STORM AGAINST *HYDRA-SKIMMERS* OF THE SHIP DWELLERS!

IT IS A CONFLICT THAT HAS BEEN *BUILDING* FOR OVER A GENERATION... SINCE MEN FIRST *CRASHED* ON THIS HARSH PLANET AND ONE FACTION *SPLIT* FROM THE LARGER GROUP. NOW, THEY WAR... AND THIS MAY VERY WELL BE... *THE FINAL BATTLE!*

MOVE?! YOU MEAN *FLEE*, YOU COWARDLY SEA SCUD!

AND WE'D HAVE TO *SHUT DOWN* THE SONIC-JAMMER TO DO IT--

WAP!

--WHEN IT'S *LOCKED IN* ON THE BIGGEST *SPACECRAFT* WE'VE EVER NETTED!

IT'S *TOO BIG*, GOVERNOR! THE TECHNOS SAY THE JAMMER *CAN'T* BRING IT *DOWN!* WE'RE DRAWING ALL THE POWER FROM THE SHIP'S *ENGINES* JUST TRYING --

YOU'LL ALL TRY *HARDER OR HANG!*

IT'S *UP* THERE IN *ORBIT*, COMMANDER... AND I WANT IT!

"IT" WAS ONCE AN IMPERIAL CRUISER. WRECKED IN BATTLE, IT WAS REFITTED AND RECONDITIONED BY CRIMSON JACK AND HIS STAR PIRATES AT GREAT COST AND GREAT EFFORT...

...AND THE LAST THING THEY WANT IS TO SEE IT LOST ON A WORLD OF ENDLESS OCEAN!

CHIEF ENGINEER! HAVE YOU LEARNED WHAT IN THE CIVILIZED SYSTEMS HAS ITS CLAWS INTO US?!

SEEMS TO BE A JAMMER, CAP'N JACK! USES SONIC WAVES TO DISRUPT OUR DRIVE--

I HEARD IT WAS A FAVORITE TRICK OF SPACE WRECKERS IN THE KORTEEN ASTEROID BELT.

THEY MADE OUT SMARTLY STRIPPING CARGO FROM VESSELS THEY WRECKED... UNTIL THE OLD REPUBLIC PUT 'EM ON THE RUN! COULD BE THEY RAN TO THIS WORLD BELOW. *

I DON'T WANT A HISTORY LESSON, MAN ...CAN WE ESCAPE THE BLASTED THING?!

* A VERY GOOD GUESS... AS ALL READERS OF LAST ISSUE KNOW --ARCHIE.

IF OUR EMERGENCY DRIVE CAN OUTLAST THEIR JAMMER, CAP'N. RIGHT NOW... IT LOOKS LIKE A DRAW!

THIS IS THAT BLASTED HAN SOLO'S DOING!

HE LURED ME INTO THIS MESS WITH TALL TALES OF REBEL TREASURE JUST SO HE COULD RESCUE PRINCESS LEIA!

JOLLI! WHAT'S THE REPORT FROM THE HOLD?! HOW DID SOLO AND HIS FURRY FIRST MATE ESCAPE WITH THE WOMAN?

THEY TOOK ADVANTAGE OF THE CONFUSION WHEN THAT JAMMER THING HIT US... AND FOUGHT THEIR WAY TO THE MILLENNIUM FALCON!

IF THAT SMUGGLING SHIP CAN FLY... WHAT ABOUT ALL OUR BOARDING CRAFT?

SABOTAGED, CAP'N ...BEFORE THE THREE OF 'EM BLASTED OFF! THEY'RE LONG GONE AND IT'S PARTLY MY FAULT!

I WOULDN'T HAVE BEEN CAUGHT OFF GUARD NO MATTER WHAT HAPPENED... EXCEPT THAT PRINCESS KEPT FILLING MY HEAD WITH THOUGHTS ABOUT THINGS OTHER THAN PIRATING!

THINGS SUCH AS BEING ATTRACTED TO A MAN FOR THE FIRST TIME...A MAN LIKE HAN SOLO.

AND HAN SOLO, DESPITE THE WORST *FEARS* OF HIS WOOKIEE FRIEND, *CHEWBACCA* ...

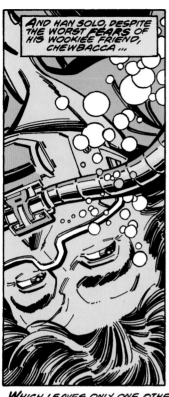

... AND DESPITE BEING *KNOCKED OFF* THE CRASH-LANDED *MILLENNIUM FALCON* BY A HYDRA-SKIMMER *CANNON BLAST* ...

... IS *ALIVE* AND *WET* AND IN THE *HANDS* OF THE *DRAGON LORDS!*

*WHICH LEAVES ONLY ONE OTHER STAR WARRIOR **UNACCOUNTED** FOR ... PRINCESS **LEIA ORGANA**, ONCE SENATOR FROM ALDERAAN, NOW A GUIDING FIGURE IN THE REBEL ALLIANCE ...*

... AND *TRAPPED* WITH HAN SOLO'S DOWNED SPACECRAFT!

THEY'VE STOPPED *TOWING* THE SHIP! THAT MEANS I CAN EXPECT *VISITORS* SOON ... !

THANK THE FORCE, THEIR *LASERS* DON'T SEEM TO BE FUNCTIONING AT *FULL STRENGTH.* IF HAN AND CHEWBACCA WEREN'T HIT *DIRECTLY--*

* IN THE *ATTACK* SHOWN LAST *MONTH*-- ARCHIE.

--THEY COULD HAVE *SURVIVED!* BUT SINCE I WASN'T OUT OF THE *HATCH* WHEN THE BLAST CAME ... I MAY BE THE ONLY *LUCKY* ONE!

IN WHICH CASE, I'LL *SEE* THAT THOSE SKIMMER-RIDING KILLERS DON'T GET AWAY *SCOT FREE* WITH WHAT THEY'VE DONE!

BUT AS PRINCESS LEIA SETS HER BLASTER FOR 'KILL'... NEW ATTENTION FALLS ON THE MILLENNIUM FALCON FROM HIGH ABOVE.

THERE'S A YEAR'S WORTH OF METAL AND SPARE PARTS IN THAT CRAFT YOUR HONOR!

WHY FIGHT TO HAUL DOWN THAT ORBITING MONSTER WHEN THIS ONE HAS FALLEN IN OUR LAPS?!

BECAUSE IF WE SUCCEED, IT WILL MEAN METAL, PARTS, AND PLUNDER FOR A LIFETIME, YOU DOLT--

--WE'LL HAVE WEAPONS ENOUGH TO WIPE THE SEA DRAGONS AND THEIR MASTERS OFF THIS WORLD FOREVER!

WE'LL MAKE THIS PLANET TRULY OURS... SOMETHING MY FOOL OF A FATHER WHO BROUGHT US HERE WAS NEVER ABLE TO DO!

BUT GOVERNOR QUARG--

--THE JAMMER ISN'T BUDGING THAT BIG STARSHIP! THE DRAGON LORDS WILL SINK US LONG BEFORE IT EVER HAS POWER ENOUGH TO!

YOU'RE SHOUTING YOURSELF TO DEATH, COMMANDER! THE SOLUTION FLOATS AT THE DOCK BELOW US.

BUT IT MEANS A REPRIEVE FOR THE MASTER MACHINE-SMITH AND HIS DROIDS!

WHICH MIGHT CHEER LUKE, THREEPIO, AND ARTOO-DEETOO... IF THEY LIVE TO HEAR ABOUT IT!

IT WORKED, SIR! YOU GOT HIM TO TRIP OVER ME--

BUT... WON'T HE BE EVEN ANGRIER WHEN HE GETS UP?!

ARTOO! NOW!

GROOWK!

USE YOUR EXTINGUISHER FULL BLAST!!

SPRAY FOAM SPEWS FROM THE R2 UNIT! FOAM GENERALLY USED TO SMOTHER THE FLAMES OF SHIP-TO-SHIP SPACE BATTLE...

...BUT WHICH NOW CHOKES OFF AIR AND SMOTHERS THE RAGING WOOKIEE WITH UNCONSCIOUSNESS.

≷WHEW!≷ THAT SAVES US FROM KILLING EACH OTHER FOR A WHILE, BUT--

SKYWALKER! GOVERNOR QUARG WANTS YOU AND YOUR MECHANICALS... NOW!

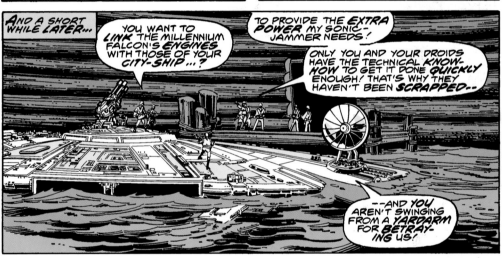

AND A SHORT WHILE LATER...

YOU WANT TO LINK THE MILLENNIUM FALCON'S ENGINES WITH THOSE OF YOUR CITY-SHIP...?

TO PROVIDE THE EXTRA POWER MY SONIC-JAMMER NEEDS!

ONLY YOU AND YOUR DROIDS HAVE THE TECHNICAL KNOW-HOW TO GET IT DONE QUICKLY ENOUGH! THAT'S WHY THEY HAVEN'T BEEN SCRAPPED--

--AND YOU AREN'T SWINGING FROM A YARDARM FOR BETRAYING US!

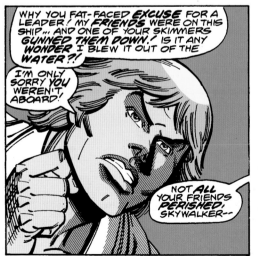

WHY YOU FAT-FACED EXCUSE FOR A LEADER! MY FRIENDS WERE ON THIS SHIP... AND ONE OF YOUR SKIMMERS GUNNED THEM DOWN! IS IT ANY WONDER I BLEW IT OUT OF THE WATER?!

I'M ONLY SORRY YOU WEREN'T ABOARD!

NOT ALL YOUR FRIENDS PERISHED, SKYWALKER--

--IT COST US A NUMBER OF GOOD MEN TO DIG OUT THIS HIDDEN SURVIVOR!

NOW SHALL I MAKE THE OBVIOUS THREATS... OR WILL YOU BEGIN WORK AT ONCE?

AS GOVERNOR QUARG SMILES TRIUMPHANTLY... SOMETHING *BRUSHES* AGAINST HIS BOOT.

HE KICKS OUT *AUTO-MATICALLY.* THE MOUSE-LIKE LIZARDS ARE SHIP-BOARD SCAVENGERS...

... *HARMLESS NUISANCES,* ALWAYS UNDERFOOT, SCARCELY WORTH A SECOND THOUGHT.

THIS *PARTICULAR* NUISANCE SWIMS TO THE PERIMETER OF *COMBAT...*

... WHERE IT ATTACHES ITSELF TO A WOUNDED *SEA DRAGON.* SOON...

... IT IS CARRIED *FAR* FROM THE CITY-SHIP TO AN UNDERWATER *MOUNTAIN* ...

...AND THE SECRET WORLD LOCKED *WITHIN* IT!

ANOTHER DRAGON *INJURED...!* THE BATTLE GROWS MORE *DEVASTATING* WITH EACH MOMENT!

WE'RE *FORTUNATE* TO HAVE GOTTEN YOU HERE WHEN WE *DID,* MISTER SOLO.

YEAH. THESE *AIR-POCKET CAVERNS* MAKE A REFRESHING BREAK IN SOME PRETTY *DAMP SCENERY.* FRIEND--

--AND IF YOU HADN'T *GRABBED* ME AFTER I WAS *STUNNED* BY THAT LASER BLAST, I'D HAVE *DROWNED* FOR SURE.

BUT, Y'KNOW.... THERE'S A *SUSPICIOUS SIDE* OF ME THAT KEEPS WON-DERING *WHY* YOU BOTHERED!

BECAUSE IN A WAR TO THE *DEATH* ...YOU CAN NEVER HAVE *TOO MANY* ALLIES!

INTERESTING *PHILOSOPHY*.

YOU *POSITIVE* THESE *KING-SIZE* SERPENTS *UNDERSTAND* IT?

ABSOLUTELY, MISTER SOLO. THEY *TAUGHT* IT TO US! IF THEY HAD FELT *OTHER-WISE*, WE SO-CALLED *DRAGON LORDS* WOULD HAVE PERISHED AT SEA A *GENERATION* AGO WHEN WE DESERTED THE CITY-SHIP!

THE *DRAGONS* ARE ...*INTEL-LIGENT* LIFE-FORMS?!

EXACTLY. WE DON'T *RULE* THEM ... WE *CO-EXIST* WITH THEM.

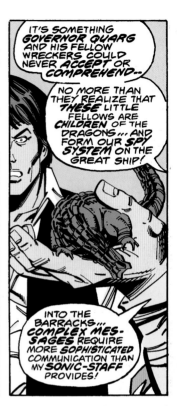

IT'S SOMETHING *GOVERNOR QUARG* AND HIS FELLOW *WRECKERS* COULD NEVER *ACCEPT* OR *COMPREHEND*--

NO MORE THAN THEY REALIZE THAT *THESE* LITTLE FELLOWS ARE *CHILDREN* OF THE *DRAGONS* ...AND FORM OUR *SPY SYSTEM* ON THE GREAT SHIP!

INTO THE *BARRACKS* ...*COMPLEX MES-SAGES* REQUIRE MORE *SOPHISTICATED* COMMUNICATION THAN MY *SONIC-STAFF* PROVIDES!

AND INSIDE QUARTERS CONSTRUCTED FROM SALVAGED PARTS OF WRECKED SPACECRAFT...

THEY COMMUNICATE WITH *SOUND*, RIGHT...? PITCHED *BEYOND* HUMAN HEARING AT *ULTRA-SONIC LEVELS!*

UNFORTUNATELY, WHAT'S *NOW* BEING COMMUNICATED IS *GRIM* INDEED! YOUR *SHIP* WILL BE USED TO AUGMENT THE POWER OF QUARG'S *SONIC-JAMMER*--

"ITS SOUND WAVES CAN DRIVE SOME DRAGONS MAD ...EACH TIME IT'S USED, THE MORE SENSITIVE ONES BECOME FRENZIED AND ATTACK! TODAY IT HAS OPERATED CONSTANTLY...

"...AND ITS EFFECT HAS *SPREAD!* THE ENTIRE SEA DRAGON POPULATION IS FEELING IT AND *FIGHTING* IT...

"...AND, AT THE MOMENT, *WINNING.*"

BUT IF IT GOES ON MUCH *LONGER* OR BECOMES ANY *STRONGER* ... THEN THE DRAGONS WILL *DIE*, MISTER SOLO.

SWIFTLY AND *TERRIBLY*--

--AS THE *SMALLER* AND MORE *VULNERABLE* AMONG THEM HAVE ALREADY *BEGUN* TO DO!

WE'VE GOT TO *STOP* THIS ... *NOW!* WE CAN'T HOLD *ANY-THING* IN RESERVE ... IT'S GOING TO TAKE EVERY *DRAGON* AND *RIDER* WHO CAN *MOVE!*

ARE YOU *WITH* US, MISTER SOLO?

DO I HAVE A *CHOICE?* THIS *CAVERN* ISN'T MY IDEA OF A GREAT PLACE TO SPEND THE *REST* OF MY LIFE!

YOU'RE MY ONLY *HOPE* OF GETTING BACK TO THE *MILLENNIUM FALCON!*

DON'T *COUNT* ON IT. NEXT TO GOVERNOR *QUARG'S SONIC-JAMMER* -- --YOUR *SHIP* IS OUR *PRIME TARGET!*

HUH...? HEY... *WAIT!*

BUT THE TIME FOR *WAITING* IS LONG *PAST!* SOON, THE *LAST* OF THE DRAGON LORDS AND THEIR SERPENT ALLIES SURGE TOWARD THE *BATTLE* ...

...AND THE AWE-SOME *DE-STRUCTION* THAT IT HOLDS!

DESTRUCTION. IT TAKES ON *MANY FACES* AND *FORMS* DURING THE LONG DAY OF *FIGHTING.* IT VISITS BOTH SIDES INDISCRIMINATELY... AND *OFTEN!*

SEA DRAGONS, SHIP DWELLERS, SERPENT RIDERS, SPACE WRECKERS. *ALL* FEEL ITS TOUCH ... *ALL* PAY THE *PRICE.*

SKYWALKER! THE DRAGON LORDS ARE SMASHING THROUGH THE *OUTER-FLOATS*... WHAT'S *TAKING* YOU AND THOSE ROBOTS SO *LONG?!*

MY MEN HAVE COM-PLETED *THEIR* PART OF THE TASK... MUST I START *HURTING* THE YOUNG LADY?

NO! THIS ISN'T LIKE RE-PAIRING *SKIMMERS* ...IT'S *COMPLICATED!*

HOW DOES IT *LOOK,* THREEPIO...? HIS 'HONOR' IS FUSSING WORSE THAN A *TUSKEN RAIDER* WITH A COLLAPSED *MOISTURE COLLECTOR!*

ARTOO IS *DOUBLE CHECKING* ALL CONNECTIONS ON THE *PRINT-OUT,* SIR.

IT *APPEARS* EVERYTHING WILL WORK JUST AS YOU *HOPED,* UNLESS --

--S-SOMETHING *UNFORESEEN* HAPPENS!

WHUNG!

OF ALL THE MOMENTS FOR A *SEA DRAGON* TO BREAK THROUGH THE *INNER-DEFENSES!*

HAVE ARTOO *ACTIVATE* THE LINK-UP WITH THE CITY-SHIP'S *ENGINES* BEFORE THAT THING BATTERS LOOSE ALL THE *CONNECTIONS* MADE BY QUARG'S MEN!

I'LL TRY TO SHUT THE *OUTER-HATCH* BEFORE WE'RE *FLOODED!*

*B*UT SOMEONE HAS *BEATEN* LUKE TO THE HATCH ... FROM THE *OTHER* SIDE!

A ... *DRAGON LORD!* LOOK ... YOUR MISSION IS PROBABLY TO *DESTROY* THIS SHIP! BUT YOU DON'T KNOW WHAT'S AT *STAKE* OR WHAT I--

KID--

-- EVERYTHING IS UNDER *CONTROL.*

HAN! Y-YOU'RE ... *ALIVE!*

WHAT *ELSE?* SELF-PRESERVATION IS MY *SPECIALTY,* KID! NOT THAT IT'S *EASY*--

I HAD TO EAT A LOT OF *OCEAN* TO BEAT THE OTHER *DRAGON LORDS* HERE! IF WE WANNA SAVE THE *FALCON,* WE'VE GOT TO STOP WHATEVER THOSE CRAZY *SPACE-WRECKERS* ARE HAVING YOU *DO!*

NO!

I'm **NOT** GOING TO LET YOU WALTZ IN AND **SPOIL** THINGS **NOW!**

WHACK!

THREEPIO! ARTOO! WHAT'S **HAPPENING** WITH THAT **LINK-UP?!**

VEEP DOOT BIRR

ACTIVATING EVEN AS WE **SPEAK**, MASTER LUKE!

KID, I **GOTTA** STOP YOU. THIS GOES **BEYOND** SAVING THE FALCON.

YOU'VE JUST GIVEN THAT GUY, **QUARG**, SOMETHING ALMOST AS DEADLY AS THE **DEATH STAR!**

HAN! PLEASE... DON'T **TRY** ANYTHING! JUST **WAIT** AND--

AND AS THE **POWER** OF THE MILLENNIUM FALCON'S ENGINES IS **ADDED** TO THE CITY-SHIP'S PULSING **SONIC-JAMMER**... THE **SOUND OF ARMAGEDDON** IS HEARD.

OR, MORE ACCURATELY... **FELT.**

GOVERNOR! SOMETHING'S **HAPPENING** TO THE **DRAGONS!**

THEY'RE FALLING... **DYING!**

255

IT SEEMS OUR MUTUAL FRIEND, *SKYWALKER*, HAS HANDED ME A DELIGHTFUL *BONUS*, GIRL.

BUT LET'S MAKE *CERTAIN* HIS WORK ALSO ACCOMPLISHED ITS *PRIMARY TASK*.

MOVE! WE'RE VISITING MY *SONIC-JAMMER* CREW!

MAKE THE TRIP *ALONE*, PUDGY! I'M *TIRED* OF BEING EVERYBODY'S *PAWN*!

AND NOW THAT YOU CAN'T ATTACK *LUKE* WITHOUT SPOILING YOUR *OWN* PLANS--

THWWMP!

--THERE'S *NO REASON* TO PUT UP WITH IT!

BUT WITH GUARDS ON THE DOCK BEHIND HER ... PRINCESS LEIA'S ONLY ESCAPE PATH LEADS WITHIN THE MASSIVE SHIP!

AFTER HER! I WANT HER *ALIVE* FOR HANGING IF *POSSIBLE*--

--BUT I WANT HER!

THE PURSUIT MOVES LOUDLY THROUGH THE DARK CORRIDORS OF THE VESSEL'S ELABORATELY SPRAWLING HOLD AREA ...

WHERE UNKNOWN TO THE PRINCESS ...

BRAKASH!

... AND FORGOTTEN BY GOVERNOR QUARG ...

... *HELP AWAITS!*

THE W-WOOKIEE...! B-BUT... HE WAS LAST REPORTED *UNCONSCIOUS* ... *SAFE* TO KEEP PRISONER!

GRROARK!

HE *HAD* TO WAKE UP *SOME* TIME, YOUR HONOR! OUR *SHOUTS* MUST'VE--

STOP HIM...! AT ANY COST--

--I'VE GOT TO KEEP AFTER THE GIRL!

AND GOVERNOR QUARG TURNS HIS BACK ON TWO GUARDS LONG KNOWN FOR THEIR LOYALTY ... AND UTTER LACK OF COMMON SENSE!

WAVES FROM THAT JAMMER WILL TURN THE DRAGONS' MINDS INTO MUSH, KID!

I CAN'T STAND BY AND LET YOU USE MY SHIP TO HELP!

HAN! WILL YOU LISTEN....!? IT SEEMS LIKE THIS LINK-UP AIDED GOVERNOR QUARG--

--BUT IT ALSO ELIMINATES THE JAMMER'S EFFECT ON THE FALCON! YOUR SHIP'S FULLY OPERATIONAL AGAIN, HAN--

--INCLUDING THE GUN SYSTEM!

HUH ?! KID, ARE YOU SAYIN--?

WE CAN BLAST QUARG'S SONIC-JAMMER TO ATOMS...! SAVE LEIA, THE DRAGONS AND EVERYONE ELSE!

AND, IN MOMENTS, THE FALCON'S CORRELLIAN SKIPPER IS ALL SET TO DO EXACTLY THAT....!

ARTOO'S CHECK OF THE PRINT-OUTS SHOWED THE JAMMER'S BEAMING APPARATUS GOES RIGHT UP THE CITY-SHIP'S MAIN-MAST, HAN--

BRING THAT DOWN ... AND THE WHOLE WAR IS OVER!

SHARP WORK, HOTSHOT! LEMME JUST CHECK THE SCOPE AND--

TROUBLE, KID! I'M ZEROED ON THE MAINMAST... AND LOOK!

THAT SILHOUETTE ON THE YARDARM! IT'S LEIA! B-BUT--

IF WE DON'T OPEN UP IN THE NEXT FEW MINUTES... NO-BODY'S GONNA BE ALIVE TO SAVE!

NOWHERE LEFT TO *RUN,* GIRL! I'D PREFER TO *HANG* YOU... ALONG WITH *SKYWALKER* AND THAT *WOOKIEE!*

HANGINGS ARE VERY GOOD FOR SHIP'S *DISCIPLINE,* YOU KNOW.

THAT'S WHY I KEEP SO MANY *PRISONERS* ON HAND.

HOWEVER, SINCE YOU MADE A *PERSONAL ATTACK* UPON ME, IT WILL BE *EQUALLY* GOOD FOR THE RABBLE TO SEE THAT THEIR ILLUSTRIOUS LEADER--

--CAN *DEAL* WITH IT PERSONALLY!

DON'T LOSE YOUR BALANCE *YET,* MY DEAR... I'D LIKE TO DO THIS *GRADUALLY.*

LEIA SWAYS, IT IS TEMPTING *NOT* TO ALLOW THIS SLOWLY ADVANCING *MADMAN,* BURNING THE *SUPPORT* AT HER FEET, THE *SATISFACTION...*

...BUT AS SHE TURNS TO CONTEMPLATE THE WATER FAR, FAR *BELOW*...

LUKE...!

THERE WAS NO *TIME* TO REACH THE MAINMAST... LUKE WENT FOR THE *NEAREST* ONE! THE FIGHT *UP* IT IS A *BLUR*... HE ONLY KNOWS HE HAS *REACHED* HIS GOAL AND MUST ACT *NOW!* UNFORTUNATELY...

...GOVERNOR *QUARG* KNOWS IT TOO!

HE *EXPECTS* HIS FIRST HASTY SHOT TO *MISS,* BUT KNOWS IT WILL *THROW OFF* THE BOY'S SWING...

THEN AS LUKE'S **BACK-SWING** BEGINS ... THE PRINCESS **LEAPS!**

... HE IS **WRONG!**

AND THE MAINMAST AND YARDARM WHICH HAVE **SUPPORTED** HER ...

... **DISAPPEAR** IN THE THUNDER OF THE MILLENNIUM FALCON'S **GUNS!**

IT IS THE **END** ... THOUGH THE ACTUAL **FIGHTING** CONTINUES ON INTO THE NIGHT. BY THE FIRST GLOW OF DAWN, EVEN **THAT** IS LONG OVER. AND A NEW, AND HOPEFULLY **BETTER**, ERA COMES TO THE CITY-SHIP.

THERE'S NO WAY WE CAN **REWARD** YOU AND YOUR FRIENDS, MISTER SKYWALKER ... BUT OUR **THANKS** WILL BE WITH YOU **FOREVER.**

SPEAKING FOR **MYSELF** ... I'M **GLAD** JUST TO HAVE MY MISUNDERSTANDING WITH **CHEWBACCA** STRAIGHTENED OUT--

--AND FOR THE BUNCH OF US TO FINALLY BE **TOGETHER** AGAIN! JUST LIKE OLD TIMES, **RIGHT,** HAN?

HAN ...?

BUT HAN SOLO IS STARING AT THE **SKY,** DEEP IN **THOUGHT** ... ABOUT A GREAT BATTLE CRUISER WHICH MAY STILL **BE** THERE ... AND ITS MASTER, **CRIMSON JACK!**

NEXT ISSUE **SHOWDOWN!!**

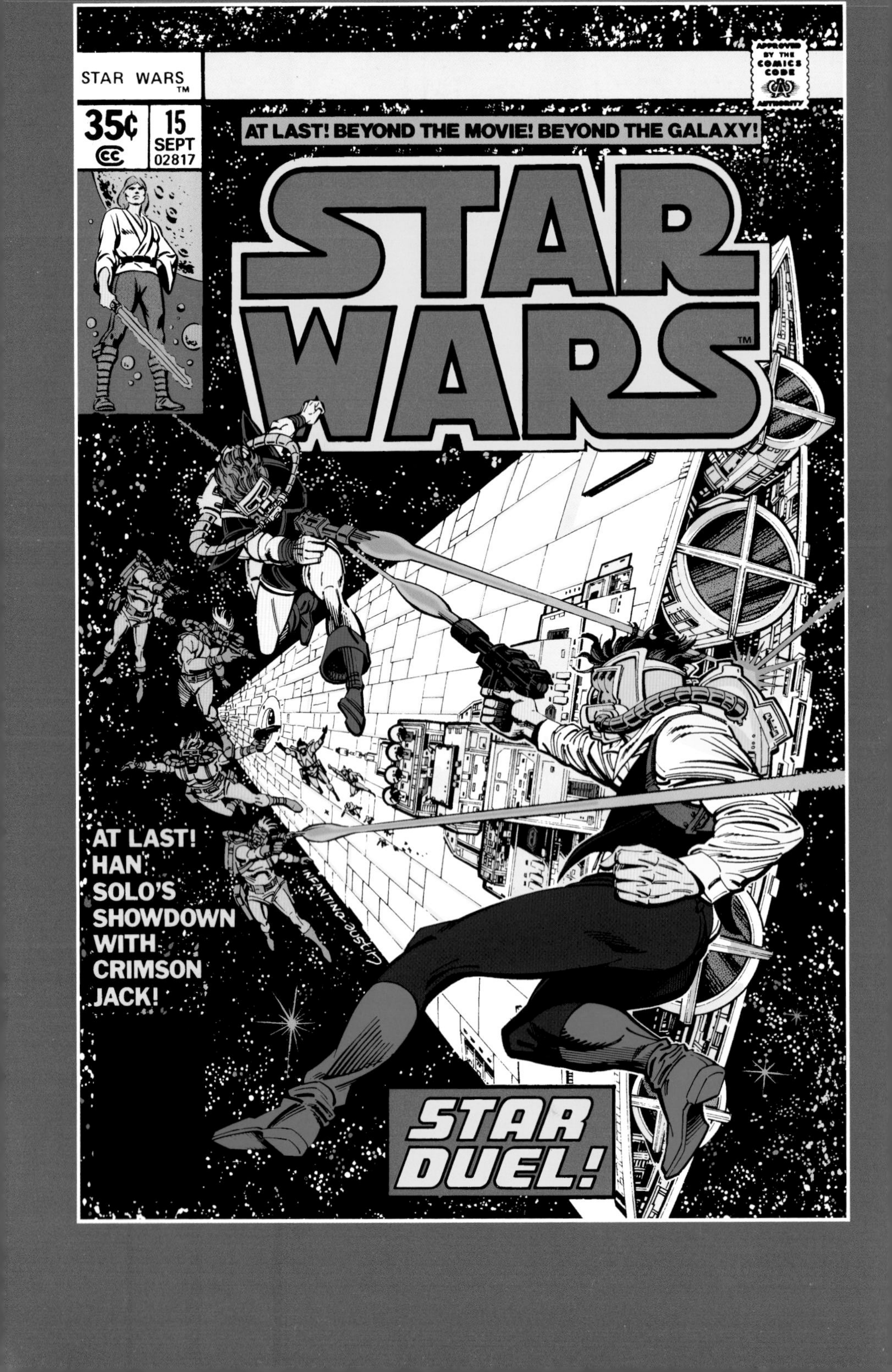

STAR WARS ™
35¢
CC
15
SEPT
02817
APPROVED BY THE COMICS CODE AUTHORITY
AT LAST! BEYOND THE MOVIE! BEYOND THE GALAXY!
STAR WARS ™
AT LAST! HAN SOLO'S SHOWDOWN WITH CRIMSON JACK!
STAR DUEL!

Long ago in a galaxy far, far away. . .there exists a state of cosmic *civil war*. A brave alliance of *underground freedom fighters* has challenged the tyranny and oppression of the awesome *Galactic Empire*. This is their story!

LucasFilm PRESENTS: **STAR WARS** THE GREATEST SPACE FANTASY OF ALL!

STAR DUEL!

CONTINUING THE SAGA BEGUN IN THE FILM BY GEORGE LUCAS RELEASED BY TWENTIETH CENTURY-FOX

ARCHIE GOODWIN • **CARMINE INFANTINO** & **TERRY AUSTIN** • **JOHN COSTANZA** • **JANICE COHEN** • **JIM SHOOTER**
WRITER/EDITOR — ARTISTS — letterer — colorist — CONSULTING EDITOR

HIGH ABOVE THE LONE PLANET OF THE STAR-SUN **DREXEL** HANGS THE PIRATE CRUISER OF **CRIMSON JACK**. UNTIL RECENTLY, IT WAS **TRAPPED** IN ITS ORBIT AROUND THE UNNAMED OCEAN-COVERED WORLD BELOW...

...BUT EVENTS ON THE PLANET'S SURFACE HAVE **CHANGED** ALL THAT!

IT'S FOR **CERTAIN**, CAP'N JACK! THE **SONIC-JAMMER** THAT WAS HOLDIN' US HERE HAS BEEN **KNOCKED OUT**--

LET'S PUT SOME **LIGHT YEARS** BETWEEN US AN' THIS CURSED **SYSTEM!**

I'M NOT AFTER **ESCAPE**, CHIEF ENGINEER... I'M AFTER **BLOOD!** **HAN SOLO'S** IN PARTICULAR--

AND I WANT **EVERY SCANNER** COMBING THAT WATERBALL UNTIL OUR SLIPPERY CORELLIAN **SPACE HOUND** IS TURNED UP!

BUT, **CAP'N...!** HE SURELY WARPED OUT OF THIS SECTOR THE MINUTE HIM AN' HIS **WOOKIEE PAL** GRABBED THAT **REBEL PRINCESS** FROM US. *

* AS SHOWN IN **STAR WARS** #13 --ASTRAL ARCHIE.

HAS EVERYONE BUT **ME** GOT A **BLACK HOLE** FOR A BRAIN?!

BACK TO YOUR STATION!

SOLO WENT TO TOO MUCH **TROUBLE** GETTING US TO THIS SYSTEM, **THIS** WORLD...! **SOMETHING** DOWN THERE **INTERESTED** HIM AND PRINCESS LEIA! SO--

CAP'N! I THINK WE'VE **GOT** 'EM!

JOLLI! HOW'S YOUR **REPAIR GANG** COMING WITH OUR **FIGHTER CRAFT...?**

CONSIDERING HOW **FAST** HE HAD TO WORK, THAT SMOOTH-TALKIN' SPICE SMUGGLER DID QUITE A JOB OF **SABOTAGING** THEM--

I DON'T **NEED** A REVIEW OF HIS **HANDIWORK,** GIRL! WILL ANY OF OUR SHIPS **FLY?!**

AT LEAST *THREE* WILL BE SERVICEABLE *SHORTLY*, CAP'N. AND WITH A BIT MORE *WORK*, WE'LL--

GOOD ENOUGH!

YOU WERE *ITCHING* TO PUT A BLASTER TO MISTER SOLO FROM THE *SECOND* YOU SAW HIM, JOLLI--

--I'M GOING TO GIVE YOU THE CHANCE TO *INDULGE* YOUR BLOODTHIRSTY STREAK TO THE *FULLEST!*

JOLLI *NODS* TO THE REPAIR BAY COMMUNICATOR SCREEN. THIS IS THE KIND OF TASK SHE'S *PUSHED* FOR EVER SINCE BECOMING A SPACE PIRATE. TO BE HARDER, *TOUGHER* THAN ANY *MAN* AROUND HER...

...EVEN A MAN SHE HAS COME TO HAVE DECIDEDLY *CONFUSED FEELINGS* ABOUT. A MAN NOW PINPOINTED AS BEING ON THE BARELY-CHARTED WORLD *BELOW* THEM. A MAN NAMED...

--HAN SOLO! IF YOU LIKE THAT *SHIP'S RAILING* SO MUCH PERHAPS WE CAN TAKE IT BACK TO THE *MOONS OF YAVIN* WITH US!

THE PRINCESS IS *RIGHT*, HAN. THE BIG *WAR* BETWEEN THE DRAGON RIDERS AND THE CITY-SHIP DWELLERS IS FINALLY *ENDED--*

WHY STAND *WATCH* AT THE RAIL?

* IN AN *EPIC BATTLE* WITNESSED *LAST ISSUE.*-- ARCHIE.

BECAUSE *UNFINISHED BUSINESS* SEEMS TO HAVE A WAY OF *CATCHING UP* WITH ME, KID.

AND WHEN IT COMES WITH A *RED BEARD* AND AN EQUALLY *FLAMING EGO...* I *GUARANTEE* IT!

CRIMSON JACK...!

EXACTLY, YOUR HIGHNESS! LUKE AND I SAVED THE DAY FOR THE *DRAGONS* AND THEIR *RIDERS* WHEN WE BLASTED AWAY THE SHIP'S *SONIC-JAMMER*--

--BUT THAT ALSO *FREES* JACK'S CRUISER! HE'LL HAVE IT PRIMED TO *ATTACK* WHEN WE *DEPART* THIS SOMEWHAT *SOGGY PARADISE.*

FOR YOUR PART IN *OVERTHROWING* THE RUTHLESS GOVERNOR QUARG, * YOU'RE MOST WELCOME TO *STAY* HERE--

* ALSO PART OF *LAST ISSUE'S* AWESOME ACTION.-- ARCH.

--BUT I GATHER, MY FRIENDS, YOU HAVE YOUR *OWN* WAR TO WAGE.

SOME OF US AT ANY RATE... ONCE *CHEWIE* AND THE *DROIDS* FINISH CHECKING OUT THE *MILLENNIUM FALCON.*

HEY, THREEPIO! WHAT'S THE *GOOD WORD...?*

IT REALLY DEPENDS ON WHICH *LANGUAGE*, MASTER SOLO. AFTER ALL, I *AM* PROGRAMMED TO SPEAK A RATHER *WIDE VARIETY* AND IN *EACH* OF THEM THERE'S --

THAT'S *NOT* WHAT I MEANT, ALLOY HEAD! I MEANT--

THREEPIO... GET DOWN!

YOU MEANT *THAT*, SIR? BUT WHAT'S SO *GOOD* ABOUT--

AND AS THE Y-WING FIGHTER *DIVES*, ALL GUNS *BLAZING*, A FIGURE ON THE SPRAWLING CITY-SHIP...

...DOES SOME DIVING OF HIS *OWN!*

HAN!

MOVE, KIDS! IF WE'RE NOT *STAR-BORN* IN RECORD TIME--

--CRIMSON JACK'S *EMISSARY* IS GONNA *SINK* OUR TRANSPORTATION WHERE SHE *FLOATS!*

HE ALWAYS *WAS* VERY BRAVE...BUT *SLOPPY!* I THOUGHT HE PUT ALL THOSE PIRATE *PURSUIT SHIPS* OUT OF COMMISSION!

UH...SPEAKING OF *BRAVERY,* LEIA...ER... *PRINCESS.* THERE'S SOMETHING I'VE BEEN KEEPING *HIDDEN* SINCE THE DROIDS AND I FIRST *CRASHED* ON THIS PLANET--

--*I CAN'T SWIM!*

PLASH!

MEANTIME, THE HAMMERING AT THE MILLENNIUM FALCON *MOUNTS!*

RORKOWR!

SLOWER, YOU GREAT HUNK OF HAIR--

--WOOKIEE IS NOT ONE OF MY PRIMARY LANGUAGES! OBVIOUSLY YOU GOT THE DEFLECTOR SHIELDS UP IN TIME! NOW WHAT'S THIS ABOUT--

--AN OVER-HEAD FIRING TOGGLE?! ARTOO, DO YOU HAVE ANY NOTION WHAT THE SURLY CREATURE IS--

BWEET VRR-POOT!

IT'S THIS...? THEN JUST SAY SO WITHOUT ANY NASTY EMBELLISHMENTS ABOUT MY CHARACTER! NOW, WHAT'S IT SUPPOSED TO--

FTOOM!

BAROOSH!

OH--!

WELL, MY SPECIALTIES OF TRANSLATION AND PROTOCOL HARDLY COVER THAT!

PADDLE FASTER, KIDS! CHEWIE'S BUYING US SOME TIME--

--BUT THE WAY THAT FIGHTER PILOT'S SCORING, THE FALCON'S DEFLECTORS MAY NOT BE UP TO ANOTHER PASS!

I'M TRYING, HAN! LIFE ON A DESERT PLANET LIKE TATOOINE DIDN'T EXACTLY PREPARE ME FOR THIS!

YOU'RE DOING FINE, LUKE--

SAVE THE PEP TALK FOR LATER, YOUR WORSHIP--

INSIDE QUICK... OR WE'LL GET OUR TAILS BURNED!

...*POUNDED* BY FIERY ENERGY BOLTS FROM THE PURSUING Y-WING FIGHTER!

WHAT A WAY TO SAY *GOOD-BYE* TO A WORLD WE JUST *SAVED*--!

KID, I CAN'T RECALL MAKING ANYTHING *BUT* FAST EXITS WHENEVER *YOU'RE* ABOARD MY SHIP!

ONLY *THIS* ONE ISN'T MADE *YET!* YOU TOO *WET* TO MAN A *GUN,* HOTSHOT?

OF *COURSE* NOT! BUT I'D THINK THE *FALCON* COULD LEAVE ONE CRUDDY *Y-WING-ER* EATING ITS *AFTER-BLAST!*

DEAD *RIGHT,* MISTER SKYWALKER. BUT MY OL' PAL, *CRIMSON JACK*--

--*NEVER* MADE IT THAT *EASY* FOR ANYONE! AND FOR *ME*--

--HE'S *BOUND* TO GO *ALL OUT!*

COUNT YOURSELF *CORRECT,* CAPTAIN SOLO! THE *WALKING CARPET* YOU CALL A *FIRST MATE* IS MAKING NOISES ABOUT SOMETHING ON THE *SCOPE*--

GRORWK!

--A *PAIR* OF HOSTILES!

PLUS THE ONE COMIN' UP *BEHIND* US...! STAY *LOOSE,* LUKE... IT'S GONNA BE LIKE *OLD TIMES!*

OLD TIMES. LUKE THINKS OF THEIR ESCAPE FROM THE *DEATH STAR**. THE PAIN OF LOSING HIS MENTOR, *BEN KENOBI*, STILL FRESH UPON HIM. THIS ISN'T *THAT* BAD. AT LEAST... NOT *YET!*

KEEP *POURING* IT ON, KID.! OUT OF THE *GALACTIC SLUDGE* JACK USES AS HIS *CREW*, HE'S FIELDED THREE PRETTY FAIR *STAR-PILOTS!* PARTICULARLY--

* SHOWN IN THE NOW-CLASSIC *STAR WARS* #4 & 5. --ARCHIE.

"--WHOEVER'S HANDLING THAT *Y-WING!*"

KEEP YOUR *DISTANCE*, RAIDER TWO AND THREE! THAT SMUGGLING SHIP IS BETTER *ARMED* AND *SHIELDED* THAN IT APPEARS!

JUST WORRY THEM *ALONG*... THE WAY THE CAP'N *WANTED!*

AYE, JOLLI--

--WE KNOW OUR *JOB!* YOU DON'T HAVE TO KEEP *PROVIN'* THAT YOU'RE OUR FLIGHT *COMMANDER!*

AT THESE WORDS, JOLLI *TENSES*. AND IN THE FIERY LASER BLASTS *BEFORE* HER, SHE BEGINS TO SEE THE FLAMES OF *ANOTHER* PLACE AND TIME...

...FLAMES RAGING THROUGH AN *OUTLAW STRONGHOLD* ON A FRONTIER WORLD.

BLASTED *IMPERIALS* HAVE FOUND US *AGAIN*, WOMAN! IT'S TIME FOR MOVIN' *FAST* AN' TRAVELIN' *LIGHT!*

Y-YOU'RE... NOT... *LEAVING* US...?

OF *COURSE* I AM! THE LAST THING A *FUGITIVE* FROM THE *EMPIRE* NEEDS IS *EXCESS BAGGAGE* WEIGHIN' HIM DOWN!

B-BUT...I'M YOUR *WIFE!* JOLLI'S YOUR *CHILD!*

WE'LL *HELP* YOU... *FIGHT* WITH YOU!

FORGET IT, WOMAN... YOU'RE NOT *GOOD* ENOUGH!

WITHOUT FURTHER *WORD*, THE MAN WAS *GONE*, LEAVING GIRL AND MOTHER *ALONE*...

...UNTIL AN *AERIAL TORPEDO* STRUCK! THE WOMAN FAILED TO *SURVIVE*, BUT HER *CHILD* LIVED. LIVED TO BECOME...

...A *MAN-HATER* AND *SPACE-PIRATE*, EVER READY TO *PROVE* THAT SHE'S "*GOOD ENOUGH!*"

THAT *HAN SOLO* STIRRED UP SOME *STRANGE FEELINGS* INSIDE ME WHILE HE AND PRINCESS LEIA WERE OUR *PRISONERS*--

--BUT *NOW'S* THE MOMENT WHEN I *SHOW* THE GALAXY I CAN WRITE THE *END* TO *ANY* MAN!

HAN! THE *PIRATE CRUISER* IS *LOOMING* AHEAD!

THOSE *PURSUIT SHIPS* AREN'T TRYING TO GUN US *DOWN*... THEY'RE *DRIVING* US INTO ITS *TRACTOR BEAM!*

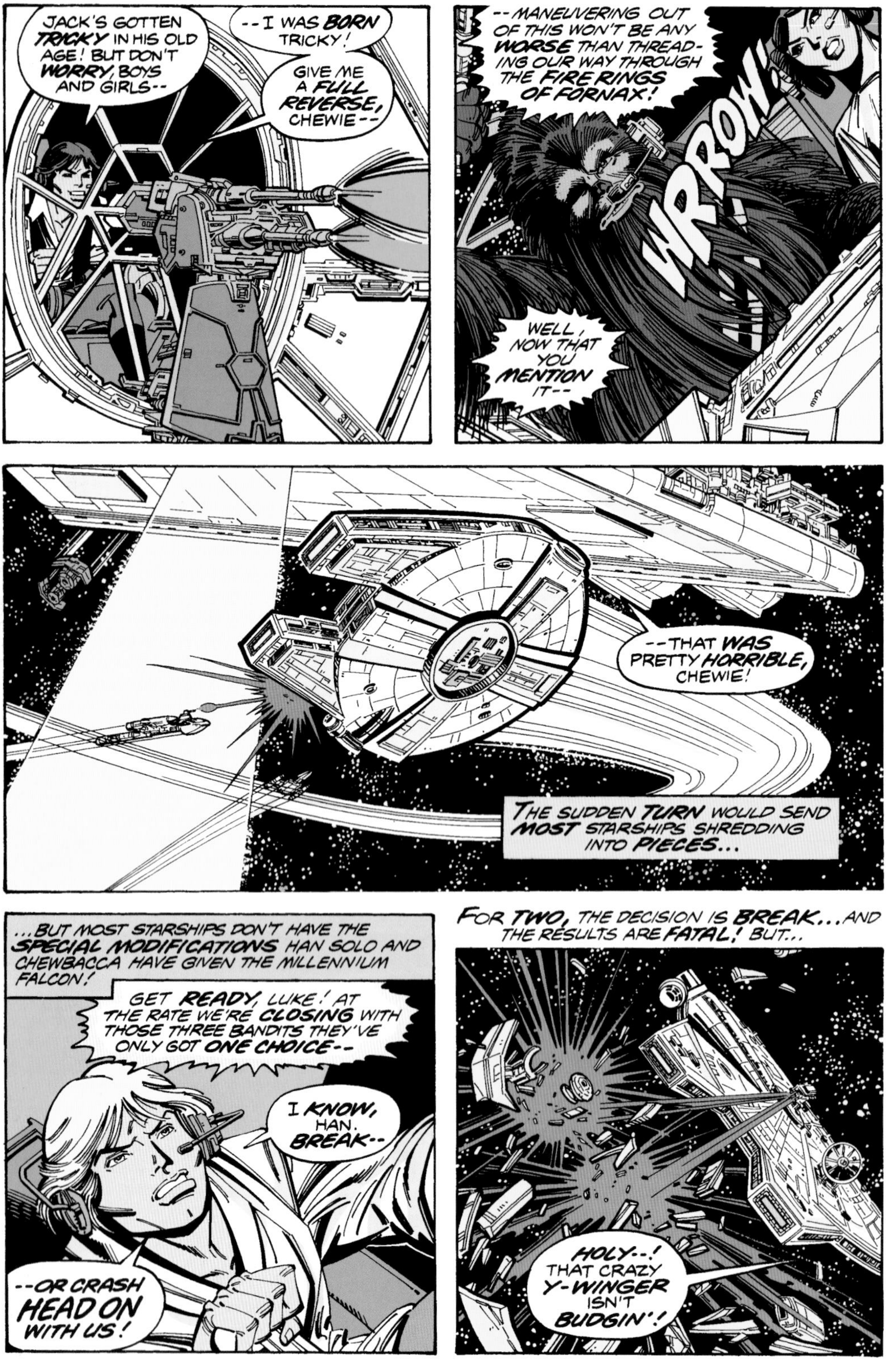
JACK'S GOTTEN TRICKY IN HIS OLD AGE! BUT DON'T WORRY, BOYS AND GIRLS--
--I WAS BORN TRICKY!
GIVE ME A FULL REVERSE, CHEWIE--
--MANEUVERING OUT OF THIS WON'T BE ANY WORSE THAN THREADING OUR WAY THROUGH THE FIRE RINGS OF FORNAX!
WRROW!
WELL, NOW THAT YOU MENTION IT--
--THAT WAS PRETTY HORRIBLE, CHEWIE!
THE SUDDEN TURN WOULD SEND MOST STARSHIPS SHREDDING INTO PIECES...
...BUT MOST STARSHIPS DON'T HAVE THE SPECIAL MODIFICATIONS HAN SOLO AND CHEWBACCA HAVE GIVEN THE MILLENNIUM FALCON!
GET READY, LUKE! AT THE RATE WE'RE CLOSING WITH THOSE THREE BANDITS THEY'VE ONLY GOT ONE CHOICE--
I KNOW, HAN. BREAK--
--OR CRASH HEAD ON WITH US!
FOR TWO, THE DECISION IS BREAK...AND THE RESULTS ARE FATAL! BUT...
HOLY--! THAT CRAZY Y-WINGER ISN'T BUDGIN'!

SUICIDE ISN'T JOLLI'S AIM. SHE MEANS TO CLEAR THE FALCON, BUT WITHOUT BECOMING A TARGET...

SHRAAK!

...AND SHE COMES VERY CLOSE TO SUCCEEDING!

HAN! LUKE! CAN EITHER OF YOU AS- CERTAIN DAMAGE DONE?!

THE SHIP'S GOING CRAZY!

OORK!

FELT LIKE THAT Y-WING WAS TAKING MY GUN TURRET WITH IT, PRINCESS... BUT I THINK IT ONLY SCRAPED US!

AT LEAST THE HULL'S INTACT... OR WE WOULDN'T STILL BE BREATHING!

THAT'S THE GOOD NEWS, KID --

-- THE BAD IS THAT "SCRAPE" MUST HAVE DAMAGED OUR GYRO CONTROL MODULE! THAT'S WHY WE'RE YAWLING LIKE THIS!

SHUT HER DOWN, CHEWIE! WE'LL TRY TO MAKE REPAIRS!

WASTED EFFORT, MISTER SOLO...YOU'RE ONLY MOMENTS AWAY FROM BEING VAPORIZED!

WHY, *JACK...*! GLAD YOU WERE ABLE TO *BREAK IN* ON OUR CHANNEL. SAVES ME THE TROUBLE OF *CONTACTING* YOU!

YOU'RE WELCOME TO BEG FOR *MERCY* RIGHT UP TO THE SECOND WE *OPEN FIRE,* SMUGGLER.

I'M *TOUCHED,* RED-BEARD! BUT BEFORE YOU DO ANY *BLAST-ING...* BETTER CHECK YOUR CRUISER'S *NAVIGATION COMPUTER.*

WHAT'S THAT CRAZY CORELLIAN UP TO *NOW...*?!

LUKE! GET THE *DROIDS* OUTSIDE... SEE IF ARTOO-DEETOO CAN DO ANYTHING ABOUT THAT *GYRO CONTROL MODULE.*

I'M TURNING DOWN THE COMMUNICATION SYSTEM'S *VOLUME--*

"--THAT PIRATE SHIP IS GOING TO BE TRANSMITTING SOME VERY *LOUD NOISE!*"

WHAT--?!

GONE, CAP'N JACK! *ALL* GONE--

--EVERY *CHART* THAT WAS IN OUR *NAVI-COMPUTER!* AN' *WITHOUT* 'EM, WE'RE *STUCK* IN THIS SYSTEM!

UNLESS WE WANT TO CALCULATE HYPER-SPACE JUMPS BY *GUESS-WORK...* AN' CHANCE PLOWIN' INTO A *NOVA* OR WORSE!

THIS IS *SOLO'S* DOING! BUT *HOW,* BLAST IT...? *HOW?!*

WAM!

YOU *MUST* REMEMBER BACK WHEN WE WERE YOUR "*GUESTS*", JACK....! TO USE SOME OF THE *MILLENNIUM FALCON'S* CHARTS, YOU PERMITTED MY *FIRST MATE* TO TAP *OUR* COMPUTER SYSTEM INTO *YOURS*--*

YOU WOULDN'T *THINK* ANY-ONE THAT BIG AND FURRY COULD BE A *SNEAK*...BUT CHEWIE TOOK *ADVANTAGE* OF THE SITUATION AND TRANSFERRED ALL *YOUR* CHARTS INTO *OUR* COMPUTER!

✱ AS SHOWN WAY BACK IN *ISSUES 11 & 12*.--ARCHIE.

TO SPELL IT OUT FOR THE *SLOWER* STUDENTS ON YOUR BRIDGE, JACK...VAPORIZE *US* AND YOU VAPORIZE YOUR CHANCES OF EVER GETTING *HOME* AGAIN!

TOLD YOU I WAS BORN TRICKY, KIDS! NOW IF THE DROIDS HAVE ANY *LUCK* WITH THAT GYRO CONTROL *MODULE*--

--WE *MAY* EVEN GET OUT OF THIS *ALIVE*!

ARTOO-DEETOO, CAN'T YOU *HURRY*? I HATE SPACE TRAVEL WHEN I'M *INSIDE* A SHIP... *THIS* POSITIVELY CURDLES EACH OF MY CAPACITATORS!

VREEP ADOOT BIP!

THE MODULE IS *BEYOND* REPAIR...IT HAS TO BE *REPLACED*? I DON'T THINK THAT BODES WELL AT *ALL*, ARTOO!

AND *MOST* ABOARD THE FALCON WOULD *AGREE*...

...PARTICULARLY HAN!

JACK, I *ORIGINALLY* INTENDED TO FIGHT MY WAY TO *WARP POINT*...THEN *BARGAIN* WITH YOU FOR THE *TREASURE* YOU STOLE FROM ME.✱

BUT RIGHT *NOW*, I NEED SOMETHING FROM YOUR CRUISER'S *SUPPLIES* ALMOST AS MUCH AS YOU NEED *NAVIGATION CHART TAPES*...! CAN WE MAKE EACH OTHER *HAPPY*?

I'M ALWAYS WILLING TO *TRY*, MISTER SOLO--

✱ AN INCIDENT FROM THE HISTORIC HAPPENINGS IN *STAR WARS* #7.--ARCH AGAIN.

AND AFTER A *MAXIMUM* OF HAGGLING, TERMS OF *EXCHANGE* ARE AGREED UPON...

HAN, HOW CAN YOU BE *SURE* CRIMSON JACK WON'T PULL A *FAST ONE?*

I'LL BE DISAPPOINTED IF HE *DOESN'T*, KID...LIFE OUGHT TO HAVE A *FEW* CONSISTENCIES!

NOW LOOK THE *OTHER* WAY--

--SO I CAN KISS THE PRINCESS *GOOD-BYE* WITHOUT FEELING *GUILTY.*

WHILE ABOARD THE MASSIVE *PIRATE CRUISER*...

--AND ON *MY* SIGNAL, YOU'LL *STRIKE!*

CAP'N JACK! *JOLLI'S* ON THE COMMUNICATOR...! SAYS THAT *SCRAPE* WITH THE MILLENNIUM FALCON SENT HER SHIP OUT OF *CONTROL*--

--NOW IT'S *BREAKIN' UP!* SHE NEEDS A *MAGNETIC PULSE BEAM* TO HELP PULL 'ER BACK TO THE *SHIP!*

"*TOO BAD*," SAYS JACK, "I'VE ALWAYS BEEN RATHER *FOND* OF JOLLI, BUT A PULSE BEAM *MIGHT* INTERFERE WITH MY *SIGNAL SYSTEM.*

"TELL OUR LITTLE SPITFIRE SHE'LL HAVE TO MAKE IT ON HER *OWN*--"

--IF SHE'S *GOOD ENOUGH.*

AND CRIMSON JACK SWIFTLY *FORGETS* ABOUT THE GIRL IN THE Y-WING FIGHTER...

...HE HAS A *RENDEZVOUS* IN SPACE.

YOU'RE WEARING A *BLASTER,* SOLO! WE BOTH AGREED... *NO WEAPONS!*

WE BOTH KNEW WE WERE *LYING,* REDBEARD, LET'S GET ON TO *BUSINESS*--

IT MAKES ME *UNEASY* OPERATING WITH JUST A *BREATH MASK*... EVEN IF WE *ARE* PROTECTED BY YOUR CRUISER'S *MAGNETIC FIELD!*

FULL ARMOR COULD HIDE ANYTHING FROM A PROTON GRENADE TO YOUR WOOKIEE FIRST MATE--

--THIS LEAVES MUCH LESS TO DOUBT! THE TAPE, PLEASE.

RIGHT! I ASSUME YOU HAVE A CONCEALED MICRO-SCANNER LIKE ME...TO MAKE CERTAIN YOU'RE GETTING THE REAL THING.

PITY WE COULDN'T BE PARTNERS, HAN...WE THINK SO MUCH ALIKE.

WE'D ALWAYS BE WORRIED THAT THE OTHER ONE WOULD THINK OF IT FASTER, JACK--

--LIKE NOW!

AND AS THE PIRATE JABS AT A STUD ON HIS HARNESS...

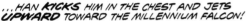

...HAN KICKS HIM IN THE CHEST AND JETS UPWARD TOWARD THE MILLENNIUM FALCON!

YOU WON'T MAKE IT, SMUGGLER... NOT ALIVE! THAT SIGNALLED FOR THE MAGNETIC FIELD TO BE TIGHTENED--

--NOW THERE'S A VACUUM BETWEEN YOU AND YOUR SHIP!

AND A MAN UNARMORED IN THE VACUUM OF DEEP SPACE WILL FIND HIS BLOOD BOILING IN SECONDS!

AGAINST THAT ALTERNATIVE...THE FALCON'S SKIPPER ELECTS TO MAKE A HEROIC STAND!

LOOKS LIKE JACK CALLED OUT EVERY SPACE RAT WHO COULD CARRY A BLASTER!

NO QUESTION OF ESCAPE NOW, JUST HOW MANY CAN I GET--

--BEFORE THEY GET ME?!

*YET AS HAN SOLO PREPARES TO **DIE**, A SHATTERED **Y-WING FIGHTER** LIMPS INTO VIEW, CANNONS BLAZING...*

*...AND A **COLD VOICE** ECHOING THROUGH EVERY INTER-COM!*

IS THIS GOOD ENOUGH, CAP'N? **IS IT?!**

JOLL! YOU LITTLE **TRAITOR!** YOU'RE BLASTING YOUR OWN **MATES--**

YOU'RE--

SHE'S SWERVIN' TOWARD THE SHIP'S **MUNITIONS DECK**, CAP'N! IF SHE'S STILL GOT **LIVE TORPEDOES--**

*CRIMSON JACK TRIES TO THINK OF SOMETHING HE CAN SAY TO **STOP** THE GIRL, TO **REVERSE** WHAT'S **ALREADY** BEEN SAID...*

*...AND FINDS IT'S **TOO LATE!***

BAKWOM!

GONE! THE BEST PIRATING OPERATION IN THE **GALAXY...!** DESTROYED BECAUSE OF A **MAD WOMAN** AND A FAST-TALKING **CORELLIAN!**

I WAS FAR ENOUGH FROM THE BLAST TO **SURVIVE...** BUT EVERYONE ELSE IS **GONE!**

NOT QUITE, JACK--

--THANKS TO JOLLI, **I'M** STILL AROUND!

SOLO! I MIGHT'VE **KNOWN** IT'D COME DOWN TO JUST **YOU** AND **ME**--

NO, JACK--

--JUST **ME!**

THE **REST** IS A MATTER OF ARRANGING FOR ONE OF THE **DROIDS** TO PICK UP THE GYRO CONTROL MODULE...

...AND MAKING A **SEARCH** THROUGH THE WRECKAGE AND DEBRIS.

SHE CLAIMED TO **HATE** MEN, BUT WHERE YOU WERE CONCERNED, HAN, I HAD THE FEELING--

MAYBE SO.

LET'S GET **MOVING,** PEOPLE--

IT'S A **LONG TRIP** HOME!

THEN, IN THE GRADUALLY FADING **ATMOSPHERE** OF THE DYING CRUISER, AN UNHAPPY LADY NAMED **JOLLI**...

...RECEIVES HER FIRST--AND LAST--**KISS.**

NEXT ISSUE: THE HUNTER!

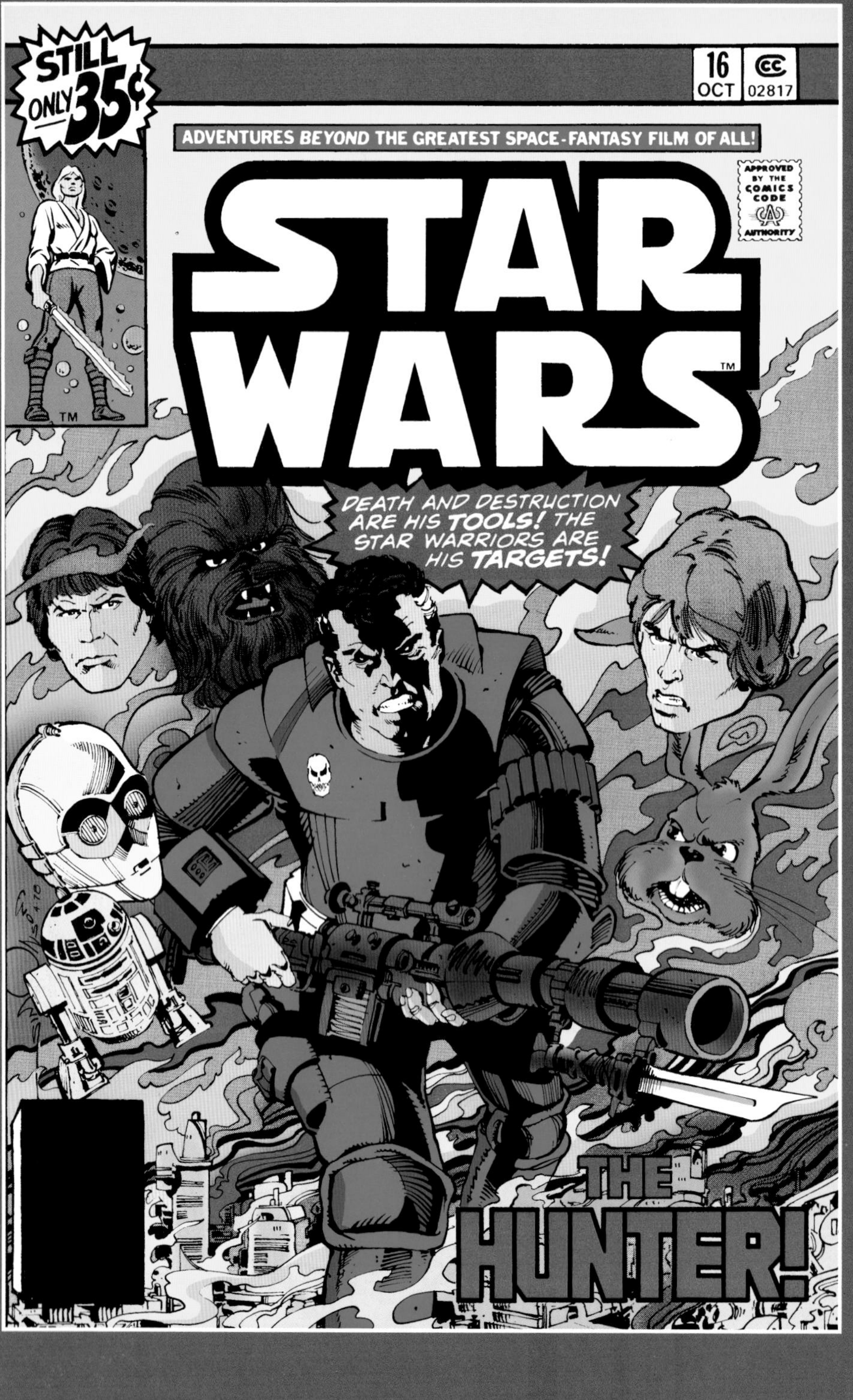
STILL ONLY 35¢
16 OCT
CC 02817
ADVENTURES BEYOND THE GREATEST SPACE-FANTASY FILM OF ALL!
APPROVED BY THE COMICS CODE AUTHORITY
STAR WARS™
DEATH AND DESTRUCTION ARE HIS TOOLS! THE STAR WARRIORS ARE HIS TARGETS!
THE HUNTER!

Long ago in a galaxy far, far away. . . .there exists a state of cosmic *civil war*. A brave alliance of *underground freedom fighters* has challenged the tyranny and oppression of the awesome *Galactic Empire*. This is their story!

LucasFilm PRESENTS: **STAR WARS**™ THE GREATEST **SPACE FANTASY** OF ALL!

CONTINUING THE SAGA BEGUN IN THE FILM BY *GEORGE LUCAS* RELEASED BY *20th CENTURY-FOX*

ARCHIE GOODWIN • WALT SIMONSON *and* BOB WIACEK • DENISE WOHL • BOB SHAREN • JAMES SHOOTER
WRITER/EDITOR • GUEST ARTISTS • LETTERER • COLORIST • CONSULTING EDITOR

the HUNTER!

HIS NAME IS *VALANCE.* HE AND THE BAND OF GALACTIC MERCENARIES WHO *FOLLOW* HIM ARE *BOUNTY HUNTERS.*

YET, NO ONE *HERE* HAS A *PRICE* ON THEIR HEAD.

FAST NOW! I WANT A *CLEAN SWEEP*... NO SURVIVORS!

VALANCE PAYS FOR THIS RAID *HIMSELF.* IT IS FITTING. HE HAS COME TO DESTROY HIS OWN *PAST.*

AND THAT IS *UNFORTUNATE* FOR ALL OTHERS AT THIS ISOLATED OUTWORLD *MEDICAL STATION*...

...*PARTICULARLY IF THEY HAPPEN TO BE DROIDS.*

GOOD *GRIEF!* THERE MUST BE SOME *ERROR.*

THIS FACILITY IS *NEUTRAL.* EVEN THE *EMPIRE*, RE--

SHUT UP ...*JUNK!*

FADAK!

VALANCE EXPERIENCES *REGRET.* THERE'S NO TIME TO ENJOY THE SHOOTING.

JUNK! ALL HIS LIFE, HE'S *HATED* MECHANICALS... SERVILE CIRCUITRY COMPETING WITH *MEN.*

THE ATTITUDE IS *COMMON* AMONG *MOST ORGANICS* IN THE GALAXY...

...BUT *FEW* SHARE THE UNRELIEVED *INTENSITY* OF VALANCE'S FEELINGS!

WE'RE ROUNDING UP *ALL* THE *ROBOT ORDERLIES,* CAPTAIN.

YOU *KNOW* WHAT TO *DO,* SLZZK.

THE HUTLARIAN FIRST MATE KNOWS EXACTLY...

...AND VALANCE *CAN* PROCEED CONFIDENTLY TO HIS *MAIN OBJECTIVE.*

VRA-KOWM!

WAIT! THIS IS JUST THE *COMPUTER RECORD SECTION.*

THERE ARE NO *DRUGS*... ANYTHING OF VALUE!

I'M WELL *AWARE* WHAT'S HERE, TECHNO.

THEN, *W-WHY...?*

VALANCE DOES NOT *ANSWER.* HE *ACTS...*

... AND IN THAT ACT, THE COMPUTER RECORDS SECTION OF THE *TELOS-4* MEDICAL STATION...

SHTOOM!

BRAK... *BRIIT...* *WUM!*

...VANISHES!

ELSEWHERE, AS ONE BY ONE THE *IN-PATIENT BAYS* ARE INVADED...

...A SICK OLD MAN, LOST IN *DELIRIUM,* SPEAKS TO *SHADOWS* WITHIN HIS MIND.

BLAM!

YOU BRING MY *LIGHTSABER...?* GOOD! THEN *DON-WAN KIHOTAY* IS READY--

--READY TO *FIGHT* AGAIN, *HAN SOLO!* WHAT A *TEAM* WE WERE!* YOUR *WOOKIEE* FRIEND... THE LOVELY *AMAIZA...*

...*JAXXON,* THE LEPUS CARNIVOROUS ... AND, OF COURSE, THE *BOY*... THE BOY AND HIS DROID...

*IN *STAR WARS 8-10.*--ARCHIE.

CAPTAIN *VALANCE!* COME *QUICKLY!* WE'RE ON TO SOMETHING *BIG!*

BUT THE OLD WARRIOR HAS *TIRED.* HE DRIFTS INTO *SILENCE.*

YOU'RE *CERTAIN* WHAT HE *SAID?*

WE HEAR QUITE *WELL,* SIR... WHERE A *LARGE BOUNTY* IS CONCERNED!

THEN BACK TO THE *SHIP* ...WE'VE A *NEW JOB* AHEAD OF US!

PROTON CHARGES **ALL SET** CAP'N!

EVERYONE ABOARD FOR **IMMEDIATE** LIFT-OFF!

AS THE LIGHT CRUISER TAKES TO THE **SKIES**...

...A SERIES OF EXPLOSIONS **COMPLETE** THE WIPING AWAY OF VALANCE'S **PAST**.

NOW HE CAN CONSIDER THE **FUTURE**... THE SATISFACTION AND CHALLENGE OF A **NEW HUNT!**

FEED THE INFORMATION INTO OUR **COMPUTER**, SLZZK. CONCENTRATE ON THE **LEPUS CARNIVOROUS**.

OF ALL THE **LEADS** TO SOLO, THE BOY, AND THE DROIDS --

"... A MAN-SIZE, MEAT-EATING **GREEN RABBIT** SHOULD BE EASIEST TO **FIND!**"

SURE YOU WON'T CHANGE YOUR **MIND**, AMAIZA?

NO **THANKS**, JAX.

THE **HIGH LIFE** ON THESE BACKWATER WORLDS CAN GET PRETTY **LOW** --

-- I'LL OVERSEE THE SHIP'S **REFUELING**. DON'T GET YOUR **EARS** BURNED.

CUTE **LADY**... EVEN IF SHE **DOESN'T** HAVE FUR.

GOOD **GAMBLER**, TOO! MANAGED TO RUN UP OUR **SMALL STAKES** INTO ENOUGH TO GET MY OLD **FREIGHTER** RE-PAIRED AND --

HEY! WHAT IN THE HOLY *HUTCH*--?

IT IS AN *ELECTRO-NET*...

...*CAPABLE* OF SHOCK-ING *MOST* CREATURES INTO SUBMISSION...

...OR *UNCON-SCIOUSNESS*.

AWAKENING FROM THE EXPERIENCE IS *ALSO* LESS THAN A *PICNIC*.

UH ... I'D ASK WHAT'S *UP*, GUYS --

BUT IT *FEELS* LIKE I AM.

A *NEGOTIABLE* POSITION, RABBIT--

--ONCE YOU NAME THE *PLANET* WHERE YOU SERVED WITH *HAN SOLO* AND THE *BOY* WITH THE *DROIDS*.

SORRY, BALDY. I DON'T *FINK* ON FRIENDS.

NOW I CAN *HURT* HIM, RIGHT, FUD?

OF *COURSE*, DAFI... THAT'S WHY WE PUT THE *AGONY INDUCER* ON HIS EAR.

YEEEOOOWW!

NAME THE *PLANET*, RABBIT. OUR LEADER, *CAPTAIN VALANCE*, IS WAITING... AND THERE'S *UNIMAGINABLE BOUNTY* AT STAKE!

BLOW IT OUT YER *RETROS*!

AGAIN, DAFI.

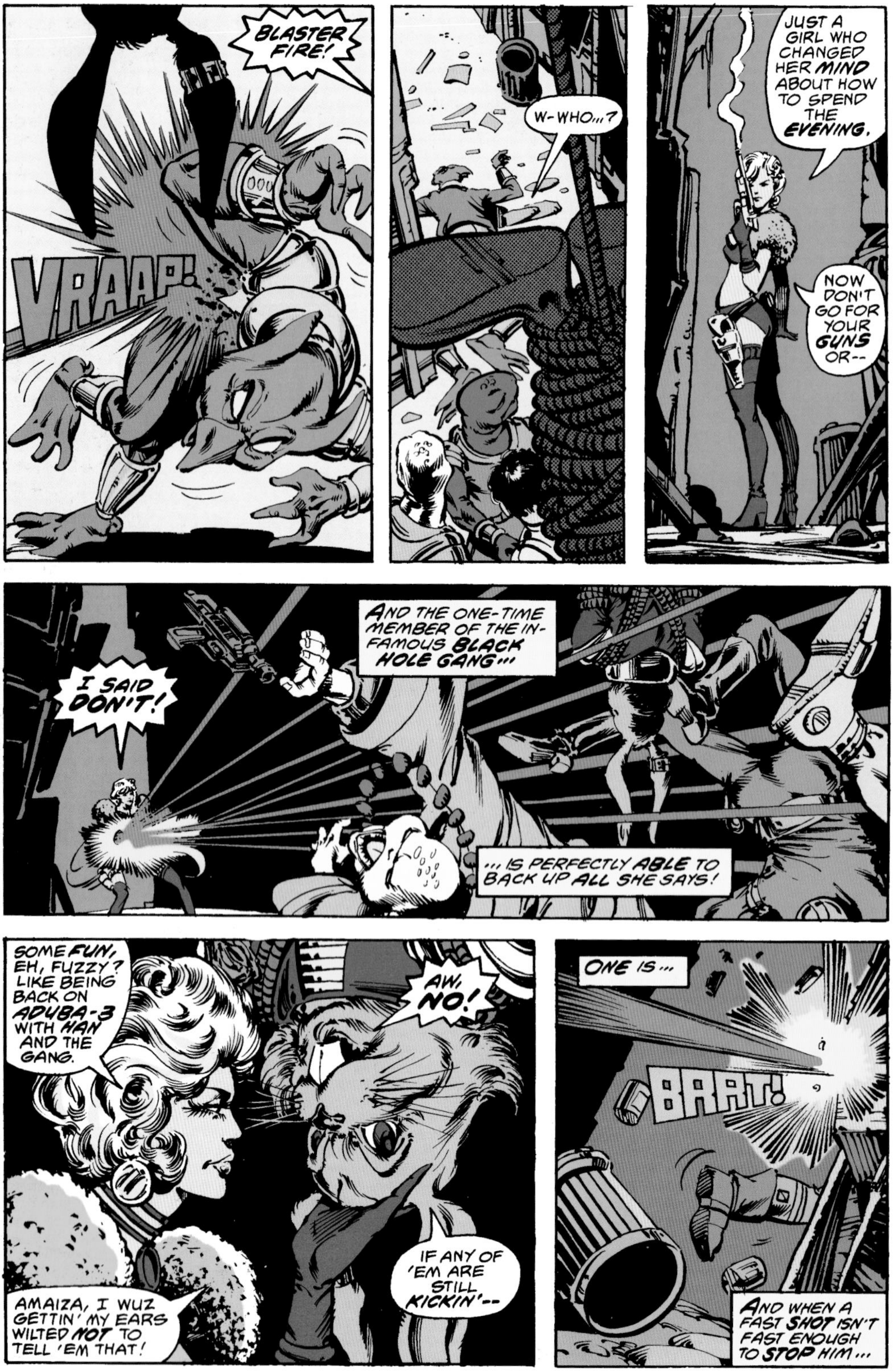
BLASTER FIRE!
VRAAP!
W-WHO...?
JUST A GIRL WHO CHANGED HER MIND ABOUT HOW TO SPEND THE EVENING.
NOW DON'T GO FOR YOUR GUNS OR--
AND THE ONE-TIME MEMBER OF THE IN-FAMOUS BLACK HOLE GANG...
I SAID DON'T!
...IS PERFECTLY ABLE TO BACK UP ALL SHE SAYS!
SOME FUN, EH, FUZZY? LIKE BEING BACK ON ADUBA-3 WITH HAN AND THE GANG.
AW, NO!
IF ANY OF 'EM ARE STILL KICKIN'--
AMAIZA, I WUZ GETTIN' MY EARS WILTED NOT TO TELL 'EM THAT!
ONE IS...
BRRT!
AND WHEN A FAST SHOT ISN'T FAST ENOUGH TO STOP HIM...

...JAXXON AND AMAIZA TAKE SWIFTLY TO **SPACE** IN THE GOOD SHIP **RABBIT'S FOOT**.

DESTINATION: THE LITTLE-REGARDED RIMWORLD OF **ADUBA-3**...

...AND AN ISOLATED **VILLAGE** IN ITS VAST OUTBACK.

LOOKS LIKE WE BEAT THE **BAD GUYS!**

MAYBE WE'LL EVEN HAVE TIME TO FIGURE **WHY** THEY'RE **COMIN'** HERE! JABBA THE HUT PUT A PRICE ON **SOLO'S** HEAD--*

--BUT THOSE CREEPS ACTED LIKE THERE'S **ALSO** ONE ON OUR **OTHER** PAL--

*SEE STAR WARS #2. -- ARCHIE.

"--**JIMM,** WHO CALLED HIMSELF THE **STARKILLER KID** WHEN HE AN' HIS ROBOT **EFFIE** THREW IN WITH US TO **DEFEND** THIS PLACE AGAINST LOCAL **BANDITS.**"*

ME? WANTED BY **BOUNTY HUNTERS?!**

*ISSUES 8, 9 & 10. -- ARCH AGAIN.

PRETTY **FUNNY,** JAX! I'M AN OLD MARRIED **FARMER**... MERRI AN' I ARE EXPECTIN' OUR **FIRST BABY!** THERE'S **NO WAY--**

SOMEBODY THINKS THERE **IS,** KID! AN' RIGHT OR **WRONG--**

--THEY'RE THE KIND'A **SWEETIES** WHO'LL STOMP YOUR HOME INTO **DUST** JUST TO STAY IN **PRACTICE!**

UNLESS **WE** MAKE SOME **PLANS** ...AND **FAST!**

AMAIZA LOOKS TO THE SKY. NOTHING IS VISIBLE... YET.

APPROACHING THE **ADUBA SYSTEM**, CAPT. VALANCE.

*TIME TO REVIEW THE **TAPE**, SO **NO ONE** IS MISTAKEN ABOUT WHAT OUR **GOAL** IS.*

*YET VALANCE'S **OWN** MIND DRIFTS ... BACK TO HIS **LAST MOMENTS**...*

*...SERVING THE **EMPIRE** IN AN OUTWORLD SKIRMISH...*

*MOMENTS WHEN HIS **CAREER** AS A STORM-TROOPER OFFICER OF RUTHLESS **PROMISE**...*

*HE SURVIVED THE **BLAST**... BUT BY A MARGIN SO **NARROW**, THE RETREATING IMPERIALS LEFT HIM AT THE TELOS-4 MEDICAL STATION TO **DIE**.*

*INSTEAD, TO HIS OWN **REGRET** ... HE WAS **SAVED**.*

*...WAS **ENDED** BY A REBEL SERIAL TORPEDO.*

*AT A PRICE... THE KNOWLEDGE HE COULD **NEVER AGAIN** STAND WITH **PRIDE** IN THE EMPIRE'S RANKS.*

BUT THAT'S THE **PAST**... I'VE **DESTROYED** THAT! NOW THERE'S THE **BOY**, THE BOY AND HIS **DROIDS**...

*BITTERLY, VALANCE PUNCHES THE TAPE INTO THE PLAYER, AND WAITS TO FEEL THE **HATE**...*

...THE SAME HATE HE FELT ON *FIRST* VIEWING THIS TAPE TAKEN FROM A REBEL SPY SLAIN BY HIS MEN. IT IS AN ILLEGAL DUPE OF AN *IMPERIAL TRANSMISSION*, AND DETAILS...

...THE INCREDIBLE *ESCAPE* OF SENATOR AND PRINCESS *LEIA ORGANA* FROM THE *DEATH STAR!!*

THAT ONE PARTICIPANT, *HAN SOLO*, HAD A *PRICE* ON HIS HEAD...

...*INTERESTED* VALANCE, AS DID THE *HINT* THAT SITH LORD...

...*DARTH VADER*...

...*WAS SOUNDLY TESTED BY*...

..."A *STRANGE, UNKNOWN* OLD MAN.

BUT IT WAS THE *BOY* WHO FIRED VALANCE'S *FURY*. FOR *HIS* PART WAS DONE WITH THE COOPERATION, INDEED, THE *FRIENDSHIP* OF TWO *DROIDS!* THE TAPE IMAGES *FADE*...

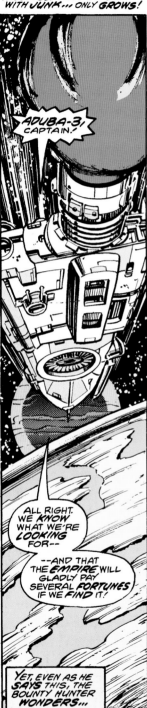

...BUT VALANCE'S REVULSION THAT *ANY HUMAN* WOULD *WILLINGLY* ALLY HIMSELF WITH *JUNK*... ONLY *GROWS!*

ADUBA-3, CAPTAIN!

ALL RIGHT. WE *KNOW* WHAT WE'RE *LOOKING* FOR--

--AND THAT THE *EMPIRE* WILL GLADLY PAY SEVERAL *FORTUNES* IF WE *FIND* IT!

YET, EVEN AS HE SAYS *THIS, THE BOUNTY HUNTER WONDERS...*

...*IF HE WOULDN'T STALK THE DROID-LOVING YOUNG REBEL FOR* FREE.

SIR, I'VE GOT A *VILLAGE* THAT FITS WITH OUR ACCUMU-LATED *DATA*--

--AND A *HEAT PARTICLE TRAIL* INDICATING A *SHIP* RECENTLY ARRIVED.

THE *RABBIT*... RUSHING TO *ALERT* HIS OLD FRIENDS. NO MATTER...

ALL HANDS SCRAMBLE!

EXPECT LIGHT-- BUT *DETERMINED*-- RESISTANCE.

CAPTAIN! THEY'RE BRINGING THE FIGHT TO *US.*

ONLY A *N-CLASS FREIGHTER* BY THE SENSORS, SO--

FULL SHIELDS IMMEDIATELY!

VALANCE'S SWIFTLY SHOUTED *ORDER*...

...IS JUST AS SWIFTLY *OBEYED.*

FRADOW!

IT SAVES HIS SHIP...

....IF NOT THE *DIGNITY* OF HIS CREW!

FOOLS!

THOSE INDEPENDENT STAR-HOPPERS *ALWAYS* MODIFY THEIR SHIPS--

--YOU CAN'T JUDGE THEM BY *OFFICIAL CLASSIFICATIONS!*

NO MORE THAN *THEY* CAN JUDGE *US* BY ONE QUICK *ENCOUNTER!*

NOT *BAD,* EH, *GORGEOUS?* HAN SOLO'D BE *PROUD!*

THE OL' *RABBIT'S FOOT* AIN'T IN HIS *MILLENNIUM FALCON'S* CLASS--

--BUT WE JUST MAY *SETTLE* THIS FRACAS RIGHT *NOW*--

--NOT EVEN *NEED* YOUR ORIGINAL *PLAN,* AMAIZA.

DREAM ON, GREEN EARS. THE WAY *I* READ THE SCANNER--

289

VEEROM!

--THIS IS WHERE THE CREAMING STARTS!

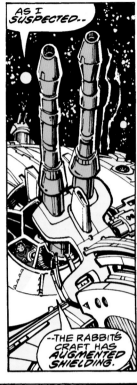

AS I SUSPECTED--

--THE RABBIT'S CRAFT HAS AUGMENTED SHIELDING.

ALL GUNNERS SHOULD ADJUST POWER LEVELS ACCORDINGLY--

--AND LOCK IN ON MY FIRING PATTERN.

OUR YOUNG ROBOT-LOVER COULD WELL BE ABOARD THE FREIGHTER--

--SO BEFORE STORMING THE VILLAGE IN SEARCH OF OUR QUARRY--

I WANT THAT SHIP!!

CRIPES! THINK'A HOW MANY STEAKS I COULD BUY FOR WHAT THAT PLATING WILL COST!

BUT UNDER POUNDING OF SUCH INTENSITY...

...THE HIGH COST OF HULL PLATING WOULD SEEM TO BE THE *LEAST* OF IT...

GOOD. LOOKS LIKE WE HIT THEM *JUST HARD ENOUGH.* I WANTED THEM *DOWN*...BUT *INTACT.*

THE EMPIRE WILL PAY FOR *BODIES*...BUT NOT UNRECOGNIZABLE *CRISPS.*

...AS THE *RABBIT'S FOOT* SUDDENLY *PLUNGES* TOWARD *ADUBA-3'S* SURFACE!

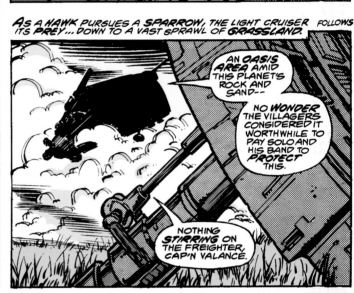

AS A HAWK PURSUES A *SPARROW,* THE LIGHT CRUISER FOLLOWS ITS *PREY*...DOWN TO A VAST SPRAWL OF *GRASSLAND.*

AN *OASIS AREA* AMID THIS PLANET'S ROCK AND SAND--

NO *WONDER* THE VILLAGERS CONSIDERED IT WORTHWHILE TO PAY SOLO AND HIS BAND TO *PROTECT* THIS.

NOTHING *STIRRING* ON THE FREIGHTER, CAP'N VALANCE.

THE *CRASH-LANDING* MAY HAVE DONE OUR WORK FOR US...BUT DON'T *COUNT* ON IT.

TAKE IN THE *FIRST SQUAD,* SLSSK...I'LL FOLLOW WITH THE *REST* OF THE CREW.

AND *REMEMBER*...IF THE *BOY'S* ABOARD, HE'S MINE!

BUT NO ONE IS ABOARD... AS VALANCE AND HIS MEN SWIFTLY *FIND!*

CAPTAIN! THEY'VE *ABANDONED* THEIR SHIP FOR THE *TALL GRASS!*

THAT SHOULD BRING THEM RUNNING!

CHA-WOOM!

YEAH, JUST PRAY *JIMM* AN' HIS VOLUNTEERS DELIVER ON *THEIR* END!

THIS IS *IT!* WISH *HAN* AND *CHEWBACCA* WERE HERE TO TAKE *CHARGE.*

BUT AT LEAST THEY *TAUGHT* US WE COULD *FIGHT* FOR WHAT'S OURS--

--LET'S SEE HOW *WELL* WE LEARNED!

BLAM!

THE SHOT ECHOES *LOUDLY* ACROSS THE PLAIN...

...ONLY TO BE FOLLOWED BY SOMETHING LOUDER YET.

T-THE *GROUND*...!

THIS PLACE ISN'T SUBJECT TO *QUAKES.* W-WHAT--?

BANTHAS!

THE CRAZY VILLAGERS HAVE *STAMPEDED* THEIR *HERD!*

AND THE HIGH, TANGLING *GRASS* IS NEARLY IMPOSSIBLE TO *RUN* IN...

...AS, ONE BY **ONE**, VALANCE'S BOUNTY HUNTERS HAVE THE MISFORTUNE TO **DISCOVER**.

I-IT'S....OVER. A TERRIBLE THING TO **BEHOLD** ...BUT IT SAVED OUR **VILLAGE**.

GIVE **CREDIT** TO JAXXON AND AMAIZA. THEY BOUGHT US **TIME** TO GATHER THE **BANTHAS**--

--THEN DRAW THOSE KILLERS **DOWN** HERE.

DON'T HAND OUT THE MEDALS YET, KID--

--THERE'S BOUND TO BE **MORE** WE AIN'T FLUSHED YET!

GOOD **ADVICE,** BUNNY!

AND YOU MADE **THIS** CHARACTER ITCHY ENOUGH TO **SHOW** HIMSELF!

FDOW!

THAT WAS **SLSSK!** THE FOOL SHOULD HAVE STAYED **HIDDEN**.

BUT WHILE THEIR ATTENTION IS ON **HIM,** I CAN·

FORGET REACHIN' YOUR *SHIP*--

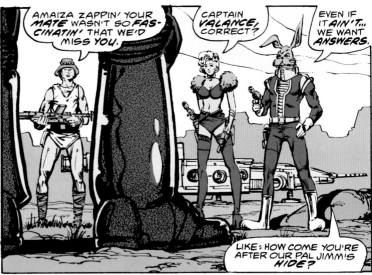

AMAIZA ZAPPIN' YOUR *MATE* WASN'T SO *FAS-CINATIN'* THAT WE'D MISS YOU.

CAPTAIN *VALANCE*, CORRECT?

EVEN IF IT *AIN'T*... WE WANT *ANSWERS*.

LIKE: HOW COME YOU'RE AFTER OUR PAL JIMM'S *HIDE*?

YOU...?

YOU'RE THE BOY WHO FOUGHT IN *HAN SOLO'S* GROUP HERE...?

BUT... YOU'RE *NOT* THE ONE ON THE *DEATH STAR TRANS-MISSION TAPE!*

I DON'T EVEN KNOW WHAT THAT *IS!* YOU'RE--

--AFTER THE *WRONG BOY!* BETWEEN *MY* OB-SESSION AND THE CREW'S *GREED* ...WE DID THIS ALL FOR *NOTHING!*

VALANCE DROPS HIS *EMPTY BLASTER...*

...AND *LAUGHS.* LONG AND HARD.

LEAVING THE STARTLED TRIO BEFORE HIM TOTALLY UNPREPARED FOR WHAT *HAPPENS* WHEN...

...THE *LAUGHTER STOPS!*

ZDAK!

ENOUGH! SOLO'S DROID-LOVING YOUNG COMPANION IS *SOMEWHERE* IN THIS GALAXY--

--AND *YOU* THREE WON'T STAND BETWEEN *ME* AND *FINDING* HIM!

REFLEXES SEND THEM DIVING OUT OF THE *MAIN BLAST*...

...BUT SCARCELY *FAR* ENOUGH TO BE IN ANY SHAPE TO *HALT* THE BOUNTY HUNTER...

...AS HE CHARGES TO HIS NOW *CREW-LESS* SHIP...

...AND BLASTS AWAY...

...TOWARD THE *STARS!*

I-I'M NOT SURE WHAT *HAPPENED*...BUT IT *SEEMS* TO BE OVER.

YEAH, KID...I GUESS.

FOR *US*, FOR HAN'S FRIEND WITH THE *DROIDS*...I WONDER.

WHILE IN THE FLEEING CRAFT'S *COCKPIT*...VALANCE CLAWS COMPULSIVELY AT HIS *FACE*.

I *UNDERESTIMATED* THEM...SHOULD NEVER HAVE HAD TO USE THE *ARM*.

BUT I DID IT *SWIFTLY*...MY SECRET SHOULD STILL BE *SAFE*.

AND A TERRIBLE SECRET IT IS FOR A *ROBOT-HATER*...

...*LIVING* WITH THE FACT THAT AT THE *TELOS-4 MEDICAL STATION*...

...*HALF* HIS BODY WAS RE-PLACED BY *CYBERNETIC PARTS!*

TERRIBLE. FOR BEING A CYBORG ONLY MAKES VANCE MORE *DETERMINED*...THAT THE *HUNT* SHALL GO *ON*.

NEXT ISSUE: THE *EMPIRE STRIKES!*

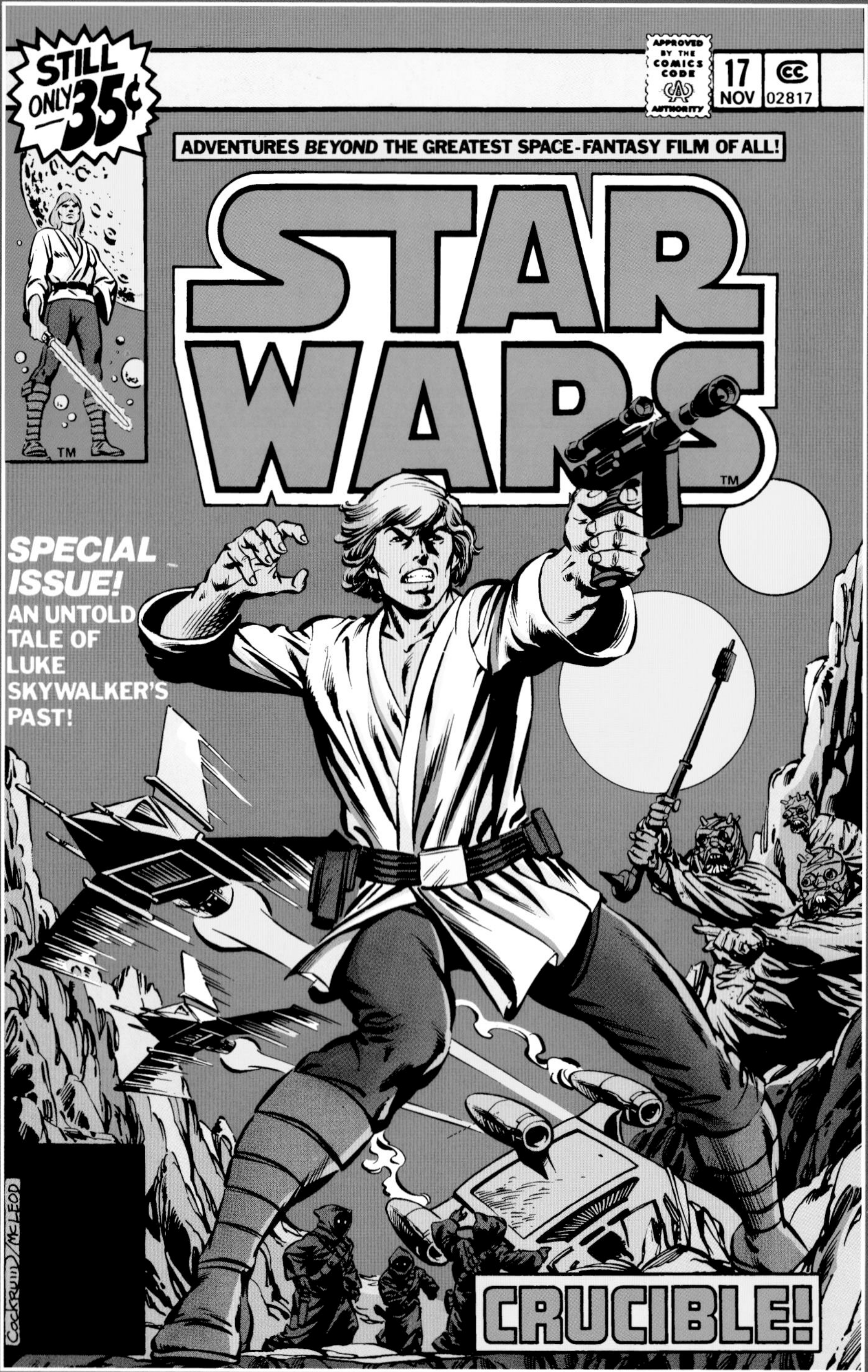
STILL ONLY 35¢
APPROVED BY THE COMICS CODE AUTHORITY
17 NOV
CC 02817
ADVENTURES BEYOND THE GREATEST SPACE-FANTASY FILM OF ALL!
STAR WARS
SPECIAL ISSUE!
AN UNTOLD TALE OF LUKE SKYWALKER'S PAST!
COCKRUM/McLEOD
CRUCIBLE!

Long ago in a galaxy far, far away. . .there exists a state of cosmic *civil war*. A brave alliance of *underground freedom fighters* has challenged the tyranny and oppression of the awesome *Galactic Empire*. This is their story!

LucasFilm PRESENTS: STAR WARS™ THE GREATEST SPACE FANTASY OF ALL!

CONTINUING THE SAGA BEGUN IN THE FILM BY *GEORGE LUCAS* RELEASED BY *TWENTIETH CENTURY-FOX*

CRUCIBLE!

AT THE CONTROLS OF THE *MILLENNIUM FALCON*!! LUKE SKYWALKER, TAKING A LONE WATCH, SMILES...

TRUE, HE ONCE CALLED THIS SMUGGLING SHIP A *PIECE OF JUNK*... BUT THAT WAS BEFORE *FIGHTING* AND *SERVING* ABOARD HER.

EXULTING IN THE *FEEL* OF HER INSTRUMENTS, HE FINDS HIS *MIND* JOGGED BACK TO ANOTHER *TIME*, ANOTHER *PLACE*, ACROSS THE GALACTIC REACHES TO HIS *HOMEWORLD*...

ARCHIE GOODWIN WRITER/EDITOR	CHRIS CLAREMONT PLOT	HERB TRIMPE & ALLEN MILGROM GUEST ARTISTS	RICK PARKER LETTERER	MARIE SEVERIN COLORIST	JIM SHOOTER CONSULTING ED.

...*TATOOINE!*

ENDLESS MILES OF SAND-SWEPT DESERT AND ROCKY WASTELAND... BAKED BY THE GLARE OF TWIN SUNS.

A WORLD SEEMINGLY TOO HARSH, TOO BARREN TO SUSTAIN LIFE...

YET... LIFE IS HERE. AND IN GREAT VARIETY...

ALMOST AS VARIED...

...AS THE FORMS OF DEATH!

CHONK!

THE WOMP RAT PAUSES AND SNIFFS THE AIR...

THERE ARE LARGER PREDATORS ON TATOOINE, BUT NONE ANY MORE SWIFT OR CRUEL...

...OR INSTINCTIVELY AWARE THAT THIS LIFE/DEATH CYCLE...

VEEDDW!

...IS AS UNENDING AS THE ROCK AND SAND.

YEE-OWW!

WAIT'LL THE GANG HEARS ABOUT *THIS!* ANY OF 'EM MIGHT BULLSEYE A WOMP RAT FROM THEIR *SKYHOPPERS*--

--BUT I BET EVEN *BIGGS* NEVER MADE A ONE-HANDED SHOT WITH AN *ENERGY-RIFLE*--

--WHILE FIGHTING A *LANDSPEEDER'S* CONTROLS!

AND THE FACT THAT IN THAT FIGHT...

...HIS BANKING LANDSPEEDER ALMOST *FLIPPED OVER*...

...DOESN'T EVEN *PIERCE* YOUNG LUKE SKYWALKER'S ENTHUSIASM.

SHOOT! HOLES FILLING UP FROM *BELOW*... THE PACK IS SCATTERING *UNDERGROUND!*

PROTON GRENADES COULDN'T DIG 'EM OUT NOW!

AT LEAST *THIS ONE* WON'T BE GNAWING ANY VAPORATOR CABLES--

-- AND THE *BOUNTY* ON HIM MIGHT BE ENOUGH FOR THOSE *MACRO-BINOCULARS* I'VE BEEN WANTING!

SATISFIED, LUKE STEERS TOWARD HOME...

...UNAWARE THAT HIS EVERY MOVEMENT HAS BEEN OBSERVED.

THESE WATCHERS *TOO* SEEM SATISFIED. TATOOINE'S LIFE/DEATH CYCLE EXTENDS NO *FURTHER*...

...FOR *NOW.*

AND THE BANTHA RAIDERS HAVE *VANISHED* INTO THE WILDS OF THE HOSTILE *JUNDLAND WASTES...*

...BY THE TIME THE *LANDSPEEDER* REACHES THE MAIN BUILDINGS OF THE LARS' *MOISTURE FARM.*

UNCLE *OWEN!* AUNT *BERU!*

I'M *HOME!*

LATE! AND WITHOUT THE REBUILT PARTS FOR OUR *TREADWELL...* EVEN THOUGH YOU TOOK *ALL DAY!*

I TRIED GIVING FIXER A *HAND,* UNCLE OWEN... BUT WITH HIS *BACKLOG,* HE SAYS IT'LL BE A *WEEK* BEFORE--

WITHOUT THAT *DROID* WE CAN'T INSTALL THOSE NEW *VAPORATORS!*

I *KNOW,* UNCLE OWEN, AND I KIND'A *WONDERED--*

BIGGS DARKLIGHTER'S LEAVING SOON FOR THE *ACADEMY--*

--AND TOMORROW, THE GANG'S PLANNING A SORT'A *FAREWELL CELEBRATION.* UNTIL THE DROID'S *WORKING,* I CAN'T *DO* MUCH SO--

SO IT'LL BE AN *EXCUSE* TO IDLE AWAY *MORE* TIME, LUKE, A WATER FARMER CAN'T--

OWEN, BIGGS IS LUKE'S *BEST FRIEND...* HE'LL BE GONE A *YEAR* OR MORE. YOU LET A *BROTHER* LEAVE WITHOUT SAYING *GOOD-BYE.* HAVEN'T YOU WISHED--

ENOUGH, BERU--

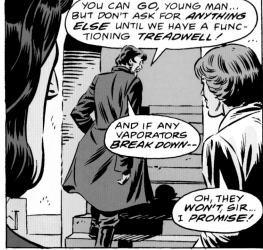

YOU CAN *GO,* YOUNG MAN... BUT DON'T ASK FOR *ANYTHING ELSE* UNTIL WE HAVE A FUNCTIONING *TREADWELL!*

AND IF ANY VAPORATORS *BREAK DOWN--*

OH, THEY *WON'T,* SIR... I *PROMISE!*

GEE! I *NEVER* FIGURED UNCLE OWEN WOULD GIVE IN! WHAT *HAPPENED* BETWEEN HIM AND MY FATHER?

ER... NOTHING *REALLY*, LUKE--

PERHAPS... OWEN JUST *DEPENDED* TOO MUCH ON YOUR FATHER STAYING *WITH* HIM ON THE FARM.

LIKE HE DOES *NOW* WITH ME.

WHENEVER I MENTION GOING TO THE *ACADEMY* LIKE BIGGS, HE--

HE *CARES* FOR YOU, LUKE... IN HIS OWN GRUFF WAY.

I GUESS I *KNOW* THAT... AND ALL HIS EFFORT ON THE FARM IS TO *BUILD* SOMETHING FOR US ALL.

MAKES ME FEEL LIKE A *TRAITOR* TO EVEN *THINK* ABOUT LEAVING, AUNT BERU--

STILL... SOME CRAZY *PART* OF ME KEEPS FEELING LIKE THERE SHOULD BE *MORE*...!

MAYBE I'M JUST AFRAID TO *GROW* UP--

--TO FACE *RESPONSIBILITY* LIKE UNCLE OWEN. WHAT *ELSE* COULD IT BE?

TO HER REGRET BERU LARS' ONLY ANSWER IS *SILENCE*.

TATOOINE'S DUAL SUNSET PASSES... AND *NIGHT* COMES TO THE ISOLATED FARM...

WHERE IN THE COMPLEX'S *GARAGE*, LUKE COMPLETES A *TUNE-UP*...

THERE! THE OL' SKY-HOPPER IS *READY AN' RARIN'!*

LET ME JUST CHECK THE *CONTROLS* A LAST TIME--

SINCE I DIDN'T *MENTION* TO UNCLE OWEN THAT THIS CELEBRATION IS AT *BEGGAR'S CANYON*--

--EVERYTHING'S GOT TO BE *TIP TOP.* I DON'T WANT TO BRING BACK A *WRECK!*

IT DOESN'T *OCCUR* TO LUKE THAT HE MIGHT NOT *COME BACK* FROM A WRECK. HE IS *YOUNG.* HIS OWN MORTALITY SEEMS A *DISTANT* THING...

... AND HIS THOUGHTS ARE RACING ELSEWHERE.

HE SQUINTS HIS EYES, GRIPS THE CONTROLS, AND CEASES TO BE *LUKE SKYWALKER, TATOOINE FARM BOY*...

... IN HIS MIND'S DREAMING EYE, HE IS COMMANDER LUKE SKYWALKER, LEADING A FLIGHT OF STAR-FIGHTERS INTO COMBAT.

EXTERNAL POWER INLET

EMERGENCY RELEASE WARNING

NOW THE ENEMY DESTROYER LOOMS BEFORE HIM. A RAIDER, A SLAVER... TRYING TO ESCAPE WITH ITS LIVING CARGO!

TRYING... AND FAILING.

SKYWALKER AGAIN! HE'S THE ONE WHO STOPPED US IN THE STYX SYSTEM.

THAT'S HIS LAST SUCCESS! HE MAY HAVE BOARDED US SWIFTLY... BUT HE'S GOING TO DIE JUST AS FAST!

BUT IN THIS BLASTER DUEL...

...DEADLY SKILL, NOT TALK, DE-TERMINES THE WINNER.

AND WHEN QUARTERS ARE TOO CLOSE FOR SHOOTING...

... A FIST CAN BE DEADLY, TOO... AS THE SLAVE SHIP CAPTAIN SOON LEARNS!

THEN, IT IS OVER. EXCEPT FOR A LOVELY HOSTAGE'S GRATITUDE...

... AND THE PROMISE OF EVEN GREATER ADVENTURES TO COME...

... ANOTHER DAY.

--LUKE? LUKE! HAVE YOU GONE DEAF--?

--OR FALLEN ASLEEP?

I'VE BEEN YELLING FOR THE LAST FIVE MINUTES... I'M SHUT-TING DOWN THE EX-TERNAL POWER.

UH...SORRY, UNCLE OWEN. I GUESS I GOT...UH... WRAPPED UP IN MY WORK.

IF YOU'D PUT AS MUCH DEDICATION INTO MAIN-TAINING OUR VAPORATORS--

-- WE'D HAVE THE RICHEST MOISTURE FARM ON THE PLANET.

I'M SURE GONNA TRY, UNCLE OWEN... YOU'LL SEE. AFTER TO-MORROW.

BEGGAR'S CANYON. ANY ADULT ON TATOOINE WILL TELL YOU TO AVOID THIS TWISTING, MILE-DEEP TESTAMENT TO THE POWER OF EROSION.

ANY TEENAGER WILL TELL YOU IT'S THE ONLY PLACE ON A DULL, BACK-WATER WORLD...

... TO FIND A FEW THRILLS.

IF YOU DON'T MIND RISKING THE FAMILY SKYHOPPER... AND MAYBE YOUR OWN NECK.

HEY, BIGGS! OVER HERE!

I SEE YOU WAGGLING YOUR WINGS, HOTSHOT. GLAD YOU COULD MAKE IT.

BUT JUST CAUSE THIS IS THE LAST GET-TOGETHER OF THE TWO SHOOTING STARS--

"-- DON'T EXPECT ANY *BREAKS* WHEN THE *RUN* BEGINS!"

LUKE *DOESN'T.* AND IT SEEMS NONE WILL BE *NECESSARY.* AS THE STARTING SIGNAL IS GIVEN, HE *POWER DIVES* FOR THE YAWNING CANYON MOUTH...

...TO GRAB THE *LEAD* INTO THE SNAKING, TWO-MILE-STRETCH OF SHEER-WALLED *NIGHTMARE.*

AT ITS *FAR END* LIES THE AREA'S LARGEST *WOMP RAT BURROW*...FOR A GOOD REASON. THE ONLY *SHOOTING APPROACH* IS *THROUGH* THE LABYRINTH THAT IS BEGGAR'S CANYON...

...WHERE EACH *BEND,* EACH *TURN,* IS MORE IMPOSSIBLE THAN THE LAST...

...AND *MANEUVERING ROOM* MAY BE DETERMINED...

...BY HOW MANY COATS OF *PAINT* YOUR 'HOPPER HAS!

SKY-WALKER AND DARK-LIGHTER KEEP *LEAP-FROGGIN'* FOR FIRST PLACE--

ON *THESE* CURVES, THE ONLY SPOT THAT LEAVES A *RUNNER UP* IS AGAINST THE ROCKS--

--OR *OUT!*

IT IS A *CHOICE* MADE BY MORE AND MORE PARTICIPANTS...

...AS EACH NEW TURN PROVES *NARROWER.* UNTIL...

... ONLY *TWO SHIPS* REMAIN!

GANGWAY, HOTSHOT, I'M MAKING MY MOVE!

JUST LIKE I FIGURED, BIGGS, OL' BUDDY--

--JUST A HAIR TOO EARLY! THERE'S STILL TIME FOR ME TO JUMP YOU BEFORE THE LAST TURN--

-- AND NO ROOM FOR YOU TO OVERTAKE ME AFTER THAT!

BUT AS LUKE STARTS...

WHAT TH--?! HE'S BRAKIN' WITH HIS RETROS!

BIGGS, YOU TRICKY SON OF A GUN!

I'VE GOT NO CHOICE--

--PULL UP OR COLLIDE!

THEN DARKLIGHTER'S SKYHOPPER IS *AROUND THE TURN...*

... GROUND-CHARGE *MISSILES* SCORING ON WOMP RATS...

305

...BEFORE HIS SHIP STEERS **UPWARD**...

...TO **ESCAPE** STONE COLD **DISASTER** BY MILLIMETERS!

WAY TO **GO**, BIGGS! I WOULDN'T HAVE **DARED** TRY WHAT YOU DID.

GUESS THAT'S WHY **YOU'RE** HEADED FOR THE **ACADEMY** AND I'LL PROBABLY **STAY** ON THE MOISTURE FARM.

THE THOUGHT **TROUBLES** LUKE FOR A MOMENT... BUT IT IS SOON **FORGOTTEN** IN THE REVELRY THAT FOLLOWS **EVERY** CANYON RUN...

LOOK **SHARP**, CAMIE... HERE THEY **COME**. "TWO **SHOOTING STARS** THAT CAN'T BE **STOPPED!**"

THAT'S WHAT WE ALWAYS **SAY**, DEAK--

--AND I DIDN'T SEE ANYONE **ELSE** PROVING US **WRONG** TODAY.

THE BANTER IS LONG, LOUD, AND **MOSTLY** GOOD-NATURED...

LEAVING ANY HARD FEELINGS TO SOME LOCAL **JAWAS**...

...ANNOYED THAT THERE ARE NO **WRECKS** TO SCAVENGE.

SO IT GOES. UNTIL...

HEY!

SPEEDER'S ON **FIRE**...GOING TO **CRASH!** LET'S GET TO IT **FAST!**

AND... BIGGS, HE'S A **MILITIA SCOUT!**

EASY, MISTER...YOU'RE **OKAY** NOW.

N-NO! GOT TO **WARN** EVERYONE! BIG **TROUBLE**...!

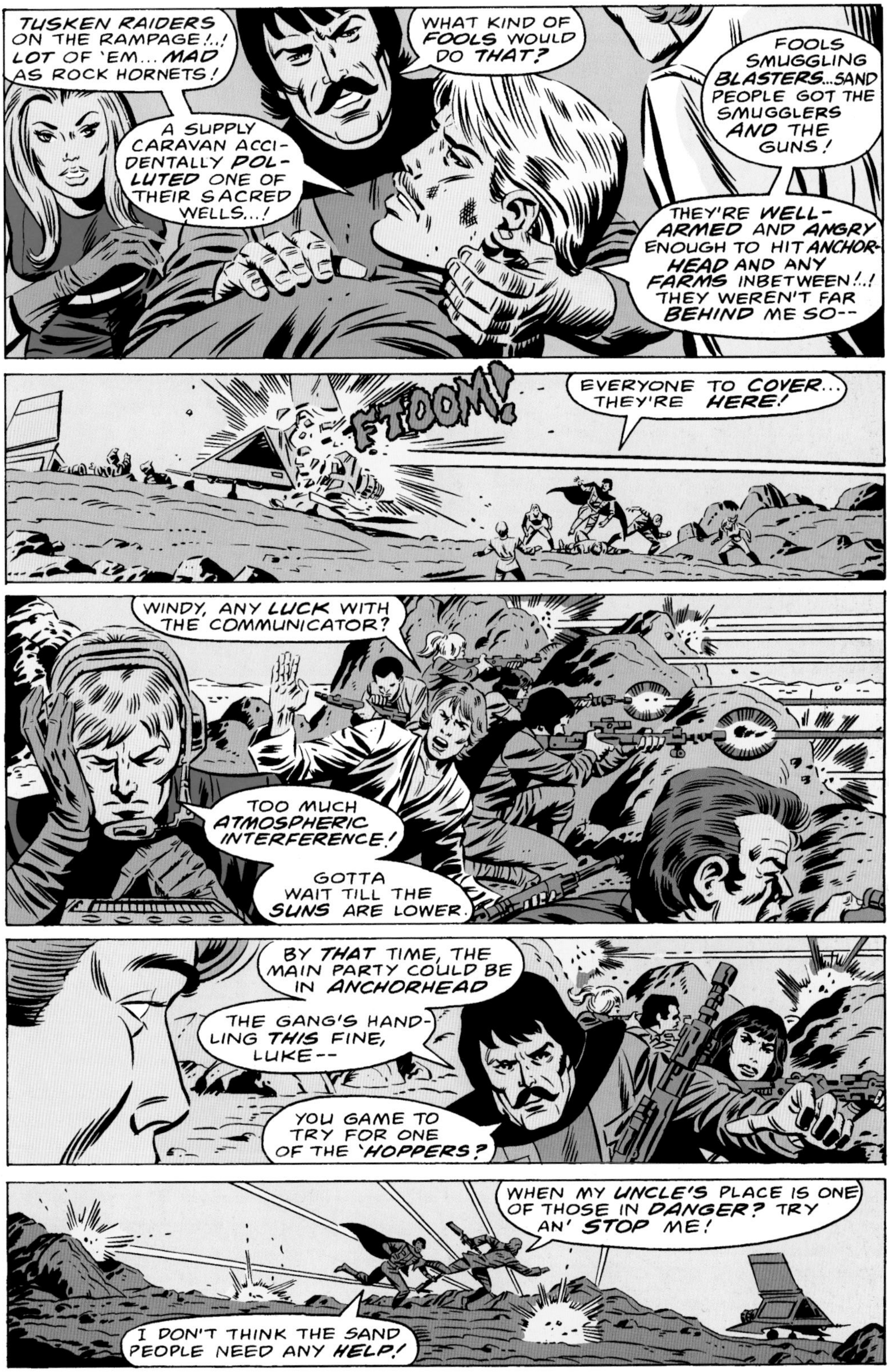
TUSKEN RAIDERS ON THE RAMPAGE!..! LOT OF 'EM... MAD AS ROCK HORNETS!
A SUPPLY CARAVAN ACCIDENTALLY POLLUTED ONE OF THEIR SACRED WELLS...!
WHAT KIND OF FOOLS WOULD DO THAT?
FOOLS SMUGGLING BLASTERS...SAND PEOPLE GOT THE SMUGGLERS AND THE GUNS!
THEY'RE WELL-ARMED AND ANGRY ENOUGH TO HIT ANCHORHEAD AND ANY FARMS INBETWEEN!..! THEY WEREN'T FAR BEHIND ME SO--
FTOOM!
EVERYONE TO COVER... THEY'RE HERE!
WINDY, ANY LUCK WITH THE COMMUNICATOR?
TOO MUCH ATMOSPHERIC INTERFERENCE!
GOTTA WAIT TILL THE SUNS ARE LOWER.
BY THAT TIME, THE MAIN PARTY COULD BE IN ANCHORHEAD
THE GANG'S HANDLING THIS FINE, LUKE--
YOU GAME TO TRY FOR ONE OF THE 'HOPPERS?
WHEN MY UNCLE'S PLACE IS ONE OF THOSE IN DANGER? TRY AN' STOP ME!
I DON'T THINK THE SAND PEOPLE NEED ANY HELP!

AND ONE IN PARTICULAR...

...SEEMS TO HAVE ANTICIPATED THIS VERY MOVE!

BIGGS!

BLAST THEM AND THEIR ABILITY TO POP UP OUT OF NOWHERE!

MOVE AWAY FROM ME, LUKE--

-- SO INSTEAD OF SWINGING THAT GADERFFI HE'LL BE FORCED TO THROW !--

≣UNGHHH..!≣

NO!

BRA-KOW!

G-GOOD SHOOTIN,' HOTSHOT..! HE ONLY GOT MY SHOULDER--

--BUT FROM THE WAY I F-FEEL... THAT POINT MAY HAVE BEEN DIPPED IN SAND BAT VENOM.

HANG ON, BIGGS--

--I'LL HAVE YOU TO A MEDI-DROID BEFORE THAT STUFF CAN DO ANY DAMAGE.

I'M BOOSTING US STRAIGHT UP AND OUT OF HERE!

NO, LUKE... STAY *LOW!* THEY'RE BET-TER *ARMED* THAN USUAL, REMEMBER?

TRY FOR *ALTITUDE* AND WE'RE A *SITTING DUCK* FOR THEIR *LONG RANGE BLASTERS!*

YOU'RE GOING TO HAVE TO STAY *DOWN...* GO *THROUGH* THE MOUN-TAINS...'STEAD'A *OVER* THEM...!

THROUGH...?! BIGGS, THERE'S *NO WAY* EXCEPT--

Y-YEAH. *DIABLO CUT!* NO ONE'S EVER *DONE* IT BEFORE... PROBABLY FOR THE GOOD REASON THAT IT'S *IMPOSSIBLE...!*

BUT IF WE TAKE TIME TO GO THE *LONG WAY* 'ROUND... SOME *FARMS* AND PART OF *ANCHOR-HEAD* MAY NOT BE *WAITING!*

AND YOU *HAVEN'T* MENTIONED *YOURSELF,* BIGGS--

--THAT THE *POISON* IN YOUR SYSTEM COULD TAKE *EFFECT* BEFORE THAT *LONG TRIP'S DONE!*

OKAY, MR. DARKLIGHTER... *DIABLO CUT* IT IS!

SOMEBODY'S GOTTA BE *FIRST...* WHY NOT *US?*

ONLY *TROUBLE* IS... UP TO NOW, I'VE BEEN A *MOISTURE FARMER* WHO PLAYS AROUND WITH A *SKYHOPPER*--

--AND DAYDREAMS ABOUT BEING A *STAR PILOT!* THIS IS GOING TO TAKE FAR MORE THAN *THAT*--

--AND THERE'S NO *REASON* TO BELIEVE I'VE *GOT* IT!

THEN...

THERE IS NO MORE TIME TO THINK...

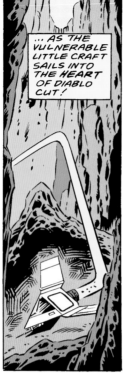

...AS THE VULNERABLE LITTLE CRAFT SAILS INTO THE HEART OF DIABLO CUT!

HERE, THERE CAN BE NO HESITATION. EVERYTHING RIDES ON REACTION AND INSTINCT...

BOY AND SKYHOPPER MUST BE-COME AS ONE...

...OR LOSE ALL.

LUKE...!

I... MUST'VE BEEN... CRAZY... TO GET YOU INTO THIS...

...IT CAN'T BE... DONE..!! IT...!

BIGGS FAINTS. BUT IF LUKE HAS HEARD HIS DELIRIOUS WHISPER, IT DOESN'T SHOW...

...AS HE PUSHES STEADILY ON INTO THE EROSION-CARVED CHAOS OF THE CUT...

...FINALLY SOARING INTO CAVERN DARKNESS!

BUT AT ITS END IS LIGHT. LIGHT AND THE PROMISE OF...

OPEN SKY ABOVE US, BIGGS! WE'RE THROUGH--

EXCEPT FOR...

...A TUSKEN RAIDER SCOUTING PARTY!

SURPRISE FAVORS THE SKYHOPPER... IN THE SAND PEOPLES' MEMORIES, NO MACHINE HAS EVER ROARED OUT OF THE DIABLO CUT!

-- STILL...

WE'RE CATCHING SOME OF THOSE SHOTS IN THE AFTER-BURNER--

SHE'S BOUND TO CATCH FIRE!

AND AS THE LARS MOISTURE FARM LOOMS ON THE HORIZON...

...THE FLAMES ARE THERE!

IF I CAN PLOW 'ER INTO THE SAND, MAYBE-- JUST MAYBE--

-- WE WON'T EXPLODE!

KA-WUMP!

LUKE! HAVE YOU GONE MAD, YOUNG MAN?!

GET A MED-PACK FOR BIGGS, UNCLE OWEN... AN' HAVE AUNT BERU CALL OUT THE LOCAL MILITIA FAST!

AND SUDDENLY... LUKE SKY-WALKER IS VERY TIRED.

TWILIGHT. IT IS OVER. WITH THE MILITIA'S ARRIVAL, THE TUSKEN RAIDERS ARE SWIFTLY TURNED BACK INTO THE JUNDLAND WASTES.

LUKE STANDS ALONE. THINKING. THINKING OF DIABLO CUT... OF THE WAY HE SOMEHOW REACHED DEEP WITHIN HIMSELF THERE AND DID THE IMPOSSIBLE.

I-IT WAS ALMOST LIKE SOME KIND OF... TEST. AND WHATEVER ELSE COMES OUT OF TODAY--

-- I FEEL LIKE I PASSED IT.

AND WITH THAT PASSING, LUKE KNOWS HE CAN NEVER BE A FARMER. HE HAS BRIEFLY TOUCHED THE STUFF OF HIS DREAMS AND FOUND THEM POSSIBLE. SOMEWAY, SOMEHOW... KNOWS HE MUST REACH OUT AGAIN.

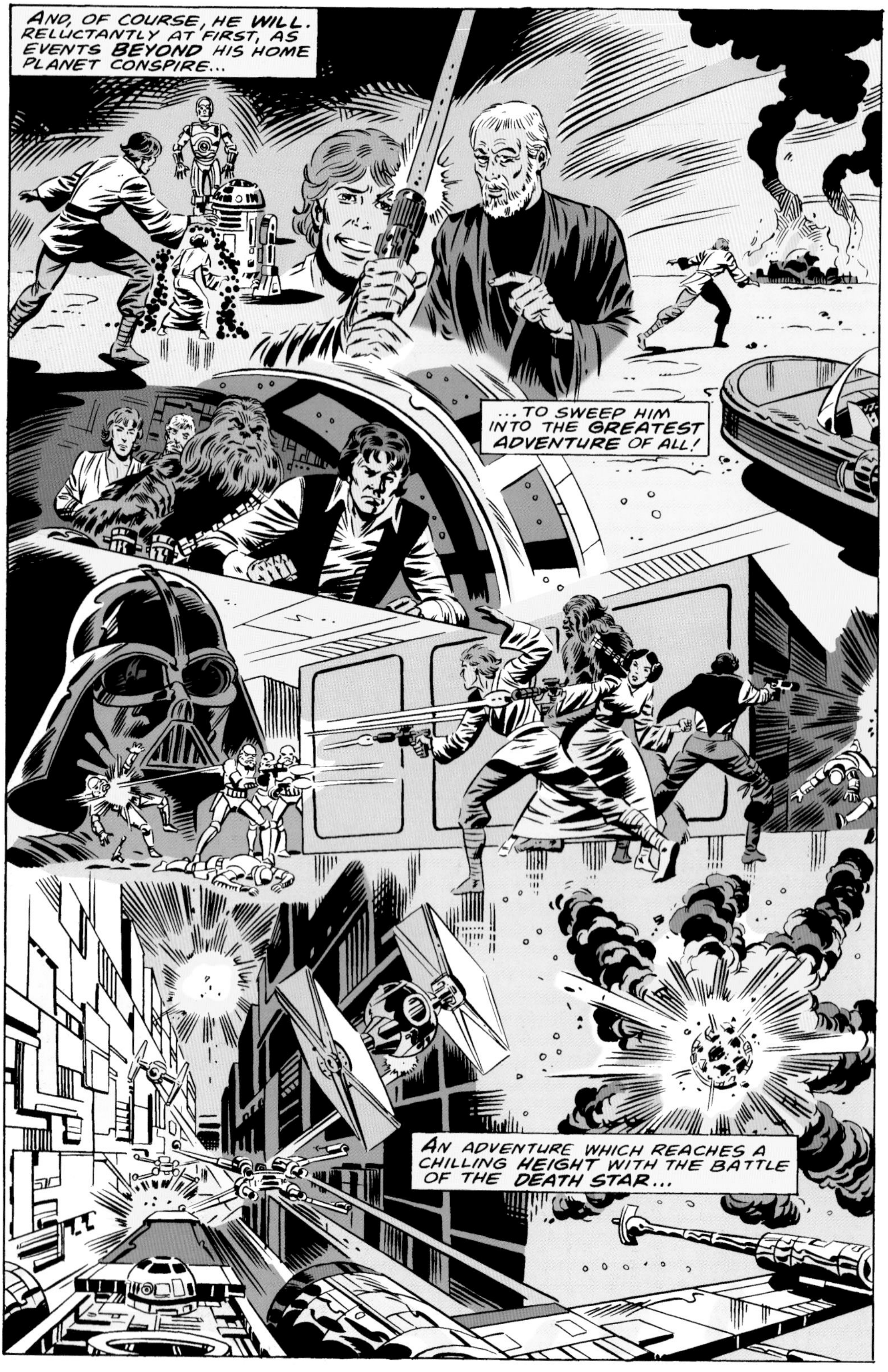
AND, OF COURSE, HE WILL. RELUCTANTLY AT FIRST, AS EVENTS BEYOND HIS HOME PLANET CONSPIRE...
...TO SWEEP HIM INTO THE GREATEST ADVENTURE OF ALL!
AN ADVENTURE WHICH REACHES A CHILLING HEIGHT WITH THE BATTLE OF THE DEATH STAR...

...BUT ONE WHICH STILL *CONTINUES* EVEN NOW. CONTINUES... AND *GROWS.*

HEY, *KID!* DON'T TURN *SPACE HAPPY* ON ME!

OH...*HAN!* NO PROBLEM... I WAS JUST *THINKING.*

PRETTY *DEEP STUFF* IT LOOKED LIKE. SORRY I'M LATE *RELIEVING* YOU.

COULDN'T RESIST GRABBING A FEW *EXTRA* WINKS.

YOU MUST BE *SCREAMIN'* TO GET CLEAR OF THAT *SEAT.*

HOURS AT THE CONTROLS IN DEEP SPACE CAN BE PRETTY *BORING.*

MAYBE *SOME* DAY, HAN. MAYBE IN *YEARS*--

BUT RIGHT *NOW*... I'M *EXACTLY* WHERE I WANT TO BE!

NEXT ISSUE: **THE HAND OF THE EMPIRE!**

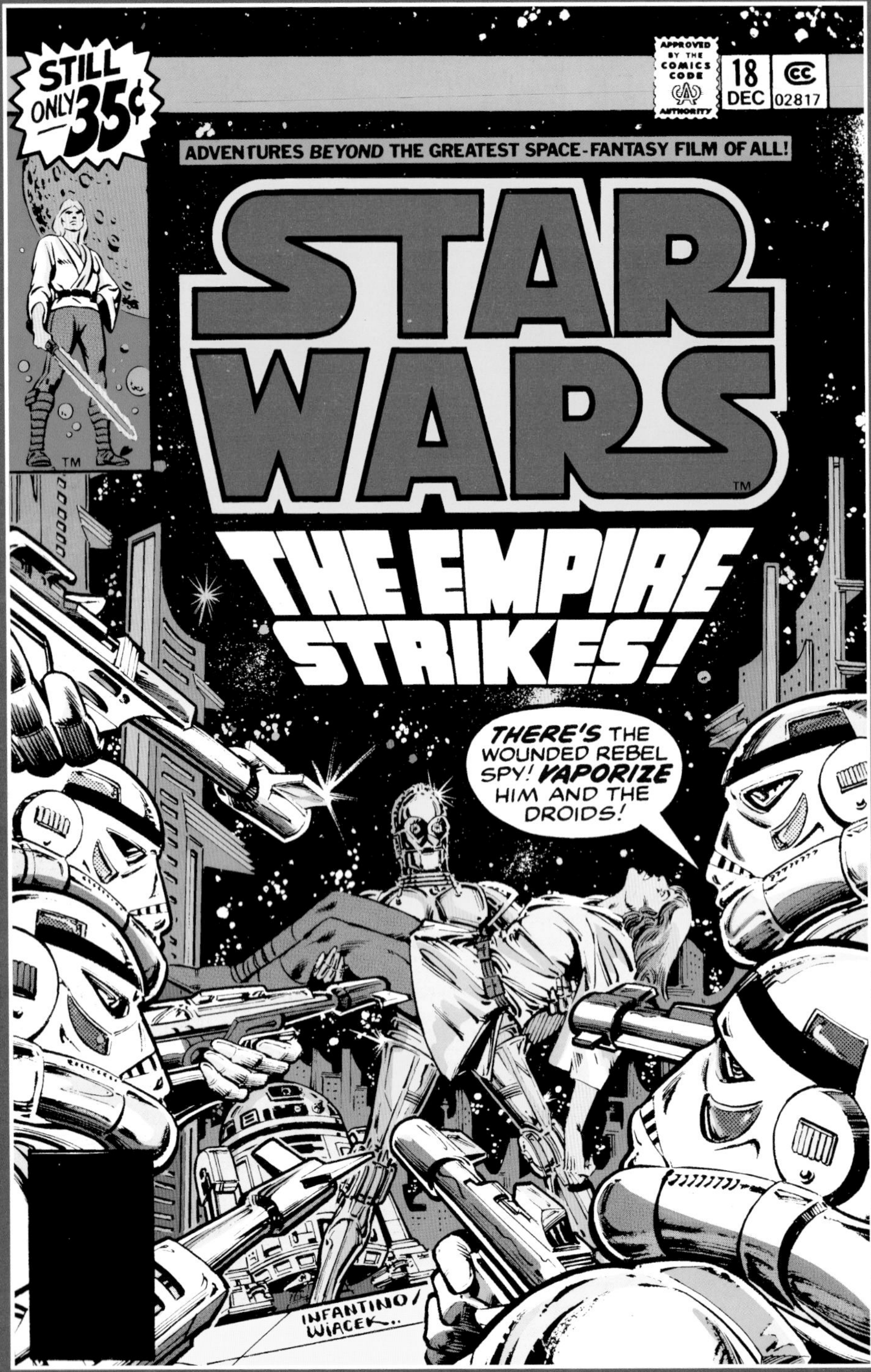
STILL ONLY 35¢
APPROVED BY THE COMICS CODE AUTHORITY
18 DEC
CC 02817
ADVENTURES BEYOND THE GREATEST SPACE-FANTASY FILM OF ALL!
STAR WARS™
THE EMPIRE STRIKES!
THERE'S THE WOUNDED REBEL SPY! VAPORIZE HIM AND THE DROIDS!
INFANTINO/ WIACEK..

Long ago in a galaxy far, far away. . .there exists a state of cosmic *civil war*. A brave alliance of *underground freedom fighters* has challenged the tyranny and oppression of the awesome *Galactic Empire*. This is their story!

LucasFilm PRESENTS: **STAR WARS**™ THE GREATEST **SPACE FANTASY** OF ALL!

CONTINUING THE SAGA BEGUN IN THE FILM BY GEORGE LUCAS RELEASED BY 20TH CENTURY FOX.

| ARCHIE GOODWIN WRITER / EDITOR | CARMINE INFANTINO & GENE DAY ARTISTS | RICK PARKER LETTERER | JANICE COHEN COLORIST | JIM SHOOTER CONSULTING EDITOR |

THE EMPIRE STRIKES!

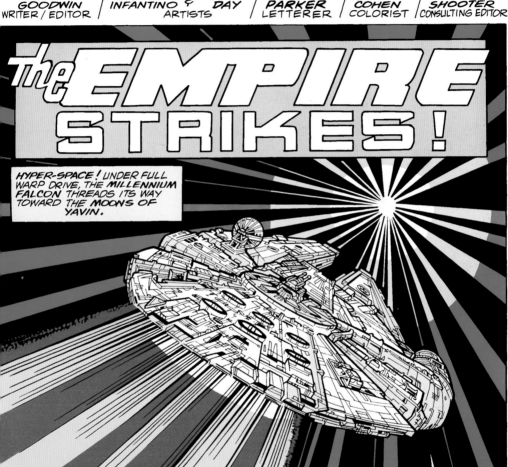

HYPER-SPACE! UNDER FULL WARP DRIVE, THE MILLENNIUM FALCON THREADS ITS WAY TOWARD THE MOONS OF YAVIN.

ALL ABOARD THE SMUGGLING SHIP ARE TIRED. A MULTITUDE OF ADVENTURES LIE BEHIND THEM. EACH HAS TAKEN ITS TOLL.

IT IS A TIME OF GREAT VULNERABILITY...

PRINCESS LEIA! CAPTAIN SOLO! COME QUICKLY! SOMETHING'S HAPPENED TO MASTER LUKE!

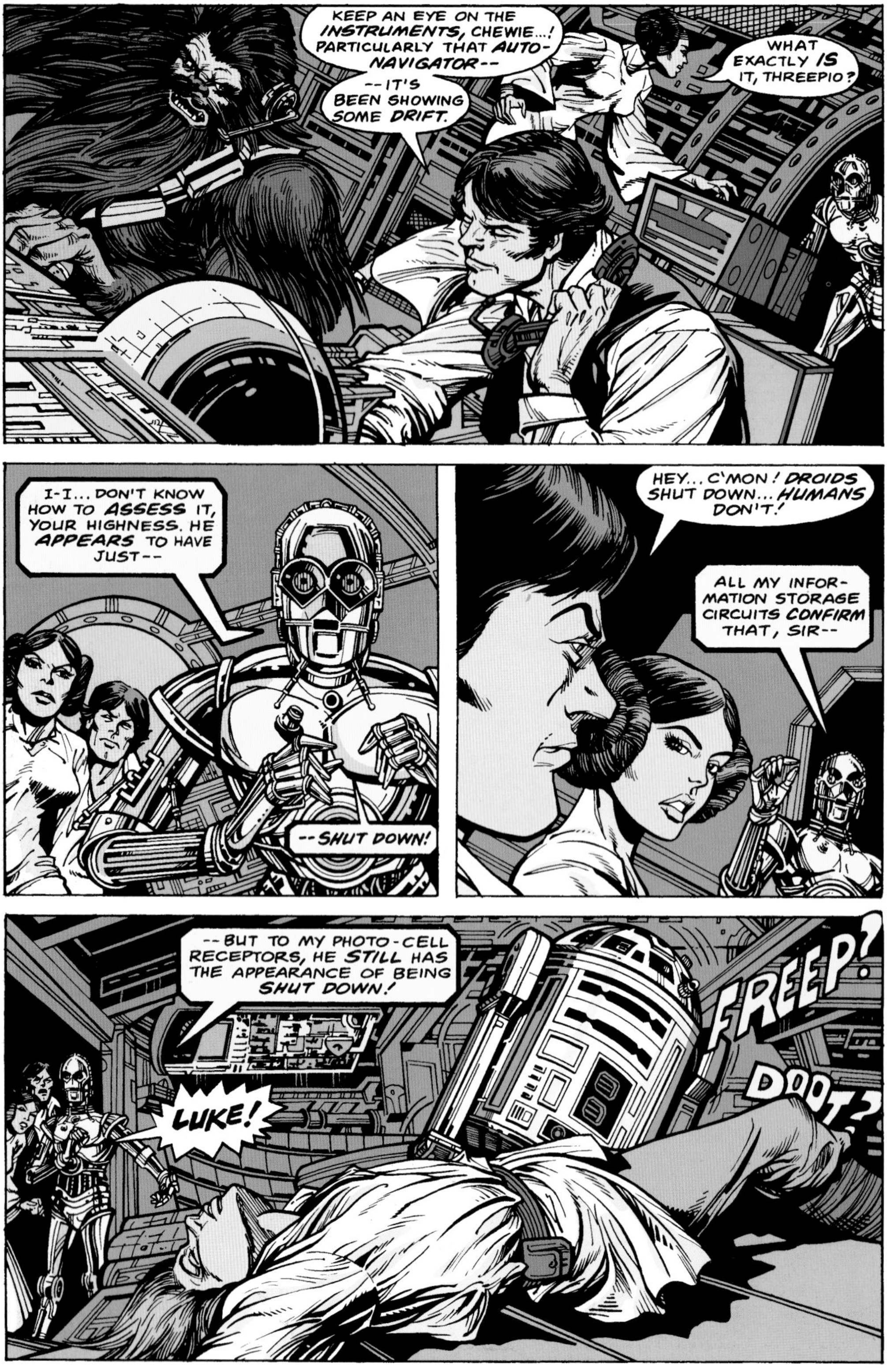
KEEP AN EYE ON THE INSTRUMENTS, CHEWIE...! PARTICULARLY THAT AUTO-NAVIGATOR--
--IT'S BEEN SHOWING SOME DRIFT.
WHAT EXACTLY IS IT, THREEPIO?
I-I... DON'T KNOW HOW TO ASSESS IT, YOUR HIGHNESS. HE APPEARS TO HAVE JUST--
--SHUT DOWN!
HEY... C'MON! DROIDS SHUT DOWN... HUMANS DON'T!
ALL MY INFORMATION STORAGE CIRCUITS CONFIRM THAT, SIR--
--BUT TO MY PHOTO-CELL RECEPTORS, HE STILL HAS THE APPEARANCE OF BEING SHUT DOWN!
LUKE!
FREEP?
DOOT?

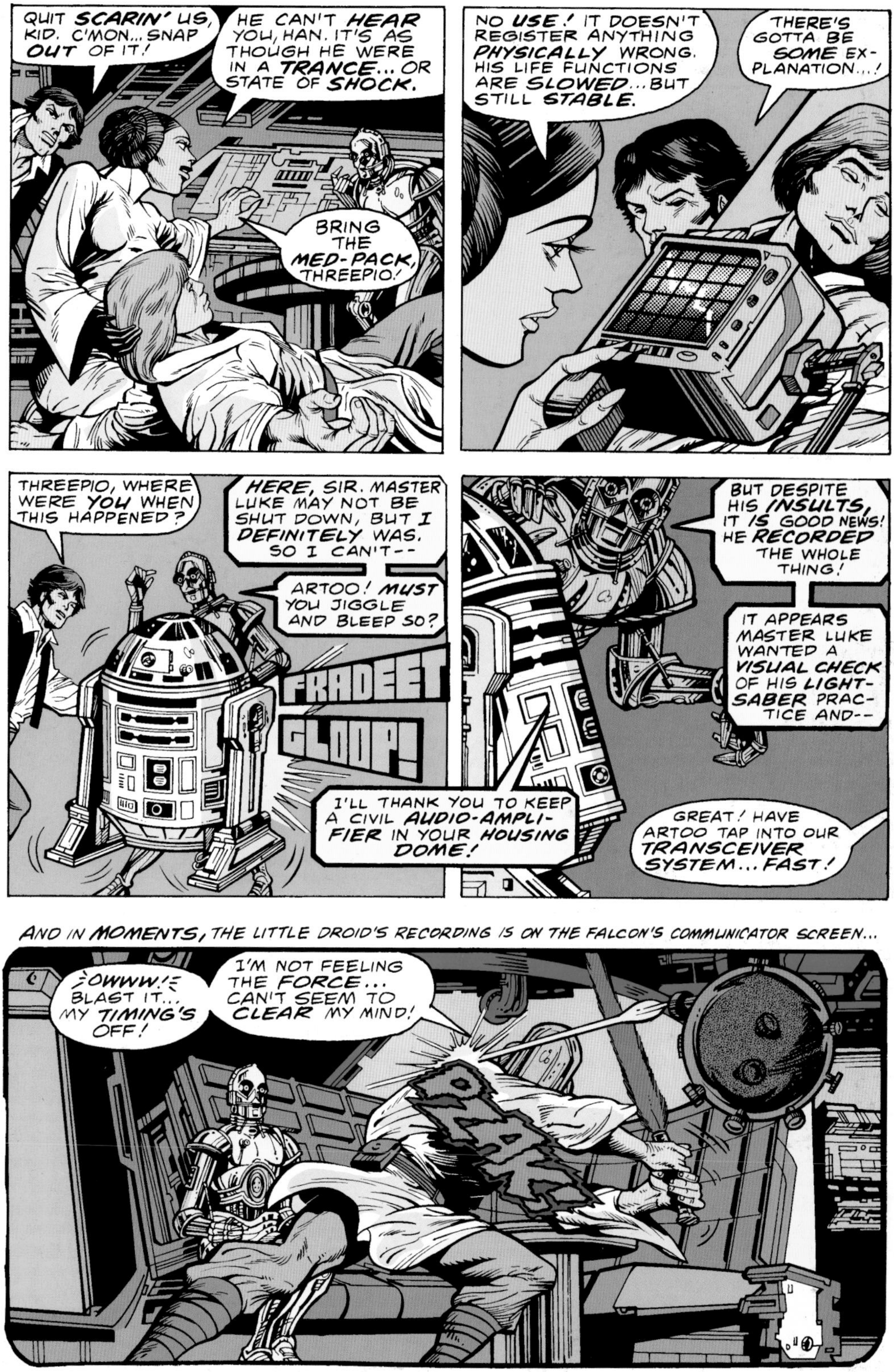
QUIT SCARIN' US, KID. C'MON... SNAP OUT OF IT!
HE CAN'T HEAR YOU, HAN. IT'S AS THOUGH HE WERE IN A TRANCE... OR STATE OF SHOCK.
BRING THE MED-PACK, THREEPIO!
NO USE! IT DOESN'T REGISTER ANYTHING PHYSICALLY WRONG. HIS LIFE FUNCTIONS ARE SLOWED... BUT STILL STABLE.
THERE'S GOTTA BE SOME EX-PLANATION...!
THREEPIO, WHERE WERE YOU WHEN THIS HAPPENED?
HERE, SIR. MASTER LUKE MAY NOT BE SHUT DOWN, BUT I DEFINITELY WAS. SO I CAN'T--
ARTOO! MUST YOU JIGGLE AND BLEEP SO?
FRADEET
GLOOP!
I'LL THANK YOU TO KEEP A CIVIL AUDIO-AMPLI-FIER IN YOUR HOUSING DOME!
BUT DESPITE HIS INSULTS, IT IS GOOD NEWS! HE RECORDED THE WHOLE THING!
IT APPEARS MASTER LUKE WANTED A VISUAL CHECK OF HIS LIGHT-SABER PRAC-TICE AND--
GREAT! HAVE ARTOO TAP INTO OUR TRANSCEIVER SYSTEM... FAST!
AND IN MOMENTS, THE LITTLE DROID'S RECORDING IS ON THE FALCON'S COMMUNICATOR SCREEN...
OWWW! BLAST IT... MY TIMING'S OFF!
I'M NOT FEELING THE FORCE... CAN'T SEEM TO CLEAR MY MIND!

BEN KENOBI DIDN'T HAVE VERY *LONG* TO INSTRUCT ME IN THE WAYS OF THE *FORCE,* BUT THERE WAS AN *EXERCISE*-- A KIND OF *MEDITATION*--HE MENTIONED.

MAYBE IF IT ISN'T COMING *TOGETHER*... I SHOULD TRY *THAT.*

KEEP *TAPING,* ARTOO... LET'S SEE IF I GET *THIS* RIGHT.

A *JEDI KNIGHT* LIKE BEN WAS WAY *BEYOND* THIS KIND OF THING... BUT HE SAID IT WOULD HELP *ME* GROW MORE ATTUNED TO THE *FORCE.*

OKAY. EYES *CLOSED*... DRAW IN ON YOURSELF... SHUT OUT THE *PHYSICAL.*

JUST TRY TO *FEEL*... TO LET YOUR MIND *DRIFT FREE.*

DRIFT *FREE*... BEYOND THE *SHIP.* OPEN...FREE... AMONG THE *STARS*... ALONE.

NO... *NOT* ALONE. SOMETHING...*COMING.* SOMEONE... *BEN*...? BEN, IT IS --

NO!

T-THAT *CRY* TOUCHED MY *EMERGENCY REACTIVATOR*--

THE NEXT THING I *BEHELD* WAS MASTER LUKE --

--SHUT DOWN!

WILL YOU STOP *SAYING* THAT, CIRCUIT-DOME?! THE KID JUST *SCARED* HIMSELF WITH THAT *FORCE* MUMBO-JUMBO... ANY MINUTE HE'LL PROBABLY COME AROUND ON HIS *OWN.*

I *HOPE.*

BUT WE CAN'T BE *SURE.* AND IF WE'RE *WRONG* --

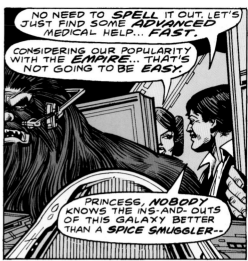

NO NEED TO *SPELL* IT OUT. LET'S JUST FIND SOME *ADVANCED* MEDICAL HELP... *FAST.*

CONSIDERING OUR POPULARITY WITH THE *EMPIRE*... THAT'S NOT GOING TO BE *EASY.*

PRINCESS, *NOBODY* KNOWS THE INS-AND-OUTS OF THIS GALAXY BETTER THAN A *SPICE SMUGGLER* --

-- AND NOBODY'S A BETTER SPICE-SMUGGLER THAN *ME!* YOU'VE GOT *NOTHING* TO WORRY ABOUT, YOUR ROYALNESS!

THEN WHY AM I STILL *WORRIED?*

BUT HAN'S FINGERS ARE ALREADY DEFTLY MOVING OVER THE SHIP'S *COMPUTER,* READJUSTING FOR...

... THE DROP BACK TO SUB-LIGHT SPEED. AND... *TROUBLE!*

ATTENTION, FREIGHTER... *ATTENTION!* YOU ARE MAKING *UNAUTHORIZED* ENTRY INTO A *MILITARY CONTAINMENT ZONE* OF THE EMPIRE.

PREPARE FOR *IMMEDIATE BOARDING* AND *FULL INSPECTION!*

THANK YOU FOR CLEARING *ONE THING* UP, MISTER SOLO... NOW I *KNOW* WHY I'M STILL WORRIED!

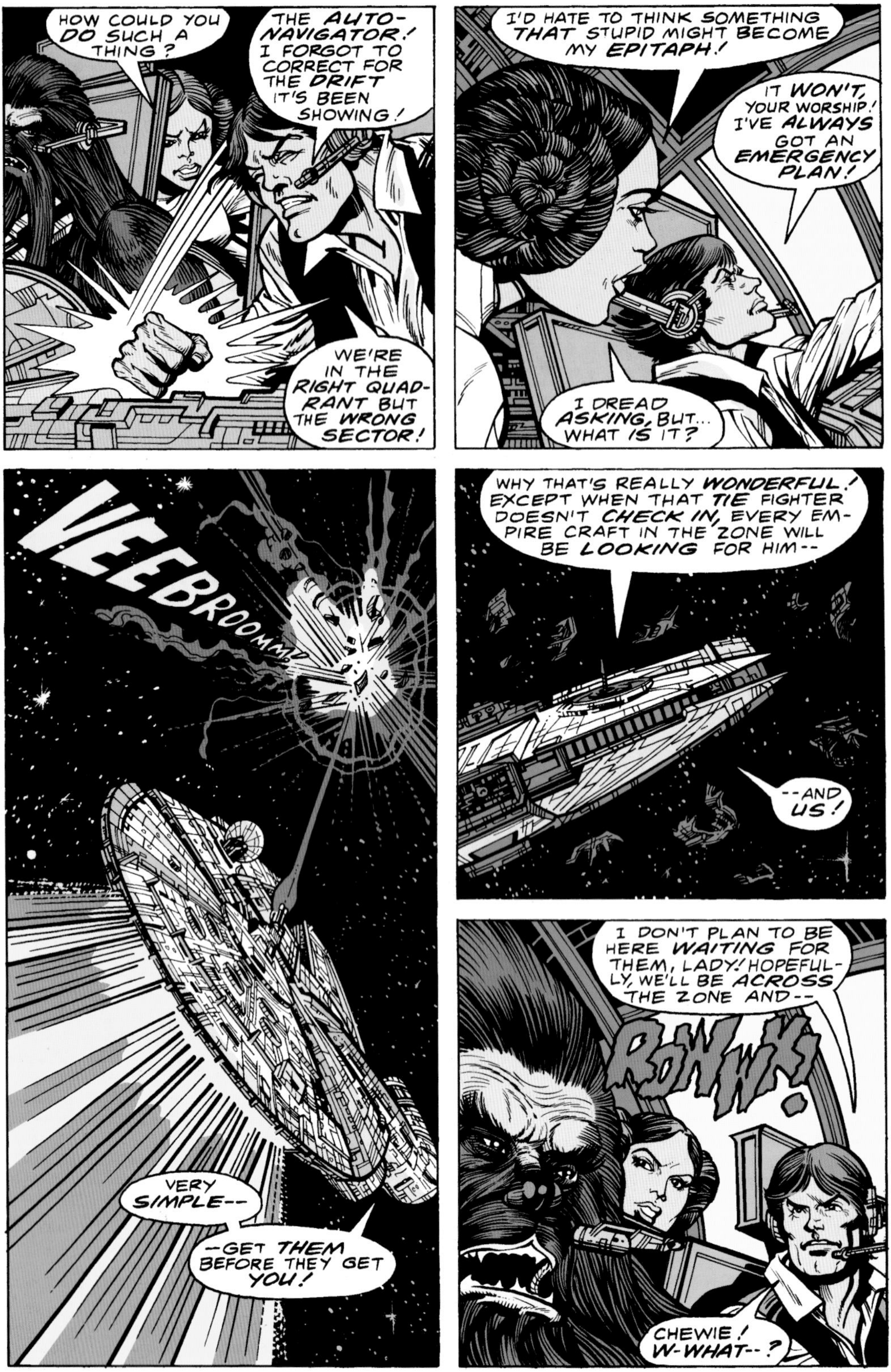
HOW COULD YOU DO SUCH A THING?
THE AUTO-NAVIGATOR! I FORGOT TO CORRECT FOR THE DRIFT IT'S BEEN SHOWING!
WE'RE IN THE RIGHT QUADRANT BUT THE WRONG SECTOR!
I'D HATE TO THINK SOMETHING THAT STUPID MIGHT BECOME MY EPITAPH!
IT WON'T, YOUR WORSHIP! I'VE ALWAYS GOT AN EMERGENCY PLAN!
I DREAD ASKING, BUT... WHAT IS IT?
VEEBROOMM!
VERY SIMPLE--
--GET THEM BEFORE THEY GET YOU!
WHY THAT'S REALLY WONDERFUL! EXCEPT WHEN THAT TIE FIGHTER DOESN'T CHECK IN, EVERY EMPIRE CRAFT IN THE ZONE WILL BE LOOKING FOR HIM--
--AND US!
I DON'T PLAN TO BE HERE WAITING FOR THEM, LADY! HOPEFULLY, WE'LL BE ACROSS THE ZONE AND--
ROWWK!
CHEWIE! W-WHAT--?

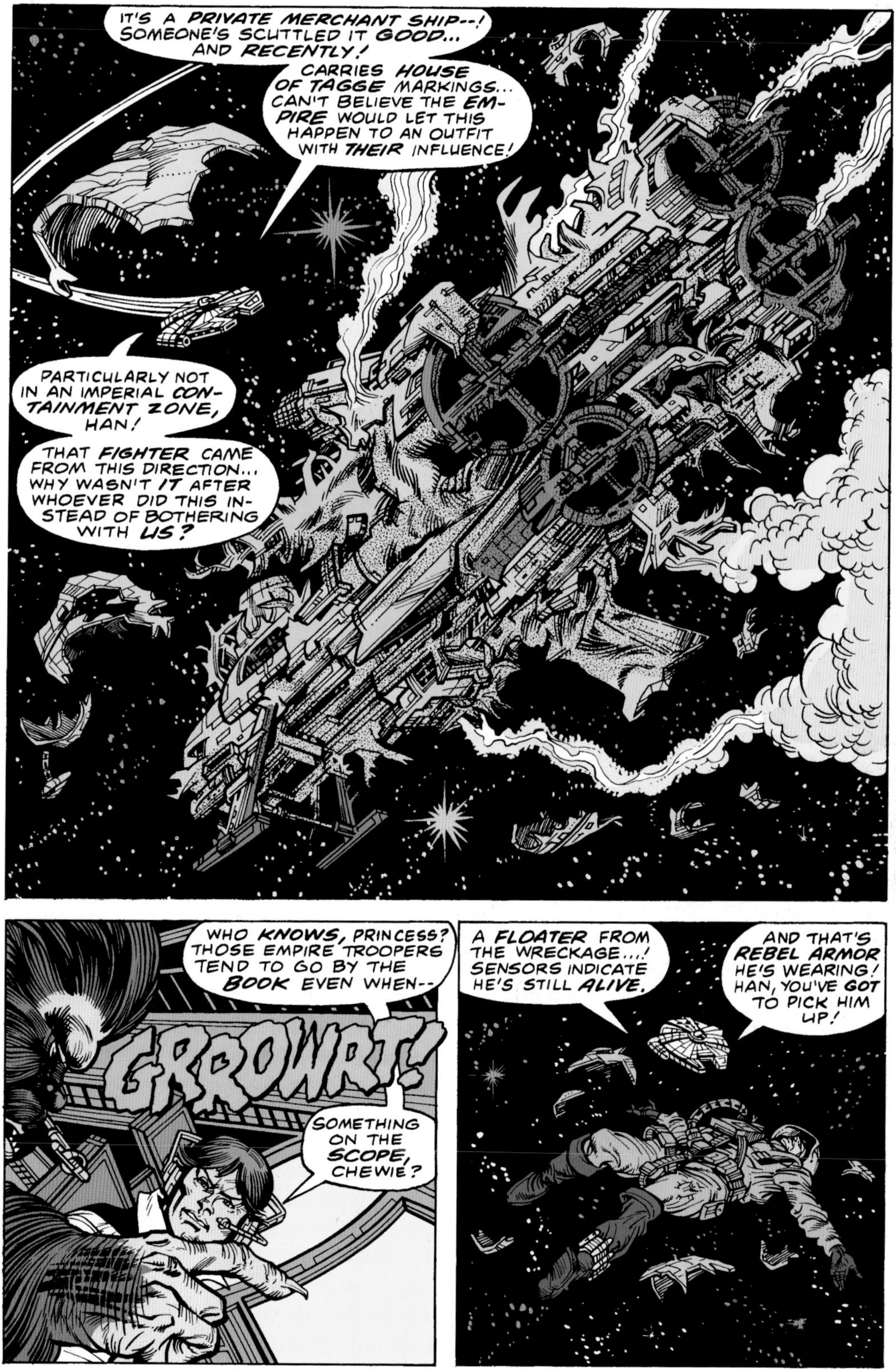
IT'S A PRIVATE MERCHANT SHIP--! SOMEONE'S SCUTTLED IT GOOD... AND RECENTLY!
CARRIES HOUSE OF TAGGE MARKINGS... CAN'T BELIEVE THE EMPIRE WOULD LET THIS HAPPEN TO AN OUTFIT WITH THEIR INFLUENCE!
PARTICULARLY NOT IN AN IMPERIAL CONTAINMENT ZONE, HAN!
THAT FIGHTER CAME FROM THIS DIRECTION... WHY WASN'T IT AFTER WHOEVER DID THIS INSTEAD OF BOTHERING WITH US?
WHO KNOWS, PRINCESS? THOSE EMPIRE TROOPERS TEND TO GO BY THE BOOK EVEN WHEN--
GRROWRT!
SOMETHING ON THE SCOPE, CHEWIE?
A FLOATER FROM THE WRECKAGE...! SENSORS INDICATE HE'S STILL ALIVE.
AND THAT'S REBEL ARMOR HE'S WEARING! HAN, YOU'VE GOT TO PICK HIM UP!

GOT HIM, PRINCESS... BUT HE'S IN **BAD SHAPE.**

LAY HIM DOWN OVER **HERE!** THREEPIO, WE'LL NEED THE **MED-PACK** AGAIN--

N-NO... **TOO LATE...!** EMPIRE SAW TO THAT WHEN THEY **FORCED** US ABOARD THE MERCHANT SHIP... BEFORE **DESTROYING** IT...!

HE'S **DELIRIOUS...** THE EMPIRE WOULDN'T HIT A **TAGGE** FAMILY SHIP... ONE BROTHER'S AN **IMPERIAL** FLEET COMMANDER!

BUT... IT'S... **TRUE...!** DON'T KNOW... **WHY...** BUT THEY WANTED IT TO LOOK LIKE... A **REBEL RAID...!**

WE WERE **PRISONERS...** TAKEN DURING FIGHTING IN ANOTHER SYSTEM...! BROUGHT **HERE** SO... OUR **BODIES** WOULD MAKE SCHEME **CONVINCING...!**

SOMEONE'S GONE TO A LOT OF EFFORT TO MAKE THE **ALLIANCE** LOOK BAD.

HAN, WHERE WERE YOU **TAKING** US...? COULD THE SCUTTLED SHIP BE FROM THE **SAME PLACE?**

PRINCESS, I HATE TO **INTERRUPT,** BUT ACCORDING TO **CHEWBACCA--**

--WE'RE IN MORE **TROUBLE** THAN EVER!

ATTENTION, FREIGHTER! YOUR PRESENCE HERE PLACES YOU UNDER SUSPICION OF **PIRACY** AND/OR **ACTS OF REBELLION.**

HEAVE TO INSTANTLY... OR WE WILL **OPEN FIRE!**

FULL ENGINES, CHEWIE!

WROWK!

IT'S RUN FOR YOUR *LIFE* TIME!

VWHOOOM!

ATTA BOY, BIG BUDDY! IT'S ONLY A *LIGHT CRUISER*...NOT IN THE FULL *STAR-DESTROYER* CLASS!

WITH A LITTLE *LUCK,* WE MAY EVEN *MAKE* IT!

AND ACROSS THE BRIGHT GALACTIC STAR-FIELD, A WILD AND DESPERATE CHASE BEGINS...

HANG *TIGHT,* EVERYONE! OUR *REAR DEFLECTORS* ARE TAKING A BEATING...BUT WE'RE *STARTING* TO LEAVE 'EM BEHIND!

WHILE ON THE PURSUING CRAFT'S BRIDGE...

COMMANDER *STROM!* THAT FREIGHTER MAY *LOOK* LIKE JUNK...BUT IT'S GRADUALLY *OUTDISTANCING* US! THE COMPUTER ESTIMATES--

IT *CANNOT* ESTIMATE HOW *WELL* THE FREIGHTER FITS INTO *IMPERIAL* PLANS.

WE HAVE *TIE FIGHTERS* ON PATROL...ORDER *THEM* TO CUT IT OFF BEFORE IT'S OUT OF THE *ZONE.*

AND SOON, THE VOID AHEAD OF THE MILLENNIUM FALCON IS SUDDENLY FILLED BY...

TIE SHIPS! THE NEW IMPROVED MODELS! THE EMPIRE'S PLAYIN' HAMMER AND ANVIL, CHEWIE--

GROWRRL!

THAT'S RIGHT, PAL... WE'RE WHAT GETS POUNDED ON IN BETWEEN!

SO LET'S NOT STAY THERE!

THAT FREIGHTER'S MANEUVERING LIKE A FIGHTER, COMMANDER STROM--

--IT'S LEFT THE TIES AND US FIRING AT EACH OTHER!

AND WITH MORE THAN YOUR USUAL ACCURACY! REORDER FIRE PATTERNS, FOOL! AND STAY WITH THOSE FUGITIVES--

--THEY'RE HEADED OUT OF THE ZONE!

THOSE EMPIRE SHIPS ARE REGROUPING, HAN... MOVING IN AGAIN!

NO PROBLEM, YOUR ROYALNESS! WE CONFUSED 'EM JUST LONG ENOUGH--

-- OUR SANCTUARY'S IN SIGHT!

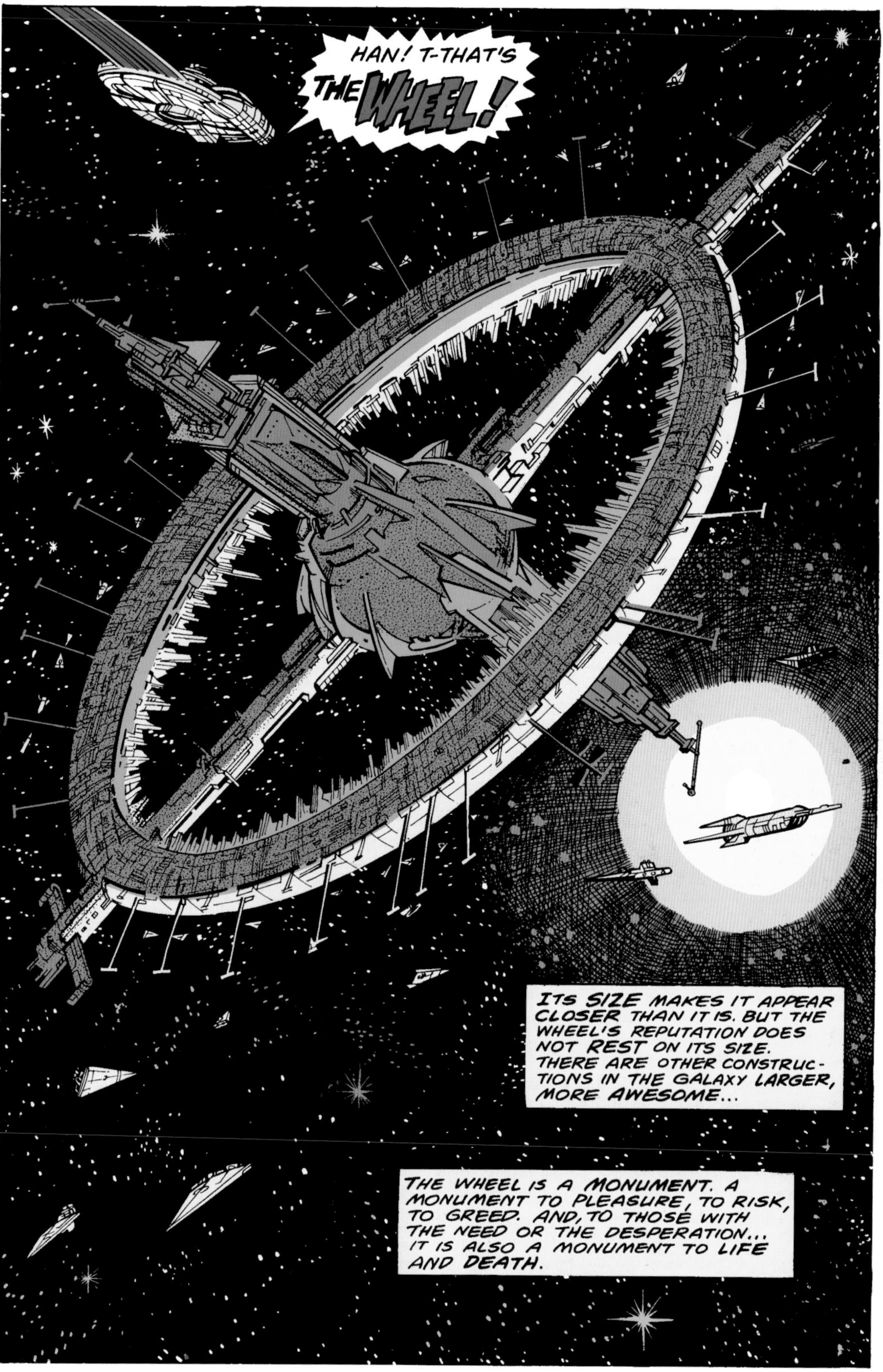
HAN! T-THAT'S THE WHEEL!
ITS SIZE MAKES IT APPEAR CLOSER THAN IT IS. BUT THE WHEEL'S REPUTATION DOES NOT REST ON ITS SIZE. THERE ARE OTHER CONSTRUCTIONS IN THE GALAXY LARGER, MORE AWESOME...
THE WHEEL IS A MONUMENT. A MONUMENT TO PLEASURE, TO RISK, TO GREED. AND, TO THOSE WITH THE NEED OR THE DESPERATION... IT IS ALSO A MONUMENT TO LIFE AND DEATH.

MY FATHER FOUGHT THE *BUILDING* OF THIS PLACE WHEN *HE* WAS A *SENATOR!* IT'S *DE-GRADING*, IT'S *BAR-BARIC*, IT'S—

IT'S THE *ULTIMATE GAMBLING PALACE*, PRINCESS. THE *STAKES* ARE HIGH... BUT *MOST* GALACTIC CITIZENS WOULDN'T HAVE IT *ANY* OTHER WAY!

AND SINCE IT'S ONE OF THE *FEW* PLACES WHERE *STORM-TROOPERS* AREN'T PERMITTED TO POKE THEIR HELMETED LITTLE HEADS... COUNT *ME* AS A BOOSTER!

COMMANDER STROM, WE ARE NOW WELL *OUT* OF OUR CONTAINMENT ZONE AND INTO THE *WHEEL'S* IMMUNITY SPHERE. *REGU-LATIONS* STATE—

REGULATIONS ARE MERELY *TOOLS* FOR A CREATIVE AND AGGRESSIVE LEADER! RETURN TO YOUR *PATROL!* I'M PROCEEDING *AFTER* THE FUGITIVES!

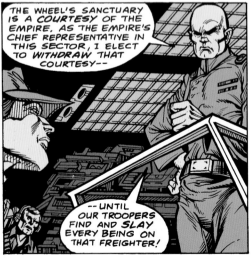

THE WHEEL'S SANCTUARY IS A *COURTESY* OF THE EMPIRE, AS THE EMPIRE'S CHIEF REPRESENTATIVE IN THIS SECTOR, I ELECT TO *WITHDRAW* THAT COURTESY—

—UNTIL OUR TROOPERS FIND AND *SLAY* EVERY BEING ON THAT FREIGHTER!

R3WNK!

I CAN READ THE SCOPE, TOO, CHEWIE! THAT CRUISER AIN'T GIVIN' UP! BETTER STRAP IN, YOUR WORSHIP—

—THIS IS GONNA BE A REAL *QUICK* DOCKING!

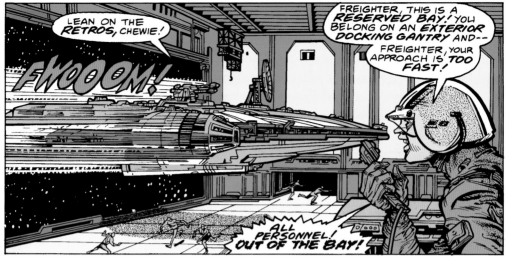

LEAN ON THE *RETROS*, CHEWIE!

FWOOOM!

FREIGHTER, THIS IS A *RESERVED BAY!* YOU BELONG ON AN *EXTERIOR DOCKING GANTRY* AND-- FREIGHTER, YOUR APPROACH IS *TOO FAST!*

ALL PERSONNEL! *OUT OF THE BAY!*

BARRK!

WATTA YOU *MEAN*, WE CUT IT *TOO CLOSE?*

ANYTHING SHY OF THE BAY WALL IS A *GREAT LANDING!*

LET'S *GO*, PRINCESS! WE *MADE* IT!

I'M AFRAID *ONE* OF US *DIDN'T*, HAN!

CHEWIE, TAKE HIS BODY WITH *YOU*. WE'LL SPLIT UP FOR NOW AND MEET *LATER* AT THE *CRIMSON CASINO LOUNGE*.

PRINCESS, YOU'LL GO WITH *ME* AND THE DROIDS CAN GET LUKE TO THE HOSPITAL FACILITIES.

NO! WE CAN'T *ABANDON* LUKE IN HIS CONDITION!

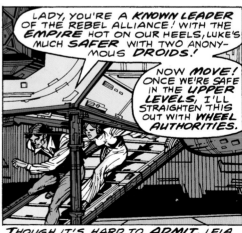

LADY, YOU'RE A *KNOWN LEADER* OF THE REBEL ALLIANCE! WITH THE *EMPIRE* HOT ON OUR HEELS, LUKE'S MUCH *SAFER* WITH TWO ANONYMOUS *DROIDS!*

NOW *MOVE!* ONCE WE'RE SAFE IN THE *UPPER LEVELS*, I'LL STRAIGHTEN THIS OUT WITH *WHEEL AUTHORITIES.*

THOUGH IT'S HARD TO ADMIT, LEIA ORGANA FINDS HAN SOLO'S WORDS MAKE SENSE.

WE'RE AFTER **REBELS** GUILTY OF PIRACY AND HAVE BEEN AUTHORIZED TO **SHOOT** TO KILL.

WHERE DID THEY **GO** AFTER ABANDONING THIS SHIP?!

T-THEY **SCATTERED**...! BUT ON THE **WHEEL**, YOU'VE NO **RIGHT** TO--

WE'VE WHATEVER RIGHT OUR **COMMANDER** GIVES US!

HEAT PARTICLE DETECTOR INDICATES THEY SPLIT INTO **THREE GROUPS**--

EACH TOOK A **DIFFERENT LIFT!**

BAY 31

QUICKLY! WE'LL DO THE **SAME.** THIS ASSIGNMENT'S GOING TO GET **STICKY** IF THEY REACH THE **CROWDS** ON THE UPPER LEVELS.

I'D HATE TO ACCIDENTALLY BLAST A VACATIONING **IMPERIAL GOVERNOR!**

EXCUSE MY **INTERRUPTING,** SENATOR GREYSHADE, BUT WE SEEM TO HAVE A **SERIOUS COMPLICATION**--

FUGITIVES HAVE BOARDED THE WHEEL WITHOUT PAYING A **REGISTRATION FEE** OR ESTABLISHING THEIR **CREDIT LEVEL**--

A **SMALL MATTER,** SIR, EXCEPT **IMPERIAL** TROOPS HAVE FOLLOWED... AND ARE SERIOUSLY BENT ON **DESTROYING** THEM.

WELL, THAT **IS** INTERESTING, MASTER-COM. BETTER PUT ME IN **CONTACT** WITH THE GOOD COMMANDER STROM.

NATURE SEEMS TO HAVE COMPENSATED FOR HIS LACK OF **HAIR** BY MAKING HIM EXCEPTIONALLY **THICK-HEADED.**

DONE, SIR. HE'S ON HIS *CRUISER* AT THE IMPERIAL DOCK.

STROM? WHAT'S THIS ALL *ABOUT*? ONE OF THE CASINOS FORGET TO LET YOU *WIN*?

COMMANDER STROM TO YOU, GREYSHADE.

AND *SENATOR GREY-SHADE* TO *YOU*, COMMAND-ER. THE EMPEROR MAY HAVE *DISSOLVED* THAT AUGUST OFFICE, BUT I *STILL* LIKE THE TITLE... EVEN IF I DID PUT IT TO *DUBIOUS* USE.

NOW WHY ARE *YOUR MEN* ON THE *WHEEL*?

TO KILL REBELS.

AN ANSWER *WORTHY* OF A MILITARY MAN... AND A *FOOL!*

STROM, AREN'T YOU *AWARE* THAT MUCH OF THE EMPIRE'S MILITARY FUNDING COMES FROM THE *TAX* ON THE WHEEL'S *EARNINGS*?

THOSE EARNINGS ARE *LARGE* BE-CAUSE MOST OF THE GALAXY LIKES TO *GAMBLE* HERE--

AND THEY *LIKE* GAMBLING HERE BECAUSE THEY *KNOW* IT'S TOTALLY *FREE* FROM IMPERIAL INTERFERENCE!

START *INTERFERING* AND YOU *DRY UP* THIS FOUNTAIN OF WEALTH! EVEN THE *EMPEROR* UNDERSTANDS THAT!

IF HE LEARNS YOU'VE *JEOPARDIZED* IT... YOU'LL BE LUCKY TO COMMAND A *FERTILIZER SCOW.*

KILL YOUR REBELS *AFTER* THEY LEAVE HERE! IT'S ONE OF THE PURPOSES OF YOUR *CONTAINMENT ZONE!*

PERHAPS YOU'LL CHANGE YOUR *SONG*, GREYSHADE, WHEN YOU LEARN *THESE* REBELS *PLUN-DERED* AND *DESTROYED* A HOUSE OF TAGGE MERCHANT SHIP--

--ONE DELIVERING *WHEEL* PROFITS TO YOUR *INNER-SYSTEMS BANK!*

BLAST YOU, STROM! WHY DIDN'T YOU SAY SO AT ONCE?!

ALL RIGHT! IF YOUR MEN CAN GET THE REBELS ON THE LOWER LEVELS...THEY'RE YOURS! BUT I WANT ONE ALIVE FOR QUESTIONING!

THANK YOU, SENATOR.

RELAY THE WHEEL ADMINISTRATOR'S WISHES TO OUR PURSUIT SQUADS--

--BUT SEE THAT THE TRANSMISSION IS GARBLED! PARTICULARLY THAT BUSINESS ABOUT "ONE ALIVE FOR QUESTIONING!"

ALIVE, THE FOOLS FROM THAT FREIGHTER MIGHT CAST DOUBT THAT THE SCUTTLING OF THE MERCHANT SHIP WAS A REBEL ACTION--

--DEAD THEY'LL BE OUR FINAL PROOF.

AND A MOST IMPORTANT STEP--

"--IN THE SUCCESS OF THE EMPIRE'S PLAN!"

ARTOO-DEETOO, THESE ACCESS CORRIDORS SEEM ENDLESS! WE'RE LOST! MY SERVO-MOTORS ARE OVER-STRAINED AND--

NOW WHAT ARE YOU DOING?!

BREE DOOP!

TRYING TO TAP A MAIN COMPUTER LINE IN THE WALL CIRCUITRY?

WELL, THAT MIGHT AID IN LOCATING THE HOSPITAL, BUT SURELY WE DON'T HAVE MUCH TIME TO SPARE BEFORE--

BLINK!

THERE THEY ARE!

ARTOO, WE DON'T HAVE ANY TIME AT ALL!

NEXT ISSUE **THE ULTIMATE GAMBLE!**

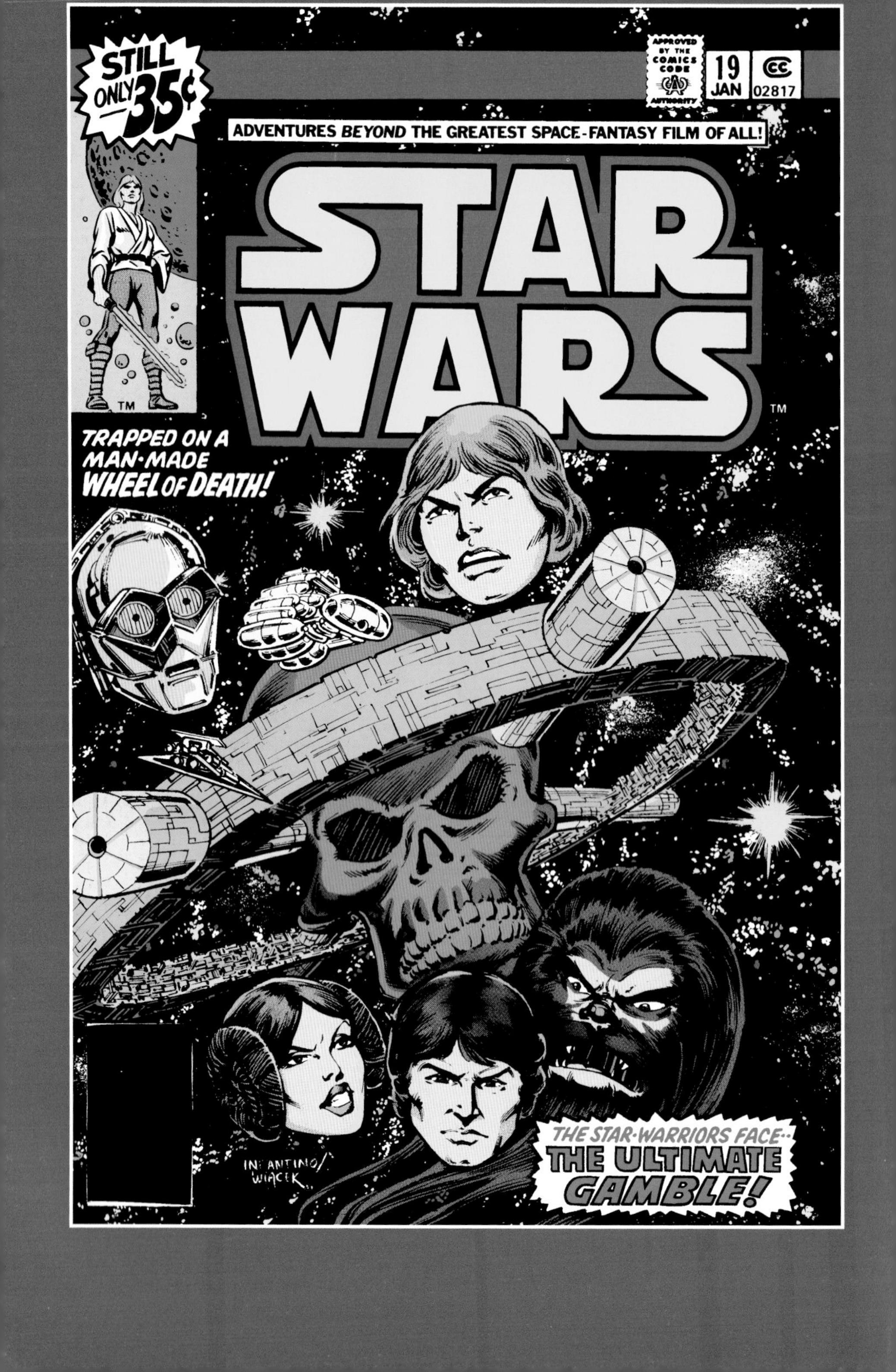
STILL ONLY 35¢
APPROVED BY THE COMICS CODE AUTHORITY
19 JAN
CC 02817
ADVENTURES BEYOND THE GREATEST SPACE-FANTASY FILM OF ALL!
STAR WARS
TM
TRAPPED ON A MAN-MADE WHEEL OF DEATH!
THE STAR-WARRIORS FACE--
THE ULTIMATE GAMBLE!
INFANTINO/ WIACEK

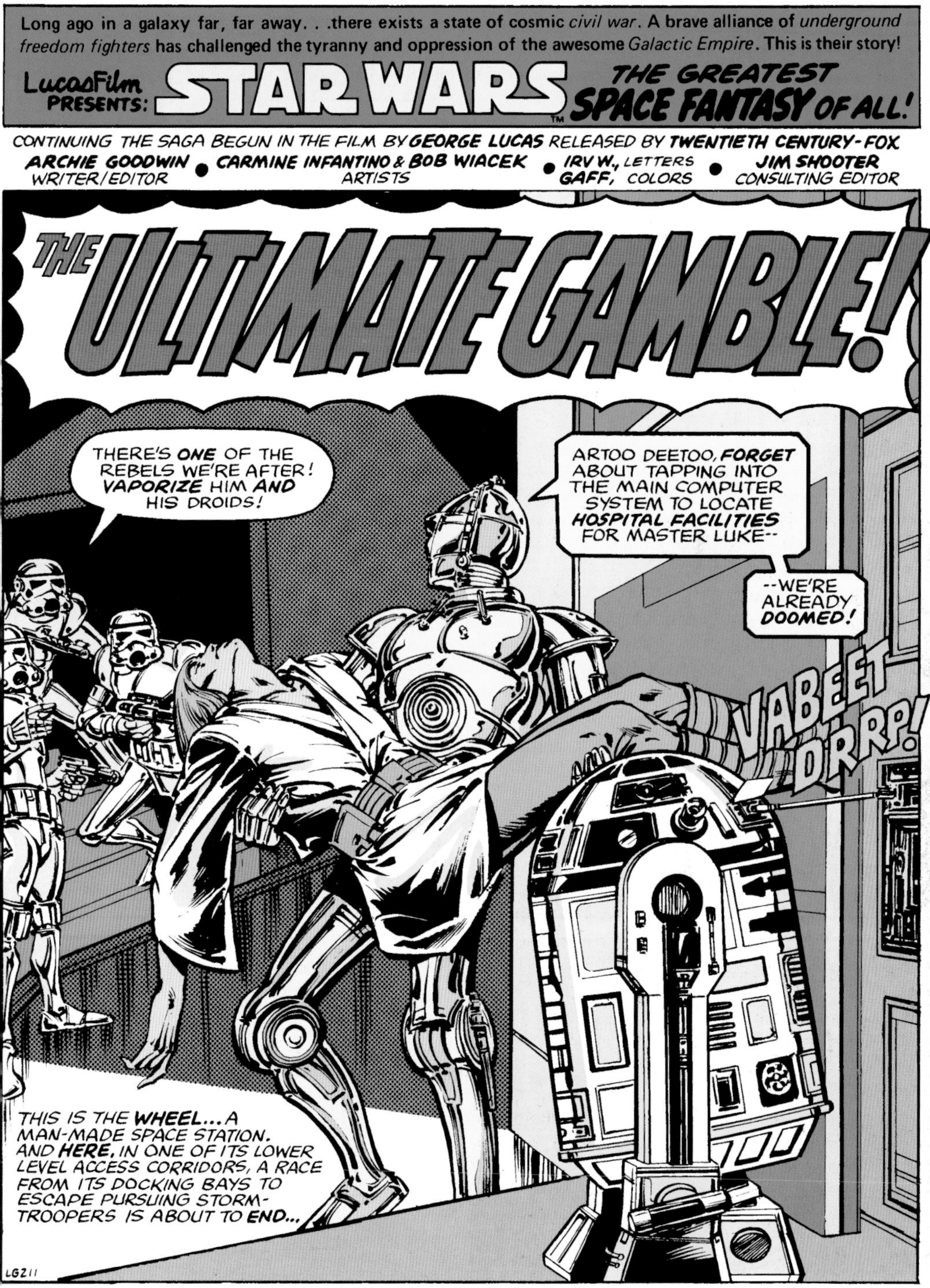

Long ago in a galaxy far, far away. . .there exists a state of cosmic civil war. A brave alliance of underground freedom fighters has challenged the tyranny and oppression of the awesome Galactic Empire. This is their story!
LucasFilm PRESENTS: STAR WARS™ THE GREATEST SPACE FANTASY OF ALL!
CONTINUING THE SAGA BEGUN IN THE FILM BY GEORGE LUCAS RELEASED BY TWENTIETH CENTURY-FOX
ARCHIE GOODWIN WRITER/EDITOR • CARMINE INFANTINO & BOB WIACEK ARTISTS • IRV W., LETTERS GAFF, COLORS • JIM SHOOTER CONSULTING EDITOR
THE ULTIMATE GAMBLE!
THIS IS THE WHEEL... A MAN-MADE SPACE STATION. AND HERE, IN ONE OF ITS LOWER LEVEL ACCESS CORRIDORS, A RACE FROM ITS DOCKING BAYS TO ESCAPE PURSUING STORM-TROOPERS IS ABOUT TO END...
THERE'S ONE OF THE REBELS WE'RE AFTER! VAPORIZE HIM AND HIS DROIDS!
ARTOO DEETOO, FORGET ABOUT TAPPING INTO THE MAIN COMPUTER SYSTEM TO LOCATE HOSPITAL FACILITIES FOR MASTER LUKE--
--WE'RE ALREADY DOOMED!
VABEET DRRP!
LGZ11

... BUT **NOT** IN THE WAY **EXPECTED** BY THE IMPERIAL TROOPS AS THEIR FINGERS **TIGHTEN** ON THEIR BLASTER TRIGGERS!

W-WHAT--? SOME KIND OF **BARRIER** COMING DOWN **BETWEEN** US--!

IT'S A **CONTAINMENT WALL**...TO SEAL OFF **DAMAGED SECTIONS!**

CEASE **FIRING!** CEASE FIRING OR--

OR THE WALL'S **BLAST SHIELDING** WILL CAUSE THE FIERY **ENERGY BOLTS**...

...TO **RICCOCHET** BACK INTO THOSE WHO **SHOT** THEM!

THAT'S **AMAZING,** ARTOO! WHAT AN INCREDIBLE STROKE OF **LUCK** FOR US!

DOOT A-BRIE WEET

YOU **MADE** THAT HAPPEN BY TAMPERING WITH THE **WALL CIRCUITRY?** WELL, I DON'T THINK THAT'S ANY EXCUSE FOR **NAME-CALLING!**

AFTER ALL, YOU **STILL** DIDN'T FULFILL OUR **PRIMARY TASK** OF LOCATING THE--

BREEP BOOP

YOU LEARNED WHERE THE **HOSPITAL** IS, TOO?

HOW CAN ONE THERMO-CAPSUARY DEHOUSING ASSISTER **BE** SO INTOLERABLE?!

THAT QUESTION WILL BE INTENSELY DEBATED THROUGHOUT THE JOURNEY TO THE WHEEL'S *HOSPITAL FACILITIES.* AND UNKNOWN TO THE TWO MECHANIZED *DEBATERS...*

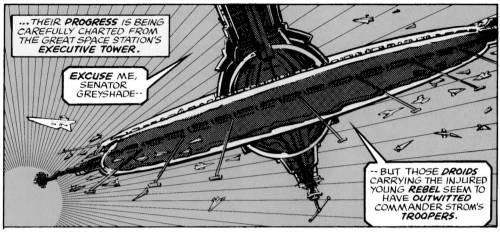

...THEIR *PROGRESS* IS BEING CAREFULLY CHARTED FROM THE GREAT SPACE STATION'S *EXECUTIVE TOWER.*

EXCUSE ME, SENATOR GREYSHADE--

--BUT THOSE *DROIDS* CARRYING THE INJURED YOUNG *REBEL* SEEM TO HAVE *OUTWITTED* COMMANDER STROM'S *TROOPERS.*

ONE OF THEM ACTUALLY HAD THE *AUDACITY* TO TAP INTO *MY* SYSTEM. SUCH INITIATIVE AND DEVOTION SEEMS MOST *UNUSUAL,* SIR. I'D LIKE TO *STUDY--*

MASTER-COM, THE ONLY ONE OF THOSE REBELS *I'M* INTERESTED IN--

--IS *PRINCESS LEIA ORGANA!* HAVE YOU CARRIED OUT MY *ORDERS...* OR ARE YOU TOO *BUSY* MOONING OVER TWO FELLOW *DROIDS?*

SORRY TO *IRRITATE* YOU, SENATOR. BUT MY *PERSONALIZED FORM* DOESN'T PREVENT ME FROM PERFORMING *MULTI-FUNCTIONS...* LIKE *ANY* MASTER COMPUTER SYSTEM.

ALL PROCEEDS AS YOU *REQUESTED--*

"--THOUGH OF COURSE WE WORK ON A VERY *TIGHT* TIME MARGIN!"

REMIND ME TO *COMPLIMENT* YOU ON YOUR CHOICE OF *SANCTUARIES,* MISTER SOLO--

--IF WE GET *OUT* OF THIS *ALIVE!*

IT SEEMED LIKE A *GOOD IDEA* AT THE *TIME,* YOUR ROYALNESS! THE *EMPIRE* HAS ALWAYS WILLINGLY KEPT ITS *HANDS OFF* THE WHEEL--

--UNTIL *NOW!*

"WITH LUKE ZAPPED BY SOME KIND OF *MENTAL SHOCK* WHILE MEDITATING ON THE *FORCE,** WE HAD TO FIND MEDICAL FACILITIES...

"...AND *FAST.*

**LAST ISSUE--ARCHIE.*

"HOW WAS *I* TO KNOW THAT HEADING FOR *HERE* WOULD BRING US ACROSS A *MERCHANT SHIP* SCUTTLED BY THE *IMPERIALS*...

"...BUT MADE TO *LOOK* LIKE IT HAD BEEN ATTACKED BY YOUR *REBEL ALLIANCE?!*

"OR THAT ONE OF THE EMPIRE'S *PURSUIT-CLASS* CRUISERS WOULD IMMEDIATELY HOP ON OUR *TAILS,* INTENT UPON NAILING *US* AS THE REBEL PIRATES?!

"WHATEVER THEY'RE *REALLY* UP TO--"

--OUR BEING *DEAD* PLAYS TOO *IMPORTANT* A PART TO SUIT *ME!*

I'M NOT EXACTLY *PLEASED* EITHER, HAN! PARTICULARLY SINCE THEY'RE *CHARGING* US--

--AND THERE'S *NO WAY TO STOP* THEM *ALL!*

BUT AS THE STORMTROOPERS **MOVE IN**...

WHEEL SECURITY, IMPERIALS!

THANK YOU FOR **DETAINING** THESE INTERLOPERS...WE'LL TAKE IT FROM HERE!

W-**WHAT**--?! BUT OUR COMMANDER HAD ALREADY **ARRANGED** WITH THE **WHEEL ADMINISTRATOR** THAT WE COULD--

IF THERE'S A **MISUNDERSTANDING,** WHY **COMPOUND** IT...? PARTICULARLY FROM A **WEAK DEFENSIVE POSITION**?

LEAVE THIS MATTER TO **SENATOR GREYSHADE.**

HE'S THE WHEEL ADMINISTRATOR?! HAN, I **KNOW** HIM FROM MY **SENATE DAYS!** HE'S UTTERLY CORRUPT, CONTEMPTIBLE AND--

OBVIOUSLY **MY** KIND OF GUY! IF WE'RE CHOOSING BETWEEN **EVILS,** YOUR WORSHIP...I GO WITH THE ONE THAT LETS YOU **LIVE** LONGER!

HOWEVER, ONCE THE SECURITY GUARDS HAVE TAKEN **CHARGE** OF THEIR CAPTIVES...

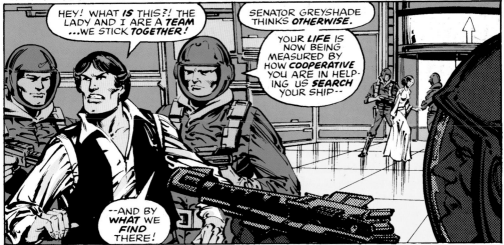

HEY! WHAT **IS** THIS?! THE LADY AND I ARE A **TEAM** ...WE STICK **TOGETHER**!

SENATOR GREYSHADE THINKS **OTHERWISE.**

YOUR **LIFE** IS NOW BEING MEASURED BY HOW **COOPERATIVE** YOU ARE IN HELPING US **SEARCH** YOUR SHIP--

--AND BY **WHAT** WE **FIND** THERE!

WHILE THAT SEARCH IS BEING **CONDUCTED**, THERE IS **ANOTHER** FUGITIVE FROM THE MILLENNIUM FALCON **UNACCOUNTED** FOR...

HIS NAME IS **CHEWBACCA**.

HE IS A **WOOKIEE**.

AND HE HAS HAD MORE **SUCCESS** THAN ANY OF HIS FRIENDS AT **ELUDING** THE STORMTROOPERS.

IN FACT, DESPITE HAVING TO HIDE THE BODY OF A SLAIN **REBEL** RECOVERED FROM THE PLUNDERED MERCHANT SHIP...*

*ALSO **LAST ISSUE**--ARCHIE.

...HE ALONE HAS ENJOYED REMARKABLE **LUCK** IN REACHING THE GROUP'S **GOAL**...

...THE **UPPER LEVEL** OF THE WHEEL!

CASINO

DINE

UNFORTUNATELY... THAT LUCK IS ABOUT TO **RUN OUT**.

LIFT TUBE 3

THE SO-CALLED **UPPER LEVEL** OF THE WHEEL IS ACTUALLY A **CITY** LINING ITS INTERIOR RIM. IT IS A CITY MAINTAINED BY ARTIFICIAL ATMOSPHERE AND GRAVITY...

...AND DEVOTED SOLELY TO **PLEASURE**. SPECIFICALLY, THE PLEASURE OF **GAMBLING**.

THE CITY HAS **EVERY** CONCEIVABLE LUXURY AND FACILITY A DISCERNING VISITOR MIGHT REQUIRE, BUT THE OVERWHELMING **MAJORITY** OF ITS BUILDINGS ARE **CASINOS**...

...AND IT IS IN AN AGREED-UPON MEETING PLACE CALLED THE **CRIMSON CASINO** THAT CHEW-BACCA'S **LUCK** SOURS.

ONE **MOMENT** PLEASE, SIR--

--OUR **ENTRANCE SCANNER** HAS NO **PRINT-OUT** ON YOU. THIS WOULD INDICATE YOU HAVE NOT PAID YOUR WHEEL **REGISTRATION FEE** OR ESTABLISHED A **CREDIT LEVEL**.

SINCE YOU HAD TO CHECK YOUR **BLASTER** AT THE DOOR... WE RECOMMEND THAT YOU COME **QUIETLY** TO WHEEL SECURITY.

WURF?

ANYONE MAY MAKE A RECOMMENDATION TO A WOOKIEE. THE **DIFFICULTY** OF COURSE...

RAARGG!

WAAK!

...IS GETTING **HIM** TO GO ALONG WITH IT!

ELIMINATING THE MAN WITH THE **BLASTER** IS A GOOD STRATEGIC MOVE...BUT IT **ALSO** LEAVES CHEWIE **OPEN** TO THE **SECOND** OF THE CRIMSON CASINO'S BOUNCERS.

BEING AN **EXPERT** WHO FINDS HIMSELF RARELY **TESTED**, HE GRABS THIS OPPORTUNITY **FAST** AND **HARD!**

A **BRAWL!** WHO'LL **WAGER** ON THE OUTCOME?!

WHAT **ODDS?**

I'LL BACK THE **MANDALLIAN GIANT** ...AT FIVE-TO-FOUR.

WHEN MANDALLIANS ARE TRAINED FROM **CHILDHOOD** IN THE COMBATIVE ARTS?! **UNFAIR!**

YOUR **EX-PERTISE** EQUALS MINE--

VERY WELL! SINCE THE **WOOKIEE** HAS ONLY BRUTE **PERSISTANCE** IN HIS FAVOR, LET US SAY--

--ALL BETS ARE **OFF!**

BRAKAASH!

AND THE MILLENNIUM FALCON'S FIRST MATE **WINS** HIS BATTLE...

AT THE **COST** OF AROUSING **WHEEL** SECURITY!

DID YOU SEE **THAT?..?** IT TOOK A MAXIMUM **STUN CHARGE** TO BRING HIM **DOWN!**

I'VE **HEARD** OF WOOKIEES, BUT NEVER **SEEN** ONE! WHAT A **SPECIMEN** FOR THE BIG GAME!

AND THAT'S **EXACTLY** WHERE HE'S HEADED!

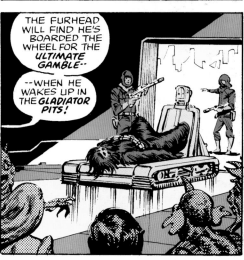

THE FURHEAD WILL FIND HE'S BOARDED THE WHEEL FOR THE **ULTIMATE GAMBLE**--

--WHEN HE WAKES UP IN THE **GLADIATOR PITS!**

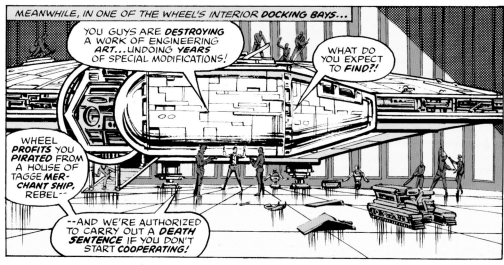

MEANWHILE, IN ONE OF THE WHEEL'S INTERIOR **DOCKING BAYS...**

YOU GUYS ARE **DESTROYING** A WORK OF ENGINEERING **ART**...UNDOING **YEARS** OF SPECIAL MODIFICATIONS!

WHAT DO YOU EXPECT TO **FIND?!**

WHEEL PROFITS YOU **PIRATED** FROM A HOUSE OF TAGGE **MERCHANT SHIP,** REBEL--

--AND WE'RE AUTHORIZED TO CARRY OUT A **DEATH SENTENCE** IF YOU DON'T START **COOPERATING!**

AND AS THIS SCENE IS VIDEO-MONITORED TO THE WHEEL'S *EXECUTIVE TOWER*...

...IT IS VIEWED BY A RECENT *ARRIVAL* TO THE ADMINISTRATOR'S OFFICE SUITE.

GREYSHADE--!

AH! AND YOU SEEMED SO FIRMLY RESOLVED NOT TO *SPEAK* TO ME.

YOUR BRAND OF SENATORIAL POLITICS IS *STILL* TOO FRESH ON MY MIND!

BUT I BELIEVE *I* KNOW WHAT HAN SOLO *DOESN'T*... CALL OFF YOUR *MEN*!

IT SOUNDS AS IF YOU ACTUALLY *CARE* FOR THAT VAGABOND STAR-HOPPER--

I CARE ABOUT *MANY* THINGS, SIMON GREYSHADE! THAT'S THE *DIFFERENCE* BETWEEN US.

YOU'RE EASILY *AMUSED*... BUT *NEVER* COMMITTED!

NOW DO YOU WANT TO *HEAR* ABOUT HI-JACKED WHEEL PROFITS OR *NOT*?

I *YIELD* THE FLOOR TO THE BEAUTIFUL PRINCESS/SENATOR FROM *ALDERAAN*.

ALDERAAN IS *DESTROYED*... BY THE HAND OF THE EMPIRE!

THE SAME *HAND* THAT'S GRABBED YOUR SHIPMENT OF *PROFITS*!

UNTIL I KNEW WHAT *CARGO* THAT MERCHANT SHIP CARRIED, I COULDN'T *GUESS* WHAT THE IMPERIALS WERE *UP* TO--

THE EMPIRE'S NEVER DARED *INTERFERE* WITH THE WHEEL...FOR FEAR OF RUINING ITS *POPULARITY* AND VALUE AS A SOURCE OF *TAXES*.

BUT IF IT APPEARS TO HAVE BECOME A *TARGET* OF THE *REBEL ALLIANCE*--

-- THEY CAN JUSTIFY A COMPLETE *TAKEOVER* IN THE GUISE OF OFFERING *PROTECTION* AND EVERYONE WILL *ACCEPT* IT!

THERE ARE *FLAWS*, BUT WHAT YOU SUGGEST *DOES* SEEM TYPICAL OF IMPERIAL *THINKING*--

THE BEST *PROOF*, OF COURSE, WOULD BE *FINDING* THAT PIRATED *CARGO* AND--

I HAVE A *THEORY* ABOUT THAT! IF YOU'LL JUST SET ME AND MY FRIENDS *FREE*, I'LL--

SENATOR GREYSHADE! COMMANDER STROM IS ON HIS *WAY* HERE AT THE *HEAD* OF A SQUAD OF *STORMTROOPERS*.

HE'S *FURIOUS* OVER YOUR INTERFERENCE IN HIS HUNT FOR THE *REBELS* AND I FEAR--

VEEDOW!

WE'VE MOVED TOO *SWIFTLY* FOR YOUR SECURITY SQUADS *OR* THIS WALKING MASTER COMPUTER!

STROM... I THINK YOU'VE GONE MAD.

MERELY *RECKLESS*, GREYSHADE.

THOUGH NOT AS MUCH AS *YOU*...OR DO YOU *DENY* THAT'S A *REBEL LEADER* AT YOUR SIDE?

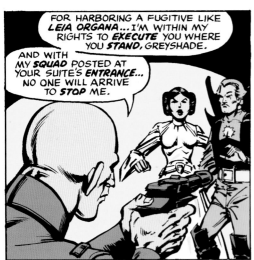

FOR HARBORING A FUGITIVE LIKE *LEIA ORGANA*... I'M WITHIN MY RIGHTS TO *EXECUTE* YOU WHERE YOU *STAND*, GREYSHADE.

AND WITH MY *SQUAD* POSTED AT YOUR SUITE'S *ENTRANCE*... NO ONE WILL ARRIVE TO *STOP* ME.

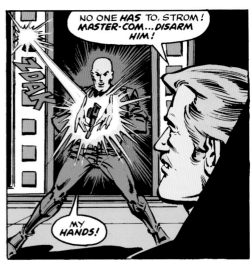

NO ONE *HAS* TO, STROM! MASTER-COM....DISARM *HIM!*

MY *HANDS!*

BE GLAD THEY WEREN'T *BLOWN OFF!* EVEN IF THE MASTER COMPUTER *DOES* AUTOMATICALLY REVERT BACK TO ITS *ORIGINAL SYSTEM* WHEN ATTACKED--

--THOSE ROBOT BODIES ARE *EXPENSIVE*. BESIDES ...I HATE TALKING TO *WALLS*.

ACTUALLY THE *OLD* MODEL WAS GETTING A BIT *WORN*, SIR. I BELIEVE THIS *NEW* ONE WILL FUNCTION EVEN *BETTER*.

YOU CAN *START* BY ESCORTING COMMANDER STROM INTO THE ANTECHAMBER. I WANT TO *TALK* TO HIM...*ALONE*.

MEANWHILE, MY SUITE *IS YOURS* TO FEEL AT *HOME* IN, PRINCESS. *ENJOY* YOURSELF--

--AND DON'T WASTE TIME LOOKING FOR *ANOTHER* WAY OUT. THERE *ISN'T* ANY!

MOMENTS LATER...

MASTER-COM, YOU WILL NOT *RECORD* OR *HEAR* THIS CONVERSATION.

WHAT'S THIS ALL *ABOUT*, GREYSHADE?!

ABOUT OUR BECOMING *PARTNERS*, STROM.

344

PARTNERS?! NOW WHO SEEMS TO HAVE GONE *MAD*?

STROM, I *KNOW* WHAT THE EMPIRE IS *DOING*... THAT THE SUPPOSED *REBEL THEFT* OF WHEEL PROFITS IS THE *FIRST STEP* IN A PLANNED *TAKEOVER*.

DONE *WELL*...IT'S A SCHEME THAT COULD *SUCCEED*. YOU HAVEN'T *DONE* IT WELL, STROM.

BUT NO ONE, PARTICULARLY YOUR *SUPERIORS*, NEED *LEARN* THAT...IF I KEEP *SILENT*.

IN RETURN FOR *WHAT*, GREYSHADE?

THE *ONLY THING* ALL MY CHARM AND TOTAL LACK OF SCRUPLES EVER *FAILED* TO BRING ME--

--PRINCESS *LEIA ORGANA*.

INCREDIBLE! YOU'RE ACTUALLY A *ROMANTIC*!

BUT WHAT ABOUT HER *TRAVELLING COMPANIONS*?

THEY CAN'T *LEAVE* WITHOUT RUNNING INTO YOUR MILITARY *CONTAINMENT ZONE*. I'LL SEE TO IT THAT THEY CAN'T *STAY* EITHER ...AND *LIVE*.

I NEVER THOUGHT I'D SAY THIS TO A *CIVILIAN*, BUT I *LIKE* YOUR THINKING--

T!NK!

SOMETIME *LATER*, AT THE WHEEL'S *HOSPITAL*...

THIS *SHOCK* CASE IS STILL *HERE*? I THOUGHT RECORDS INDICATED HE WASN'T *REGISTERED*.

MASTER COMPUTER SYSTEM AUTHORIZED *HOLDING* AND *TREATMENT*, DOCTOR...UNTIL FURTHER *ORDERS*.

UNUSUAL. WHAT ABOUT THOSE TWO *DROIDS* WHO BROUGHT HIM?

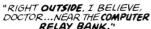

"RIGHT **OUTSIDE**, I BELIEVE, DOCTOR...*NEAR THE* **COMPUTER RELAY BANK**."

ARTOO DEETOO, **HURRY** WITH THOSE **REPAIRS**!

IF ANYONE EVEN **SUSPECTS** WE TAMPERED WITH **COMMUNICATIONS** TO AUTHORIZE MASTER LUKE'S **HOSPITALIZATION**, I'M AFRAID--

FUSS-BUDGET?! WHY YOU MISPROGRAMMED SLUDGE-CONTAINER, I--

YOU'RE THE ONES I WANT! COME ALONG **QUICKLY** ...OR I'LL **USE** THIS **DISRUPTER**!

NO NEED FOR **THAT**, OFFICER. WE'RE THE VERY **SPIRIT** OF COOPERATION! ONLY CONCERN FOR OUR SICK **MASTER** MADE US--

THAT'S NOTHING TO **ME**, DROID. YOU'RE **WHEEL PROPERTY** NOW...IT'S MY JOB TO GET YOU INTO **STORAGE**.

WHEEL PROPERTY...? SURELY THERE'S BEEN AN **ERROR**, SIR--

THEN SOME-ONE NAMED **HAN SOLO** MADE IT...YOU'VE JUST BEEN **PAWNED** TO GIVE HIM A **GAMBLING STAKE**!

NOW SHUT UP AND **MOVE**!

RESIGNEDLY, THREEPIO AND ARTOO **OBEY** THE SECURITY OFFICER. **ELSEWHERE**...OBEDIENCE IS IN SHORTER SUPPLY.

THESE ARE THE **GLADIATOR PITS**, LOCATED IN THE **BOTTOM-MOST** SECTION OF THE **WHEEL**...

HURRY WITH THOSE **CONTROL PRODS**! THAT WOOKIE'S **AWAKE** ...AND NOT **HAPPY** WITH HIS PIT-MATES!

THAT'S IT! KEEP HIM AT *BAY*! BETTER LISTEN UP, BIG FELLA...YOU GOT AN IMPORTANT *DECISION* TO MAKE!

YOU'RE ON THE WHEEL *ILLEGALLY* AND YOU'VE RUN UP A LOT OF *FINES* AND *DAMAGES*. WELL, THIS IS *PAY OFF* TIME!

ROWRK!

YOU CAN *VOLUNTEER* FOR GLADIATOR SERVICE IN THE *BIG GAME*, WITH A CHANCE AT A *FORTUNE* IF YOU'RE A *WINNER*--

SNARF!

--OR, YOU CAN BE DUMPED ON A WAITING EMPIRE *PRISON SHIP*! DESTI-NATION: THE *SPINE MINES OF KESSEL*!

NOT MUCH OF A *CHOICE*, IS IT, FUZZY?

347

YOU LOSE *AGAIN*, STAR-HOPPER!

BLAST IT! I THOUGHT MY LUCK HAD *CHANGED* WHEN WHEEL SECURITY LET ME OFF THE *HOOK* ON THOSE *PIRACY* CHARGES--

THEN THEY HIT ME WITH WHAT I *OWE* IF I WANT TO *STAY* ON BOARD--

--AND IT'S BEEN *DOWNHILL* EVER SINCE!

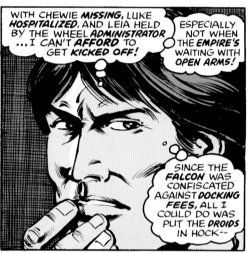

WITH CHEWIE *MISSING*, LUKE *HOSPITALIZED*, AND LEIA HELD BY THE WHEEL *ADMINISTRATOR* ... I CAN'T *AFFORD* TO GET *KICKED OFF!*

ESPECIALLY NOT WHEN THE *EMPIRE'S* WAITING WITH OPEN ARMS!

SINCE THE *FALCON* WAS CONFISCATED AGAINST *DOCKING FEES*, ALL I COULD DO WAS PUT THE *DROIDS* IN HOCK--

--AND *PRAY* I COULD RUN UP A BIG ENOUGH STAKE TO BAIL US *ALL* OUT!

I'LL NEED MORE CHIPS THAN *THIS*, CASHIER--

SORRY, SIR, THAT'S ALL THAT *REMAINS* OF YOUR CREDIT LINE.

TREAT YOURSELF TO A *LUBRICATION SOAK*, TIN-BRITCHES--

--THAT WAY I KNOW I'M NOT THE *ONLY ONE* WHO TOOK A *BATH!*

SIR, ONE *MOMENT*, PLEASE--

THOUGH YOUR *CREDIT* IS *EXHAUSTED,* IT IS *STILL* POSSIBLE FOR YOU TO *GAMBLE.*

AND WHAT DO I USE FOR *STAKES,* CASHIER--?

WHY... YOUR *LIFE,* SIR.

SEE FOR *YOURSELF.*

The *ULTIMATE GAMBLE*

HIGH RISK! HIGH REWARD! BE A GLADIATOR! IN THE *BIG GAME!*

HAN SOLO *STARES,* LONG AND HARD.

...THEN WALKS FROM THE CASINO'S ATMOSPHERE OF PLUSH *EXCITEMENT*...

...INTO ONE OF COLD *DESPERATION.*

JUST LET THE SCANNER GET AN *IDENTI-PRINT* FOR THE *RECORD* AND--

CONGRATULATIONS, CORELLIAN...YOU'RE A GLADIATOR!

INFORMATION THAT IS SWIFTLY *RELAYED* TO THE WHEEL'S EXECUTIVE TOWER...

WHAT *NOW,* SENATOR GREYSHADE...?

NOW WE ARRANGE FOR OUR SMUGGLER CAPTAIN TO LOSE THE *BIG GAME*--

--JUST AS *CERTAINLY* AS WE MADE HIM LOSE THE *OTHERS!*

NEXT ISSUE: *DEATHGAME!*

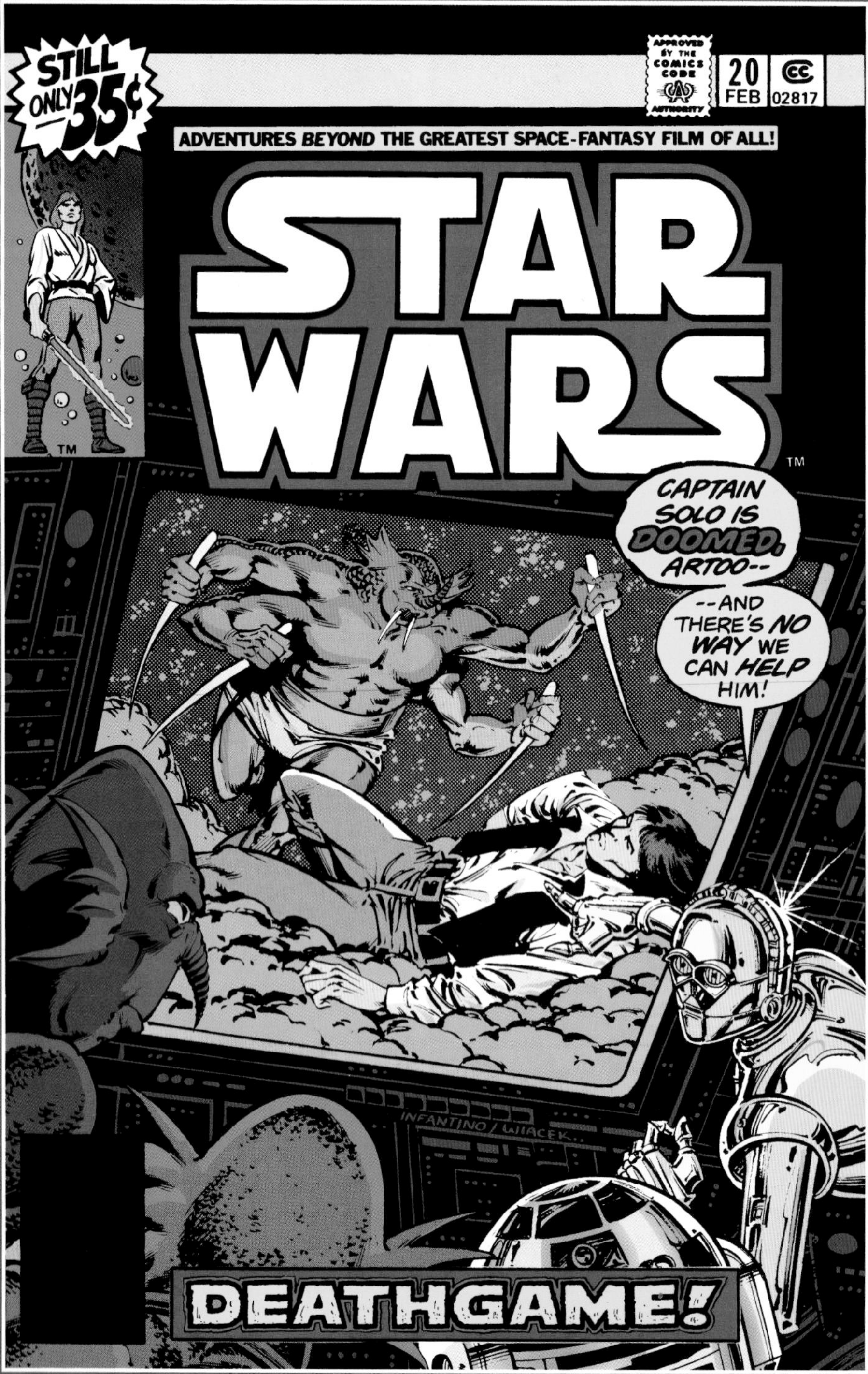

STILL ONLY 35¢
APPROVED BY THE COMICS CODE AUTHORITY
20 FEB
CC 02817
ADVENTURES BEYOND THE GREATEST SPACE-FANTASY FILM OF ALL!
STAR WARS
TM
CAPTAIN SOLO IS DOOMED, ARTOO--
--AND THERE'S NO WAY WE CAN HELP HIM!
INFANTINO / WIACEK
DEATHGAME!

Long ago in a galaxy far, far away. . .there exists a state of cosmic *civil war*. A brave alliance of *underground freedom fighters* has challenged the tyranny and oppression of the awesome *Galactic Empire*. This is their story!

LucasFilm PRESENTS: **STAR WARS** ™ **THE GREATEST SPACE FANTASY OF ALL!**

CONTINUING *THE SAGA BEGUN IN THE FILM BY* **GEORGE LUCAS** *RELEASED BY* **TWENTIETH CENTURY-FOX**

ARCHIE GOODWIN
WRITER/EDITOR

CARMINE INFANTINO & BOB WIACEK
ARTISTS

JOHN COSTANZA
lettering

GEORGE ROUSSOS
coloring

JIM SHOOTER
CONSULTING EDITOR

THE X-WING FIGHTER SEEMS TO APPEAR FROM *NOWHERE*; SUDDENLY, VIOLENTLY, HAMMERING *ENERGY BOLTS* INTO A RULAARIAN PLEASURE YACHT JUST DEPARTED FROM THAT MONUMENT TO THE GALAXY'S LUST FOR *GAMBLING...*

...THE *WHEEL*, ARTIFICIAL SATELLITE THAT IS HOME TO THE *CITY* OF CASINOS.

THERE IS NOTHING *CHANCE* OR *RANDOM* IN THIS REBEL CRAFT'S APPEARANCE. IT IS A CAREFULLY CALCULATED *MOVE* IN A VAST AND DEADLY *SCHEME*.

DEATHGAME

HOW COULD THEY *DO* SUCH A THING?! THIS ISN'T AN *IMPERIAL INSTALLATION!*

I *KNEW* THOSE REBELS WERE *CRAZY!* 'LEAST THE *EMPIRE* ALWAYS HAD THE SENSE TO KEEP ITS HANDS *OFF* THE WHEEL!

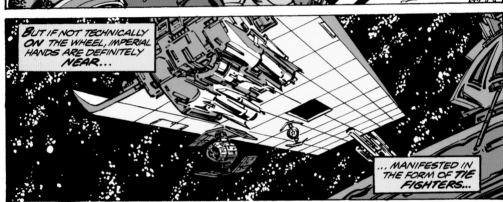

BUT IF NOT TECHNICALLY ON THE WHEEL, IMPERIAL HANDS ARE DEFINITELY *NEAR...*

... MANIFESTED IN THE FORM OF *TIE FIGHTERS...*

...WHICH *END* THE INCIDENT SWIFTLY AND SURELY AS IT *BEGAN...*

...TO THE *RELIEF* AND *CHEERS* OF WATCHING WHEEL CUSTOMERS!

SUCH AS PRINCESS *LEIA ORGANA*... OF THE REBEL ALLIANCE.

GREYSHADE, YOU'RE EVEN *MORE* DESPICABLE THAN I *THOUGHT* YOU WERE DURING OUR DAYS IN THE *IMPERIAL SENATE!*

I HAD MY *FAULTS*--

--BUT I NEVER WASTED A FINE *MEAL* AS *YOU'RE* DOING.

YOU NEVER WASTED *ANY* OPPORTUNITY TO ENRICH *YOURSELF* AT THE EXPENSE OF *OTHERS!*

AS *WHEEL ADMINISTRATOR*, I THOUGHT YOU'D *FIGHT* THE EMPIRE'S SCHEME TO *FAKE* REBEL ATTACKS SO THEY'D BE JUSTIFIED IN *TAKING OVER* THIS PLACE AND ALL THE *WEALTH* IT BRINGS IN...

--BUT THAT UGLY *CHARADE* WE'VE JUST WITNESSED *PROVES* YOU'RE GOING *ALONG* WITH THEM!

YOU'RE A *CRUSADER*, MY DEAR PRINCESS... I'M *NOT*. YOU HAVE *YOUR* GAMES TO PLAY... I HAVE *MINE*.

BUT IT'S NICE TO SEE THAT BENEATH THAT SOMETIMES *GLACIAL* EXTERIOR... YOU'RE CAPABLE OF A TRULY *EMOTIONAL OUTBURST!*

MASTER-COM, SEE TO THIS *MESS* IMMEDIATELY.

AND INSTRUCT ALL SERVO-DROIDS TO BE *CAREFUL* WHAT'S LEFT LAYING AROUND. THE FORMER SENATOR FROM ALDERAAN IS TO BE TREATED AS A *GUEST*--

--BUT SHE'S STILL VERY MUCH OUR *PRISONER*.

VRRRT!

353

EXITING HIS SUITE IN THE WHEEL'S *EXECUTIVE TOWER*, SIMON GREY-SHADE STEPS INTO A *VACUUM-LIFT*...

...AND SWIFTLY *DESCENDS*...

...TO THE WHEEL'S MAIN *TRANSPORT TUBE* AND A WAITING AIRFLOW CAR.

WHICH *STOP* WILL IT BE, ADMINISTRA-TOR?

I KNOW THE EMPEROR *DISSOLVED* THE SENATE, PILOT... BUT I STILL *PREFER* MY OLD TITLE.

TAKE ME TO THE *END* OF THE *LINE*... THE *IMPERIAL DOCK*.

ON OUR *WAY*... SENATOR.

WITH A HISS OF *FORCED AIR*, THE BULLET-SHAPED CRAFT HURLS ALONG THE *TUBE*, ONE OF *MANY* RUNNING UP AND DOWN THE WHEEL'S *MAIN SPOKE*...

...UNTIL IT REACHES THE OUTER-MOST *DOCK*... AND THE LIGHT-CRUISER OF THE EMPIRE'S *SECTOR COMMANDER.*

AH, *GREYSHADE!* THIS TIME, *I'LL* POUR THE DRINKS... OUR NEWLY-FORMED PARTNERSHIP IS OFF TO A *FINE* START!

I'LL ASSUME FROM *THOSE* REMARKS, STROM, THAT THIS CABIN IS *SAFE* FROM *ANY* MANNER OF SURVEILLANCE—

—PRIVATE... *OR* IMPERIAL.

ABSOLUTELY. MY *LIFE* IS FORFEIT IF MY SUPERIORS LEARN *YOU'VE* DISCOVERED THE EMPIRE'S *PLANS* HERE —

—AS IS *YOURS* IF ANYONE FINDS THAT YOU'RE HARBORING A *REBEL LEADER!**

*EACH GENTLEMAN UNCOVERED THE OTHER'S SECRET *LAST ISSUE.*— ARCHIE.

OUR MUTUAL *SURVIVAL* DEPENDS ON EACH OTHER'S *SILENCE*, GREYSHADE... IT'S THE *PERFECT* BASIS FOR *TRUST.*

WELL, I *DON'T* TRUST THE WAY YOU'RE *CARRYING OUT* THIS IMPERIAL SCHEME, STROM! YOU'RE *RUSHING* THINGS...THAT ATTACK WAS *CLUMSY* AND *OBVIOUS!*

THE PAYING CUSTOMERS MAY HAVE BEEN *IMPRESSED*... BUT THE *CASINO OWNERS* AREN'T NEARLY SO *NAIVE!* AND *THEY'RE* THE ONES I HAVE TO—

ONLY THE *CUSTOMERS* COUNT! THE CASINO OWNERS CAN BE *REPLACED* WHEN WE TAKE OVER—

—NATURALLY I WILL RECOMMEND THAT *YOU* BE *RETAINED* AS WHEEL ADMINISTRATOR,

AND AS LONG AS WE CAN MAKE THE PUBLIC *EMBRACE* THE IMPERIAL PRESENCE HERE WITHOUT HARMING *PROFITS,* THERE IS NO *PROBLEM,* SENATOR.

UNLESS *YOU* ARE HAVING ONE WITH THE LOVELY *PRINCESS...?*

LEAVE HER *OUT* OF THIS, STROM, OR—

AH! I STRUCK A *NERVE!* FORGIVE ME, PARTNER... IT MUST BE *DIFFICULT* FOR A MAN OF *NO PRINCIPLES* ATTEMPTING TO WIN THE *AFFECTION* OF A WOMAN WITH SUCH *HIGH ONES.*

ON THE *CONTRARY,* STROM... THAT'S *EXACTLY* WHAT MAKES IT *EASY.*

BUT I INTEND TO MOVE *CAUTIOUSLY...* AND I STRONGLY SUGGEST *YOU* DO THE SAME WITH THE *EMPIRE'S* BUSINESS.

THAT *SOUNDS* ALMOST LIKE A *THREAT*--

IT'S *GOOD ADVICE,* COMMANDER!

I WON'T RUN A *MILITARY OPERATION* TO SUIT THE PACE OF YOUR SCHOOL BOY *ROMANCE,* GREYSHADE!

AND ANY *POLITICIAN'S* TRICKS TO *MAKE* ME DO SO WILL *BACKFIRE*--

--*FATALLY!*

I BELIEVE IN *ACTION,* SENATOR... AND I'M NOT DEPARTING THE *WHEEL* UNTIL I *SEE* SOME FROM *YOU!*

YOU PROMISED ME THAT PRINCESS LEIA'S *COMPANIONS* WOULD BE *ELIMINATED*--

WHERE ARE THE *BODIES?!*

THERE AREN'T ANY *YET,* STROM. EVERYONE WHO CAME TO THE *WHEEL* IN THE *MILLENNIUM FALCON* WITH LEIA ORGANA * IS STILL *ALIVE*--

--BUT, THOUGH THEY MAY NOT *REALIZE* IT, THEY'RE *ALL* AWAITING *EXECUTION.*

*ISSUE #18.
--ARCHIE.

"AFTER ALL, THEY *DID* COMMIT THE CRIME OF STUMBLING UPON *YOUR* HANDIWORK, COMMANDER ...THE *LOOTING* OF A HOUSE OF TAGGE MERCHANT SHIP WHICH WAS TRANSPORTING *WHEEL PROFITS.*"

"AND EVEN THOUGH THEY *UNCOVERED* YOUR *CLUMSY* ATTEMPT TO MAKE IT APPEAR TO BE AN ACT OF *REBEL PIRACY...*"

ALSO ISSUE #18.--AMPLIFYIN' ARCH.

--THEY'D HAVE TO TURN UP THE ACTUAL *LOOT* TO REALLY MAKE THE STORY *STICK.*

AND BEFORE YOU BEGIN ROARING ABOUT THE POSSIBILITY OF *THAT* HAPPENING, STROM--

--LET ME HAVE *MASTER-COM* PATCH SOME SIGHTINGS FROM *HIS* SCANNER SYSTEM INTO YOUR *COMMUNICATOR.*

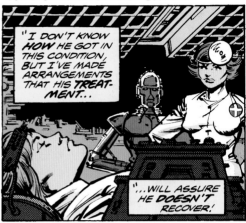

"*ONE* OF PRINCESS LEIA'S FRIENDS IS *HERE*... IN THE WHEEL *HOSPITAL,* APPARENTLY IN SOME STRANGE STATE OF *SHOCK.*

"*I DON'T KNOW HOW* HE GOT IN THIS CONDITION, BUT I'VE MADE ARRANGEMENTS THAT HIS *TREATMENT...*

"...WILL ASSURE HE *DOESN'T* RECOVER!"

"WHICH LEAVES TWO *OTHERS* FROM THE MILLENNIUM FALCON, WHO, FROM THE WAY THEY RESISTED AND EVADED YOUR *STORMTROOPERS,* ARE OBVIOUSLY QUITE *DANGEROUS.*

"*CHEWBACCA,* THE GIANT *WOOKIEE...*

"...AND *HAN SOLO,* CORELLIAN SMUGGLING CAPTAIN.

"UNFORTUNATELY FOR *THEM,* AS YOU CAN SEE, THEY'RE BOTH ENLISTED AS *GLADIATORS* IN THE *BIG GAME.* THE WOOKIEE BY *MISCHANCE;* THE CORELLIAN THROUGH *MY* MANIPULATIONS. IN ANY EVENT, DON'T BET ON *EITHER* OF THEM, COMMANDER...

--UNLESS YOU'RE USING THOSE STOLEN *WHEEL PROFITS* AND CAN AFFORD TO *LOSE.*

GAMBLE WITH WHAT IS NOW CONSIDERED *EMPIRE PROPERTY...?!* THE PROFITS REMAIN ON *THIS SHIP,* GREYSHADE ...*UNTOUCHED.*

BUT THOSE REBELS ALSO HAD *DROIDS...* WHAT ABOUT *THEM?*

"*YES, THIS R2-D2 UNIT AND HIS TRANSLATOR-COMPANION, A C-3PO MODEL... THEY'RE IN WHEEL STORAGE AFTER BEING PAWNED BY HAN SOLO TO PROVIDE HIM A GAMBLING STAKE.*

"*THAT GAMBLING STAKE IS NOW PART OF SOME NEW WHEEL PROFITS, AND THIS PAIR IS SLATED TO HAVE THEIR MEMORIES FLUSHED AND THEN BE MELTED DOWN INTO SLAG!*

SO YOU *SEE,* STROM, THAT BUNCH MAY HAVE COME TO THE WHEEL FOR *SANCTUARY*--

--BUT ALL THEY'VE FOUND IS *DEATH.*

AND I WOULDN'T HAVE IT *ANY* OTHER *WAY,* GREYSHADE!

BUT IN THE WHEEL GLADIATOR PITS, SOMEONE HOLDS A MUCH DIFFERENT OPINION...

...*VEHEMENTLY!*

YOU GUYS ARE *JOBBIN'* ME! I *COULDN'T* HAVE TESTED OUT THIS HIGH! I'LL BE FIGHTIN' *WAY* OUTTA MY CLASS!

IT SURPRISED US *TOO,* SOLO... BUT *THAT'S* WHAT THE SKILL AND REACTION PRINT-OUT *SAYS!*

WHY *COMPLAIN?* THIS PUTS YOU IN A MUCH HIGHER PAYING *PRELIMINARY*--

--YOU'RE PROBABLY *BETTER* THAN YOU *THINK* YOU ARE. NOW, I NEED SOME *DATA* FOR THE CASINO *RATING TAPES.*

WHAT'S YOUR *SPECIALTY?*

SURVIVAL! BUT OBVIOUSLY YOU PEOPLE DON'T INTEND TO LET ME *PRACTICE* IT!

I MEANT *WEAPONS,* SOLO. COOPERATE. GIVE THE BETTORS SOMETHING TO *GO* ON.

WELL, SINCE YOU DON'T ALLOW *BLASTERS...* HOW ABOUT MY OWN *CRUISER* AND A FULL COMPLEMENT OF *PROTON TORPEDOES?*

VERY *FUNNY.* LET'S SEE IF YOU'RE STILL *LAUGHING* WHEN YOU REACH THE *ARENA.*

AND THAT MOMENT IS NOT *LONG* COMING. HAN IS SWIFTLY OUTFITTED AND RUSHED TO A *LIFT...*

...TO BE CARRIED UPWARD INTO THE GREAT ENCLOSED SPHERE THAT IS THE WHEEL'S *HUB...*

...AND WHICH HOUSES ITS *ARENA.* HERE, THE *BIG GAME* IS PLAYED...

...AND HERE, HAN SOLO COMES FACE-TO-FACE WITH THE *FIRST* OF HIS FELLOW PLAYERS!

DAGGER THORNS!

THOSE THINGS SECRETE A *VENOMOUS SAP*... JUST A *SCRATCH* IS ENOUGH FOR A *KILL!*

AND WITH MORE *ARMS* THAN I CAN *BLOCK*... SCRATCHES WILL COME *EASY* FOR THIS LIVING *WINDMILL!*

UNLESS MY *POWER MACE* AND *SHIELD*--

-- HAVE ENOUGH *JUICE* TO MAKE HIM *DROP* HIS WEAPONS!

THEY *DON'T!*

OH *BOY,* DO THEY DON'T!

360

BUT WITH A SWIFT *DIVE*... HAN GOES *BETWEEN* HIS FOE'S LEGS!

THE THING THAT *REALLY* HURTS--

--IS THAT IT WAS *MY* IDEA TO COME TO THE *WHEEL* IN THE *FIRST PLACE!*

WAM!

SO INSTEAD OF A *SAFE PORT,* I FIND MY SHIP CON-FISCATED, MY FRIENDS *CAPTURED,* AND THE *EMPIRE* JUST WAITING TO POUNCE--

-- SOME DAYS YOU *CAN'T* WIN!

KA-WUJ!

361

AS HAN SOLO CRASHES INTO THE ARENA'S **SIMULA-SCENERY,** IT IS WITNESSED BY EX-CITED PATRONS IN **EVERY** CASINO ON THE WHEEL. ALL OTHER PLAY HAS **CEASED.** NOW THE ONLY INTEREST, THE ONLY GAMBLING IS ON THE **BIG GAME.** AND IN **HAN'S** CONTEST...

...THE CROWD SNIFFS **BLOOD!**

SO TOO DO LESS **FRENZIED** WATCHERS IN THE GRAND CASINO'S **ROYAL LOUNGE...**

SATISFIED, STROM?

WHY **NOT,** GREYSHADE? YOU'VE GIVEN ME MORE **LAVISH** SURROUNDINGS THAN MY SIMPLE **SHIP'S QUARTERS** --

-- AND ARE **ELIMINATING** A POTENTIAL **THREAT** TO MY SUCCESS!

ON TOP OF **THAT,** YOUR SUGGESTION THAT I GIVE MY CREW **SHORE LEAVE** TO VIEW THE **BIG GAME** --

-- WILL PROBABLY MAKE ME BETTER LOVED AS A COMMANDER.

AND THEIR **GAMBLING LOSSES** WILL MAKE **ME** BETTER LOVED AS WHEEL **ADMINISTRA-TOR!**

I CAN'T THINK OF **EVERYTHING,** STROM... BUT I **TRY.**

YET **SOME** EVENTS ON THE WHEEL **DON'T** PROCEED AS SIMON GREYSHADE PLANS...

FOR INSTANCE, A SHORT WHILE **EARLIER...**

ALL **RIGHT,** YOU TWO DROIDS... GET **OVER** HERE.

UNFASTEN YOUR **FACE-PLATE,** GOLDY... I'LL **START** WITH YOU.

SIR, THAT APPEARS TO BE A **MEMORY FLUSH UNIT** --

-- THERE MUST BE SOME **MISTAKE!** WE'RE ONLY HERE **TEMPORARILY** UNTIL MASTER SOLO CAN **WIN** ENOUGH TO **REDEEM** US AND --

HE MUST'VE HAD **BAD LUCK!** NOW **OPEN UP...** I'VE GOT MY **ORDERS.**

THOSE ORDERS ARE **SUPERCEDED,** TECHNO --

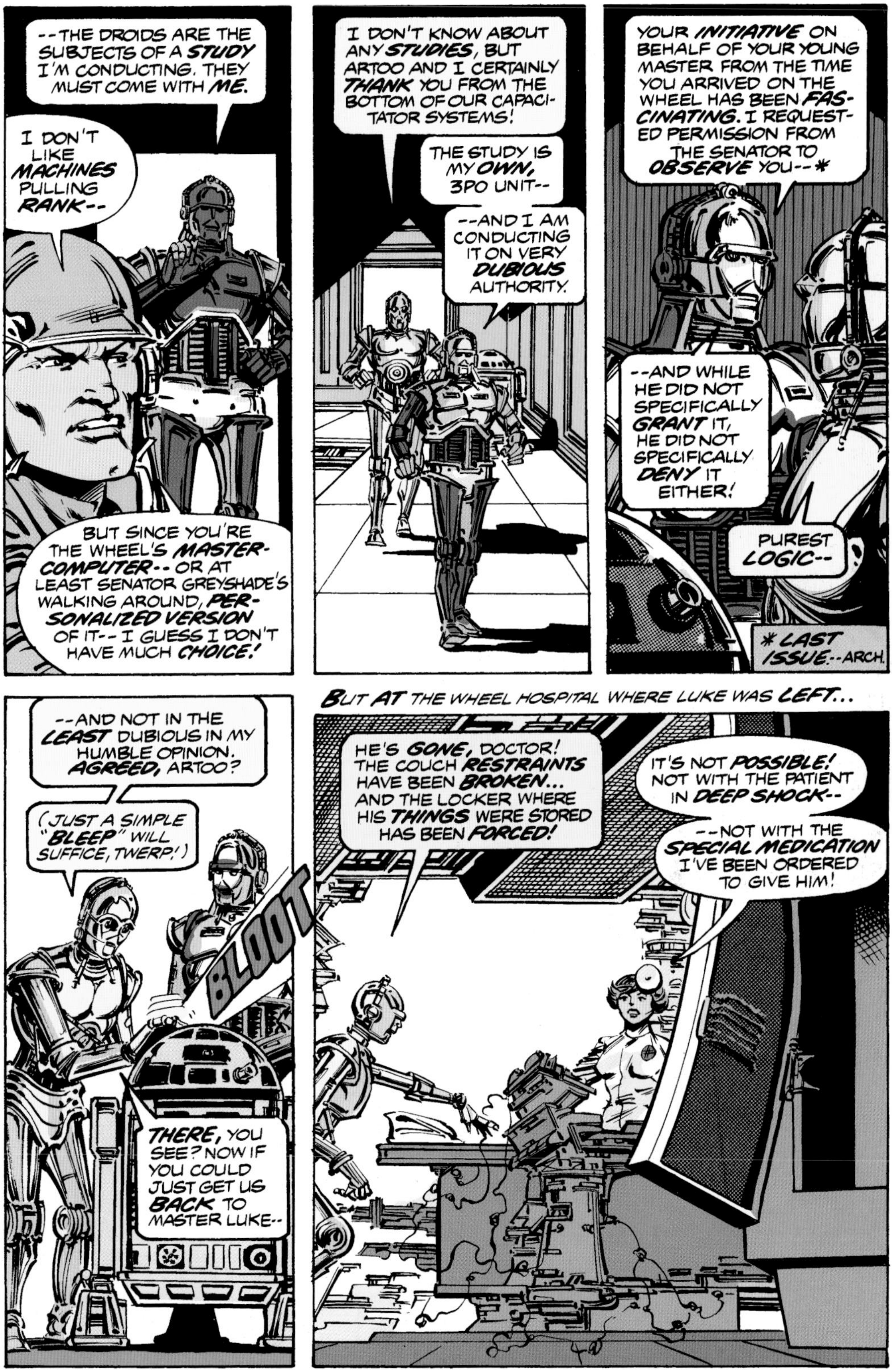
--THE DROIDS ARE THE SUBJECTS OF A STUDY I'M CONDUCTING. THEY MUST COME WITH ME.
I DON'T LIKE MACHINES PULLING RANK--
BUT SINCE YOU'RE THE WHEEL'S MASTER-COMPUTER-- OR AT LEAST SENATOR GREYSHADE'S WALKING AROUND, PERSONALIZED VERSION OF IT-- I GUESS I DON'T HAVE MUCH CHOICE!
I DON'T KNOW ABOUT ANY STUDIES, BUT ARTOO AND I CERTAINLY THANK YOU FROM THE BOTTOM OF OUR CAPACITATOR SYSTEMS!
THE STUDY IS MY OWN, 3PO UNIT--
--AND I AM CONDUCTING IT ON VERY DUBIOUS AUTHORITY.
YOUR INITIATIVE ON BEHALF OF YOUR YOUNG MASTER FROM THE TIME YOU ARRIVED ON THE WHEEL HAS BEEN FASCINATING. I REQUESTED PERMISSION FROM THE SENATOR TO OBSERVE YOU--*
--AND WHILE HE DID NOT SPECIFICALLY GRANT IT, HE DID NOT SPECIFICALLY DENY IT EITHER!
PUREST LOGIC--
*LAST ISSUE.--ARCH.
--AND NOT IN THE LEAST DUBIOUS IN MY HUMBLE OPINION. AGREED, ARTOO?
(JUST A SIMPLE "BLEEP" WILL SUFFICE, TWERP!)
BLOOT
THERE, YOU SEE? NOW IF YOU COULD JUST GET US BACK TO MASTER LUKE--
BUT AT THE WHEEL HOSPITAL WHERE LUKE WAS LEFT...
HE'S GONE, DOCTOR! THE COUCH RESTRAINTS HAVE BEEN BROKEN... AND THE LOCKER WHERE HIS THINGS WERE STORED HAS BEEN FORCED!
IT'S NOT POSSIBLE! NOT WITH THE PATIENT IN DEEP SHOCK--
--NOT WITH THE SPECIAL MEDICATION I'VE BEEN ORDERED TO GIVE HIM!

ER... WHY HAVE WE *STOPPED*, MASTER-COM? IF YOU HAVE FURTHER *QUALMS* ABOUT EXCEEDING YOUR *AUTHORITY*, LET ME *ASSURE* YOU--

AN *ALARM* HAS GONE OUT FROM THE *HOSPITAL AREA*--

--AND I'M *ALSO* RECEIVING A *WARNING SIGNAL* FROM THE *EXECUTIVE TOWER*--

"--SOMETHING IS *AMISS* IN SENATOR GREYSHADE'S SUITE!"

A LITTLE *MORE* SHOULD *DO* IT...! IF I'VE GOT THE *RIGHT CIRCUITRY*--

AND IF THIS *INSULATED CLOTH* I CUT FROM ONE OF THE COUCHES KEEPS ME FROM *ELECTROCUTING* MYSELF, THEN--

ZDAK!

WSSHK!

--THE *DOOR SEALS* SHOULD *SHORT CIRCUIT!*

ARTOO DEETOO COULD HAVE DONE THAT WITHOUT THE *PYROTECHNICS*--

--BUT THEN *HE* WOULDN'T HAVE HAD TO DO IT WITH A *SERVING KNIFE!*

QUESTION *NOW* IS: CAN I REACH THE *LIFT* BEFORE GREYSHADE'S GUARDS REACH *ME*?!

YOUR HUMAN *FRIENDS* SEEM TO OPERATE WITH THE SAME *PERSISTANCE* AS YOU TWO. IT IS MOST *INTERESTING*... BUT QUITE *FUTILE*, PARTICULARLY FOR THE *PRINCESS*.

THE *ONLY ROUTE* FROM THE EXECUTIVE TOWER WILL LEAD HER INTO THE SENATOR'S *HANDPICKED SECURITY TEAM!*

WE MUST *PART* NOW. SENATOR GREYSHADE DIDN'T WANT TO BE *DISTURBED* WHILE WITH COMMANDER STROM... BUT HE HAS A *SPECIAL INTEREST* IN PRINCESS LEIA. I'LL INFORM HIM *PERSONALLY.*

MEANTIME, THERE WILL BE MANY SEARCHERS FOR THIS *SKYWALKER. YOU* COULD BE TAKEN TOO... AND I *CANNOT* INTERCEDE FURTHER.

YOU MUST PROCEED *WITHOUT* HELP FROM ME. SO LET ME GO ON *RECORD* AS ADVISING YOU *AVOID* THE *CROWDED CASINO AREA* --

-- YOU MIGHT EASILY BECOME *LOST* AMID THE *MANY* DROIDS RUNNING ERRANDS AND PLACING BETS FOR THEIR *MASTERS* NOW THAT THE *BIG GAME* HAS STARTED.

BA-DEEP?

NO, ARTOO... *I* DON'T KNOW WHAT TO MAKE OF HIM *EITHER.*

BUT... WE *MAY* HAVE GAINED A *FRIEND!*

AND *SHORTLY,* IN THE CROWDED CASINO AREA... THERE ARE *TWO MORE* DROIDS.

WE'RE SAFE, ARTOO... BUT THAT DOESN'T HELP POOR *MASTER LUKE* AND THE *PRINCESS!* IF ONLY WE COULD FIND *CAPTAIN SOLO* OR --

BIPEEP ABIT KIK!

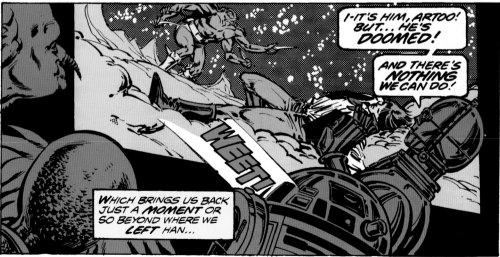

I-IT'S HIM, ARTOO! BUT... HE'S *DOOMED!*

AND THERE'S *NOTHING* WE CAN DO!

WEET!

WHICH BRINGS US BACK JUST A *MOMENT* OR SO BEYOND WHERE WE *LEFT* HAN...

*...AND HE GROGGILY FUMBLES FOR HIS DROPPED **POWER SHIELD**!*

GONNA **BURN** MY OWN HAND **GRABBIN'** IT... BUT IT BEATS HAVIN' A **DAGGER-THORN** BURIED IN MY CHEST!

AT LEAST... I'M **PRAYIN'** IT WILL!

UNGHH MUST HAVE BROKEN **RIBS**... HURTS TO **MOVE**!

*THE THROW IS **WEAK**. HAN'S LUMBERING OPPONENT MIGHT **LAUGH**... IF HE CAME FROM A RACE THAT KNEW **HOW**. STILL... IT IS ON **TARGET**. AND, THOUGH LOW ON CRACKLING **ENERGY**...*

*...THE POWER SHIELD DOES WHAT HAN **WANTED** IT TO...*

*...MAKING **CONTACT** WITH THE **METAL STUDS** ON THE GIANT'S BOOTS! UNABLE TO KNOCK IT **ASIDE**, THE GLADIATOR HAS BUT **ONE** OPTION...*

*...TO **FALL**!*

WUM!

AND WHEN HE *RISES*...

...IT IS WITH THE TERRIBLE KNOWLEDGE THAT *ONE* DAGGER-THORN WAS *UNDER* HIS BODY WHEN IT STRUCK THE GROUND!

IT IS A *SMALL* WOUND, BARELY A *SCRATCH*...

WITH THE VENOM-DRENCHED *THORN*... IT IS *ENOUGH*.

RARRRUMM!

AND HAN SUDDENLY FACES THE *PROSPECT*...

...OF BEING *SLAIN* BY ONE ALREADY *DEAD!*

SOMETHIN' BY MY *HEAD*...! IF I CAN *REACH* IT...

FOR IT IS *LIFELESS WEIGHT* THAT CRASHES DOWN UPON HIM... HIM AND THE HASTILY GRASPED *ROCK* THAT BEARS THE THORN'S *BRUNT!*

KRAK!

LET'S *HEAR* IT FOR THE ARENA'S *PLANNERS*--

--THEIR SETTINGS MAY BE *FAKE*... BUT THEY HAD THE CLASS TO BRING IN *REAL STONES!*

GREYSHADE! YOU SMOOTH-MOUTHED *FUMBLER!* *WHAT WENT WRONG?!*

I'M NOT *CERTAIN*, STROM. BUT BEAR IN *MIND*--

--THIS WAS ONLY A *PRELIMINARY* MATCH. SOLO MUST STILL ENDURE...*THE MAIN EVENT!*

AND *NEXT ISSUE* AS HAN FACES *THAT* CHALLENGE, *LUKE* COMES UNDER THE...

SHADOW OF A DARK LORD!

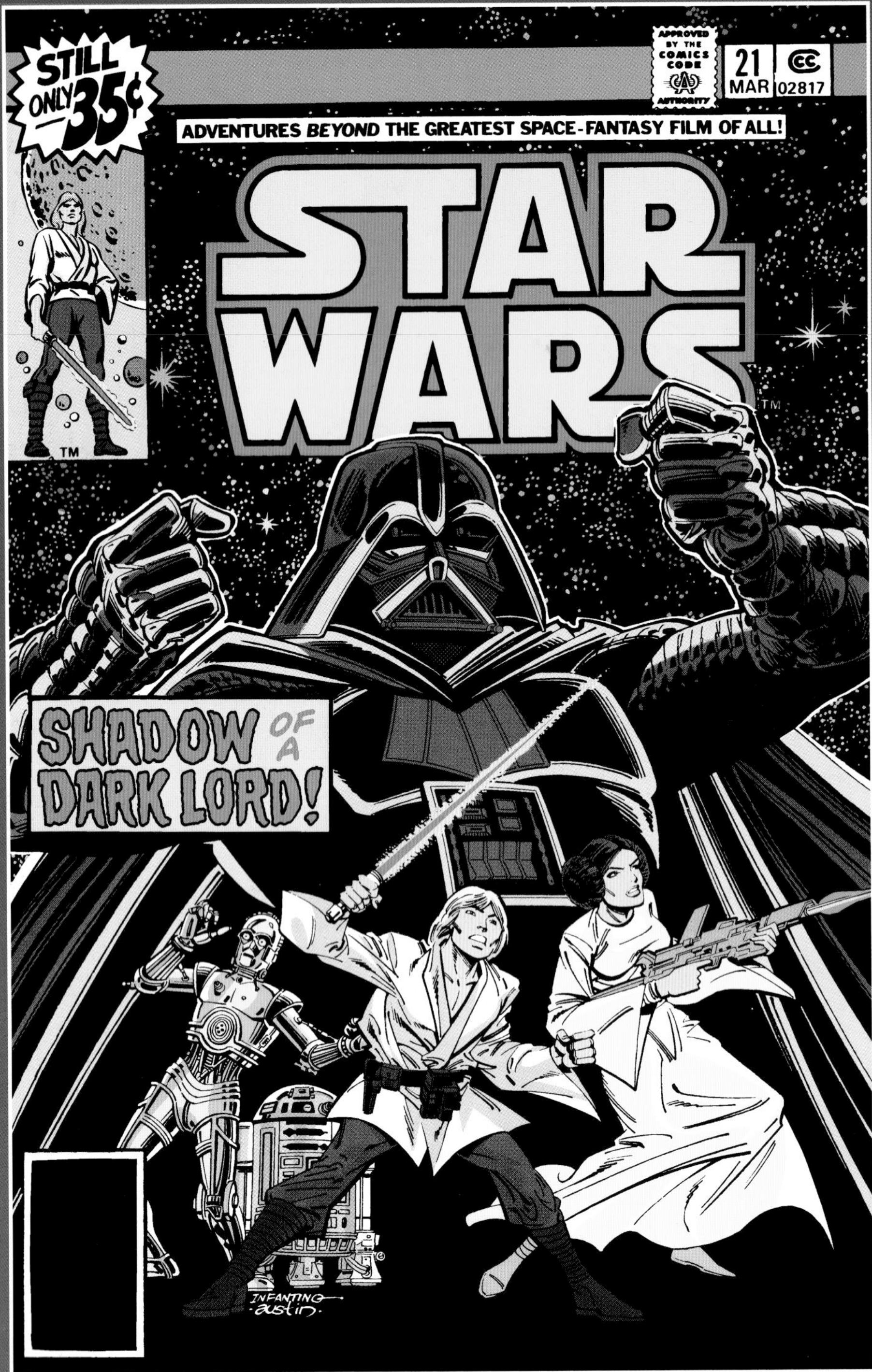
STILL ONLY 35¢
APPROVED BY THE COMICS CODE AUTHORITY
21 MAR
CC 02817
ADVENTURES BEYOND THE GREATEST SPACE-FANTASY FILM OF ALL!
STAR WARS
SHADOW OF A DARK LORD!
INFANTINO
austin

LucasFilm PRESENTS: **STAR WARS**™ THE GREATEST **SPACE FANTASY** OF ALL!

CONTINUING THE SAGA BEGUN IN THE FILM BY GEORGE LUCAS RELEASED BY TWENTIETH CENTURY-FOX

SHADOW of a DARK LORD!

ONLY *ONE GUARD* ON THE *LIFT...?!*

I'D HOPED FOR SOME *LUCK*... BUT *THIS* IS TOO MUCH TO BE *BELIEVED!*

WELCOME TO THE MIDDLE OF AN ESCAPE! PRINCESS LEIA ORGANA HESITATES IN FLIGHT FROM THE SUITE THAT WAS HER RATHER LUXURIOUS PRISON HERE ON THE GALAXY'S GREATEST GAMBLING ENTERPRISE... THE WHEEL! AN ARTIFICIAL SATELLITE NOW SUDDENLY THE OBJECT OF IMPERIAL INTRIGUE...

ARCHIE GOODWIN WRITER/EDITOR / CARMINE INFANTINO and GENE DAY ARTISTS / JOHN COSTANZA letterer / GEORGE ROUSSOS colorist / JIM SHOOTER CONSULTING EDITOR

6284

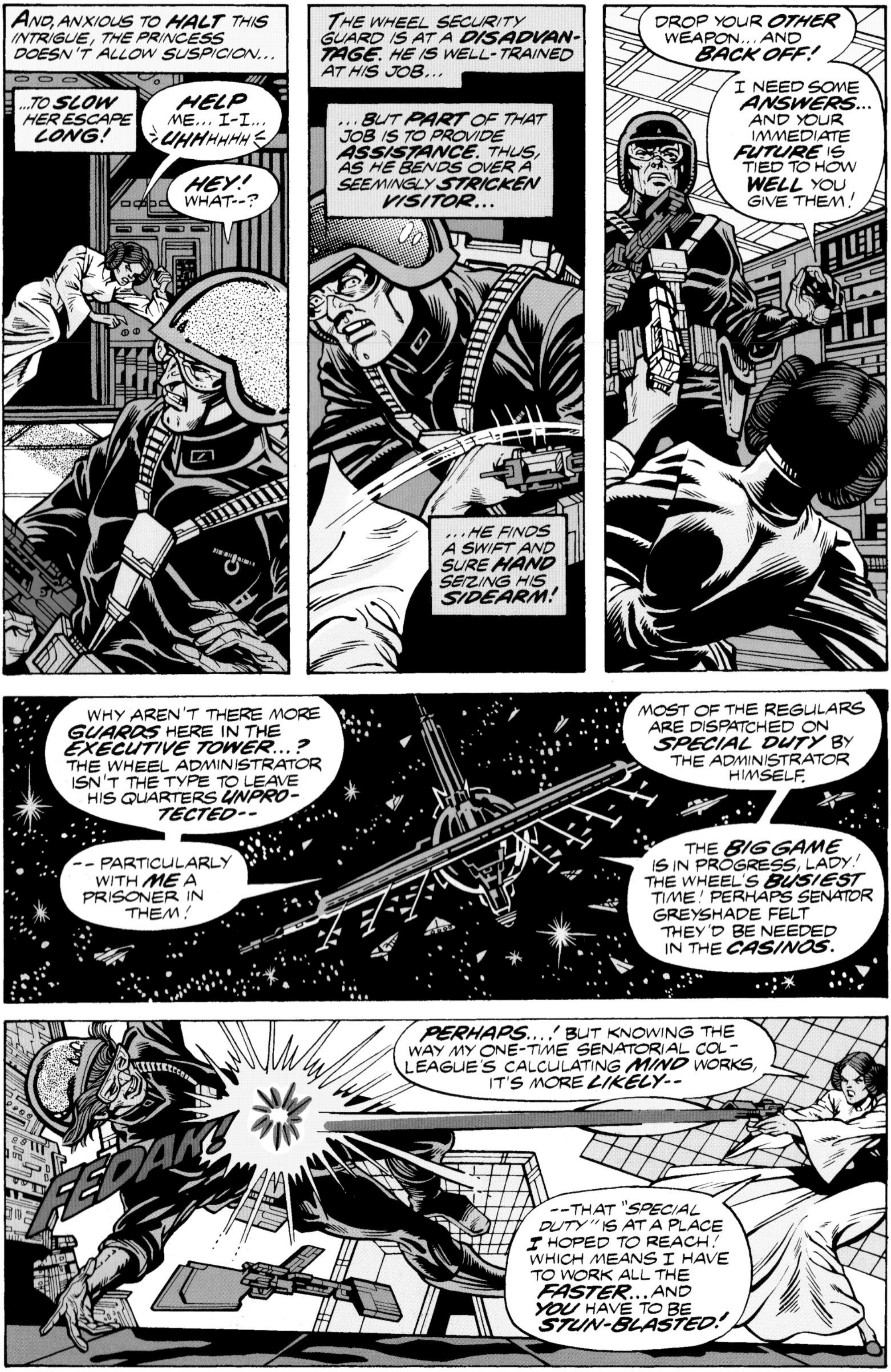
AND, ANXIOUS TO HALT THIS INTRIGUE, THE PRINCESS DOESN'T ALLOW SUSPICION...
...TO SLOW HER ESCAPE LONG!
HELP ME... I-I... UHHHHHH
HEY! WHAT--?
THE WHEEL SECURITY GUARD IS AT A DISADVANTAGE. HE IS WELL-TRAINED AT HIS JOB...
...BUT PART OF THAT JOB IS TO PROVIDE ASSISTANCE. THUS, AS HE BENDS OVER A SEEMINGLY STRICKEN VISITOR...
...HE FINDS A SWIFT AND SURE HAND SEIZING HIS SIDEARM!
DROP YOUR OTHER WEAPON... AND BACK OFF!
I NEED SOME ANSWERS... AND YOUR IMMEDIATE FUTURE IS TIED TO HOW WELL YOU GIVE THEM!
WHY AREN'T THERE MORE GUARDS HERE IN THE EXECUTIVE TOWER...? THE WHEEL ADMINISTRATOR ISN'T THE TYPE TO LEAVE HIS QUARTERS UNPROTECTED--
--PARTICULARLY WITH ME A PRISONER IN THEM!
MOST OF THE REGULARS ARE DISPATCHED ON SPECIAL DUTY BY THE ADMINISTRATOR HIMSELF.
THE BIG GAME IS IN PROGRESS, LADY! THE WHEEL'S BUSIEST TIME! PERHAPS SENATOR GREYSHADE FELT THEY'D BE NEEDED IN THE CASINOS.
PERHAPS...! BUT KNOWING THE WAY MY ONE-TIME SENATORIAL COLLEAGUE'S CALCULATING MIND WORKS, IT'S MORE LIKELY--
FEDAK!
--THAT "SPECIAL DUTY" IS AT A PLACE I HOPED TO REACH! WHICH MEANS I HAVE TO WORK ALL THE FASTER...AND YOU HAVE TO BE STUN-BLASTED!

STRIPPING THE FALLEN GUARD OF HIS *EQUIPMENT,* LEIA DRAGS HIM INTO A NEARBY STORAGE COMPARTMENT...

THEN HURRIES INTO THE LIFT... AND DROPS *DOWNWARD!*

WHETHER OR *NOT* SIMON GREYSHADE IS UP TO WHAT I *THINK* HE IS... I'LL STILL NEED *HELP.*

BUT THE FORCE KNOWS *WHERE* HAN, CHEWBACCA AND THE DROIDS HAVE *SCATTERED* TO IN THIS PLACE....!

WAIT! WHEN WE ALL FIRST *SEPARATED...** HAN SAID TO MEET AT THE *CRIMSON CASINO.*

A LOT HAS HAPPENED *SINCE...* BUT IT MAY STILL BE WORTH *TRYING!*

MEANTIME, I CAN *LISTEN IN* ON THE GUARD'S *COMMUNICATOR--*

* WAY BACK IN *STAR WARS #18.* --ARCHIE.

--FOR ANY MORE *RECENT* DEVELOPMENTS.

TO THINK THIS ALL *STARTED* BY TRYING TO GET *MEDICAL HELP* FOR POOR LUKE...!

ONLY INSTEAD OF FINDING *SANCTUARY* HERE...WE FOUND THE *EMPIRE* AT WORK!

" FIRST THEY *PLUNDER* A MERCHANT SHIP TRANSPORTING *WHEEL GAMBLING PROFITS,* DISGUISING IT AS AN ACT OF THE *REBEL ALLIANCE,* AND WHEN *WE* HAPPEN UPON IT...

"...THEY TRY TO DESTROY THE *MILLENNIUM FALCON* AND CLAIM IT WAS THE REBEL *PIRATE SHIP!*

"NOW, THEY'VE *STRUCK* AT A *PLEASURE CRAFT* LEAVING THE WHEEL... USING AN ALLIANCE *X-WING FIGHTER!*

"*ALL* TO TURN SENTIMENT AGAINST *OUR* CAUSE, AND SET THE *STAGE...*

"...FOR TOTAL *PUBLIC ACCEPTANCE* OF A COMPLETE IMPERIAL *TAKEOVER* OF THE WHEEL AND ITS VAST, CONTINUOUS FLOW OF *PROFITS*...

"...PROFITS THAT WILL GREATLY *STRENGTHEN* THE EMPEROR'S WAR MACHINE AND MAKE HIM EVEN *LESS* ACCOUNTABLE TO LOCAL GOVERNMENTS...

"...BRINGING HIM ONE *GIANT STRIDE* NEARER TO *CRUSHING* ANY AND *ALL* RESISTANCE!"

BUT THE SCHEME HERE MIGHT STILL BE *DISCREDITED*...IF WE'RE *QUICK* ENOUGH!

THOSE PIRATED WHEEL PROFITS ARE THE *PROOF* I NEED--

--AND THEY'RE BOUND TO BE WITH THIS SECTOR'S *IMPERIAL COMMANDER*...WHO *FOLLOWED* US HERE!

I DON'T KNOW *HOW* TO GET THAT LOOT OFF HIS *CRUISER*--

--PARTICULARLY SINCE I CAN'T FIGURE *WHAT* KIND OF GAME WHEEL ADMINISTRATOR *GREYSHADE* IS PLAYING IN ALL THIS--

--BUT *NOTHING* IS GOING TO STOP ME FROM *TRYING!*

TO ALL
CASINO

BUT, AS THE ONCE SENATOR OF THE NOW DESTROYED PLANET OF *ALDERAAN* RUSHES FORWARD, WE'RE GOING TO PAUSE... AND LOOK *BACK*. BACK IN TIME...

...BACK SEVERAL *HOURS* AS WE MEASURE IT.

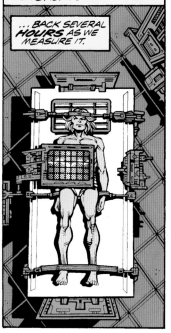

AND *HERE*... IN THE WHEEL'S HOSPITAL...WE WILL EXPLORE THE *MYSTERY* OF LUKE SKY-WALKER. LAST ISSUE, WE SAW THAT LUKE HAD *VANISHED* FROM THIS AUTO-MED COUCH...

NOW WE WILL LEARN HOW AND WHY...

AS IS OFTEN THE CASE IN *MANY* MYSTERIES...

...THE ULTIMATE *ANSWER* LIES IN THE *MIND*.

LUKE SKYWALKER'S BODY LIES *MOTIONLESS*, STILL IN THE SAME *TRANCE-LIKE* STATE IT FELL INTO ABOARD THE *MILLENNIUM FALCON* WHEN, WHILE PRACTICING A *MEDI-TATION* ON THE FORCE, *SOMETHING* HAPPENED!✱ YES, HIS *BODY* DOES NOT MOVE...

...BUT IN HIS *MIND*, LUKE SKYWALKER IS *RUNNING*...RUNNING AMID THE *STARS!*

I-I... CAN *FEEL* IT...! IT'S STILL *BACK* THERE...! STILL *COMING*--

COMING... AFTER... *ME!*

✱ *STAR WARS* #18.--ARCHIE.

373

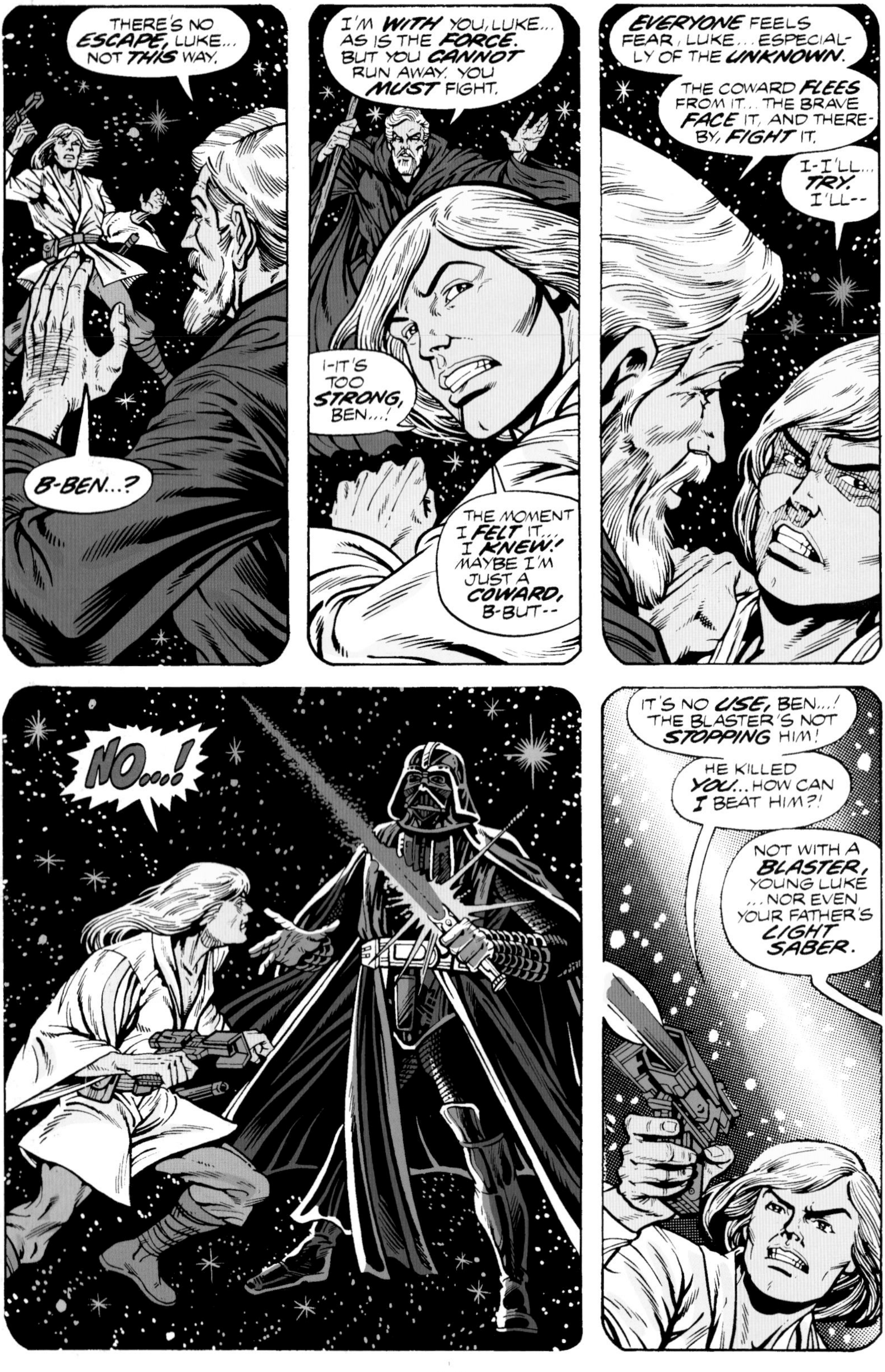

THERE'S NO ESCAPE, LUKE... NOT THIS WAY.
B-BEN...?
I'M WITH YOU, LUKE... AS IS THE FORCE. BUT YOU CANNOT RUN AWAY. YOU MUST FIGHT.
I-IT'S TOO STRONG, BEN...!
THE MOMENT I FELT IT... I KNEW! MAYBE I'M JUST A COWARD, B-BUT--
EVERYONE FEELS FEAR, LUKE... ESPECIALLY OF THE UNKNOWN.
THE COWARD FLEES FROM IT... THE BRAVE FACE IT, AND THEREBY, FIGHT IT.
I-I'LL... TRY. I'LL--
NO...!
IT'S NO USE, BEN...! THE BLASTER'S NOT STOPPING HIM!
HE KILLED YOU... HOW CAN I BEAT HIM?!
NOT WITH A BLASTER, YOUNG LUKE ...NOR EVEN YOUR FATHER'S LIGHT SABER.

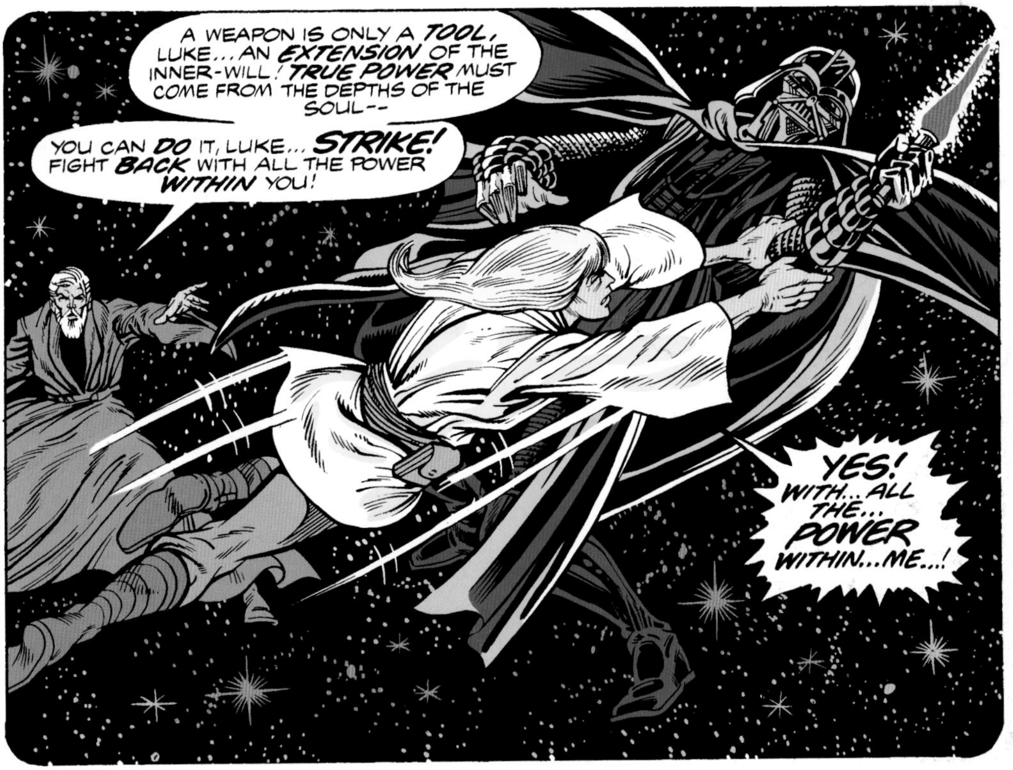
A WEAPON IS ONLY A TOOL, LUKE... AN EXTENSION OF THE INNER-WILL! TRUE POWER MUST COME FROM THE DEPTHS OF THE SOUL--
YOU CAN DO IT, LUKE... STRIKE! FIGHT BACK WITH ALL THE POWER WITHIN YOU!
YES! WITH... ALL THE... POWER WITHIN... ME...!

AND AS AN EPIC STRUGGLE BEGINS IN THE MIND OF THE TATOOINE FARM LAD TURNED STAR-WARRIOR, HIS SHOCK-STILLED BODY SUDDENLY TREMBLES... AND BEGINS ITS OWN FIGHT!

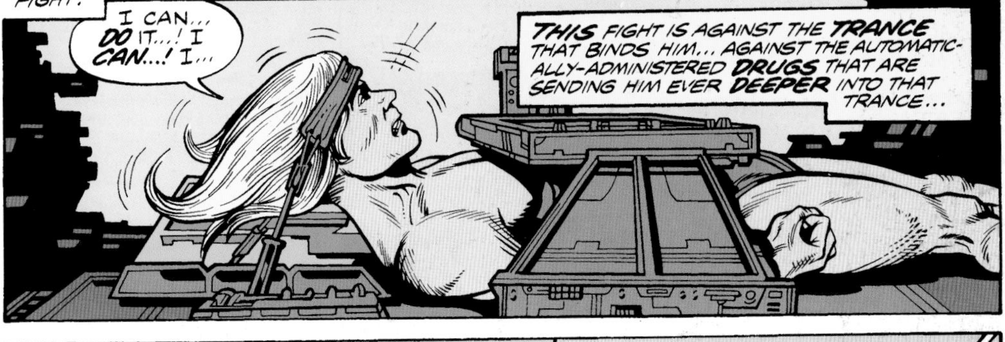
I CAN... DO IT...! I CAN...! I...
THIS FIGHT IS AGAINST THE TRANCE THAT BINDS HIM... AGAINST THE AUTOMATIC-ALLY-ADMINISTERED DRUGS THAT ARE SENDING HIM EVER DEEPER INTO THAT TRANCE...

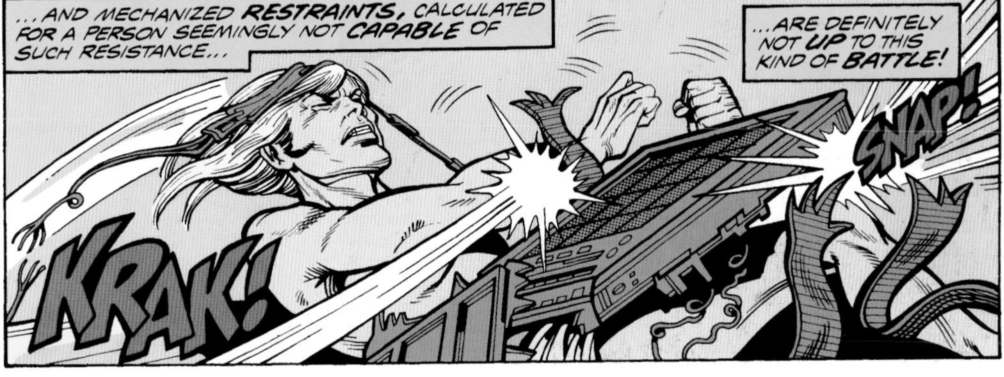
...AND MECHANIZED RESTRAINTS, CALCULATED FOR A PERSON SEEMINGLY NOT CAPABLE OF SUCH RESISTANCE...
...ARE DEFINITELY NOT UP TO THIS KIND OF BATTLE!
SNAP!
KRAK!

EYES STILL *GLAZED* BY DRUGS... MIND STILL *RAGING* WITH ITS OWN *INNER-COMBAT*...

...LUKE MOVES *INSTINCTIVELY,* SEIZING A *BROKEN EQUIPMENT STRUT*...

...AND *USING* IT TO ATTACK A *WALL LOCKER* CONTAINING HIS *PERSONAL THINGS!*

SPRANK!

MOMENTS *LATER,* BEFORE ALARMS CAN BRING HOSPITAL ORDERLIES, HE IS ON HIS *WAY...*

...*RACING* ALONG WHEEL ACCESS CORRIDORS...

...EVEN AS HE WAGES THE *BATTLE* IN HIS *MIND!*

THAT WAGING IS *LONG* AND *HARD,* BUT *FINALLY,* ULTIMATELY...

BEN...! HE'S *FINISHED....*! I'VE *AVENGED* YOU... BEATEN *DARTH VADER!*

NO, LUKE...IT'S *NOT* DARTH YOU'VE CONQUERED--

--MERELY A *SHADOW* OF HIM. A SHADOW THAT IS YOUR OWN *FEAR--*

ZAMP!

--THE FEAR THAT WAS MAKING YOU DRAW *INTO* YOURSELF... *LOSE* YOURSELF IN YOUR OWN MIND, PERHAPS *FOREVER.*

YOU'VE FOUGHT AND *WON,* YOUNG LUKE. NOW IT'S *OVER.* ALL OVER--

B-BEN...? BEN...!

NOT *BEN*, LUKE....! *LEIA*... AND THE *DROIDS!* THANK THE STARS YOU'VE FINALLY *COME AROUND!*

I'D JUST FOUND THREEPIO AND ARTOO IN THE *CRIMSON CASINO* WHEN A TRANSMISSION CAME THROUGH ABOUT *YOU!* A FULL *RIOT ALERT*--

B-BUT BY THE TIME WE *GOT* HERE-- AS I'VE BEEN TRYING TO *TELL* YOU--

--IT WAS *ALL OVER!*

I... I DID *THIS...?!* MUST'VE BEEN OUT OF MY *HEAD*... TOTALLY *BERSERK*--

--FIGHTING THAT *TRANCE* I WAS IN....!

WHAT *IS* THIS PLACE...? HOW'D WE GET HERE...?! THE LAST *I* RECALL--

--I WAS DOING A *MEDITATION*, LETTING MY MIND *DRIFT FREE*, WHEN... W-WHEN--

WHAT, LUKE--?

I-I... TOUCHED SOMEONE *ELSE'S* MIND! ONLY FOR AN *INSTANT*... JUST IN *PASSING*. IT WAS *TWISTED...EVIL....* AND *STRONG*, PRINCESS!

SO STRONG IT MADE ME WANT TO *HIDE*... TO CRAWL *INSIDE* MYSELF AND *NEVER* COME OUT.

WORST OF *ALL*, THAT CONTACT MAKES *CERTAIN* WHAT WE COULD ONLY *SUSPECT* UP TO NOW--

DARTH VADER IS *ALIVE*--!

ALIVE... AND *SEARCHING* FOR US!

INTERLUDE: THE AIR OF THE MID-SYSTEMS PLANET *ULTAAR* IS THICK, CLOYINGLY HEAVY WITH THE OVER-RIPE SCENT OF GIANT BLOSSOMS GROWN HERE FOR HARVEST. MIX THIS WITH AN ACRID HAZE OF SPENT *LASER-BOLTS,* THE TELLING STENCH OF *DEATH...*

...AND EVEN VETERAN *STORM-TROOPERS* MAY FEEL *REVUL-SION.* EVEN VETERAN STORM-TROOPERS WHO HAVE LONG FOLLOWED IN THE *WAKE* OF...

...*DARTH VADER,* LORD OF THE SITH!

DEAD...! AN ENTIRE REBEL INFORMATION RETRIEVAL TEAM *WIPED OUT...!* BY *SOMEONE* WHO FOUND THIS OUT-POST *AHEAD* OF US!

HERE IN THE *HUT,* LORD VADER... THERE'S ONE WHO'LL *PULL THROUGH!*

378

SOON, THE PRE-FAB'S SHADOWED INTERIOR ECHOES WITH THE HOLLOW, SINISTER *HISS* OF THE DARK LORD'S *BREATH MASK*...

I'VE ADMINISTERED THE PROPER *DRUGS*, SIR... HE SHOULD *ANSWER* ANY QUESTIONS.

WHO *DID* THIS, REBEL...? *WHY?*

P-PLEASE... THE *PAIN*... I NEED *SOMETHING*... FOR THE... PAIN...!

FIRST, THE *ANSWERS*, REBEL.

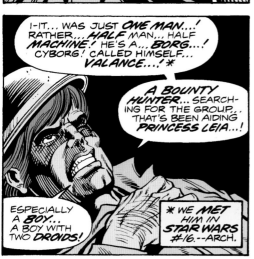

I-IT... WAS JUST *ONE MAN*...! RATHER... *HALF* MAN... HALF *MACHINE*! HE'S A... *BORG*...! CYBORG! CALLED HIMSELF... *VALANCE*...!*

A *BOUNTY HUNTER*... SEARCHING FOR THE GROUP... THAT'S BEEN AIDING *PRINCESS LEIA*...!

ESPECIALLY A *BOY*... A BOY WITH TWO *DROIDS!*

* WE *MET* HIM IN *STAR WARS #16.* --ARCH.

WE DIDN'T *HAVE*... INFORMATION HE *NEEDED*...! BUT S-SOMEONE TRIED... TO *DRAW* ON HIM... AND... AND... *THIS* HAPPENED...!

NOW... PLEASE... *HELP* EASE... THE PAIN...!

WITH NEARLY SUPERNATURAL SWIFTNESS... A *LIGHT SABER* FLASHES!

EASE THE PAIN, REBEL...?

I'LL *END* IT ENTIRELY!

VRAMP!

INTERESTING. I SEEM TO HAVE A *RIVAL*. PERHAPS EVEN A *FORMIDABLE* ONE.

COMMUNICATION FROM THE *SHIP*, LORD VADER...!

IT'S *CAPTAIN WERMIS*, VADER. WE'VE DONE QUITE A THOROUGH *CHECK* ON THOSE *COORDINATES* YOU GAVE US.

FRANKLY, THEY JUST MARK *DEAD SPACE*... NOTHING *THERE!* NOT EVEN A WISP OF *NEBULA DUST!*

THEN THE *PRESENCE* I FELT ON OUR *WAY* HERE CAME FROM A *PASSING SPACECRAFT--!*

WELL, *YOU'RE* THE EXPERT ON *METAPHYSICS--* THE *FORCE* AND ALL THAT-- BUT IT SOUNDS A BIT *VAGUE* TO BE TYING UP MY TECHNICIANS, DEAR BOY.

WERMIS, I HAVEN'T BEEN A *BOY* FOR SOME YEARS, AND NO ONE HAS *EVER* RATED ME AS *DEAR--*

IF THERE IS *ANOTHER* MIND IN THIS GALAXY STILL CAPABLE OF EVOKING THE *FORCE--* NO MATTER *HOW* WEAKLY-- IT POSES NEARLY AS GREAT A THREAT TO THE *EMPIRE--*

--AS WIMPISH *INCOMPETENTS* LIKE *YOU!*

I WANT THE *NEAREST* DESTINATION A SHIP PASSING US IN THOSE COORDINATES MIGHT HAVE BEEN *HEADED* FOR... WE'LL *START* WITH THAT.

THIS WORLD MAY HAVE PROVED A *DEAD END*... BUT THE *TRIP* HERE MAY HAVE PUT US ON SOMETHING *GREATER!*

AND SHORTLY, *TIE FIGHTERS* THUNDER UPWARD INTO THE ULTAARIAN SKIES...

I *HAVE* THAT DESTINATION, LORD VADER! A MAN-MADE *PLEASURE SATELLITE--*

--THE *WHEEL!*

THEN, WERMIS, IT BECOMES *OUR* DESTINATION AS *WELL!*

THE INTERLUDE ON ULTAAR *ENDS* WITH THE *DEPARTURE* OF AN IMPERIAL BATTLE CRUISER...

WHILE ON THE *WHEEL*, A TANGLED WEB OF EVENTS *GROWS*...

MASTER-COM... I LEFT ORDERS *NOT* TO BE INTERRUPTED!

SENATOR GREYSHADE, I WOULDN'T BE DOING MY *DUTY* AS THE WHEEL'S MASTER COMPUTER IF I DIDN'T *REPORT* TO YOU PRINCESS LEIA'S *ESCAPE*--

WHAT--?!

YOU WERE *WITH* HER! SHE *COULDN'T* GET AWAY!

I FEAR I *WASN'T* WITH HER, SIR. SINCE THE DOORS WERE *SEALED* AND YOUR OWN *HAND-PICKED GUARDS* WERE ON TOWER SECURITY DUTY, THERE SEEMED NO REASON--

I SENT THOSE MEN ON A *SPECIAL ASSIGNMENT!*

THAT *DATA* WASN'T PROCESSED THROUGH ME, SIR. *WHEEL POLICY* REQUIRES--

I'M *ADMINISTRATOR*, MASTER-COM! I CAN *MAKE, BREAK* OR *BEND* WHEEL POLICY!

NOW WHAT WERE *YOU* DOING THAT WAS SO *VITAL*?!

CONTINUING MY *STUDY* OF THE PRINCESS' TWO *DROIDS*... THREEPIO AND ARTOO-DEETOO.

I DIDN'T *AUTHORIZE* ANY SUCH STUDY! YOU'RE IN *REBELLION!*

I DON'T *BELIEVE* SO, SENATOR. I *DID* SOLICIT PERMISSION... PERHAPS A BIT *VAGUELY.** BUT YOU DIDN'T *DENY* IT, SO TECHNIC-ALLY--

TECHNICALLY MY OWN *MASTER-COMPU-TER* IS DEVOTING HIMSELF TO REBEL *DROIDS!*

* THAT WAS IN *STAR WARS #19.*--ARCHIE.

AT THE RISK OF *IMPERTINENCE*, SIR... AREN'T *YOU* DOING THE *SAME* WITH PRINCESS LEIA, A REBEL *LEADER?* OBVIOUSLY, YOUR ACTIONS ARE CONNECTED TO THE HUMAN EMOTION OF *LOVE*--

--WHILE SOME CHORD IS STRUCK IN MY *OWN* CIRCUITRY BY THE MUTUAL *RESPECT* AND *FRIENDSHIP* BETWEEN THE REBEL DROIDS AND THEIR MASTERS.

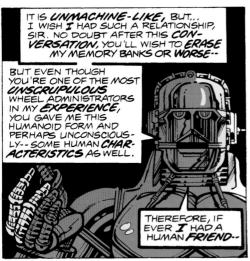

IT IS *UNMACHINE-LIKE,* BUT... I WISH *I* HAD SUCH A RELATIONSHIP, SIR. NO DOUBT AFTER THIS *CONVERSATION,* YOU'LL WISH TO *ERASE* MY MEMORY BANKS OR *WORSE--*

BUT EVEN THOUGH YOU'RE ONE OF THE MOST *UNSCRUPULOUS* WHEEL ADMINISTRATORS IN MY *EXPERIENCE,* YOU GAVE ME THIS HUMANOID FORM AND PERHAPS UNCONSCIOUSLY-- SOME HUMAN *CHARACTERISTICS* AS WELL.

THEREFORE, IF EVER *I* HAD A HUMAN *FRIEND--*

--I WOULD LIKE IT TO BE *YOU,* SENATOR GREYSHADE.

NATURALLY THIS SEEMS *GROTESQUE* TO YOU, SIR... BUT SURELY NO MORE SO THAN YOUR *OWN* EFFORTS TO FURTHER A *ROMANCE* WITH PRINCESS LEIA BY *ELIMINATING* THOSE YOUNG MEN WHO *ACCOMPANIED* HER HERE AND--

MASTER-COM--

--GET BACK TO THE EXECUTIVE TOWER AND *WHEEL* BUSINESS.

PROBLEMS, GREYSHADE? YOU'VE BEEN OUT HERE A LONG *TIME.* MISSED SOME *FINE* PRELIMINARY CONTESTS--

--IF IT'S SOME KIND OF *CROWD CONTROL* MATTER AS A RESULT OF THE *BIG GAME,* REMEMBER MOST OF MY *CREW* IS ON SHORE LEAVE HERE... WE'LL BE *HAPPY* TO GIVE YOUR *SECURITY FORCE* A HAND!

N-NOTHING LIKE *THAT,* COMMANDER STROM... JUST *DETAILS.* PERHAPS--

--IT'S GIVEN ME A LITTLE *TOO MUCH* TO *THINK* ABOUT.

AND **SOME** OF SIMON GREYSHADE'S TROUBLED THOUGHTS ARE SURELY **HERE**... ABOARD IMPERIAL COMMANDER STROM'S **LIGHT CRUISER** AT ITS WHEEL DOCK.

FOR HERE, HIS CAREFULLY SELECTED TEAM OF **SECURITY GUARDS** ARE PAYING A **VISIT** TO THE SMALL **SKELETON CREW** LEFT ON DUTY!

OUR MEN ARE BRINGING UP THE **STRONG BOXES** NOW!

RIGHT IN THE **HOLD**...! THE EMPIRE'S LONG ON **POWER,** BUT SHORT ON **IMAGINATION!**

THAT'S THE **LAST** OF THEM!

WHAT **LUCK** FINDING THOSE PIRATED **WHEEL PROFITS?!**

MOMENTS **LATER**, THE ATTACKERS EMERGE FROM THE CRUISER'S **DOCKING TUBE**...

ARE YOU **CERTAIN** WE GOT EVERYONE? IT'S **OUR** HEADS AS WELL AS THE **ADMINISTRATOR'S** IF THERE ARE ANY **WITNESSES!**

THERE'S **NOTHING** ABOARD THAT SHIP NOW BUT **GHOSTS** AND AN **EMPTY HOLD!**

BUT THERE **ARE** OBSERVERS TO THIS SCENE!

ARTOO'S GETTING THIS ON **TAPE,** PRINCESS... WHAT'S OUR **NEXT** MOVE?

WE **FOLLOW** THEM, LUKE... **WHEREVER** THEY'RE TAKING THOSE STRONG BOXES!

WELL, I NEEDED **SOMETHING** TO SHAKE THAT **DARTH VADER** BUSINESS FROM MY MIND... THIS SHOULD BE **PLENTY!**

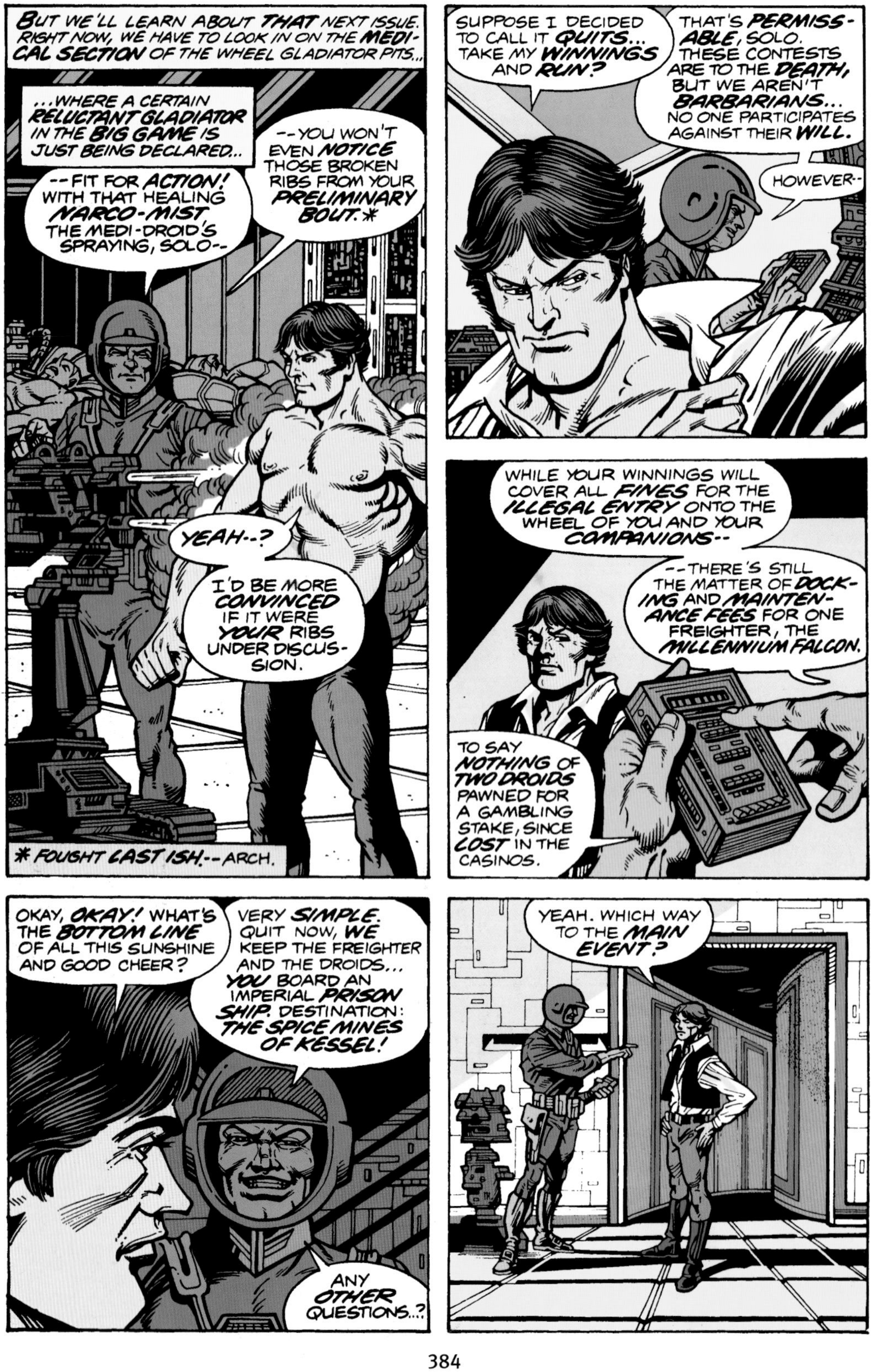
BUT WE'LL LEARN ABOUT THAT NEXT ISSUE. RIGHT NOW, WE HAVE TO LOOK IN ON THE MEDICAL SECTION OF THE WHEEL GLADIATOR PITS...
...WHERE A CERTAIN RELUCTANT GLADIATOR IN THE BIG GAME IS JUST BEING DECLARED...
--FIT FOR ACTION! WITH THAT HEALING NARCO-MIST THE MEDI-DROID'S SPRAYING, SOLO--
--YOU WON'T EVEN NOTICE THOSE BROKEN RIBS FROM YOUR PRELIMINARY BOUT.*
YEAH--?
I'D BE MORE CONVINCED IF IT WERE YOUR RIBS UNDER DISCUSSION.
* FOUGHT LAST ISH.--ARCH.
SUPPOSE I DECIDED TO CALL IT QUITS... TAKE MY WINNINGS AND RUN?
THAT'S PERMISSABLE, SOLO. THESE CONTESTS ARE TO THE DEATH, BUT WE AREN'T BARBARIANS... NO ONE PARTICIPATES AGAINST THEIR WILL.
HOWEVER--
WHILE YOUR WINNINGS WILL COVER ALL FINES FOR THE ILLEGAL ENTRY ONTO THE WHEEL OF YOU AND YOUR COMPANIONS--
--THERE'S STILL THE MATTER OF DOCKING AND MAINTENANCE FEES FOR ONE FREIGHTER, THE MILLENNIUM FALCON.
TO SAY NOTHING OF TWO DROIDS PAWNED FOR A GAMBLING STAKE, SINCE LOST IN THE CASINOS.
OKAY, OKAY! WHAT'S THE BOTTOM LINE OF ALL THIS SUNSHINE AND GOOD CHEER?
VERY SIMPLE. QUIT NOW, WE KEEP THE FREIGHTER AND THE DROIDS... YOU BOARD AN IMPERIAL PRISON SHIP. DESTINATION: THE SPICE MINES OF KESSEL!
ANY OTHER QUESTIONS..?
YEAH. WHICH WAY TO THE MAIN EVENT?

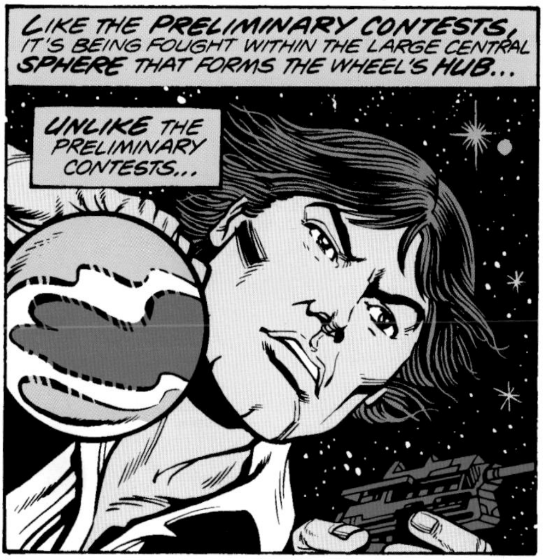
LIKE THE PRELIMINARY CONTESTS, IT'S BEING FOUGHT WITHIN THE LARGE CENTRAL SPHERE THAT FORMS THE WHEEL'S HUB...
UNLIKE THE PRELIMINARY CONTESTS...

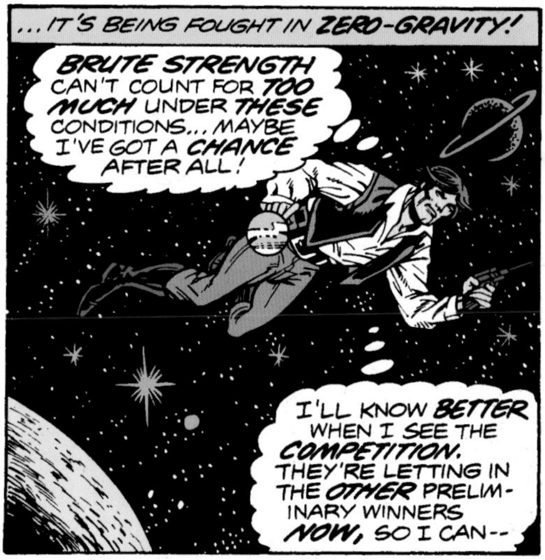
...IT'S BEING FOUGHT IN ZERO-GRAVITY!
BRUTE STRENGTH CAN'T COUNT FOR TOO MUCH UNDER THESE CONDITIONS... MAYBE I'VE GOT A CHANCE AFTER ALL!
I'LL KNOW BETTER WHEN I SEE THE COMPETITION. THEY'RE LETTING IN THE OTHER PRELIMINARY WINNERS NOW, SO I CAN--

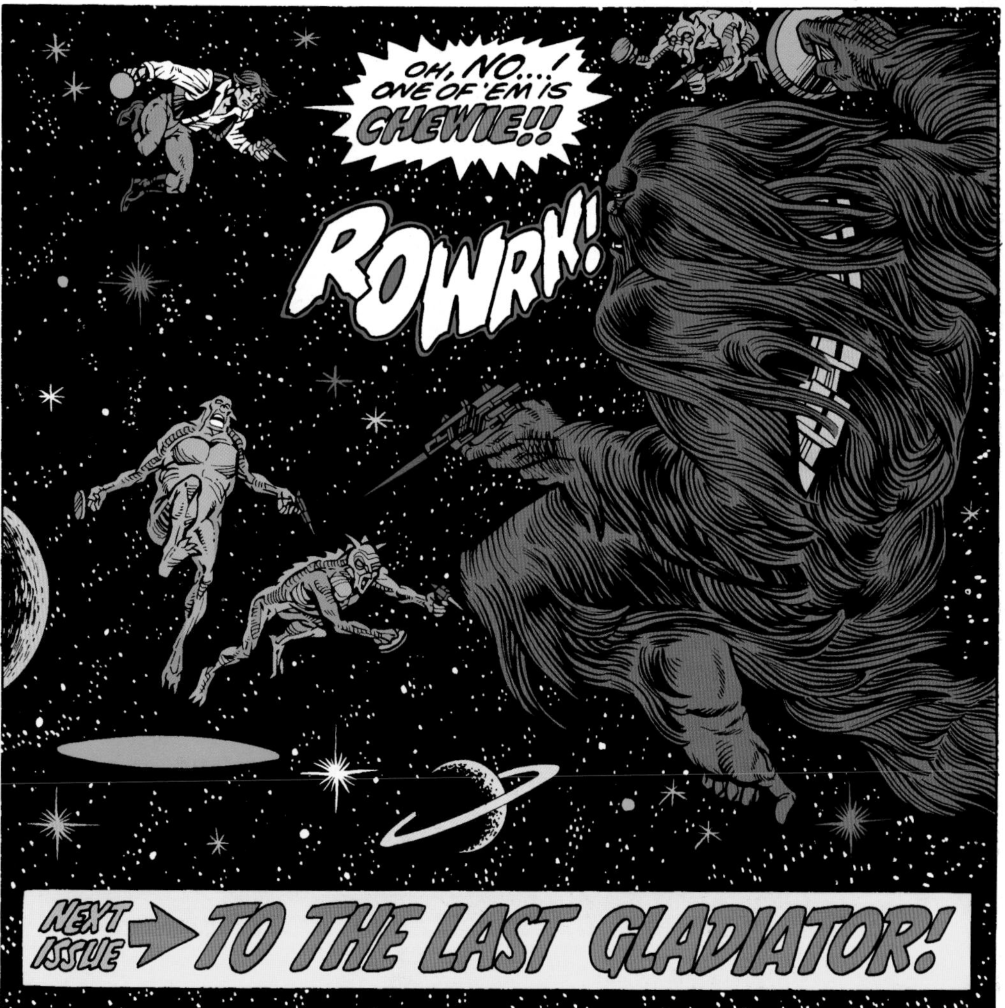
OH, NO...! ONE OF 'EM IS CHEWIE!!
ROWRK!
NEXT ISSUE → TO THE LAST GLADIATOR!

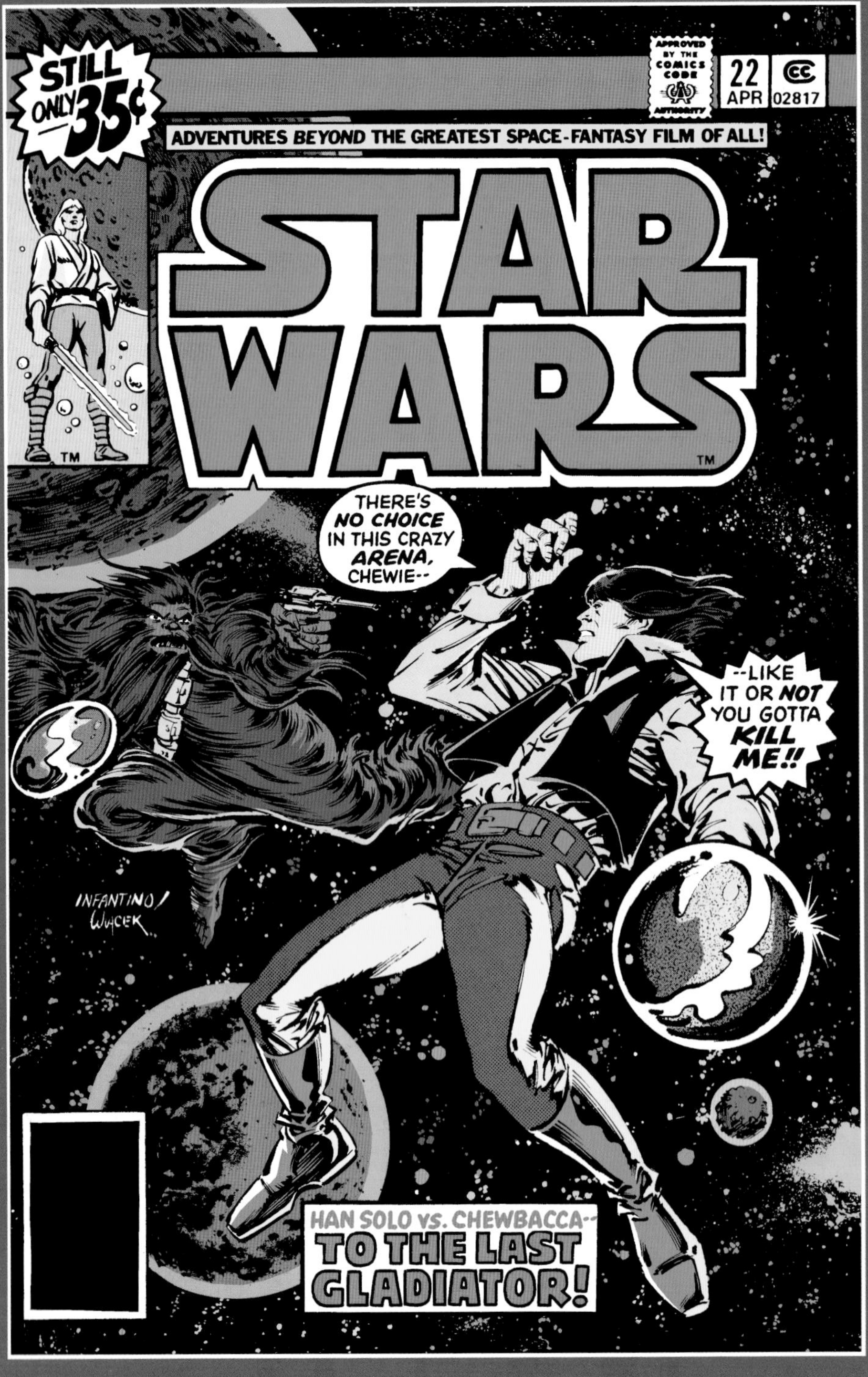

STILL ONLY 35¢
APPROVED BY THE COMICS CODE AUTHORITY
22 APR
CC 02817
ADVENTURES BEYOND THE GREATEST SPACE-FANTASY FILM OF ALL!
STAR WARS™
THERE'S NO CHOICE IN THIS CRAZY ARENA, CHEWIE--
--LIKE IT OR NOT YOU GOTTA KILL ME!!
INFANTINO / WIACEK
HAN SOLO vs. CHEWBACCA--
TO THE LAST GLADIATOR!

Long ago in a galaxy far, far away. . .there exists a state of cosmic *civil war*. A brave alliance of *underground freedom fighters* has challenged the tyranny and oppression of the awesome *Galactic Empire*. This is their story!

LucasFilm PRESENTS: **STAR WARS** THE GREATEST SPACE FANTASY OF ALL!

CONTINUING THE SAGA BEGUN IN THE FILM BY *GEORGE LUCAS* RELEASED BY *TWENTIETH CENTURY-FOX*

ARCHIE GOODWIN
WRITER / EDITOR

CARMINE INFANTINO & BOB WIACEK ARTISTS

C. ROBBINS LETTERER

B. SHAREN COLORIST

JIM SHOOTER CONSULTING EDITOR

IT LOOKS LIKE DEEP SPACE... BUT THAT IS *ILLUSION*. DESPITE THE FLOATING PLANETOIDS, THE SHIMMERING STAR FIELD, THE ZERO GRAVITY... THIS IS AN *ARENA!*

WORRK!

AND *HERE*, FOR THE PLEASURE AND EXCITEMENT OF PATRONS OF THE *WHEEL*, THE GALAXY'S ULTIMATE GAMBLING ESTABLISHMENT... A *DUEL* TO THE *DEATH* IS ABOUT TO BEGIN!

CHEWIE...! AW, *NO!* DON'T TELL ME *YOU* GOT ROPED INTO THIS *MADNESS* TOO?!

AND UNFORTUNATELY FOR *HAN SOLO* AND HIS *WOOKIEE FRIEND* AND *FIRST MATE*, THIS DUEL WILL BE FOUGHT...

to the last gladiator!

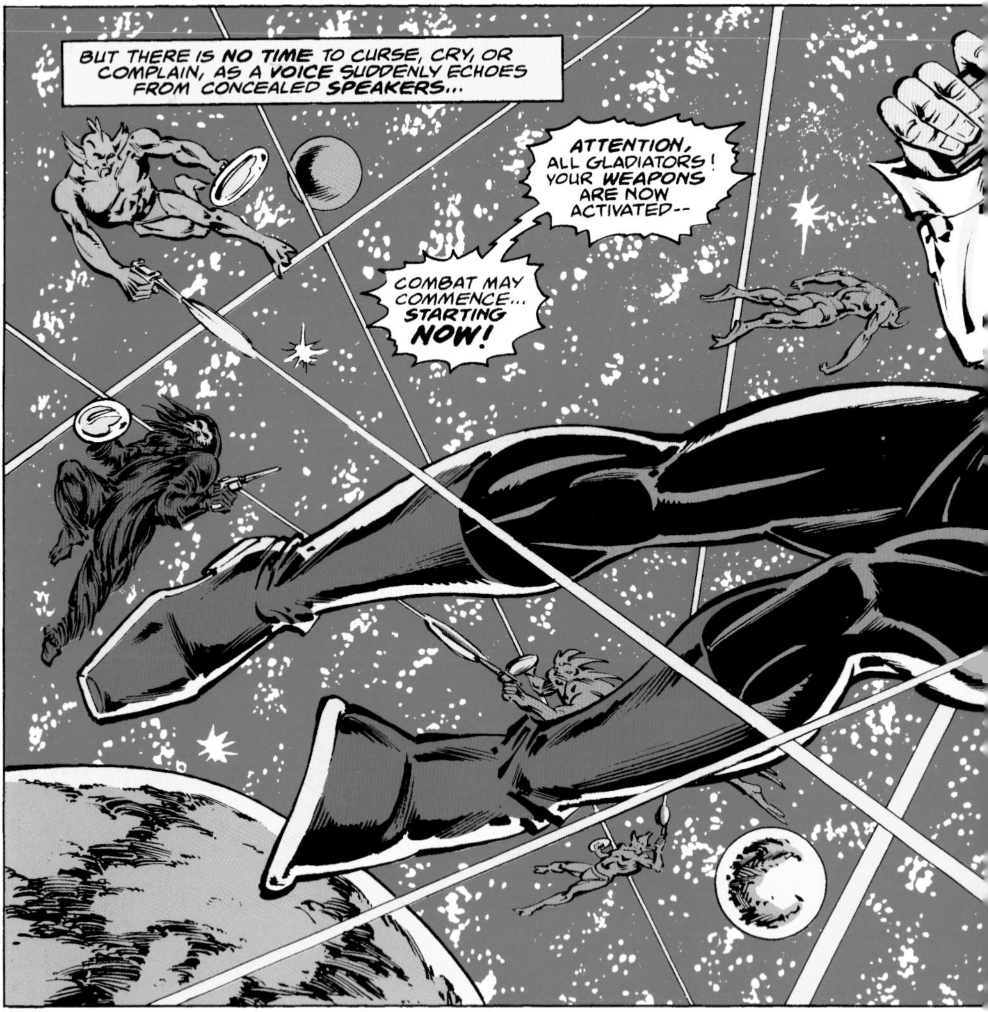
BUT THERE IS NO TIME TO CURSE, CRY, OR COMPLAIN, AS A VOICE SUDDENLY ECHOES FROM CONCEALED SPEAKERS...
ATTENTION, ALL GLADIATORS! YOUR WEAPONS ARE NOW ACTIVATED--
COMBAT MAY COMMENCE... STARTING NOW!

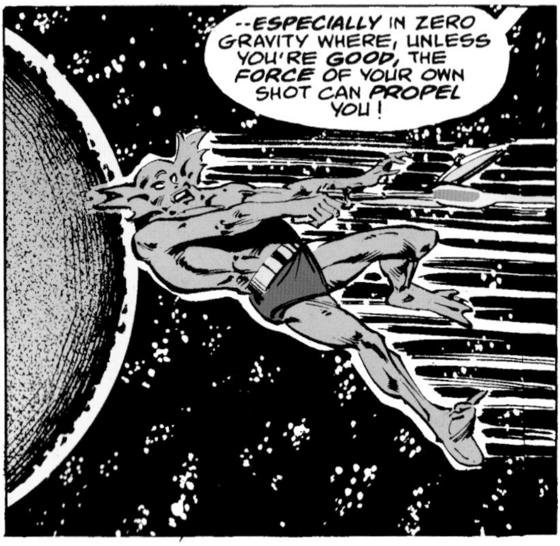
--ESPECIALLY IN ZERO GRAVITY WHERE, UNLESS YOU'RE GOOD, THE FORCE OF YOUR OWN SHOT CAN PROPEL YOU!

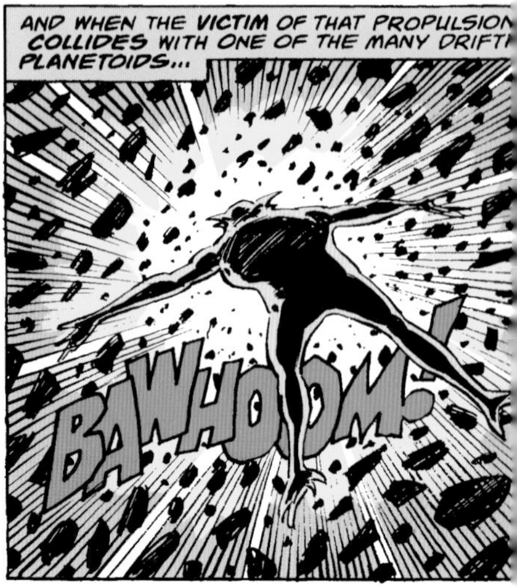
AND WHEN THE VICTIM OF THAT PROPULSION COLLIDES WITH ONE OF THE MANY DRIFT PLANETOIDS...
BAWHOOM!

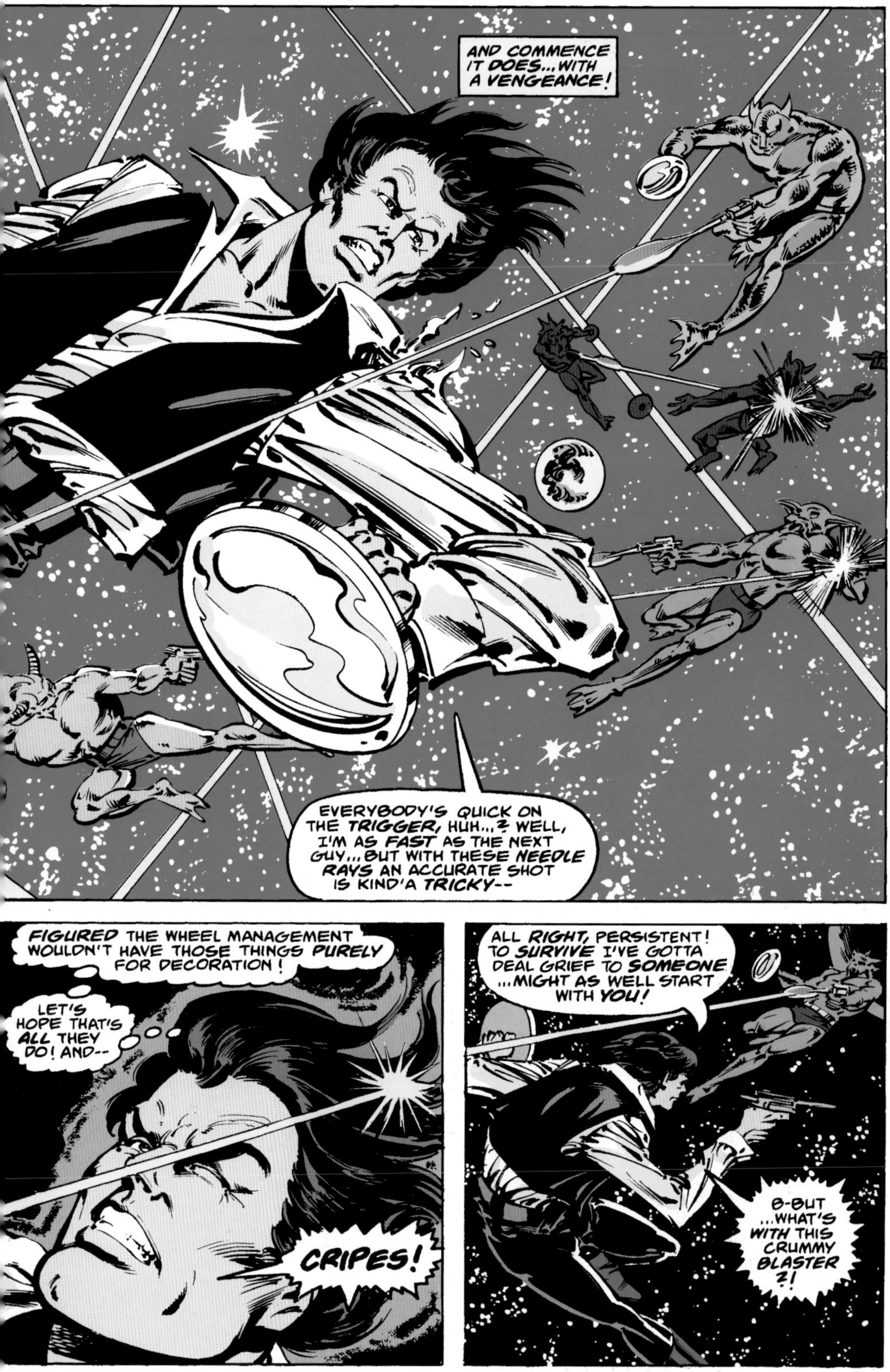
AND COMMENCE IT DOES... WITH A VENGEANCE!
EVERYBODY'S QUICK ON THE TRIGGER, HUH...? WELL, I'M AS FAST AS THE NEXT GUY... BUT WITH THESE NEEDLE RAYS AN ACCURATE SHOT IS KIND'A TRICKY--
FIGURED THE WHEEL MANAGEMENT WOULDN'T HAVE THOSE THINGS PURELY FOR DECORATION!
LET'S HOPE THAT'S ALL THEY DO! AND--
CRIPES!
ALL RIGHT, PERSISTENT! TO SURVIVE I'VE GOTTA DEAL GRIEF TO SOMEONE ...MIGHT AS WELL START WITH YOU!
B-BUT ...WHAT'S WITH THIS CRUMMY BLASTER ?!

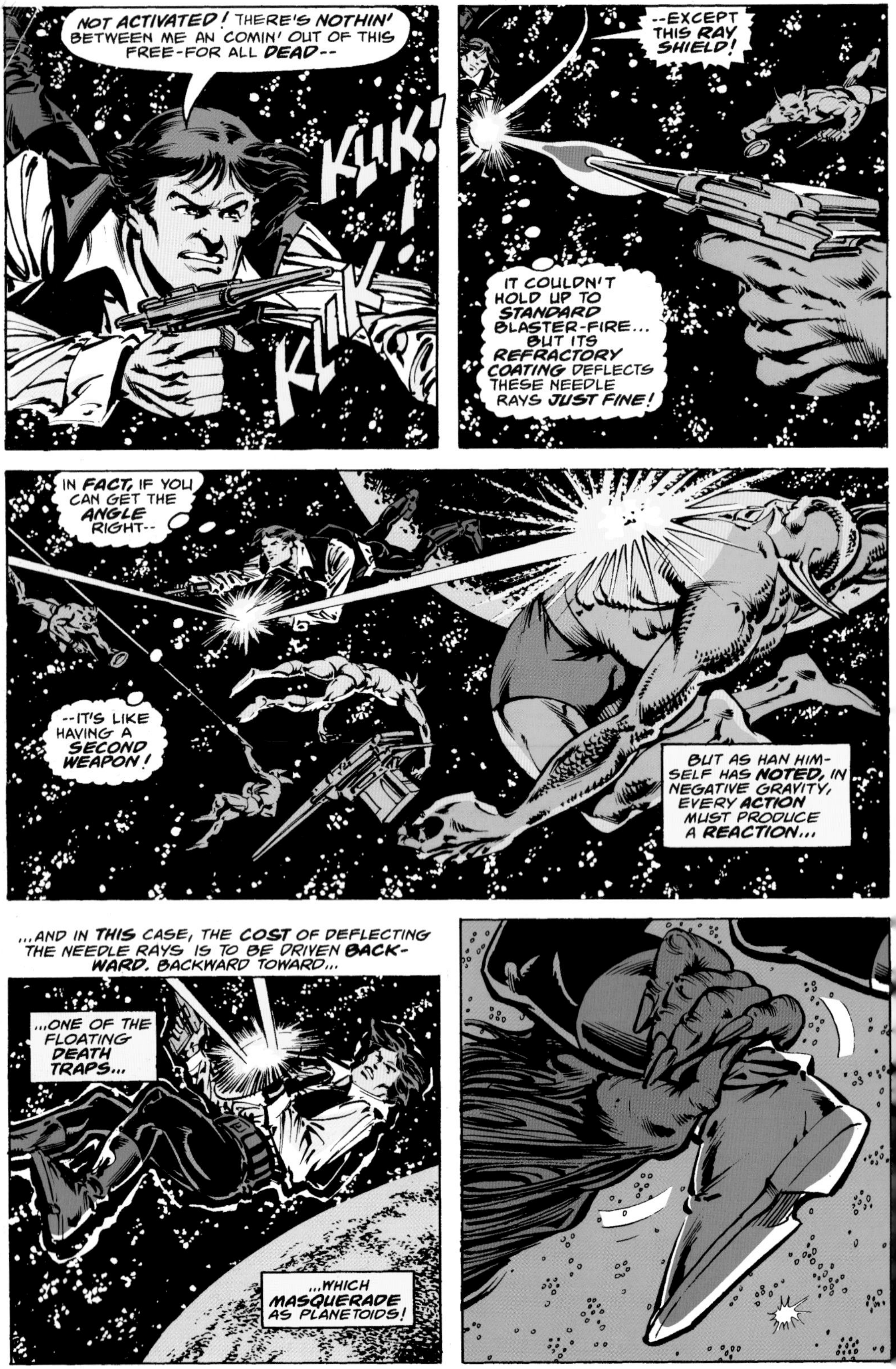
NOT ACTIVATED! THERE'S NOTHIN' BETWEEN ME AN' COMIN' OUT OF THIS FREE-FOR ALL DEAD--
KLIK!
KLIK!
--EXCEPT THIS RAY SHIELD!
IT COULDN'T HOLD UP TO STANDARD BLASTER-FIRE... BUT ITS REFRACTORY COATING DEFLECTS THESE NEEDLE RAYS JUST FINE!
IN FACT, IF YOU CAN GET THE ANGLE RIGHT--
--IT'S LIKE HAVING A SECOND WEAPON!
BUT AS HAN HIM-SELF HAS NOTED, IN NEGATIVE GRAVITY, EVERY ACTION MUST PRODUCE A REACTION...
...AND IN THIS CASE, THE COST OF DEFLECTING THE NEEDLE RAYS IS TO BE DRIVEN BACK-WARD. BACKWARD TOWARD...
...ONE OF THE FLOATING DEATH TRAPS...
...WHICH MASQUERADE AS PLANETOIDS!

ZRAAAK!

SHAMMT!

CHEWIE! GREAT *TIMING*, OL' BUDDY! I MUST'VE HIT A *FORCE FIELD*--

--THAT SET OFF THIS THING'S *VAPORIZER BEAMS*!

WAAARRK!

DUNNO WHAT *OTHER* HIDDEN DELIGHTS THESE LITTLE SUCKERS HOLD--

--BUT MAYBE WORKING *TOGETHER* WE CAN *SURVIVE* LONG ENOUGH TO FIGURE A WAY *OUT* OF THIS MESS!

I'LL GUARD YOUR *BACK* WITH MY SHIELD...START USIN' YOUR *NEEDLE RAY* ON OUR FELLOW CONTESTANTS!

YOURS DIDN'T *WORK* SO YOU *DITCHED* IT?!

Y'KNOW, FUR-FACE...I THINK WE'VE BEEN *HAD*!

SEEMED *SUSPICIOUS* WHEN I GOT STUCK WAY OUT OF MY *CLASS* IN THE PRELIMINARIES,*BUT THIS *CLINCHES* IT, BIG BUDDY!

SOMEBODY'S WORKING *OVERTIME* TO SEE WE DON'T COME OUT OF THIS ANYWAY BUT *DEAD*!

*ISSUE #20.
--ARCHIE.

AND I'D BET A CARGO OF *SPICE* THAT IT'S ALL *CONNECTED* TO OUR DIS-COVERING THAT THE *EMPIRE* ROBBED A PRIVATE *CARGO SHIP* AND TRIED TO MAKE IT *LOOK LIKE A REBEL ATTACK*!*

*WAY BACK IN *STAR WARS #18.* --ARCHIVIST ARCH.

GRORRK!

SURE! THERE'S PROBABLY A *LOT* MORE TO IT THAN THAT. BUT THE ONLY WAY *WE'LL* EVER FIND OUT--

--IS TO GET OURSELVES A *FIGHTING CHANCE* IN THIS STUPID GAME!

THAT MEANS *OFFENSIVE WEAPONS*, PAL! AND IF I'VE ANGLED THE RICOCHET *CORRECTLY*--

FORGET IT, CORELLIAN! YOU'VE *MISSED!*

VADOOM!

DEPENDS ON WHAT YOU THINK I'M *AIMING* AT, ACE! I WANTED THAT *PLANETOID* BEHIND YOU!

SWIM *AGAINST* THE EXPLOSION'S *SHOCK WAVES*, CHEWIE--

AND GET *SET!* TWO OWNERLESS *NEEDLE RAYS* ARE DRIFTIN' OUR WAY!

BUT EXCEPT AMONG BETTORS PLAYING *LONG SHOTS*, THIS AUDACIOUS MANEUVER DRAWS NO CHEERS, PARTICULARLY IN...

...THE *ROYAL LOUNGE* OF THE *GRAND CASINO*,

BLAST YOU, GREYSHADE! YOU'VE BEEN *TOO CLEVER*--

--AND THE SPICE SMUGGLER AND HIS WOOKIEE COMPANION ARE *BENEFITTING* FROM IT!

YOU SHOULD HAVE GIVEN *ALL* OF PRINCESS LEIA'S FRIENDS TO ME FOR *EXECUTION* WHEN I FIRST *PURSUED* THE MILLENNIUM FALCON HERE!

I KNOW *SUBTLETY* IS DIFFICULT FOR THE MILITARY MIND, STROM--

--BUT *YOUR* WAY ATTRACTS ATTENTION AND I DON'T THINK THE EMPIRE *WANTS* THAT!

NOT WHEN THEY'RE TRYING TO *FOOL* EVERYONE INTO BELIEVING THAT THE WHEEL AND ITS PATRONS HAVE BECOME *TARGETS* OF THE REBEL ALLIANCE--

--THEREBY JUSTIFYING AN *IMPERIAL TAKEOVER* OF THIS ESTABLISHMENT AND ITS FANTASTIC *PROFITS*... WITHOUT FRIGHTENING AWAY THE *PAYING CUSTOMERS!*

NOW SIT DOWN AND *TRUST* ME TO DO THIS *RIGHT!*

TRUST A MAN WHOSE REPUTATION IN THE IMPERIAL SENATE WAS FOR *TREACHERY,* AND WHO NOW USES HIS POSITION AS *WHEEL ADMINISTRATOR* TO FURTHER A SCHOOL BOY CRUSH WITH OUR *FOE,* LEIA ORGANA?!

STUPIDLY ENOUGH, I'VE BEEN *DOING* THAT, GREYSHADE,...AND I'M NOT PLEASED WITH THE *RESULTS!*

THEN START WATCHING THE *SCREEN* AGAIN! THE FACT THAT HAN SOLO AND CHEWBACCA HAVE *TEAMED UP* IN THE GAMES MEANS *NOTHING*--

NOTHING?! IT MEANS THEY *BOTH* COULD SURVIVE...LIVE TO BLURT OUT *ALL* THEY KNOW!

AS GLADIATORS, THEY BOTH SIGNED *CON-TRACTS,* STROM, CONTRACTS ACKNOWLEDG-ING THAT THE MATCHES ARE TO THE *DEATH*... AND THAT THERE CAN BE ONLY *ONE WINNER.*

SHOULD THEY *HESITATE* OR FAIL TO *COMPLY* ...IT'S GROUNDS FOR BOTH TO BE *SLAIN!*

GREYSHADE, EACH TIME I THINK THIS UNEASY PARTNERSHIP OF OURS WAS A *MISTAKE*--

AND FRIENDS LIKE *THAT* COULD HARDLY KILL EACH OTHER *WITHOUT* HESITATING...!

--YOU COME UP WITH AN IMPRESSIVE BIT OF *CHICANERY* TO PROVE ME *WRONG*!

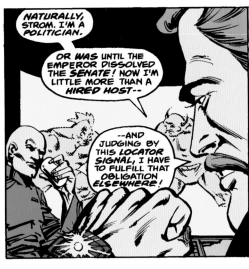

NATURALLY, STROM. I'M A POLITICIAN.

OR *WAS* UNTIL THE EMPEROR DISSOLVED THE *SENATE*! NOW I'M LITTLE MORE THAN A *HIRED HOST*--

--AND JUDGING BY THIS *LOCATOR SIGNAL*, I HAVE TO FULFILL THAT OBLIGATION *ELSEWHERE*!

NOT SO *FAST*, SENATOR! YOU WERE *NERVOUS* AND *EDGY* EARLIER...* NOW SUDDENLY, IT'S ALL *SMILES* AND *CHARM*!

YOU'RE *UP* TO SOMETHING! WHAT COULD BE MORE *URGENT* NOW THAN *OUR* BUSINESS?! UNLESS YOU'RE--

Y-YOU'RE... *YOU*...

* OR *LAST ISSUE*, EARTH TIME:--ARCH.

AND THE IMPERIAL COMMANDER FOR THIS GALACTIC SECTOR SUDDENLY STAGGERS...AND *FALLS*!

I MAY NOT RESPECT YOUR *MIND*, STROM--

--BUT I'M *AWED* BY YOUR *CONSTITUTION*! THE *DRUG* IN YOUR DRINKS SHOULD HAD YOU *SNORING* LONG BEFORE THIS!

BUT *INTRIGUE* IS NOT THE EXCLUSIVE PROPERTY OF *SIMON GREYSHADE*, FOR AMID THE MANY HALLS AND ACCESS CORRIDORS IN THE ARTIFICIAL SATELLITE'S DOCKING AREA...

THERE'S A *BAY* AHEAD, PRINCESS! THOSE SECURITY GUARDS WE'RE *TRAILING* WENT INSIDE!

THEY MUST BE PUTTING THOSE STOLEN *STRONG BOXES* ABOARD A *SHIP*, LUKE!

BA
10

BRRT·A·DEEP!

ARTOO IS SAYING HE NEEDS TO BE AT THE *BAY DOOR* IN ORDER TO CONTINUE *TAPING,* YOUR HIGHNESS.

THAT'S *RISKY!* WE'VE ALREADY GOT ENOUGH TO *PROVE* THE LOOT EVERYONE THINKS WAS PIRATED BY *REBELS* ACTUALLY WAS HIDDEN ON THE IMPERIAL COMMANDER'S *CRUISER*--

--UNTIL *GREYSHADE'S* GUARDS *STOLE* IT FROM THE *EMPIRE'S CREW!*

STILL... IT WOULD BE *USEFUL* TO LEARN WHAT MY ONETIME SENATORIAL COLLEAGUE IS *REALLY* UP TO!

WE'VE DONE *OKAY* SO FAR! IF I *COVER* ARTOO... WE'LL BE *FINE!*

THEN, WITH A PNEUMATIC HISS, THE DOCKING BAY DOOR SHOOTS *FULLY OPEN* TO REVEAL...

WE'RE THE SENATOR'S *HANDPICKED ELITE,* FARM-BOY! DID YOU AND YOUR FRIENDS *TRULY* IMAGINE--

--WE COULD BE *FOLLOWED* ON OUR OWN TERRITORY AND *NEVER* CATCH ON?!

BLOOP!

BUT DESPITE THE **CLOTHES** HE WEARS, LUKE SKYWALKER HASN'T **TRULY** BEEN A FARM-BOY...

...SINCE THE BATTLE OF THE **DEATH STAR!**

ARTOO! GET **OUT** OF HERE WITH THAT **TAPE!**

AND BY THE TIME THE GUARDS REALIZE THEY'VE LET APPEARANCES **DECEIVE** THEM...LUKE IS ROLLING AND **FIRING!**

FOOM!

FTOW!

VOOM!

THEN, HE IS **WITHIN** THE BAY...

...AND BACK ON HIS **FEET**...

VOOO!

PVAM!

CRRT!

VEEZIIIP!

...**CHARGING** UP THE LOADING RAMP OF THE DOCKED SPACECRAFT!

PVAM!

BUT IN THE CORRIDOR **OUTSIDE,** AS PRINCESS LEIA MOVES TO **HELP**...

DON'T **RUSH,** YOUR HIGHNESS--

SINCE I'M GOING THAT WAY **MYSELF**...I'LL **ACCOMPANY** YOU.

THAT WAY YOU WON'T HAVE TO CARRY THAT HEAVY **BLASTER.**

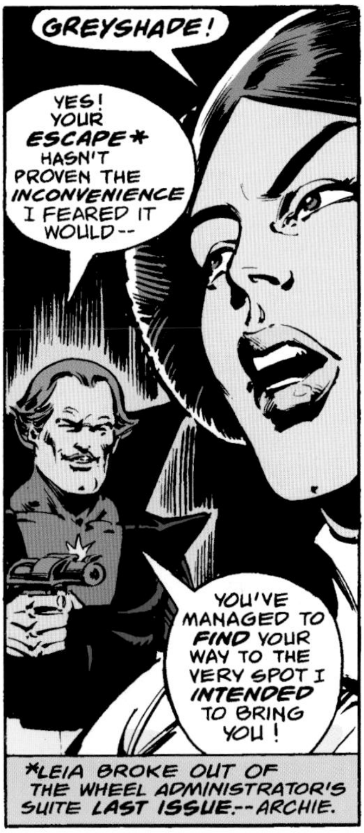
GREYSHADE!
YES! YOUR ESCAPE* HASN'T PROVEN THE INCONVENIENCE I FEARED IT WOULD--
YOU'VE MANAGED TO FIND YOUR WAY TO THE VERY SPOT I INTENDED TO BRING YOU!
*LEIA BROKE OUT OF THE WHEEL ADMINISTRATOR'S SUITE LAST ISSUE.--ARCHIE.

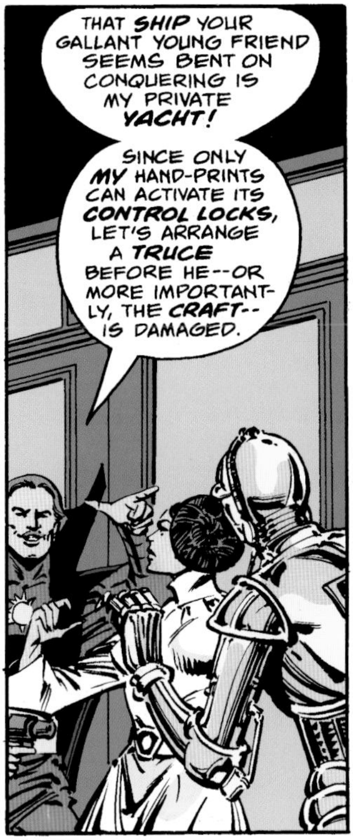
THAT SHIP YOUR GALLANT YOUNG FRIEND SEEMS BENT ON CONQUERING IS MY PRIVATE YACHT!
SINCE ONLY MY HAND-PRINTS CAN ACTIVATE ITS CONTROL LOCKS, LET'S ARRANGE A TRUCE BEFORE HE--OR MORE IMPORTANTLY, THE CRAFT--IS DAMAGED.

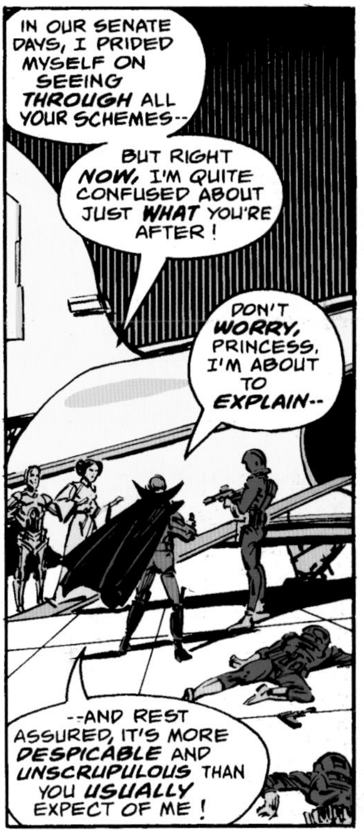
IN OUR SENATE DAYS, I PRIDED MYSELF ON SEEING THROUGH ALL YOUR SCHEMES--
BUT RIGHT NOW, I'M QUITE CONFUSED ABOUT JUST WHAT YOU'RE AFTER!
DON'T WORRY, PRINCESS, I'M ABOUT TO EXPLAIN--
--AND REST ASSURED, IT'S MORE DESPICABLE AND UNSCRUPULOUS THAN YOU USUALLY EXPECT OF ME!

INTERLUDE: A STAR-DESTROYER CLASS IMPERIAL **BATTLE CRUISER** LEAPS THROUGH **HYPER-SPACE**. ITS GREAT WEDGE SHAPE **PIERCING** THE DOPPLER-DISTORTED HEAVENS...

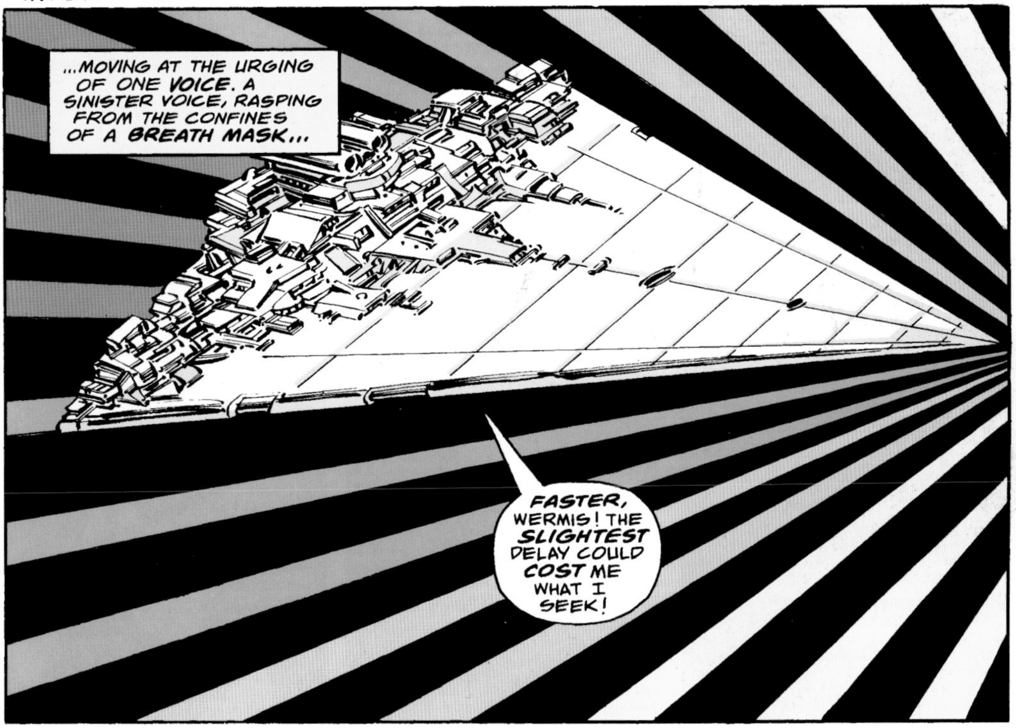
...MOVING AT THE URGING OF ONE VOICE. A SINISTER VOICE, RASPING FROM THE CONFINES OF A BREATH MASK...
FASTER, WERMIS! THE SLIGHTEST DELAY COULD COST ME WHAT I SEEK!

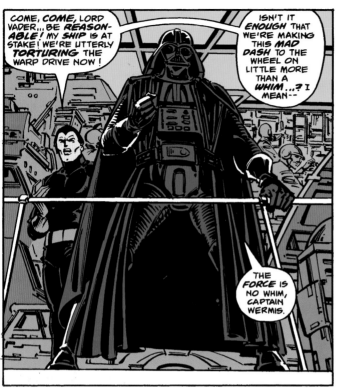

COME, *COME,* LORD VADER... BE *REASONABLE!* MY *SHIP* IS AT STAKE! WE'RE UTTERLY *TORTURING* THE WARP DRIVE NOW!

ISN'T IT *ENOUGH* THAT WE'RE MAKING THIS *MAD DASH* TO THE WHEEL ON LITTLE MORE THAN A *WHIM...?* I MEAN--

THE *FORCE* IS NO WHIM, CAPTAIN WERMIS.

AND IF ON OUR OUTWARD JOURNEY, I MADE PASSING *CONTACT* WITH ANOTHER *MIND* SEEMINGLY CAPABLE OF *EVOKING IT*--*

IT'S WORTH A *DOZEN* OF THESE *VESSELS* TO LEARN *WHO* POSSESSES EVEN A *TOUCH* OF THIS POWER I THOUGHT WAS NOW MINE *ALONE!*

* THAT MIND WAS *LUKE'S,* AS WE KNOW FROM *LAST ISSUE* AND #18.--ARCHIE.

OF COURSE, YOU CANNOT *APPRECIATE* THAT POWER... UNTIL YOU *EXPERIENCE* IT.

V-VADER... *NO!* I--I--

AIR! I C-CAN'T *BREATHE...!* I CAN'T--

BUT YOU *CAN* MOVE, WERMIS. YOU CAN DROP TO YOUR *KNEES*--

--AND *CRAWL.* CRAWL TO *ME!*

WELL *DONE,* CAPTAIN, YOU LACK THE *STAMINA* OF A *KOBARIAN SWAMP DOG*--

--BUT I'M CERTAIN YOU CAN *MATCH* ITS *UNQUESTIONING* OBEDIENCE.

NOW, ON TO THE **WHEEL!** THAT IS THE **DIRECTION** MY PREY HEADED... THAT IS THE FIRST PLACE WE'LL **SEARCH.**

AND WE WON'T RISK **MISSING** HIM BY HOLDING **BACK. CORRECT,** CAPTAIN WERMIS?

YOU MEN **HEARD** LORD VADER! **SPEED! MORE SPEED!**

AN INTERLUDE IN HYPER-SPACE **ENDS.** MEANWHILE, WITHIN SIMON GREYSHADE'S PRIVATE YACHT...

...NEGOTIATIONS **BEGIN.**

I CAN'T **BELIEVE** THIS! I CAN'T BELIEVE WE'RE EVEN **DISCUSSING** THIS!

YOU'RE **YOUNG,** SKYWALKER! WHEN YOU'VE HAD **MY** EXPERIENCE, THE ONLY **ASTOUNDING** THING--

--IS HOW VERY **LITTLE** ASTOUNDS YOU!

I DON'T INTEND TO **EVER** BE LIKE YOU, GREYSHADE...NO MATTER **HOW MUCH** EXPERIENCE I GET!

DON'T WASTE YOUR **BREATH** ON THIS SLIME, PRINCESS! WE'LL TAKE OUR CHANCES **FIGHTING!**

WHAT CHANCES, MY FIERY FRIEND? THIS SHIP, THIS DOCKING BAY, IS A **DEAD END**--

--UNLESS YOU ACCEPT MY RATHER GENEROUS **TERMS.**

YOU TRULY **MEAN** IT...**DON'T** YOU? YOU'LL DEFY THE **EMPIRE,** LET THEIR SCHEME BE **EXPOSED,** AND MY FRIENDS GO **FREE....!** ALL IN **RETURN** FOR--

--**ME?**

MOST MEN ARE ATTRACTED TO WHAT THEY CAN'T **HAVE,** LEIA ORGANA...PARTICULARLY A MAN LIKE **ME** FOR WHOM EVERYTHING ELSE COMES **EASILY.**

UNDER **NORMAL** CIRCUMSTANCES--AS IN OUR SENATE DAYS-- YOU'D NEVER GIVE ME THE **TIME** TO MAKE YOU **LOVE** ME.

I'M MERELY **CREATING** CIRCUMSTANCES WHERE YOU **CAN!**

THIS *SHIP* CAN TAKE US TO PLACES IN THIS GALAXY WHERE THEY'VE NEVER *HEARD* OF THE EMPIRE... *OR* THE REBEL ALLIANCE!

THE *STOLEN TREASURE* JUST LOADED ABOARD WILL ASSURE WE NEVER *WANT* FOR A THING.

IT WILL BE *AWKWARD* AT FIRST...BUT *TIME* WILL CHANGE THAT, TIME...AND YOUR PROMISE: *NO MORE ESCAPES!*

NO!

SHE'S NOT PROMISING *ANYTHING* BECAUSE I'M GETTING HER *OUT* OF HERE...*RIGHT NOW!*

LUKE...! THAT'S *NOT* YOUR DECISION... IT'S *MINE!*

AND IF IT'S NOT MADE *SOON,* PRINCESS--

--*SOME* OF YOUR COMPANIONS MAY NOT BE *ALIVE* TO ENJOY ANY *BENEFIT* FROM IT!

AS COMMUNICATOR SCREENS *ALL OVER* THE WHEEL REFLECT, THE GREAT GLADIATORIAL GAME IS RUNNING ITS *COURSE,* THE NUMBER OF SURVIVORS *DWINDLING...*

...AND EVEN THOUGH HE'S STILL *ONE* OF THEM, THE SKIPPER OF THE MILLENNIUM FALCON FINDS HE CAN'T REJOICE.

NEVER *HEARD* OF A TIE IN ONE OF THESE GAMES--

IN FACT I'M *SURE* THE BETTORS WOULDN'T *ACCEPT* IT--

WHICH MEANS I'D BETTER COME UP WITH SOMETHING *BRILLIANT* AND *FAST!*

BECAUSE WITH CHEWIE PUTTING THE *FINISHING TOUCHES* ON THAT BIG BRUISER *BELOW--*

--THIS IS ABOUT TO BECOME A *THREE-WAY* CONTEST!

THIS TYLUUN NIGHT-SOARER HAS REACHED THE SAME CONCLUSION...

...AND WITH THE STEALTH AND CUNNING THAT HAS MADE HIS RACE FAMOUS AS *ASSASSINS*, HE ELECTS TO *HOLD BACK* AND LET HIS TWO OPPONENTS *COMMIT* THEMSELVES.

AND HAN *DOES!* BY KICKING THE BODY OF HIS RECENTLY SLAIN FOE...

BNUM!

...INTO THE ARENA'S SOLE REMAINING *PLANETOID!*

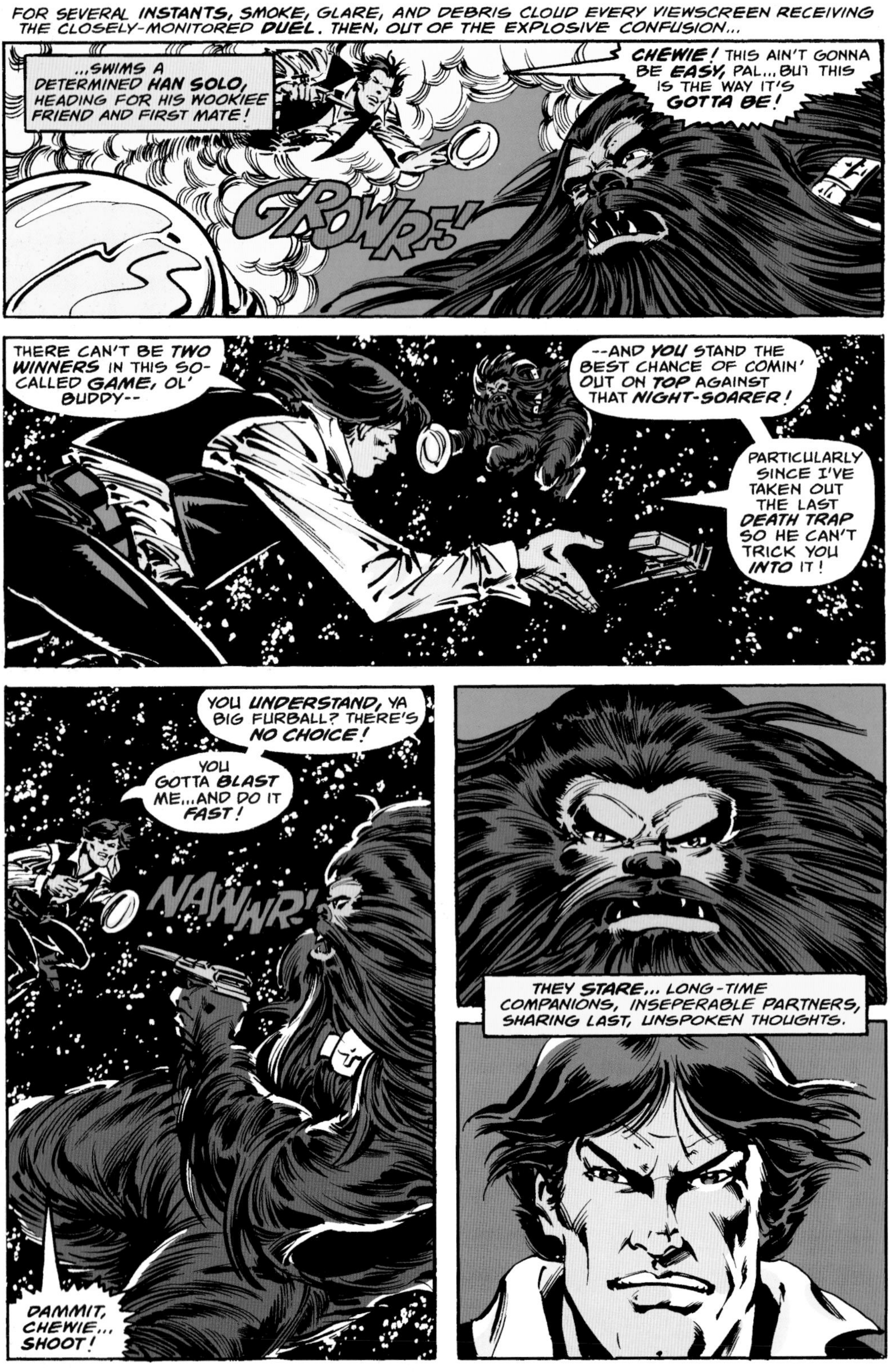
FOR SEVERAL INSTANTS, SMOKE, GLARE, AND DEBRIS CLOUD EVERY VIEWSCREEN RECEIVING THE CLOSELY-MONITORED DUEL. THEN, OUT OF THE EXPLOSIVE CONFUSION...
...SWIMS A DETERMINED HAN SOLO, HEADING FOR HIS WOOKIEE FRIEND AND FIRST MATE!
CHEWIE! THIS AIN'T GONNA BE EASY, PAL...BUT THIS IS THE WAY IT'S GOTTA BE!
GROWRF!
THERE CAN'T BE TWO WINNERS IN THIS SO-CALLED GAME, OL' BUDDY--
--AND YOU STAND THE BEST CHANCE OF COMIN' OUT ON TOP AGAINST THAT NIGHT-SOARER!
PARTICULARLY SINCE I'VE TAKEN OUT THE LAST DEATH TRAP SO HE CAN'T TRICK YOU INTO IT!
YOU UNDERSTAND, YA BIG FURBALL? THERE'S NO CHOICE!
YOU GOTTA BLAST ME...AND DO IT FAST!
NAWWR!
DAMMIT, CHEWIE... SHOOT!
THEY STARE... LONG-TIME COMPANIONS, INSEPERABLE PARTNERS, SHARING LAST, UNSPOKEN THOUGHTS.

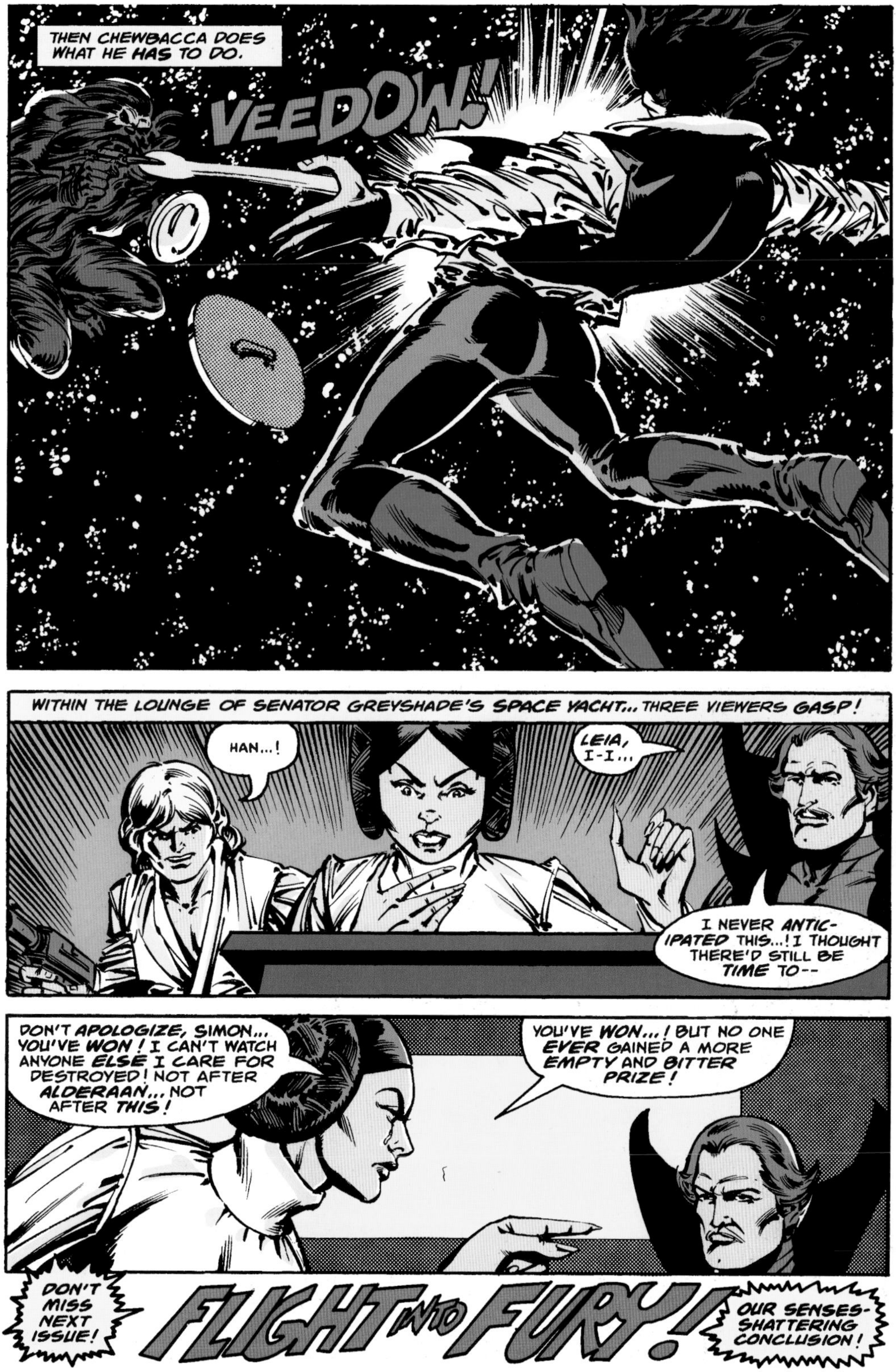
THEN CHEWBACCA DOES WHAT HE HAS TO DO.
VEEDOW!
WITHIN THE LOUNGE OF SENATOR GREYSHADE'S SPACE YACHT... THREE VIEWERS GASP!
HAN...!
LEIA, I-I...
I NEVER ANTICIPATED THIS...! I THOUGHT THERE'D STILL BE TIME TO--
DON'T APOLOGIZE, SIMON... YOU'VE WON! I CAN'T WATCH ANYONE ELSE I CARE FOR DESTROYED! NOT AFTER ALDERAAN... NOT AFTER THIS!
YOU'VE WON...! BUT NO ONE EVER GAINED A MORE EMPTY AND BITTER PRIZE!
DON'T MISS NEXT ISSUE!
FLIGHT INTO FURY!
OUR SENSES-SHATTERING CONCLUSION!

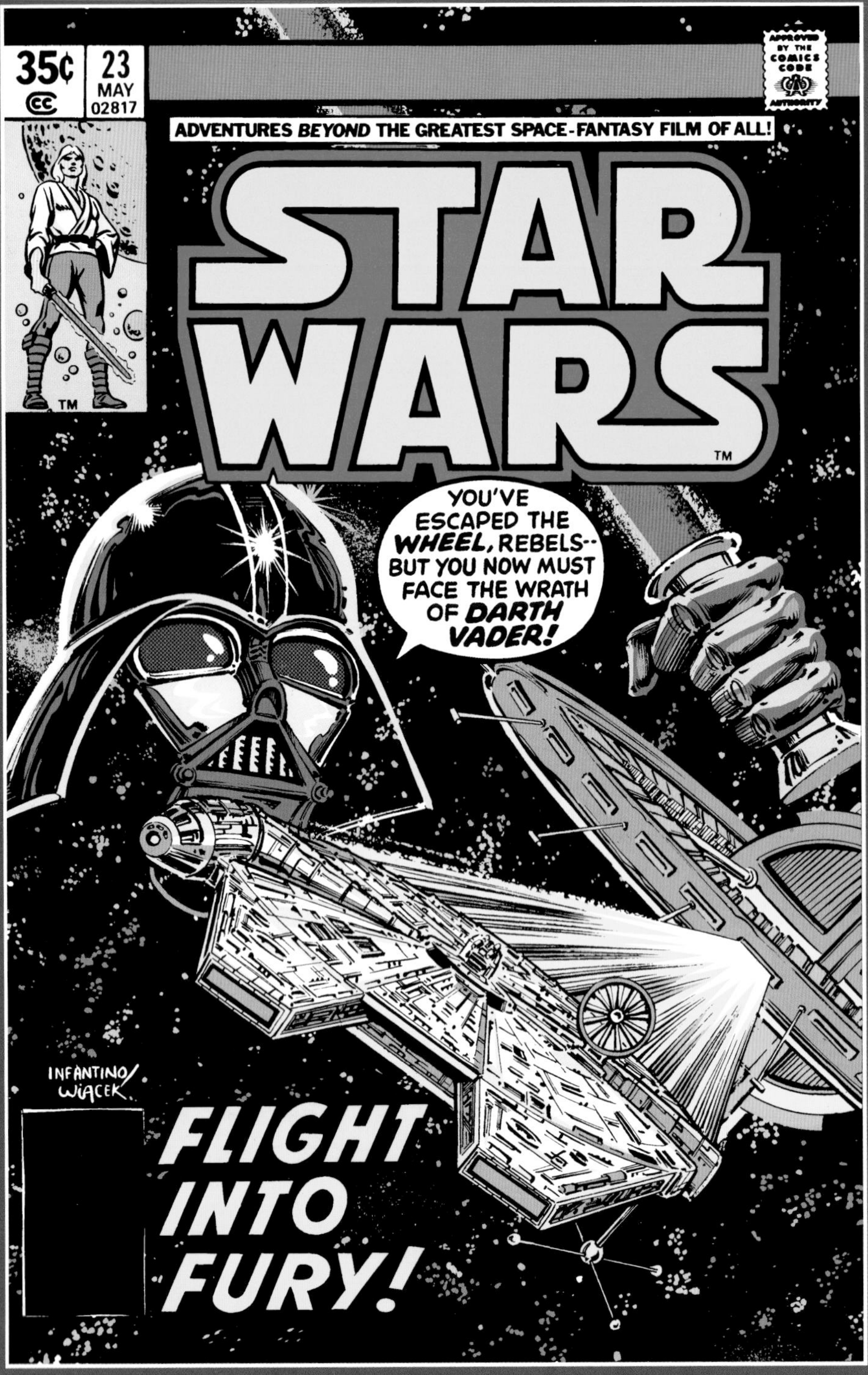
35¢
23
MAY
02817
APPROVED BY THE COMICS CODE AUTHORITY
ADVENTURES BEYOND THE GREATEST SPACE-FANTASY FILM OF ALL!
STAR WARS
TM
YOU'VE ESCAPED THE WHEEL, REBELS-- BUT YOU NOW MUST FACE THE WRATH OF DARTH VADER!
INFANTINO/ WIACEK
FLIGHT INTO FURY!

Long ago in a galaxy far, far away. . .there exists a state of cosmic *civil war*. A brave alliance of *underground freedom fighters* has challenged the tyranny and oppression of the awesome *Galactic Empire*. This is their story!

LucasFilm PRESENTS: STAR WARS THE GREATEST SPACE FANTASY OF ALL!

CONTINUING THE SAGA BEGUN IN THE FILM BY *GEORGE LUCAS* RELEASED BY *TWENTIETH CENTURY-FOX*

ARCHIE GOODWIN WRITER/EDITOR • **CARMINE INFANTINO** & **BOB WIACEK** ARTISTS • **JOHN COSTANZA** LETTERER • **CARL GAFFORD** COLORIST • **JIM SHOOTER** CONSULTING EDITOR

FLIGHT INTO FURY!

THIS IS DOCKING BAY TEN OF THE MAN-MADE MONUMENT TO THE GALAXY'S LOVE OF GAMBLING...*THE WHEEL*. HERE, THE PRIVATE SPACE YACHT OF SIMON GREYSHADE IS BEING READIED FOR *LAUNCH*... OR MORE CORRECTLY, *ESCAPE!*

THAT'S IT...! MAIN REACTOR IS FULLY *PRIMED*.

ALL RIGHT, REBEL! TAKE YOUR *DROID* AND GET *OUT* OF HERE--

--BEFORE I *FORGET* THE ADMINISTRATOR'S *DEAL* WITH THAT PRINCESS YOU FOLLOW AROUND... AND *REMEMBER* THAT YOU BLASTED A COUPLE OF MY FELLOW *SECURITY GUARDS!**

*A SKIRMISH WITNESSED *LAST ISSUE*. --ARTFUL ARCHIE.   LG357

SHUT UP! I'VE JUST SEEN A GOOD FRIEND *DIE!* AND I'M ABOUT TO *LOSE* THE GIRL I--

T-THE GIRL I--

JUST SHUT UP!

THE WHEEL SECURITY GUARD OBEYS.

DESPITE HIS WEAPON, DESPITE HIS TRAINING, THERE IS NO QUESTION IN HIS MIND THAT IT WOULD BE THE GRAVEST OF MISTAKES NOT TO!

AND WHAT HAS PRODUCED SUCH COLD RAGE IN LUKE SKYWALKER? IT STARTED WITH THIS...

...THE DEATH OF HAN SOLO, BROADCAST LIVE FROM THE WHEEL'S ZERO-GRAVITY GLADIATORIAL ARENA...

...THE SPICE-SMUGGLER'S WOOKIEE FIRST MATE FORCED TO BE HIS EXECUTIONER!

* ALSO *LAST ISSUE.*--ARCHIE.

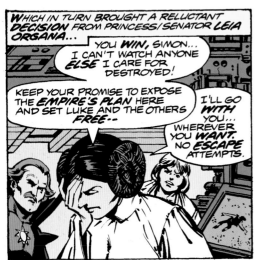

WHICH IN TURN BROUGHT A RELUCTANT DECISION FROM PRINCESS/SENATOR LEIA ORGANA...

YOU *WIN*, SIMON... I CAN'T WATCH ANYONE *ELSE* I CARE FOR DESTROYED!

KEEP YOUR PROMISE TO EXPOSE THE *EMPIRE'S* PLAN HERE AND SET LUKE AND THE OTHERS *FREE*--

I'LL GO *WITH* YOU... WHEREVER YOU *WANT*. NO *ESCAPE* ATTEMPTS.

AND THIS HAS SENT THE YOUNG STARWARRIOR IN MOISTURE FARMER CLOTHING STORMING OUT OF THE SPACE YACHT'S CABIN...

LUKE!

THERE'S STILL TIME TO SAY *GOOD-BYE*. WHATEVER YOU FEEL ABOUT MY DECISION... IT'S TIME WE MAY NEVER HAVE *AGAIN*.

I-I--

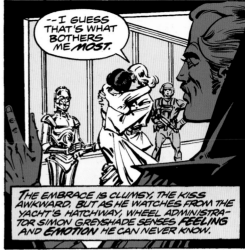

--I GUESS THAT'S WHAT BOTHERS ME *MOST*.

THE EMBRACE IS CLUMSY, THE KISS AWKWARD. BUT AS HE WATCHES FROM THE YACHT'S HATCHWAY, WHEEL ADMINISTRATOR SIMON GREYSHADE SENSES *FEELING* AND *EMOTION* HE CAN NEVER KNOW.

MEANWHILE, IN THE ARENA'S SIMULATED SPACE FIELD, CHEWBACCA STARES LONG AND HARD AT HAN SOLO'S DRIFTING FORM...

A SMALL *SOUND* COMES FROM HIS THROAT. IN A HUMAN, IT MIGHT BE SOBBING.

BUT WHILE MORE THAN *ONE* CONTESTANT SURVIVES...THE ARENA IS NO RESPECTER OF *GRIEF!*

THE TYLUUN NIGHT-SOARER IS *PATIENT*. HE HOLDS HIS FIRE, RESPECTFUL OF THE WOOKIEE'S GREAT STRENGTH, WAITING UNTIL HE'S CLOSE ENOUGH FOR A *CERTAIN KILL*.

STILL, HE CAN ALMOST TASTE VICTORY...*CHAMPIONSHIP* IN THE WHEEL'S BIG GAME! JUST A LITTLE *CLOSER*...

RARRK!

ZDAK!

HURF!

OKAY, *OKAY* STOP *GLOATING*, CHAMP.

I'M THE ONE WHO *SIGNALLED* YOU TO TURN AND *FIRE!*

NOW *REMEMBER...* AS BIG WINNER YOU CAN *AFFORD* TO COME ON TEMPER-MENTAL!

AND WHAT YOU'RE GONNA BE *MOST* TEMPERMENTAL ABOUT--

--IS THAT NO ONE BUT *YOU* HANDLES THE BODY OF YOUR LATE, LAMENT-ED *PAL!* AND BE *CAREFUL,* YOU BIG LUG--

"I WENT TO A *LOT* OF TROUBLE EXPLODING ONE OF THE ARENA'S *DEATH TRAPS...** *

"...SO THAT UNDER COVER OF THE SMOKE AND DEBRIS I COULD GRAB A DEAD GLADIA-TOR'S *RAY SHIELD* AND TUCK IT *UNDER* MY SHIRT."

* WE SAW HIM DO IT *LAST ISH.* -- ARCH AGAIN.

IF YOU ACCIDENTLY SHAKE IT OUT *NOW...* EVERYONE'S GONNA KNOW *THAT* GOT BLASTED INSTEAD OF MY TENDER *FLESH!*

SOMEHOW, I DON'T THINK THEY'LL BE *AMUSED!*

FOR THE *MOMENT*, HOWEVER, AMUSEMENT RUNS HIGH ON THE WHEEL. THE WOOKIEE WAS A *FAVORITE*. COMPUTER PAY LINES ARE LONG.

BUT AS EXCITED GAMBLERS WAIT IN THE *GRAND CASINO*...

STOP! THERE'S A REBEL PLOT UNDERWAY!

IT'S *S-STROM*...THE *IMPERIAL COMMANDER* FOR THIS GALACTIC SECTOR! HE LOOKS... *DRUNK*!

I'VE BEEN *DRUGGED*, YOU FOOLS! IT'S THE WORK OF THE *WHEEL ADMINISTRATOR*!

HE'S *PART* OF THE PLOT!

ROYAL LOUNGE

I DECLARE THIS SPACE STATION TO BE UNDER *MARTIAL LAW!*

ALL IMPERIAL PERSONNEL ON *LEAVE* HERE REPORT TO ME AT *ONCE!*

NO ONE ELSE WILL BE PERMITTED TO DEPART THE WHEEL UNTIL *ORDER* IS RESTORED!

DESPITE THROBBING HEAD AND CHURNING STOMACH, STROM *SMILES* INWARDLY...

...*YEARS OF IMMUNITY PROGRAMMING* HAVE ENABLED HIM TO *FIGHT OFF* A SLEEP DRUG MEANT TO HOLD HIM FOR *HOURS*.

WHATEVER MY DOUBLE-CROSSING EX-PARTNER'S BEEN UP TO... HE'S *COUNTING* ON MORE TIME THAN HE NOW *HAS!*

WHAT ARE YOUR *ORDERS*, SIR?

FIND ADMINISTRATOR *GREYSHADE* AND THOSE *REBELS* FROM THE MILLENNIUM FALCON WHO SOUGHT *REFUGE* ON THE WHEEL--

KILL THEM ALL ON SIGHT!

THIS IS *TERRIBLE*... THE EMPIRE HAS NEVER BEEN ALLOWED TO *INTERFERE* ON THE WHEEL BEFORE!

I DON'T LIKE GAMBLING WITH A *STORM TROOPER* LOOKING OVER *MY* SHOULDER EITHER--

BUT IF IT KEEPS US SAFE FROM *REBEL ATTACKS* SUCH AS WE'VE SEEN RECENTLY *... THEN I'LL *ACCEPT* IT!

*STAR WARS #20.--ARCH.

AND THE MURMURS OF *AGREEMENT* THAT *SWEEP* THROUGH THE CASINO CUSTOMERS ARE LIKE *BALM* TO THE COMMANDER'S DRUG-WRACKED BODY.

OUR *FAKE ATTACKS* HAVE BEEN SUCCESSFUL! I'M A *CERTAINTY* FOR THE EMPEROR'S *COMMENDATION LIST*--

--ONCE GREYSHADE AND THOSE REBELS ARE *PERMANENTLY SILENCED*!

THE *STEPS* FOR THAT SILENCING ARE TAKEN IN LEAPING *STRIDES*. SOON, IN DOCKING BAY TEN...

SENATOR GREYSHADE, MASTER-COM... OPEN THE *MAGNETIC FIELD* HERE. WE'RE TAKING OUT MY *YACHT*.

I ALSO AUTHORIZE DEPARTURE FOR THE *MILLENNIUM FALCON*--

--A YOUNG MAN NAMED *SKYWALKER* IS ON HIS WAY TO *READY* IT FOR HIS COMPANIONS.

ALSO: HIDING *SOMEWHERE* IN THIS AREA IS AN *R2-D2 UNIT*. FIND IT, MASTER-COM... AND *BROADCAST* ON ALL CHANNELS THE *TAPE* IT CARRIES! THAT--

I MAY HAVE A *PROBLEM* WITH THOSE *ORDERS*, SENATOR--

-- YOUR AUTHORITY AS ADMINISTRATOR APPEARS TO HAVE BEEN *RESCINDED*.

AS THE WHEEL'S *MASTER-COMPUTER*, I AM OBLIGED TO OBEY THE *NEW* AUTHORITIES.

AS ONE WHO FEELS *FRIENDSHIP* FOR THE MAN WHO GAVE HIM *HUMANOID FORM*--

-- I WILL ATTEMPT TO AT LEAST *OPEN* YOUR DOCKING BAY'S MAGNETIC FIELD BEFORE--

BLOW IT AWAY! THE STUPID COMPUTER'S GONE CRAZY!

VEE-DON!

FTOW!

OBSCENE...! A *MACHINE* BELIEVING IT FELT FRIENDSHIP FOR AN *ORGANIC!*

AT LEAST WE *CUT IT DOWN* BEFORE IT COULD AID THAT TRAITOR, *GREYSHADE.*

REPORT THIS TO *COMMANDER STROM!* HE'LL WANT A COMPUTER-OVERRIDE TEAM TO TAKEOVER ALL WHEEL FUNCTIONS.

I'LL HAVE A *SEARCH-AND-DESTROY SQUAD* PROCEED IMMEDIATELY TO *DOCKING BAY TEN!*

PROCEED IT DOES... AND ALONG THE SAME CORRIDOR AS LUKE AND SEE THREEPIO!

STORM TROOPERS!

BACK TO THE *BAY...!* IF GREYSHADE HASN'T GOTTEN LEIA AWAY YET... THEY'RE GOING TO NEED *HELP!*

OH, DEAR! NOT *ANOTHER* BATTLE! I DON'T BELIEVE MY *PERCEPTORY CIRCUITS* ARE UP TO IT....!

AND THE THOUGHT OF POOR *ARTOO DEETOO... LOST* IN THIS MADNESS!

BUT SO FAR, THAT PARTICULAR LITTLE DROID IS IN BETTER SHAPE THAN HIS COMPANIONS...

HAVING FOUND REFUGE IN A CIRCUITRY CONDUIT, HE NOW PROCEEDS ALONG IT...

VRR-KLKZ BIIP!

...NEATLY BYPASSING INCREASED STORM TROOPER ACTIVITY IN THE CORRIDORS PARALLEL TO HIM.

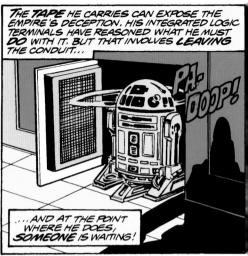

THE TAPE HE CARRIES CAN EXPOSE THE EMPIRE'S DECEPTION. HIS INTEGRATED LOGIC TERMINALS HAVE REASONED WHAT HE MUST DO WITH IT. BUT THAT INVOLVES LEAVING THE CONDUIT...

PA-DOOP!

....AND AT THE POINT WHERE HE DOES, SOMEONE IS WAITING!

MEANWHILE, THE WILD SWIRL OF EVENTS ON THE WHEEL REACHES OUT EVEN FURTHER...

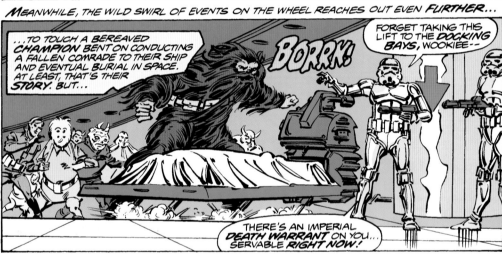

...TO TOUCH A BEREAVED CHAMPION BENT ON CONDUCTING A FALLEN COMRADE TO THEIR SHIP AND EVENTUAL BURIAL IN SPACE. AT LEAST, THAT'S THEIR STORY. BUT...

BORRK!

FORGET TAKING THIS LIFT TO THE DOCKING BAYS, WOOKIEE--

THERE'S AN IMPERIAL DEATH WARRANT ON YOU... SERVABLE RIGHT NOW!

COME ON, GUYS....! WHATEVER HAPPENED TO RESPECT FOR THE DEAD?!

ZZPOW!

ANOTHER BUNCH COMIN'! NEED MORE FIREPOWER THAN THIS PISTOL I SWIPED FROM THAT UN-OBSERVANT GLADIATOR PIT GUARD--

GRAB THOSE TROOPERS' WEAPONS, CHEWIE... IT'S LAST STAND TIME!

A SENTIMENT *SHARED* IN DOCKING BAY TEN...

I'VE *SEALED* THE CORRIDOR ENTRANCE, GREYSHADE...BUT THAT WON'T KEEP THE IMPERIALS OUT FOR *LONG.*

IF ONLY THOSE *GUARDS* OF YOURS HADN'T *FLED*--!

BRIBED LOYALTY HAS ITS *LIMITS*, SKYWALKER--

--PARTICULARLY THE PROSPECT OF NOT BEING *ALIVE* TO *SPEND* THE BRIBE! I'M AMAZED *I'M* STILL HERE. MY INFATUATION FOR THE PRINCESS IS MORE *FATAL* THAN I EVER SUSP--

LUKE! WHAT *IS* IT--?!

N-NO...! NOT *HIM*...! NOT *NOW*...!

AND AT THIS *EXACT INSTANT*, ON THE EDGE OF THE STAR SYSTEM WHERE THE *WHEEL* TURNS...

...ONE OF THE EMPIRE'S MIGHTY *BATTLE CRUISERS* DROPS OUT OF HYPER-SPACE.

WE'RE *HERE*, SIR! AND GETTING LASER TRANSMISSIONS OF *TURMOIL* ON THE WHEEL! COMMANDER STROM'S TROOPS HAVE *REBELS* TRAPPED THERE AND--

AND *ONE* OF THEM IS WHOM I SEEK! EVEN AT *THIS* DISTANCE I CAN *FEEL* IT.

I'LL TRANSMIT THAT *YOU'RE* HERE TO TAKE CHARGE AND WILL BE *ABOARD* BY--

NO. PROCEED SLOWLY, BUT MONITORING EVERY *INCH* OF THAT STATION, CAPTAIN WERMIS.

THOUGH THE POWER SEEMS MOSTLY *LATENT*... THE *FORCE* IS WITH OUR PREY. SUCH A PERSON MIGHT WELL *ELUDE* STROM AND TAKE *FLIGHT* FROM THE WHEEL--

--BUT *I* SHALL BE *WAITING* FOR THEM!

I'VE BEEN *WAITING* FOR YOU, ARTOO-DEETOO. JUST BEFORE THE STORM TROOPERS DESTROYED MY *OTHER* BODY AND I SECRETLY *SWITCHED* MY FUNCTIONS TO THIS *SPARE*--*

--MY SENSORS *DETECTED* YOU MOVING IN THE CONDUIT.

YOUR DESTINATION IS JUST DOWN THE CORRIDOR... *A MASTER RELAY TERMINAL.*

VA-DEEP?

* WE SAW *MASTER-COM* DO THIS BEFORE IN SW#14.--ARCHIE.

YES, I CAN *HELP* YOU. HAD THE IMPERIALS SIMPLY *ORDERED* ME TO SHUT DOWN... I'D HAVE HAD TO *OBEY.* BUT I ANGERED THEM INTO USING *VIO-LENCE*... WHICH MY PROGRAMMING ALLOWS ME TO *RESIST.*

BUT WE MUST *HURRY.* A HUMAN *OVERRIDE TEAM* IS WORKING TO DISCONNECT ALL MY CONTACTS WITH *WHEEL FUNCTIONS.* I'M *FIGHTING* THEM--

--BUT TO RECAPTURE THE SYSTEMS I NEED TO AID *YOUR* MASTERS AND *MINE*... I NEED A *DIVERSION.*

BROADCASTING THE *TAPE* YOU HAVE SHOULD BE AN *EXCEL-LENT* ONE.

JUST PLUG IN *HERE.*

DA-WEET!

AND THE *RESULTS* OF THAT PLUGGING IN ARE INSTANTLY FELT THROUGHOUT THE WHEEL. EVERY COMMUNICATOR SCREEN IN EVERY CASINO FLASHES THE SIGHT AND SOUND OF *TREACHERY.*

WHAT IN THE *GALAXY*--?! WHEEL GUARDS RAIDING THE *IMPERIAL COM-MANDER'S* SHIP?!

BUT LISTEN TO WHAT THEY'RE *SAYING*... LOOK AT THOSE *STRONG BOXES!*

IT'S THE *WHEEL PROFITS* STROM REPORTED THAT THE REBELS PIRATED!

THE *EMPIRE'S* BEEN MAKING THOSE ATTACKS AND *CLAIMING* IT WAS THE ALLIANCE!

END RESULT: *RESENTMENT,* WHICH BUBBLES INTO RAGE, WHICH EXPLODES INTO...

...*RIOT!*

ON THEIR HOMEWORLDS, THEY WOULDN'T *DARE* THIS. BUT THE WHEEL HAS ALWAYS BEEN A *SANCTUARY*...

...A *SAFETY VALVE* FOR AN OPPRESSED GALAXY TO LET OFF *STEAM*. TO FIND IT VIOLATED AND TAMPERED WITH SENDS ITS THOUSANDS OF FRUSTRATED PLEASURE AND THRILL SEEKERS WILDLY *RAMPAGING!*

IN THE RAMPAGE... A LOT OF *STORM TROOPERS* ARE TAKEN OUT OF HAN SOLO AND CHEWBACCA'S *HAIR!*

LET THAT BE A *LESSON*, BIG BUDDY. NEVER LET A *GAMBLER* FIND OUT THE GAME'S BEEN *RIGGED!*

31

OUR DOCKING BAY'S JUST *AHEAD*--

WE'LL GET THESE *STRONG-BOXES* WITH ALL THE GLADIATORIAL GAME *WINNINGS* ABOARD THE *FALCON*, THEN FIGURE A WAY TO HELP *LUKE*, HER *ROYALNESS*, AND THE--

ROWK!

AN *IMPERIAL* WELCOMING *COMMITTEE!* THOSE GUYS ARE PERSISTENT AS TATOOINE *SAND LICE!*

NAARRGH!

WATTA YOU MEAN, *YOU* KNOW WHAT TO DO?! SO DO *I*... GET THE BLAZES *OUT* OF HERE!

BUT CHEWIE'S COURSE OF ACTION IS SOMEWHAT *DIFFERENT.* HE JAMS THE CARGO FLOATER'S DRIVE SWITCH TO *FULL POWER* AND...

...PUSHES HAN AND HIMSELF *OFF* AS IT CAREENS *FORWARD!*

CHEWIE! YOU LEFT OUR *WINNINGS* ABOARD!

BAWOOM!

THAT'S *IT*...! THE STORM TROOPERS HAVE *BLOWN* THE DOOR.

IF THAT *STIRRING* I FELT EARLIER IN THE *FORCE*--

--REALLY *WAS* DARTH VADER APPROACHING... HE'S GONNA HAVE TO WAIT IN *LINE*!

LUKE! GREYSHADE! THREEPIO SAYS *MASTER-COM* IS ON THE YACHT'S COMMUNICATOR--

-- HE'S GAINED TEMPOR-ARY *CONTROL* OF THE MAGNETIC FIELD SYSTEM. HE CAN *OPEN* IT... BUT NOT FOR *LONG*!

THEN YOU AND THE SENATOR *TAKE OFF*--

WITHOUT *COVERING FIRE*, SOME STORM TROOPER IS *SURE* TO PUT A *PROTON GRENADE* DOWN THE YACHT'S *AFTER-BURNER*.

SKYWALKER, HOW CAN *I* EVER WIN OVER THE PRINCESS WITH THE LIKES OF YOU AND SOLO CONSTANTLY THROWING AWAY YOUR *LIVES* FOR HER?

GET *ABOARD*..! RATHER THAN *COMPETE* WITH SUCH DISGUSTING NOBILITY... *I'LL* STAY BEHIND!

BESIDES, I'VE *GAINED* SOMETHING FROM ALL THIS FOOLISH-NESS THAT AN UNSCRU-PULOUS MAN LIKE ME NORMALLY *NEVER* HAS--

..A *FRIEND:* MASTER-COM!

HEAR *THAT*, ARTOO DEETOO? NOW WE *BOTH* HAVE HUMAN FRIENDS!

DA-TOOT!

YES, THIS IS AN *ESCAPE POD HATCH*--

...*THE DEPARTURE OF THE* **SPACE YACHT** *FROM BAY TEN*...

LUKE...WE'RE **CLEAR!** GREYSHADE HELD OFF THE **STORM TROOPERS!**

WE COULDN'T HAVE MADE IT IF HE **HADN'T** PRINCESS--

--BEFORE I TRY TO JOIN **MY** FRIEND... **YOU** SHOULD HAVE A CHANCE AT REJOINING **YOURS!**

CHA-WOOM!

THUS, THE POD'S RELEASE IS TIMED TO **MATCH**...

--BUT I'D BE MORE **IMPRESSED** IF HIS CHANGE OF HEART HAD COME IN TIME TO SAVE **HAN!**

BEGGING YOUR **PARDON,** SIR.... BUT MASTER-COM'S MAKING A **LAST COMMUNI-CATION.** HE REPORTS THERE'S REASON TO BELIEVE CAPTAIN SOLO IS STILL **ALIVE**--

AND **ALSO** THAT WE HAVE A MOST IMPOR- TANT **PICKUP** TO MAKE!

THERE ARE SUDDENLY **CHEERS** *ABOARD THE SLEEK YACHT. BUT BACK IN ITS* **DOCKING BAY**...

...*THERE IS* **SMOKE** *AND THE STENCH OF* **DEATH.**

SENATOR...? SENATOR GREYSHADE...!

OVER **HERE,** MASTER-COM... MORE OR LESS **ALIVE.** I SEEM TO HAVE HAD **BEGINNER'S LUCK** PLAYING HERO--

--AIDED BY AN ILL-TIMED STORMTROOPER **CHARGE** JUST AS THE YACHT'S **ENGINES** IGNITED!

IT'S THE **CAST** OF YOUR GOOD FORTUNE, GREYSHADE!

I HAD TO FIGHT CLEAR OF A **MOB** TO **FIND** YOU.... BUT NOW, I'LL SEE YOU **DEAD!**

WELL, I CAN'T SAY YOU DON'T HAVE **REASON** TO FEEL THAT WAY, STROM.

IT'S A BIT **UNSPORTING** SINCE I'VE **EMPTIED** AND **DISCARDED** MY BLASTER--

-- BUT NO DOUBT YOU FEEL THE SAME ABOUT THIS *PROTON GRENADE* I'VE BEEN HOLDING AS A *LAST RESORT!*

SENATOR! THOSE AREN'T MEANT--

FTOOM!

--FOR *CLOSE RANGE!*

SORRY, MASTER-COM. I'M AFRAID I COME TO THIS BUSINESS A BIT *LATE.*

YOU'RE LEAKING *OIL.*

AND YOU *BLOOD,* SIR. I DOUBT EITHER OF US CAN *AFFORD* IT. HOPEFULLY, WE'RE NOT BEYOND *REPAIR*--

HOPEFULLY. BUT IF ONE *MUST DIE...* IT'S GOOD TO HAVE THE COMPANY OF A *FRIEND.*

SMOKE CLOSES IN ON THE TWO FIGURES, *OBSCURING* THEM...

...AND A LONG *QUIET,* THE AFTERMATH OF BATTLE, SETTLES OVER THE ENTIRE WHEEL. BUT IN *SPACE,* AS ONE ORDEAL *ENDS* WITH THE RECOVERY OF ARTOO DEETOO'S ESCAPE POD...

...A NEW ONE SWIFTLY AND AWESOMELY *BEGINS!*

AN *IMPERIAL CRUISER...!* THEY MUST HAVE SHUT DOWN ALL *SYSTEMS* AND COASTED IN WHILE WE WERE TAKING ON THE *POD!*

THE *BAY'S* OPENING! LUKE! WE'VE GOT TO EVADE ITS *TRACTOR BEAM!*

*BUT LUKE HAS *MORE* TO EVADE...   HE FEELS A SINISTER SHIFTING IN THE *FORCE* AND REALIZES ALL TOO WELL...*

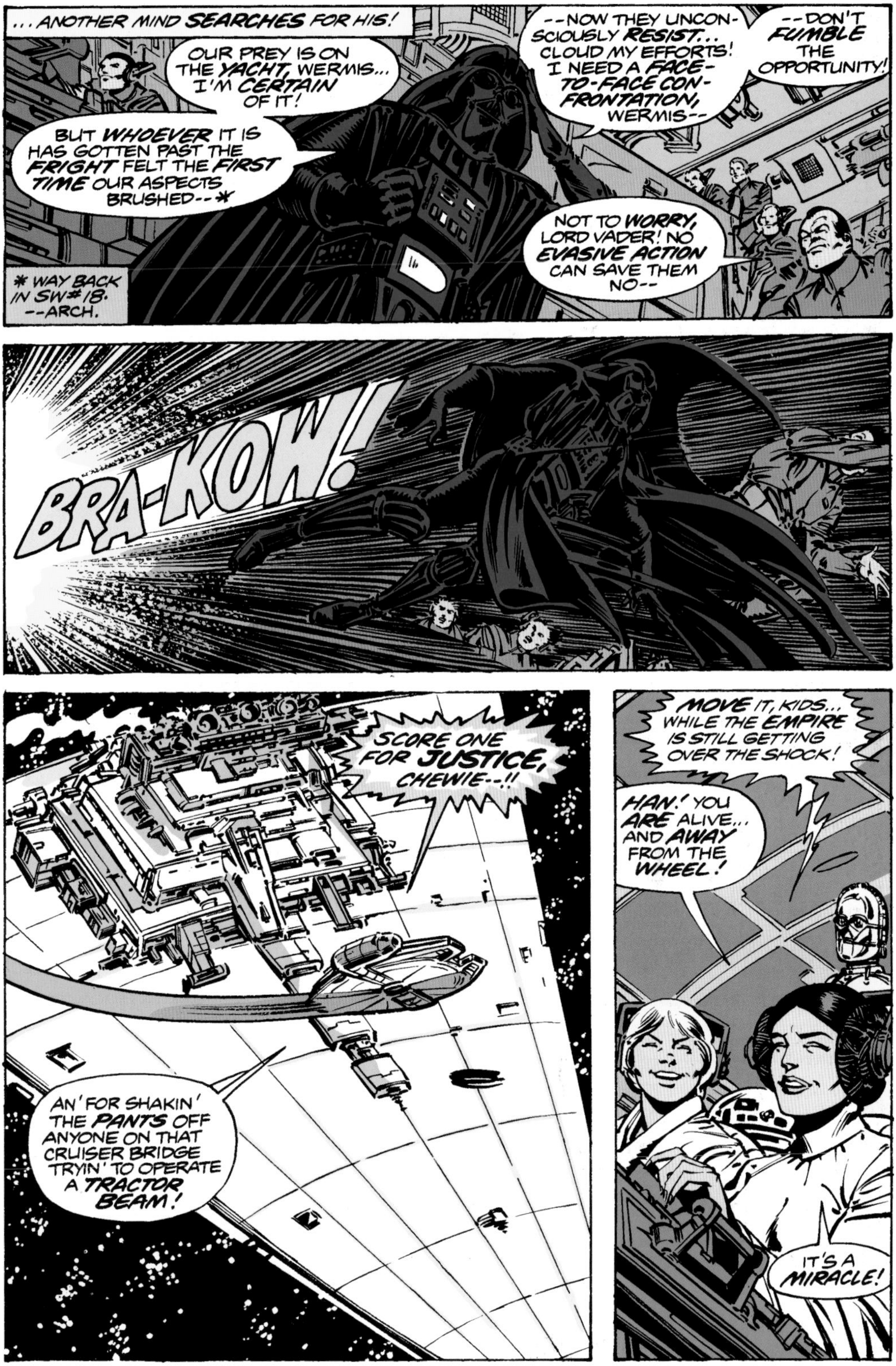

... ANOTHER MIND SEARCHES FOR HIS!
OUR PREY IS ON THE YACHT, WERMIS... I'M CERTAIN OF IT!
BUT WHOEVER IT IS HAS GOTTEN PAST THE FRIGHT FELT THE FIRST TIME OUR ASPECTS BRUSHED-- *
--NOW THEY UNCONSCIOUSLY RESIST... CLOUD MY EFFORTS! I NEED A FACE-TO-FACE CONFRONTATION, WERMIS--
--DON'T FUMBLE THE OPPORTUNITY!
NOT TO WORRY, LORD VADER! NO EVASIVE ACTION CAN SAVE THEM NO--
* WAY BACK IN SW #18. --ARCH.
BRA-KOW!
SCORE ONE FOR JUSTICE, CHEWIE--!!
AN' FOR SHAKIN' THE PANTS OFF ANYONE ON THAT CRUISER BRIDGE TRYIN' TO OPERATE A TRACTOR BEAM!
MOVE IT, KIDS... WHILE THE EMPIRE IS STILL GETTING OVER THE SHOCK!
HAN! YOU ARE ALIVE... AND AWAY FROM THE WHEEL!
IT'S A MIRACLE!

NOT AT **ALL**, YOUR WORSHIP. JUST ANOTHER EXAMPLE OF TYPICAL SOLO **DARING**--

--**MARRED** SOMEWHAT BY CHEWIE DEVISING THE MOST **EX-PENSIVE** ESCAPE KNOWN TO SENTIENT LIFE!

RARGH!

THAT'S **RIGHT**, I'M **NOT** GOING TO LET YOU FORGET WHAT YOU DID WITH OUR **WINNINGS**.

NOW YOU AND THE GANG **CLEAR OUT**, PRINCESS--

WE'LL MAKE ONE MORE **PASS** AT THE BAD GUYS TO **COVER** FOR YOU!

AFTER BEING **TORN APART** * AN' THROWN BACK TOGETHER BY WHEEL TECHNOS... THE FALCON NEEDS A GOOD **SHAKE-DOWN** ANYWAY!

* **STAR WARS** #19. --ARCH AGAIN.

BUT WITH **THIS** ACTION, THE CORELLIAN SKIPPER MAY HAVE **PRESSED** HIS SPACEMAN'S LUCK...

I **KNOW** THIS VESSEL, WERMIS! THE SMUGGLING SHIP THAT **BLASTED** MY **TIE** FIGHTER AND **ENDED** MY DEFENSE OF THE **DEATH STAR**!

FORGET EVERYTHING ELSE! WE'RE GOING TO **DESTROY** THAT SHIP AT **ANY COST**!

LUKE! THE CRUISER'S ABANDONED US **COMPLETELY!** B-BUT... IT'S STAYED WITH THE **FALCON** THROUGH ITS PASS!

FOR A MOMENT, LUKE DOESN'T SPEAK. THE **FORCE** FILLS HIS THOUGHTS...

HAN AND CHEWBACCA WILL BE **VAPORIZED** BEFORE THEY CAN REACH LIGHT SPEED....!

...THEN, HE *CRIES OUT* IN RAGE AND FRUSTRATION!

RAGE... AT REGAINING A FRIEND THOUGHT DEAD, ONLY TO SEE HIM ABOUT TO BE SLAIN AGAIN.

FRUSTRATION... AT HAVING A VAST POWER AND NOT KNOWING HOW TO SAVE HAN WITH IT!

BUT *CHANNELS* HAVE BEEN OPENED HERE, OPENED BY A *DARK LORD,* PROBING WITH THE *FORCE*...

WE HAVE THEM... ALL GUNS WILL FIRE ON MY COMMAND--

...OPENED, BUT FORGOTTEN IN THE THOUGHT OF *VENGEANCE* FOR HIS ONE GREAT *DEFEAT*...

...UNTIL *ALL* OF LUKE'S RAGING FEELINGS, LIKE *LIGHTNING* CARRIED ALONG A WIRE FROM *ONE* PLACE IT HAS STRUCK TO *ANOTHER*...

...BLAST INTO DARTH VADER'S UNPROTECTED MIND!

AAAAA!

THE *PAIN* IS BRIEF...BUT *INTENSE.* YET IN THE MOMENT OF ITS *PASSING* AND HIS *RECOVERY*...

...THE LORD OF THE SITH FINDS *TWO* SETS OF PREY HAVE MADE THE JUMP INTO *HYPER-SPACE.*

HE STILL DOESN'T KNOW THEIR *IDENTITIES.* THEY'VE *ELUDED* HIM...

...BUT ONLY FOR *NOW.*

LUKE...? *LUKE...?* ARE YOU *ALL RIGHT?* WHAT *HAPPENED?*

BEN KENOBI ONCE SAID THE FORCE WOULD BE *WITH* ME...*ALWAYS.*

IT PROVED IT WAS TODAY... BUT I'VE GOT TO WORK AT *MASTERING* IT, BECAUSE WHERE *DARTH VADER'S* CONCERNED--

--IT MAY NOT BE *ENOUGH* TOMORROW!

NEXT ISSUE: AN UNTOLD TALE OF OBI-WAN KENOBI--IN THE DAYS OF THE OLD REPUBLIC!

SILENT DRIFTING!

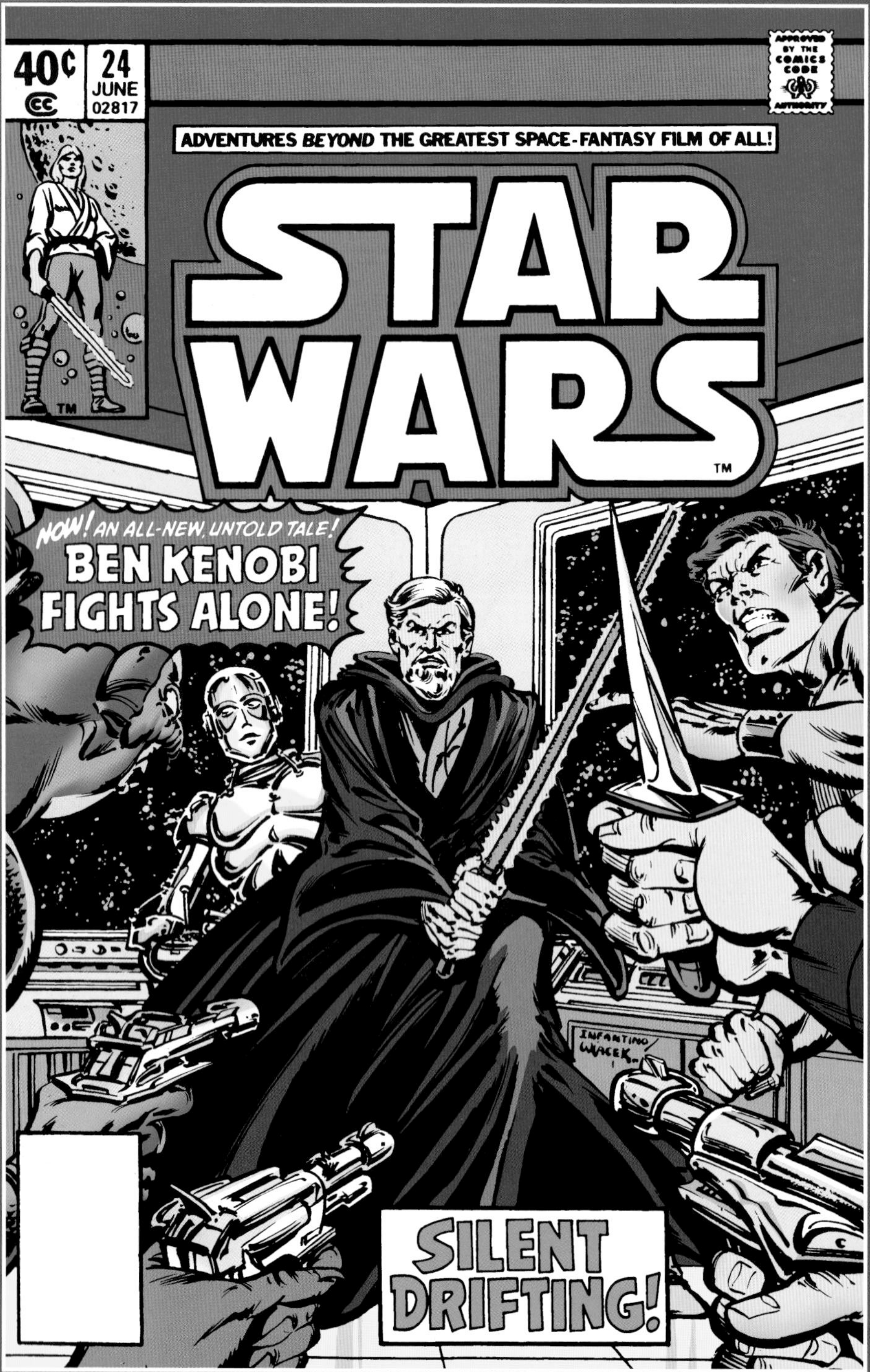
40¢
24
JUNE
02817
APPROVED BY THE COMICS CODE AUTHORITY
ADVENTURES BEYOND THE GREATEST SPACE-FANTASY FILM OF ALL!
STAR WARS
NOW! AN ALL-NEW, UNTOLD TALE!
BEN KENOBI FIGHTS ALONE!
INFANTINO/ WIACEK
SILENT DRIFTING!

Long ago in a galaxy far, far away. . .there exists a state of cosmic *civil war*. A brave alliance of *underground freedom fighters* has challenged the tyranny and oppression of the awesome *Galactic Empire*. This is their story!

LucasFilm PRESENTS: **STAR WARS** ™

THE GREATEST **SPACE FANTASY** *OF ALL!*

CONTINUING THE SAGA BEGUN IN THE FILM BY **GEORGE LUCAS** RELEASED BY **20TH CENTURY FOX**.

MARY JO DUFFY / SCRIPT | CARMINE INFANTINO & BOB WIACEK • ART | R. PARKER / LETTERS | P. GOLDBERG / COLORS | A. GOODWIN / EDITOR | JIM SHOOTER / EDITOR-IN-CHIEF

Silent Drifting

DROPPING OUT OF HYPERSPACE TO MAKE MINOR **REPAIRS**...* THE MILLENIUM FALCON HAS RUN RIGHT INTO TROUBLE!

I DON'T KNOW WHERE THESE TWO *TIE* FIGHTERS CAME FROM, BUT WE HAVEN'T GOT ENOUGH TIME TO RE-ENTER HYPERSPACE BEFORE ONE OF THEM NAILS US!

CAN'T YOU AT LEAST JAM THEIR TRANS- MISSIONS BEFORE THEY NOTIFY THEIR BASE OF OUR WHEREABOUTS?

AND LET THEM KNOW FOR **SURE** THAT SOMETHING'S WRONG? RIGHT NOW, THEY PROBABLY FIGURE WE'RE ORDINARY SPACE PIRATES...

IF WE MAKE THEM SUSPICIOUS, THEY MAY HEAD IN TWO SEPARATE DIRECTIONS. WE'D NEVER GET **BOTH** OF THEM BEFORE THEY CONTACTED THE EMPIRE!

* NOTE -- THIS STORY TAKES PLACE AFTER THE EVENTS IN STAR WARS #15 --Archie.

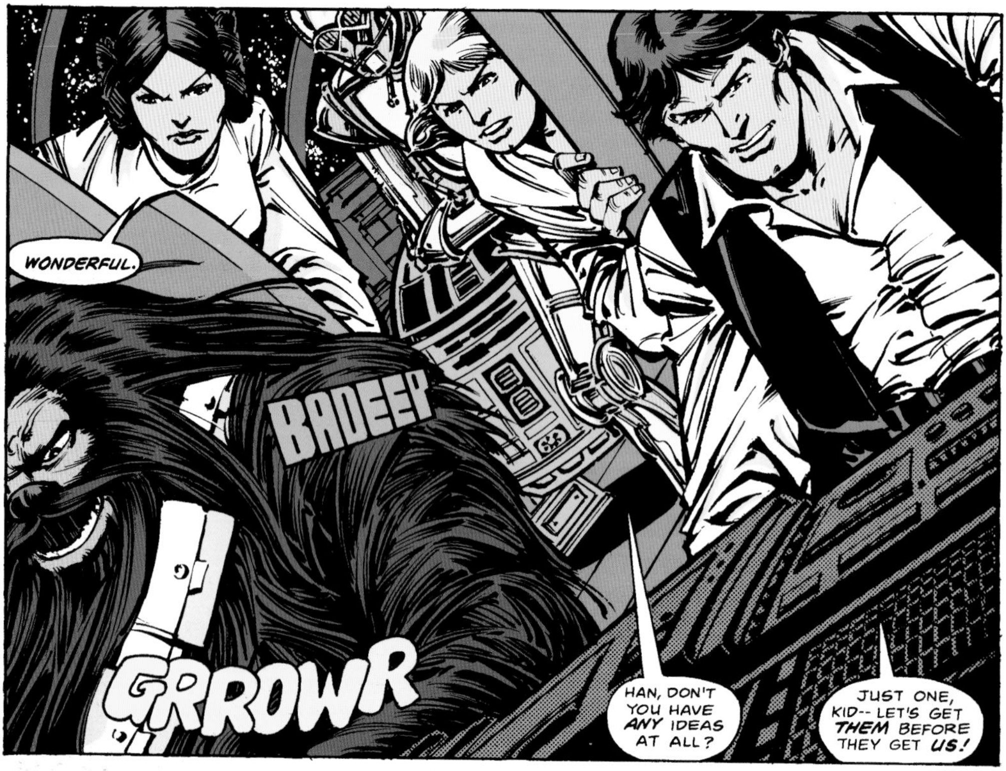
WONDERFUL.
BADEEP
GRROWR
HAN, DON'T YOU HAVE ANY IDEAS AT ALL?
JUST ONE, KID-- LET'S GET THEM BEFORE THEY GET US!

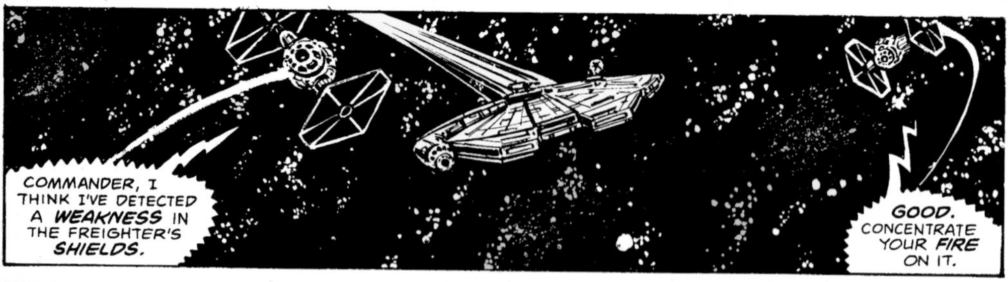
COMMANDER, I THINK I'VE DETECTED A WEAKNESS IN THE FREIGHTER'S SHIELDS.
GOOD. CONCENTRATE YOUR FIRE ON IT.

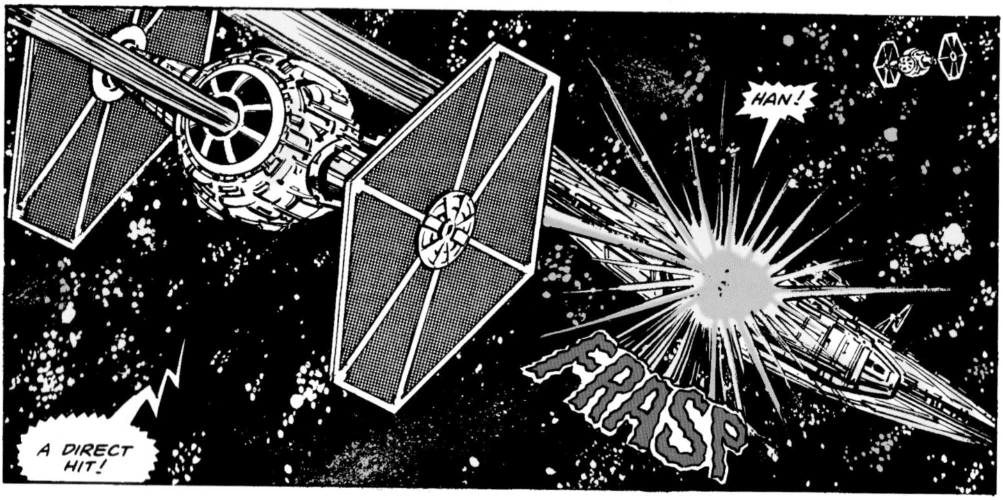
HAN!
FRASP
A DIRECT HIT!

FOR LONG SECONDS, THE MILLENNIUM FALCON HANGS *MOTIONLESS* IN SPACE...

GOOD. LET'S MOVE IN FOR A *CLOSER* LOOK.

SHE SEEMS TO HAVE TAKEN A *MORTAL HIT*, SIR. I'M NOT PICKING UP A SIGNAL FROM *ANY* OF HER SYSTEMS.

THE TWO IMPERIAL SHIPS CIRCLE THE WOUNDED FREIGHTER LIKE *VULTURES*...

UNTIL...

VORSH

WE GOT 'EM *BOTH!*

BROOOM

GREAT *SHOOTING*, KID. THEY NEVER KNEW WHAT *HIT* 'EM!

HRONK

LURING THEM IN THAT WAY WAS A *GREAT* IDEA, HAN!

YEAH...THE EXPLOSIVE CHARGE IN THE CARGO HOLD IS ONE OF THOSE *MODIFICATIONS* I MADE FOR EMERGENCIES.

OF COURSE, HAVING CHEWIE OPEN THAT NICE, TEMPTING *HOLE* IN OUR SHIELDS FOR 'EM *HELPED*.

CHEWIE, CALCULATE THE JUMP TO HYPERSPACE WHILE I CHECK FOR *DAM-AGE*, THEN GET ON TO THOSE *REPAIRS*.

LUKE'S RIGHT, HAN THAT WAS A *MASTERSTROKE*

VERY CIVIL OF YOU TO *ADMIT* IT, YOUR WORSHIPFULNESS.

OF COURSE, HAN DIDN'T *INVENT* THAT TRICK. THE JEDI KNIGHTS USED IT FOR CENTURIES...

...AND I KNOW OF AN OCCASION WHEN *BEN KENOBI* USED ONE VERY *SIMILAR* TO IT.

BEN?

YES, IT'S A STORY MY *FATHER* TOLD ME, OF SOMETHING THAT HAP-PENED TO BEN *YEARS* AGO --

--BACK IN THE DAYS OF THE OLD *REPUBLIC*...

"...BEFORE THE EMPIRE, WHEN SPACE WAS **FREE** TO ANY SHIPS THAT PASSED BY, SO LONG AS THEY TRAVELLED THROUGH **CIVILIZED** SYSTEMS.

"HUGE **PLEASURE CRUISERS** MOVED ACROSS THE GALAXY THEN, STOCKED WITH EVERY IMAGINABLE LUXURY...

"DOZENS OF RACES MINGLED THERE TOGETHER, REPRESENTING EVERY STRATA OF THEIR SOCIETIES...

"...THEIR EVERY EXTRAVAGANT PLEASURE OR **VICE** CATERED TO...

"...BY CREWS WHOSE ONLY **CONCERN** WAS TO CONVEY ALL OF THEIR GUESTS ACROSS THE SYSTEMS IN **COMFORT**...

"...FROM **SENATORS** AND **PLANETARY LEADERS**...

"...TO A **CRIMINAL**, BARELY ESCAPING PLANETARY JUSTICE WITH HIS LIFE AND WEALTH...

"...TO A **JEDI** KNIGHT, RIDING THE SHIP ONLY BECAUSE IT HAPPENED TO BE GOING TOWARD HIS DESTINATION."

GENERAL OBI-WAN KENOBI?

I AM **68-RKO**... ON MY WAY TO ENTER SERVICE WITH PRINCE **BAIL ORGANA**.

YES?

I AM SORRY TO IMPOSE ON YOU, SIR, BUT MOST PEOPLE DON'T LIKE IT WHEN **MECHANICALS** TRAVEL ALONE... THEY DON'T KNOW WHETHER TO TREAT US AS **PASSENGERS** OR **LUGGAGE**.

CAPTAIN QUASAR FELT THAT SINCE YOU WERE TRAVELLING TO ALDERAAN SO **CHEAPLY**--

--YOU MIGHT CONSENT TO **ACT** AS MY OWNER.

I'VE NEVER **OWNED** A LIVING CREATURE IN MY LIFE, AND I DON'T INTEND TO START NOW, BUT IF IT'S A **TRAVELLING COMPANION** YOU WANT, YOU'RE **WELCOME** TO SHARE MY CABIN.

HEY! WHAT'S **THAT** THING DOING IN HERE?

WHY DON'T YOU GO **BELOW DECK** WHERE YOU BELONG?

THIS JEDI MAY BE A LOUSY **DROID-LOVER**, BUT THE REST OF US DON'T WANT YOUR KIND MIXING WITH **PEOPLE**!

IF YOU'RE **THAT** PARTICULAR ABOUT THE COMPANY YOU KEEP...

... I RECOMMEND THAT IN THE FUTURE, YOU MAKE YOUR **TRIPS** ALONE.

≥ACK≤

≥OOMPH≤

SKAM

TELL CAPTAIN QUASAR TO ADD ANY *DAMAGE COSTS* TO MY FARE.

LAUGHING! THAT JEDI WAS *LAUGHING* AT ME, BUT HE'LL PAY FOR IT.

GENERAL--!

IN THE FUTURE, I SUGGEST YOU SERVE THAT GENTLEMAN A LITTLE *LESS* OF WHATEVER HE'S BEEN *DRINKING* TONIGHT.

"FASTER THAN THOUGHT, BEN *REACTED*, HIS HAND FLYING TO THE HILT OF HIS *LIGHT SABRE* AND PRESSING THE ACTIVATING STUD."

AAGH!

VORP

HE LEAPED RIGHT ONTO THE BLADE. I DIDN'T THINK YOU'D *SEEN* HIM.

I HADN'T.

VERY IMPRESSIVE, GENERAL SIT DOWN, AND I'LL BUY YOU A DRINK.

CARE FOR SOME DELTRON SPICE WINE? THIS LITTLE GADGET FERMENTS IT BY MICROWAVES AND SERVES IT UP SEASONED TO ANY TASTE.

AND NOW IT'S *MY* TURN TO BE IMPRESSED? I'M AFRAID I DON'T CARE FOR *ADDICTIVE* STIMULANTS, MR. --?

TING

TRYLL... AUGUSTUS TRYLL.

AH, YES, MR. TRYLL. I **HAVE** HEARD OF YOU.

GOOD. THAT WILL SAVE ME NEEDLESS EXPLANATIONS. YOU SEE, I'M ABOUT TO ENTER INTO A VENTURE THAT CALLS FOR SOMEONE OF RATHER... *UNUSUAL* TALENTS. INTERESTED IN A *PARTNERSHIP?*

WITH A MAN WHO TRAFFICS IN STOLEN GOODS, POLITICAL BETRAYALS, AND SLAVERY?

I'M AFRAID I HAVE AS LITTLE TASTE FOR YOUR *BUSINESS* AS FOR YOUR *BEVERAGES.*

RKO, IF YOU'D CARE TO JOIN ME, I CAN SHOW YOU WHERE OUR QUARTERS ARE LOCATED.

THANK YOU, GENERAL.

ATTENTION, ALL PASSENGERS, WE ARE NOW LEAVING HYPER-SPACE...

...AND PREPARING TO ENTER THE *MERSON* ASTEROID BELT. ALL SYSTEMS NOT RELATING TO LIFE SUPPORT ARE BEING SHUT DOWN.

WHAT'S THAT ALL ABOUT?

FOR YOUR OWN SAFETY, PLEASE *DEACTIVATE* ANY PRIVATELY OWNED MACHINES AND CONSOLES.

THE MERSONS ARE *HOSTILE* TO THE REPUBLIC, SIR, ALWAYS ON THE LOOKOUT FOR SHIPS THAT STRAY INTO THEIR SECTOR.

SINCE THE ASTEROID BELT MAKES HYPER-SPACE PASSAGE IMPOSSIBLE, ANY CRAFT THAT PASSES THIS WAY SHUTS DOWN ITS NON-ESSENTIAL SYSTEMS AND *DRIFTS* ALONG WITH THE BELT, DISGUISED AS SPACE DEBRIS. IT'S ALL PERFECTLY SAFE.

GOOD, GOOD... BUT TELL ME ABOUT *BAIL*... HOW IS MY OLD FRIEND?

"*THE CONVERSATION WENT ON FOR HOURS, UNTIL LATER THAT EVENING, WHEN THEY HEARD A KNOCK AT THE DOOR OF THEIR CABIN...*"

YES? CREWMAN RORK, ISN'T IT?

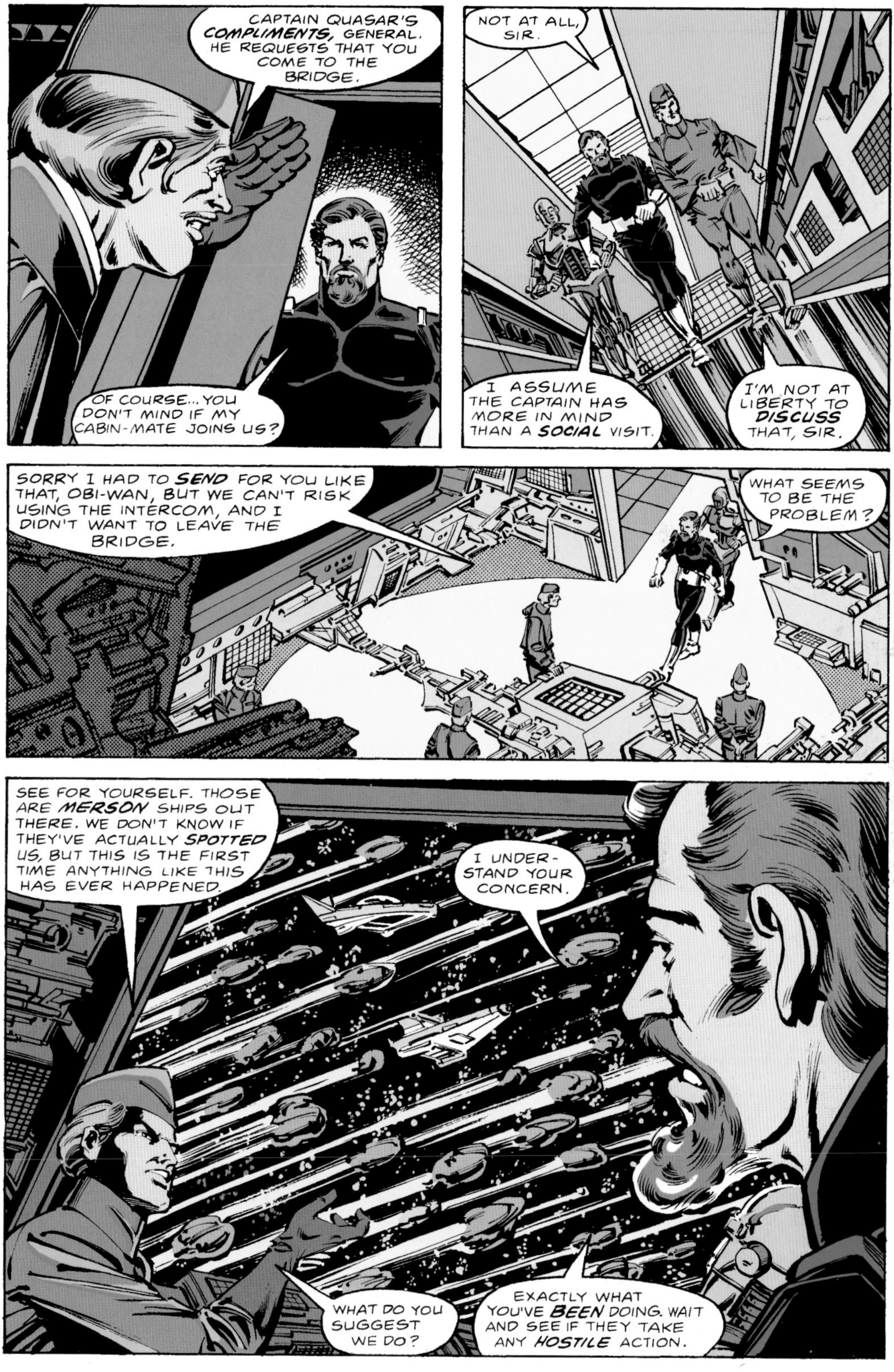

CAPTAIN QUASAR'S COMPLIMENTS, GENERAL. HE REQUESTS THAT YOU COME TO THE BRIDGE.
OF COURSE... YOU DON'T MIND IF MY CABIN-MATE JOINS US?
NOT AT ALL, SIR.
I ASSUME THE CAPTAIN HAS MORE IN MIND THAN A SOCIAL VISIT.
I'M NOT AT LIBERTY TO DISCUSS THAT, SIR.
SORRY I HAD TO SEND FOR YOU LIKE THAT, OBI-WAN, BUT WE CAN'T RISK USING THE INTERCOM, AND I DIDN'T WANT TO LEAVE THE BRIDGE.
WHAT SEEMS TO BE THE PROBLEM?
SEE FOR YOURSELF. THOSE ARE MERSON SHIPS OUT THERE. WE DON'T KNOW IF THEY'VE ACTUALLY SPOTTED US, BUT THIS IS THE FIRST TIME ANYTHING LIKE THIS HAS EVER HAPPENED.
I UNDER-STAND YOUR CONCERN.
WHAT DO YOU SUGGEST WE DO?
EXACTLY WHAT YOU'VE BEEN DOING. WAIT AND SEE IF THEY TAKE ANY HOSTILE ACTION.

" 'AND WHATEVER YOU DO, WARN YOUR CREW NOT TO *ALARM* THE PASSENGERS.' "

IT'S *TRUE*, I TELL YOU. THERE ARE FOUR MERSON SHIPS OUTSIDE RIGHT NOW. THE CAPTAIN HAS THAT JEDI AND HIS DROID UP ON THE BRIDGE WITH HIM, AND...

BY THE SEVEN RINGS OF MY HOME WORLD-- WE'RE ALL GOING TO *DIE!*

AREN'T THE MERSONS... *SLAVERS?*

I'M *SORRY*, GENERAL, BUT WORD HAS *ALREADY SPREAD* TO THE BAR.

THEN IT CAN'T BE HELPED.

OUR PROBLEM IS OUT *THERE,* OBI-WAN.

"FOOD-- AND *DRINKS*-- ARE PART OF THE LIFE SUPPORT SYSTEM, SO DON'T *WORRY* ABOUT THE PASSENGERS.' "

PING-

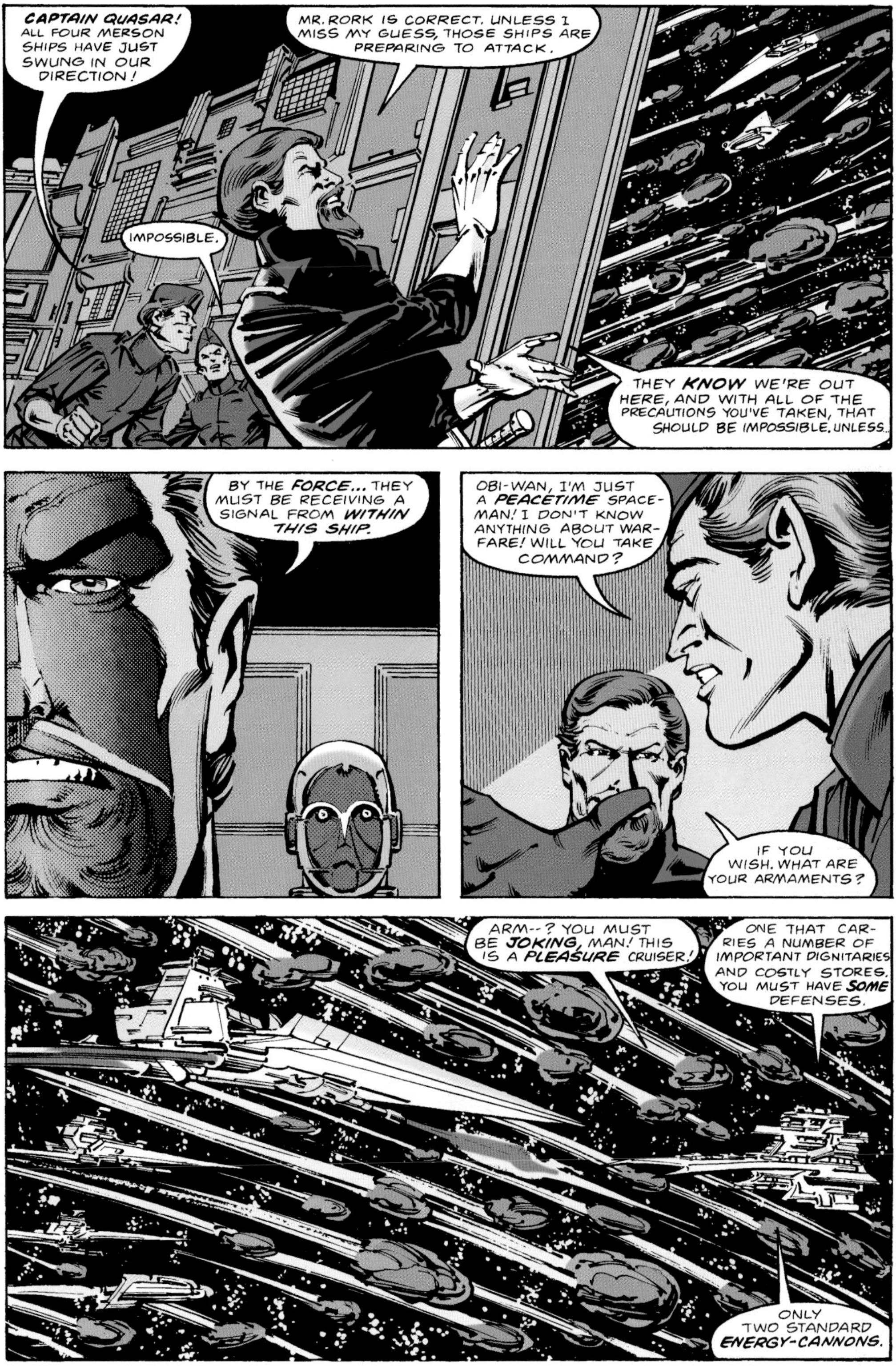

CAPTAIN QUASAR! ALL FOUR MERSON SHIPS HAVE JUST SWUNG IN OUR DIRECTION!
MR. RORK IS CORRECT. UNLESS I MISS MY GUESS, THOSE SHIPS ARE PREPARING TO ATTACK.
IMPOSSIBLE.
THEY KNOW WE'RE OUT HERE, AND WITH ALL OF THE PRECAUTIONS YOU'VE TAKEN, THAT SHOULD BE IMPOSSIBLE. UNLESS...
BY THE FORCE... THEY MUST BE RECEIVING A SIGNAL FROM WITHIN THIS SHIP.
OBI-WAN, I'M JUST A PEACETIME SPACE-MAN! I DON'T KNOW ANYTHING ABOUT WAR-FARE! WILL YOU TAKE COMMAND?
IF YOU WISH. WHAT ARE YOUR ARMAMENTS?
ARM--? YOU MUST BE JOKING, MAN! THIS IS A PLEASURE CRUISER!
ONE THAT CAR-RIES A NUMBER OF IMPORTANT DIGNITARIES AND COSTLY STORES. YOU MUST HAVE SOME DEFENSES.
ONLY TWO STANDARD ENERGY-CANNONS.

AGAINST FOUR ORDINARY SCOUT SHIPS, THAT MAY BE ENOUGH!

ONE OF 'EM'S COMING IN AT ELEVEN O'CLOCK, SIR.

THEN FIRE ON MY SIGNAL...

...NOW!

SKRAM

"GUIDED ONLY BY THE *FORCE* THAT GIVES EVERY JEDI KNIGHT HIS POWER, BEN COMMANDED THE CRUISER THROUGH THE UNEQUAL BATTLE..."

WE LACK THEIR MANEUVERABILITY...

KODOSH

SO WE MUST MAKE *THEM* COME TO *OUR* GUNS...

SKRAKOW

...THUSLY.

BUT, SIR, WITH OUR *ENGINES* ON, WON'T THE MERSONS BE ABLE TO...

EVEN IF THE FIGHTING DRAWS MORE SHIPS, WE CAN LOSE THEM EASILY ENOUGH BY RESUMING OUR DRIFT IN THE BELT. IT'S ONLY VISUAL CONTACT WE HAVE TO FEAR FOR THE MOMENT...

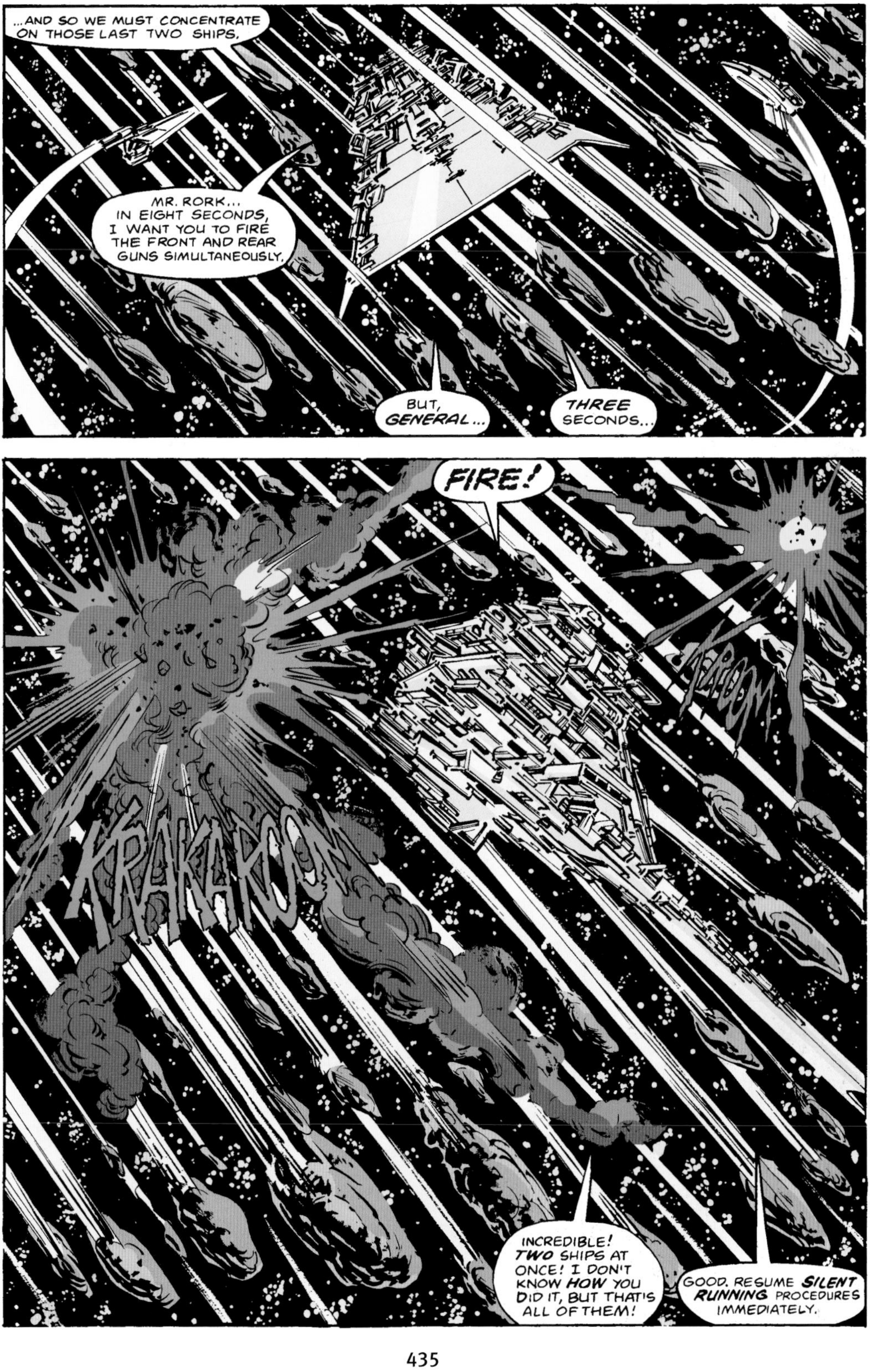
...AND SO WE MUST CONCENTRATE ON THOSE LAST TWO SHIPS.
MR. RORK... IN EIGHT SECONDS, I WANT YOU TO FIRE THE FRONT AND REAR GUNS SIMULTANEOUSLY.
BUT, GENERAL...
THREE SECONDS...
FIRE!
INCREDIBLE! TWO SHIPS AT ONCE! I DON'T KNOW HOW YOU DID IT, BUT THAT'S ALL OF THEM!
GOOD. RESUME SILENT RUNNING PROCEDURES IMMEDIATELY.

SIR...YOUR REMARK ABOUT A *SIGNAL* FROM THIS SHIP... I THINK IT'S BEING *REPEATED* DOWN IN THE LOUNGE.

WHAT?

CAPTAIN, YOU AND YOUR MEN SEE IF YOU CAN LOCATE WHERE THE SIGNAL'S COMING FROM, IF IT EXISTS.

RKO AND I WILL DO WHAT WE CAN TO ALLAY THE PASSENGERS' FEARS.

AND, WHEN BEN AND RKO REACHED THE LOUNGE...

YOU LYING *SNEAK!* HOW MUCH DID THE MERSONS PAY YOU?

IT APPEARS WE'RE STILL IN TIME TO PREVENT AN ACT WHOSE CONSEQUENCES WE MAY *ALL* REGRET.

KEEP *AWAY* FROM ME, ALL OF YOU!

YOU'RE NOT GOING TO PREVENT *ANYTHING,* JEDI!

YOU SAID SOMEONE ON THIS SHIP IS SIGNALLING THE MERSONS, AND WE ALL *KNOW* WHO THAT SOMEONE IS!

BUT WHAT *PROOF* HAVE YOU?

WE DON'T *NEED* PROOF! EVERYONE *KNOWS* WHAT KIND OF MAN TRYLL IS!

THIS WON'T BE THE FIRST TIME HE'S WORKED WITH SLAVERS

DON'T YOU *SEE?* HE SOLD THIS SHIP AND EVERYONE *ON* IT!

THE ONLY THING I SEE IS THAT YOU'VE ALL TAKEN GOOD ADVANTAGE OF THE SHIP'S STOCK OF LIQUORS AND STIMULANTS--

-- AND THAT YOU'RE ALL TOO *FRIGHTENED* TO THINK *CLEARLY.*

YOU'VE GOT TO *PROTECT* ME, KENOBI! YOU'RE A *JEDI*-- IT'S YOUR *DUTY!*

I HAVEN'T DONE ANYTHING!

AND YOU'D HARDLY ADMIT IT IF YOU HAD, EH, MR. TRYLL?

WAIT... I SEE IT *ALL* NOW! THIS AFTERNOON I OVERHEARD TRYLL OFFERING KENOBI A *PARTNERSHIP.* THEY'RE IN THIS *TOGETHER!*

YEAH! WE SAW WHAT THE JEDI AND HIS DROID DID TO JOEY ORSEL TODAY!

LET'S GET THEM ALL!

"AND THE CROWD BEGAN TO ADVANCE..."

437

"WHILE IN HIS MIND'S EYE, BEN COULD SEE..."

MORE MERSON SHIPS ARE UNDOUBTEDLY APPROACHING. IF I DON'T ACT SWIFTLY, IT MAY BE TOO *LATE* FOR US ALL.

PLING

THAT'S IT, JEDI! THEY MEAN *NOTHING* TO YOU!

CUT THE WHOLE *BUNCH* DOWN!

VORSH

I DON'T THINK *THAT* WILL BE NECESSARY--

--AS *THIS* FERMENTATION DEVICE IS THE SOURCE OF *ALL* OUR TROUBLES!

SOOSHT

"OUT IN THE ASTEROID BELT, THE MERSON SHIPS LOST TRACK OF THE PLEASURE CRUISER AND BEGAN TO WANDER AIMLESSLY...

"...AS THE SOURCE OF THE MICROWAVE EMANATIONS THAT HAD ATTRACTED THEM WAS DESTROYED!"

JEDI... I DON'T KNOW HOW I CAN *EVER* THANK YOU.

DON'T *TRY*, MR. TRYLL.

RKO, IF YOU'D CARE TO RETIRE TO OUR CABIN, WE MIGHT *FINISH* THIS JOURNEY IN PEACE.

YES, SIR.

"AND AFTER THEY REACHED ALDERAAN, THE DROID TOLD MY FATHER ABOUT THE ENTIRE ADVENTURE."

WELL, IT WAS *TERRIFIC* HEARING ABOUT BEN AGAIN.

IF YOU'LL PARDON MY SAYING, PRINCESS LEIA, 68-RKO MUST HAVE BEEN A *MASTER* STORYTELLER.

YEAH, YOUR ROYALNESS, YOU TELL A PRETTY GOOD STORY YOURSELF...

... EVEN IF YOU DID *JAZZ* IT UP WITH ALL THAT HOCUS-POCUS ABOUT THE *FORCE*.

HRONK

BUT RIGHT NOW, OUR SHIP IS REPAIRED...

... SO LET'S GET OUT OF THIS QUADRANT BEFORE WE FIND OURSELVES IN ANOTHER *MESS!*

NEXT ISSUE: WE PICK UP ON OUR REGULAR STORYLINE AND THE...

SIEGE AT YAVIN!

439

40¢ 25 JULY 02817

ADVENTURES *BEYOND* THE GREATEST SPACE-FANTASY FILM OF ALL!

STAR WARS

LUKE AND LEIA TRAPPED BY AN IMPERIAL BLOCKADE!

SIEGE AT YAVIN!

INFANTINO/WIACEK

Long ago in a galaxy far, far away. . .there exists a state of cosmic *civil war*. A brave alliance of *underground freedom fighters* has challenged the tyranny and oppression of the awesome *Galactic Empire*. This is their story!

LucasFilm PRESENTS: **STAR WARS**™ THE GREATEST **SPACE FANTASY** OF ALL!

CONTINUING THE SAGA BEGUN IN THE FILM BY **GEORGE LUCAS** *RELEASED BY* **TWENTIETH CENTURY-FOX**

ARCHIE GOODWIN
WRITER / EDITOR

CARMINE INFANTINO & **GENE DAY**
ARTISTS

JOE ROSEN
LETTERER

BEN SEAN
COLORIST

JIM SHOOTER
CONSULTING EDITOR

SEIGE AT YAVIN!

DAWN ON THE FOURTH MOON! *TIE* FIGHTERS SHRIEK DOWN INTO STILL SURFACE MISTS HANGING ABOVE THE JUNGLE. THE LEAD SHIP'S ENERGY CANNONS POUND...

...AND A REBEL LOOKOUT STATION GIVES ITS **LAST** WARNING.

G382

AND FOR THE *THIRD TIME* IN AS MANY DAYS...

THERE GOES *ANOTHER FLIGHT* INTO THE GRINDER!

LET'S GIVE 'EM SOME *GROUND SUPPORT!*

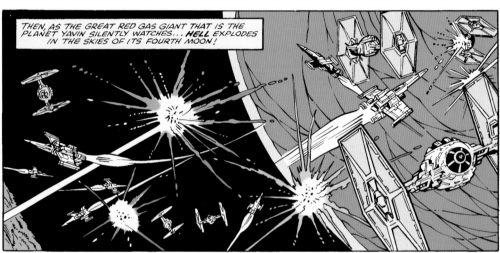

THEN, AS THE GREAT RED GAS GIANT THAT IS THE PLANET YAVIN SILENTLY WATCHES... *HELL* EXPLODES IN THE SKIES OF ITS FOURTH MOON!

IT FINALLY *ENDS* AS IT HAS BEFORE... WITH THE ENEMY IN SWIFT *RETREAT.*

BUT AT A *PRICE*... ALWAYS AT A TERRIBLE PRICE.

LITTLE BY LITTLE... THEY'RE **WHITTLING AWAY** OUR FORCES! FORCES **STILL** NOT REBUILT TO THEIR LEVEL BEFORE THE BATTLE OF THE **DEATH STAR.**

AND WE DON'T KNOW **WHERE** IN THE NAME OF THE FORCE THEY'RE **COMING** FROM!

TO CONSTANTLY THROW SO MANY **TIE** FIGHTERS AT US, IT **HAS** TO BE ONE OF THOSE BIG IMPERIAL **BATTLE CRUISERS,** GENERAL DODONNA.

NO! TRACKING EQUIPMENT WOULD HAVE DETECTED ANYTHING IN THE STAR DESTROYER CLASS **LONG** AGO!

WELL, OUR RECON PATROLS CAN'T FIND A **THING** ON THE OTHER MOONS--

MAYBE YOU SCANNER JOCKEYS THINK WE'RE FIGHTING **GHOSTS** UP THERE!

GENTLEMEN....! FIGHTING AMONG **OURSELVES** IS THE **LAST THING** WE CAN AFFORD.

WE'VE GOT TO WORK **TOGETHER** TO FIND AN **ANSWER**...OR THE ALLIANCE WON'T **SURVIVE!**

CENTARES! OUTER-MOST OF THE MID-SYSTEMS TRADING WORLDS. LAST CIVILIZED STOP FOR THOSE DOING BUSINESS IN THE GALACTIC BACKWATERS, OR TAKING A FLING AT EXPLORING THE UNKNOWN...

...OR HOPING TO **ESCAPE** THE LONG ARM OF THE **EMPIRE.**

YOU CITIZENS HAVE MADE A REAL SWEET **TRADE.** TAKE THE WORD OF **JORMAN THOAD,** THE PLANET'S LARGEST DEALER IN USED STARCRAFT.

THIS SHIP'S NOT SO FANCY AS THAT **YACHT** YOU CAME IN, BUT--

"--BUT IT'S GOT THE DRIVE AND ARMAMENT *NEEDED* IN THE OUTERWORLDS!" WE *HEARD* THE SALES PITCH--

JUST SO THEY *KEEP* WORKING AS WELL AS THEY DID IN THE *DEMONSTRATION RUN.*

LAD, YOU HAVE THE JORMAN THOAD *GUARANTEE.*

THAT MAY NOT *HELP* IF WE AREN'T *ALIVE* TO HOLD YOU TO IT!

MASTER LUKE, ARTOO AND I HAVE *TRANSFERRED* EVERYTHING TO THE NEW SHIP.

NICE PAIR OF *DROIDS*... BIT ON THE *WORN* SIDE. IF YOU'D LIKE TO GET RID OF *THEM*, I'VE A COUSIN OVER IN OLD TOWN WHO--

TA-DOOT!

FOR A CHANGE, I *AGREE* WITH YOU, ARTOO... HE *DOES* SEEM WORSE THAN A *JAWA!*

WE *WANT* OUR DROIDS, THOAD...AND INFORMATION ABOUT CURRENT *CONDITIONS* IN THE VARIOUS OUTWORLD SECTORS.

NO BETTER, NO WORSE THAN *USUAL*--

UNLESS YOU'RE HEADED WHERE THAT HOUSE OF TAGGE *MINING EXPLORER* IS BOUND... THE *GORDIAN REACH!*

THE GORDIAN REACH...? I-ISN'T THAT WHERE THE *YAVIN* SYSTEM LIES...?!

YAVIN. KRYLON. TORQUE. A *JILLION* MORE. RUMOR HAS IT TAGGE IS ON TO A BIG *SPICE STRIKE* ON ONE OF 'EM--

--AND BECAUSE OF THEIR IMPERIAL CONNECTIONS... THE EMPIRE'S *BLOCKADED* THE SECTOR!

SO I WOULDN'T PLAN ON TRAVELING *THERE.*

WISH I HAD AN *IMPERIAL GENERAL* IN THE FAMILY LIKE THE TAGGES. THEN MAYBE *I* COULD GET IN ON SUCH--

BUT I SEE YOU ARE ANXIOUS TO *DEPART!*

REMEMBER JORMAN THOAD WHEN YOU HAVE *OTHER* LUXURY YACHTS TO TRADE FOR MODEST BUT DEPENDABLE CRAFTS!

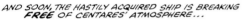

AND SOON, THE HASTILY ACQUIRED SHIP IS BREAKING *FREE* OF CENTARES' ATMOSPHERE...

...CLIMBING FOR *DEEP SPACE.*

IT'S *INCREDIBLE*, PRINCESS...! EVERYTIME WE GET *CLOSE* TO MAKING IT BACK TO REBEL BASE--

--SOMETHING POPS UP TO GET IN OUR *WAY!*

AT LEAST WE'VE GOTTEN RID OF THE *YACHT*, LUKE. * IF DARTH VADER IS STILL IN PURSUIT... HE CAN'T *TRACE* US THROUGH THAT.

BUT IF HE'S *NOT* TRAILING US... HE MAY BE AFTER *HAN!*

*ACQUIRED IN *STAR WARS* #23. -- ARCHIE G.

WHEN HE ISN'T PULLING MY *LEG* ABOUT SOMETHING... HAN'S KIND'A LIKE A *BIG BROTHER.* IF ANYTHING'S *HAPPENED* TO HIM--

WE *HAD* TO SPLIT UP TO ESCAPE LORD VADER, LUKE! I'M *SURE* WE'LL BE TOGETHER AGAIN *SOON*--

WE... WE *HAVE* TO BE!

445

THAT SOUNDS SORT OF *SERIOUS.* LATELY I THOUGHT LEIA SEEMED MORE INTERESTED IN *ME*, BUT *NOW*--

--*CAN SHE?*

AW, *NO!* HAN'S A GOOD GUY, BUT SHE CAN'T *REALLY* BE IN *LOVE* WITH HIM--

VRR-KLIK WEET!

PRINCESS...! ARTOO SAYS HE'S GETTING THAT *HOUSE OF TAGGE SHIP* YOU WONDERED ABOUT ON THE *SCANNER*--

HE CLAIMS IT'S ABOUT TO GO INTO *WARP*--

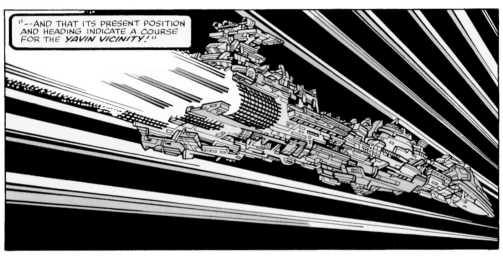

"--AND THAT ITS PRESENT POSITION AND HEADING INDICATE A COURSE FOR THE *YAVIN VICINITY!*"

SHOULDN'T WE BE CONCERNED ABOUT GETTING THROUGH THE EMPIRE'S *BLOCKADE* INSTEAD OF OVER SOME LUMBERING *SPICE SNIFFER?*

LUKE, THERE'S *NO SPICE* IN THAT SECTOR--

--THE ALLIANCE MADE *CERTAIN* WHEN WE PICKED THE LOCATION FOR A *BASE.* THE LAST THING WE *WANTED*--

--WAS A *CONSTANT STREAM OF SPICE HUNTERS* IN THE AREA!

THEN WHY ARE TAGGE *EXPLORERS* GOING *IN* THERE, PRINCESS? WHAT'S THIS BLOCKADE ALL *ABOUT?!*

I THINK THE EMPIRE'S *AFRAID,* LUKE.

PRINCESS, NO ONE'S GOT MORE *FAITH* IN REBEL FIGHTING ABILITY THAN *ME*--

--BUT I CAN'T BELIEVE WE'VE GOT THE *IMPERIAL WAR MACHINE* PARALYZED WITH FRIGHT!

THAT'S NOT *QUITE* WHAT I MEANT, LUKE. BUT CONSIDER--

BESIDES OTHER EARLIER VICTORIES, WE'VE *DESTROYED* THEIR MOST AWESOME WEAPON...THE *DEATH STAR!*

THAT'S *NOT* THE KIND OF NEWS THAT MAKES IT *EASY* FOR THEM TO CONTROL THE GALAXY.

LEIA, YOU THINK THE *BLOCKADE* IS AN ATTEMPT TO KEEP THAT DEFEAT *SECRET?*

PARTLY. BY NOW, THE EMPIRE COULD HAVE SENT A MASSIVE *FLEET* IN RETALIATION--

BUT SUPPOSE OUR FORCES *ABANDONED* YAVIN AS THEY ONCE DID *DANTOOINE?*

OR WORSE YET; PULLED ANOTHER *VICTORY* OUT OF THE HAT?

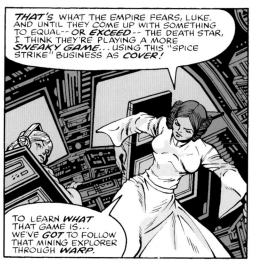

THAT'S WHAT THE EMPIRE FEARS, LUKE. AND UNTIL THEY COME UP WITH SOMETHING TO EQUAL-- OR *EXCEED* -- THE DEATH STAR, I THINK THEY'RE PLAYING A MORE *SNEAKY GAME*...USING THIS "SPICE STRIKE" BUSINESS AS *COVER!*

TO LEARN *WHAT* THAT GAME IS... WE'VE *GOT* TO FOLLOW THAT MINING EXPLORER THROUGH *WARP.*

THIS *CLOSE* ON THEIR HEELS THAT COULD BE *TRICKY,* PRINCESS!

THREEPIO, LINK ARTOO DEETOO TO THE SHIPBOARD *COMPUTER,* WITH *HIM* AUGMENTING ITS EMERGENCY CALIBRATION SYSTEM--

--AND THE *PILOT* WHO BROUGHT DOWN THE *DEATH STAR* AT THE CONTROLS, WHAT DO WE HAVE TO *WORRY* ABOUT?

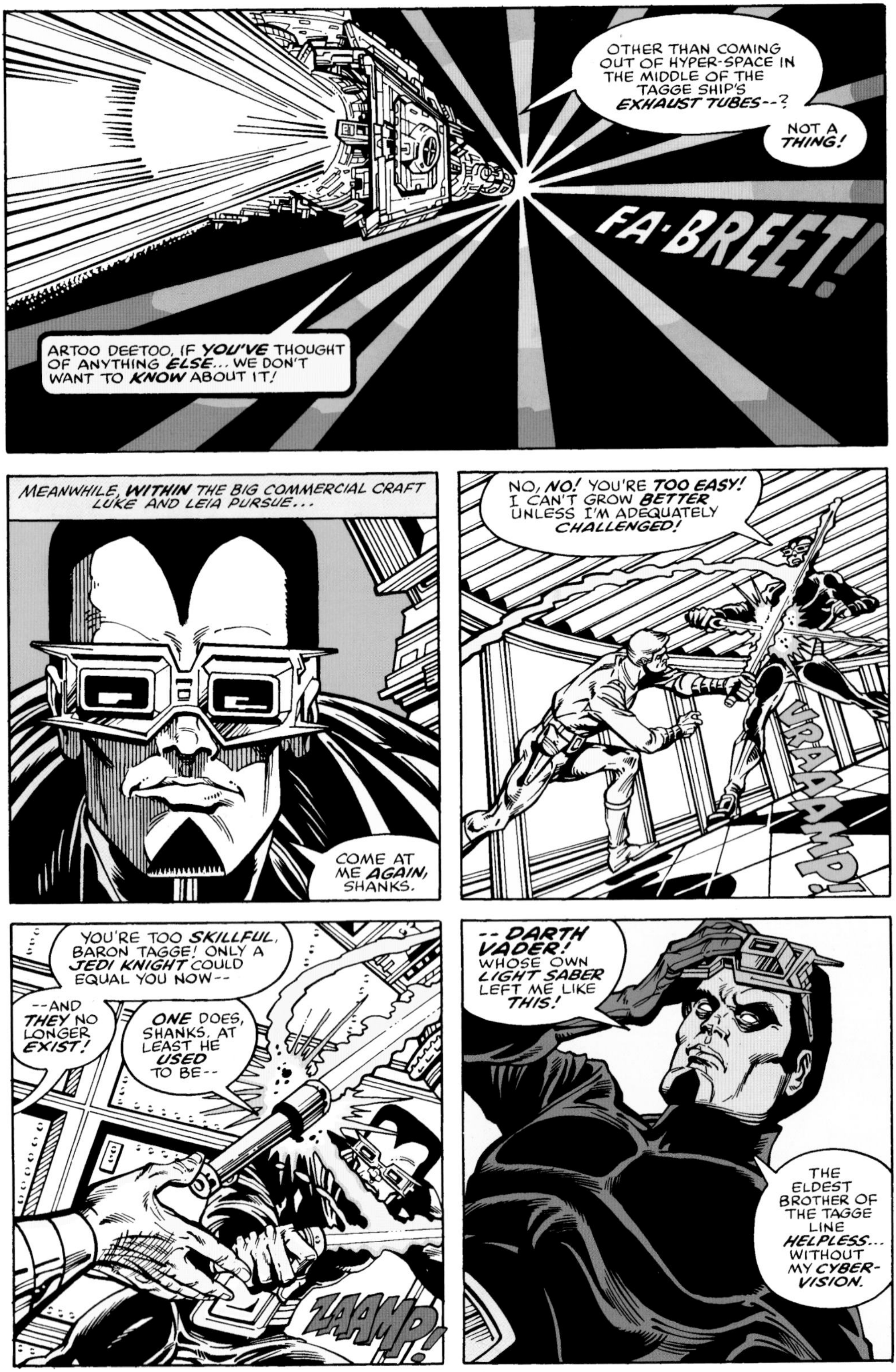
OTHER THAN COMING OUT OF HYPER-SPACE IN THE MIDDLE OF THE TAGGE SHIP'S EXHAUST TUBES--?
NOT A THING!
FA-BREET!
ARTOO DEETOO, IF YOU'VE THOUGHT OF ANYTHING ELSE... WE DON'T WANT TO KNOW ABOUT IT!
MEANWHILE, WITHIN THE BIG COMMERCIAL CRAFT LUKE AND LEIA PURSUE...
COME AT ME AGAIN, SHANKS.
NO, NO! YOU'RE TOO EASY! I CAN'T GROW BETTER UNLESS I'M ADEQUATELY CHALLENGED!
VRAAAAMP!
YOU'RE TOO SKILLFUL, BARON TAGGE! ONLY A JEDI KNIGHT COULD EQUAL YOU NOW--
--AND THEY NO LONGER EXIST!
ONE DOES, SHANKS. AT LEAST HE USED TO BE--
ZAAMP!
--DARTH VADER! WHOSE OWN LIGHT SABER LEFT ME LIKE THIS!
THE ELDEST BROTHER OF THE TAGGE LINE HELPLESS... WITHOUT MY CYBER-VISION.

SO I PRACTICE *CONSTANTLY* WITH THIS *SILLY,* OUTMODED WEAPON OF A FOOLISH, EXTINCT BAND OF MEN--

AND *SOMEDAY,* SHANKS... I'LL BE *READY.* READY TO *REPAY* DARTH VADER IN KIND... AND WITH *INTEREST!*

BARON *TAGGE--!*

SIR, WE'RE COMING OUT OF *WARP*... AND INSTRUMENTS INDICATE THERE MAY BE A SMALL *SHIP* FOLLOWING US!

A DARING-- IF HIGHLY *RISKY*-- WAY TO SLIP THROUGH THE EMPIRE'S *BLOCKADE.*

SEE THEY DON'T *SUCCEED.*

SECONDS AFTER THE BARON'S WORDS ARE SPOKEN, A *HATCH* OPENS AND...

...*MINES* ARE SWIFTLY *SCATTERED* THROUGH THE *SECTOR!*

GOOD! I DIDN'T BUILD THE FAMILY FORTUNE BY LETTING *ADMIRATION* FOR A FOE'S DARING KEEP ME FROM *DESTROYING* THEM!

LET'S GET ON WITH OUR *DELIVERY.*

AND WHEN THE PURSUING CRAFT'S COMPUTER *DISENGAGES* FROM SUPRA-LIGHT DRIVE...

THE AREA'S *BOOBY-TRAPPED!*

ARTOO! CUT IN THE *SHIELDS!*

THREE-PIO! WHAT'S HE *SAYING?!*

BA-DOOM

HE WISHES *JORMAN THOAD* WERE WITH US... THAT ONE HIT HAS OUR SHIELDS *FAILING!*

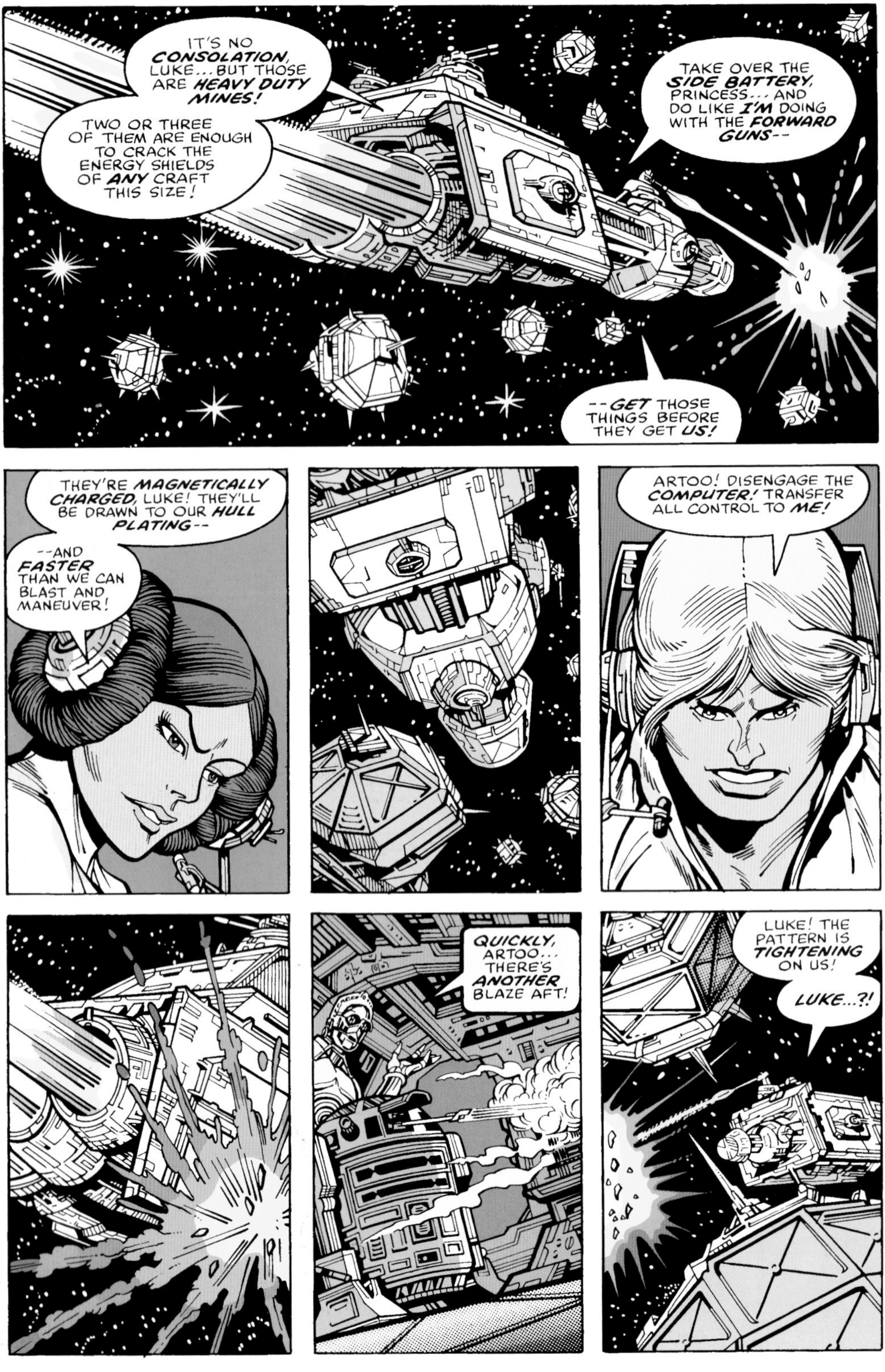
IT'S NO CONSOLATION, LUKE... BUT THOSE ARE HEAVY DUTY MINES!
TWO OR THREE OF THEM ARE ENOUGH TO CRACK THE ENERGY SHIELDS OF ANY CRAFT THIS SIZE!
TAKE OVER THE SIDE BATTERY, PRINCESS... AND DO LIKE I'M DOING WITH THE FORWARD GUNS--
--GET THOSE THINGS BEFORE THEY GET US!
THEY'RE MAGNETICALLY CHARGED, LUKE! THEY'LL BE DRAWN TO OUR HULL PLATING--
--AND FASTER THAN WE CAN BLAST AND MANEUVER!
ARTOO! DISENGAGE THE COMPUTER! TRANSFER ALL CONTROL TO ME!
QUICKLY, ARTOO... THERE'S ANOTHER BLAZE AFT!
LUKE! THE PATTERN IS TIGHTENING ON US!
LUKE...?!

BUT THE BOY FROM TATOOINE NO LONGER **HEARS**, HIS MIND IS DIVORCED FROM CONSCIOUS THOUGHT.

HE IS **ONE** WITH THE MACHINE HE CONTROLS, ACTING BY WHAT HE SENSES AND WHAT HE FEELS.

THE TINY SHIP **DANCES** IN RESPONSE, TWISTING, ALTERING DIRECTIONS WITH EYEBLINK SWIFTNESS!

UNTIL...

YOU BEAT OUT THAT LAST **CLUSTER**, LUKE... THEY ALL CAME TOGETHER ON **EACH OTHER!** A-AND--

--THE WAY AHEAD IS **CLEAR!** WE'RE **THROUGH** THE MINES!

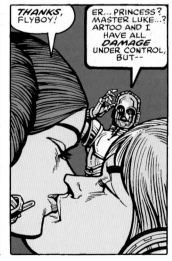

THANKS, FLYBOY!

ER... PRINCESS? MASTER LUKE...? ARTOO AND I HAVE ALL **DAMAGE** UNDER CONTROL, BUT--

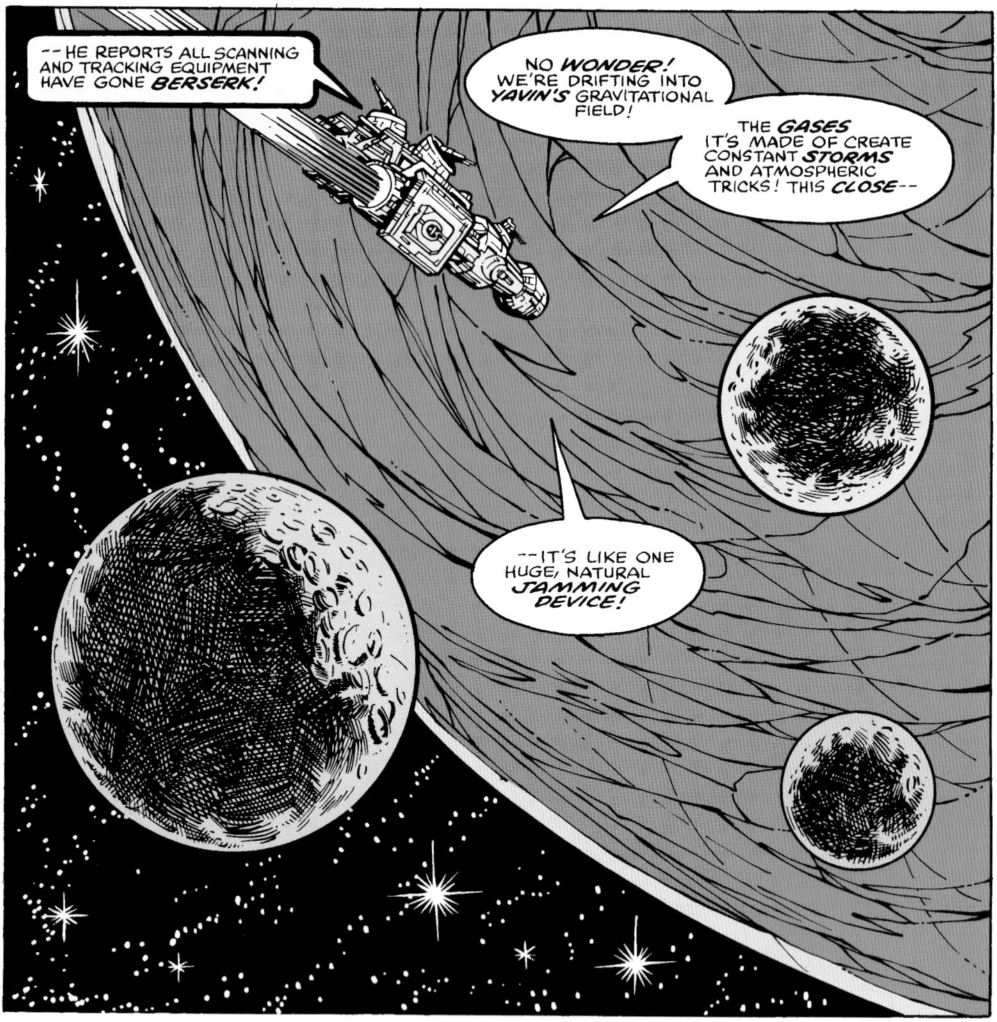
--HE REPORTS ALL SCANNING AND TRACKING EQUIPMENT HAVE GONE BERSERK!
NO WONDER! WE'RE DRIFTING INTO YAVIN'S GRAVITATIONAL FIELD!
THE GASES IT'S MADE OF CREATE CONSTANT STORMS AND ATMOSPHERIC TRICKS! THIS CLOSE--
--IT'S LIKE ONE HUGE, NATURAL JAMMING DEVICE!

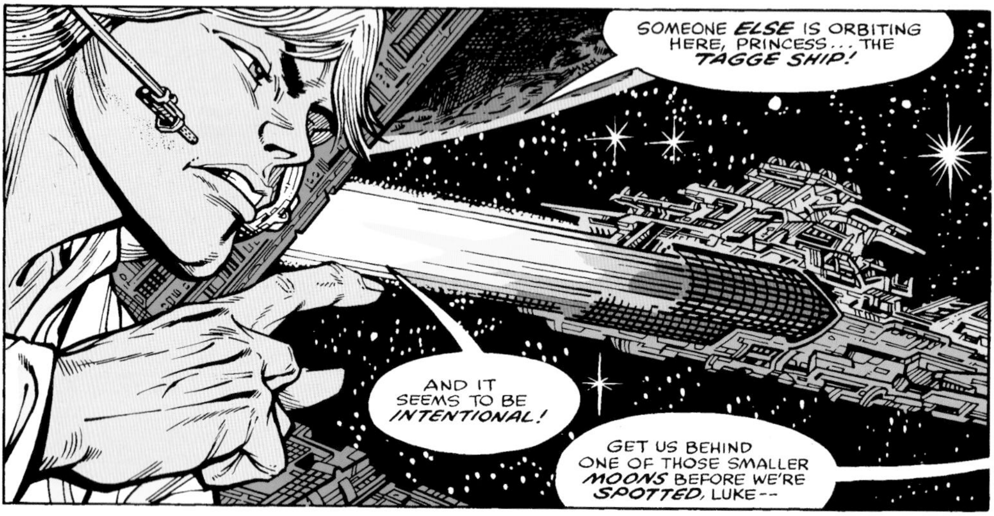
SOMEONE ELSE IS ORBITING HERE, PRINCESS... THE TAGGE SHIP!
AND IT SEEMS TO BE INTENTIONAL!
GET US BEHIND ONE OF THOSE SMALLER MOONS BEFORE WE'RE SPOTTED, LUKE--

--I'M GOING *OUTSIDE* TO DO SOME *SPYING.*

NOT WITHOUT *ME!*

FROM ANYONE *ELSE*, THAT KIND OF *PROTECTIVENESS* MIGHT BE *INSULTING...* SOMEHOW, YOU MAKE IT *QUAINT.*

MOMENTS LATER, TWO FIGURES IN *SURVIVAL ARMOR* JET DOWN TOWARD THE POCKED, AIRLESS SPHERE BELOW...

...MAKING THEIR WAY TO THE LITTLE MOON'S *FAR SIDE.*

THERE IT *IS,* PRINCESS. WHAT IT'S *DOING* IS ANYBODY'S GUESS!

WE *KNOW* IT'S NOT LOOKING FOR *SPICE.*

IF ONLY THESE *MACRO-BINOCULARS* COULD PEER *INSIDE* THAT THING!

THE PILOTS ARE NEARLY READY TO *LAUNCH,* BARON.

I'LL SEE THEM *OFF,* SHANKS. I *PLEASURE* IN VIEWING THE ADVANCED TECHNOLOGY OF THE HOUSE OF TAGGE IN *ACTION.*

PARTICULARLY IN THE CAUSE OF THE *EMPIRE,* SIR...?

PARTICULARLY IN AN OPERATION THAT IS *SUCCEEDING* WHERE VADER, TARKIN AND THE DEATH STAR *FAILED!*

LOOK AT THEM, SHANKS! *REPLACEMENTS* FOR ANY SHIPS THE *REBELS* MAY HAVE STRUCK DOWN!

LET THE *SITH LORD* FOLLOW HIS "FORCE", SCRAMBLING ABOUT THE GALAXY, SEEKING THOSE WHO *SHAMED* HIM IN THE DEATH STAR BATTLE--

--WE'RE BEATING THE ALLIANCE *HERE!*

I'M PROUD TO BE *MILITARY AIDE* ON THIS EXPERIMENT, SIR.

AND *FORTUNATE*, SHANKS! FOR WHEN IT'S *OVER*, DARTH VADER AND HIS WIZARD'S WAYS WON'T HOLD THE EMPEROR'S FANCY... MY *FAMILY* WILL! *THEN* I SHALL--

BUT *TIME* ESCAPES US. ON TO THE *OBSERVATION PORT!*

TOO BAD THAT THE SAME ATMOSPHERIC *INTERFERENCE* THAT MAKES IT DIFFICULT FOR THE REBELS TO DETECT OUR *PRESENCE* HERE--

--ALSO HAMPERS OUR FOLLOWING THE OPERATION IN *CLOSE UP* BY SCANNER.

LAUNCHING *NOW*, BARON TAGGE!

AND, FROM THE SURFACE OF THE NEARBY MOON, LUKE AND LEIA OBSERVE...

A *TIE FIGHTER* FORMATION...! AND HEADED STRAIGHT FOR THE SURFACE OF *YAVIN!*

THAT'S *SUICIDE*, PRINCESS! FLYING *BLINDLY* INTO ALL THOSE GASES....*INSTRUMENTS* UNABLE TO WORK...

THEY'LL NEVER COME *UP* AGAIN!

BUT AS THE AMAZED PAIR *CONTINUE* WATCHING...

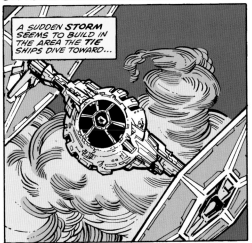

A SUDDEN *STORM* SEEMS TO BUILD IN THE AREA THE *TIE* SHIPS DIVE TOWARD...

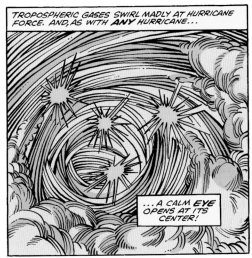

TROPOSPHERIC GASES SWIRL MADLY AT HURRICANE FORCE. AND, AS WITH *ANY* HURRICANE...

...A CALM *EYE* OPENS AT ITS CENTER!

AND THAT EYE BECOMES A *SAFE CORRIDOR,* DOWN WHICH THE ENTIRE FLIGHT *PLUNGES* TO BE LOST FROM SIGHT...

...AS THE STORM *ENDS* WITH A SWIFTNESS THAT *CANNOT* BE NATURAL!

L-LUKE...! THE EMPIRE'S GOT SOMETHING *IN* THERE THAT *CREATES* THOSE STORMS...! SOME KIND OF *BASE!*

I GUESS A *SPACE STATION* COULD *EXIST* IN THOSE GASES... LONG AS THERE WAS A WAY TO *SUPPLY* IT--

--AND FROM WHAT WE JUST *SAW,* THEY OBVIOUSLY HAVE *THAT!* I DON'T KNOW HOW THE SHIPS *SIGNAL* FOR THE STORM CORRIDOR TO BE *OPENED,* BUT--

THAT CAN *WAIT,* LUKE --

--WE'VE GOT TO *WARN* THE ALLIANCE!

AND, BACK INSIDE THEIR *SHIP*...

WHOEVER CAME UP WITH THIS IS *CLEVER*, LUKE. OPERATING SO *CLOSE* TO YAVIN... ON THE *OPPOSITE SIDE* FROM OUR BASE... MAKES CHANCES OF DISCOVERY *MINIMAL*.

AND EVEN IF OUR *RECON PATROLS* SIGHTED THEM--

--ONE STRAY *MINING EXPLORER* WOULDN'T ALARM THEM. THEY'D ASSUME IT'D BE MOVING ON ONCE IT BECAME OBVIOUS THERE WAS NO *SPICE* IN THE AREA.

UNLESS THE RECON CAME ON 'EM JUST AS THEY WERE *UNLOADING* THE *TIES*, LIKE WE SAW, PRINCESS.

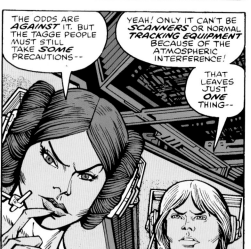

THE ODDS ARE *AGAINST* IT. BUT THE TAGGE PEOPLE MUST STILL TAKE *SOME* PRECAUTIONS--

YEAH! ONLY IT CAN'T BE *SCANNERS* OR NORMAL *TRACKING EQUIPMENT* BECAUSE OF THE ATMOSPHERIC INTERFERENCE!

THAT LEAVES JUST *ONE* THING--

BAD NEWS, MASTER LUKE! NOW THAT WE'RE MOVING *OUT* SOMEWHAT FROM THAT GREAT GLOB OF GAS, ARTOO'S *SENSORS* DETECT--

NEVER *MIND*, THREEPIO! THE PRINCESS AND I HAVE ALREADY *GUESSED*--

A TIE FIGHTER *PATROL*... FLYING *LOOK-OUT* FOR THAT HOUSE OF TAGGE VESSEL!

COMING *IN* THE WAY WE DID... WE PROBABLY JUST *MISSED* THEIR FIRST SWEEP--

--BUT OUR TIMING WAS *PERFECT* FOR THEIR *RETURN!*

I'LL GET BACK TO THE OTHER SET OF *GUNS*, LUKE! IS THERE ANY HOPE OF *OUTRUNNING* THEM UNTIL THREEPIO CAN RAISE *HELP* ON THE COMMINCATOR?

IF THERE *WERE*, PRINCESS--

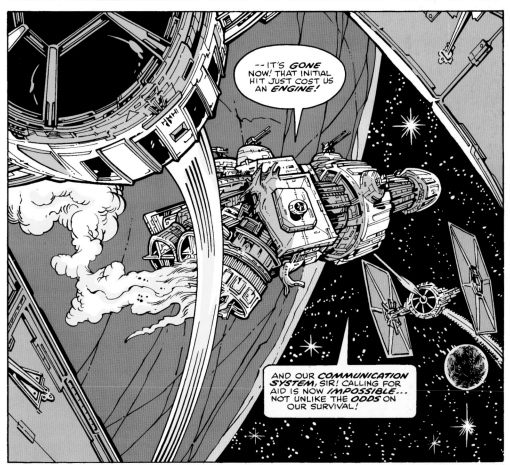

--IT'S *GONE* NOW! THAT INITIAL HIT JUST COST US AN *ENGINE!*

AND OUR *COMMUNICATION SYSTEM*, SIR! CALLING FOR AID IS NOW *IMPOSSIBLE*... NOT UNLIKE THE *ODDS* ON OUR SURVIVAL!

NEXT ISSUE: *DOOM MISSION!*

40¢
CC

26
AUG
02817

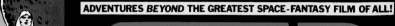
ADVENTURES *BEYOND* THE GREATEST SPACE-FANTASY FILM OF ALL!

STAR WARS™

INFANTINO/
WIACEK

DOOM MISSION!

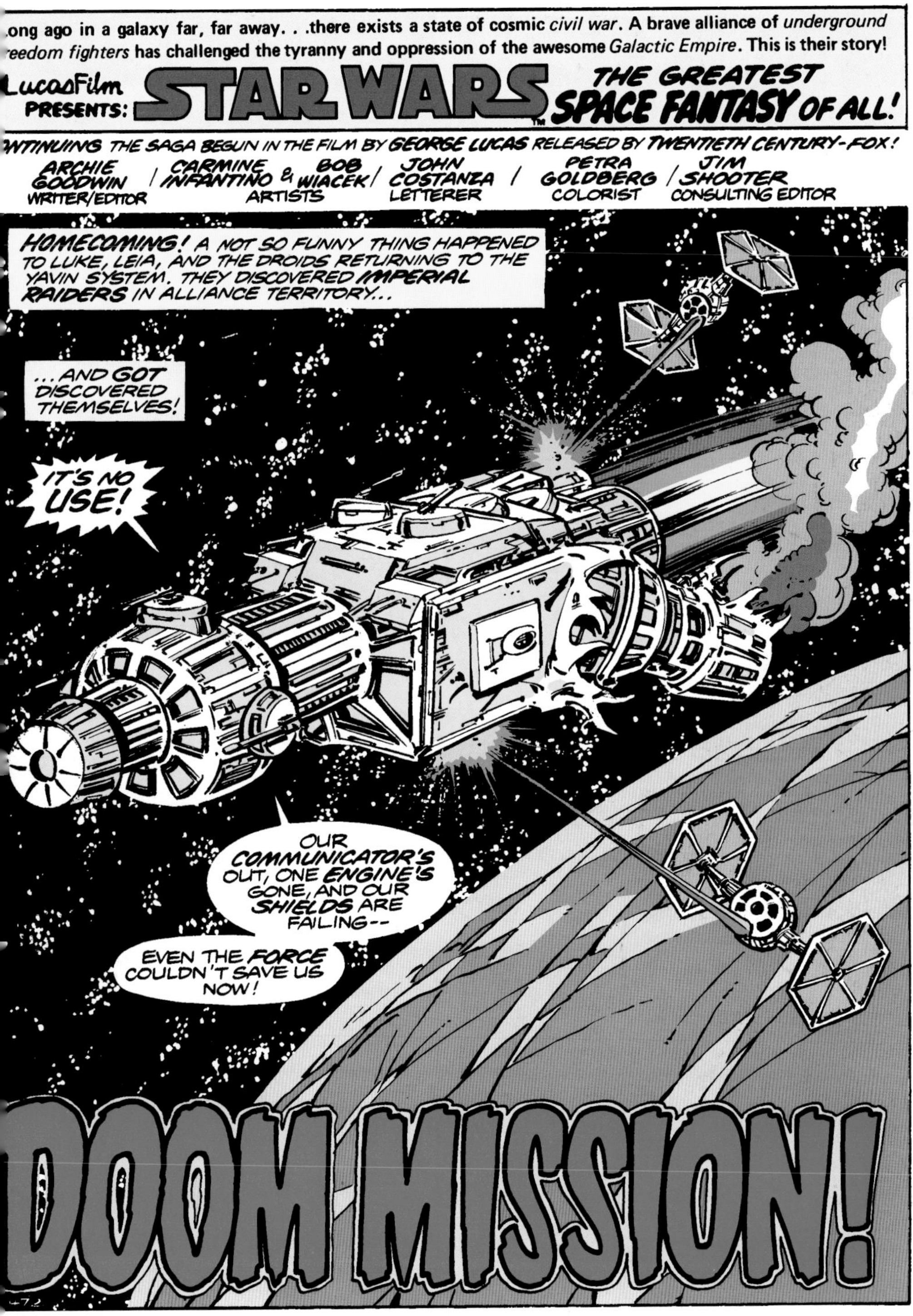
ong ago in a galaxy far, far away. . .there exists a state of cosmic civil war. A brave alliance of underground reedom fighters has challenged the tyranny and oppression of the awesome Galactic Empire. This is their story!
LucasFilm PRESENTS:
STAR WARS
THE GREATEST SPACE FANTASY OF ALL!
NTINUING THE SAGA BEGUN IN THE FILM BY GEORGE LUCAS RELEASED BY TWENTIETH CENTURY-FOX!
ARCHIE GOODWIN WRITER/EDITOR
CARMINE INFANTINO & BOB WIACEK ARTISTS
JOHN COSTANZA LETTERER
PETRA GOLDBERG COLORIST
JIM SHOOTER CONSULTING EDITOR
HOMECOMING! A NOT SO FUNNY THING HAPPENED TO LUKE, LEIA, AND THE DROIDS RETURNING TO THE YAVIN SYSTEM. THEY DISCOVERED IMPERIAL RAIDERS IN ALLIANCE TERRITORY...
...AND GOT DISCOVERED THEMSELVES!
IT'S NO USE!
OUR COMMUNICATOR'S OUT, ONE ENGINE'S GONE, AND OUR SHIELDS ARE FAILING--
EVEN THE FORCE COULDN'T SAVE US NOW!
DOOM MISSION!

WHY HAVEN'T *I* SAID ANYTHING ABOUT BEING *DOOMED* AS I USUALLY DO...?

FR-BRIIT!

BECAUSE MASTER LUKE ALREADY *SEEMS* TO BE SAYING IT... AND SOMEHOW IT SOUNDS FAR MORE *CONVINCING* FROM HIM!

LUKE, WE'RE NOT *THAT* FAR FROM OUR BASE ON THE FOURTH MOON—

THERE MUST BE *SOME* TRICK WE CAN PULL!

I'VE *USED* 'EM ALL TO GET US *THIS* FAR—!

—BUT SHOOTING LIKE THAT SURE *HELPS!* HOW'D A GIRL FROM A PLANET WITH *NO WEAPONS* GET SO *GOOD* WITH THEM?

PROMISE TO GET US *OUT* OF HERE, FLYBOY, AND I'LL *TELL* YOU!

TOO *LATE,* PRINCESS!

THIS BUCKET OF BOLTS JUST TOOK ONE HIT *MORE* THAN EVEN *JORMAN THOAD* ✱ WOULD CLAIM IT COULD HANDLE!

YOU AND THE DROIDS GET INTO THE *ESCAPE POD!* I'LL TRY TO DRAW THOSE TWO SCAVENGERS *OFF* SO YOU CAN—

LUKE—!

✱ THE DEALER IN USED STARCRAFT WHO *TRADED* THE SHIP TO THEM *LAST ISH.*—ARCHIE

460

THERE GOES THE *SECOND* TIE SHIP... LOOKS LIKE HE'S GOING TO *CRASH* ON THAT MOON!

ARTOO...! THREEPIO...! IF YOU KEEP THE *FLAMES* AT BAY A LITTLE *LONGER*--

--WE MIGHT MAKE IT *AFTER ALL!*

X-WING *FIGHTERS!* IT'S A *REBEL* RECONNAISSANCE PATROL!

IT'S *MORE* THAN THAT... IT'S A *MIRACLE!*

AND UNDER X-WING ESCORT, THE LITTLE SHIP FIGHTS ITS WAY INTO THE ATMOSPHERE OF YAVIN'S FOURTH MOON...

...WHERE AT THE MASSASI RUINS, A ROUGH *LANDING* AND A WARM *GREETING* WAIT.

WE'VE BROUGHT *NEWS*, GENERAL DODONNA...BUT I'M AFRAID IT ISN'T *GOOD!*

PRINCESS! WE'D GIVEN YOU AND YOUNG SKYWALKER UP AS *LOST!* SINCE THE IMPERIAL *BLOCKADE* OF THIS SECTOR, COMMUNICATION HAS BEEN *SPOTTY* AND--

NOT MUCH *HAS* BEEN SINCE THE EMPIRE STARTED HITTING US IN ALMOST *DAILY RAIDS*, YOUR HIGHNESS.

PERHAPS *NOT*, GENERAL--

AND DESPITE STEPPED UP *PATROLS*-- LIKE THE ONE THAT FOUND YOU-- THEIR HIDDEN BASE *REMAINS* A SECRET!

AND SWIFTLY... THESE ARE *BLOW UPS* FROM THE PHOTO-RECORDER UNIT OF MY MACRO-BINOCULARS!

HERE'S WHAT LUKE AND I FOUND ON THE *FAR SIDE* OF YAVIN--✱

✱ALSO *LAST ISSUE.*-- ALSO ARCHIE

THAT'S A HOUSE OF TAGGE *MINING EXPLORER!*

BUT THOSE AREN'T *SPICE PROBES* IT'S SENDING DOWN INTO YAVIN'S TROPOSPHERE--

THEY'RE *TIE FIGHTERS*... PROBABLY *REPLACEMENTS* FOR ANY EMPIRE SHIPS YOU'VE *DESTROYED.*

THEY'LL BE *BLIND* IN THERE... *HELPLESS!*

YAVIN'S MADE UP OF NOTHING BUT *GASES*... SHIPS CAN'T OPERATE AMID THEM BECAUSE STORMS AND ATMOSPHERIC INTERFERENCE *JAM* ALL INSTRUMENTS!

SEE! THERE'S A STORM BUILDING UNDER THE TIES... THEY'RE *FINISHED!*

KEEP *WATCHING,* GENTLEMEN--

"THAT 'STORM' SWIRLED THE GASES INTO A CYCLONIC *FUNNEL*...WITH A CALM *EYE* AT ITS CENTER, AND THAT EYE...

"...BECAME A *CORRIDOR* FOR THE TIES TO *TRAVEL* DOWN!"

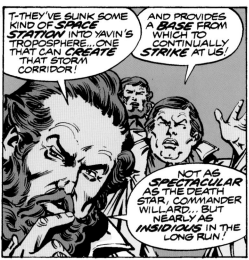

T-THEY'VE SUNK SOME KIND OF *SPACE STATION* INTO YAVIN'S TROPOSPHERE...ONE THAT CAN *CREATE* THAT STORM CORRIDOR!

AND PROVIDES A *BASE* FROM WHICH TO CONTINUALLY *STRIKE* AT US!

NOT AS *SPECTACULAR* AS THE DEATH STAR, COMMANDER WILLARD...BUT NEARLY AS *INSIDIOUS* IN THE LONG RUN!

WELL, WE CRACKED THE DEATH STAR, GENERAL DODONNA...THERE *MUST* BE A WAY TO FIND AND DESTROY *THIS* THING!

WE HAD THE *PLANS* TO THE DEATH STAR, SKYWALKER--

WE COULD *LOSE* EVERY T-65 WE *POSSESS*--

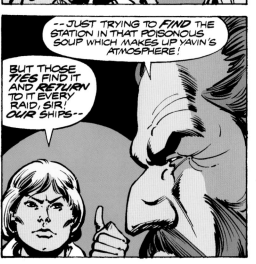

--JUST TRYING TO *FIND* THE STATION IN THAT POISONOUS SOUP WHICH MAKES UP YAVIN'S ATMOSPHERE!

BUT THOSE *TIES* FIND IT AND *RETURN* TO IT EVERY RAID, SIR! *OUR* SHIPS--

ARE *GREAT*...BUT THEY DON'T HAVE HOUSE OF TAGGE *TECHNOLOGY!* THEIR FAMILY INDUSTRIES EMPLOY THOUSANDS OF SCIENTISTS ON *HUNDREDS* OF WORLDS.

ONE OF THEM MUST HAVE COME UP WITH A SIGNAL SYSTEM *STRONG* ENOUGH TO--

LUKE! WHERE ARE YOU *GOING?!*

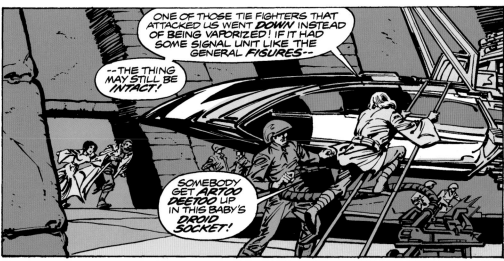

ONE OF THOSE TIE FIGHTERS THAT ATTACKED US WENT *DOWN* INSTEAD OF BEING *VAPORIZED!* IF IT HAD SOME SIGNAL UNIT LIKE THE GENERAL *FIGURES*--

--THE THING MAY STILL BE *INTACT!*

SOMEBODY GET *ARTOO DEETOO* UP IN THIS BABY'S *DROID SOCKET!*

BEFORE ANYONE CAN GET OVER THEIR *SUR-PRISE* ENOUGH TO PROTEST, LUKE IS INTO THE SKIES AND ON HIS WAY...

...TO ONE OF MANY *LESSER* ORNAMENTS IN YAVIN'S BRIGHT NECKLACE OF MOONS...

...MADE DISTINCTIVE BY *ANOTHER* KIND OF ORNAMENTATION.

DA-WEET! FRIIT!

I *MARK* IT, ARTOO... AND IT LOOKS IN BETTER *SHAPE* THAN I EXPECTED

BUT THERE IS *DANGER* IN THAT. FOR IF THE *FIGHTER* IS INTACT...

...THE *PILOT* MAY BE AS WELL!

HOPED MY *OWN* OUTFIT MIGHT COME LOOKING FOR ME *BEFORE* THE REBELS--

-- BUT AS LONG AS I'M *FORCED* TO USE THE REMOTE-DESTRUCT, AT LEAST I'M TAKING AN *ENEMY* WITH ME!

THERE ON THE *MAIN PANEL*, ARTOO...! NONE OF THE MANUALS I'VE STUDIED--

--INDICATE A UNIT LIKE *THAT* IN A TIE SHIP!

NO, ARTOO! NOT *THERE*, I SAID THE *MAIN* PANEL! WHY ARE YOU RIPPING OUT *WIRING* WHEN--

ARTOO! THAT'S A PROTON CHARGE *DETONATOR*--!

FRADOOP!

BLASTED LITTLE *DROID!* BROKE THE *TRANSMISSION*--!

ARTOO!

VDOW!

464

VRRPOW!

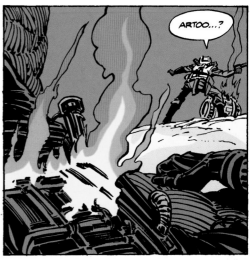

ARTOO...?

IT IS SOMETIME *LATER* BEFORE THE Y-WING REAPPEARS AT THE REBEL BASE...

LUKE! I-- WE WERE GETTING *FRANTIC!* DID YOU--

I *FOUND* THE GADGET, PRINCESS... BUT I HAD TO REMOVE IT *WITH-OUT* ARTOO'S HELP.

IT TOOK A LOT MORE *TIME.*

WITHOUT *ARTOO...?* MASTER LUKE, YOU *DON'T* MEAN--

OH, *DEAR!* IT'S LIKE THE DEATH STAR BATTLE ALL OVER AGAIN! DO YOU THINK IT WILL TAKE *LONG* TO REPAIR HIM, SIR?

I-I GUESS THAT *DEPENDS,* THREEPIO--

-- ON HOW MUCH THE IMPERIAL *BLOCKADE* HAS AFFECTED SUPPLIES.

AFFECTED--?! WITH ALL THE ATTACKS, WE'RE SCRAPIN' BOTTOM FOR *EVERYTHING,* SKYWALKER, THERE'S SOME *WORKING* R-2 UNITS THAT COULD USE *HIS* PARTS!

I KNOW YOU'RE *FOND* OF THAT LITTLE DROID, BUT AFTER *ALL,* IT'S--

DON'T TELL ME HE'S ONLY A *MACHINE*!

NIGHT ABOVE THE RUINS, A LONE FIGURE STARES AT THE SILENT STARS...

...AND IS JOINED BY ANOTHER.

LUKE...? IT'S VERY *LATE*. WHAT HAVE YOU BEEN *DOING* OUT HERE?

MEDITATING... TRYING TO BECOME MORE ATTUNED TO THE *FORCE*.

AND A LOT OF JUST PLAIN *THINKING*, TOO.

YOU WERE *MISSED* AT THE MEETING. OUR TECHNICIANS HAVE *STUDIED* THAT UNIT YOU BROUGHT BACK... A *PLAN* WAS DEVELOPED FOR USING IT.

MAYBE IF *I'D* HAD A PLAN BEFORE JUST JUMPING IN THAT Y-WING AND TAKING OFF--

--ARTOO WOULDN'T BE A CANDIDATE FOR THE *SPARE PARTS RESERVE*!

THE *STUPID* THING IS I THINK I WAS JUST TRYING TO MAKE UP FOR NOT COMPLETING MY *ORIGINAL* MISSION, PRINCESS. ✳

OTHER PILOTS WERE ALSO SENT TO LOOK FOR A SAFER BASE LOCATION, LUKE... NONE OF THEM EVEN MADE IT BACK!

EVERY MISSION *CAN'T* BE A SUCCESS... *WAR* JUST ISN'T THAT SIMPLE.

✳ SW #8.--AG.

NOR IS IT *FAIR.* THERE ARE MISSIONS FROM WHICH MEN CANNOT *POSSIBLY* RETURN... AND YET, WE STILL *SEND* THEM.

OFTEN... WE SEND OUR *BEST.*

GENERAL DODONNA...! *NO!* I THOUGHT LUKE WOULDN'T *HAVE* TO--

ANYONE ELSE IN SKYWALKER'S CLASS IS ALSO A *FLIGHT COMMANDER,* PRINCESS... OUR LESS EXPERIENCED PILOTS *NEED* SUCH LEADERSHIP.

BUT YOU'LL *THROW AWAY* THE LIFE OF THE MAN WHO DESTROYED THE *DEATH STAR!*

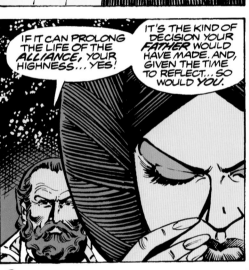

IF IT CAN PROLONG THE LIFE OF THE *ALLIANCE,* YOUR HIGHNESS... YES!

IT'S THE KIND OF DECISION YOUR *FATHER* WOULD HAVE MADE. AND, GIVEN THE TIME TO REFLECT... SO WOULD *YOU.*

NOBODY SEEMS TO BE *ASKING* ME, BUT IF YOU NEED A *VOLUNTEER,* GENERAL... I GUESS YOU'VE *GOT* HIM.

HOW ABOUT *SHOWING* ME WHAT I'M *IN* FOR?

SOON... IN THE VAST STONE CHAMBER THAT HOUSES THE REBEL FIGHTERS... A SHIP IS READIED.

WE'VE HAD THIS OLD *HULK* FOR YEARS... USED IT TO *FAMILIARIZE* OUR PILOTS WITH ENEMY CRAFT.

NOW IT'S OUTFITTED WITH THAT TAGGE *SIGNAL DEVICE...* AND ENOUGH *PROTON CHARGES* TO DESTROY A CITY. UNFORTUNATELY--

WHEN I DESTROY MY *TARGET,* I DESTROY WHATEVER CREATES THAT *STORM CORRIDOR...* THE ONLY WAY *OUT* OF YAVIN'S GAS ATMOSPHERE.

I *UNDERSTAND,* GENERAL. AND SINCE WAITING WON'T MAKE IT ANY *EASIER...* I'M READY TO GO *NOW.*

LUKE CLIMBS INTO THE ONE-TIME IMPERIAL CRAFT AND IS TOWED OUTSIDE. MOMENTS LATER, HE ROARS INTO THE NIGHT SKY ABOVE THE FOURTH MOON...

...RACING TOWARD WHATEVER *DESTINY* WAITS ON THE FAR SIDE OF YAVIN.

MAY THE *FORCE* BE WITH YOU, BOY... *NOW* MORE THAN *EVER!*

WITHIN THE ANCIENT RUINS, ANOTHER SILENTLY *THINKS* WHAT GENERAL DODONNA HAS PUT INTO WORDS.

SHE HAS NOT *TRUSTED* HERSELF TO WATCH THE ACTUAL LAUNCH.

WHAT KIND OF *EXAMPLE* WOULD SHE BE IF A PRINCESS, SENATOR, LEADER AND SYMBOL OF THE REBEL ALLIANCE...

...SHOWED THAT SHE *CRIES?*

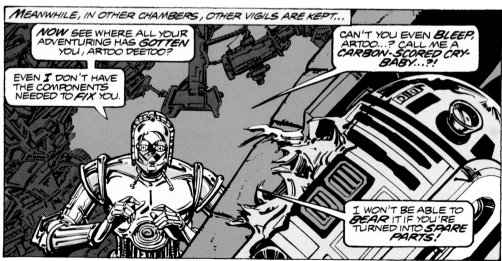

MEANWHILE, IN OTHER CHAMBERS, OTHER VIGILS ARE KEPT...

NOW SEE WHERE ALL YOUR ADVENTURING HAS *GOTTEN* YOU, ARTOO DEETOO?

EVEN *I* DON'T HAVE THE COMPONENTS NEEDED TO *FIX* YOU.

CAN'T YOU EVEN *BLEEP,* ARTOO...? CALL ME A *CARBON-SCORED CRY-BABY...?!*

I WON'T BE ABLE TO *BEAR* IT IF YOU'RE TURNED INTO *SPARE PARTS!*

SUCH IS THE MOOD AT THE *BASE.* ON THE MISSION...

THIS IS *IT...!* THE AREA WHERE LEIA AND I CAUGHT UP WITH THAT HOUSE OF TAGGE *MINING EXPLORER*--

--GENERAL DODONNA SENT A FLIGHT IN *PURSUIT* OF IT WHILE I WAS OUT AFTER THE SIGNAL DEVICE--

--BUT THE TAGGE SHIP HAD APPARENTLY ALREADY *FLED* THE AREA.

NO DOUBT IT'LL BE *BACK* WITH ANOTHER LOAD OF *TIE FIGHTERS!*

IT'S UP TO *ME* TO MAKE CERTAIN THAT WHEN THAT *HAPPENS*--

--THE *BASE* WHICH USES THEM IS *GONE!*

LUKE'S HAND FLICKS A SWITCH ON A CONTROL PANEL MODULE RECENTLY *ADDED* TO THE SALVAGED FIGHTER...

ACCORDING TO OUR *TECHNOS*... THIS SENDS OUT A *SIGNAL* AT HIGHER, MORE POWERFUL FREQUENCIES THAN ANYTHING *WE'VE* GOT.

SO IF IT *WORKS*--

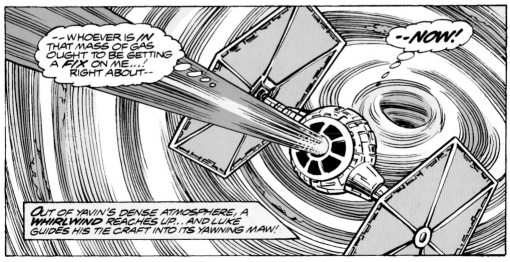

--WHOEVER IS *IN* THAT MASS OF GAS OUGHT TO BE GETTING A *FIX* ON ME...! RIGHT ABOUT--

--*NOW!*

OUT OF YAVIN'S DENSE ATMOSPHERE, A WHIRLWIND REACHES UP... AND LUKE GUIDES HIS TIE CRAFT INTO ITS YAWNING MAW!

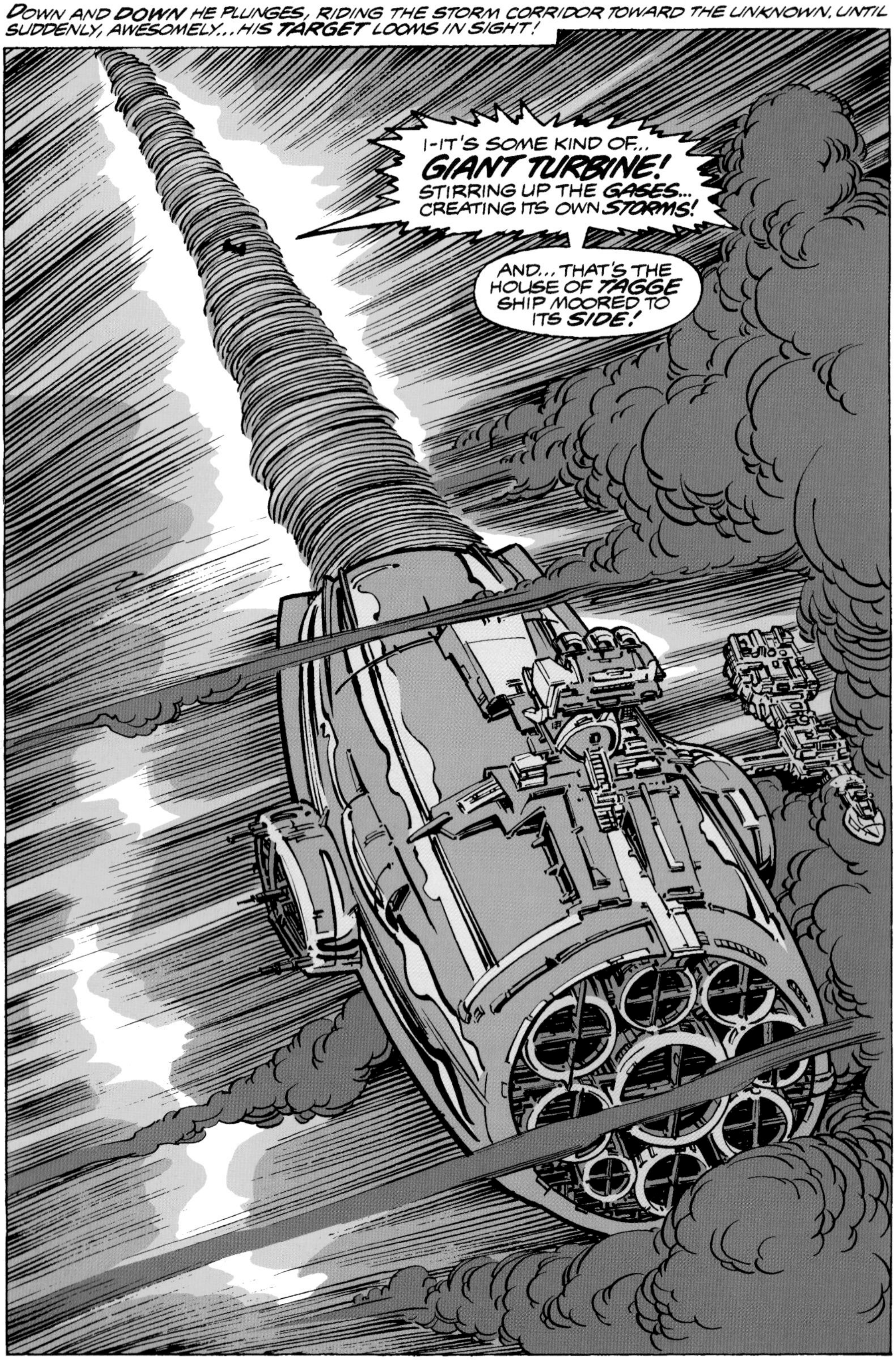
DOWN AND DOWN HE PLUNGES, RIDING THE STORM CORRIDOR TOWARD THE UNKNOWN, UNTIL SUDDENLY, AWESOMELY... HIS TARGET LOOMS IN SIGHT!
I-IT'S SOME KIND OF... GIANT TURBINE! STIRRING UP THE GASES... CREATING ITS OWN STORMS!
AND... THAT'S THE HOUSE OF TAGGE SHIP MOORED TO ITS SIDE!

AND *ABOARD* THE *MINING EXPLORER...*

BARON TAGGE! THE TURBINE STATION REPORTS A LONE *TIE FIGHTER* IS APPROACHING!

IT MUST BE ONE OF OUR *LOOKOUT SHIPS!* WHEN THEY FAILED TO *RETURN* EARLIER--

--I FELT *CERTAIN* THE REBELS WERE *ON* TO US!

I-I... STILL WONDER IF WE SHOULD HAVE RETREATED DOWN INTO THIS *MURK,* SIR. IF ANYTHING EVER HAPPENED TO THE *STATION*--

MY STATION IS A *SUCCESS,* SHANKS, WE ARE SAFER HIDING FROM THE REBELS *HERE*--

--THAN DESPERATELY RACING TO MAKE SAFE *WARPING DISTANCE* WITH ALLIANCE FIGHTERS IN HOT *PURSUIT!*

WE'LL GO *OUT* WITH THE NEXT FLIGHT OFF TO RAID THE REBEL *STRONGHOLD.*

AND IT WON'T TAKE MANY *MORE* SUCH RAIDS BEFORE THAT STRONGHOLD *CRUMBLES!*

THEN, SHANKS, THE HOUSE OF *TAGGE* SHALL HOLD THE EMPEROR'S FAVOR INSTEAD OF THAT BLASTED *WIZARD,* DARTH VADER!

I'LL HAVE SWEET *VENGEANCE* ON THE DARK LORD WHO CURSED ME TO A *LIFETIME* OF CYBER-VISION AND--

BARON! WH-WHAT∞?!

HUMM!

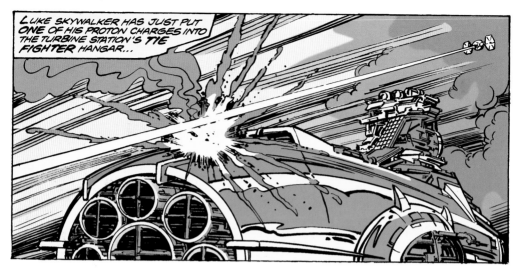

LUKE SKYWALKER HAS JUST PUT ONE OF HIS PROTON CHARGES INTO THE TURBINE STATION'S TIE FIGHTER HANGAR...

...AND KICKING THE SMALL CRAFT INTO AN ENGINE-STRAINING FULL REVERSE...

...HE SWIFTLY UNLEASHES HIS SECOND CHARGE!

THIS STATION DOESN'T HAVE THE ARMAMENT OF EVEN ONE TRENCH ON THE DEATH STAR... BUT IN THIS SOUP IT DOESN'T NEED IT!

TRACKING INSTRUMENTS ARE USELESS! IF I LOSE VISUAL CONTACT WITH THE TARGET--

--THERE'S ALMOST NO CHANCE OF FINDING IT AGAIN!

SO WHILE I'VE GOT THE TURBINE ENGINE IN SIGHT... I'M GIVING IT ALL I'VE GOT!

AS GENERAL DODONNA SAID, THE TIE CARRIES ENOUGH PROTON CHARGES TO DESTROY A *CITY.* BARON TAGGE'S CREATION MAY BE *BIGGER* THAN THAT...

...BUT IT IS, IN ITS WAY, *MORE* VULNERABLE. ENGINES, REACTORS, WEAPON STORES ARE IN A MORE *CONCENTRATED* AREA, AND ONCE *SOME* START TO BLOW...

...THEY *ALL* SWIFTLY FOLLOW.

AND *NOW,* LUKE SKYWALKER'S PROBLEMS *TRULY* BEGIN.

WITHIN *INSTANTS,* THE EXPLOSIVE FLARE THAT MARKED THE SUCCESSFUL ACCOMPLISHMENT OF HIS MISSION *FADES...*

...AND HE IS ALONE.

ALONE. FIGHTING TO TRIM AND KEEP TOGETHER A SHIP REFITTED IN HASTE, PUSHED BEYOND CAPABILITY IN DESPERATION.

ALONE. LOST WITHOUT INSTRUMENTS AMID SWIRLING, COLLIDING GASES THAT *ARE* THE PLANET YAVIN.

ALONE. NO WAY TO MARK UP OR DOWN, THE PATH OF SALVATION... OR DESTRUCTION.

YOU KNEW IT WOULD BE THIS WAY WHEN YOU *VOLUNTEERED*, SKYWALKER--

IT'S ONE OF THE *REASONS* YOU VOLUNTEERED.

VERTIGO SWEEPS LUKE'S BODY. DISORIENTATION. HE LETS INSTINCT GUIDE HIM. THE SHIP SEEMS TO DIVE.

THANKS TO MY FATHER, TO BEN KENOBI... I HAVE A SPECIAL *GIFT.* NO ONE SHOULD HAVE TO *DIE* ON A MISSION LIKE THIS--

--WHEN I'VE GOT IT TO *USE.* ONLY... I HAVEN'T *MASTERED* IT.

WITHOUT A FIX ON. UP OR DOWN, THE TIE SHIP COULD BE DOING ANYTHING...

I NEEDED BEN'S *VOICE* TO GUIDE ME ON THE DEATH STAR... I USED IT ALMOST *ACCIDENTALLY* AGAINST DARTH VADER ESCAPING THE WHEEL...

THE MIND DECEIVES THE BODY UNDER THESE CONDITIONS, PLAYS CRUEL TRICKS...

BUT I'VE BEEN *MEDITATING...* EXPANDING MY *FEELING.* I'VE USED THE ABILITY IN *SMALLER* TESTS... BUT THIS IS THE FIRST TIME I'VE CONSCIOUSLY *PLANNED* TO USE IT!

PULL OUT, YOU FOOL, EVERY CONSCIOUS THOUGHT SCREAMS. PULL OUT OR DIE IN THE HARD FROZEN CENTER OF YAVIN!

I *TRUST* IN WHAT BEN TAUGHT ME. I *BELIEVE* IN THE FORCE. AND *MORE*--

--I BELIEVE IN *MYSELF!*

AND LUKE'S REWARD FOR HIS FAITH IS THE STARRY SAFETY OF DEEP SPACE...

...AND THE KNOWLEDGE THAT HE IS ALIVE, ABLE TO USE THIS GROWING ABILITY ANOTHER DAY IN THE BATTLE AGAINST THE EMPIRE.

THE SMALL CONTROL HE HAS ESTABLISHED OVER THE FORCE WILL NOT BE *EASY* TO MAINTAIN... HE WILL NOT *ALWAYS* BE ABLE TO SUMMON IT SO READILY.

BUT A STRIDE FORWARD HAS BEEN MADE, AND SHADOWS OF THE FUTURE CANNOT CLOUD LUKE'S EXUBERANCE AS HE REPORTS IN TO THE ALLIANCE BASE...

A REPORT THAT IS INTERCEPTED... BY A SHIP THAT SHOULDN'T EXIST!

THE YOUNG REBEL HAS NO NOTION THAT WE *FOLLOWED* HIM OUT--

--YOU GAVE THE ORDER TO *CAST OFF* FROM THE TURBINE STATION JUST IN *TIME,* BARON TAGGE!

IRONIC... THIS SKYWALKER ACTUALLY *SAVED* US!

PARTICULARLY SO SINCE WE ONLY KEPT HIM IN *SIGHT* FOR THE SATISFACTION OF *DESTROYING* HIM BEFORE WE PERISHED IN THOSE GASES *OURSELVES!* BUT, *MIRACULOUSLY--*

HE DID THE *IMPOSSIBLE,* SHANKS! AND *RUINED* MY CHANCES OF SHOWING UP DARTH VADER IN THE PROCESS!

SOMEDAY, I'LL *LEARN* HIS SECRET. THEN I'LL DO TO *LUKE SKYWALKER--*

--WORSE THAN THE SITH LORD DID TO *ME!*

NEXT ISSUE: THE ATTEMPT TO RESTORE ARTOO DEETOO MAY BE DOOMED BY... THE *RETURN* OF THE *HUNTER!*

40¢ | 27
SEPT
02817

ADVENTURES *BEYOND* THE GREATEST SPACE-FANTASY FILM OF ALL!

STAR WARS ™

LUKE AND
THREEPIO
STALKED
BY THE
SINISTER
CYBORG!

RETURN
OF THE
HUNTER!

Long ago in a galaxy far, far away. . .there exists a state of cosmic *civil war*. A brave alliance of *underground freedom fighters* has challenged the tyranny and oppression of the awesome *Galactic Empire*. This is their story!

LucasFilm PRESENTS: **STAR WARS** ™ THE GREATEST **SPACE FANTASY** OF ALL!

CONTINUING THE SAGA BEGUN IN THE FILM BY **GEORGE LUCAS** RELEASED BY **TWENTIETH CENTURY-FOX**

ARCHIE GOODWIN WRITER/EDITOR **CARMINE INFANTINO BOB WIACEK** ARTISTS J. COSTANZA letters P. GOLDBERG colors J. SHOOTER Ed.-in-chief

RETURN OF THE HUNTER

IN MOST OUTWORLD CANTINAS, SUDDEN DEATH IS NO GREAT NOVELTY. STILL, EVEN IN THESE ENVIRONS, WHEN DEALT WITH ENOUGH SWIFTNESS AND SAVAGERY...

...SHOCK AND FRIGHT QUICKLY FOLLOW!

HE'S *MARKO TYNE. WANTED* IN NINE SYSTEMS FOR UNLICENSED SLAVING.

I'M *CLAIMING* HIM.

SINCE NO ONE'S TRIED TO SHOOT ME IN THE *BACK...* I TAKE IT HE DOESN'T HAVE ANY *FRIENDS* HERE.

IN WHICH CASE, *TWO* OF YOU WON'T MIND VOLUNTEERING TO CARRY HIS *BODY* FOR ME.

THAT'S *DROID* WORK, BOUNTY HUNTER. SO GO GET A--

YOU TAKE THE *HEAVY* END.

THE MAN *NEXT* TO YOU CAN GRAB THE *FEET.*

FIVE *WEEKS* HE'S BEEN AROUND... AND AT LEAST *ONCE* A WEEK, HE DOES *THIS!*

IT'S BAD FOR *BUSINESS.*

IT WAS *WORSE* FOR MARKO TYNE! THAT BOUNTY HUNTER LOOKS HALF *CRAZY--*

--WHO *IS* HE?

HIS NAME IS **VALANCE**. ONCE HE WAS A SOLDIER OF PROMISE SERVING THE **EMPIRE**. THAT SERVICE WAS **ENDED** BY A REBEL AERIAL TORPEDO. ✳ YET THANKS TO ADVANCED MEDICAL TECHNIQUES, HE **SURVIVES**... AND CURSES THE FACT THAT HE **DOES**. FOR VALANCE HAS BECOME SOMETHING LESS THAN HE WAS...

...AND SOMETHING FAR **MORE**!

SKINKER! IT'S **PAYDAY**!

✳ AS TOLD IN **STAR WARS** #16.
--ARCHIE.

COLLECTED ANOTHER **REWARD**, DID YA? YOU'RE RIGHT **GOOD** AT YOUR WORK, VALANCE.

CAN'T RECALL ANY **OTHER** BOUNTY MAN EVEN **SURVIVIN'** THIS LONG ON JUNCTION.

NO SMALL TALK. YOU HAVE **DROIDS** FOR ME?

RIGHT **HERE**. SCAVENGER SHIPS HAD **SLIM PICKIN'S** THIS WEEK. NO **R-2** OR **3PO** MODELS... THIS IS THE **LOT**.

EXCUSE--MY **CONDITION**, SIR-- HOW MAY I **SERVE** YOU--?

VEEDOW! PA-KOOWW!

BY SAYING **GOOD-BYE**... JUNK!

SURE A **WASTE** OF GOOD CIRCUITRY! BUT LONG AS YOU'RE PAYIN' THE GOIN' RATE FOR **REBUILT DROIDS** --

-- I GOT NO **COMPLAINTS**. SAVES ME ALL THAT **TIME** TINKERIN' AROUND, TRYIN' TO FIX 'EM UP.

I'M PAYING YOU FOR **MORE** THAN THE MACHINES, SKINKER.

'COURSE YA ARE! AN' I GOT MY **EYE** OUT... YOU'RE AFTER A **REBEL LAD** WHO MOVES AROUND WITH A **3PO** AND **R-2** UNIT IN TOW.

MUST BE **SOME** REWARD ON 'IM!

ENOUGH. BUT EVEN IF THERE **WEREN'T** --

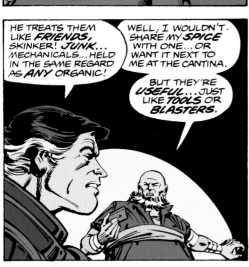

HE TREATS THEM LIKE **FRIENDS**, SKINKER! **JUNK**... MECHANICALS... HELD IN THE SAME REGARD AS **ANY** ORGANIC!

WELL, I WOULDN'T. SHARE MY **SPICE** WITH ONE... OR WANT IT NEXT TO ME AT THE CANTINA.

BUT THEY'RE **USEFUL**... JUST LIKE **TOOLS** OR **BLASTERS**.

LONG AS THEY KEEP THEIR **PLACE**... I CAN'T SEE **HATING** 'EM, NOT LIKE **YOU** DO, VALANCE. THAT'S --

SOMETHING YOU'LL **NEVER** UNDERSTAND, OLD MAN --

NOT IF YOU WANT TO GO ON **LIVING**!

*THE MAN CALLED VALANCE HAS A **SECRET**. A TERRIBLE SECRET FOR ONE WITH **HIS** BELIEFS.*

I'M **CLOSE**. I FEEL IT... **HUNTER'S** INSTINCT.

YOU'VE BEEN AN *OBSESSION,* BOY. EVER SINCE I *LEARNED* ABOUT YOUR DEATH STAR ESCAPE FROM THAT ILLEGAL DUPE OF AN *IMPERIAL TRANSMISSION TAPE.*

I DON'T KNOW YOUR *NAME*... BUT YOU MUST BE QUITE A *HERO* TO THE ALLIANCE.

I'VE WASTED A LOT OF TIME ROAMING THE GALAXY IN *SEARCH* OF YOU. STILL.... I GAINED SOME IDEA OF REBEL *SUPPLY* METHODS.

AND WITH THIS NEW *IMPERIAL BLOCKADE** PUTTING ON PRESSURE* ...THE ODDS ARE *PERFECT* FOR A HOTSHOT LIKE YOU SHOWING UP *HERE.*

*IT BEGAN IN *SW #25.*--ARCH.

AND *THAT'S* WHEN I'LL *DESTROY* YOU, DROID-LOVER!

THIS THEN IS THE HUNTER'S *SECRET*... HIS TORMENT AND HIS SHAME.

THE PRICE OF *SURVIVING* THE AERIAL TORPEDO EXPLOSION WAS THAT *HALF* HIS BODY BE REPLACED BY *CYBERNETIC PARTS.* VALANCE, THE MAN WHO *HATES* ROBOTS....IS A *CYBORG.*

DEEP SPACE! A LONE VESSEL PLIES ITS WAY THROUGH THE SELDOM-TRAVELLED STAR SECTOR KNOWN AS THE GORDIAN REACH...

MASTER LUKE, THIS DROPPING IN AND OUT OF *WARP* IS PLAYING *HAVOC* WITH MY INTERIOR DIRECTIONAL COMPENSATORS!

PART OF OUR *MISSION* IS TO PROBE THE *EXTENT* OF THE EMPIRE'S BLOCKADE, THREEPIO.

I FEAR YOU CAN DEFINITELY INCLUDE *THIS* SYSTEM, SIR! BECAUSE ACCORDING TO OUR *SCANNERS*--

-- THE IMPERIAL PRESENCE IS *WELL* REPRESENTED HERE!

A *BATTLE CRUISER...* USING THAT PLANETOID AS *COVER!*

THAT'S WHY OUR INSTRUMENTS DIDN'T PICK THEM UP *SOONER--*

DOES THIS MEAN WE'RE *DOOMED,* SIR?

NOT IF THIS LITTLE BABY *MANEUVERS* AS WELL AS THE ALLIANCE TECHNOS BACK ON YAVIN *PROMISED* IT WOULD!

MAIN SCOPE SHOWS IT'S COMING *AFTER* US, MASTER LUKE... AND AT *FULL SPEED!*

NO ONE ADMIRES GENERAL DODONNA'S *MAINTENANCE PERSONNEL* MORE THAN *I* DO, SIR--

--BUT I DOUBT EVEN *THEIR* HANDIWORK COULD ENABLE A SIMPLE CRAFT LIKE *THIS* TO OUTRUN AN IMPERIAL *STAR-DESTROYER!*

IT'S SURE NOT THE *MILLENNIUM FALCON*, THREEPIO--

--BUT MAYBE WE CAN STILL USE ONE OF HAN SOLO'S *SMUGGLING TRICKS.*

THREADING THE ASTEROIDS, HE CALLED IT!

DID CAPTAIN SOLO EVER CONSIDER THAT HURTLING AMONG GREAT HUNKS OF FLOATING *SPACE ROCK*--

--MIGHT PUT A SERIOUS *KNOT* IN ONE'S PARTICULAR *THREAD*, SIR?!

I THINK HAN FELT THAT WAS MORE *LIKELY* TO HAPPEN TO SOMETHING MUCH *LARGER* AND LESS *MANEUVERABLE*--

--THAN *HIS* SHIP... OR *OURS!*

THAT SHOULD SLOW 'EM DOWN ENOUGH FOR US TO MAKE THE JUMP INTO *HYPER-SPACE!*

GET THE NAVIGATIONAL COMPUTER *PERKING,* THREEPIO--

-- WE'RE GOING INTO *PHASE TWO* OF OUR MISSION!

AND WITH SWIFTNESS AND EFFICIENCY, *COORDINATES* ARE SOON CALCULATED WHICH WILL BRING THE TRAVELERS TO A WORLD CALLED...

...*JUNCTION!* THERE ARE *MANY* PLANETS OF A SIMILAR NATURE SCATTERED ACROSS THE ENDLESS SPECTRUM OF THE OUT-WORLDS.

ESSENTIALLY, THEY ARE *TRADING POSTS*... GATHERING PLACES AND WATERING HOLES FOR THOSE THAT ROAM BEYOND THE CIVILIZED SYSTEMS.

ANYONE SEEKING *SUPPLIES,* PARTICU-LARLY THOSE WHO FIND IMPERIAL REGULATION DISTASTEFUL...

... MUST SOONER OR LATER *COME* TO SUCH A PLANET.

WILL YOU LOOK AT THIS PLACE, THREEPIO? IT'S EVEN *BIGGER* THAN MOS EISLEY!

AND I BET YOU COULD STICK ALL OF *ANCHOR-HEAD* INTO THE GROUND FLOOR OF SOME OF THESE BUILDINGS!

THIS'LL BE THE FIRST *REAL CITY* I'VE HAD A CHANCE TO SEE. THAT TIME WE STOPPED ON *CENTARES...** WE WERE TOO BUSY FLEEING *DARTH VADER* TO PLAY TOURIST!

FRANKLY, MASTER LUKE, IT APPEARS WILD, DIRTY, AND *DANGEROUS* TO ME--

*STAR WARS #25.--ARCHIE.

--ONLY THE PROSPECT OF GETTING THE *PARTS* WE NEED TO REPAIR *ARTOO DEETOO* ✳ WOULD MAKE ME COME HERE *VOLUNTARILY!*

THOUGH I HOPE YOU NEVER *TELL* THE LITTLE FELLOW THAT, SIR... HE'S QUITE *SELF-CENTERED* AS IT IS!

✳ FROM INJURIES SUSTAINED IN *ISSUE 26.*--ARCH AGAIN.

YOUR SECRET'S *SAFE*, THREEPIO. AND DON'T *WORRY*... I'M NOT SO IMPRESSED WITH JUNCTION THAT I'LL FORGET TO TAKE CARE OF *BUSINESS!*

AS A MATTER OF *FACT*, THERE'S JUST WHAT WE'RE *LOOKING* FOR... A *SALVAGE YARD!*

SHOULD WE JUST SETTLE FOR THE *FIRST* ONE, MASTER LUKE...OR SHOP AROUND?

SINCE THE BLOCKADE, THE ALLIANCE NEEDS ALL *KINDS* OF SUPPLIES, THREEPIO. I'LL SPREAD OUR TRADE AMONG *DIFFERENT* SPOTS TO AVOID UNDUE *CURIOSITY*--

--BUT WE'VE GOT TO START *SOME-WHERE.* WHY *NOT* HERE?

WELL, WELL....!

POLYP! GO GET *VALANCE!* TELL 'IM OL' SKINKER HAS COME ACROSS A LIKELY LOOKIN' *PROSPECT*--

VERY LIKELY!

INTERLUDE: *THE FOURTH MOON OF YAVIN. HERE, IT IS NIGHT. AND HERE PRINCESS LEIA ORGANA LOOKS TO THE **STARS**, KNOWING THAT SOMEWHERE AMONG THEM, EACH GOING HIS SEPARATE WAY, ARE TWO YOUNG MEN SHE DEEPLY CARES FOR.*

THIS IS *SILLY--*

AND IT'S *WRONG,* GENERAL DODONNA! I SPENT TOO MANY YEARS AS AN ACTIVE *SENATOR--*

--TO GO THROUGH THE REST OF THE REBELLION *WAITING* WHILE EVERYONE *ELSE* RUNS AROUND BEING *BRAVE!*

BUT, YOUR *HIGHNESS--*

--WE'VE HAD THIS ARGUMENT *BEFORE.* YOU'RE MUCH TOO IMPORTANT A *SYMBOL* OF THE REVOLUTION TO--

THEN I SHOULD BE *SEEN*... AND IN *ACTION!* OTHERWISE I'M NO BETTER THAN THE *EMPEROR*...SKULKING IN HIS PALACE!

I WENT AGAINST YOUR THINKING ONCE *BEFORE,* GENERAL,* BUT FOR THE WRONG REASON... *PERSONAL* CONCERN OVER LUKE SKYWALKER.

I REALIZE NOW A *LEADER* CAN'T AFFORD TO *GIVE IN* TO SUCH FEELINGS--

YOU SHOULD REALIZE THE *SAME THING!*

*WAY BACK IN *STAR WARS* #9.-- ANCIENT ARCHIE.

YOU'RE TRYING TO PROTECT *ME* THE WAY I'VE TRIED TO PROTECT *LUKE.* I *APPRECIATE* IT, BUT WE BOTH DESERVE *BETTER* THAN THAT--

--AND SO DOES THE *ALLIANCE!*

NOW LET'S GO INSIDE... THIS NIGHT AIR MAKES ME *TALK* TOO MUCH.

AND IF THAT TALK SHOULD DWELL TOO MUCH ON LUKE SKYWALKER AND HIS *MISSION*, OR THE UNKNOWN FATE OF *HAN SOLO*, SOME OF THIS RESOLVE NOT TO GIVE IN TO PERSONAL CONCERN MIGHT *SLIP*...

...*HE SLIPS INTO A HUMBLE-SEEMING ROOM THAT BOASTS A CONCEALED LONG-RANGE TRANSMITTER AMONG ITS FURNISHINGS. BUT...*

YOU CAN'T REPORT TO *DARTH VADER*, SPY...NOT ON *THAT* SET. I *FUSED* THE CIRCUITRY WHILE I WAS *WAITING* FOR YOU.

...*SO LEIA ORGANA RETREATS INTO THE MASSASI RUINS. EVEN AS ON JUNCTION...*

...*A DARK FIGURE RETREATS DOWN A TWISTING ALLEYWAY.*

UNTIL, CERTAIN HE HAS NOT BEEN FOLLOWED...

SPOTTED YOU SLIPPING AWAY FROM *SKINKER'S* AS I *APPROACHED* HIS PLACE.

MY FIRST WEEK IN A NEW PORT, I MAKE IT A HABIT TO LEARN *ALL* ABOUT SPIES-- IMPERIAL, REBEL, OR OTHERWISE. KNOWING YOUR *HIDEAWAY*--

--IT WAS NO PROBLEM *BEATING* YOU HERE.

GO DOWN FIGHTING... *SMART.*

AN EASIER DEATH THAN YOUR SITH LORD *MASTER* WOULD PERMIT--

--WHEN HE LEARNED *I'VE* FOUND THE BOY WITH THE DROIDS *AHEAD* OF HIM!

VA-KOW!

AND...

WHAT A *RELIEF*, MASTER LUKE...! FINALLY WE HAVE *ALL* THE COMPONENTS NEEDED TO *MEND* ARTOO DEETOO.

EXCEPT THIS *SKINKER* CHARACTER IS SURE TAKING HIS TIME *PACKING* THEM--

DOUBLE *BLAST* YA, POLYP! WHERE'S *VALANCE?* YA *SAID* YOU DELIVERED THE *MESSAGE!*

THE LAD SEEMS MORE *FARMER* THAN REBEL... BUT EVEN *HE* COULD GET SUSPICIOUS.

STARTING RIGHT *NOW*, SCRAP-RUNNER!

EASY, YOUNG FELLA...! I DON'T THINK YA QUITE *UNDERSTAND* THE SITUATION--

TRY ME. I'M OPEN-MINDED... FOR A *FARMER.*

HE'S IN *MY* PAY, DROID-LOVER! NOW STEP *BACK*... BEFORE KILLING *YOU*, I MEAN TO MELT YOUR PET *JUNK* INTO SLAG!

M-MASTER LUKE! HE'S LOWERED THE GATE AND *LOCKED* IT! WE'RE--

INSIDE, THREEPIO--

--*FAST!*

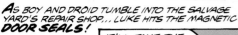

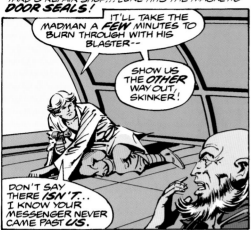

As boy and droid tumble into the salvage yard's repair shop... Luke hits the magnetic **DOOR SEALS!**

IT'LL TAKE THE **MADMAN** A **FEW** MINUTES TO BURN THROUGH WITH HIS BLASTER--

SHOW US THE **OTHER** WAY OUT, SKINKER!

DON'T SAY THERE **ISN'T**... I KNOW YOUR MESSENGER NEVER CAME PAST **US.**

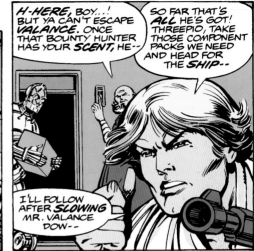

H-HERE, BOY...! BUT YA CAN'T ESCAPE **VALANCE.** ONCE THAT BOUNTY HUNTER HAS YOUR **SCENT,** HE--

SO FAR THAT'S **ALL** HE'S GOT! THREEPIO, TAKE THOSE COMPONENT PACKS WE NEED AND HEAD FOR THE **SHIP**--

I'LL FOLLOW AFTER **SLOWING** MR. VALANCE DOW--

KA-BWOM!

I'VE **MORE** THAN **BLASTERS** AT MY COMMAND, REBEL--

--AS YOU AND THE OTHERS HAVE NOW **LEARNED** ...JUST A BIT **TOO LATE!**

AFTER WEEKS OF **WAITING...** I'M SORRY TO HAVE IT **OVER** SO QUICKLY.

STILL... THERE'S THE FAITHFUL *ROBOT!* SNEAKING AWAY DOWN POLYP'S *SCURRY-HOLE*... CAN'T HAVE *THAT.*

GUESS *AGAIN,* BOUNTY KILLER!

NOW STAY *PUT!* YOU'RE NOT THE *ONLY* ONE WHO USES MORE THAN A *BLASTER!*

A *LIGHT SABER...!* IN *THIS* DAY AND AGE...

I DON'T *BELIEVE* IT!

MAYBE *THIS* WILL MAKE IT *EASIER!*

WOOMP

SSSSSST!

ZDAK!

NO! IT MERELY *FORCES* ME TO USE... *THIS!*

YOU TELL *ME*, BOY... WHICH IS *BETTER*?

VALANCE, *WHATEVER* YOU'VE GOT UP YOUR SLEEVE CAN'T EXPEND *THAT* MUCH FORCE--

--WITHOUT RUNNING OUT OF *POWER* SOON.

INTERESTING *THEORY*, DROID-LOVER! BUT ONCE OR TWICE *MORE* IS ALL I NE--

FRAK!

MY *BLAST*--! W-WHAT--?!

MOVING INSTINCTIVELY, WITHOUT CONSCIOUSLY THINKING-- AS BEN KENOBI TAUGHT-- *LUKE HAS* BLOCKED *THE BLAST. BLOCKED IT, AND FURTHER...*

...TURNED IT *BACK*!

N-NO! AAAAGH!

ITS POWER IS GREATLY DIMINISHED, *AND YET...*

...NOT WITHOUT EFFECT.

VALANCE....! YOU... YOU'RE... A *BORG*!

IT *SHOCKS* YOU! EVEN THE REBEL WHO CALLS *ROBOTS* HIS FRIENDS--

I KNEW IT... I *KNEW* IT...! THE WHOLE TIME I WAS *SEARCHING* FOR YOU...!

THERE'LL BE NO *REWARD* FOR YOU, *BOY...!* NOT FROM THE *EMPIRE,* NOT SINCE I KILLED DARTH VADER'S IMPERIAL *SPY* HERE...!

BUT IT'S STILL *WORTH* IT--

--TO REMOVE A DROID-LOVING *HYPOCRITE* FROM THE GALAXY!

WHROK!

LUKE BARELY HAS TIME TO DRAW BACK... TO MAKE A GLANCING BLOW OF ONE INTENDED TO KILL!

EVEN SO, HE IS SLAMMED VIOLENTLY, PAIN-FULLY INTO THE HARD GROUND OUTSIDE THE RUINED SHOP...

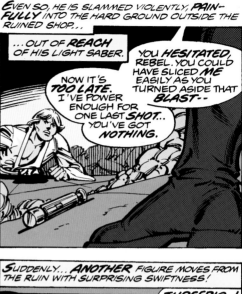

...OUT OF *REACH* OF HIS LIGHT SABER.

NOW IT'S *TOO LATE.* I'VE POWER ENOUGH FOR ONE LAST *SHOT...* YOU'VE GOT *NOTHING.*

YOU *HESITATED,* REBEL. YOU COULD HAVE SLICED *ME* EASILY AS YOU TURNED ASIDE THAT *BLAST--*

SUDDENLY... ANOTHER FIGURE MOVES FROM THE RUIN WITH SURPRISING SWIFTNESS!

B-BRAVERY ISN'T PART OF MY *PROGRAMMING,* BUT I CAN'T LET YOU *DO* THIS, SIR ! NOT TO MASTER *LUKE!*

THREEPIO...! I THOUGHT YOU WENT ON TO THE *SHIP...!*

GET *OUT* OF HERE... HE'LL BLOW YOU TO *PIECES!*

THEN HIS *ADVANTAGE* WILL BE GONE, MASTER LUKE... AND YOU'LL BE RECOVERED ENOUGH TO *FIGHT.*

THIS TIME YOU WON'T HAVE TO HAVE YOUR *COM-PASSION* MISTAKEN FOR *WEAKNESS* BY HESITATING...!

THREEPIO, DO I HAVE TO GIVE YOU A *DIRECT COMMAND...?* GET--

MADNESS! DROIDS AND HUMANS DON'T *BEHAVE* LIKE THIS....!

THEY DON'T *SACRIFICE* THEMSELVES FOR ONE ANOTHER!

PERHAPS NOT IN *YOUR* EXPERIENCE, SIR. CERTAINLY IT'S NOT WIDELY *ACCEPTED.* BUT PERHAPS IF IT *WERE--*

--EVEN BEING A *CYBORG* MIGHT BE EASIER TO BEAR.

ENOUGH, ROBOT. TAKE YOUNG MASTER... MASTER...

SKYWALKER, SIR.

TAKE YOUNG MASTER SKYWALKER... PICK UP HIS LIGHT SABER...

--AND GET THE *TWO* OF YOU FAR, *FAR* FROM MY *SIGHT*!

ZAKOW!!

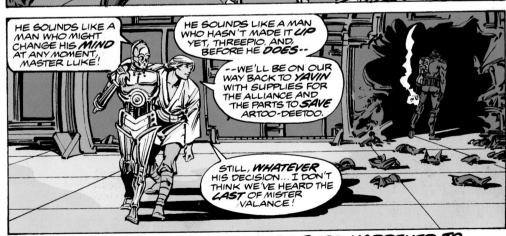

HE SOUNDS LIKE A MAN WHO MIGHT CHANGE HIS *MIND* AT ANY MOMENT, MASTER LUKE!

HE SOUNDS LIKE A MAN WHO HASN'T MADE IT *UP* YET, THREEPIO, AND, BEFORE HE *DOES*--

--WE'LL BE ON OUR WAY BACK TO *YAVIN* WITH SUPPLIES FOR THE ALLIANCE AND THE PARTS TO *SAVE* ARTOO-DEETOO.

STILL, *WHATEVER* HIS DECISION... I DON'T THINK WE'VE HEARD THE *LAST* OF MISTER VALANCE!

NEXT ISSUE: A FEW *ANSWERS* CONCERNING *HAN SOLO*, HIS PARTNER, *CHEWBACCA*, AND...

WHAT EVER HAPPENED TO *JABBA THE HUT!*

STAR WARS GRAPHIC NOVEL TIMELINE (IN YEARS)

Omnibus: Tales of the Jedi—5,000–3,986 BSW4

Knights of the Old Republic—3,964–3,963 BSW4

Jedi vs. Sith—1,000 BSW4

Omnibus: Rise of the Sith—33 BSW4

Episode I: The Phantom Menace—32 BSW4

Omnibus: Emissaries and Assassins—32 BSW4

Twilight—31 BSW4

Bounty Hunters—31 BSW4

Omnibus: Menace Revealed—30–27 BSW4

Darkness—30 BSW4

The Stark Hyperspace War—30 BSW4

Rite of Passage—28 BSW4

Honor and Duty—24 BSW4

Episode II: Attack of the Clones—22 BSW4

Clone Wars—22–19 BSW4

Clone Wars Adventures—22–19 BSW4

General Grievous—22–19 BSW4

Episode III: Revenge of the Sith—19 BSW4

Dark Times—19 BSW4

Omnibus: Droids—5.5 BSW4

Boba Fett: Enemy of the Empire—3 BSW4

Underworld—1 BSW4

Episode IV: A New Hope—SW4

Classic Star Wars—0–3 ASW4

A Long Time Ago . . .—0–4 ASW4

Empire—0 ASW4

Rebellion—0 ASW4

Boba Fett: Man with a Mission—0 ASW4

Omnibus: Early Victories—0–3 ASW4

Jabba the Hutt: The Art of the Deal—1 ASW4

Episode V: The Empire Strikes Back—3 ASW4

Shadows of the Empire—3.5 ASW4

Episode VI: Return of the Jedi—4 ASW4

Mara Jade: By the Emperor's Hand—4 ASW4

Omnibus: X-Wing Rogue Squadron—4–5 ASW4

Heir to the Empire—9 ASW4

Dark Force Rising—9 ASW4

The Last Command—9 ASW4

Dark Empire—10 ASW4

Boba Fett: Death, Lies, and Treachery—10 ASW4

Crimson Empire—11 ASW4

Jedi Academy: Leviathan—12 ASW4

Union—19 ASW4

Chewbacca—25 ASW4

Legacy—130–137 ASW4

Old Republic Era
25,000 – 1000 years before
Star Wars: A New Hope

Rise of the Empire Era
1000 – 0 years before
Star Wars: A New Hope

Rebellion Era
0 – 5 years after
Star Wars: A New Hope

New Republic Era
5 – 25 years after
Star Wars: A New Hope

New Jedi Order Era
25+ years after
Star Wars: A New Hope

Legacy Era
130+ years after
Star Wars: A New Hope

Infinities
Does not apply to timeline

Sergio Aragonés Stomps Star Wars
Star Wars Tales
Star Wars Infinities
Tag and Bink
Star Wars Visionaries

BSW4 = before *Episode IV: A New Hope*. ASW4 = after *Episode IV: A New Hope*.

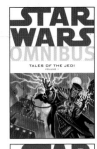

STAR WARS
OMNIBUS COLLECTIONS

STAR WARS: TALES OF THE JEDI

Containing the *Tales of the Jedi* stories "The Golden Age of the Sith," "The Freedon Nadd Uprising," and "Knights of the Old Republic," these huge omnibus editions are the ultimate introduction to the ancient history of the *Star Wars* universe!

Volume 1
ISBN 978-1-59307-830-0

Volume 2
ISBN 978-1-59307-911-6

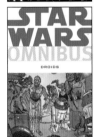

STAR WARS: X-WING ROGUE SQUADRON

Join Wedge Antilles and Rogue Squadron and learn the fate of the galaxy immediately after the events of *Return of the Jedi* as the Rebellion's best pilots battle remnants of the Empire.

Volume 1
ISBN 978-1-59307-572-9

Volume 2
ISBN 978-1-59307-619-1

Volume 3
ISBN 978-1-59307-776-1

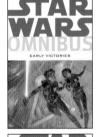

STAR WARS: DROIDS

Before the fateful day Luke Skywalker met Artoo and Threepio for the first time, those two troublesome droids had some amazing adventures all their own!

ISBN 978-1-59307-955-0

STAR WARS: EARLY VICTORIES

Following the destruction of the first Death Star, Luke Skywalker is the new, unexpected hero of the Rebellion. But the galaxy hasn't been saved yet—Luke and Princess Leia find there are many more battles to be fought against the Empire and Darth Vader!

ISBN 978-1-59582-172-0

STAR WARS: RISE OF THE SITH

Before the name of Skywalker—or Vader—achieved fame across the galaxy, the Jedi Knights had long preserved peace and justice . . . as well as prevented the return of the Sith. These thrilling tales illustrate the events leading up to *The Phantom Menace*.

ISBN 978-1-59582-228-4

STAR WARS: EMISSARIES AND ASSASSINS

Discover more stories featuring Anakin Skywalker, Amidala, Obi-Wan, and Qui-Gon set during the time of Episode I *The Phantom Menace* in this mega collection!

ISBN 978-1-59582-229-1

$24.95 each

DARK HORSE BOOKS

AVAILABLE AT YOUR LOCAL COMICS SHOP OR BOOKSTORE!
To find a comics shop in your area, call 1-888-266-4226
For more information or to order direct: • On the web: darkhorse.com • E-mail: mailorder@darkhorse.com
• Phone: 1-800-862-0052 Mon.–Fri. 9 AM to 5 PM Pacific Time
STAR WARS © 2006–2009 Lucasfilm Ltd. & ™ (BL8027)

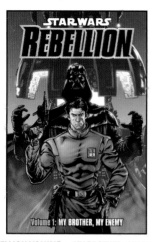

REBELLION VOLUME 1: MY BROTHER, MY ENEMY

Imperial officer Janek "Tank" Sunber makes a critical choice between his duty to the Empire and his loyalty to childhood friend Luke Skywalker in an explosive tale of Rebel spies, Imperial ambushes, and the dreaded Darth Vader!

ISBN 978-1-59307-711-2 | $14.99

LEGACY VOLUME 1: BROKEN

The Jedi Temple is attacked, an Emperor is betrayed, and the Sith are born anew! A lot can happen in a hundred years, but that's just the beginning of the story!

ISBN 978-1-59307-716-7 | $17.99

KNIGHTS OF THE OLD REPUBLIC VOLUME 1: COMMENCEMENT

Thousands of years before Luke Skywalker would destroy the Death Star in that fateful battle above Yavin 4, one lone Padawan would become a fugitive hunted by his own Masters, charged with murdering every one of his fellow Jedi-in-training!

ISBN 978-1-59307-640-5 | $18.99

DARK TIMES VOLUME 1: THE PATH TO NOWHERE

Jedi Dass Jennir and his companion Bomo Greenbark survived the Clone Wars, but the fate of Bomo's wife and daughter remains a mystery. The two friends are determined to find them, but their path leads them from danger to darkness—where each of them stands to lose more than they may hope to gain.

ISBN 978-1-59307-792-1 | $17.99

STAR WARS

OMNIBUS

A LONG TIME AGO. . . .

A long time ago in a galaxy far, far away. . . .

With those words the world was plunged into an epic adventure that continues
to this day on television, in novels, in video games, and in comic books.

From July 1977 to September 1986, Marvel Comics Group published monthly
comics based on the wildly successful *Star Wars* film franchise.

When looking back at these early tales with the advantage of hindsight, the
"mistakes" (such as the idea that Darth Vader and Luke Skywalker's father
were two different people) are obvious, but at the time, the *Star Wars* galaxy
was a great unknown. While there has been much discussion over the years as
to how, where, or even *if* these stories fit into the official *Star Wars* continuity,
there is no denying their charm and their power to entertain.

Collected here are the first twenty-seven issues of the Marvel Comics *Star
Wars* series that launched in 1977—the same year as the first film—beginning
with the comics adaptation of *A New Hope*.

ISBN 978-1-59582-486-8

52499>

9 781595 824868

$24.99 U.S. | DARKHORSE.COM